Karl McCarty: *The Last One Standing*

The Last One Standing

By

Karl D. McCarty

I have been blessed by those who have influenced my thinking in the past and present, and whose opinion I will no doubt rely on in the future. Special thanks to:

- Laura McCarty, Mary Thompson, and Craig Ellenbecker for taking the time to read the manuscript.
- Amy Thurk, a high school and college friend for proofreading.
- Lori and Larry Wilhelm for their creativity and patience with the cover.
- Jim Vollmer, a retired English teacher from Campbellsport High School for proofreading and advice.
- Kelly Rybold, for her support and listening throughout.
- Bill McConkey, my mentor and friend who has always reminded me real leadership is about serving the people.

I would like to thank Rick and Barb Heisler, two very influential people in my life who have been so patient in all their help. Lastly, I would like to thank Jim and Deb McCarty, my parents.

ISBN: 0-9714497-3-2

The Last One Standing

Copyright©: 2007

Karl D. McCarty
Quiet Side Publishing Co.
All rights reserved.

~For Kay Beisbier~

Karl McCarty: *The Last One Standing*

Table of Contents

Introduction (5)

Forward (6)

Part I: The Democrats (7)
Senator Evan Bayh (8)
Senator Joe Biden (13)
Retired General Wesley Clark (22)
Senator Hillary Rodham Clinton (25)
Former Senator Tom Daschle (33)
Senator Chris Dodd (36)
Former Senator John Edwards (40)
Senator Russ Feingold (45)
Former Senator Mike Gravel (53)
Former Vice President Al Gore (58)
Senator John Kerry (63)
Representative Dennis Kucinich (76)
Senator Barack Obama (79)
Governor Bill Richardson (90)
Former Governor Tom Vilsack (96)
Former Governor Mark Warner (103)

Part II: The Republicans (112)
Former Senator George Allen (113)
Senator Sam Brownback (126)
Former Senate Majority Leader Bill Frist (136)
Former Governor Jim Gilmore (145)
Former House Speaker Newt Gingrich (148)
Former New York Mayor Rudy Giuliani (152)
Senator Chuck Hagel (164)
Former Governor Mike Huckabee (170)
Representative Duncan Hunter (176)
Senator John McCain (182)
Representative Ron Paul (192)
Former Governor George Pataki (198)
Former Governor Mitt Romney (207)
Representative Tom Tancredo (215)
Former Senator Fred Thompson (219)
Former Governor Tommy Thompson (223)
Former Senator Rick Santorum (227)
New York Mayor Michael Bloomberg (233)

Afterword (236)

Introduction

American voters are force fed a constant series of sound bytes, slogans, blogging biases and sports metaphors. From all of that they try to become informed citizens.

I hope this book provides an important service, a carefully documented report and unbiased analysis of nearly three-dozen candidates for the U.S. Presidency in 2008. Every credible candidate is included to illustrate the length and severity of the "invisible primary" before the Iowa Caucus. Some folks were left out; Al Sharpton, Mark Sanford, Ed Rendell, Haley Barbour, Frank Keating, Dick Armey, and Jeb Bush, just to name a few. It could be argued that others should have been included and some excluded; but my list is what it is and I think it will be helpful.

This book is not meant in any way to slant the reader's view towards Republicans, Democrats or Independents. Truth is hard to find and is not owned by any one; neither are hopes, humor, tragedies, mistakes or ideas.

Karl McCarty
Campbellsport
Fond du Lac County
Wisconsin
October 11, 2007

Forward

The consent of the governed is a powerful, yet dangerous idea. Americans select folks to govern through the nomination and election process. These people then have our consent to go and do things. Some of the things they do in our name are good things; some are not.

We are often disappointed and we are often misled. We almost always select our politicians without enough information to make an intelligent choice. The blame lies primarily with the print journalists and their newspapers and television newscasts. They feed us far too little information and far too many slogans and photo-ops. The candidates share the blame also for following rather than leading and parroting rather than educating. And, as citizens, we do not demand nearly enough hard information.

Karl McCarty has done a great service with this book. He gives us a great deal of information, with detailed documentation.

I was an instructor of Karl McCarty's at the University of Wisconsin in Oshkosh. He is an extremely bright young man, a great researcher and writes a book that is easy to read. It is also an important one.

William C. McConkey, Ph.D.
Baileys Harbor
Door County
Wisconsin

Part I: The Democrats

Bayh
Biden
Clark
Clinton
Daschle
Dodd
Edwards
Feingold
Gravel
Gore
Kerry
Kucinich
Obama
Richardson
Vilsack
Warner

Senator Evan Bayh

The Bayh name was familiar to Iowans, as Evan's father Birch ran for the 1976 Democratic nomination. Evan also helped his dad in his last U.S. Senate campaign in 1980, when Birch lost to the young Dan Quayle (R-IN) during the 1980 Republican landslide.[1] Birch Bayh was a leading advocate in the Senate for ethanol production and helped Indiana become a leader in the grain-derived fuel.[2] The younger Bayh has been one of the most conservative Democrats in the Senate. He is not like his liberal father.[3]

He was elected governor in 1998, and was the first Democrat in two decades to hold that Indiana office, and became the youngest chief executive in the country at the age of 33.[4] He was often called a "Republicrat' who worked the center, and "He never raised taxes and he left office with a humming state economy, low unemployment and a record budget surplus."[5] By the time his tenure ended he had a 79 percent approval rating.[6] Bayh was asked to give the keynote address at the 1996 Democratic National Convention, and then was elected to the Senate in 1998.[7] *US News & World Report* (Feb.2001) also reported his outstanding record as governor: "Bayh does have what many of his [possible presidential] competitors would lack, namely a record as governor when he cut taxes, Medicare spending, and welfare rolls and left the state with a then record budget surplus. One television ad during his 1998 Senate campaign was titled 'Conservative,' and it proudly pitched him as a 'real fiscal conservative.'"[8]

Bayh had long-held presidential ambitions

Bayh had already considered running in 2004 but opted out. Ironically, a *US News & World Report* article from February 2001 could have been cut and pasted four years later for an article on the 2008 presidential campaign. The article reported "history and hunches" said Bayh was running for president: he had emerged as "a prominent dissenting Democratic voice" in the early days of President Bush's first term, and Bayh had voted against Attorney General John Ashcroft's confirmation, then attacked the Bush tax cuts.[9] He had experience in positioning to the left and would do so again after the 2004 elections. Also, in his first testing-the-water experience for the presidency, Bayh had been buoyed for being mentioned as Gore's running mate, and in February 2001 had "recently ascended" to the Democratic Leadership Council chair.[10] Bayh released a biography in 2003, *From Father to Son: A Private Life in the Public Eye.*[11] His young twin boys were cited as the first reason he did not run in 2004.

He was considered for vice president in 2004, but this may have been more by pundits than by John Kerry. Indiana went Republican in presidential races and the state may only have moved to a 'swing' state if Bayh had been given the vice presidential nomination. Considering John Edwards did not win his home state of North Carolina for Kerry in 2004, Bayh would not likely have carried Indiana for Kerry. The majority of voters don't vote for vice presidents; they vote for the presidential nominee.

Bayh hugs the center

Evan Bayh was interviewed by the *Terre Haute Tribune-Star* in August 2005. His answers displayed a concerted effort to appeal to values. "It's my belief that being a good candidate and perhaps serving as a good president is consistent with being a good father...If I ever conclude that it's not and I've got to choose, I'll choose being a good father," said Bayh.[12] If his mom were alive, Bayh said she would say, "'Make sure your children and your wife are taken care of. And once you do that, if you can serve your country, that would be a noble thing to do.'"[13] *US News & World Report* said (Feb. 2001) his approach "may represent the return of the family-values Democrat, a potent antidote to the Clinton era."[14] He irritated regular Democratic constituencies by voting for the partial birth abortion ban in 1999 and for Permanent Normal Trade Relations (PNTR) with China in 2000.[15]

Within days after the 2004 election, a moderate Democrat organization officially sprouted with Bayh's help. The Third Way believed "Conservative ideas now dominate not only in their traditional strongholds, like the South and the mountain west, but also in central Pennsylvania, upstate New York, southwestern Oregon, and virtually all of rural, suburban and exurban Michigan, Illinois and Minnesota."[16] And "Progressives must find new policies and messages that better connect with moderate and middle class Americans, particularly in those places where our ideas have lost resonance."[17] Bayh was named an Honorary Senate Chair for the organization. Quoted in the *Washington Post*, Bayh stated (11.11.04), "The answer to the ideological extremes of the right has to be more than rigid dogma from the left."[18] Did that mean Bayh felt John Kerry's campaign had too much rigid dogma? Joining Bayh with Third Way were Southern Democratic Senators Mary Landrieu (LA), Blanch Lincoln (AR), and Mark Pryor (AR).[19]

Third Way was an organization very similar to the Democratic Leadership Council, which started in 1985 with the help of Indiana native Al From after Walter Mondale's loss to Ronald Reagan in 1984. The DLC eventually spawned a think tank, the Progressive Policy Institute; and a political advocacy organization called the New Democratic Network.[20] Ties to the DLC and the Third Way meant a concerted effort by Bayh to be moderate. Evan Bayh led the DLC since 2001. In November 2004, as he laid the groundwork for 2008, Bayh still held the position (in July 2005, Tom Vilsack became DLC chair).[21] He also was a member of the Senate Centrist Coalition—a group of moderates from both parties that met regularly to find compromise.[22]

Bayh is still seen as a centrist. An *ABC News/AP* report called him (12.3.06) a senator who "has charted a relatively centrist course in the Senate."[23] *Reuters* said he was "considered more moderate than some of the other likley" candidates "such as" Clinton and Obama, and labeled him "more conservative than many of the other" Democrats running.[24]

Bayh was on his way to declaring
  Bayh did not immediately announce his candidacy after the 2006 midterms, and basically told reporters (11.9.06) the country did not know what his party stood for despite winning on Nov. 7: "It's up to us to prove that we're something better than just a mirror image of the people they voted against. And if we serve up a highly partisan, ideologically extreme, Democratic version of what they just voted against, we're not going to do very well."[25] Bayh's words were a slap in the face to Democrats who were just anti-status quo rather than offering an agenda.
  Monetarily, he was much closer to Hillary Clinton in comparing Senate campaign accounts, but Bayh's coffers compared to Clinton because she unloaded tons of cash in her 2006 Senate race—not because of Bayh's success in fundraising. Clinton had $13 million in her Senate account, compared to Bayh's $10.5 million as of September 30, 2006.[26] Evan Bayh, like Kerry, was criticized for not giving $1 million to the Democratic Senatorial Campaign Committee.[27] So he consolidated his midterm donations to his home state, and gave Indiana's Democratic Party $100,000 for three important House races.[28] As of December, he had a formidable crew in Iowa as reported by the *Des Moines Register* (12.17.06): "Bayh had put two dozen campaign staffers - paid by his political action committee - to work on Iowa legislative campaigns during the fall election season and had visited the state nine times in the past two years."[29]
  Bayh appeared on ABC's *This Week* (12.3.06), and was coy on his eventual ambitions: "As the people get to know me, I think we'll do very well. I've been a successful two-term governor with a record of delivering results. I now have national security experience from my presence in the Senate...Is this a little bit like David and Goliath? A little bit, but as I recall, David did OK."[30] He announced he would set up an exploratory committee and after the holidays make a final decision.[31] The show billed the interview with Bayh as an 'exclusive.'[32] After his appearance on *This Week*, Bayh went to Iowa, then New Hampshire.[33]

The end of Bayh
  So it was a shocker when Evan Bayh told the *Indianapolis Star* he was leaving the presidential race.[34] The *International Herald Tribune* said the decision "stunned many Democrats."[35] The *Des Moines Register* reported the decison "surprised Iowa party activists."[36] Indeed, Iowa state representative Janet Petersen (Des Moines) talked to Bayh (12.4.06) and told the *Register*, "They were still talking about getting ready to announce."[37] His departure on December 16 came when only a handful of candidates on the Democratic side had officialy entered the 2008 race (Tom Vilsack, Dennis Kucinich, and Mike Gravel).[38]

Why did he leave the race?
  1) Some cited his lack of charisma. The *Indianapolis Star* reported of Bayh's shortcomings, "including a cautious personality that lacks star power, [which] could be a challenge if he tries to compete on a national stage."[39]
  2) Obama completely overshadowed Bayh. The Democratic field was crowded, particularly with Obama entering the presidential race informally by late

2006. In his All America PAC statement e-mailed to supporters, Bayh said "Whether there were too many Goliaths or whether I'm just not the right David, the fact remains that at the end of the day, I concluded that, due to circumstances beyond our control, the odds were longer than I felt I could responsibly pursue."[40] Of course, days earlier Bayh recalled 'David did OK.'

The *Indianapolis Star* reported (12.3.06) in an article on Bayh's exploratory committee that "The candidates most expected to dominate the field if they run include" Clinton and Obama.[41] Obama was weeks fresh; Bayh was a tired candidate having already invested heavily in trips to Iowa and New Hampshire.

Bayh's investment had little return. When Bayh was speaking to Democrats from Keene and Cornish N.H. (12.10.06), the *AP* noted Obama, "a potential rival in the 2008 Democratic primary, drew much larger crowds Sunday in Portsmouth and Manchester."[42] A posting on *Boston.com* noted, "while staff members for Bayh may have to scramble to find 50 people to show up for his three events, Obama has a guaranteed audience of 2,225," and people from 13 states showed up at the Obama rallies.[43] The *AP* reported (12.16.06), "...his appearance was barely noticed as Obama delivered two speeches to sold-out crowds and drew hordes of media."[44] The *Washington Post* reported (12.24.06): "As Bayh drew small crowds on his seventh trip to the Granite State, Obama enjoyed sold-out audiences and saturation coverage on his first."[45] Bayh scored only three percent in the *NBC News/Wall Street Journal* nationwide poll (12.8-11.06)—and that finish was high for Bayh.[46]

To make matters worse, when Obama went to New Hampshire he said the country's foreign policy should be "tough and smart,"[47] and stole Evan Bayh's phrase on foreign policy used months earlier. Bayh's connection to strategist Anita Dunn, and Dunn's conection to Obama adds to the belief the Bayh dropped out because of Obama—or Bayh certainly knew in the inside channels how hot the Illinois Senator was. The *International Herald Tribune* reported (12.17.06), "To some extent, Bayh's withdrawal reflects the degree to which Obama and Clinton have dominated the early going of this race, threatening to soak up campaign contributions and, as Bayh witnessed last weekend, news coverage."[48] But Bayh's aides said no specific rival forced him out.[49] In comparison to Bayh, John Edwards had comparable crowds to Obama in New Hampshire when he visited days after Bayh dropped out. So the problem was not necessarily Obama, but Bayh.

3) Bayh supported the 2003 invasion. Bayh was "one of the first Democrats to support military action in Iraq. But in December 2005, he changed his position, saying he would not have supported legislation" for the authorization if the facts used by the White House had been presented accurately.[50] Of course, Sens. Ted Kennedy (MA), Russ Feingold (WI), Dick Durbin (IL), and twenty other Senators intially voted against authorization for force in Iraq in October 2002.

Is Bayh a strong VP candidate?

Despite his vote for the war, Evan Bayh could have offered a strong path for Democrats to win in Republican leaning states, and also exemplified how to be strong on defense while being critical of the war. He dropped out of the presidential contest in December 2006 before many realized his campaign existed, but the early exit may have raised his chances as a vice presidential candidate.

An op-ed in the *Indianapolis Star* by Ken Bode (12.22.06) said Bayh was "solid" as running mate material, because in the VP slot Bayh's "charisma deficit will actually be an asset," not to mention the geography of Bayh as a Midwesterner, and "his strong election record in Indiana raises the possiblity that on the ticket, he might turn his home state blue."[51] Bayh's appearance as a strong family man make him a viable vice president as well.

At the very least, Bayh appeared remarkably honest in his departure, and left the field gracefully. In his weekly commentary, CBS's Bob Schieffer lauded Bayh's comments on the Goliaths of 2008:

> In other words, he took a look, realized he had no chance and decided not to waste his time or the country's. How refreshing! None of this "I decided I wanted to spend more time with my family," or the catalogue of excuses we've come to expect from usual wanna-bes — or even worse, one of those ego trip campaigns that all involved know is headed nowhere except to get some TV time for the candidate. Bayh just concluded it wasn't to be and said so. The one downside is, that is just the kind of straight talk we need more of in politics. A man so candid about himself and his chances might have had some interesting thoughts on other subjects. In a way, I'm sorry we won't get to hear them.[52]

The *Des Moines Register* reported (rather complimentarily) he was the "second centrist Democrat with proven fund-raising ability and who had made inroads in Iowa to decide not to run for president [with Mark Warner being the first]."[53] But Bayh's vice presidential hopes may be dimming. Bayh has considered running for president twice. He is not the rising star anymore.

Senator Joe Biden

Joe Biden was elected to the US Senate from Delaware in 1972, but weeks later his wife and daughter died in an auto accident, and his two boys were injured.[54] He decided to stay in politics. Biden himself may be forming into an icon in the Senate, and ironically gave legendary Sen. Strom Thurmond's eulogy in July 2003.[55] In 2006, his son Beau was elected Delaware Attorney General, the state's second most powerful position.[56] Sen. Biden commutes to Washington D.C. everyday from Wilmington, Delaware by Amtrak—an 80 minute ride.[57]

Biden gained notoriety when he became a force on the Judiciary Committee in the 1980s. He was the ranking Democrat on the committee from 1981-1987 and 1995-1997, and in between those two time frames he was the chairman.[58] He retained his senior member spot on the Judiciary Committee after the 2006 midterms.[59]

Biden had a moderate-to-liberal voting record.[60] With successful credit card companies (MNBA) in Delaware, he often sided with the industry in bankruptcy bills.

Biden became the ranking member of the Foreign Relations Committee in 1997 and chairman in 2001 (just before 9/11),[61] and was ranking member until January 2007, when he reassumed the chair. This committee helped Biden mold his moderate image as a Democrat who could aggressively address foreign policy issues. Biden has worked well with Chair/Ranking Republican Dick Lugar (R-IN) over the years on the committee.

Biden himself had never ruled out a second run for the White House, even for 2004. Given the Democrats hesitance to give another northeastern liberal the nomination in 2008, in hindsight, perhaps Biden should have run in 2004.

What happened in the 1988 Biden campaign?

In 1987, Biden ran for the 1988 Democratic nomination. The campaign was cut short when a video, made by a staffer on Massachusetts Governor Michael Dukakis's campaign, showed Biden using British Labour Party leader Neil Kinnock's words without crediting him.[62] Politicians use similar words from others to paraphrase other politicians. For example, as Bill Whalen of *The Weekly Standard* found, Biden was also criticized for mimicking Robert F. Kennedy's 1968 words. RFK said, "The gross national product ... does not include the beauty of our poetry or the strength of our marriages, the intelligence of our public debate or the integrity of our public officials. It measures neither our wit nor our devotion to our country."[63] Biden said in 1987 "This standard ... doesn't measure the beauty of our poetry, the strength of our marriages, the intelligence of our public debate, the integrity of our public officials. It counts neither our wit nor our wisdom, neither our compassion nor our devotion to our country."[64] Biden's borrowing of RFK's words may not be entirely ethical, but it is frequent in politics.

But can you borrow another person's biography? Biden did. Kinnock asked:

> Why am I the first Kinnock in a thousand generations to be able to get to university? Was it because our predecessors were thick? Was it because they were weak, those people who worked eight hours underground and then come up and play football, weak? It was because there was no platform upon which they could stand.[65]

Biden questioned:

> Why is it that Joe Biden is the first in his family to ever go to a university? Was it because our fathers and mothers were not bright? Is it because they didn't work hard, my ancestors who worked in the coal mines of northeast Pennsylvania and would come up after 12 hours and play football for four hours? It's because they didn't have a platform upon which to stand.[66]

As Bill Whalen wrote, "the Kinnock mimicry was more grievous offense since Biden used his words to reinvent his own biography. In reality, Biden grew up in suburban Wilmington, the son of a car salesman and grandson of a Pennsylvania state senator."[67]

The Dukakis campaign secretly distributed the video to news outlets showing Biden and Kinnock's speeches.[68] The Dukakis campaign denied any part in the recording's disbursement, but the truth became evident so Dukakis fired the two who constructed the attack: his campaign manager, John Sasso, as well as his political director, Paul Tully.[69] Dukakis said he had no prior knowledge of Tully's and Sasso's actions.[70]

When the Biden campaign fell apart, Biden was working on the controversial Robert Bork Supreme Court confirmation hearings in Washington D.C. Biden was at the height of both his presidential campaign and his Senate career when he crashed. "Its time for me to assess my mistakes and make sure that I don't make them again," stated Biden on the day he withdrew from the campaign.[71] Rhodes Cook described the plagiarism ordeal:

> The episode cut short a promising candidacy. At the time of his candidacy, Biden had raised more money than any other Democrat except Dukakis. After a slow start, he also was showing progress in the Iowa polls. But, like [Gary] Hart, Biden lacked a dedicated personal constituency to act as a safety net in his time of political crisis. Of the Democratic candidates [for 1988], only [Jesse] Jackson had run for president before and only he had an identifiable constituency, among fellow blacks, whose support he could count on through thick and thin."[72]

Would voters disregard the plagiarism in 2008? In the fall of 2006, he was still commenting on 1988. He told the *Providence Journal*, "Twenty years ago, I made a mistake. Twenty years ago, I learned a whole hell of a lot getting up off my knees."[73] An *AP* article (12.25.06) said Biden was behind Clinton, Obama, Edwards, and Kerry in a NBC/*Wall Street Journal* poll, rehashed the Neil Kinnock episode, and hinted Biden "can also be a little long-winded."[74]

The only good that came out of 1988 was Biden's health. He was beginning the onset of a brain aneurysm and might have died had he been campaigning instead of seeing a doctor.[75] The cerebral aneurysm occurred on the eve of the 1988 New Hampshire primary.[76]

Biden was never coy about seeking the nomination, and in 2005 he all but said he was running for 2008; some suggest he threw his hat in the ring in December 2004 during an interview on *Imus in the Morning*. Perhaps Biden immediately entered the race (though unofficially) right after the 2004 elections so the media would re-cover his 1988 campaign saga (in Biden introductory stories) so his disgrace would be watered down by 2008.

Biden 'compliments' Indian Americans

In a July 2006 trip to New Hampshire, Biden said "In Delaware, the largest growth of population is Indian Americans, moving from India. You cannot go to a 7/11 or a Dunkin' Donuts unless you have a slight Indian accent. I'm not joking."[77] The comments aired on C-SPAN's *Road to the White House* series.[78]

Biden really did not apologize. He told MSNBC (7.7.06), "It was meant as a compliment."[79] The same day, he told CNN's *The Situation Room*, "I could have said that 40 years ago about walking into a delicatessen and saying an Italian accent in my state."[80] Biden's spokeswoman did not apologize either:

> The point Senator Biden was making is that there has been a vibrant Indian-American community in Delaware for decades. It has primarily been made up of engineers, scientists and physicians, but more recently, middle-class families are moving into Delaware and purchasing family-run small businesses. These families have greatly contributed to the vibrancy of the Indian-American community in Delaware and are making a significant contribution to the national economy as well.[81]

At the very least, Biden's comments brought back clips of Hillary's famous gaffe in January 2004. While campaigning for Nancy Farmer's Senate campaign in Missouri, Clinton quoted Gandhi "He ran a gas station down in St. Louis," and when laughs died down, said "No, Mahatma Gandhi was a great leader of the 20th century," then actually quoted Gandhi, "First they ignore you, then they laugh at you, then they fight you, then you win."[82] Clinton apologized and said the comments were "a lame attempt at humor."[83]

Let's give a hand to Delaware: a slave state!

How did he rank with southernors like Mark Warner and John Edwards in 2008? Biden said (8.27.06), "Better than anybody else. You don't know my state. My state was a slave state. My state was a border state. My state has the eighth-largest black population in the country," and Delaware is anyting but "a Northeast liberal state."[84] As one blogger sarcastically translated: "My state also has a fine history of hating black people and we still got a lot of them to put up with. Southern white racists will come to think of Deleware as just like home."[85]

Biden clearly bashed Obama

On the day Joe Biden announced his candidacy for president on the internet, a *New York Observer* interview got him in trouble.[86] The Biden quote on Obama which was often showed on news reports was: "I mean, you got the first sort of mainstream African-American. Who is articulate and bright and clean and a nice-looking guy. I mean, that's a storybook, man."[87]

What really occurred? Biden said "I mean, you got the first sort of mainstream African-American." A man [the reporter from the Observer] affirmed with a "Yes." And Biden continued with "Who is articulate and bright and clean and a nice-looking guy. I mean, this—that's a storybook, man."[88]

In a conference call (1.31.07) Biden said "My mother has an expression: clean as a whistle, sharp as a tack. That's the context. He's crisp and clear."[89] By the end of the night, he tried to laugh it off. Biden told *The Daily Show*, "Look, the other part of this thing that got me in trouble is using the word clean. I should have said fresh. What I meant was that he's got new ideas, he's a new guy on the block..."[90] The *AP* reported "But then Biden trailed off as he stared into Stewart's deadpan face. 'It's not working, right?'"[91] Biden told Stewart "I spoke to Barack today...," and Stewart replied, "I bet you did."[92] Biden said he also spoke to the Rev. Al Sharpton, Stewart added, "And Michael Jordan and anybody you could get your hands on. The Jackson Five. Who else?"[93]

Obama 'staffed up'

Wasn't Biden just trying to say Obama was the most credible black candidate in US history? How did Obama respond? Initially on the day Biden's quote went public, Obama said "I mean, you would have to ask Senator—Senator Biden what—what he was thinking. I don't spend too much time worrying about what folks are talking about during the campaign season."[94] Biden said (2.2.07), "Well, I heard his first statement saying he understood what I meant. And then I heard his second statement..."[95] Chris Matthews told Biden, "Then he [Obama] got staffed up, right?"[96]

Hours later, Obama said he did not take "Senator Biden's comments personally, but obviously they were historically inaccurate. African-American presidential candidates like Jesse Jackson, Shirley Chisholm, Carol Moseley Braun, and Al Sharpton gave a voice to many important issues through their campaigns, and no one would call them inarticulate."[97] Biden said, in response to Matthew's suggestion whether Obama was staffed up, "Well, I don't know about that..."[98] Matthews rehashed the same argument later in the interview: "Yes. Well, he was careful. But he issued a statement two [hours] after the first one. The first one was beneficial to you. Two hours later he said, obviously, historically you were inaccurate because you suggested and this is where his judgment came in politically—he put you in a position of saying people like Jesse Jackson and Al Sharpton are not articulate, the one thing their worst enemies would say they are. So he was using your statement to get you, wasn't he? He was playing hardball here."[99] Biden said "Well, look, it's a hardball game."[100]

The media ripped Biden apart. Keith Olbermann said (1.31.07), "He calls Senator Obama the first 'mainstream African-American, who is articulate and bright and clean and a nice-looking guy.' He blasts John Edwards about Iraq, calls Senator Clinton's plan about Iraq a disaster, and right now, this man knows his disasters."[101] Chris Matthews asked "Is this 'gotcha' journalism jumping on your back?"[102] And Matthews told Biden, in reference to the criticism of Biden attacking Clinton and Edwards on Iraq, "There seems to be some new standard out there which I don't understand or like, which you can't criticize your opponent."[103] Should Biden drop out of the race ASAP? *Washington Post* reporter Dana Milbank opined: "Well, let's hope he doesn't. We could have a year and a half of these, and we treasure every one of them, going back when he used so many words in his last run for president, he ran out of them, and he had to start... quoting Neil Kinnock, the British labor leader, using his speeches."[104]

Wilmington was a base of Biden's support, and Delaware was in the top ten states with the highest African-American population.[105] The truth was Biden's political career was aided by his support for civil rights.

What are Biden's strengths?

1) Foreign policy. Had John Kerry won in 2004, Biden was on a shortlist to be Secretary of State.[106] The *AP* described him as "one of his party's most experienced spokesmen on international affairs."[107]

When the Senate surprisingly went Democratic with the 2006 midterms, it meant Joe Biden would lead the Senate Foreign Relations Committee, which he last chaired in 2003.[108] As NBC's Chip Reid reported (11.9.06), "And if you think you've seen a lot of Senator Joe Biden, get ready for a lot more when he becomes chairman of the Foreign Relations Committee."

2) Biden can connect with voters. Republican pollster Frank Luntz tested Iowa and New Hampshire opinions of the Democratic candidates for '08 in the Spring of 2006 with focus group audiences and found "Biden and Warner were the only ones they wanted to hear more from."[109] Luntz said Biden was the only Democratic candidate whose ratings did not plummet when he mentioned the topic of religion or faith.[110] This is opposed to Tom Vilsack, who did so poorly on religion with the focus groups—even in Iowa, as Luntz said "Democrats don't want to hear about your church. If they really cared, they'd be Republican."[111] Clinton, for example, told an audience (6.25.06) "that as a child attending Sunday school she would baby-sit the children of migrant workers so that their older siblings could join their parents at work."[112] That may have very well been the case. But what did secular Democrats think? And did she throw the 'migrants' in there to appeal to Latinos? Biden came across as authentic, and not pushy.

Biden knows how to sprinkle religion into his repertoire without having listeners role their eyes. He once opened a speech (9.10.01): "My mother wanted me to be a priest or a politician, and for the longest time I didn't think you could do both. But you can. Any rate, obviously not a lot of Irish-Catholics in this room."[113] In Dover, New Hampshire (6.17.06), Biden continued his message of what the Democratic nominee needed in 2008: "they'd better be able to ante up …two things: security and faith…..If we can't negotiate the faith issue, we won't win."[114] When he discused Iraq on *FOX News Sunday* (8.27.06), three different times he said he prayed things were turning around in Iraq; the three 'prays' were followed by 'buts' (…but… I don't think there's any reasonable prospect…but I'm doubtful of that….but look what we've had to do).[115]

Luntz said when Biden "looks people in the eye and tells a joke, he connects. When he reads, he doesn't. In an effort to demonstrate intelligence, he loses on the charisma, and it's clear he could have both."[116] Luntz concluded that Kerry and Feingold bashed the president too much, Warner was polished, Clinton was "highly partisan, overly negative," Bayh did not make an impression, Edwards was seen as charismatic to some, and "too slick" by others; and Richardson had big ideas on domestic programs, but some found him boring and one focus member said he should lose weight.[117]

3) Biden's personal life is of role-model quality. Biden lacks the promiscuity of Gingrich, Dodd, Giuliani, and others. Biden "was never linked with actresses, models or late-night carousing. Five years later [after the death of his first wife], Biden remarried and had another daughter."[118] Unfortunately his 1988 campaign tarnishes some of his credibility on moral issues.

4) Biden is one of the few who want to talk about Iraq. In May 2006, Joe Biden announced his de-centralization plan for Iraq, and to give local control to Sunnis, Shiites, and Kurds. Into February 2007, Biden was still saying, "To those who disagree with my plan, I have one simple question: what is your alternative?"[119] And in April 2007, Biden still said the country was "faced with two false choices in Washington. One, stay the course with Bush, and hand it off, or leave, and hope for the best."[120] His descriptions were a bit simplistic, but he heightened a glaring weakness of his party.

Biden had asked Howard Dean, the Democratic National Committee chair, to support a presidential debate to be devoted solely to Iraq.[121] His website posted it proudly, and posted quotes from other news outlets. The *Concord Monitor* said (5.2.07), Biden was "absolutely right about one thing: 60 seconds is not enough time to debate the future of Iraq," and supported his suggestion.[122] The *Des Moines Register*'s David Yepsen wrote (5.8.07), a debate should be held on Iraq and America's role in the world.[123] And Biden's website included a quote from Obama's spokesman, who told CNN (4.27.07) after the South Carolina debate, "Obviously we're dealing with big issues. It's sometimes not easy to compress how to fix Iraq into a 60-second answer."[124]

Biden held the Iraq-only debate on June 6, 2007. What was the result? Only Dennis Kucinich and Mike Gravel showed up, but Biden had an immigration debate in the Senate, so he had to cede the stage to Gravel for 40 minutes.[125] In that eternity on stage, Gravel "repeatedly" called himself "the crazy uncle," and compared Gen. Petraeus to Gen. Westmoreland.[126] Kucinich was also late, but came before Biden. Biden arrived at nine o'clock, and the crowd, according to an *AP* report, was relieved after being "somewhat restless and befuddled."[127] Biden's debate on Iraq was more like a sideshow. Why did Biden give in so early with his Iraq-only debate in June 2007?

The Democrats held a presidential debate on black issues, and a forum on gay rights. A debate on the most pressing issue for the country: Iraq…well, that was too much to ask from Clinton, Obama, and Edwards.

Weaknesses for Biden

1) Can he win liberal voters in the primaries? Would he continue being a moderate Senator or be pushed to the left during the primaries? Biden told the *Delaware News Journal* (April 2006) that "I may not be what the party is looking for….I may be too 'muscular' on foreign policy. I may not be 'pure' enough about abortion rights [he voted to ban the so-called partial birth abortion procedure]. I may not have been energetic enough about gay marriage [he voted for a 1996 congressional resolution against gay marriage]."[128]

He named his PAC 'Unite Our States' for a reason. But when he visited Iowa (10.31), he said Republicans were more interested in tax cuts than paying for homeland security.[129] Yet, even as late as January 2007 he was still complimented by Republicans. Sen. Lindsey Graham (R-SC) said (1.7.07) "He plays well in South Carolina," but added "I don't want to hurt his chances."[130]

The *Delaware News Journal* reported (5.7.06) "The online activists who gave Howard Dean's campaign such a boost in 2004 tend to ignore him or lambaste him as 'Biden (D-MBNA)'—a dig at his support for the unpopular bankruptcy bill championed by Delaware's credit card industry, and MBNA, which was bought out in January [2006] by Bank of America."[131] Biden's initial support for the Iraq war did not help his rapport with online activists either.[132]

2) Biden has no rock star status. If he did, it was in 1988. In the polls, Biden is far from the front tier Democrats. A Rasmussen report (released 1.12.07) showed Biden losing extensively to Giuliani (54-35) and McCain (48-36).[133] Biden was viewed favorably by 35 percent, unfavorably by 38 percent, and 27 percent did not have an opinion.[134]

How many chances does one get to run for president? Often many get only one—and if it they get two, it seldom happens 20 years after the first. Critics wondered who would vote Rip Van Winkle for President. There was no Biden-mania—Clinton, Gore, and Obama would take up valuable media hype. But Kerry was clearly slipping in the polls after the 'botched joke,' and was getting in Biden's range to pass. Then Kerry dropped out of the race. The loss of Evan Bayh and Tom Vilsack from the field also helped Biden, as the Indiana Senator pulled national security support and the Iowa Governor was a centrist.

However, Bill Richardson offers many similarities to Biden, and Richardson's strengths on foreign policy may cancel Biden's prowess on international issues.

3) Biden bluntly criticizes other Democrats. In August 2003, Biden said "The guy I'm most inclined to support would be John Kerry. But John, I think, has to become, quite frankly, more decisive...I think John's being sort of modulated by a lot of the 'pros' around him instead of just saying what he thinks."[135]

Numerous times on the Iraq issue, he has all but laughed at his colleagues' proposals. Some respect his honesty, but others within the party may think he crosses the line in criticism. Biden is a rare candidate most often on offense, and recognizes primaries should be about debate.

4) Biden's verbosity. In the Sam Alito confirmation hearings in January 2006, as a member of the Judiciary Committee, Biden, "asked just five questions of Alito and spent the rest of his allotted 30 minutes talking."[136] Biden told *Hardball* "these hearings don't generate much of anything any more...you know, it's pretty well staged, there's a refusal to answer..."[137] True, but Biden himself was the problem at the hearings.

Biden put on Princeton (Alito's alma mater) hat during the questioning. And he recollected his Grandpa Finnigan to give a personal touch to the hearing.

Seriously. As Dana Milbank wrote, Biden "spoke about his own Irish American roots, his 'Grandfather Finnegan,' his son's application to Princeton (he attended the University of Pennsylvania instead, Biden said), a speech the senator gave on the Princeton campus, the fact that Biden is 'not a Princeton fan,' and his views on the eyeglasses of Sen. Dianne Feinstein (D-Calif)."[138]

Chris Matthews asked if Robert Bork was the "last honest man to testify in a confirmation hearing, because he told the truth and you guys bounced him for it. Now these guys come along slippery as greased pigs and you say they should be more honest, but the price of honesty is rejection. The benefit of dishonesty, of slipperiness is confirmation. Aren't you teaching these guys how to dance?"[139] Biden answered "Well, I guess…that's true."[140] Biden appeared on the *Today Show* and told Katie Couric the confirmation process is "kind of broken," but when Couric mentioned Robert Bork was rejected for his candor, Biden agreed Bork was forthcoming, "and the American people didn't agree with his views."[141]

In a *Newsweek* article titled 'Joe Biden: It's Time to Change the Conversation,' Biden said "we oughta just go straight to the Senate [for a vote on Supreme Court judges]."[142] *Newsweek* failed to point out Biden was the reason the 'conversation' was so bad, but discussed his ambitions as an 'aide to a Democratic senator' said the public, in looking at 2008, would think Biden was a "blowhard among blowhards" in the Senate.[143] Biden took the high road. "If my Achilles heel has to be 'I talk too much,' versus 'I'm a womanizer' or 'I'm dishonest' or whatnot, its fine, I set myself up for that."[144] This statement implied Biden was honest, a somewhat odd description coming from a plagiarizer.

Despite complementing Biden's abilities, Richard Cohen of the *Washington Post* called Biden an "anatomical disaster. His Achilles' heel is his mouth."[145] David Brooks, too, complimented Biden in an editorial titled "In praise of Joe Biden,"[146] in which the senator was praised for his "emotive vitality" and "by making candor the core of his self image, he has preserved the ability to think independently and to be honest with himself."[147] But *The Daily Show* ran a competition asking who was the "most long-winded," and divided the screen into quadrants timing Sens. DeWine, Biden, Leahy, and Kennedy at the Alito hearings. Who spoke the longest at the hearing before asking a question? Actually, Biden was not first, talking *only* 8 minutes, 39 seconds before asking a question (DeWine went over 9 minutes).[148]

Senators wanted airtime just as much as the judicial nominee's wanted to dodge questions. Biden's 'candor' could be confused with arrogance. In a one-segment-long interview on *Hardball* (1.19.06), Biden said, 'I,' 'I'm,' 'I think,' 'I really think,' 'I don't think,' about 40 times.[149] He told the *Delaware News Journal* he achieved the 2005 objectives he set to be on track to run for the 2008 nomination, including the goal of raising $2 million (surpassing it by $1 million).[150] Who would have thought Biden would admit reaching the goals he set for himself?

5) Biden is low on cash. Biden, who ended 2004 with just over half a million in his war-chest, stated (June 2005), "They tell me the ante just to get into

Iowa is $40 million" and said he would run for president and re-election to the Senate for 2008 simultaneously.[151] At the end of 2006 he had $3.5 million in his Senate account.[152]

His fundraising problems are quite evident, even though he had "strong debate performances."[153] In July 2007, even Richardson and Dodd had twice as much money as Biden. The *National Journal* said (7.23.07) Biden was running "an 'I'll just how up for the debates' campaign."[154] Running such a campaign won't make a frontrunner, and that critique signals a bad ending for Joe Biden's ambitions. But the *National Journal*'s assessment is really a sad commentary on the status of American politics. The *New York Observer* (Aug.2007) said, "It's a shame, but it looks like the only way Mr. Biden will make history when this campaign is over is as a curiosity: the candidate who won no delegates, but every debate."[155]

Retired General Wesley Clark

Clark entered the 2004 campaign in September 2003. The late start caused the General to skip the Iowa Caucus. Clark's candidacy ascended from a Draft Clark drive by supporters who thought Clark's background would solve the party's problems with the weak-on-foreign-policy stereotype. The cartoon *Doonesbury* gave a whole week's worth of Clark's run, including one of its character's reading a newspaper article: "'A brilliant, telegenic, Southern Rhodes Scholar, decorated Vietnam hero and ex-Supreme Commander of NATO.' Whew! I wonder if Bush has the slightest clue what he may be up against."[156]

An unclear message in 2004

But Clark made immediate mistakes after declaring his candidacy, and within days stated he 'probably' would have voted for the congressional resolution that authorized force in Iraq.[157] In addition, Clark spent a lot of his pre-candidacy days commenting on *CNN* and writing op-eds. On April 10, 2003 he wrote to the *London Times*: "Already the scent of victory is in the air,"[158] a much different sentiment than Clark's attitude when he decided he was 'probably' against the war. Hence, in an October 2003 presidential debate, Joe Lieberman said Clark "took six different positions on whether going to war was the right idea."[159]

Clark had other mishaps. He said "If I'm president…we are not going to have one of these incidents [terrorist attacks]."[160] But on *Meet the Press* (1.25.04) he said "no one can guarantee that there can't be another attack," but "we won't use fear as…a political agenda."[161] Having endorsed Clark, filmmaker Michael Moore told Clark supporters (1.17.04), "The general vs. the deserter [Bush]! That's the debate."[162] Clark's response was poor. Was there any evidence Bush was a deserter? Clark said, "I've never looked into those… I've heard those allegations."[163] So Clark was a presidential candidate repeating rumors. Clark called Moore "a man of conscience" and "he's done a lot of great things for ordinary people, working people, across America."[164]

Character concerns

Army Gen. Tommy Franks, who lead day-to-day operations in Iraq, said Clark would "absolutely not" make a good president.[165] When Franks and Barry McCaffrey were leading men on the battlefield in Desert Storm, Clark merely commanded the Army's national training center in California: his request for commanding battle was denied.[166] Why?

The *New Yorker* later reported that before he was a candidate, Clark stated he was leaning toward the Democratic Party because Bush strategist Karl Rove did not return his calls: "He later said he'd been joking, but some believe that Clark himself would have been happy to have had a role in Bush's war on terror."[167] Retired Gen. Hugh Shelton said "Wes won't get my vote."[168]

And in 1994, Clark was warned not to meet with Serbian officials suspected of ordering ethnic cleansing, but Clark, despite State Department protests, met with Serbian General Ratko Mladic, a war crimes suspect.[169] A picture was taken in which the men wore each other's hats; Clark said (11.16.03) "It was a mistake to accept gifts....And at the time, of course, Mladic was not an indicted war criminal."[170] On Mladic, then-Sec. of State, Lawrence Eagleburger said he was a suspected war criminal at the time the Clark-Mladic photo was taken.[171] And why did Clark apologize for accepting gifts if he made excuses for meeting with Mladic?

In the same 2003 interview, Clark admitted his intentions to testify before The Hague at Slobodan Milosevic's trial in December 2003.[172] So in 2003, Clark testified against a war criminal, but a decade earlier he posed for pictures with one.

A rising star exploded

Clark was the only Rhodes Scholar in the 2004 presidential race.[173] But it wasn't reflected in his decision to skip the Iowa Caucus.

Howard Dean was the frontrunner, but as Dean later summarized, "we got in a fight with Dick Gephardt and we both ended up third and fourth instead of first and second."[174] If only Clark was in Iowa when the brawl erupted, but Kerry and Edwards filled the gap. Clark was climbing fast in other states. Days before the Iowa Caucus, polls had Clark second to Dean (28) in New Hampshire with 20 percent, a point above Kerry and double Edwards' margin.[175] As Dan Balz of the *Washington Post* observed (1.18.04), "Things are moving. Wes Clark has had a very good few weeks up there. He has benefited from essentially having the state to himself," (while all the other candidates were in Iowa).[176] Kerry's military record, for some reason, hinted at credibility in foreign policy—which was Clark's message. The Clark campaign sunk. By the time Clark won the Oklahoma primary, his only victory, he was essentially out of the race.

In December 2006, Clark still owed $260,000 from his 2004 campaign, and according to the *AP,* he was waiting for the outcome of a federal audit before retiring his debt.[177]

Was Clark running for president in 2008?

His political action committee is called WESPAC, and he held his first fundraiser to fund the PAC in August 2005, when about 50 supporters gave $1,000 each.[178] When asked if he would run for President in 2008, he stated (Fall 2005) "I haven't given it any thought. I haven't ruled anything out."[179]

Clark visited Oklahoma in October 2005, and according to the *AP*, "at one point in his speech…Clark walked away from the podium and held up a nearby American flag and said it doesn't belong to the Republican Party."[180] Was this action appropriate for a retired General?

He continued to be a major contributor to *FOX News* as a military analyst. In the month of October 2005, for example, Clark appeared on *The O'Reilly Factor* (October 3), *At Large with Geraldo Rivera* (October 9), *Forbes on Fox* (October 15), and *Hannity and Colmes* (October 19).[181]

Clark campaigned hard for Democrats in 2006, but particularly veterans. It was evident he was still running for president in September 2006 when Carol Shea-Porter won the Democratic primary for Congress in New Hampshire, and

Clark immediately called her.[182] (Though the *PoliticsNH.com* headline was "I'd love to talk, Wes, but I've got Chris Dodd on hold…")[183] In October, he campaigned for Vietnam Veteran and Rep. Leonard Boswell in Iowa, and joked he "should've been here earlier last time [in 2004, when Clark skipped the Iowa caucus]."[184] He also told the *AP* (Dec.2006), "I think it was clear that I got in too late last time."[185]

He campaigned for Virginia's US Senate candidate Jim Webb with Michael J. Fox (an actor suffering from Parkinson's, and supporter for embryonic stem cell research) days before the midterms.[186] The headlines he drew in New Hampshire were all Iraq related. Campaigning for Carol Shea-Porter for Congress, the *Hampton Union* (10.25.06) read "Clark: A failing Mission," the *Portsmouth Herald* (10.21.06) article was titled "Clark Bashes Bush," as he campaigned for himself; and the *New Hampshire Union Leader* said "Shea-Porter, Clark blast Bush on Iraq Policy" in what was another stop for Shea-Porter in Manchester the same day Clark was in Portsmouth.[187] In Portsmouth, Clark said "Anyone want to quibble over whether (Iraq) is a civil war or not? It is. What we're doing is losing traction and losing troops."[188] Clark also appeared in a Ned Lamont commercial (Lamont, an anti-war Democrat, challenged Sen. Joe Lieberman in the August 2006 Connecticut primary).[189] This was the Clark who 'probably' would have voted for the war.

By December 2006, Palgrave Macmillan announced a deal with Clark for his third book, to be called *America's Son* with a scheduled release of fall 2007, which hinted he was still running for president.[190] And in January 2007, he administered the oath of office to Agriculture and Industries Commissioner Ron Sparks in Alabama.[191]

As a *National Review Online* blog asked (1.13.07), Was "this a brilliant use of below-the-radar grassroots outreach, collecting chits to be cashed in later? Or is this a sign that Clark has not much else to do in mid-January?"[192] The evidence in the above paragraphs is important because it is not clear whether Clark was running for President. He remained in the public eye, but was not as overtly running for president as Joe Biden or John Edwards had been.

Yahoo! News reported (2.5.07) Clark was "The only candidate who has not officially announced a candidacy or set up an 'exploratory' committee."[193] In an interview that was published July 1 by the *New York Times*, Wes Clark sounded like he was running for president again. "I haven't said I won't. I think about it every day."[194]

In September 2007, Gen. Clark endorsed Hillary Clinton for president. It is conceivable what Clark really wanted, as he toyed with running for president a second time, was a position as Secretary of State or Secretary of Defense for the next Clinton administration.

Senator Hillary Clinton

In February 2000, with polls showing she was at best even with Rudy Giuliani, she formally announced her candidacy for Senate.[195] In April, Giuliani announced his prostrate cancer, in May he announced his separation from his wife and days later he left the race.[196] Rick Lazio replaced Giuliani, but lost (43-55) despite raising $40 million.[197] Speculation was already rampant of her presidential ambitions, but she focused on her duties as Senator. For example, she turned down many national appearances, and did not appear on *Meet the Press* until the December after 9/11, and she built a reputation of respect in upstate New York by visiting it over 100 times by June of 2002.[198] Quinnipiac tracked Clinton's approval rating within the state of New York: which was below 40 percent in February 2001; it steadily increased to over 60 percent by September 2004.[199]

On the road to 2008

She created her political action committee, HILLPAC, in February 2001 with Harold Ickes as its chairman.[200] HILLPAC raised $3.2 million for the 2002 cycle and gave $1 million to Democrats nationwide ($21,000 in Iowa, $15,000 in New Hampshire);[201] of that $1 million, she gave nearly $600,000 to House candidates and over $240,000 to Senate candidates.[202] In 2004, the PAC gave $10,000 each to Bayh, Feingold, Dodd and Daschle's 2004 re-election bids, as well as Obama's campaign.[203] Some thought HILLPAC was a sign Clinton would run in 2004. John Kerry avoided her during his campaign. At the 2004 Democratic convention, Kerry did not allow her to speak in the prime-time lineup; he said Sen. Clinton simply did not ask to speak (she did introduce her husband).[204]

In August 2005, Jeanine Pirro announced she would run against Hillary Clinton for U.S. Senate. Pirro's husband was a convicted felon. Her kick off speech was brilliant. She reached the point of the address in describing her opponent. "Hillary Clinton:" At which point thirty seconds of embarrassment passed because Pirro was missing a page of her speech. "Do I have page 10?" asked Pirro. Ahh…no. Someone else obviously had it. When asked what was going through her head when she could not find the page, Pirro responded "Yeah, things happen. But 32 seconds or whatever it was doesn't compare to 5 years of [Clinton's] unaswered and unmet promises."[205] What a great idea for Pirro to restate the time that elapsed during the incident. The Democrats mocked Pirro in a poltical ad within days, concluding: "…Without a Script….She is Speechless."[206]

Pirro turned out not to even run for the Senate nomination after deciding she was more qualified to run for state attorney general. When a GOP candidate surfaced, Clinton obliterated her opponent. The amount spent was astronomical: Clinton exhausted $7 million in September 2006 while Sen. Feinstein, representing the larger state of California, spent $1.36 million in the same month, even though polls showed she was "in a closer race than Clinton."[207] But Clinton won convincingly. She had to.

There was never a surprise Hillary was running for president. As Jay Leno said (6.11.06), "Hey, did you see what happened? This weekend, a person was caught trying to jump over the White House fence after throwing a package over it. Turns out it was just Hillary Clinton with carpet samples. But it was scary, scary for a minute there."[208]

Hillary the Hawk

Clinton was the first New York Senator to sit on the Senate Armed Services Committee and the *National Journal* found that her voting record in 2004 on foreign policy issues was more conservative than all but five Democratic Senators in 2005.[209] The position padded the 'tough on defense' label she wanted.

She looked hawkish in her questioning of Vice Admiral Lowell Jacoby of the Director of the Defense Intelligence Agency (4.28.05). The grilling was replayed on *Meet the Press* (5.1.05), and a similar sound bite was played on ABC's *This Week*. Clinton asked Jacoby if North Korea had "the ability to arm a missile with a nuclear device?" Jacoby answered yes.[210] Clinton prodded: "Do you assess that North Korea has the ability to deploy a two-stage intercontinental nuclear missile that could successfully hit U.S. territory?"[211] Jacoby conceded this too. Clinton released a statement, calling Jacoby's remarks "the first confirmation, publicly, by the administration that the North Koreans have the ability to arm a missile with a nuclear device that can reach the United States…Put simply, they couldn't do that when George Bush became president, and now they can."[212] Senator Clinton continued to look tough on defense. And her comments came after the Robb-Silverman commission weeks earlier had stated that "the intelligence community knows disturbingly little about the nuclear programs of many of the world's most dangerous actors."[213]

So many questions for a 2008 candidate

1) Did front runner status help Clinton? Hillary Clinton evolved as the frontrunner for 2008 almost immediately after the 2004 election. The Democratic Party had a history of losing frontrunners. John Kennedy was not the Democratic frontrunner in 1960. In 1968, incumbent President Johnson, was stunned by Eugene McCarthy in New Hampshire. Edmund Muskie was the favorite before McGovern won the nomination in 1972. Walter Mondale's frontrunner status had fierce competition from Gary Hart in 1984. Bill Clinton was not the Party's initial choice in 1992. Howard Dean led just before he collapsed in the Iowa Caucus in 2004.

But even after the hype of 'Obama Mania' in late 2006, Sen. Clinton was still the frontrunner into the fall of 2007.

2) Would she be a good majority leader? Caught up in the Obama mania, the *Washington Post* reported (12.8.06), "her reluctance to hog the spotlight has earned her considerable goodwill—to the extent that some of her colleagues have speculated that she might become the top Democratic leader someday, should her presidential bid falter."[214] *The Sunday Times* (UK) claimed (9.3.06) "some" of Sen. Clinton's "closest advisors say she might opt out of the White House race and seek to lead her party in the Senate," and suggested Clinton could take over as the Senate minority leader in 2009 "from the lackluster Harry Reid."[215] The *Washington Note* said Reid privately told Clinton she could have the job if she did not run for president.[216] But in August 2006, she told *Nightline* she hoped America was ready for its first female president: "It just depends on when and if that happens…Stay tuned."[217]

3) Would Nancy Pelosi's leadership as Speaker affect Sen. Clinton? The *New York Times* reported on Pelosi's liberalism: "Aided by a highly partisan House, she has overseen the most uniform voting record of any Democratic caucus since the 1950s," and added, "….her voting record is among the most liberal in Congress," (10.31.06).[218] Is it beneficial for Clinton to be compared to the other most powerful woman in politics (a San Francisco liberal)?

4) What match-up best serves Clinton? When Michael Goodwin told her he thought 2008 would be Clinton vs. Rudy, "With that, she broke into a broad smile, slapped the tabletop in front of her with an open palm and said, eyes twinkling, 'Well, then, we would finish what we started.'"[219]

If Hillary Clinton wins the nomination early, and the GOP is undecided, will a more partisan, anti-Hillary Republican be the GOP nominee?

5) Is she too mechanical? Hillary Clinton supported legislation to criminalize the desecration of the US flag—but she still opposed a constitutional ban on flag attacks. She was a co-sponsor of Bob Bennett's (R-Utah) bill, which outlawed a protester intimidating one by burning the flag, burning someone else's flag, or desecrating it on federal property.[220] Some argued it was throwing a bone to those on the right, but in reality, Clinton said in the summer of 2004 that she did not support a constitutional ban, but supported a federal law to make it a crime to desecrate the flag.[221] Critics argued criminalizing burning the flag (free speech) was unconstitutional, and therefore Clinton's legislation was just as stupid as a constitutional amendment.

When she went to Iowa for the first time, the *Milwaukee Journal Sentinel* reported she "took her carefully planned and staged show on the road."[222] And "The event seemed to be the work of a seasoned team," with "campaign buttons galore. A get-your-juices-flowing song. And even an oversized 'Hillary for President' rug for her to stand on."[223] That giant rug had a table setting with a flap that said "LET THE CONVERSATION BEGIN!"[224] The conversation on Iraq had been going on for four years regardless of Clinton's January 2007 invitation to talk.

6) Can a woman be president? The analysis of the Marist polling (Feb.2006) argued "a women candidate for president from either party would have a lot of convincing to do."[225] Twenty-seven percent of registered voters said they were not likely to vote for a women regardless if she were a Democrat or Republican?[226] In a January 2006 *CBS News/New York Times* poll, adults were asked "if your party nominated a woman for president, would you vote for her if she were qualified for the job?" 92% said yes.[227] But when asked if America was "ready to elect a woman president, or not?" 38 percent said no, with the highest amount coming from Republicans (44%) and women (42%).[228] In a December

2006 CNN poll, a majority (60%) of Americans thought the country was ready for a woman president, though this number was higher with blacks (67) than whites (58).[229]

In addition, ABC premiered *Commander in Chief* on September 27, 2005.[230] In the plot Mackenzie Allen, played by Gina Davis, was an Independent Vice President as President Bridges was about to undergo emergency surgery.[231] Bridges wanted the Speaker of the House—a male—to be his replacement if things went bad, and "after sitting through an insulting and sexist conversation" with the Speaker, Mackenzie decided "to forge ahead and assume the presidency, despite the obstacles that lie ahead."[232] Indeed, as tv.com explained, "Not only will she take charge of a grieving nation, but also the care of her own household."[233] The series was a fascinating story about a woman being president. It was so fascinating, that by June 2006, the series was dead.

Still, from December 2006 to August 2007, Hillary Clinton, according to ABC *News/Washington Post* polling, had been solidly the Democratic frontrunner by at least ten points over Obama.[234]

7) What should she do with Bill? Former President Clinton has tried to laugh away the question, noting the Scottish tell him he would be "First Laddie." But Lynne Duke of the *Washington Post* wrote of the Hillary-Bill awkwardness on the Senator's reelection night, "So the former president stood pokerfaced. He clasped his hands. He held his head high. He clapped when appropriate. He smiled ever so faintly."[235]

As Barack Obama campaigns for a new political order, does the Democratic Party want to go back to the 1990s?

Nobody likes Hillary

Are Hillary's negative qualities over reported? She appeared on the cover of *Time* (8.28.06) with an empty check box infront of "LOVE HER" and "HATE HER," with the subtitle "The presidential ambitions of Hillary Clinton."[236] *Time* included a report titled "How Americans View Hillary: Popular but Polarizing."[237] Fifty-seven percent of Democrats agreed Clinton should have stayed with her husband after the Monica Lewinsky scandal, and only a third of Republicans said the same thing.[238] Only 35 percent of independents thought Clinton put her own political interests ahead of what she actually believed; the Republicans (60%) felt she was much more calculated.[239]

An August 2006 *Boston Herald* column was particlulary harsh, and although the author said "I usally don't like reporting such personal remarks but in this case you can hardly understand the situation without them," he still qouted New Hampshire Democrats calling her a "lying bitch," "political whore," "megalomaniac," and "Satanic."[240] Good luck finding a similar story on Barack Obama.

Jerry Falwell said (9.24.06) "I certainly hope that Hillary is the candidate....because nothing will energize my (constituency) like Hillary Clinton. If Lucifer ran, he wouldn't."[241] And although Falwell said his comments at the Value Voter Summit was "totally tongue-in-cheek," Clinton's press secretary

Philippe Reines said "Working for someone who believes in the Golden Rule, we're not going to engage in such vitriolic discourse—but it seems that a new low has been reached in demonizing political opponents."[242]

In the *Milwaukee Journal Sentinel* report of Mark Warner's decision not to run for president in October 2006, the paper reported "Privately, some Democratic strategists worry about Clinton as the party's candidate, in part because her time as first lady made her into a polarizing figure nationally."[243]

McCain likes Hillary

The *New York Times* reported on a vodka-drinking contest between Sens. Clinton, Graham, Collins, and McCain while traveling to Estonia in 2004.[244] Maureen Dowd wrote, "The after dinner drinks went so well—memories are a bit hazy on who drank how much—that McCain…later told people how unexpectedly engaging he found Mrs. Clinton to be."[245] McCain denied a drinking contest days later, but when Joshua Green, for an *Atlantic Monthly* article in the Fall of 2006, asked McCain about the competition he "lit up at the recollection," Green wrote, as McCain said "It's been 50 years since I'd been in a drinking game…She can really hold her liquor."[246]

But the McCain camp told Maureen Dowd in October 2006 that "After dinner, they had drinks. It was not a drinking contest, the way you and I think of a drinking contest. John had two drinks."[247] Dowd said McCain staffers had since "put a stop to their boss' inviting Clinton on trips" to appeal to the conservative base.[248] On *Hardball* (10.18.06), McCain said, "What happens in Estonia stays in Estonia," and "Nothing [happened]. We had dinner there and we went to a restaurant afterwards with Senator Lindsey Graham and Senator Susan Collins, and we had a—and I think Sununu also—and we had a couple of drinks after dinner. That's it. I'm sorry it's not more exciting. I'd love to tell you that I ran up and down the square."[249] And "I promise you it's been about 50 years since I've been in a drinking contest. I wish it was sooner."[250]

Before McCain ended the trips with Hillary Clinton, they took another road trip in August 2005. This time it was to Alaska and Canada. Susan Collins (R-Maine) and Lindsay Graham (R-SC) came along in an effort to question the effects of global warming [Notice the same characters went along as the Estonia trip]. McCain and Clinton's overwhelming belief in the negative effects of global warming were communicated in their visit. As of the August trip, McCain and Joe Lieberman were sponsoring legislation limiting greenhouse gas emissions from utilities and industry.[251] The Climate Stewardship and Innovation Act would cap U.S. emissions at levels recorded in 2000.[252] The Senators flew over Canada's Yukon Territory to see forests decimated by the spruce bark beetle, which were believed to be increasing due to warm weather.

Clearly Alaska was warming, but even Alaska's congressional delegation was not convinced (at least in the public eye, given Alaska's oil industry). Republican Sens. Ted Stevens and Lisa Murkowski, and Congressmen Don Young had previously opposed emission standards, arguing they were not convinced it was caused by humans.[253] The three members of Alaska's congressional delegation did not accompany the visitors.[254] But Hillary Clinton said the "science is overwhelming," and McCain was convinced of "the overwhelming scientific evidence" of climate change and human's role in it.[255] McCain's stance on global warming made him a populist. He stated that on this topic, "It's the special interests versus the people's interest."[256] Why does McCain no longer unite with Clinton on issues?

McCain told *Esquire Magazine* (July 2006) "I think the biggest mistake we could make is to underestimate Hillary Clinton. She's smart and she's tough. She's very disciplined in all ways—unlike her husband—and I think she's formidable. Plus, she already has $20 million in the bank."[257] *Vanity Fair* (Feb.2007) quoted McCain on Hillary: "People underestimate her political intelligence and her antennae. She's not her husband—no one's her husband. But she's good. And I like her. I know you're not supposed to say that, but I do."[258] But he no longer takes trips with her.

Clinton's ties to Wal-Mart

Clinton has a long history with Wal-Mart. She served as one of Wal-Mart's Board of Directors (1986-1992), was the first female on the board and earned an annual salary of $18,000.[259] And Mrs. Clinton was a partner at the Rose Law Firm, which handled many of Wal-Mart's legal affairs.[260]

Sam Walton and the Clinton's had a good working relationship. As the *AP* reported (Mar.2006), Hillary Clinton got Walton's help in 1983 for the Blue Ribbon Commission on Education in Arkansas, and Bill Clinton "persuaded" Walton to save 200 jobs at an Arkansas plant and essentially helped initiate the Made in America campaign.[261] Sam Walton donated to Clinton's 1992 campaign.[262] And in the '92 campaign, Bill Clinton "came proudly to the rescue of a local [New Hampshire] company called American Brush Co. by helping it become a Wal-Mart supplier."[263] When Walton died, President Clinton called him "a wonderful family man and one of the greatest citizens in the history of the state of Arkansas."[264] By 1993 Hillary Clinton had at least $100,000 in Wal-Mart stock.[265]

Fast forward a decade. She appeared to be blatantly grasping for the base of the Party when she gave back $5,000 from Wal-Mart after their late 2005 donation.[266] But she kept her check from Jerry Springer.[267] (She has standards.) The *New York Times* reported (8.17.06) that "she did so to protest Wal-Mart's health care benefits, and she has continued to distance herself from the policies of a company she was close to when she was the first lady of Arkansas."[268] In February 2006, Clinton's spokeswoman Ann Lewis said the $5,000 was returned "because of serious differences with the current company practices."[269]

Sen. Clinton told the U.S. Conference of Mayors (Jan.06) that "Cities and states are saying we can't keep holding the bag here," and cited the new Maryland law that required Wal-Mart to spend 8 percent of payroll into health benefits or contribute to insurance plans for the poor.[270] Though Clinton did not "explicitly" endorse the Maryland law, she did say she "certainly" understood "their need to try to take some action because the burden is getting shifted onto the taxpayer."[271]

When *Newsday* covered Clinton's address to the mayors, it reported she could not "recall if she pushed for worker benefits during six years as a paid board member for the nation's largest retailer."[272] She told reporters "Well, you know, I, that was a long time ago...have to remember..." and added she "obviously" believed "every company should" contribute to benefit plans.[273] In early 2006, a spokesman for Clinton said "Her tenure on the board ended nearly 14 years ago, and it's a very different company now."[274]

Wal-Mart changed. When did the Clintons?

The strongest argument for Clinton on Wal-Mart is that the company changed. In 1986, it had just under $12 billion in net sales, but by 2006, in had over $312 billion in sales with 1.3 million U.S. workers.[275] The huge corporation was sued over 4,800 times in 2000 alone.[276] Still, who changed? Sebastian Mallaby of the *Washington Post* wrote (9.3.06), "...The Wal-Mart of the early 1990s mainly bought American, where as today's irresponsible monster buys cheap stuff from China. But this argument merely illustrates how far Democrats have come. Since when did the party's centrist believe that trading with China is evil? It was the Clinton administration that brought China into the World Trade Organization."[277]

The problem is as Wal-Mart supposedly changed, the Clintons did little to complain about it. In 2004, "during the peak of the presidential campaign," Bill Clinton signed copies of his memoir at a Fayetteville, Arkansas Wal-Mart.[278] And in 2004, Sen. Clinton told the National Retail Federation that her time on the Wal-Mart board "was a great experience in every respect."[279]

Not to mention she actually laid low in August 2006 when the rest of her party was lambasting the company. Clinton's aides told the *New York Times* scheduling conflicts prevented the Senator from attending the rallies that others attended.[280] But many of those rallies occurred in August 2006, when Congress was in recess. Edwards, Bayh, Biden, and Richardson all campaigned against Wal-Mart during the month.[281] Joe Biden spent half that month in Iowa. In March 2006, her communications director turned down the *AP* for an interview with Sen. Clinton.[282] Nor would Wal-Mart say much about Clinton's time on the board, nor release any of the minutes during her tenure.[283]

Her stance against Wal-Mart may have been aligned with New York. In October 2005, New York City passed a law directed at Wal-Mart, which required large grocery stores to pay most of their workers a health care benefit of about $2.50-$3.00 an hour and slowed the corporations' plans to move into the city.[284] But the likely reversal of Clinton's opinions of Wal-Mart mirror labor unions' animosity towards the non-unionized company.

Clinton promises the world to middle class

Hillary Clinton has a "Strengthening the Middle Class" page in her 'Issues' portion of her website (8.1.07)[285] She promises a lot. "As president, Hillary will:"

- Make health care affordable and accessible to every American.
- Reduce the cost of energy and make us energy independent.

- Expand access to affordable, high-quality child care.
- Make college more affordable.
- Protect families from predatory lenders and help them avoid foreclosures.
- Increase the minimum wage.
- Create good jobs with good wages to expand the middle class.
- Balance the federal budget so we don't pass today's massive debts to the next generation.
- Reward savings, protect pensions, and provide greater retirement security.

Hillary Clinton says she "will" do all of the above. And she would do these things while balancing the budget? Some of the above is not even possible. There is no way Hillary Clinton will "make us energy independent." If the US is energy independent, the country has to be 100% off foreign oil. How can we be using only US oil by the eighth year of a Clinton Presidency? Sen. Clinton should call her plan "Eliminating the middle class," because if she accomplished all those bullet points, the middle class would be aristocrats.

The Onion has pointed out such promises with John Edwards. In a July 2007 front-page article, the sarcastic paper's headline was "John Edwards Vows To End All Bad Things By 2011."[286] The story's picture showed John Edwards speaking in front of a fabricated sign saying "John Edwards 08 - BAD THINGS ARE BAD."[287]

Former Senator Tom Daschle

Tom Daschle served four terms in the House representing South Dakota until 1987, when he moved to the Senate after winning election in 1986.[288] Daschle was elected Senate Democratic Leader in 1994, and only Lyndon Johnson served less years in the Senate before getting the position.[289] He was very close to President Clinton, and they frequently jogged together.[290] His office suffered an anthrax attack a month after 9/11.[291]

Daschle narrowly lost reelection in 2004, which ended an 18 year career in the Senate. Daschle joined with former Majority Leaders George Mitchell, Bob Dole, and Howard Baker to create the Bipartisan Policy Center in 2007.[292]

Daschle the Obstructionist

When Sen. George Allen (R-VA) was asked (8.22.04) why the Bush administration poured in everything to defeat Daschle, Allen said:

> Because he's the chief obstructionist on so many issues, whether it's tax cuts, whether it's energy policy, whether it is fair consideration of judges. The people of South Dakota, yeah, they do know Tom Daschle. And he has spent $9 million--$9 million--since January of last year and can't break 50 percent. It's about 48-45 right now. And for $9 million, for a state like Virginia, that would be like $90 million being spent and can't break 50. John Thune is a positive, constructive leader who will represent South Dakota values... Tom Daschle has to carry the water for Hillary Clinton and Ted Kennedy and all of these views that are so contrary to the values of the people of South Dakota. The fact that Bill Frist went into South Dakota shows that a leader is vulnerable. When in history has a leader of any party ever been so vulnerable? You didn't see folks going in against Bob Dole because no one's going to beat Bob Dole.[293]

Allen's justifications were the classic conservative staple answers in 2004, but the GOP machine wiped Daschle off the political map.

Daschle was liked by Republicans

His appearance on *Meet the Press* (12.26.06) was very humbling, as he and Oklahoma Sen. Don Nickles reflected on their time in the Senate (Nickles retired). The *New York Times* reported, Sen. Lott "was the first Republican to call to offer condolences after Mr. Daschle's defeat. Other Republicans called as well, he said, but only surreptitiously. …'I can't tell you how many Republicans have called and said, 'If you ever tell anybody I called you, I'll deny it.' I just don't know what to say about that. Why is it that this town has to be so mean that a guy can't even call and say, 'I'm sorry you lost?'"[294] Daschle said, "I just felt sorry for them that they felt somehow as if they had to ask me to keep this conversation private."[295]

Daschle ran for president, however quietly

In the beginning of 2006, Daschle was quoted in the *National Journal* that he was "taking a look" at the 2008 nomination, but told the *Sioux Falls Argus* major factors in his decision would be "family and our mutual decision to consider the rigors of a campaign and re-entry into public life."[296] He visited Iowa State University (2.1.06), which had followed trips to California and New York City to solicit funds for his PAC; meanwhile his political advisor Steve Hildebrand refused to address Daschle's national ambitions.[297] Hildebrand helped

Al Gore defeat Bill Bradley in Iowa six years earlier.[298] In his visit to Iowa, Daschle endorsed Iowa Sec. of State Chet Culver for the Democratic nomination for governor.[299]

Planning to visit Iowa, New Hampshire, and Michigan in June 2006, Daschle told the *AP* Hillary Clinton was "in a class by herself. In many cases she's like an incumbent. But I've learned after all these years in politics that what looks like a certainty one day could be a complete turnabout the next." [300] In New Hampshire, Daschle said the Bush administration "have got to be the most arrogant crowd I ever worked with."[301] Daschle contributed to candidates, including Virginia's Jim Webb (By May 2006)—even though Mark Warner held back from endorsing Webb during the Democratic primary for Senate.[302]

Daschle's small success was that he received 3% in a spring 2006 *Des Moines Register* poll. No doubt South Dakota's proximity to Iowa helped. Daschle said (June 2006) he planned to make a decision to run at the end of 2006: "It's a big decision and one you can't take lightly, so I don't take it lightly, I'm going to be very carefully considering this over the course of the next several months."[303]

An issueless candidacy

Why was he running for president? All the concerns Daschle took up were already somebody else's issue. For example, the *AP* covered (June 2006) Daschle New Hampshire trip and what he spoke: "Daschle criticized Bush for launching the war in Iraq, secret domestic wiretapping and a national debt that he argued will be passed on to future generations. He complained that the administration is too cozy with oil companies and has ignored the threat of global warming."[304] A *Reuters* report (7.3.06) said "Early polls show him with scant support," and his priorities included "upgrading schools, expanding health care, energy independence and cutting 'the growing gap between rich and poor.'"[305]

But what Democratic candidate had not criticized Bush on Iraq? The secret domestic wiretapping program was Feingold's issue. The national debt was a problem—but the public's priorities were Iraq, Iran, and immigration in the spring of 2006. The administration was too cozy with oil companies? Really. The Democrats didn't need Tom Daschle to tell them that line. Global warming was Gore's issue.

Why on earth was Daschle running for president? Did he have a chance? An *AP* report in the *Black Hills Pioneer* said "Democrats attending his speech privately asked that question, wondering if he can come back from his loss to [John] Thune to run a strong enough campaign" for president.[306] *Hotline* reported (5.19.06), Daschle also underwent "a large detachment" of his political kitchen cabinet, including his longtime communications director Dan Pfeiffer, and, Anita Dunn, who both went to other presidential teams.[307] In July 2006, he resigned from the board at Apollo Investment Corporation after serving three months on the job as the company said the resignation was due to other commitments.[308]

Daschle dropped out

Tom Daschle announced on December 2, 2006, he would not run for president, and "he told *Keloland News*" he would not run, as his former campaign manager said there was many factors including the task of raising $50 million.[309] He did take trips to Iowa and New Hampshire,[310] but he was never an intense polticial candidate. Trying to Google his dropped bid was difficult. Keloland reported it—obviously: the news outlit is from South Dakota. So too did *WISTV* out of Columbia, South Carolina. The coverage did not compare to Russ Feingold's withdrawal—and was not even close to Evan Bayh's decision. The fact that *KELO-TV* was the major outlet that found out about Daschle's ambitions spoke for itself.[311]

It was almost as if Daschle received more attention *days after* he announced he would not run. Indeed, the *New York Times* included his comments in an article featuring Dennis Kucinich's run (12.12.06). Daschle said "There is a level of intrigue that goes with being a potential presidential candidate," and that he had been introduced thousands of times as a 'potentional presidential candidate' in the past and generally that was a good thing.[312] Dashcle added that "I think, at a certain point, you'd need to become more discriminating about who's viable."[313]

Dashcle never was.

Senator Chris Dodd

On Jan. 11, 2007, Chris Dodd became the fifth Democrat to enter the race after Gravel, Vilsack, Kucinich, and Edwards.[314] The Dodd name is familiar in Connecticut. His father, Thomas Dodd was censured by the Senate in 1967 for using campaign funds for personal purposes.[315]

After serving time in the House, Chris Dodd was elected to the Senate in 1980. His landmark legislation was the Family and Medical Leave Act during the Clinton administration.[316] Besides the Banking Committee chair, Dodd currently holds the senior position on the Foreign Relations Committee; and a spot on the Health, Education, Labor and Pensions Committee.[317]

Dodd flirted with leadership before. As the general chairman of the DNC for two years in the 1990s, Dodd was known by party activists.[318] The *New York Times* noted Dodd "long expressed a desire for higher office," as he lost to Daschle for the Senate Leadership post in 1994, and "explored" a run for the minority leadership post for the 109th Congress, but Harry Reid already had sewed up support.[319] He considered running for president in 2004, but Joe Lieberman (D-CT) entered.[320] Joe Lieberman was not running for president in 2008, and Dodd would not be up for re-election until 2010, so the green light for his chance at the presidency was 2008.[321]

Weaknesses for Dodd

1) **The Ditching of Lieberman.** The *New York Observer* called Dodd (12.4.06), "one of the most personally well-liked members of the Senate."[322] But when Dodd's fellow senator from Connecticut, Joe Lieberman, lost the August 2006 Democratic primary for Senate, Dodd switched his support to anti-war candidate Ned Lamont and hung his longtime colleague out to dry. Even in a trip to Iowa (Sept.2006) Dodd "seemed to be caught off guard" when questioned about Lieberman by Iowans.[323] For voters who respected loyalty in politicians, Dodd was not their man. Then Dodd announced his presidential campaign on *Imus in the Morning*, even though Don Imus hated what Dodd did to Lieberman and had all but endorsed John McCain for 2008.

2) **Did Dodd have an issue?** The *Hartford Courant* said "Other candidates are taking definitive stands on pet issues. Feingold stresses his strong opposition to the war. Edwards talks about how he plans to ease poverty. Dodd emphasizes his work on health care and education."[324] But this was the *Hartford Courant*, and not the *New York Times*. Was Dodd to health care as Feingold was to Iraq?

If anything was Dodd's pet issue it was then-UN Ambassador John Bolton—who was eventually blocked from confirmation to keep his UN Ambassador position. But the credit for that blocked ambassadorship should go to outgoing Senator Lincoln Chafee (R-RI), who stopped Bolton in the Foreign Relations Committee before the vote was ever taken to the Senate floor.

The *Courant* reported (1.11.07), "During the campaign, Dodd will stress his 32 years in Congress, including long stints on the Senate Foreign Relations

Committee - and his detailed knowledge of Latin America - as well as his championing of major social legislation, such as the family and medical leave act."[325] The *Courant* (5.22.06) also noted Dodd had won passage of major legislation as a "skilled backroom negotiator," including "The Family and Medical Leave Act, help for minority voters and huge budget boosts for Head Start and child care."[326] The *AP* called him (1.12.07), "the chief Senate sponsor of the 1993 Family and Medical Leave Act," that allowed workers up to 12 weeks of unpaid leave for birth or adoption, or personal or family illness.[327] But the main issues in May 2006 were immigration, Iraq, Iran, and gas prices—not a 1993 law. Likewise, in the first months of his official campaign, the main issues into 2007 had been Iraq, immigration, and Alberto Gonzales' potential resignation—none of which vaulted Dodd into the spotlight.

Yahoo!News/AP reported (1.2.07: "Dodd well-positioned for White House bid") the chairmanship of the Banking Committee would be "a potential boost" for the senator who had "accepted millions" from Wall Street interests during his quarter century in the Senate.[328] The Center of Responsive Politics said Dodd received $2.8 million from securities and investment industry interests since 1989, as the *AP* report added, "Insurance industry sources gave $1.08 million, the center's statistics showed, while commercial bank interests gave $553,719."[329] Dodd was looked upon by the banking industry more than most other Democrats. Banking issues would help him with fundraising, but not necessarily with primary voters.

3) Dodd was an old insider. Dodd was no spring chicken. The *New York Observer* said he had "frosted white hair and unruly eyebrows."[330]

"In the past, experience seemed to be a liability…If you had 25 years in the Senate—sorry, you're disqualified. I think this is different…Certainly the last five years has reminded people that maybe—maybe—experience has value."[331] As a *Wall Street Journal* writer opined, "Certainly Mr. Dodd -- the son of a senator, a senator himself since 1981 and a House member six years before that -- wouldn't have a prayer if voters wanted an outsider."[332] How did the seniority card work for Kerry in 2004? Howard Fineman described him with "a boyish enthusiasm for the old-school arts of bipartisan legislating and serious debate…He's the product of, and thrives in a pre-Internet world where deals are done and votes are won in person, face to face, handshake to handshake, across party lines. Definitely old school."[333]

4) Dodd was another northeastern liberal. The *Hartford Courant* noted (1.10.07) Dodd "addressed that concern repeatedly," as he told Iowans "This is not about geography. This is about who you are."[334] He based his campaign out of Connecticut, and had the state's Attorney General Richard Blumenthal act as the state chair while Rep. Rosa L. DeLauro, from Connecticut's 3rd Congressional District, was the national co-chair.[335]

5) Dodd's past. After Dodd officially declared his candidacy, Stan Simpson's column in the *Hartford Courant* started with "He's got a playboy past…"[336] The *Courant* said (1.11.07), "In the 1980s, when he was single, he was one of the tabloids' favorite political figures."[337] The *New York Times* said (1.12.07), "….Dodd's interest in family issues was once viewed as incongruous: His personal life—including a period of well-publicized womanizing in the 1980s" with Ted Kennedy "at a time when both senators were divorcees—was the stuff of tabloid chatter."[338] A *Hartford Courant* analysis (5.22.06) suggested another "…problem may be his 1980s image as one of the tabloids' favorite senators," and Dodd was "known as a ladies' man."[339] The *New York Observer*, rehashing some of his past, said:

> After Mr. Dodd's 12-year marriage ended in divorce in 1982, he began making a name for himself as one of Washington's most eligible bachelors. He danced nearly into the small hours with a woman in a Budapest hotel and dated Bianca Jagger and Carrie Fisher. According to the *Hartford Courant*, his late-night carousing with Mr. Kennedy earned them the reputation in Washington as the 'Playboys of the Western World.' Whether all this is helpful biographical material for a Presidential candidate is certainly open to debate. But Mr. Dodd professes to be unconcerned.[340]

Dodd told the *Observer*, "People have a lot more problems on their minds than worrying about some newspaper article or comment by a social columnist about 20 years ago. Let them talk about that if they want to; it's their business. I'm going to be talking about the world we live in. There are a lot more serious things."[341] Dodd remarried and has two young children.[342]

6) Dodd clearly started late. The *Hartford Courant* (5.22.06) said Dodd had "decided to do all the things…necessary to prepare to seek the presidency in 2008."[343] Dodd himself said in January 2007, "I have thought about it [running] over the last six months since I first started to explore it…"[344] So May 2006 is when Dodd decided to run for president. Seriously, there was really no coyness before May. As late as April 2006, Chris Dodd told *Fox News Sunday*, when asked about running for president, "I was in New Haven this week, not New Hampshire, and around Danbury rather than in Dubuque, so that ought to tell you something…."[345]

By the time Dodd went to Iowa in the fall of 2006, Edwards had made ten trips since 2004 and Bayh made seven.[346] Dodd was the ninth Democrat to campaign in Iowa (Sept.2006), with Clinton the only holdout.[347] Where others' out-of-state visits totaled 30-something states since 2004, Dodd had been to a dozen states between May and October 2006 (the first four contested states and Ohio, Penn., Maine, Vermont.).[348]

When a local TV station polled Iowa State Fair goers in August 2006, Edwards and Clinton tied with 33% each, but Dodd was not included with the 10 other candidates.[349] Dodd was not included in the *Des Moines Register* June 2006 poll, which Edwards won.[350] As a result, the Environmental Defense poll taken in October 2006 (but released in December) showed Dodd "received too little support to be expressed as a percentage."[351] A November Quinnipiac poll did not even include him.[352]

7) From the start, Dodd had an uphill climb. The *New York Observer* said it was "something of a stretch to say that he's on the same stage, politically speaking, as John Edwards" and was "not in the same universe as Hillary

Clinton."[353] But he did not hide from it, and told the *AP* he was a dark horse candidate.[354] When he went to Iowa in September 2006, David Lightman wrote that in between his breakfast with Tom Vilsack and the Johnson County barbeque, Dodd "learned that he's someone who has flashed only fleetingly, if at all, into the minds of most Iowans, and could be quickly forgotten almost immediately."[355]

The *Bristol Press* had a headline: "Local reaction to Dodd bid great choice, but no chance."[356] *Wonkette*, a sarcastic website, said "some guy named Chris Dodd (he's a member of some sort of legislating body?) is running for President" as the Senator was taking requests for his DoddPod playlist of songs.[357] On the first day of his annoucment, he featured Jon Fogerty's song with the lines *Put me in coach, I'm ready to play, today*.[358] *Wonkette* requested The Heartbreakers' *Born to Lose*.[359] The criticism got worse when a posting suggested Chris Dodd got crabs in the late 1990s, and was "Still Not Cool":

> I hope you are able to track down this tip! In 1997 or 1998, Pop Smear magazine ran an article by a woman who was a regular of the NYC music scene. Her article was about how crabs (pubic lice) used to be a lot more common in the music scene, but no one seems to get them anymore.
> She got crabs from John Doe of the band "X" and then passed them on to her boyfriend at the time, who was Chris Dodd's son. He then went home to visit Dad and Dad (Chris Dodd) caught the crabs from the bed that Chris had slept in.[360]

This story was a bit false given his oldest child was 5.[361]

Hotline (June 2006) was not enthusiastic on Dodd '08, as its top five contenders for the Democratic nomination were Clinton, Edwards, Warner, Bayh and Kerry; as Dodd was described a "great orator" yet "we don't see him doing much more right now than creating some interesting staff quandaries for other contenders."[362] As one blogger at the *New Republic* asked (6.16.06), "WHY IS CHRIS DODD RUNNING FOR PRESIDENT?: Seriously, **why**?"[363]

The *Hartford Courant* said, "…the five-term senator has serious hurdles as he enters a crowded field of Democratic hopefuls. Dodd is perceived as a New England liberal, does not have the kind of cash on hand that others have, and will have to take on" Clinton, Obama, and Edwards, "all of whom are viewed as top-tier candidates."[364] The same article quoted former Iowa party chair Gordon Fischer that it was going to be hard for Dodd to "get any oxygen" if Clinton and Obama made the race.[365] And "On the national political radar Dodd is barely a blip. A Gallup survey of nationwide Democrats in December found Dodd the choice of 1 percent, while an *ABC News/Washington Post* survey listed him 11th with less than 1 percent."[366]

In a Quinnipiac July 2007 poll of Connecticut's registered Democrats, Dodd garnered six percent and placed fifth behind Clinton (28), Obama (20), Gore (13), and Edwards (8).[367] Dodd's poor showing in his home state was despite the fact he had a 60 percent approval rating in the same poll.[368] Dodd had $6.3 million on hand half way through 2007, which put him fifth place on the Democratic side.[369] Dodd is liked by Democrats and has some money to spend: but in terms of presidential ambitions, all directions point to nowhere.

Former Senator John Edwards

John Edwards has experienced hardship. His son was killed in a car crash in 1996, and his wife Elizabeth announced she had breast cancer immediately after the 2004 elections, but the disease returned in 2007. But his rise in politics within ten years has been monumental.

Edwards beat incumbent Lauch Faircloth in North Carolina's US Senate race in 1998. An attractive man from the South, Edwards was actually in the running to be Al Gore's running mate in 2000. Political consultants Bob Schrum and Tad Devine tried to convince Gore to pick Edwards.[370] Nonetheless, in an indication of his foresight, Edwards spoke to delegates from big donor states at the 2000 Democratic convention (despite having just been overlooked by Gore) and even met with Iowa's delegation.[371]

Edwards and Kerry gave their 2004 concession speeches at Faneuil Hall in Boston (11.4.04). Edwards stated as he introduced Kerry, "This fight has just begun… This campaign may end today. But the battle for you and the hardworking American who built this country rages on."[372] When he left the race in February 2004, Edwards said he had decided to "suspend" his campaign for the presidency. He was telling the truth by not using "end."[373] Edwards has been running for president for seven years.

A moderate no more

The Bush team feared Edwards in 2003, as the *Almanac for American Politics* wrote, and thought Edwards' "southern background, his moderate voting record on many issues and his attractive persona might put into play some Southern and Northern states which would be safe for Bush against other possible nominees."[374] Having been picked as Kerry's running mate, the *New York Times* said Edwards would be dispatched "to rural areas in critical states across the Midwest and the West."[375] And the Kerry campaign hoped Edwards would be particularly useful in rural spots in Ohio, Pennsylvania, Missouri, West Virginia, Iowa, and New Mexico.[376] A July 2004 poll done by the University of Pennsylvania's National Annenberg Election Survey showed 19% of rural voters thought of Edwards unfavorably while 43% viewed Kerry unfavorably; and 36% of rural voters viewed Kerry favorably, with Edwards basically tied (37%).[377] The Annenberg survey indicates that although Edwards did not hurt Kerry, he may not have helped. In the Wisconsin primary, Edwards defeated Kerry among Independent voters (40-28) and narrowly lost the state.[378] But with Edwards on the Kerry ticket, Bush still won North Carolina by 13 points, the same margin as 2000.[379] So how moderate did voters actually perceive Edwards to be? Could he bring southern states to the Democratic fold for 2008? *Time* reported (12.19.06) Edwards was "running as a much more liberal candidate now."[380]

What were Edwards' weaknesses?

1) Foreign policy. The *AP* reported his "liabilities" included "a lack of political and foreign policy experience"—and this was reported *after* the 2004 elections.[381] As he was "boning up on foreign affairs so much he seemed downright thrilled to drop the names of leaders of Iran and North Korea in responding to one question in New Orleans," as *Time* added (12.29.06) that he had to overcome "a reputation as a lightweight."[382] His perception of a pretty boy does not make him appear stronger on defense.

2) Is he superficial? In one podcast he said, "I'd rather be successful or unsuccessful based on who I really am. Not based on some plastic Ken-doll."[383] His campaign against poverty took a hit when his expensive haircuts were reported.

In April 2007, his campaign reported it had paid for two hair cuts at $400 each, and "the political damage was immediate."[384] According to the *Washington Post*, Edwards claimed he was embarrassed at the cost and said he "didn't know it would be that expensive."[385] He did. Edwards has had the same Beverly Hills hairstylist since 2003. Many of the initial 16 cuts were free, but the hairstylist had to start charging for each cut's airfare and hotels when Edwards was on the campaign trail and not in California.[386] One cut cost Edwards nearly $1,300 because the stylist lost two days of work.[387]

Jay Leno claimed (7.20.07), "John Edwards has a new TV commercial touting him as a tough guy. His wife says he has unbelievable toughness. And he is tough. Like in the ad, sometimes it says he shampoos his hair and then skips the conditioner completely."[388] Days later, Leno joked (7.24.07), "Edwards is continuing his poverty tour around America. Today, he visited a group of people who get their haircut in a place called a 'barber shop.' He was horrified to hear that story."[389] Then there was the YouTube two-minute clip in which the former Senator combs his hair; the clip was called "John Edwards Feeling Pretty."[390]

Along the lines of appearing superficial, critics have questioned Edwards past as a lawyer. He amassed a fortune of at least $20 million as a trial lawyer. In January 1997, he won the largest personal injury verdict in North Carolina history when he won $25 million in compensatory damages for a girl injured by a faulty swimming pool drain.[391] In the 2004 presidential campaign, critics joked that Edwards was an ambulance chaser. He sided with lawyers in the US Senate, and did not accept a $4 million limit on pain and suffering damages in 2002.[392] According to the Center for Responsive Politics, lawyers gave Democrats over $107 million in 2004, but only $39 million to Republicans.[393] Legislation capping civil damage rewards would choke income to trial lawyers, among the most generous contributors to Democrats.[394]

3) Edwards would increase taxes. *Time* reported (12.29.07) Edwards had "essentially promised to raise taxes, although he would focus the hikes on the wealthy and the profits of oil companies, to pay for expensive programs like universal health care."[395] This is true, as the *AP* also reported "he would tax oil company profits and eliminate President Bush's tax cuts to pay for" the priorities.[396]

4) What is the role for Elizabeth Edwards? On one hand, Edwards has an appealing wife. Elizabeth Edwards spent the fall of 2006 promoting her book,

Saving Graces: Finding Solace and Strength from Friends and Strangers.[397] Her story of battling cancer is inspiring.

But Elizabeth Edwards is fighting her husband's political battles. In October 2006, Elizabeth Edwards talked about Sen. Clinton, and said "She and I are from the same generation. We both went to law school and married other lawyers, but after that we made other choices. I think my choices have made me happier. I think I'm more joyful than she is."[398] In July 2007, Elizabeth Edwards noted of Sen. Clinton: "sometimes you feel you have to behave as a man and not talk about women's issues."[399] As one blogger opined, "Having your wife not-so-slyly raise questions about Hillary Clinton's femininity is simply bizarre and inevitably counterproductive."[400]

At what point is Elizabeth Edwards too involved in her husband's campaign? She then said (Aug.2007), "We can't make John black; we can't make him a woman. Those things get you a certain amount of fundraising dollars."[401] In a September 2007 *Time* article, she continued to fight the former First Lady, and argued Clinton's unpopularity would help fire up Republicans in the general election if she were the Democratic nominee: "I want to be perfectly clear: I do not think the hatred against Hillary Clinton is justified…I don't know where it comes from. I don't begin to understand it. But you can't pretend it doesn't exist, and it will energize the Republican base. Their nominee won't energize them, Bush won't, but Hillary as the nominee will. It's hard for John to talk about, but it's the reality."[402] It's so 'hard for John to talk about' he makes his wife do it.

Edwards' Strengths

1) Edwards has an issue. Poverty was not the major issue for Edwards in 1998 in his run for Senate, but by 2004, his stump speeches focused on the inequality of "two Americas."[403] In 2005, Edwards helped start the Center on Poverty, Work and Opportunity at the University of North Carolina.[404] Edwards call's poverty "the great moral issue of our day."[405] *McClatchy* described (11.14.06) Edwards as "a consistent voice for the poor."[406] He also traveled to Uganda to bring attention to that country's plight.

2) Edwards has a Democratic base to lean on. He spent 2005 and 2006 advocating for minimum wage increase initiatives across the country, and is continually seen as a favorite for unions. His email list by the end of 2006 was over 700,000, and union leaders were "enamored of his populist message."[407] His union ties will help him in the second presidential contest in Nevada, which is loaded with service workers who are union members.

3) Edwards has distanced himself from Kerry. The *AP* reported (10.30.05) the "simmering rivalry" that was "ignited" by Edwards's comments after the 2004 election that he told Kerry to fight back against the Swift Boat Veterans for Truth.[408] Citing the competitive speeches Edwards and Kerry gave the same day in September 2005 on similar topics (Hurricane Katrina), the *AP* reported when Edwards came to Massachusetts in November, "he made a special point to call" Ted Kennedy "to tell him he was in the state. No such call was made to Kerry…"[409]

Edwards said (12.12.06) he "wasn't crazy about" running as V.P., and added "There's something about not being able [to] just freely say exactly what you think."[410] When asked if he had been 'used' by Kerry, Edwards said "I'll let you guys talk about that."[411] When asked about Kerry's botched joke on President Bush and Iraq, Elizabeth Edwards creatively interrupted her husband from explaining Kerry by saying "Don't go there," and the crowd applauded.[412] Elizabeth said "there are not many politicians who are actually good at jokes. John [Edwards] spoke one time and I said I wouldn't even go because it was—he was supposed to be funny and I didn't think he could carry it off."[413]

Edwards (12.28.06) did not deny that he promised John Kerry he would not run in 2008 if Kerry did, instead Edwards said he did not talk about "private conversations" with Kerry.[414]

4) Edwards helped out Democratic candidates in a different route. *Roll Call* reported (Mar.2006) Edwards was the only person considering a run in 2008 who had not donated to another campaign, and avoided the tradition of spending PAC money in Iowa and New Hampshire. Instead, Edwards spent his money trying to help others raise money with his appearances. "Aides to Edwards said this approach is far more beneficial to candidates and state and local committees than simply cutting a $5,000 or $10,000 check from One America's downtown Washington D.C. headquarters."[415]

5) The primary calendar is in his favor, and Iowa looks good. The early Democratic schedule is the Iowa Caucus, Nevada Caucus, and New Hampshire Primary, followed by the South Carolina primary. The Edwards plan is possible: win Iowa because of dedicated stops and a second place finish in 2004, win Nevada because of the labor unions in the hotel/casino industry, stay alive in New Hampshire; then win South Carolina, the sister to his home state.

As of Labor Day 2007, the Democratic National Committee stipulated only New Hampshire, Iowa, Nevada and South Carolina could hold contests before Feb. 5, 2008.[416] However, Michigan, among other states, have tried to buck the trend (The Michigan primary for the GOP will be the third contest).[417] The states could still run primaries earlier than the Democratic National Committee's liking, but the DNC can void a state's delegates for the Democratic Convention in 2008.

The polls look good for Edwards. Although Giuliani and McCain swept their four Democratic rivals (Clinton, Kerry, Edwards, and Vilsack) in a September 2006 *Des Moines Register* poll, Edwards was the only one to give "them a close battle," and unlike Clinton actually beat Frist and Romney.[418] More Iowans viewed Clinton negatively than favorably (49-43), as Edwards was overwhelmingly favorable (54-30).[419]

A poll conducted by Environmental Defense (10.12-19.06), and released in December 2006 showed Edwards with a clear lead in Iowa again with 36 percent, followed by Clinton (16), Obama (13), Vilsack (9), Kerry 6), Biden (5), Clark (3), Richardson (2), and Bayh and Dodd "received too little support to be expressed as a percentage."[420] Even more favorable to Edwards, Environmental

Defense had another poll in October 2006 which looked at the opinions of the Democratic county chairs, and according to the *Des Moines Register*, "the poll found even more enthusiasm for Edwards (40) and a stronger sentiment for Vilsack (15)."[421] Then, a *KCCI-TV* poll released in December 2006 of likely caucus goers, had Edwards in first, tied with Obama (22), followed by Vilsack (12), Clinton (10), Gore (7), Kerry (5), Clark (4), Kucinich (4); and Biden, Bayh, and Richardson all at a percentage point.[422]

Edwards's is low on the expectations list. On the *NBC Nightly News* (12.11.06), a report by Chip Reid labeled Bayh, Vilsack—and Edwards "second tier candidates."[423] Edwards is not a second tier candidate. Edwards continued to lead in a July 2007 CNN Poll (for Iowa) with 27 percent, followed by Clinton (22), Obama (16), Richardson (11), Biden (3), Kucinich and Dodd (2), and Gravel (1).[424] In September 2007, Edwards was still competitive in Iowa. But according to *Newsweek*'s poll and a *Real Clear Politics* polling average in September 2007, Edwards is not the clear, unequivocal frontrunner in the state. He is competitive, but Clinton and Obama are just as viable.

Edwards has to win Iowa, but he has some things going for him. Bill Clinton never ran in the Iowa Caucus in 1992 because Sen. Tom Harkin (D-Iowa) ran for president, and accordingly, Sen. Clinton's campaign lacks the stout Iowa organization it has in New Hampshire. And if the media continues to show the Obama v. Clinton news stories and lower the expectations on Edwards, he could get a major bump after winning Iowa. However, Edwards will struggle in raising enough money to go all the way to the nomination.

Senator Russ Feingold

Feingold was a Rhodes Scholar and Harvard Law School graduate who was narrowly elected to the Wisconsin legislature at age 29.[425] His political career began in 1982, when he defeated Wisconsin State Senator Cy Bidwell (R) by 31 votes; once in the state legislature, he garnered attention for his belief that bovine growth hormone should be banned.[426]

He beat two notable Democrats in the 1992 US Senate primary by avoiding negative campaigning and running humorous ads (one of which was a tour of his house, specifically his closet: "Look, no skeletons.")[427] Another commercial in the senate primary consisted of Elvis Pressley's endorsement.[428] Feingold won the primary with 70% of the vote, then beat two term incumbent Bob Kasten.[429]

Feingold was the only Democrat in the US Senate to vote against Robert Byrd's (D-WV) resolution to dismiss the impeachment case against President Clinton before hearing it.[430]

He was the chairman of the Constitution Subcommittee of the Judiciary Committee when he made his vote against the Patriot Act, the only 'no' vote in the U.S. Senate (it passed 96-1 in late 2001).[431] "Preserving our freedom is the reason that we are now engaged in this new war on terrorism," said Feingold in a speech on the Patriot Act (10.12.01), "We will lose that war without firing a shot if we sacrifice the liberties of the American people."[432] "The leadership of both parties wanted to take this bill, which was never considered or voted on in the Judiciary Committee, and ram it through the U.S. Senate without a single amendment being offered."[433]

More importantly, he voted against the authorization for force in Iraq. He was re-elected to the Senate in 2004, despite competition against a Republican challenger much in favor of the Patriot Act and Iraq War.

The divorce

Feingold hit a rough spot in April 2005, when Feingold's office left a 31-word statement indicating he and his wife Mary were "separating amicably, and intend to remain very good friends."[434] Would it kill his presidential hopes? On an online chat (8.11.06) he was asked about the country never having a single, twice divorced, Jewish president; and "If you were to run for president, how much of your personal life do you think would 'play' into a national campaign?" Feingold said "I think my personal life is sufficiently boring and the issues facing America are so compelling that people will focus on the latter, if I end up running."[435]

Feingold to Bush: 'You're Naughty'

Russ Feingold secured an interview on ABC's *This Week* (3.12.06) to announce his resolution seeking a censure of President Bush over the NSA wiretapping program. "This conduct is right in the strike zone of the concept of high crimes and misdemeanors."[436] Censure of the President was rare and is only a symbolic chastisement. Impeachment is the House's indictment (allowed in the

Constitution) that goes to the Senate, who decides for acquittal or removal from office.[437] Given Feingold's accusation above, why did he merely call for a slap on the wrist?

Bill Frist followed the interview of Feingold and told George Stephanopoulos Feingold "is just wrong, he is flat wrong, he is dead wrong."[438] In classic Frist partisanship, the Majority Leader claimed Feingold would send a "terrible, terrible signal" to enemies of the US overseas.[439] This made perfect sense because merely questioning the President aided our enemies. Frist urged Democrats to either allow a "vote or move on to addressing the real threats facing our national security."[440] This urgent vote put Democrats leaders on the spot and they objected, and the immediate vote stalled.[441]

An awkward position

When Feingold proposed the resolution on March 13, 2006, the Democrats in the Senate dodged commenting. Obama said he had not read it, Clinton's spokesman said ask Clinton "after lunch"—but she "fled the lunch out a back door as if escaping a fire."[442] Kerry said he couldn't answer questions right now, "an excuse that fell apart when Kerry was forced into an awkward wait as Capital Police stopped an aide at the magnetometer."[443] Earlier, Kerry said he was "interested in it [censure]."[444] Mark Dayton (D-MN) said "it's an overreaching step by someone who is grandstanding and running for president at the expense of his own party and his own country."[445] Feingold did not warn his party leaders of his proposal.[446]

The Daily Show had (3.15.06) a segment called "RussellMania06 [a spoof on Wrestle Mania]," and Jon Stewart sarcastically added the censure "…only happened once before to Andrew Jackson and he was never heard from again," upon which the backdrop showed a twenty dollar bill.[447] Then a clip showed fellow Democrats (Obama, Kerry, and Kennedy) silent after Feingold proposed the resolution.[448] The Republican National Committee called it "Feingold's Folly."[449] Feingold was hung out to dry by both political parties.

Carl Levin (D-MI) said (3.26.06) it was "premature to reach any conclusion about censure."[450] Joe Lieberman called it a "very unusual measure," and McCain called it "unfortunate and wrong."[451]

Take for instance how the situation was reported by the *Milwaukee Journal Sentinel*: "…the debate in Congress has focused much more on whether laws need to be changed to accommodate the policy than on whether the administration should be rebuked or sanctioned for going beyond the law."[452] The *Washington Post* (3.15.06) displayed the stink bomb mentality: Democratic senators leaving their caucus lunch "looked as if they'd seen a ghost."[453]

The *Washington Post* reported (3.15.06) "Democratic views were mixed" as Dodd "dismissed the proposed censure as 'getting way down the road on this issue.'"[454] The *Post* did not point out that Dodd's father, Sen. Thomas J. Dodd, was censured by the Senate in 1967 for using campaign funds for personal purposes.[455]

In defense of Feingold

However, Joe Biden deserved some credit for not throwing Feingold to the wolves. Asked if Feingold was grandstanding for 2008, Biden said "No, I think it's more of an intense frustration. Do any of you in the news media or any of us have any idea what the president is doing [with the NSA program]?"[456] By the end of March 2006, only Sens. Barbara Boxer (CA) and Tom Harkin (IA) signed on to Feingold's resolution.[457]

The *New Republic* called him the "Hillary Slayer"; *Vogue* labeled him "The Man of the Moment"—but such victories were apparently tabulated by media attention, and not results.[458] Then he appeared on *The Daily Show* (3.22.06) where Jon Stewart complimented the Senator: "this feels like some accountability…because it seems like the worse you screw up with these guys [the Bush Administration], the bigger the trophy they give you."[459] Feingold's appearance boded well, as Stewart jokingly told the senator he hoped "that your colleagues let you still eat at the lunch table."[460] After a clip of Rep. John Boehner's statement suggesting Feingold was "more interested in the safety and security of the terrorists as opposed to the American people," Stewart asked Feingold "How long have you been working with the terrorists? And are they nicer than they seem?"[461]

Feingold's censure: poor logic

Hurting Feingold's logic was his own statement. In an op-ed to the *Milwaukee Journal Sentinel*, Feingold wrote (3.18.06): "Contrary to the president's misleading rhetoric, no one questions whether the government should wiretap terrorists. Of course it should, and it can under current law. The issue is whether the president is going to follow the laws that Congress passed to ensure that as we wiretap terrorists, we also protect innocent Americans from unjustified government intrusion."[462] Such an argument blurred whether Feingold felt wiretapping was completely wrong. The *Milwaukee Journal Sentinel*, which had been complimentary to the senator in other editorials, said censure was "premature, unfair." [463] The paper itself reported Feingold "wants to make one thing perfectly clear—he's for wiretapping terrorists. He just wants it done legally."[464]

Feingold blatantly suggested his colleagues were weak. Even after the Patriot Act renewal, "If Democrats can't stand up on something like this when the president's poll numbers are 34%, I just wonder how much right we have to govern the country. You've got to show people you believe in something, not just that you're gaming the issues."[465]

If Feingold labeled his fellow Democrat's weak, he was the one who appeared to be 'gaming the issues.' Indeed, he was the first senator to ask for a timetable for troop withdrawal. About 130,000 US troops were still in Iraq. He was not calling for a censure of the president on a war Feingold himself thought never should have been started. It might have made more sense to censure the president on false intelligence on WMD in Iraq, which was exactly what Moveon.org and other liberal groups called for in February 2004.[466]

Feingold could tolerate the President misleading the country into the war, but wiretapping…well…that was a completely different story. Michigan Rep. Jon Conyers offered a censure of Bush on Iraq in December 2005.[467] But censure was unlikely because only 44 Democrats were in the Senate in the spring of 2006.

The Polls & Censure

Rasmussen Reports (3.15-16.06) found 38% of Americans thought Bush should be censured for the NSA wiretapping program; Feingold's name recognition was initially low (15% favorable/23% unfavorable), but when respondents were told Feingold was the advocate his numbers jumped (32%/41%)—a bigger proportional gain occurred with the favorable rating.[468] A *Newsweek* poll (3.16-17.06) showed 42% favored the program, 50% opposed; but 60% of Democrats supported it.[469] In averaging polls, those supporting was usually around the low-40s, those against were around 50, and a clear majority of Democrats supporting the measure.[470] Still, a Pew poll found 43 percent never heard of Feingold (4.7-16.06).[471]

Feingold's hearing: We don't know enough, but NSA certainly illegal

When Feingold held his hearing on censure before the Judiciary Committee (3.31.06), Ted Kennedy, Joe Biden, Dianne Feinstein, Chuck Schumer, and Dick Durbin did not show up.[472] Feingold was allowed two witnesses. He chose John Dean from Nixon's administration and Bruce Fein of Reagan's.[473] Former Nixon White House Counsel John Dean made his first appearance before Congress since the 1970s Watergate hearings on March 31 in testimony which "conjured up old political ghosts and added a theatrical edge to a long and unusual hearing on Sen. Russ Feingold's resolution to censure the president."[474] The hearing was as unusual as the *Milwaukee Journal Sentinel* reported.

Sen. Cornyn (R-TX) protested the Judiciary Committee gave a forum to a "convicted felon," and Lindsey Graham (R-SC) said Nixon-comparisons were "apples and oranges" to the NSA debate as Graham then debated Dean on the meaning of the Watergate scandal.[475] Arlen Specter (R-PA) did not support censure, but it was he who decided to hold the censure hearing and did not go as far to say the reprimand was "frivolous."[476] Despite skepticism on Feingold's censure, Lindsey Graham was still unsure about the president's rationale of the program and even complimented Specter for having the hearing.[477]

Feingold appeared on *FOX News Sunday* (4.2.06) to discuss the censure. He did not shy away from his previous comment that the NSA program was "one of the greatest attempts to dismantle our system of government in history."[478] He reinforced his belief the situation was "worse" than Watergate, and rehashed the proverbial description of an "imperial presidency."[479] Feingold cited conservative columnist George Will and his leeriness of the program, and even though Feingold said the president's "personal conduct" was not "as serious" as Watergate, it was "more dangerous to our system of government, to our republic,…it weakens us in the fight against terrorism, to have a president who's thumbing his nose at the laws of this country."[480] Feingold himself threw the weakness-card into the fray.

"I am absolutely convinced, after five hearings, three in the Judiciary Committee, two in the intelligence Committee, that there is no legal basis for this. I may not know all the details, but its clear from everything we've heard that you can't sort of create a new law or a new statute or a new constitutional provision."[481] How could one be 'absolutely convinced' if he may not know all the details? Lindsey Graham followed up Feingold's appearance on *FOX News Sunday* and argued a censure would "weaken the presidency. And to bring up the ghost of Watergate here is really absurd."[482]

A brief flirtation with 2008

In March 2005, the *Wisconsin State Journal* reported that his Senate campaign registered the domain name for the Web Site www.russfeingold08.com.[483] Feingold also re-visited Alabama in late March, as the headlines stated "Feingold in Dixie on mission of diplomacy,"[484] and "Southern strategy for Feingold."[485] Tom Curry, MSNBC's national affairs writer, wrote an editorial (3.30.05) which offered great arguments for Feingold's candidacy for president. Curry noted Feingold's position on the Senate Judiciary Committee could give him strong media attention as revising the USA Patriot Act would begin in early April 2005; the same committee membership would be valuable when a Supreme Court vacancy appeared.[486] And unlike Kerry or Edwards, Curry noted that Feingold voted against the bill to grant permanent normal trade relations (PNTR) to China in 2000.[487] The *AP* reported Russ Feingold's PAC had about a total of $100,000 for the first quarter of 2005.[488]

He was not a top tier candidate. But he raised over $1 million in the first quarter of 2006 with his two committees and surpassed Biden, Clark, Bayh, and Edwards in the time frame; Feingold's PAC raised more money in each successive month in the quarter (especially during March, and his call for censure of the president).[489] Two-thirds of his contributions came at less than $200.[490] He went to Iowa (4.29.06) and played the middle ground. He called his censure effort "moderate" and "responsible," and mentioned his 2004 Senate victory in an *AP* interview: "I carried 27 counties that George Bush carried and was elected by 300,000 votes."[491]

As 2006 began, Feingold's media coverage increased. *Newsweek* managing editor, John Meacham called (1.1.06) Feingold "a sane Howard Dean."[492] He was in Vermont (1.7.06) for Rep. Bernie Sanders' Senate campaign.[493] When *FOX News* reported Vice President Cheney's support for wiretapping, it included a quote from Feingold: "What we're not open to is the president deciding on his own that he ought to make up a law because he's frustrated that he can't do whatever he wants."[494] And by late 2005, Feingold quotes were incorporated into *AP* and other news stories on Iraq. The same was not the case in 2003.

If any candidate was internet savvy—it was Russ Feingold. In a January 2006 poll on the liberal blog *Daily Kos*, Feingold garnered 30% of 11,000 votes to place 1st in Democratic polling for 2008.[495] Likewise, this same disproportion to reality (Gallup, Cook, and *AP*/Ipsos) was displayed on the liberal blog *MyDD.com* in February: Feingold led, followed by Clark, Warner, and John Edwards—the same order as the *Daily Kos* poll.[496] Noteworthy here was Clark, who before the Jan.31 *Daily Kos* poll led the previous five bimonthly polls on the website.[497] Feingold had already posted nearly a dozen times on DailyKos by February 2006.[498]

Feingold held a national "Listening Session" online (3.10.06).[499] Feingold picked up Paul Tewes, a partner in Hildebrand Tewes consulting firm (Hildebrand was helping Tom Daschle).[500] Tewes was helping (on a volunteer basis) Feingold's assistance with Iowa candidates in the 2006 election.[501]

In nationwide polls, Feingold had gained little ground. But individual states are more important than nationwide polls. In June 2006, Clinton won Washington state (31%), followed by Gore (19), and Edwards (12), but Feingold finished a very strong fourth (11).[502] Sure, Feingold placed 11th in the May 2006 Democratic insiders poll (by the nonpartisan *National Journal*) of who had the best chance of being the nominee, and ABC's political unit gave Feingold the worst odds among contenders, but Strategic Vision's polling found otherwise. Feingold had received only 4% in Washington in September 2005; in New Jersey, he received 1% in October 2005 but 8% in June 2006—indeed the Republican polling firm found Feingold averaged 7% in Washington, New Jersey, Pennsylvania, Michigan, Florida, and Georgia—an average that put him fourth place behind Clinton, Gore, and Edwards.[503]

Feingold and Mark Warner went to New Hampshire (6.3.06). More than 800 Democrats came to St. Anselm College in Manchester in what was for New Hampshire Democrats "their biggest state convention in 30 years."[504] Feingold had a half dozen standing ovations,[505] and "applause punctuated his half-hour speech about 20 times."[506] He criticized his party on the war. "I didn't just write an op-ed about it. I didn't say after the fact, 'Hey, jeez, maybe that wasn't such a good idea.' I just plain voted against it…Why are Democrats so timid to say what everyone in America knows. . . . It's time to get the troops out of Iraq," said Feingold.[507] According to the *Concord Monitor*, "Warner's message of national unity didn't inspire much reaction….But criticism of Bush went over big."[508]

Russ Feingold dropped out of contention

On November 11, 2006, Russ Feingold became "the second Democrat to seriously explore a campaign before opting out," as Warner had been the first a month earlier.[509] *McClatchy* (11.14.07) called Feingold "the purest anti-Bush voice in the campaign," despite he had already dropped out.[510] The *AP* said Feingold "decided against a long-shot run."[511] Feingold already stated before the midterms that he would be tempted to stay in the Senate if the Democrats controlled it, or if individuals within his party had more voice.[512] The decision was not a jaw-dropper.

Why did he drop out?

Feingold told the *AP* "I never got to the point where I felt strongly I wanted to run...Then I saw the result Tuesday and thought what a great opportunity to do my work in the Senate."[513] Feingold said being an underdog was not the reason, but admitted to the *Journal-Sentinel* "It would have required the craziest combination of things in the history of American politics to make it work."[514] And it did not appeal to him. Feingold said the effort would have "dismantle[d] my professional life (in the Senate) and my personal life."[515] Was there something in his personal life that made him drop out? His latest divorce? Feingold told the *Journal-Sentinel* he had been through three US Senate campaigns: "The people I've run against have not been pansies."[516]

What was the reaction?

The country had no clue. Weeks earlier, while reporting on John Kerry, the *Boston Globe* said, "Last June he proposed, with Senator Russell D. Feingold, a July 2007 deadline to withdraw all US troops from Iraq. The amendment failed badly but marked a forward position for antiwar Democrats in Congress."[517] No one who followed Feingold closely called him 'Russell D,' i.e. Jonathon Edwards....Albert Gore. His 2004 Senate campaign slogan was "Standing Up For Us: Russ." Conan O'Brien said that having heard Feingold's announcement, it "...finally answers the question no one asked."[518]

Before the midterms "he was not traveling, fund raising or organizing with quite the same intensity as some potential candidates."[519] Eventually Feingold was all but forgotten. By December 17, the *International Herald Tribune* reported Evan Bayh was "the second Democrat who had drawn interest to announce that he was quitting the race before even beginning it" noting Mark Warner as the first.[520]

With Feingold out, who did it help?

Most likely Obama and Gore. Even Feingold himself "lauded" both before the mid-terms for their early criticism of the war and said voters in 2008 would be looking for a candidate who "had the judgment to understand (the war) was a bad idea from the beginning....I don't think it is asking a lot for people to see this was a stupid idea."[521] That line was quoted in the same article in which he said (11.3.06), "I will run if I want to run, regardless of who else is running. But I will tell you, seeing Barack Obama considering running gives me comfort. If I decided not to run, it makes me feel good, it makes me very happy to see him thinking about running...If he came up to me and asked me, should he run...I might tell him, 'It's a good thing.'"[522] Feingold was just as specific when he dropped out, noting his "first choice" for a nominee would be someone who voted against the war, and the "Second choice is somebody who at least said it was a bad idea...I would be happy if Obama or Gore ran," but added it was not an endorsement.[523]

The *Milwaukee Journal-Sentinel* suggested "there was some speculation Sunday [11.12.06] that Feingold's decision could in an odd way help Clinton, since she won't have to defend her record on the war, which has been criticized on the left, from a fellow senator who voted in the other way."[524] Maybe

Feingold's decision didn't help any candidate. Feingold often led straw polls on liberal blog sites, though only low single digits (if any) in national polls.[525]

Feingold: another censure?

In July 2007, on *Meet the Press* and a *Daily Kos* community website blog, Feingold announced his proposal of censuring the President, Vice President, and other administration officials for "misconduct relating to the war in Iraq and for their repeated assaults on the rule of law."[526] But Senate Majority Leader Harry Reid said (7.22.07), "I don't think we need a censure resolution in the Senate to prove" Bush was "the worst president we've ever had."[527]

According to Feingold's Progressive Patriots Fund website (8.1.07), Feingold considered two censure resolutions. The first would condemn the president on Iraq; and the second "will likely focus on the Bush administration's relentless refusal to abide by the rule of law. Possibly including" the wiretapping program.[528] If a Senator is thinking about censuring the president, the evidence should overwhelm. Why did Feingold use "likely" and "possibly" in asking for support for the censure?

At the very least, Feingold's proposal in July 2007 showed his suggestions for Iraq and wiretapping were not just hyped up to bolster his presidential ambitions in 2006, because Feingold was just as liberal before as he was after his presidential ambitions ended. In addition, Feingold's left-wing strategies after his presidential campaign still impact the presidential race, because they negate the anti-war campaigns of Dennis Kucinich and Mike Gravel.

Former Senator Mike Gravel

Gravel served in the Army (1951-54),[529] but by all accounts was a loser in the beginning of his political career. In 1958, he ran for what would become the Alaska Legislature, but lost; then in 1960 he lost a bid for Anchorage City Council.[530] He finally won a seat the Alaska's House in 1962, and by 1965 he was the Speaker.[531] He tried to beat the Democrat occupying Alaska's only congressional seat in 1966, but lost. So he ran for Senate in 1968 and beat Democratic incumbent Ernest Gruening.[532] Gruening was one of two Senators to vote against the Gulf of Tonkin Resolution authorizing the Vietnam conflict.[533] Salon.com observed: "Though it might come as a surprise to his newfound fans, the liberal Gravel also ran to the right of Gruening on the issue of Vietnam."[534]

In the Senate, Gravel was a staunch opponent of nuclear testing, but "his political survival required him to support resource exploitation."[535] His 1971 filibuster against the continuation of the draft "was successful" and helped end the policy by 1973.[536] A very humble man, he nominated himself for vice president during the 1972 Democratic National Convention.[537] Gravel also read into the Congressional record 4,100 pages of the 7,000-page leaked document known as the Pentagon Papers.[538]

In 1978, Gravel killed a compromise bill over huge parcels of Alaskan land controlled by the federal government despite being "the product of the almost-obsessive work of many disparate groups and, especially," Alaska Sen. Ted Stevens.[539] Salon.com said Stevens blamed the collapse of the bill and Gravel for the death of his wife, Ann, who died in a plane crash: "if that bill had passed, I might have a wife sitting at home when I get home tonight," said Stevens in 1979.[540]

Gravel lost the 1980 Democratic primary to Clark Gruening, who lost to Frank Murkowski in the general election.[541]

The National Initiative

Gravel had a quest for representative democracy, in that all major policy decisions (health care, social secuirty investments, and declaration of war) would be decided through the people by a direct vote.[542] "Our three branches of government have become like an unstable chair, a three-legged chair.The founders could not have envisioned how much money and special interests would corrupt the political process. Giving us Americans legislative power will put forth the fourth leg of our stool and make it stable."[543]

Hence, he ran on the slogan of a "National Initiative for Democracy," which would, as Gravel said, "bring all American citizens into the operations of government as lawmakers."[544] His press release said the "clarion call of his campaign" was "Let the People Decide."[545] Since the 1990s, he invested his time at his think-tank in Virginia, the Democracy Foundation.[546] Its website claimed Gravel "does not naively dismiss the negative elements of human nature, but is convinced that an improved structure for governance—direct democracy—will call forth the better side of our nature."[547]

Gravel's opinion on the declaration of war vote is noteworthy. Four months after the 2003 Iraq invasion, 69% of the public still believed Saddam Hussein was personally involved in the 9/11 attacks.[548] Even if the public were given a chance to vote for war, would it have changed the Iraq situation?

Gravel said citizens would become used to voting on issues, rather than allowing Congress to vote, and elections would be about issues, not candidates.[549] Gravel argued that once 60 million citizens directly voted for the National Initiative for Democracy, it would by virtue of Article 7 of the Constitution become law.[550] So would there be more elections if the people voted more? How much would the extra polling workers and ballots cost nationwide?

A national sales tax

His campaign focused on not only his initiative, but also eliminating the IRS and income taxes.[551] He said the current tax system "unfairness" was "only superceded by its incomprehensibility" and offered "a straight forward national sales tax with proper consideration for the necessities of life through a pre-bate."[552] His idea was not new, for he had previously advocated replacing corporate and individual income taxes with a 23% national sales tax.[553] He supported a federal sales tax at his April 2006 press conference, but a percentage was not reported.[554] Gravel said (July 2006) he thought the government should send monthly cash-flow checks for poor and middle class families: "Then, you to get your paycheck, and there are no federal deductions [except for his 23% sales tax when the check is spent]. Now that's pretty good."[555]

Gravels weaknesses

1) Clearly his age and money. He resorted to old clichés, and in the first presidential debate said of his opponents: "I won't hold their youth and inexperience against them."[556] He visited New Hampshire in late May 2006. The *Concord Monitor* said (5.29.06), "Mike Gravel doesn't talk like a 21st-century, media-savvy politician. He interrupts himself to tell political yarns from the 1970s. He meanders from one topic to the next and back. He can be impolitic."[557]

Retired Senators ran for president before. Paul Tsongas and Bill Bradley ran—but "Tsongas and Bradley were only away from politics for seven and three years, respectively, not twenty-five."[558] The candidacy came from no where. Gravel announced his long shot bid for president on April 17, 2006—months before all the other candidates. Gravel and his wife Whitney took public transportation to the news conference announcing his bid for president.[559] When he filed his papers on April 14, 2006 the FEC said it was the earliest anyone had ever filed to run.[560]

Not to mention Gravel was fiscally irresponsible. *Salon* called (5.7.07) Gravel "broke, unemployed, and happy," as his US Senate pension went to his ex-wife.[561] Gravel has also endured two bankruptcies.[562]

2) Why was he running? Historically it's hard to compare Gravel to anyone? Why was Gravel running? Was it to revive his political career? Like George McGovern, who ran for president in 1984 despite losing a presidential campaign (1972) and Senate seat (1980).[563] Was there an ego factor? Was the National Initiative the real reason he was running?

3) Gravel who? The *Washington Post* wrote (4.18.06) of his likeness to a Dennis Kucinich, Gary Bauer or Alan Keyes—to which Gravel added ('helpfully' in an interview) "And Al Sharpton."[564] When he began his candidacy announcement, Gravel ended his speech at the press conference, in which he spent $1,500 to rent a National Press Club room and a *U.S. Newswire* release. "I'm sure some of you have some questions."[565] "Nobody raised a hand. 'Who has the first question?' he repeated. Nobody did," reported the *Washington Post*, which added an *AP* reporter finally "took pity on Gravel and asked a question."[566] After his conference with reporters, where 50 people attended, he drew 30 interview requests and appeared on *Hannity & Colmes* and *C-SPAN*.[567] So Gravel received some attention. But not much. By July 2006 Gravel had been to New Hampshire, Iowa, California, Nevada and Arizona.[568] By the end of the year, when other Democrats announced their candidacies, Gravel was not mentioned as one who had already declared.

Essentially no one knew who Mike Gravel was in 2006. When Kucinich announced his candidacy, *ABC News* said he was joining Vilsack in announcing his candidacy; even though Gravel announced it months earlier.[569] The *Des Moines Register* did the same thing (12.19.06).[570] Likewise, CNN reported Kucinich as the "second Democrat to officially" announce his candidacy, after Vilsack.[571] For the most part, Gravel, in 2006, was not accepted as an official candidate for the Democratic nomination.[572]

His "Mike in the News" section of his official website was clear evidence of his lack of publicity. In December 2006, there were only five articles in the section—two of which were from June 2006, one from July 2006, and the other two were from December 2006.[573] Those two latest articles being "Journalist Ignore Democratic Pack for 2008" from the *Irregular Times*, and a *Portsmouth Herald/AP* report ("Granny D' endorses longshot hopeful").[574] Doris 'Granny D' Haddock endorsed Gravel on December 7, but the *Portsmouth Herald* did not report it until the December 9.[575] Gravel said (12.7.06) "The most important state to me in this campaign has got to be New Hampshire. This is why Doris' endorsement is so significant. She really is an icon within the state."[576] Days later Barack Obama rolled over Evan Bayh in New Hampshire. And Mike Gravel was no Evan Bayh. Gravel rented a Manchester apartment and reportedly intended to campaign hard in the state "up until the primary and beyond, if possible."[577]

4) Initially he had no traction with his war stance. Gravel asked (April 2006) for troops to be withdrawn "expeditiously, without contingency,"[578] though it was unclear how many were listening. Though an anti-war candidate, Democrats already had Feingold, Gore, and Kerry to pick from. Not to mention who was this guy? In a July trip to Connecticut, Gravel said he "would withdraw the power to declare war from the Congress."[579] In an interview with the *Portsmouth Herald News* in June 2006, Gravel said the war in Iraq was "impossible to clean up," and "We need a superpower that can impose peace. We need leadership in this country. You don't fight terrorism with war."[580] So would he have gone to Afghanistan after 9/11?

5) Gravel said things other candidates would (and could) not. Gravel was not optimistic on his time in the Senate. "I was so disgusted with the way that Congress works that when I left office, I thought I was a failure. I didn't realize that I had a record of ending the draft, of starting the nuclear critique, of creating the Alaska pipeline. ... But when I left office, I felt terrible about the system. I went in as an idealist, and I was getting corrupted by the system. And thank God, I lost and got out, and I didn't come back," (4.26.07).[581] The *New York Times* claimed (7.27.07) he "retired" in 1981.[582] The *Concord Monitor* reported (5.29.06) Gravel left Congress in 1981, and he claimed he was fed up with Washington and "disgusted with politics."[583] But Gravel didn't leave politics; he was kicked out of it. But such inaccuracies are less likely to be corrected when the candidate is perceived as a fringe candidate, and facts need to be checked from archives from the 1970s.

On a *YouTube* posted sketch in June 2007, Gravel stared into the camera for over a minute, then abruptly turned, walked to a pond, picked up a rock and chucked it in the water.[584] Gravel said, "Throwing a rock in the water was a metaphor for causing ripples and changes in society, and then walking down and disappearing—that—isn't that what life's about? We start, try to do something, and then go on."[585] If Barack Obama made such a clip, he would be labeled senile.

Gravel ruled out nuclear weapons

Mike Gravel has encouraged Iran and US relations. Gravel said there was a "brainwashing of the mainline media" in the US, where as "I've been interviewed in Tehran about five times on the radio, and we've gotten along just fine."[586] But his strongest point on Iran came in an April 2007 debate.

Gravel said of his fellow Democrats at the presidential debate: "....some of these people frighten me—they frighten me. When you have mainline candidates that turn around and say that there's nothing off the table with respect to Iran, that's code for using nukes, nuclear devices. I got to tell you, I'm president of the United States, there will be no preemptive wars with nuclear devices. To my mind, it's immoral, and it's been immoral for the last 50 years as part of American foreign policy."[587] The moderator, Brian Williams of *NBC News*, interrupted and asked who on the stage worried Gravel. Gravel said "I would say the top tier ones," to which Clinton and Obama could both be seen laughing.[588]

And the discussion of nuclear weaponry continued in the debate. Dennis Kucinich said Vice President Cheney was "already ginning up a cause for war against Iran," (4.26.07).[589] When Obama said Iran was "the largest state sponsor of terrorism" including Hezbollah and Hamas, Kucinich interrupted with "It is disputed."[590] But Kucinich's cries were muzzled by Gravel's tirade:

> No, with respect to Iran, we've sanctioned them for 26 years. We scared the bejesus out of them when the president says, "They're evil." Well, you know something? These

things don't work. They don't work. We need to recognize them [Iran]. And you know something? Who is the greatest violator of the non-proliferation treaty? The United States of America. We signed a pledge that we would begin to disarm, and we're not doing it. We're expanding our nukes. Who the hell are we going to nuke? Tell me, Barack. Barack, who do you want to nuke?

Obama said, "I'm not planning to nuke anybody right now, Mike, I promise."[591] Gravel replied, "Good. Good. We're safe then, for a while."[592] After the debate days later, he told CNN "we could cut our nuke arsenal in half, unilaterally, and it wouldn't affect one bit our capability to defend ourselves," (4.30.07).[593]

Gravel has already exceeded the expectations for his campaign.

Former Vice President Al Gore

Gore began his public career in 1976, when he was elected to Congress at the age of 28.[594] He ran for president in 1988 and 2000, and in between was Bill Clinton's Vice President. Would 2008 be his third try for the White House?

Some friends in high places

In December 2005, at Stanford's Memorial Auditorium, Gore talked to an audience of 2000, that "was filled with Silicon Valley luminaries," including Apple's Steve Jobs, Google's Larry Page and Eric Schmidt, and Yahoo's Jerry Yang.[595] Schmidt was the CEO of Google, and his wife helped organize the event.[596] Gore was no stranger to elites in the tech world. There was a lump of donors just waiting to contribute to Gore if he ran for president in 2008, primarily because after losing the 2000 election, Gore led a successful private sector life.

Gore took an advisory post with Google in 2001, joined Apple's Board of Directors in March 2003, teamed with a consortium of investors to purchase a cable TV news network for $70 million in 2004, and then joined with David Blood to form Generation Investment Management (announced November 2004).[597]

With Generation, Al Gore was one of six founding partners in a new investment firm whose research team mixed sustainability research with traditional investment.[598] The *Financial Times* reported that Generation's founders, including Blood, the former CEO of Goldman Sachs Asset Management, contributed 'double-digit' millions for startup.[599] Generation's purpose was to "integrate traditional equity analysis with sustainability research."[600] Blood was "a legend in the London investment scene," as he retired at the age of 44 as the CEO of Goldman Sachs in 2003, after growing the company's assets by $275 billion in seven years.[601]

Gore is media savvy

Though he was mocked for saying he invented the Internet, Al Gore was experienced in technology. As *American Prospect* later wrote, Gore could arguably be named

> ...the rich uncle who sent it [the internet] to college, using his seat on the Commerce, Science, and Transportation Committee [in the Senate] to ensure the fledgling technology had the financial wherewithal to make something of itself. Vinton Cerf and Bob Kahn, the two men most often given credit for birthing the Web (due to their development of the crucial TCP/IP protocols), were so appalled by the media's distortion of Gore's comments that they jointly penned a defense, writing that 'no other elected official ... has made a greater contribution over a longer period of time' than Gore.[602]

Indeed, perhaps Al Gore's most underrated quality is his knowledge and passion for understanding media. Joel Hyatt was the son-in-law to former Ohio Sen. Howard Metzenbaum and was the Democratic Party's finance chair during Gore's campaign; both Gore and Hyatt tried to buy the *New Republic* in 2001.[603]

Gore began teaching journalism at Columbia in the spring of 2001. He challenged the ethics of journalism and argued journalists goal for balance in controversial issues can give attention to even the most fringe views—which Gore said harmed media's accuracy.[604] The *American Prospect* later quoted a student who said Gore "knew more than everyone in the room. So the class basically turned against him because he was smarter than they were and they didn't like that."[605] Gore's message did not agree with the university's journalistic philosophy, and Gore did not return the following year to teach.[606]

In April 2005, Al Gore officially announced his cable network, *Current,* would debut in August of 2005. Gore stated that "We have no intention of being a Democratic channel, a liberal channel or the TV version of *Air America...*It is not in any way an ideological, much less partisan point of view in any respect. It will have the point of view of the young generation."[607] (*Air America* was the liberal radio network established a year earlier.) Despite the insistence of no political agenda, it would have to wait to see whether Gore's network would benefit the former Vice President politically. To be carried by DirecTV, Comcast and Time Warner, Gore's network was scheduled to begin by being offered in 19 million homes; Gore would serve as the venture's board chairman.[608]

An Inconvenient Truth

Al Gore wasn't always a star spokesman for the environment. Gore held the first congressional hearing on carbon-dioxide levels in 1981; though it wasn't until the end of the decade, a failed bid for the presidency (1988), and his son's near death in a car accident that he "immersed himself in global warming."[609] *Earth in the Balance* did not come out until a decade after the first hearings.

George H. W. Bush called Gore "ozone man" in 1992.[610] Eight years later, George W. Bush said Gore "likes electric cars. He just doesn't like making electricity."[611] The younger Bush asked Gore "to explain what he meant by some of the things" in Gore's book (Bush admitted he never read it).[612]

In June 2000, when Gore gave a speech in Philadelphia laying out a $150 billion, ten-year plan to address fossil-fuels, the *New York Times* placed the story on page A24.[613] In 2000, he ended up rather cautious on the environmental issues, which some critics thought "may have cost him Florida, where he was reluctant to speak out on the construction of an ecologically disastrous airport in the middle of the Everglades and Biscayne National Parks."[614]

But Gore's environmental push reached a pinnacle in the spring of 2006, when *An Inconvenient Truth* showed in theaters across the country. The *New Yorker* complimented the film, but said (4.24.06), it was a "documentary film about a possibly retired politician giving a slide show about the dangers of melting ice sheets and rising sea levels. It has a few lapses of mise en scène [movie direction] sometimes we see Gore gravely talking on his cell phone—or gravely staring out an airplane window, or gravely tapping away on his laptop in a lonely hotel room—for a little longer than is absolutely necessary."[615] But the movie did well.

As 2006 ended, Gore may not have retained the height of coverage that he received when *An Inconvenient Truth* was released in May, but he still received numerous appearances. The DVD was released November 21,[616] around the same time it had become the top 15 of 81 submitted films still in the running for an Academy Award for feature-length documentary.[617] The top five nominations were unveiled Jan. 23 for the Feb.25, 2007 ceremony.[618] MoveOn.org teamed up with Gore and organized over 1600 viewing parties nationwide (12.16.06).[619] Even JohnKerry.com co-sponsored the viewing parties, and said Gore deserved support in the global warming fight.[620] Bill Clinton hopped on the bandwagon in September 2006, as he told CNN he talked to Gore and "I said, you need to make a second movie out of that last chart [greenhouse gas emissions]. And, he's doing it I think. He's going to make another movie."[621]

The British Treasury Chief Gordon Brown said Gore would advise the British Government on climate change (10.29.06).[622] The *AP* reported (12.11.06) Gore was "waging a fierce campaign" for an Oscar, as he appeared for interviews with Jay Leno, Oprah Winfrey, and Matt Lauer.[623] Gore won his Oscar, but did not announce a candidacy for president in his acceptance speech as some suggested that he should.

In between the nomination and the Oscar, the *Today Show* reported (12.28.06) Canada's polar bear population was down 22 percent due to earlier thaws of ice in the Arctic.[624]

An inconvenient zinc mine

Peter Schweizer, thru *USA Today*, basically hinted Gore was a hypocrite in an August 2006 editorial. The Gores, according to public records, lived in two properties: the 10,000 square foot home in Nashville and a 4,000 square foot in Virginia; and they had another home in Carthage, Tennessee.[625] "For someone rallying the planet to pursue a path of extreme personnel sacrifice, Gore requires little from himself," wrote Schweizer, who noted Gore's Arlington and Nashville properties did not use the wind energy options.[626] As Howard Dean was saying "Global Warming …threatens our very existence," the Democratic National Committee did not pay the additional two pennies per kilowatt hour to green.[627] Schweizer also noted Gore still had holdings in Occidental Petroleum, which was accused of drilling ecologically sensitive areas.[628] As *An Inconvenient Truth*'s website said "Humanity is sitting on a ticking time bomb," Gore's Carthage property was on top of a zinc mine, and he received $20,000 royalties annually from Pasminco Zinc, which operated a Zinc concession on the estate.[629] Tennessee cited the company for significant amounts of zinc, iron, and barium in a nearby river.[630]

Gore has answered his critics. When *Time* asked about his critics who felt he was not as carbon-neutral as he claimed, Gore said "That's just not true. Two years ago we became a carbon-neutral family. I purchase Green Power [electricity from renewable sources], have installed new light bulbs and clock thermostats, and I'm installing solar panels. We switched to a hybrid car. I am not recommending actions that I haven't already taken myself."[631]

Gore is not alone: Arnold Schwarzenegger

Though some Republican's have been critical of Gore's movie and environmentalism, major Republican leaders believe the climate change issue is a problem. The Governor of California won re-election in 2006 over his Democratic opponent 56-39.[632] When asked to describe what it meant to be an Arnold

Republican, he said "Well, it's basically being fiscally conservative, being socially moderate and you know, being environmentally progressive."[633]

Senator Jim Inhofe (R-OK) said in August 2003, as chairman of the Environment and Public Works Committee, "With all the hysteria, all of the fear, all of the phony science, could it be that man-made global warming is the greatest hoax ever perpetrated on the American people? It sure sounds like it."[634] *On Meet the Press*, Schwarzenegger was asked what such statements did for the GOP.

> I don't think it does—it does much to the Republican Party. I think it is just, you know, there's always in history been people that are back with their thinking in the Stone Age. And I think that the key thing for us is, is to not pay any attention to those things, because as I said, the science is in, we know the facts, there's not any more debate as to global warming or not. We have global warming and the fact also is that we can do something about it. We can slow it down or we can stop it, but only if everyone is working together. The United States is, you know, 5 percent of the world population but we're using 25 percent of the oil. So I mean, you know, we are creating 25 percent of the pollution of the greenhouse gas emissions with a 5 percent population. So of course, the rest of the world is looking at us kind of, you know, in an odd way, saying, "Why are they preaching to us and why are they trying to be, you know, so righteous about all of this?" Let us all work together on this. And I think that's what we have to do.[635]

Al Gore was in line with Schwarzenegger. Gore also talked about those who doubt science in *Time* (Nov.2006):

> There's some good news here. Senator Inhofe will soon be replaced [on the Senate's environmental committee] by Senator Barbara Boxer, an advocate of solving the crisis, as chairwoman of that committee. As to why there are still skeptics--there are people who believe that the moon landing was staged in a movie lot in Arizona. Another reason is that some of the largest polluters are still putting millions of dollars a year to hire pseudo scientists to confuse people into thinking that this crisis isn't real.[636]

Why do conservatives attack climate change? Mike Huckabee (May.06) said it was better for the country "to act as if global warming" was a scientific fact because there was "no downside in conserving our resources."[637]

Gore stayed in the game

The *AP* reported (12.12.06) Clinton "is the front-runner, but a polarizing one for some Democrats," Obama "is the electrifying newcomer, but limited in his experience," and Gore "remains, for many party activists, the Democrat and popular vote-getter done wrong."[638] When asked if he missed politics, he told Jay Leno (11.29.06) "Well, there's some things I miss about it. Being able to have more of a direct influence on policy."[639] The Leno bit was an extended fifteen minute interview for Gore (two segments),[640] who sometimes struck a chord with his humor in an interview that focused mainly on his DVD. Leno showed a picture in *GQ Magazine* where Gore wore black and had a "Bono thing going there. What's that? Was that a fashion choice?"[641] To which Gore responded, "…that's from my portfolio that was made for the 10 Sexiest Men on *CSPAN*."[642] Though skeptics like *CNN*'s Jack Cafferty said "Al Gore—you know, there's just people in this world who aren't hip. And he's one of them."[643]

The *AP* reported of Gore as if he had comedic talent: "Derided in 2000 for being a wooden know-it-all, the new Gore is funny. He's done humorous turns on 'Saturday Night Live' and voiced a disembodied head on the cartoon

'Futurama,' which is being made into a movie," (12.11.06).[644] *GQ* actually made Gore one of their men of the year, and in the article Gore bashed the President with big words: "Dammit, whatever happened to the concept of accountability for catastrophic failure? This administration has been, by far, the most incompetent, inept, and with more moral cowardice and obsequiousness to their wealthy contributors, and obliviousness to the public interest of any administration in modern history, and probably in the entire history of the country!"[645]

Gore himself said in early December 2006, "I am not planning to run for president again,' while adding that he had not "completely ruled it out."[646] He told CNN's *Showbiz Tonight*, "I have no intention of being a candidate again."[647] But the *AP* reported (12.11.06) "aides say he could spend as much as $50 million of his own money to launch a credible presidential run.'[648]

Gore still had his fans

Donna Brazille, who played a major role in Gore's 2000 campaign, said "Al Gore has the right set of what I call post-9/11 skills. Strong on national security. Someone who can talk about domestic issues, as well. But you know, his No. 1 priority right now is focusing the world on the dangers of global warming. He's spent a great deal of time and resources. By the way, his DVD is out. I should give a plug for 'An Inconvenient Truth.'"[649] And although he may not have been mentioned on many news reports' lists for presidential candidacies, Donna Brazille said "Don't rule out Al Gore yet," (11.26.06).[650] By the end of the month it was the third highest grossing documentary in the history of theatrical releases."[651] Jimmy Carter told *Hardball* Gore "would still be my preference" in 2008, and said Gore would have won in 2004 had he run.[652] David Schuster said Joe Trippi wanted "to create an Internet phenomenon again like he did for Howard Dean, for Al Gore."[653] Apparently Trippi was aligning with the Gore camp, as the *AP* reported (12.11.06) Trippi "said Gore would be a formidable candidate and could probably wait longer than others to enter the field."[654]

Why wouldn't he run?

Though the documentary's release kept him in the spotlight, he was different from Clinton and Obama and had "steered far from campaign mechanics," and avoided the primary states; he was spending weekends "training environmentalists" to deliver presentations on climate change.[655] In the meantime, Gore totally dodged the Iraq issue. The *AP* (Dec.06) noted his appearances with Leno and Oprah, and how he "parried questions on Iraq from Matt Lauer."[656]

His focus has all been on climate change. In July 2007, Gore participated in Live Earth '08, as he kicked off the US portion of the worldwide concerts.[657] The same month, Gore's daughter Kristen said, "He's really not going to get in the race."[658] That may be the case, but if the Iowa Caucus turned into an Obama v. Clinton dog fight, days before the vote, Gore could announce he would allow Iowa voters to consider him. He immediately would receive double-digit support. But in the end, Gore's decision not to run might be the best evidence that the Democratic Party is on its way to a Hillary Clinton coronation.

Senator John Kerry

Why did John Kerry lose in 2004? There is not just one reason, but dozens. The beginning headings of this chapter examine why the Senator from Massachusetts could not beat a President who would eventually become as unpopular as Richard Nixon.

The bin Laden tape

Maybe the bin Laden tape hurt Kerry. In the tape released Oct.29, 2004, bin Laden said, "Your security is not in the hands of Kerry or Bush or al Qaeda. Your security is in your own hands, and each state that does not harm our security will remain safe."[659] If voters tend to stick with incumbents during war, the tape was a death sentence to Kerry's efforts.

Kerry's excuses in April 2006

Kerry once again declined to get in the specifics of his mistakes on *Meet the Press* in April 2006. However, he did say his "biggest mistake was probably not going outside the federal financing so we could have controlled our own message."[660] Having won the Democratic nomination, Kerry decided to accept federal money in 2004, along with its spending limits but the Boston nomination convention occurred over a month before Bush was re-nominated in New York City; so Kerry began spending under federal rules much sooner than the President.[661] "We had a 13-week general election, they had an eight-week general election. We had the same pot of money."[662] Kerry's regret actually garnered *AP* headlines ("Kerry: Taking Federal Money a Mistake"),[663] even though he appeared on *Meet the Press* to discuss his Iraq proposal. How did Kerry's campaign overlook the extra five weeks Kerry would have to spend the same amount as Bush?

What was the vision of the 2004 campaign? Kerry's *Meet the Press* interview (4.9.06) also brought up the *Boston Globe*'s March 2006 article which reported many Democrats remained upset about Kerry and his inability to "refine his policy positions into a coherent vision" in 2004; and Joe Klein's *Time* article suggested Kerry's political consultants told Kerry not to say something about the Abu Ghraib prison scandal.[664] "I know nothing about a focus group [which reportedly was inconclusive on what the Kerry camp should say about US soldiers abusing Iraqi prisoners] being ordered."[665]

Kerry was a waffler no Democrat would deny. His famous line that he voted for the $87 billion package to fund Iraq before he voted against it solidified him as a flip-flopper. *Boston Globe* columnist Ellen Goodman, who even admitted she voted for Kerry "six different times," wrote (4.28.06) a column titled "Don't run [in 2008], John Kerry," noting "In the end [of the 2004 campaign], the president who lied to us about war and weapons of mass destruction looked like the straight talker. That's how bad it was."[666] Paul Begala and James Carville appeared on *Meet the Press* (1.22.06) to discuss their book for Democratic success: *Take it Back*. Tim Russert read from the book, in which a Bush strategist told the authors after the 2004 election that "'From day one we talked about three things: strength, trust, and values.' In their story, Bush embodied all of those things and John Kerry had none of them."[667] Begala told Russert the Democratic Party's problem "is not ideological, it is anatomical."[668] "We need a spine. And a party that allows someone who has won five major medals, who three times has shed blood for our country, and won the bronze star and silver star to be positioned as weak and waffling and weird is—It's a sin. It's awful."[669] Kerry was still part of the problem, not the solution.

Teresa Heinz-Kerry spoke her mind

Teresa Heinz-Kerry was born in Mozambique to Portuguese parents.[670] She was married 15 years to Sen. John Heinz (R-PA), who died in a 1991 plane crash.[671] She inherited Heinz's fortune, and then married Kerry in 1995.[672] She was worth around $500 million, but she may have been most remembered in the campaign for her mouth.

On the eve of the 2004 Democratic National Convention, Theresa Heinz-Kerry accused the editorial page editor of the *Pittsburgh Tribune-Review* of misquoting her and told one of the paper's reporters to "Shove it."[673] Before those blunt words, Heinz-Kerry had said "We need to turn back some of the creeping, un Pennsylvanian and sometimes un-American traits that are coming into some of our politics."[674] Minutes later, a *Pittsburgh Tribune-Review* reporter asked her was she meant by "un American activity."[675] She said "I didn't say 'activity' or 'un-American,'" then she talked to Pennsylvania Gov. Ed Rendell, and came back and asked the reporter if she worked for the *Pittsburgh Tribune-Review*.[676] The reporter affirmed, Heinz-Kerry said "Of course," the reporter asked the question again, and she said "You said something I didn't say. Now shove it."[677] Kerry did not apologize for his wife, and said she "speaks her mind appropriately," while Kerry advisor Tad Devine said Heinz-Kerry "tells it like it is."[678] But she had not been misquoted. The Kerry campaign saw the paper as biased, (hence, her 'of course' comment) as it was owned by Richard Mellon Scaife, who donated millions to conservative causes.[679] Ironically, before the 'shove it' remark, she had told her audience "I remember a time when people in political parties in Pennsylvania talked to one another and actually got things done."[680]

Not surprisingly, when she took the stage at the 2004 convention she said, "My name is Teresa Heinz Kerry, and by now I hope it will come as no surprise to anyone that I have something to say."[681] She also told the convention, "My right to speak my mind, to have a voice, to be what some have called 'opinionated' is a right I deeply and profoundly cherish. And my only hope is that one day soon, women who have all earned a right to their opinions, instead of being called opinionated, will be called smart and well informed, just like men."[682]

But sometimes 'opinionated' came off as abrasive. In August 2004, when discussing the Republican chants of "four more years" at a Bush rally, Heinz-Kerry said, "They want four more years of hell."[683] Heinz-Kerry also said, "I don't know Laura Bush. But she seems to be calm, and she has a sparkle in her eye, which is good. But I don't know that she's ever had a real job—I mean, since she's been grown up."[684] She then had to retract: "I had forgotten that Mrs. Bush had worked as a school teacher and librarian, and there couldn't be a more important job than teaching our children."[685] In 2005, she commented on Catholic bishops' previous comments on Kerry's pro-choice views: "You cannot have bishops in the pulpit—long before or the Sunday before the election—as they did in Catholic churches, saying it was a mortal sin to vote for John Kerry."[686]

Kerry's military records and swift boating

In his 2004 convention speech he said "I'm John Kerry and I'm reporting for duty."[687] And with that statement, Kerry himself had invited speculation into his military records by making his past service a part of his campaign.

Kerry's battle with the Swift Boat Veterans For Truth, a veterans organization criticizing Kerry's service in Vietnam, continued after the 2004 elections. In a South Carolina newspaper (May 2006), William Schacte rehashed his allegation he was with Kerry when he received the injury that led to Kerry's first Purple Heart, and claimed Kerry's wound was actually self-inflicted.[688] The *New York Times* reported (May 2006) "the battle over Kerry's wartime service continues."[689] In the report, Kerry and his supporters claimed they did not have the extensive archival material to defend the Senator, which would have been too complicated to gather concurrently in the 2004 campaign; and Kerry said his opposition challenging his military service "spent something like $30 million, and we didn't. That's just a terrible imbalance when somebody's lying about you."[690]

But the fact of the matter was not the Swift Boaters' story of itself—that was for 2004. The importance of the Swift Boat story in 2006 was that the story still existed. Indeed, commenting on the *New York Times* article, *Yahoo!NEWS* had a story from *RealClearPolitics* (6.12.06) titled "John Kerry's Skimmer Scam."[691] When was this saga going to end? And why didn't it end?

Kerry said what the Swift Boat Veterans for Truth said in the 2004 campaign was "untrue" and "…the truth in its entirety will come out."[692] In his appearance on *Meet the Press* (1.30.05), Kerry said he would sign a SF 180 releasing his military records; according to Kerry's communication director David Wade, the former presidential candidate did so on May 20, 2005.[693] That was just the beginning. As Wade stated, "The next step is to send it [SF 180] to the Navy, which will happen in the next few days. The Navy will then send out the records."[694] It had been over a year since the Swift Boat Veterans had derailed Kerry's campaign, and Kerry still did not have a clear answer for them. Joan Vennochi of the *Boston Globe* commented that if the truth should come out, signing the SF 180 was the first step; releasing the entire military record was the second… "It doesn't get any plainer than that."[695]

When allegations surfaced about John McCain and Wes Clark with their military records, they opened up their files entirely.[696] John Kerry's release did not come as easily.

Pressed on his military records, Kerry authorized the *Boston Globe*, the *Los Angeles Times* and the *Associated Press* to receive a complete copy of his military and medical records directly from government archives.[697] His signing of the SF 180 in May 2005 paved the way for these releases. But what made the news was his grades at Yale. President Bush received a cumulative of a 77 in his first three years at Yale.[698] But it turned out through the Navy's records that Kerry averaged a 76 in his four years, but "the military and medical records...appear identical to what Kerry has already released."[699]

The incident posed some important questions. Why did Kerry delay the release of his records if the military part of the records was the same? A release in 2004 would have silenced his critics and the Swift Boat Veterans for Truth. And if his military records were the same, was Kerry's initial decision not to release all of his records based on his concern about looking 'dumber' than Bush? Clearly Kerry had the appearance of a better student. Indeed, a Fox News poll conducted June 14-15, 2005 showed 43% still felt Kerry got the better grades at Yale—only 27% said it was Bush.[700] Kerry's grades had already come out the week before the poll was conducted

Why did Kerry delay the release of the SF (standard form) 180? Kerry responded in writing—not orally: "The call for me to sign a 180 form came from the same partisan operatives who were lying about my record....Even though the media was discrediting them, they continued to lie. I felt strongly that we shouldn't kowtow to them and their attempts to drag their lies out."[701] If Kerry didn't want to kowtow to these 'partisan operatives,' why did he kowtow to them in June 2005 by releasing the records?

Kerry's friend Sandy Berger

In September 2006, Vice President Cheney said, "I don't know how you can explain five years of no attacks, five years of successful disruption of attacks, five years of defeating the efforts of Al Qaida to come back and kill more Americans. You've got to give some credence to the notion that maybe somebody did something right."[702] Kerry would not give the administration any credit in his response to the quote:

> Well, of course, some people have done some things right, and I give them great credit. Law enforcement officials and intelligence officials, cooperating with other countries, have succeeded in interrupting some cells. We all accept that. That is the least that we should expect.
> But the fact is the bottom line, they took eight years to prepare in between the first bombing of the World Trade Center, I think anybody in law enforcement would tell you that there's an element of luck involved and they're grateful we haven't been hit. But there's nobody in law enforcement who will tell you that we are as safe as we ought to be. [703]

Perhaps Kerry would give credit to Sandy Berger, the former National Security Advisor to President Clinton. In July 2004, Berger quit as an advisor to Kerry's presidential campaign after he was "under criminal investigation for removing copies of highly classified documents from the National Archives" related to the 9/11 Commission's investigation,[704] as the *Washington Post* reported the missing documents were apparently "five or six drafts of a critique of the government's response to the millennium terrorism threat."[705]

Berger allegedly took the documents by shoving them into his clothes and portfolio, but said he "made an honest mistake."[706] More disturbing was that the whole media outbreak occurred a week before the Democratic Convention, so President Clinton said he wished he "knew who leaked it" and noted the "interesting timing," despite that the *Denver Post* said Clinton knew about the investigation for several months.[707] If Clinton knew for months, how long did Kerry know of Berger's investigation? Kerry's spokesman said the situation appeared "to be a partisan attempt to divert attention away from the 9/11 Commission report."[708]

Didn't Berger divert information from the 9/11 Commission? Berger took the high road: "Everything that I have done all along in this process [since Oct.2003] has been for the purpose of aiding and supporting the work of the 9/11 Commission and any suggestion to the contrary is simply, absolutely wrong."[709] But Berger was clearly "reviewing the materials to help determine which Clinton administration documents to provide" the 9/11 Commission.[710] Democrats claimed it was a Republican effort to smear Kerry.[711] Why did Berger leave Kerry's campaign?

Kerry kept his organization in tact

The Presidential nominee from 2004 showed no signs of giving up after the November 2004 elections. There were some legitimate arguments for Kerry to run again. He faced Bush in a wartime election: a difficult task. Yes, Kerry was hindered by the Swift Boat Veterans for Truth in the summer of 2004, but it was a block of opposition unlikely to return in 2008. Kerry could learn from his mistakes, and also have the benefit of having already been harassed by elements of his past.

His concession speech was one of his finest speeches of the campaign, and lacked the partisanship that would encompass Kerry in the following months. Indeed, Kerry called for "the desperate need for unity and finding the common ground, coming together."[712] This unifying speech contrasted with Al Gore's month-long Florida debate after election night in 2000. Within days of his defeat, Kerry met with Democratic leaders in the House and Senate to strategize for 2005.[713] And Kerry's brother Cameron told the *Boston Globe* (11.8.04) a 2008 run was "conceivable."[714] Kerry himself said days after the election, in regard to 2008, "I'm not opening any doors, I'm not shutting any doors,"[715] a confusing statement, given that a door can never be both shut and open.

The *Pittsburgh Post-Gazette* reported days after the 2004 election, Kerry "sparked the speculation with remarks at a campaign goodbye party last weekend and he reportedly has made calls to donors to keep his organization intact. Kerry announced to reporters on the Hill that '54-plus million Americans' voted for health care, energy independence, unity in America, stem-cell research, and protecting Social Security on Nov. 2 and that he would be 'fighting for that agenda with all of the energy that I have and all the passion I brought to the campaign.'"[716] But bi-partisanship of his concession speech dissipated within two weeks: Kerry emailed three million supporters claiming Bush was "planning a right-wing assault on values and ideals we hold most deeply."[717]

Also in Kerry's favor was the Democrats' leadership vacuum. Senate Minority Leader Tom Daschle, having lost to John Thune in South Dakota, was leaving the Senate. Though Nancy Pelosi already was House Minority Leader, she was named to the position when Dick Gephardt decided to step down from the leadership to run for the 2004 Democratic nomination. Gephardt was retiring. Did this help Kerry remain a leader for the Party? There was a void of structural leadership among the Democratic Congressional caucus. And Nevada Sen. Harry Reid, Tom Daschle's replacement in the leadership post, would not adequately fill it.

What were Kerry's obstacles in 2008?

History did not suggest Kerry had a chance to be renominated, given the Democrats had avoided renominating a previous general election loser since 1956 with Adlai Stevenson, who lost the general election to Eisenhower in 1952.

Another problem for Kerry was his appearance and age, as the *Washington Post* reported bluntly (11.17.04), "Kerry no longer wears the makeup he needed for the constant campaign TV appearances. He has the baggy-eyed look of someone who is getting a lot of sleep after not getting enough."[718] One of the jokes on Kerry in 2004 was "Why the long face John?" (Kerry has a protracted head, and gray hair.) Another Kerry campaign in 2008 would rejuvenate the base?

A *Washington Post* report on Kerry (11.9.04) was much more negative, and showed the pessimistic reporting Kerry would have to deal with for 2008. According to the *Post*, a well-known operative who worked on the Kerry campaign "said opposition to Bush, not excitement about Kerry" was behind Kerry's success in fundraising.[719] The same article quoted another anonymous Kerry campaign strategy operative: "I can't imagine people are going to say, 'It worked pretty well last time. This is what we need next time."[720]

Kerry was unpopular. Throughout polling by *CBS News/New York Times* in 2004, when given the choice between "favorable, not favorable, undecided, or haven't you heard enough about John Kerry," registered voters never rated Sen. Kerry higher than 41% favorable.[721] In a *FOX News*/Opinion Dynamics poll, Kerry was so popular 43% rated him unfavorable—one percent higher than those viewing him favorably (Feb.2006). The 42% favorability was 9 points lower than December 2004.[722]

John Kerry was running for President

Hillary Clinton had visited Minnesota in the spring of 2005, and Sen. Mark Dayton (D-MN) introduced the guest as "the next great president of the United States of America." According to the *Minneapolis Star-Tribune*, John Kerry asked Dayton "What are you doing endorsing my 2008 presidential opponent?"[723] A Kerry aide stated it was "nothing but joshing," but Dayton told the paper Kerry was serious.[724]

The *AP* said (1.2.06), "It's almost as if Sen. John Kerry never stopped running for president...He still stalks the TV news show circuit, scolding

President Bush at every turn."[725] The *AP* comments were in a report—not an opinion. But it quoted Kerry's spokesman David Wade: "No other past presidential candidate, with the exception of McCain, has done what Kerry has done in terms of converting his presidential campaign into a grass-roots political and legislative operation."[726]

The *Boston Globe* reported Kerry's schedule of many appearances in important 2006 states with weeks to go before the election, and did not name, but quoted, advisors that were certain Kerry would officially re-run for president.[727] Up to October 2006, he raised $6 million through the Internet (the list of 3 million emails from 2004) and over $13 million total for candidates and campaign committees.[728] In late September, he sent an e-mail for Democratic candidates Webb (VA), Tester (Mont.) Cardin (MD) and Whitehouse (RI)—all viable Senate candidates late in the fall—and raised $400,000 for the four in three days.[729] With less than two weeks in the campaign, Kerry e-mailed his list from the 2004 campaign and his fundraising appeals with Obama garnered $900,000 in two days for Senate candidates in Missouri, Tennessee, Virginia, and New Jersey.[730] Kerry had significantly helped his party. The *Boston Globe* reported (10.9.06) Kerry's sharing of the wealth: "Over the last two years, the Kerry campaign operation generated more than $10 million for various party committees and 179 candidates for the US House, Senate, state and local offices in 42 states, according to tallies kept by his staff."[731]

An October 2006 report in the *Boston Globe* suggested he was running, opening with, "Yesterday, Senator John F. Kerry was in Iowa. Tomorrow and Wednesday, he'll be in Nevada. On Friday, he'll be in New Hampshire. After that, he'll visit 11 more states, including South Carolina, before the Nov. 7 election."[732] In addition, a consultant from New York, Edward Reilly, who in the later half of 2006 had "become one of Kerry's closest advisers," rented a Washington-area apartment in late September to devote more time to Kerry.[733]

Kerry still had the money in 2006. But some Democrats complained about it. HeyJohn.org accused Kerry for not giving Democrats enough money. They claimed, "In 2004, over 171,154 Americans donated $328,479,000 and countless hours of time to help John Kerry get elected president. Now, two years later, Democrats have a real opportunity to regain a majority in both chambers of Congress."[734] Kerry explained himself like a stump speech on ABC's *This Week*:

> Let me tell you what I've been doing, George. First of all, those facts are incorrect. We have been -- and I'm very proud of what I've been doing. I've been traveling all over the country, to some 34 states, many of which have absolutely nothing to do with the presidential political schedule.
>
> I've been campaigning with candidates and for candidates. I've been raising money for candidates and have given money to candidates. I've raised and given over $11 million to candidates, $3.5 million to my Senate colleagues alone, $2.5 million, I think, to the House candidates (ph), millions of dollars to party members and others.
>
> And it costs money to do that. We have to -- we're spending down. Unlike some folks who are out there raising money for themselves, out of cycle, I have not been doing that. I've been spending down, in order to be able to go out and help people. And I'm going to continue to do that. I'll continue to raise money. I'll continue to give money.[735]

Evan Bayh, like Kerry, was criticized for not giving $1 million to the DSCC.[736] Kerry then overtly complimented Jim Webb in Virginia and Chet Culver for Iowa governor. George Stephanopoulos interrupted Kerry and basically said he was advertising (though JohnKerry.com seemingly converted the middle of the host's sentence into an "(inaudible)."[737]

The joke

On October 30, 2006, John Kerry spoke at rally for Phil Angelides, gubernatorial candidate for California,

> Yesterday, I was in the state of Texas. As you all know, President Bush used to live there. Now he lives in a state of denial, a state of deception. I'm glad to be here with you now, I really, thank you. We're here to talk about education and I want to say something. You know education, you make the most of it, you study hard, do your homework, work hard, you do well. If you don't, you get stuck in Iraq.[738]

The joke turned out to be on John Kerry, as President Bush (and even John McCain) asked Kerry to apologize for offending the troops in Iraq. Kerry defenders claimed he was joking about Bush getting 'us' stuck in Iraq, but the 'us' was missing in Kerry's comments. So the Vietnam veteran and 2004 nominee was troop bashing? Kerry canceled midterm campaign stops until Election Day.

The consequences of Kerry's 'joke'

1) John Kerry looked stupid. David Yepsen of the *Des Moines Register* wrote a column titled "As Kerry gets stuck with a gaffe, Biden offers vision," and noted Biden was "offering specific, middle-of-the-road plans for dealing with the nation's crises overseas, especially Iraq."[739] Kerry was telling California college students jokes on the president as Biden was touting federalism for Iraq. There was glaring discrepancy in substance between the two.

The context of Kerry's joke was also important. His so-called botched-joke was preceded by his comment that Bush once lived in Texas but now lived "in a state of denial." [740] The 'botched' part of Kerry's self-described 'botched joke' would never had happened if Kerry focused on policy rather than one liners about the president.[741] Kerry merely reaffirmed the intellectual arrogance by his own stupidity, and as Chuck Todd of the *Hotline* said, Kerry talked about the president's IQ "from that place northeastern liberal Democrats sometimes do it too much."[742]

The ordeal was Kerry's fault and his fault alone. As Jonah Goldberg wrote, "If it was a joke, it was a pretty bad one. First, Bush got better grades than Kerry at Yale. More relevant, if launching the Iraq war is a sign of stupidity and a failure to do one's homework, Kerry should avoid calling attention to the fact that he voted to approve it and defended that vote throughout his 2004 campaign."[743] Maybe Kerry, too, would have gotten *us* stuck in Iraq.

He became the butt of the late night jokes. Jay Leno said, "You know, people have been wondering what the Republicans are going to use as their secret weapon to help turn the election around, you know? Who would have guessed it'd be John Kerry? It's amazing."[744] David Letterman said, "How 'bout this John Kerry controversy, ladies and gentleman? ... So he's out there in California, and he tells some kind of a joke, and it backfires. And he's now walking around saying that he botched the joke. He was trying to tell a joke about Bush. I'm telling you, this guy can lose elections he's not even in."[745]

2) Kerry was dumped by his own Party. Senator Clinton called Kerry's words inappropriate, Rep. Harold Ford Jr., running a close but eventually losing bid for US Senate in Tennessee, said Kerry should have apologized; and Bruce Braley, campaigning for Congress in Iowa, reportedly (11.1.06) "asked Kerry not to come and campaign for him as planned."[746] Even Howard Dean distanced himself from Kerry's remarks.[747] Kerry told Don Imus (11.1.06), "Yes, I'm—you know, I'm coming back to Washington today so that I'm not a distraction, because I don't want to be a distraction to these campaigns."[748] He canceled campaign stops in Minnesota, Pennsylvania, and Iowa (Braley's[749]).[750] Feingold said Kerry's words were "a very regrettable incident. That just should not have happened. I'm sure he wasn't trying to insult the troops, but that doesn't really help. You've got to be awfully careful, especially this time of year."[751]

David Schuster reported for *Hardball* (11.1.06), "The irony is that John Kerry has given more than $12 million this year to Democrat candidates and has campaigned for them in over 35 states. But the state of the Democratic Party right now is one of frustration, that John Kerry, at least for now, seemed to give Republicans an opportunity to put the attention on him and take attention away from the problems in Iraq…"[752] The title for *Hardball*'s coverage (11.1.06) was "The Kerry Factor."[753] *NBC Nightly News* (11.1.06) described the ordeal as "the biggest war of words in the 2006 campaign."[754] Coverage of Kerry's lame joke spanned three new cycles: one for the statement, the next day for Kerry's stubbornness, the third day covering his apology.

Radio Iowa ("Vilsack: Iraq no joking matter') indicated Tom Vilsack gave one of the more diplomatic defenses of Kerry which came from a Democrat:

> Governor Tom Vilsack, a Democrat who endorsed Kerry's presidential run in 2004, says it's time to stop talking about Kerry's goof, and move on. "If the issue is whether or not John Kerry can tell a joke and tell it well, I could have told you the answer to that question was 'No' a week ago," Vilsack says. "(Kerry) obviously made a mistake and it's an unfortunate mistake but you know what really is unfortunate is that we're talking about this instead of the fact that 105 American soldiers lost their lives in Iraq in October in one of the deadliest months in that war."
>
> Vilsack's advice to Democratic candidates in 2006 is to talk about charting a new course in Iraq. "The question I think that ought to be answered by politicians running for office at the federal level is 'What are we going to do about changing the course in Iraq?' That's the question and it's not a laughing or joking matter."[755]

New York Senator Chuck Schumer was not as kind, as suggested by an *abcnews.com* blog, and when the new Democratic leadership in the Senate was announced (11.14.06), Schumer whispered something to Kerry, who stayed out of the picture:

> We obviously don't know what Schumer said, but Kerry stopped in his tracks, watched the four Democratic leaders walk on without him, … then he ducked between two of the marble statues in the hallway, which leads from the old Senate Chamber to the new Senate floor. Someone trying to project might say that Schumer had told Kerry to get the heck out of the leadership shot and Kerry, after digesting the request for a moment, did it.[756]

3) Kerry proved he was wrong when he apologized. Kerry said he was not going to apologize, and preceded that statement with "Let me make it crystal clear" that he would not. [757] He did. On November 1, Kerry appeared on Don Imus, who asked the Senator "well, why not apologize for the misunderstanding?" Kerry said "Well, I did. I said it was a botched joke. Of course I'm sorry about a botched joke...."[758] As Chris Mathews stated upon Kerry's apology thru a statement, Kerry "has given his enemies exactly what they spent all day demanding out of him. He has lost this round."[759]

4) Kerry's words had absolutely no effect on the midterms. Some defended Kerry's joke, which may have been bad, but wasn't as bad as the President's decision to go into Iraq (as a *Milwaukee Journal-Sentinel*'s cartoon depicted), which finally blew up in Bush's face on Election Day.[760] *Reuters* reported Nov. 2 in the title: "Kerry slip-up not seen hurting Democrats at polls."[761] This whole ordeal had everything to do with number five.

5) The joke ended any hope for a second Kerry presidential run. How did Kerry end his presidential ambitions?

1) Ted Kennedy hung Kerry out to dry. Ted Kennedy told *This Week* (3.6.05) that he had "enormous respect for Sen. Clinton" but "my man is John Kerry."[762] Kennedy told the *AP* in October 2005 that he would support Kerry for the 2008 presidential nomination, even if Sen. Clinton would run.[763] "Every day, I think they [the American People] regret that John wasn't elected."[764] In April 2006, Ted Kennedy restated if Kerry "runs, I'm supporting him."[765]

Kerry's joke led him "to reevaluate whether to mount a run for the presidency in 2008" and led him "to delay an announcement about his decision," reported the *Boston Globe* (12.2.06) through 'Kerry associates.'[766] This lead to Ted Kennedy's support to be "indefinite" for Kerry, an odd fallout which lead Kerry to make a decision after the New Year. Indeed, before Kennedy's quasi-withdrawal of Kerry support, the *Globe* reported Kerry was "leaning toward waiting until late spring [2007] before declaring his intentions."[767] Kerry's aides said the delay would occur because the focus in early 2007 would be on the party's agenda, and the $13 to 14 million in the bank gave him time to wait to declare.[768]

On the very day Kerry turned 63, Ted Kennedy told the *Boston Globe* (12.11.06) he would not wait "indefinitely" to support Kerry for president.[769] *Globe* columnist Scot Lehigh sarcastically wrote to Kerry, "old Teddy Weathervane tossed a time bomb your way, announcing that there's an expiration date stamped on his political backing."[770] Kennedy had buyer's regret, but even Kennedy did not launch his candidacy against Jimmy Carter until the fall of 1979.[771] Kennedy now was rushed even though he did not endorse Al Gore until January 5, 2000.[772] This was the same Kennedy who told *This Week* in March 2005 that "My man is John Kerry."[773]

"Within hours" of Kennedy's comments in December 2006, the Kerry camp said a decision to run in 2008 would be made after the new year, which sufficed for Kennedy's support.[774] Kennedy's pull back was based on Kerry's

Karl McCarty: *The Last One Standing*

decision to delay an announcement of a potential run, which likely occurred because of his botched joke.[775] Kerry did not have to declare early, given his $13 million and name recognition—but now Kennedy forced Kerry to do so.[776] (Kennedy was the incoming chair on the Senate Health, Education, Labor, and Pensions Committee of which both Obama and Clinton served.)[777] Kerry now had to make a decision despite that he stated on Dec.5, "I think all this '08 stuff is way too early."[778]

But in all the flak over the joke, Kerry said (10.31.06) that "I'll be very upfront: I'm thinking about it [running]."[779] Conan O'Brien later joked that John Kerry said he was still considering running for President, and thus, "…John Kerry is still telling bad jokes."[780] That joke was told before the midterms, and by November—before Teddy's time bomb—the writing was on the wall.

Kerry appeared he was in a state of denial. When asked when he would formally announce he said could not tell "exactly when," (Nov.30).[781] He told the *Situation Room* (11.30.06) he and Teresa were writing a book on the environment.[782] A Nov. 14 *McClatchy*'s article on presidential candidates had him under "damaged goods" and noted the Democrats have not "renominated a loser" since 1956.[783] A loser.

2) The atrocious interview on *FOX News Sunday*. Kerry could not recover. He first appeared (after the 'joke') on the Sunday morning talk shows for *FOX News Sunday* on November 19. Chris Wallace began the interview, "Well, I must say — and we told you before you came on that we were going to talk some about the joke. I agree there's things to talk about after, but there are questions people have, and I'm going to ask you about them, sir."[784] That did not happen, and only in the last minute of the interview did Wallace switch to a different topic.[785] Kerry defended himself that he was still a viable candidate after the misstatement:

> Take a measure of the guy who mortgaged his house when I was at 30 points below and nobody said I could win. Take a measure of a guy who got up every morning and went to Iowa and said, "I know how to win this." Take a measure of a guy who was 10 points down and won three debates against a sitting president of the United States and put on a convention that had a great message to America about where we're going. I believe I learned a lot of lessons in that race. And one of the lessons is, when the full attack machine of the Republican Party is leveled at you, fight back. I fought back, for my honor, my integrity and for the rectitude of what I said."[786]

Wallace also showed a mother of a US soldier killed in Iraq who demanded an apology from Kerry as she suggested Kerry had dishonored soldiers. Wallace did not show a mother of a US soldier killed in Iraq who agreed Kerry made an honest mistake.[787]

3) Kerry's poll numbers were still embarrassingly low. Quinnipiac's Thermometer poll released Nov. 27 showed Kerry dead last as only 39.5 percent of the public was 'warm' to him, as the Massachusetts Senator placed five spots behind the president he 'botched' joked about.[788] The *Boston Globe* reported (12.11.06), "Early polls show him far behind the leading Democrats in potential presidential fields, and many party activists want Democrats to look for a fresh face in 2008."[789] When asked about his low poll numbers he said (11.30.06), "It's a reaction to having lost in '04 and to a lot of, you know, things that have gone on since. I don't put a lot of stock in polls at this point. I really think that we have to wait and see where we are next year and I think what the American people want us to do is do their business right now, not get caught up in this. I don't put a lot of stock in polls, as you know. I was 30 points behind for months upon months and I won. And I think I, you know, I've earned the right to say that anything right now is really not particularly meaningful."[790] A University of New Hampshire poll showed (10.12.06) Kerry's net popularity in the Granite State (percent who voted for a candidate minus the percent who said the candidate was the one they would least likely vote for) was the worst among Democratic hopefuls.[791]

By December 2006, he was no longer a double-digit candidate in national polls for Democrats in 2008, as he received between 5 and 7 percent in the ABC, CNN, FOX, and WNBC/Marist polls.[792] Kerry received 11 percent in the *NBC News/Wall Street Journal* poll (Dec.8-11), but Al Gore was not included in this poll (nor was Dodd or Clark).[793] The 2004 Democratic presidential nominee was a single digit candidate.

4) Kerry's odd observation on Iraq. Kerry had no credibility. In December 2006, the President met with Abdul Aziz al-Hakim, the leader of Iraq's largest Shiite party, but after meeting with the president, al-Hakim said the US military was not doing enough to fight the insurgency and that US strategy contributed to massacres; and he downplayed Shiite responsibility.[794] The *Washington Post* quoted al-Hakim, who said "The strikes that the insurgents are getting from the multinational forces are not hard enough to put an end to their acts, but leave them to stand up again to resume their critical acts. That means that there is something wrong on the policies taken to deal with that danger threatening the lives of Iraqis."[795] Seemingly forgetting he had been politically killed for a botched joke weeks earlier, Kerry said "I think he's insulting a lot of family in American who have lost their kids. I think he's insulting a lot of marines and a lot of Army folks who go out on some extraordinarily dangerous patrols in order to make Iraq safe for Iraqis."[796] Oh, the irony.

5) Finally! He told the Senate he was out of the running. On the Senate floor (1.24.07), Kerry announced he would not run: "I've concluded this isn't the time for me to mount a presidential campaign. It is the time for put my energy to work as part of the majority in the Senate to do all I can to end this war and strengthen our security and our ability to fight the real war on terror."[797] Joe Biden overreacted: "My initial reaction to Senator Kerry' decision is one of extreme sadness. John Kerry is a major voice in American politics and the country would be much better off today if he were president."[798]

Reuters reported he "would have faced a tough challenge overcoming the criticism of some Democrats that he ran a lackluster 2004 campaign that failed to take advantage of growing public doubts about Bush's leadership and the Iraq War."[799] Kerry said he was "proud of the campaign we ran, proud of the fact that three years ago I said Iraq was the wrong war at the wrong place at the wrong time…We came close, certainly close enough to be tempted to try again."[800] The *Reuters* report quoted Biden's 'sadness' and rehashed the 'botched joke' saga from November.[801] With Kerry's decision, the only undeclared presidential 'candidates' for the Democrats in early 2007 were Gore and Clark.[802]

Representative Dennis Kucinich

Dennis Kucinich was elected mayor of Cleveland at the age of 31, and was the youngest mayor of a major city in the country.[803] He was known as the "Boy Mayor,"[804] and also was mayor of "the first city since the Great Depression to go into default."[805] Kucinich was confrontational and nicknamed "Dennis the Menace," and he "refused to sell the city's municipal electrical system, so local banks foreclosed on the city," a failure which the *New Hampshire Union Leader* said "plagued his career for years," as he survived a recall by 236 votes but lost re-election to future Sen. George Voinovich (R).[806]

He served on the City Council beginning in 1969, as mayor (1977-79), then briefly served on the council again, then in the state senate (1994-96), before moving to the U.S. House of Representatives in 1997,[807] after his 1996 upset over incumbent Rep. Martin Hoke (R).[808] When he announced his second candidacy for the presidency, He had just been elected to his sixth term during the midterms.[809]

Before his stint in state and federal politics, he apparently dabbled in everything, as he was a clerk of municipal courts, host of a radio talk show, copyreader for the *Wall Street Journal* and *Cleveland Plain Dealer*; and a TV reporter, media consultant, and surgical technician.[810] Though if he dabbled in everything it may have been because he was desperate for a job. Indeed, the *Union Leader* said "after his ouster" as mayor, he "couldn't find employment in Cleveland, so he left the city."[811] The *Union Leader* said in the 1980s he "briefly served on the Cleveland City Council and lost or withdrew from other races."[812] Kucinich has said (1.8.07), "I am a product of the city. My parents never owned a home. I grew up in 21 different places by the time I was 17, including a few cars."[813]

The joke of the 2004 campaign

There were many jokes on Kucinich during the 2004 campaign. Jay Leno said, "The only way Dennis Kucinich is going to end up in the White House is if he moves to San Francisco and marries John Kerry."[814] Conan O'Brien said, "Consumer activist Ralph Nader announced he would run for president. When he heard about it, Dennis Kucinich was furious and said, 'He's going to steal my voter away.'"[815] Tina Fey of *Saturday Night Live* stated, "In the Rock The Vote presidential debates ….Democratic candidates Howard Dean, John Edwards and John Kerry admitted that they had smoked marijuana, while candidate Dennis Kucinich admitted that he was high right now."[816]

What were his negatives?

1) The 2008 campaign was just as thoughtless as the previous one. It was a surprise when Dennis Kucinich announced his second bid for the presidency on December 12, 2006.[817] His issue: Iraq, particularly an immediate pullout of US forces.

The *New York Times* reported (12.12.06) that in a "brief chat in his office" in early December Kucinich "mentioned that, oh, by the way, he planned to run for president again in 2008."[818] And his wife "arched her eyebrows in apparent surprise," then he left his office to inform his press aide.[819] The *Times* went on to label it a "'What the heck?' sensibility" and, "...Besides the possible Rudys, Hillarys, and Barracks, the names on the Great List now seem to include every Tom [Vilsack], Dick [Armey], or Sammy [Brownback]."[820] Kucinich said he ran "well on a sloppy track," a line he also used in 2004—in which he won no primaries.[821] Kucinich has so many one liners it is difficult to suggest he took his own campaign seriously. He told the *Times* he would be to every debate, and may show up anyway if uninvited: "This is where it comes in handy to be a vegan. I don't take up that much space."[822]

    2) Kucinich doesn't look presidential. As one blogger wrote, he was "small and boyish looking. Americans seem to prefer their leaders to be on the tall side...Bunch that up with his almost-zero name recognition, his problems as mayor of Cleveland, and his relatively low-profile job...and you have only a small-but-passionate smattering of support."[823] Stephen Colbert, after the first Democratic presidential debate in April, said "There were seven candidates up there. Seven and a half if you count woodland creature Dennis Kucinich."[824]

    Leno said (7.20.07), "Kucinich is in the hospital for food poisoning. You ever see Kucinich? Doesn't he always look like he always has food poisoning?"[825] Jimmy Kimmel claimed (7.19.07) Kucinich was fine after the food poisoning: "He was released from the Cleveland's Children's Hospital yesterday. He's now back home, resting comfortably in a hollow tree. I guess he ate out of the wrong bird feeder."[826]

    3) Kucinich's campaign has not changed the debate on Iraq. He seldom received double-digits in the 2004 primaries.[827] Though staying in the race until the end, he earned only 70 of the over 2,100 delegates he needed.[828] One blogger on *TPM Café* said: "I'll never forget when he tore into Ted Koppel at one early debate for asking too many questions about process and horse race...and not enough about policy and the war in Iraq."[829] Would Kucinich add that same value to the 2008 campaign? Feingold had dropped out after the midterms, and Howard Dean never ran...so there was room for a liberal anti-war candidate. As of December 2006, Kucinich was the only candidate calling for an immediate withdrawal,[830] because most media ignored Mike Gravel's candidacy.

    But once 2007 began, perhaps Kucinich's campaign wasn't needed for liberal activists. Mike Gravel was just as vehement against the war as Kucinich, but Gravel was a new candidate and, quite frankly, was more entertaining. And though Russ Feingold did not run for president, he did not leave the political landscape, especially on the Iraq war. In July 2007, Feingold offered his plan to censure the president on Iraq.

    4) Was the campaign an ego trip? When CNN's Andrea Koppel reported Kucinich's entry, she noted experts said "there are usually only two reasons why long shots like Kucinich go through presidential campaigns," and cited the Brooking Institution's Stephan Hess that they are either on "an ego trip" or saying something "that other's aren't saying..."[831] Immediately the

Washington Post reported (12.12.06) his campaign as "a long-shot candidacy" and said his 2004 campaign "made more headlines for his bachelorhood than his policies."[832] Indeed, he told New Hampshire audiences that he was seeking a mate, and he ate breakfast with the women who won an online contest, but as the *Washington Post* reminisced: "nothing evolved from Kucinich's breakfast date with the winner. It did earn him appearances on late-night comedy talk shows."[833] He married Elizabeth Harper in 2005,[834] she was his third wife.[835]

Kucinich's response to an ego trip was "…I heard that comment and was it an ego trip to stand up in 2002 and say there was no basis for this war, when no other person was willing to do that? I organized 125 Democrats and I took a lot of abuse on some of the talk shows with people saying what are you saying, there's no weapons of mass destruction? Kucinich, I mean don't you believe our president?"[836] As stated in the previous point (#3), Kucinich's anti-war song doesn't play well in 2008. Obama and Gravel were on record against this war before it began, Kucinich can't play up his foresight before the war like he did in 2004.

Kucinich told the *Situation Room* his run for the presidency was "about a quest for integrity."[837] And despite being the choice of one person out of 470 Democratic and Democratic leaning independents in a *USA Today* poll, Kucinich was still saying, "I expect to get the nomination," (June 2007).[838]

Along with his ego, Kucinich is never shy at getting attention. Dennis Kucinich was a voice for the poor. But not many listened when he sang *16 Tons* in a speech in New York City (1.8.07). "You load 16 tons and what do you get, another day older and deeper in debt," as the *Cleveland Plain Dealer* described the "60-year-old" Kucinich, "who is white, sang in a slow, sorrowful voice Monday to a mostly black audience of about 500 people, getting their attention and mild approval near the end of a long, somewhat rambling speech at the start of his second try at becoming president…"[839] Will Kucinich be remembered for the 2008 campaign for something beyond entertainment and ego?

Senator Barack Obama

Barack Obama was born in Hawaii (1961) to a Kansan mother and Kenyan father, who went to Harvard and returned to Kenya.[840] Obama's dad was also named Barack. Having studied economics at Harvard, the elder Barack was a university lecturer in Uganda, and eventually worked in Kenya's private sector, then joined the country's Treasury Department and became a senior economist.[841] He died in a car accident in 1982.[842]

Barack is Swahili for "Blessed by God."[843] Obama was only two when his father left, and his Kansas grandparents raised him in Hawaii.[844] His mother and stepfather took him to Indonesia for four years,[845] but Barack returned to Hawaii by high school.[846] On his return to Hawaii, Obama was largely raised by his grandparents. The *New Yorker* has said Obama was "a black child, by American lights, but his mother and his grandparents—the only family he knew—were 'white folks,' and his confusion was acute."[847]

Obama: lucky to be 2008 player

He spent four years in the Illinois Senate, and by 2000 held the position simultaneously with teaching constitutional law a the University of Chicago, but grew "impatient" and lost a Democratic Congressional primary to Rep. Bobby Rush.[848]

He won the March 2004 seven-way primary for U.S. Senate with 53% of the vote.[849] In the primary, he ran as a "proud black progressive, anti-NAFTA and anti-war, and carried areas that were considered conservative."[850] The Republican candidate to replace retiring Sen. Peter Fitzgerald, Jack Ryan, left the race after the *Chicago Tribune* showed inconvenient details of a messy divorce.[851] A former investment banker, Ryan won the primary for Illinois Republicans but dropped out after allegations he previously urged his wife to attend sex clubs against her will.[852]

The Illinois GOP's efforts to replace their first choice was a disaster.[853] They considered former Chicago Bears head coach Mike Ditka,[854] who decided not to run. Eventually Alan Keyes became the nominee. As the *Washingtonian* later wrote, "Had it not been for... allegations of Ryan's trips to sex clubs, Obama might never have stood before the Democrats in Boston that July."[855] Keyes ran for Senate twice in Maryland and ran for president in 1996 and 2000.[856] That the nomination went to Keyes was an embarrassment. Though leading the Republican Senatorial Campaign Committee, George Allen said (8.22.04), "He's going to be an articulate voice for conservative views."[857] In reality, Keyes was a diehard social conservative, who, though incredibly articulate, had no chance of getting independents (or many moderate conservatives) to vote for him in the general election.

And so, the 2004 Democratic convention address solidified Obama as a rising star even before he was elected to the Senate:

> ….there's not a liberal American and a conservative America—there's the United States of America. There's not a black America and white America and Latino America and Asian America; there's the United States of America. The pundits like to slice-and-dice

our country into Red States and Blue States; Red States for Republicans, Blue States for Democrats. But I've got news for them, too. We worship an awesome God in the Blue States, and we don't like federal agents poking around our libraries in the Red States."[858]

How did Obama become a presidential candidate?

Barrack Obama's name was tossed around, in part because Sen. Dick Durbin (D-IL) said (5.28.06) he told Obama to consider a presidential run. "I think he really has the capacity to bring a lot of red and blue states together for a change so that we start seeing common goals in this country. Younger people are in particular inspired by his message, and people like Barrack don't come along very often...As far as I'm concerned, he should seriously consider it, I think he could bring a great deal to the national race for the presidency."[859] Durbin said "I said to him, 'Why don't you just kind of move around Iowa and watch what happens?' I know what's going to happen. And I think it's going to rewrite the game plans in a lot of presidential candidates if he makes that decision."[860]

Then Obama addressed the Tom Harkin Steak Fry (9.17.06), and dropped the news that some of his staffers would be working for Iowa candidates in the fall.[861] Over 3,000 supporters paid $25 to get in to the steak fry in Warren County, Iowa.[862] In the summer and fall of 2006, in was no secret Obama was thinking about running, but it officially became apparent when the Illinois senator appeared on *Meet the Press* (10.22.06), and told Tim Russert "I'll sit down and consider it [running for president]" after the midterms.[863] In what seemed out of the ordinary, Obama's consultant David Axelrod flew from Chicago to Washington for the interview.[864]

And Obama Mania began

The *Washington Post* reported (10.23.06) he was "one of the brightest stars in the party since he electrified the 2004 Democratic National Convention with his keynote address."[865] The *Washingtonian* said "From out of nowhere, he's become DC's brightest star."[866] The *Washingtonian* did an extensive bio, and said he "was the master of the large group."[867] A group of 4,000 greeted him in Arizona (10.23.06) the day after his *Meet the Press* interview.[868]

Polticialwire.com mimicked (10.16.06) the "Obama-mania" with an excerpt of *Time*'s coverage: "The current Obama mania is reminiscent of the Colin Powell mania of September 1995, when the general...leveraged speculation that he might run for President into book sales of 2.6 million copies of his memoir, *My American Journey*."[869] *Time*'s cover was titled "Why Barack Obama Could Be The Next President."[870] He was on the cover of *GQ*.[871] Oprah Winfrey, a Chicago native, had 'her' senator on *Oprah*.

The *Christian Science Monitor* was overall favorable in reporting the Obama situation (11.15.06): "The first-term Illinois senator is currently riding a wave of 'Obama-mania,' following the publication of his second memoir and a book tour that has highlighted his appeal as a fresh face on the political scene - and his opposition to the Iraq war from the beginning, a key contrast with Clinton. The Gallup poll [Nov. 9-12] placed him second to Clinton among Democrats and Democratic leaners for the nomination, 31 percent to 19 percent."[872] Likewise,

McClatchy (11.14.06), said in the Senate, Obama "hasn't actually accomplished anything. But he gives a great let's-all-work-together speech, the news media love a new face, and he could cash in on hunger for a fresh voice and new approach for the post-Bush era."[873] The *Des Moines Register* described him as "the new star in the party."[874] The *New York Daily News* called him "The charismatic young lawmaker who has been likened to Bobby Kennedy…," and when Obama took back his pledge to finish his Senate term the result was "…setting hearts aflutter among voters looking for fresh faces."[875] The *Sunday Times* (U.K.) headline on Nov. 5 was already "Obama mania."[876]

"What's driving Obama-mania?"[877] So asked a headline for the *Christian Science Monitor*, which was apparently too naïve to consider that by having such a headline the news organization itself was partially to blame. That article reported the "attraction" to Obama "seems to be a mix" of his "own compelling personal narrative and many voters' desire for a less caustic brand of politics," and included a comment from a high school teacher in Nashua, NH who said Clinton was "too polarizing."[878] And yes, this article too said Obama "shot to superstar status after an electrifying speech" at the 2004 convention.[879] The *New Hampshire Union Leader* also said (12.11.06) he "rode to stardom virtually overnight after his speech" at the convention.[880] He said he would not 'dilly-dally' about his White House decision, and gave a "major speech" on November 20 at the Chicago Council on Global Affairs.[881] The blitz continued with a meeting with rapper Ludacris (Nov.29), an appearance on Jay Leno (Dec.1), and a stop in New Hampshire (Dec.10).[882]

The trip to New Hampshire

No other trip to New Hampshire was covered as Obama's in December 2006. A subtitle for an *MSNBC* article (11.30.06) said "Euphoria builds over Illinois senator as he plans foray to New Hampshire."[883] The *Union Leader* said "the spectacle that is 'Obama-mania' swept New Hampshire."[884] The *New York Times* said Obama "has emerged" as the party's "strongest alternative" to Clinton.[885] When Gov. Lynch introduced him in NH, he said "We originally scheduled the Rolling Stones, but we canceled them when we figured out that Senator Obama would sell more tickets, [1,500 paid $25 a pop for the rally]."[886] Obama eventually told New Hampshire his fifteen minutes of fame "has extended a little longer than 15 minutes."[887] The *Milwaukee Journal Sentinel* (12.11.06) said his trip "was a perfect storm of attention."[888]

Obama told New Hampshire audiences there was a "certain tone I've taken in my career that seems to be resonating. People are looking for something new, and I'm a stand-in for that desire on the part of voters. They want a common sense, non-ideological, practical approach to the problem they face."[889] He also was quoted similarly: "I think to some degree I've become shorthand or symbol or stand-in for a spirit that the last election in New Hampshire represented," [two incumbent congressmen lost]."[890] The event was a New Hampshire Democratic Party celebration, and Obama was the only presidential candidate invited.[891] The New Hampshire frenzy sped Evan Bayh's removal from the field.

Days after his New Hampshire visit, the website DraftObama.org announced its sponsorship of a 60 second commercial to get Obama into the race.[892] The ad was titled "Believe Again" and produced by Bud Jackson, who made Draft Clark ads in 2004.[893]

Who was Edwards?

When Adam Nagourney wrote for the *International Herald Tribune* (12.17.06) he said, "In much of the coverage by the U.S. news media, the 2008 contest has been portrayed, notwithstanding the expanse of the Democratic field, as a two-way race between Obama and Senator Hillary Rodham Clinton of New York, complicating efforts by lesser-known candidates to hire staff members, raise money and get noticed."[894] 'Much of the coverage by the U.S. news media' forgot about Edwards.

Indeed, the Clinton v. Obama stigma began. On December 24, Dan Balz's *Washington Post* article was titled "Clinton, Obama Clearing the Field" as both were "driving potential rivals to the sidelines and casting a huge shadow over all others who may run."[895] An *AP* (1.12.07) article was titled "Obama, Clinton Making 2008 Moves," and said, "Obama and Clinton would clearly be the Democratic field's heavyweights…"[896] The *Washington Post* said (12.24.06), "At this point, Clinton and Obama are eclipsing a group of Democratic heavyweights that includes the party's presidential and vice presidential nominees in 2004."[897] This despite Edwards was still winning in many Iowa polls.

Obama was the "most requested speaker" on the midterm campaign trail, as he appeared in over 30 states while selling well over a quarter million copies of his book.[898] But John Edwards was still a major player in the 2008 campaign.

What was the most important aspect of Obama Mania?

Did Obama's stances on the issues have anything to do with whether he should run for president? Durbin told the *Washington Post* (12.8.06) "Hang on tight. They ain't seen nothing yet."[899] Durbin was right. Had the public seen anything of substance on Iraq from Obama? And when Obama spoke in Chicago (Nov.20), did he have any breakthrough plan on Iraq? It was hard to see through all the media infatuation.

Oprah endorsed Obama

When asked about a follower who thought Oprah should be president, Oprah told *Larry King Live* (9.25.06), "You know what I would say to him, I would say, take your energy [they would put in an Oprah campaign] and put it in Barack Obama. That's what I would say."[900] The headline for *All Headline News* was "Oprah Supports Barack Obama For President."[901] Take a cut from her magazine's website:

> He electrified the 2004 Democratic National Convention. He's prompted cries of "first black president." He's Barack Obama, the United States Senator from Illinois.
> Surrounded by his wife, Michelle, and their two daughters, he takes a rare break from his 16-hour workday to sit down with Oprah at his Chicago home.
> "I don't consider myself political and I seldom interview politicians. So when I decided to talk with you [Barack], people around me were like, 'What's happened to you?' I said, 'I think this is beyond and above politics.' It feels like something new." — Oprah[902]

Oprah held a mansion bash for Barack Obama in September 2007, which was already sold out (at $2,300 a person) two months earlier.[903]

Why did Obama run?

Take George Will's three points of view. First, as Will wrote, "one can be an intriguing novelty only once."[904] If he passed the chance, he could end up like Gov. Mario Cuomo of New York, who passed opportunities in 1988 and 1992, then was kicked out of office by Pataki in 1994.[905] Estimates suggested it would take $25 to $35 million to campaign in the first four states of the Democratic contests, and Obama had the capacity to raise it. He spent $14 million in his 2004 Senate campaign and Hopefund PAC raised almost $4 million by mid 2006 after having been created in 2005.[906] And Chicago served as a great fundraising base for national candidates—much less a senator already from Illinois.[907]

Second, Obama tempted the public so much he had to run. Will stated, "…if you get the girl up on her tiptoes, you should kiss her." [908] Case in point, Obama's *Monday Night Football* spiel. When the Chicago Bears played the St. Louis Rams on *Monday Night Football*, he appeared in a taped segment and said he would like to make an announcement: "And tonight, after a lot of thought and a good deal of soul-searching, I would like to announce to my hometown of Chicago and all of America that I am ready—for the Bears to go all the way, baby, da-da-da-da!"[909] If he did the introduction just to taunt and eventually not run for president, Obama's non-campaign campaign would have come of as incredibly arrogant.

Third, Will said Obama was an "optimal opponent," to Hillary: "The contrast is stark: He is soothing, she is not. Many Democrats who are desperate to win are queasy about depending on her," and although the non partisan *National Journal* rated him more liberal than Clinton, Obama was similar in how Reagan handled ideology, as the 40th president "demonstrated the importance of congeniality to the selling of conservatism."[910] Keep in mind this praise for Obama came from a conservative pundit.

Another reason to run was his book. Obama was on a nationwide tour in Oct. 2006 to promote *The Audacity of Hope*.[911] This begged the question whether Obama was just cleverly pumping the coffers of his book, which is exactly what Colin Powell did in the fall of 1995, when the presidential speculation turned into over two and a half million copies of his memoir, *My American Journey*.[912] Obama's near-$2 million advance on his second book let him pay off his student loans, so he moved from an apartment to a new $1.6 million house in Chicago.[913]

Obama was also in good shape to run because he already threw out his skeletons. In *Dreams of My Father*, he admitted to using cocaine and marijuana, as well as attending socialist meetings.[914] He didn't use heroin because he said he did not like the dealer.[915] Joe Klein of *Time* concluded in Obama's second book, "I counted 28 impolitic or self-deprecating admissions," including Obama's claim he once accidentally voted against a bill to protect children from sex offenders.[916] He started smoking since the 2004 race, and smoked three Marlboros a day, but "never around his family," said the *Washingtonian* (Oct. 2006) which also said he tried regularly to stop.[917]

Obama had to run for president. The political climate was ripe for something inspiring. The midterm campaigns were turning nasty, such as the commercial connecting a loosely dressed white woman asking Senate candidate Rep. Harold Ford, Jr. to "call me." Most saw the commercial as a sleazy attempt to scare white-southern voters against Ford, an African American. Then there was radio-talk show host Rush Limbaugh's claim actor Michael J. Fox basically increased his shaking movements from his Parkinson's disease to pad his case for increased embryonic stem cell research. And in Virginia, the Senate race became 'Macaca' Allen versus 'sexist' Webb.

The timing of Obama's announced consideration was brilliant. By the end of 2005, Mark Warner was a rising star for the Party, but by the end of 2006, he had been completely forgotten. With the second-tier candidates recently breathing a sigh of relief that Mark Warner had dropped out (10.12.06), a Goliath had entered the race. As David Shuster reported (10.23.06) "…party strategists, including some advising John Kerry, John Edwards, Joe Biden, and Bill Richardson, agree that Obama could leapfrog much of the potential Democratic field and become the challenger to" Clinton.[918] Candidates unofficially running for president for two years were bypassed by a Senator who tested the water for about two months. The success of Obama led John Kerry to take responsibility for Obama's success. Kerry said (10.22.06), "I think he's a very interesting and very powerful communicator with a great deal of skill. I wouldn't have picked him if he didn't. And I'm really pleased to see the way in which the country is ratifying my judgment on that [Obama speaking at the 2004 Democratic Convention]."[919]

Is he too Young?

Obama became a presidential candidate at age 45, two years older than John F. Kennedy when he became president. But Kennedy had been in the House for six years, and the Senate for eight years.[920]

Already on his *Meet the Press* interview, Obama said "I'm not sure anybody is ready to be president before they're president."[921] With less than two years in the Senate, he was 98th in seniority, and would have been 99th if Jon Corzine had not left to be governor of New Jersey.[922] Bob Herbert of the *New York Times* called the potential run "disturbing," and added Obama "may be capable of being a great president. Someday. But one quick look around at the state of the nation and the world tells us that we need to be more careful than we have been in selecting our leaders."[923]

Did the Senator have a strong record? The *Washingtonian* (10.31.06) cited his senatorial accomplishments: a nuclear non-proliferation trip with Sen. Lugar (R-IN) to Eastern Europe and Russia, an attempt with Tom Coburn (R-OK) to make government contracts more transparent, and "a push for immigration reform with Mel Martinez."[924] But it was the Hagel-Martinez bill that heightened the immigration debate in 2006—not an Obama-Martinez bill. The *Washingtonian* also cited his African trip in August 2006.[925] Bill Clinton said Obama had to be careful about running too soon.[926]

Joe Biden was a young candidate and a rising star when he plagiarized speeches for the 1988 nomination. But it was Biden's words, not age, which doomed his candidacy. Obama's age, 47 on Election Day 2008,[927] could be a good thing, he is a younger Senator without a lengthy voting record that hurt John Kerry down 2004.

Obama was fresh, when everyone else was tired. The situation was ripe, as 77 percent thought the ads in the midterms were negative.[928] His youth seemed to be a catalyst, not a crutch.

Obama can talk the God-talk

Obama spoke at a Call to Renewal conference (6.28.06), a faith based movement for poverty, in which the *AP* reported his courting for evangelical support.[929] He said "…if we don't reach out to evangelical Christians and other religious Americans and tell them what we stand for, Jerry Falwells and Pat Robertsons will continue to hold sway," but Obama also warned of unauthentic pandering: "Nothing is more transparent than inauthentic expressions of faith: the politician who shows up at a black church around election time and claps—off rhythm—to the gospel choir."[930] Did he mean John Kerry? In 2004 he was quoted in *Atlantic Monthly*: "'Sometimes Kerry just doesn't have that oomph,' [Obama] said, punctuating the thought with a tight-lipped shake of the head and a clenched fist."[931] Obama had the oomph.

MSNBC reported (12.1.06) Obama's visit to a megachurch "follows Dem's exurbia gains."[932] According to Hotsoup.com, "In 2005, Democrat Tim Kaine became governor [of Virginia] while defeating Republican Jerry Kilgore in four fast-growing counties won by Bush just twelve months earlier. The Democrat succeeded in exurbia because he talked about his faith and quality-of-life issues in ways that showed voters he shared their values."[933] And now Obama visited "the soul of suburbia—the Orange Country mega-church run by Rick Warren."[934]

Rick Warren, the leader of the largest church in the country and best-selling author of *The Purpose Driven Life,* said he went to Obama for the AIDS summit in a moment of bi-partisanship.[935] Wiley Drake, the second vice-president of the Southern Baptist Convention said "You can't work together with people totally opposed to what you are. This kind of conference is just going to lead people astray." Warren said "If you could only work with people you agree with 100 percent, you've ruled out the entire world because I can't even get my wife to agree with me on everything."[936] The conference was for the Global Summit on AIDS and the Church at Warren's Saddleback Church in Lake Forest, California.[937] "Can Obama woo evangelicals?" asked a link on *MSNBC.com* (12.3.06).[938] He could. Rev. Rob Schenk (president of the National Clergy Council) said Obama's "policies on abortion and embryonic stem cell research" negated "his moral authority." Obama was smart enough to tactfully decline an interview request after Schenk's complaint.[939]

Rick Warren would not rescind Obama's invitation. Sam Brownback spoke at Warren's event: "Welcome to my house."[940] Obama replied, "This is my house, too. This is God's house. So I just, I just wanted to, I just wanted to be clear. I hope, I hope you don't mind that modest correction."[941] Warren later commented (12.26.06) on two very different politicians coming together on religion, and defended his support for Obama. "I called it the face of compassionate conservatism and the face of compassionate liberalism. And what they had in common was compassion, which is the Jesus part. For pro-lifers to attack me is ludicrous."[942] And Warren talked the importance of working with some interest group on one issue, even if there was a disagreement on a different subject: "...I really think in the next election, people are looking for that kind of leader, and both Sam and Barack are men of civility."[943] But make no mistake: Brownback did not receive much attention for his words at Warren's Church. The *AP* title (12.1.06) had Obama in the headline, Brownback was just part of the story—not *the* story.[944]

Obama stood strong in front of Warren's church. In fact, he declared condoms should be made more widely available to fight AIDS, as the *AP* reported he "urged unity despite political differences to fight the disease that has killed 25 million people since the first case was reported in 1981. Some 40 million currently are infected with HIV..."[945] He called the debate over condoms a "false argument," and said "I also believe we can't ignore the fact that abstinence and fidelity, although the ideal, may not always be the reality, that we're dealing with flesh and blood, men and women and not abstractions, and that if condoms and potentially things like microbicides can prevent millions of deaths, then they should be made more widely available. That's my belief."[946] He did come to press his beliefs on the church, but was bold enough to state his opinion. Obama also complimented Bush, and said he did not receive enough credit for the $15 billion he committed to Africa for AIDS/HIV over five years; and Obama also complimented Brownback's efforts toward AIDS.[947]

Obama doesn't need a religious adviser

Meanwhile Hilary Clinton had just hired a religious advisor for her campaign.[948] As Sally Quinn of the *Washington Post* opined, McCain had already hired a debate coach from Liberty University and Sen. Clinton was wearing crosses, but "....look at somebody like Barack Obama, who made this incredible speech on religion in July [2006] and everyone, Republicans and Democrats responded to that and the reason they did is because it was authentic. He really meant what he said and he was speaking as George Bush would say, from the heart." Take for example an excerpt from Obama's book, it which he clearly articulates his knowledge of religion and politics:

> It is a truism that we Americans are a religious people. According to the most recent surveys, 95% of Americans believe in God, more than two-thirds belong to a church, 37% call themselves committed Christians, and substantially more people believe in angels than believe in evolution. Books proclaiming the end of days sell millions of copies, Christian music fills the Billboard charts, and our president routinely remarks on how Christ changed his heart.

> Today, white evangelical Christians (along with conservative Catholics) are the heart and soul of the Republican party's grassroots base. It is their issues — abortion, gay marriage, prayer in schools, intelligent design, the posting of the Ten Commandments in the courthouse, and the makeup of the Supreme Court — that often dominate the headlines and serve as one of the great fault lines in American politics. The single biggest gap in party affiliation among white Americans is not between men and women, or between those who reside in so-called red states and those who reside in blue states, but between those who attend church regularly and those who don't.[949]

Here is another excerpt of Obama's delicate handling of religion in *Audacity of Hope*:

> It is my obligation, not only as an elected official in a pluralistic society but also as a Christian, to remain open to the possibility that my unwillingness to support gay marriage is misguided, just as I cannot claim infallibility in my support of abortion rights…I must admit that I may have been infected with society's prejudices and predilections and attributed them to God; that Jesus' call to love one another might demand a different conclusion; and that in years hence I might be seen on the wrong side of history.[950]

Obama and race: the eye of the beholder

Obama is the only African-American in the Senate and the fifth in American history.[951] Joe Klein of *Time* reported (10.15.06) the difference of how Obama was perceived: "The African-Americans tend to be fairly reserved—quiet pride, knowing nods and be-careful-now looks. The white people, by contrast, are out of control."[952] As conservative black commentator Shelby Steele said, "White people are just thrilled when a prominent black person comes along and doesn't rub their noses in racial guilt…White people go crazy over people like that."[953]

Obama does not play the race card. When he campaigned for Ben Cardin, the senate candidate in Maryland, he told African-Americans not to vote along racial lines (11.3.06).[954] *The Sunday Times* (UK) noted that Obama was an African and an American, and "as opposed to a descendent of slaves, he is free of historical hang-ups. He can cite the famous phrase in the Declaration of Independence about life, liberty, and the pursuit of happiness and not sound corny."[955]

He met with Ludacris in November 2006.[956] Obama met privately with the rapper, who said "We talked about empowering the youth," as he was in Chicago to launch the YouthAIDS 'Kick Me' campaign to raise awareness.[957] While Chris Bridges (his real name) said meeting Obama was like talking to a relative, "Obama declined to comment after their meeting, but walked with Bridges to the elevator as he left."[958] There was an *AP* photo showing Obama in his suit and tie, and Ludacris in his black t-shirt with a picture of Ben Franklin on a WANTED poster.[959] Why did Obama decline to comment on their discussion?

The dictatorial debate

In the July *YouTube* debate, Obama was asked if he would meet, in his first year as president without precondition, the leaders of Iran, Syria, Venezuela, Cuba, and North Korea.[960] While Obama said "I would," Clinton said, "I don't want to be used for propaganda purposes," and would first use envoys to test the waters.[961]

Former Clinton Secretary of State, Madeline Albright, who endorsed Hillary Clinton, came to the former first lady's defense (and was made available to reporters immediately after the debate): "It's a step-by-step process. It's not just some event."[962] An Obama foreign policy advisor, Anthony Lake, who was an early national security advisor in the Clinton administration, noted President Nixon negotiated with China, and Reagan did so with the Soviet Union.[963]

The day after the debate, Clinton then told the *Quad-City Times* she thought Obama's suggestion "was irresponsible and frankly naïve."[964] Clinton's 'toughness' was a joke: in truth, she herself did not rule out talking to the dictators.[965] The Democratic Party supported direct talks with Iran. How could Sen. Clinton be a proponent of direct talks with Iran, and simultaneously shoot down Obama's proposal to talk with the Iranian leader?

For Obama, another problem with the above comments was that Fidel Castro remained unpopular in Florida's Cuban-American population. However, Cuban-Americans tended to vote Republican. If Obama wanted to talk to Castro, the stance would hurt him more in the general election than a Democratic primary. In addition, days later, in what appeared to be an effort to look tough, Obama said he might send troops to Pakistan to hunt terrorists (8.1.07).[966] Jon Stewart asked, "Who put the bomb in Obama?"[967] Maybe Obama had become too aggressive.

Whoever won the early skirmish, it was clear Sen. Clinton was going to paint Obama as another weak-on-defense Democrat in the campaign. Obama has padded up his knowledge. Colin Powell, who has not ruled out endorsing a Democrat in 2008, has met at least twice with Obama.[968] But Obama's suggestion to attack terrorists thru Pakistan was also seen by John McCain as an irresponsible comment, because the current leader of Pakistan is an ally to the US. Such an attack could make Pakistani's revolt against their government, and cause a terrorist to lead Pakistan. What would President Obama do then?

Who would be Obama's running mate?

If Obama beats Clinton for the nomination, who will be his vice president? His short list of possibilities will be just that: a short list. Clinton would likely be out of the picture, as she would overshadow the nominee. She could be placated with Harry Reid's Majority Leader position in the Senate. With an Obama victory in the primaries, Edwards or Richardson would likely finish after Clinton. To put Edwards on the ticket a second time would be foolish. Why would Obama re-run Edwards in that position, after Obama himself has commented that a new political order void of Bush and Clintons should occur. Why would Obama re-nominate someone from 2004?

So the next choice would be Bill Richardson. If pollsters are worried about the first black president, more might be concerned about running the first black/Hispanic ticket. In this scenario, even possible success for Richardson in the primary might relegate his success to just a Secretary of State position (which Richardson would, no doubt, take). But Richardson may fit well as a vice presidential candidate because he could make Western states go Democrat. Yet he would be a better VP for Clinton, than Obama, because Richardson would not overshadow Clinton.

After Bill Richardson, who could Obama choose? Joe Biden is closer to Secretary of State material. Evan Bayh, like Biden, is a senator. A senator has not won a presidential election since 1960? Putting two on the ticket decreases the odds for success. Bayh has also considered running for president twice, and is no longer the rising star he once was.

And so, the best vice presidential candidate for Barack Obama may be Mark Warner. Obama has spent much of 2007 criticizing the war and pulling his Iraq stance left. As non-divisive as Obama can be, his VP needs to be a centrist to placate possible general election consequences of his liberal anti-war position. Warner is virtually untouched on the Iraq War because he quit running for president so early (October 2006). Warner would offend neither pro-war nor anti-war voters. And some have suggested a quarter of Warner's supporters are Republican leaning. Warner would reinforce the independence and bi-partisanship of an Obama candidacy.

Warner left the race for the presidency citing family concerns. But a vice-presidential campaign would last four months, and a winning campaign would not cause his family to move, as they already live in Virginia. Warner's moderate stances, coupled with Obama's non divisive tone, would likely stave off an independent presidential run by Michael Bloomberg. Bloomberg's candidacy will likely hinge on Hillary Clinton winning the Democratic nomination, because her victory could cause a polarizing political climate for the general election and leave room for an Independent's success.

To compensate Warner's deficiency in foreign policy, Obama could make Biden, Richardson, or Colin Powell Secretary of State. Powell has not ruled out voting Democrat in 2008 and has met with Obama. In the face of GOP disillusionment, is there a better combination than an Obama-Warner ticket, with occasional campaign stops from Colin Powell?

Of course, this dream scenario collapsed when Mark Warner decided to run for US Senate in September 2007. And so the question pops up again: Who would be Barack Obama's running mate?

Governor Bill Richardson

Bill Richardson was born in Pasadena and grew up in Mexico City before he attended a Massachusetts prep school.[969] He served in the US House from 1982 to 1997. Then he was appointed UN Ambassador by Bill Clinton, who then made Richardson the Energy Secretary.

In the 2002 elections, he was one of only four Clinton cabinet members running who won, as he became New Mexico's governor after promising to cut the state's income taxes and sketching a statewide water policy, "in considerable detail."[970] He took himself out of the running for the VP slot in 2004. He made headlines in July 2004 ("Richardson to Kerry: Don't pick me") for declining to run on the Kerry ticket. He gave the Kerry campaign a letter, and said he would respectfully "remove myself from the selection process and withdraw my name from consideration...,"[971] as if he was doing Kerry a favor. The reality was Richardson met Kerry for two hours days before the public 'decline.'[972]

Concerns for Richardson

1) His lifestyle. Richardson was known for his humor, and unique personality. But was he disciplined enough to handle a presidential campaign? Some did not think so, for "he was famous in Washington for his ribald sense of humor and penchant for late-night, cigar-smoking conviviality."[973] The *Denver Post* said (April 2006), Richardson was "as famous for his political skill as for his love of lavish dinner parties and inch-thick Cuban cigars."[974]

Richardson lives life in the fast lane. He said "we are going to slow down," after state Republican Party ads said (spring 2005) he was not "bothered by speed limits."[975] Two years earlier, a local TV station caught him at 100mph on a trip between Sante Fe and Albuquerque; and Richardson hit 110 mph with a *Washington Post* reporter on the way to a social event the night of the Democratic presidential debates in 2003.[976]

2) His years in the Clinton administration. Richardson had a small tie to the Monica Lewinsky scandal, as before it hit headlines, the White House asked Richardson to give Lewinsky a job at his U.N office, and he did offer, but Lewinsky declined.[977]

When Energy Secretary Federico Pena resigned, President Clinton shifted Richardson to the cabinet post. Richardson incurred some difficulties as Energy Secretary, and he fired Los Alamos scientist Wen Ho Lee in March of 1999 after it appeared the secret documents about the assembly of nuclear weapons ended up in China.[978] Richardson was embarrassed after two computer hard drives with nuclear secrets got lost at the Los Alamos National Laboratory; the drives were located behind a copy machine, "but not before Richardson had received an angry dressing down on Capital Hill."[979] In September 2000, Lee pleaded guilty to one count of downloading sensitive material.[980] Richardson later commented that the "security stuff cancelled me out" for the possibility to be Al Gore's running mate in 2000.[981]

Richardson wrote (November 2005) how Wen Ho Lee was "badly treated," but when he was interviewed by Amy Goodman in September 2005, he was more blunt: "this was a man that was convicted on several counts of tampering with classified information."[982] "Actually, Lee was convicted of only one count," wrote Steve Terrell of *The New Mexican*.[983]

Time reported (8.13.05), "a federal judge named Richardson last month as a probable source of leaks to the press about Los Alamos scientist Wen Ho Lee, who admitted mishandling sensitive data but was ultimately absolved of espionage-related charges in 2000."[984] Richardson's book did not address the allegations he leaked Lee's name to the press before Lee was even charged with crimes.[985]

Richardson's life story

November 2005 marked the official debut of Bill Richardson's book: *Between Worlds—the Making of a Political Life*. The Penguin Group's website said the book was about "A rising star of the Democratic Party tells the fascinating story of the ways his multicultural heritage and political education have shaped his dreams for America and given him vital lessons in the art of successful negotiating."[986] The book was not that sentimental. For example, did Richardson really 'tell the fascinating story'? Richardson himself said he had not written a single word, and instead gave full credit to co-author [or just author] Michael Ruby.[987] Ruby's name was in smaller font on the cover.

In addition, the *Washington Times* reported that a large number of notables stopped by a celebration for the books publication, including *Meet the Press* moderator Tim Russert, PBS' Margaret Warner (who interviewed Richardson about North Korea the month before), and Chris Matthews.[988] Was it appropriate for these news figures to be at the party? Chris Matthews was particularly fond of Richardson, and told him (2.26.07) he was one of the four (Edwards, Clinton, Obama) who had "a real shot" to get the Democratic nomination.[989]

Well…I thought I was drafted

"N.M. governor admits he wasn't drafted by baseball team" ran the *AP* headline (11.25.05).[990] Richardson admitted that his claim to have been drafted by the Kansas City Athletics in 1966 was false; it was claim used in his 1982 campaign for Congress and a White House news release in 1997.[991] The *Albuquerque Journal*'s investigation into the matter spawned the story.

Perhaps the confusion was an honest mistake. But the *AP*'s depiction of the incident was embarrassing: "'After being notified of the situation and after researching the matter…I came to the conclusion that I was not drafted by the A's,' he said….He insisted his name had appeared on 'a draft list of some kind' created by the Los Angeles Dodgers and Pittsburgh Pirates. He named team scouts, whom he said told him that he 'would or could' be drafted. The scouts have since died."[992] How does one mistakenly claim to have been a Major League Baseball draftee?

Richardson's strengths
    1) His foreign policy credentials. Was he a strong candidate? Chris Matthews asked him what he had the President Bush did not have? Richardson said:

> Foreign policy experience. When he came in as president, he traveled literally only to Mexico and Europe. I have been U.N. ambassador dealing with 185 countries. I've been secretary of energy, running with the Russians and OPEC countries. I have negotiated … in Darfur with the Sudanese on a cease fire, with the North Koreans. President Clinton used to say the bad guys like Richardson, so we will send him to deal with them. The point is that if we're going to have diplomacy as our main weapon, which we should, we should be talking to North Korea, to Syria, to Iran. We should be engaging diplomatically, and I have done it. I don't have to study. I have actually negotiated, I have been face-to-face with very tough dictators, like Saddam Hussein and the North Koreans in Bashir of Sudan. That's what I bring. And I bring a lifetime of not just a graduate degree, service in the House Intelligence Committee, U.N. ambassador, also secretary of energy. And as governor, I kind of—they say I am the only governor with a foreign policy, so I've got that portfolio. And our main objective should be to restore America's standing in the world and get out of Iraq this year.[993]

    Specifically in Sudan (Sept.2006) Richardson met with the Sudanese President in September 2006 and secured a pledge that *Chicago Tribune* correspondent Paul Salopek be freed; along with his driver and interpreter (who were from Chad, and were repatriated after the release).[994] Salopek was held in the capital of the state of North Darfur, Sudan.[995] Illinois Sens. Durbin and Obama also helped.[996] Richardson had brokered deals in Sudan before: in December 1996 he "secured the release of three Red Cross workers, including Albuquerque pilot John Early, from Marxist rebels in Sudan," reported the *AP* (9.6.06), which also rehashed Richardson's travels to Iraq, North Korea, and Cuba to "gain the release of Americans held prisoner."[997]

    In 1994, Richardson assisted to free a U.S. solder whose helicopter went into North Korea. In 1996, as a U.S. House member, he went to North Korea to release an American held for three months for spy charges. In 2003, just after starting his governorship, Richardson held talks with two North Korean envoys. The Bush administration granted the two North Koreans permission to go to New Mexico in 2003.[998] Likewise in 2005, Richardson spokesman said the governor "intends to coordinate fully with the Bush administration should the visit [another one with North Korea] take place."[999] Richardson has been an asset to the Bush administration.

    2) Richardson is a Democrat with a history of tax cutting. Bill Richardson signed a tax cut bill in April 2005, which included a yearly 'tax-holiday' to occur during the first Friday, Saturday, and Sunday in August. The *Albuquerque Tribune* stated the provision was to help families with back-to-school purchases by removing "state and local gross receipts taxes from purchases of certain items," such as clothing, footwear, computers and printers.[1000]

    In October 2006, he proposed a $69 million tax relief package which included $18 million in tax relief for the 19,000 active duty and retired military residents in New Mexico.[1001] However, as *Governing Magazine* later pointed out,

"His state is awash with revenue from oil and natural gas leases and so, in the words of Albuquerque pollster Brian Sanderoff, 'he can spend tons more on education and kids and at the same time cut taxes.'"[1002]

3) He is a governor in a field crowded by senators. And governors Vilsack and Warner had dropped out by the spring of 2006. The list was long of those Senators who ran or were still in the race: Bayh, Biden, Clinton, Dodd, Edwards, Feingold, Kerry, Gravel, Obama. Where was the executive experience?

ABC reported (12.6.06), Richardson "took a swipe" at the Democrats in Congress for not consulting with the nation's Democratic governors, telling a Washington news conferences "the Democratic Congress should listen to Democratic governors more because we have won, " and "Here in Congress, the people just float around and nothing happens."[1003] How could he blame Congressional Democrats when they did not control Congress until January 2007?

He chaired the Democratic Governors Association but Richardson did not receive the credit for the Democrats recovery of half a dozen governor's mansions in the midterms, which was largely viewed as a repudiation of the status quo in Iraq. His chair on the DGA was replaced by Kansas Gov. Kathleen Sebelius.[1004]

4) His ethnicity should help. Would he be good for the party? Exit polls in the 2004 election showed Bush getting 42% of the Hispanic vote (Bush won 35% in 2000).[1005] Richardson said (11.4.05), "the erosion of the Hispanic vote" was consistent in the last three elections in states like Nevada, Arizona, and New Mexico.[1006] "If John Kerry had carried those states, he would have been president."[1007] Was it a direct jab at Kerry? Richardson argued he was on a personal campaign to make such states "more than just flyovers," but the same *Reuters* article did not point out his push for a Western primary was an effort to make himself president. The article did not even mention his push for the Western primary. A Western Primary never developed, but Nevada Caucus was made the second competition for the Democrats.

Richardson was asked (Nov.2005) if the country was ready for a Hispanic President? "…You've got to appeal to the American mainstream. You can't run as a woman or a Hispanic. You run as an American, a healer."[1008] Richardson is a Hispanic who campaigns without saying 'Look at me, vote for me because I'm Hispanic.' The talk of Hispanics in politics was not used by Richardson as a prelude to bash the Bush Administration efforts in Latin America (Bush visited South America and had been poorly received). He said the Venezuelan relationship with the United States was "very strained"… [but] …"I'm not faulting the administration."[1009]

Bill Safire said (12.31.06), "….what we [media] have to do is come up with somebody new every couple of months. And we all swarm all over him. In a couple of months, I'm sure, it's going to dawn on somebody that the Hispanic vote is very important. And then we'll look around, and there the Democrats will have Bill Richardson. And he'll be on the cover of *Time* and *Newsweek*."[1010] As of 2007, Democrats won the struggle over Latino voters. A Richardson candidacy, even if he wouldn't win the nomination, could solidify Hispanics to vote Democrat for years to come.

5) Richardson is from the southwest. He was from the West as the region was becoming increasingly important to presidential politics: "four of the biggest swing states are now in the West—Colorado, New Mexico, Arizona, and Nevada," (4.16.06).[1011] And he was a moderate governor at a time when the Democrats were reevaluating the defeat of a 'Massachusetts liberal" in the 2004 election.

Richardson's candidacy should give voice to the southwest states and the lower Rocky Mountain region. The argument is Richardson could help make Nevada, Arizona, New Mexico, and Colorado go Democrat for 2008; especially after seeing candidates like Sen. Jon Tester (D-MT) get elected in 2006. Richardson is an advocate for the NRA, a strategy taken by few Democrats (exception: Mark Warner).

Through the Western Governors Association, Richardson sponsored a policy resolution in June 2004 in Sante Fe, New Mexico which stated the WGA would "support states and political parties in the region examining the idea of a common date for interested states and parties to hold their primaries and caucuses in order to draw attention to western issues."[1012] The Nevada Caucus was placed between the Iowa Caucus and New Hampshire primary, a move that might help Richardson succeed in the primary season.

6) Richardson thinks outside the box. In early 2005, he proposed a plan in which New Mexico would spend $800,000 a year to pay for a $250,000 life insurance policy for active National Guard members; the state would be the first to pay for a life insurance plan to Guard members.[1013] Was Richardson aligning himself for 2008 to an issue often won by Republicans? "…This is an attempt by an obviously ambitious Democratic politician to try to make the Democratic Party right with the military,"[1014] said Andrea Mitchell of *NBC News* (1.9.05).

In December 2005, British billionaire Sir Richard Branson announced the construction of "the first purpose-built commercial spaceport for the personal spaceflight industry" with the help of Richardson and state officials.[1015]

And by 2006, New Mexico paid $400,000 to a California-based consulting firm to study the feasibility of bringing an NFL team to New Mexico, perhaps with a joint effort with Albuquerque (only 800,000 residents) and the El Paso market in Texas.[1016]

On the presidential campaign trail, Richardson said (7.27.07) he would give voters a preview of his cabinet before Election Day, and that it would include "independents, Republicans and Democrats."[1017] But if he announced his cabinet (including a teacher at Education, and a union member at Labor, both of which Richardson promised), wouldn't it only invite more criticism to his campaign?

Richardson is competitive

His early rounds of ads in July 2007 bumped up his Iowa and New Hampshire numbers nicely.[1018] In Iowa, he finally reached double digit status in the polls.[1019] He had $7.1 million on hand mid-way through 2007, which put him in fourth place among the Democratic contenders.[1020] Richardson has not made the Big Three (Edwards, Clinton, Obama) the Big Four, but Richardson is edging closer to the front tier.

He has exceeded Joe Biden significantly in cash, an important separation given that both Biden and Richardson's strength is foreign policy. Dodd's campaign coffers are similar in amount to those of Richardson. But Richardson has so much more different facets to offer. The New Mexico governor is younger, Hispanic, a diplomatic trouble shooter, a former cabinet member, a UN ambassador. Chris Dodd has a lot of experience, but he is just another northeastern liberal Senator in his sixties.

Dodd helped pass the Family Medical Leave Act, while Richardson has talked to North Korean officials more than once. Richardson, as of late August 2007, was on pace to leave Dodd and Biden in the dust.

Former Governor Tom Vilsack

Thomas James Vilsack was born in 1950 and was soon placed in a Catholic orphanage, but was adopted by Bud and Dolly Vilsack.[1021] His birth name was Kenneth.[1022] Vilsack later stated he was adopted by a "troubled but loving family" as his alcoholic mother and financial unstable father sent him to preparatory school.[1023]

He met Ann Christine Bell in 1968, and married in 1973 in her hometown of Mount Pleasant, where the couple soon moved and Tom practiced law with his father in law.[1024] Then in the mid 1980s, Mount Pleasant's mayor was shot and killed at a City Council meeting and the late Mayor's father asked Tom Vilsack to run, and he was elected in 1987.[1025] Vilsack's first foray into politics offered Vilsack to appear as a hero, as the *AP* later reported (11.30.06) that Vilsack was elected mayor "and faced the task of healing the close-knit community."[1026] He was the mayor of Mount Pleasant then served two terms in the Iowa Senate.[1027]

As governor, the Iowa legislature repealed Vilsack's order that banned discrimination in state employment against sexual orientation; Vilsack vetoed the legislature's actions in the fall of 2002, but over twenty legislators sued and claimed Vilsack overstepped his powers, and a state judge agreed with the legislators.[1028] In many respects, Vilsack towed the party line as governor. He vetoed a waiting period for abortions, and teacher unions were key supporters as he helped increase their pay.[1029]

But Vilsack angered some in his party when he signed a bill making English Iowa's official language in 2002.[1030] Some felt this hurt Vilsack's chance to be Kerry's running mate in 2004.

Vilsack's representation of rural Iowa fit in with his moderate perception for 2008. Vilsack's term for governor expired in January 2007, but he was connected to the Democratic Leadership Council, a centrist organization that propelled Bill Clinton to the Presidency in 1992. In fact, after the 2004 elections, both Vilsack and Al From (of the DLC) independently stated the Democrats were impaired by "trust gaps" in security, values and ideas.[1031] Vilsack took over the two-year DLC chairmanship position in July 2005, and followed in Evan Bayh's footsteps.[1032]

Tom Vilsack had long planned his 2008 presidential run. *Des Moines Register* columnist David Yepsen wrote a half-dozen points in April 2003 suggesting the Iowa Governor was considering a White House bid. Yepsen cited Vilsack's political consultant at the time, Teresa Vilmain, who had been asked by the DNC to develop a presidential strategy for 2004; and "as a trial lawyer" Vilsack was "a member of one of the wealthiest constituency groups in the Democratic Party."[1033] Yepsen also hinted at Vilsack's oratorical skills.[1034] Vilsack's ambitions for the presidency were long discussed before the end of the November 2004 elections. In 2004, he campaigned in New Hampshire for John Lynch, the Democratic candidate for governor.[1035]

Vilsack wanted felons to vote

Tom Vilsack announced (June 2005) he would sign an order July 4 to restore the voting rights for all felons who had completed their sentences in Iowa. According to the *New York Times*, the order would make 80,000 ex-felons eligible to vote, of which 19% were black (even though just 2% of the state's population was African American).[1036] It was a great way to increase Democratic turnout in 2008 for the Iowa Caucus, though Vilsack argued research showed ex-prisoners who vote are less likely to end up in prison.[1037]

David Yepsen of the *Des Moines Register* was very critical of Vilsack. The governor's actions were more than just accepting criminals who had paid their debts to society. Indeed,

> ...why did Vilsack wait almost seven years as governor before he acted? If he were all that concerned about integrating criminals back into society, he would have taken action earlier in his term - not when he doesn't have to face voters for re-election. And he wouldn't have dropped his little political bomb on a Friday afternoon, traditionally a time when politicians unload controversial stories in the hope they'll get downplayed in the weekend news void. Yes, indeed. We've seen quite a transformation in the Tom Vilsack who while running for governor wanted to lock up all the meth dealers for 99-year prison terms to the one who now wants to hurry many of these same people to the polling booth.[1038]

Vilsack entered the race first; nobody cared

Vilsack filed papers for a presidential campaign committee on November 9, as campaign finance law required potential candidates to start an exploratory committee or a federal campaign committee to accept donations.[1039] He was immediately labeled as a long-shot. The *AP* reported (11.9.06) Vilsack was "the first Democrat to make a formal declaration for the presidency although a number of better known candidates are presumed to be running."[1040] The *Washington Post* headline was "Vilsack Faces Hurdles in 2008 Run," (11.10.06), and the story was only ten sentences long, not including the second half of the story which had nothing to do with Vilsack, but a non germane story on PACs.[1041] The story was tucked away nicely on page A13.[1042] *Wonkette* was sarcastic:

> If you woke up today all excited for no apparent reason, it's obvious that you've got a bad case of Vilsack Fever. That's right, ladies: Iowa Gov. Tom Vilsack is running for president! He's the first of approximately 270 Democrats to officially announce his sure-shot bid for the White House. ... Don't laugh off Vilsack just because you've never heard of him, or Iowa. AIPAC (the America Israel Public Affairs Committee) flew him to Israel in May, so he's a contender. And Kerry was considering him as a running mate, but decided John Edwards was 'much hotter.'[1043]

ABC News reported (11.30.06) that "Vilsack launched his long-shot bid for the presidency." *Oval Office 2008* opined, "the poor guy's only been out for five minutes and he's officially only got Mike Gravel to go up against so far, and already he's a long shot."[1044]

Vilsack on *Comedy Central*

Upon his announcement *The Daily Show* had random shots of the AFLAC Insurance duck yelling 'VILSACK' on the screen, followed up by Stephen Colbert's 'Vilsack Attack' sketch in which Colbert accused the Iowa Governor of being a liar due to having once said "There isn't nothing you can't do at the Iowa State Fair." Colbert said actually one can't ice fish, one can't go to the Nebraska State Fair, and one can't see Charley Daniels.[1045] Colbert corrected himself and said maybe Charley Daniels could be seen at Iowa's State Fair, and stated Vilsack was the frontrunner as he was the only official candidate.[1046] The 'Vilsack Attack' title on the screen was spelled with animated corncobs.

The Nightly News (12.11.07) even reported how Vilsack was compared to AFLAC.[1047] Vilsack then went on *The Daily Show* in mid December. Vilsack gave Jon Stewart a squeezable AFLAC duck, as Jon Stewart asked "So you're not going to run away from duck-related humor?"[1048] Vilsack responded, "I'm not going to duck the issue, that's right."[1049] As Eric Kleefeld of *TPM Café* wrote of Vilsack's appearance, the governor

> proved that he does sport a brisk sense of humor, albeit a low-key, deadpan one. At one point, for example, he worked in a decent crack in his description of his trip to Iraq: 'When you go over there it's a scripted trip, but every once in a while there's an unscripted moment — sort of like this show.' Jon Stewart rejoined, 'Did you just compare our show to Iraq? Because I will have you know there are a lot of stories about this show you don't hear about: The schools I'm building.'[1050]

The *Des Moines Register* said Vilsack "was loose with his sharp-witted host."[1051] And "Vilsack is a self-described serious guy, although not one without a sense of humor. Still, his humor is dry and self-deprecating. For example, in June, he told a New Hampshire audience his adopted parents chose him 'somewhat similar to how you would buy a Thanksgiving turkey,' calling himself the 'plumpest one in the orphanage.'"[1052]

Overall Vilsack's use of *Comedy Central* was a great way to increase his name recognition. But on the next day after Vilsack's appearance on *The Daily Show*, Stewart showed Vilsack's opinion of Iraq leading to a "culture of dependency." Stewart raised the question of how appropriate it was for Vilsack to suggest it was the Iraqis fault the situation was not improving in Iraq, even though the US was the country that invaded.

Still, Vilsack's' spurt on Comedy Central was the highlight of his campaign, which is a sad commentary.

Could Vilsack have won Iowa?

Vilsack was the first Iowa candidate for president since Tom Harkin in 1992, but at that time other Democrats bypassed the state.[1053] The *Des Moines Register* reported (11.10.06) Edwards and Bayh were among the likely candidates who "set their sights on competing in Iowa" despite Vilsack.[1054]

Iowa Lt. Gov. Sally Pederson served two terms with Vilsack, and stepped down as Iowa party chairwoman before Vilsack announced his candidacy.[1055] Already by December 2, the new chair of Iowa's Democratic Party announced the party would remain neutral in the caucuses, as Scott Brennan said Vilsack was "well liked in this state and should have an early advantage."[1056] However, that comment may have been a jab at Vilsack, who immediately suffered from inflated expectations, as the *AP* headline was "Iowa Dems Declare Neutrality in Caucuses," and reported:

Vilsack faces a far different political calculation than did Iowa Sen. Tom Harkin when he sought the Democratic nomination in 1992. When Harkin ran, all of his rivals skipped the Iowa caucuses to focus on New Hampshire and its leadoff primary. Harkin won a lopsided victory in his home state, but got little attention and was quickly forced out of the race.The challenge for Vilsack would be to meet expectations that he will win a lopsided victory in his home state. Anything less probably would be seen as a setback.[1057]

But an Environmental Defense poll (October 2006) of Democratic county chairs in Iowa found a "stonger sentiment for Vilsack," who placed second with 15 percent ahead of Obama (11) and Clinton (8); Edwards placed first.[1058] And the *Des Moines Register* reported "Scandals in Iowa unlikely to hurt Vilsack at caucuses," whether those issues included "From a prison break last year that attracted national media attention to a spending scandal at CIETC that attracted federal investigators, there has been a fair share of controversy in state government, …Vilsack has had to deal with it all," then the *Register* report added "Most political activists do not think the scandals and controversies will affect Vilsack's presidential ambitions in other states."[1059] The *Register* also reported in the same article (12.2.06), "It's not a primary election in which Vilsack needs a half-million votes to win. In the 2004 caucuses, Kerry won with support from about 38 percent of the 122,000 participating Democrats, or about 46,400 people."[1060] If the national media was labeling Vilsack a long shot, the *Des Moines Register* was keeping his chances alive.

After Bayh dropped out in December 2006, Craig Varoga said "All the supporters who were drawn to Senator Bayh because of his positions, but also because of his background as a Midwesterner and former governor, now have a very attractive alternative in Tom Vilsack."[1061] One had to wonder how Vilsack thought in late September 2006 compared to two or three months later after Mark Warner and Evan Bayh had dropped out.

Still, as of September 2006, 57 percent of Iowans thought it was a bad idea for Vilsack to run, while only 26 percent said it was good.[1062] The majority of Iowans were correct, or so thought Vilsack, who became both the first presidential candidate to officially declare, and officially drop out.

The sad demise of Tom Vilsack

The Democratic National Committee had a meeting in February 2006, in which ten presidential hopefuls addressed the crowd. Vilsack said, "Those who voted for the war, those who voted to continue to support the war, those who voted to continue funding the war can surely vote to stop the war…," and he endorsed an immediate end to the war.[1063] "It is time for us to clearly say the war must end and our troops must be brought home now…And let me say that I think Congress has a constitutional responsibility and a moral obligation to do it now: not a cap, an end. Not eventually, immediately."[1064] These, were the most startling words of the meeting.

Why? Not because Vilsack was loud and clear, but because nobody heard him. He had completely flopped on Iraq in a matter of months. In one year, Vilsack went from centrist Governor to vehemently anti-war. Here is the timeline.

In June 2006, Vilsack avoided questions on whether he would have voted for authorization, and did not support withdrawal. The *New York Times* reported (6.2.06) Vilsack "declined to say in an interview how he would have voted on the war."[1065] "I'm not going to get into that; this isn't about what happened in the past. If we're looking at the elections of 2006 and 2008, I think it's important to look to the future and learn from whatever mistakes we made in the past."[1066] Vilsack was vague too, as a report on a trip to New Hampshire claimed Vilsack "said a recent trip to Iraq convinced him that it would be a bad idea for the U.S. to set a deadline for withdrawing troops. He said such a deadline would encourage insurgents to hold their fire, and then unleash 'instability and chaos' after the US left."[1067] So in July 2006, Vilsack was not like some other Democrats claiming Iraq was in total chaos.

In typical moderate fashion, the local news (*WHOTV*) in Des Moines reported after Joe Lieberman's US Senate primary in Connecticut (August 2006) Vilsack said "he doesn't see a broader message for the Democratic party" in Lieberman's defeat and "…While critical of Bush's handling of the war, Vilsack has not called for withdrawing troops, nor has he sought the firing of Defense Secretary Donald Rumsfeld, who is widely perceived as being the war's architect. Despite Lieberman's loss, Vilsack says he does not need to take a tougher stance on the war."[1068] Even Hillary Clinton beat Vilsack in calling for Rumsfeld's resignation, and she waited until the fall of 2006. And no Democratic presidential hopefuls supported Lieberman after Ned Lamont won the Democratic primary, and Lieberman ran as an Independent.

By the end of 2006, Vilsack still opposed a timeline for pulling troops out of Iraq, but supported pulling troops out of Baghdad, and wanted to put them in enclaves in the northern parts of the country.[1069]

Then Vilsack became anti-war

Vilsack struggled on *Hannity & Colmes* after the President's speech on Iraq (1.10.07). Bush said "America's commitment is not open-ended" and the "Iraqi government plans to take responsibility for security in all of Iraq's provinces by November," and Sean Hannity suggested that was evidence of a suggestion on a timetable for withdrawal.[1070] Vilsack struggled with his repetitive indecisive answer to Hannity, who asked Vilsack if he supported Ted Kennedy's resolution.[1071] Vilsack called the president's new plan "a grim assessment of a grim circumstance," but *WHOTV.com* noted "the governor dueled a bit with" Hannity about Kennedy's plan to stop funding the surge."[1072] But *WHOTV.com* did not really explain the scuffle happened because Vilsack did not give an answer to whether he supported Ted Kennedy's proposal to cut the surge's funding.

Within ten days, Vilsack had asked Congress to prevent Bush from the surge by refusing to fund it [Kennedy's bill], he "also called for stricter oversight of reconstructions," and asked "Are they just going to blindly approve another $100 billion?"[1073]

At the February DNC meeting, he said the plan to cap forces [Sen. Clinton's idea] was like staying the course.[1074] He was the last candidate to speak at the meeting.[1075] On Feb. 4, he reiterated his call for immediate withdrawal of US troops on *Late Edition*, and said it could be done safely without a bloodbath.[1076] He said the withdrawal could happen "as quickly as possible," and that it was "necessary for Congress to send a message to this administration that they are not going to fund this war effort."[1077] Vilsack said "it's going to be up to the Iraqis themselves" as to when to end the conflict, and it was up to "outsiders" to tell Congress to cut funding.[1078] But which Iraqis? The Sunnis fighting Sunnis? The Shiite fighting Shiite? Or the Sunnis and Shiite fighting each other? Or the Kurds? Suddenly all Iraqis did not want to end the conflict. Yes, Vilsack told CNN (2.4.07): "… it's going to be up to the Iraqis themselves to decide when to end this conflict. It's not up to the United States."[1079]

The description in the *Des Moines Register* was disturbing (2.5.07), "He rejected arguments by members of Congress such as Sen. Dianne Feinstein, D-Calif., that the safety of troops on the ground could be endangered by a quick pullout. 'It will be done correctly,' Vilsack said, 'but we clearly need to send a message. We are going to absolutely see more of our soldiers die, more of our soldiers injured, if we continue on this course.'[1080] But it was possible more soldiers would die if another course was considered.

The *Des Moines Register* reported, "By saying Congress should stop financing the war in Iraq now, former Iowa Gov. Tom Vilsack has starkly differentiated himself from many of the other contenders for the 2008 Democratic presidential nomination."[1081] Vilsack said (2.4.07), "It's necessary for Congress to send a message to this administration that they are not going to fund this war effort," and "Congress has the constitutional responsibility and a moral obligation to do it now."[1082] He also repeated (2.4.07), "Those who voted for the war, those who voted to continue to support the war, those who voted to continue funding the war, can surely vote to stop the war."[1083] This was the same war that a half year earlier, Vilsack wouldn't even say whether he would have voted for.

Dishonorable discharge

Vilsack left the campaign before the end of February. On March 26, 2007, Vilsack endorsed Hillary Clinton.[1084] Chris Matthews told Vilsack, there was "…the pitch that you were an executive and the other candidates weren't. ….Now you're saying she is the best candidate. If executive experience and being from out of town and not part of the Washington scene were so vital to your success, why have you switched 180 now and said, what we really need is a Washington insider with only legislative experience?"[1085] When he dropped out, Vilsack said "I think we were winning the idea primary, but the money primary was the one that mattered. We obviously had a position on the war that I think was the right position….[Which position: the one from July 2006 or February 2007?] But the reality is, if you don't have the resources, you can't basically push the message, and that was the—at the end of the day, that's what it was."[1086] So he endorsed the wealthiest contestant in the race.

And he defended Clinton's vote for force in Iraq: "Hillary had information that I don't have, so I certainly wouldn't be able to try to second-guess the decision that she made."[1087] The information was so bad for Hillary, Vilsack couldn't decide nine months earlier if he would have voted for the same war.

Vilsack was asked if he supported permanent bases (as Sen. Clinton still did). Vilsack answered (3.26.07), "I think it's important for the United States to have protection of its national strategic interests in that region. Obviously, there is going to be an opportunity for us to have troops deployed throughout that region, as there has been. But the bottom line is, the war has to end. Hillary Clinton has promised and pledged to end it. I believe she will on the first day she is in office." Vilsack did not answer the question. Vilsack wanted an immediate withdrawal from Iraq but not so immediate withdrawal from bases.

After Vilsack left the race, Jay Leno joked, "…Well, you know there were signs Vilsack had had enough. Did you see what he did last night? He shaved his head [like singer Brittany Spears] and got a tattoo. That's not a good sign."[1088] Ironically, Vilsack's shifting stance on Iraq in a matter of months, to placate the liberal base of his party, came off just as desperate as Spear's head shaving.

Former Governor Mark Warner

Born in Indianapolis in 1954, Mark Warner went to George Washington University, Harvard Law School, and then worked for the Democratic National Committee. Besides Virginia, Warner spent his early years in Indiana and Connecticut, and his combined wealth made him a formidable appeal as a national candidate.[1089]

His estimated worth was $200 million by setting up a venture capital fund in 1989 called Columbia Capital which financed over 70 telecommunications and information technology firms (including Nextel).[1090] In the 1980s, the Federal Communications Commission stopped its expensive application process and gave licenses through a lottery.[1091] Warner did not enter the lottery for licenses to operate cell franchises in specific markets, but he did realize most of those lottery winners wanted to sell their licenses. Warner and a few others stepped in and managed deals between buyers and sellers (and got 5% of the sale price). He then borrowed money to buy shares in the licenses held by partnership groups, then sold these shares for higher prices.[1092] He then signed on to Columbia Capital, which focused on the wireless industry and within a decade he had made $150 million.[1093] Others described the scenario as a man who made millions mastering an industry that few could understand in the 1980s. *Atlantic Monthly* (May 2006) explained Warner's maneuverings as making his "first big money by exploiting a multibillion-dollar government giveaway in the cell-phone industry."[1094]

He was Virginia's Democratic Party chairman from 1993 to 1995, then nearly beat John Warner for Senate in 1996 by spending $10 million of his own fortune.[1095] But winning 47% against the entrenched incumbent Senator was in itself a major accomplishment for Mark Warner—many of Mark's friends initially thought he was crazy for trying.[1096]

An unorthodox Democrat

Considered a moderate, Warner was not the stereotypical Democrat. He ran for governor of Virginia in 2001 by claiming to be an entrepreneur bringing business methods to government.[1097] An understanding of this campaign for governor is crucial in respecting the viability of Warner as a presidential candidate, and now a Senate candidate for 2008. Warner avoided social issues and focused on economics—a move that got southwestern Virginians to pay attention to a Democratic candidate more than in the past.[1098] Roanoke real estate developer Dave "Mudcat" Saunders told Warner to focus on 'kitchen table' issues: economics and education.[1099] Warner spent another $5 million of his own money, opposed new gun control measures, and sponsored a NASCAR race truck.[1100]

He campaigned so successfully on the gun issue that the NRA did not back a candidate in the campaign; a "Sportsmen for Warner" campaign was launched and 10,000 4-by-8 signs covered southwest Virginia[1101] The year before, there was a state wide ballot initiative allowing a constitutional amendment to protect the rights to hunt and fish, so Warner picked up the support of the women who led the initiative and succeeded in blocking the NRA from endorsing the Republican candidate.[1102] His business prowess made him a moderate. "Many of his friends in the high-tech community—some of whom donated more than $100,000 to his gubernatorial campaign—are either political independents or outright Republicans."[1103]

As a young governor, he argued that the globalizing high tech economy was making rural economies in southern Virginia irrelevant as textile industries (in Martinsville in 2002, for example) lost massive amounts of jobs. So Warner's administration started programs getting the unemployed GED's and high school diplomas within three months.[1104] Then, he recruited NASCAR part's manufacturers in the southwestern portions of the state.[1105] A businessman himself, Warner was instrumental in starting four regional venture capital funds started across Virginia, and encouraged his business partners to invest in Virginia.[1106]

There was one problem. Virginia is the only state to constitutionally limit governors to one term, so Warner would be out of office by January 2006. What could he do to keep himself active on the national stage? He would be unemployed sooner than other 2008 candidates.

Early praise

Zell Miller—the senator from Georgia who defected his party in 2004 to support President Bush—put Warner in a group of "very, very good candidates," for president.[1107] Warner held the chairmanship of the National Governors Association, and was named as public official of the year by *Governing Magazine* in November 2004.[1108] Quoted in a *Washington Post* article after the 2004 elections, DLC founder Al From said Warner's "biggest contribution to our party can be redefining our brand and what it stands for."[1109] The same article said Mike Huckabee was "one of Warner's closest friends," while the Arkansas governor said he was "glad" Democrats "didn't turn to him this time [2004], Frankly, it might mean all my friends in Washington would be looking for jobs."[1110]

Warner scored a big victory when the February 2005 edition of *Governing Magazine* rated all the state governments in the nation and stated that there was "little" that Virginia did not do well in government management.[1111] *Governing* said Virginia had an "ethos of good management," and despite a Council on Virginia's Future absent from Warner's control, Warner was still able to make his own mark and "got off to a running start by instituting performance contracts for top officials throughout state government. These 'executive agreements' provide a clear and measurable way to communicate priorities to the 10 cabinet secretaries and roughly 100 agency heads."[1112] *Governing* commented on Virginia's decision to raise taxes. "Raising taxes by a sufficient amount to stabilize the state's fiscal condition wasn't a choice the legislature made easily, or even—for many members—willingly. It required rancorous special sessions that lasted long beyond the General Assembly's normal adjournment time....Other states in similar fiscal condition shirked their responsibilities."[1113]

Warner was praised by the *Roanoke Times* for his bi-partisanship (4.8.05), "...Warner and a critical number of responsible Republican lawmakers worked together during the Democrat's term to save Virginia's finances from ruin."[1114] The *Washington Post* reported (7.9.05) Warner "cultivated an image of fiscal discipline and bipartisanship" that was "catapulting him into the ranks of 'the mentioned' among Democrats."[1115]

Though his first two years as governor were mired by budget cuts and other failures, "things changed in 2004" as Warner got a tax increase to pass with the help of the Republican legislature in an effort coalesced by business executives, lobbyists, and local officials.[1116] Adversaries said he successfully convinced Virginians of the tax proposal despite a mending economy, they could point out that Warner lied in his 2001 gubernatorial campaign to not raise taxes.[1117] In November 2005, *Time* named Mike Huckabee and Warner in the top five governors in the country.[1118]

The 2005 Elections were Warner's

The elections of 2005 might have helped Warner the most. Newt Gingrich said the "big winner" on election night was Warner: "He's followed a relatively centrist policy, clearly far to the right of the left-wing of his party. He's had the courage to go and lead the state the way he wanted to....and it paid off..."[1119] However, Warner was not on the ballot, but rather his lieutenant governor.

Having influenced Governor-elect Tim Kaine's election in Virginia, Mark Warner was interviewed on *Face the Nation*. Days after the interview, Warner made his first trip to New Hampshire and unveiled a website for his Forward Together PAC.[1120] He then received a favorable op-ed from David Broder of the *Washington Post*, and ended the month in New York discussing Asia's influence in the world.[1121] Warner agreed that there was a lesson to be learned from the 2005 elections for the Democratic Party; he listed successes in Virginia and said the lesson was "results matter. Efficiency matters."[1122] On the flip side, Jerry Kilgore, the GOP candidate to be Virginia's governor, ran a "social hot-button campaign," while the winning message was bipartisan.[1123] Once again Warner affiliated himself with a campaign avoiding divisive social issues. When asked if President Bush's visit to Virginia hurt Kilgore, Warner said he would "leave it to the pundits to make that determination."[1124]

Warner raised taxes: did Virginia benefit?

Warner used the time on *Face the Nation* to display what he did as governor. But he raised taxes. As a Democrat, how would Warner explain what he did?

> What we did in Virginia was we started with cutting spending...We got rid of close to 5,000 positions in state government. We eliminated 70 boards and agencies. Then we launched a major reform of state government in terms of how it operates...And then we ended up saying, 'Hey, we still have a structural budget imbalance,' because like most states in the late '90s, in the go-go days, we either cut taxes too much or started spending too much. We launched a tax reform plan that lowered some taxes, raised others.[1125]

This was the plan to combat his tax credibility. First, argue that he slashed the government bureaucracies. Second, the tax reform (as oppose to calling it a 'tax hike') was a solution that both raised and lowered different taxes. In an overall perspective, the "tax reform" was a $1.4 billion increase in taxes supported by Warner and a legislature controlled 2 to 1 by Republicans.

Virginia was a great state economically, and Warner's reputation as governor shined only brighter. (See the opinion by *Governing* in early 2005 mentioned above.) In August 2006, *Forbes* magazine said Virginia was the best state for business, as it "dominated our rankings, placing in the top ten in each of the six categories we examined: business costs, economic climate, growth prospects, labor, quality of life and regulatory environment," as no other state placed in the top ten for 4 or more categories.[1126] Virginia's business costs were 9% under the national average—they were "very low," said *Forbes*, "particularly tax and energy costs, which are seventh and ninth lowest in the country."[1127]

Although it did not specifically mention taxes, *Forbes* described an ideal situation for businesses. MeadWestvaco, a packaging and office products firm, searched a year and a half and decided to move its $6 billion-in-sales and 400 jobs from Connecticut to Richmond.[1128]

Edwards criticized Moderates; Bayh & Warner responded

The *Des Moines Register* reported (7.12.06) Warner's comments "sets him apart from" Edwards, who went to Iowa a week before Warner, "accused moderates of forsaking the party base."[1129] In a July 2006 trip to Iowa, Edwards said "I don't believe in a party that's trying to navigate its way to the political center and to see how careful we can be."[1130] But Warner's comments were borderline offensive to leftists: "My feeling is if you are a hard-core ideologue at either end of the spectrum, basically you've got all of your answers because you've got a predetermined position on every issue."[1131]

Like Warner, Evan Bayh made efforts to question the party's ideology. Bayh said (7.17.06) "We may consider ourselves the party of the middle class, but too many middle class Americans no longer consider us their party. They have left the Democratic Party in droves—costing us the last two presidential elections and the last six congressional elections, and if we don't learn some lessons, we'll lose in 2006 and 2008 too."[1132] "Implicit" in Bayh's comments, was a critique on Gore's 2000 message of the 'people vs. the powerful' and Edwards post-2004 campaign on poverty.[1133] Furthermore, Joe Biden said (July 2006) the next Democrat for 2008 had to be "tough" on national security, "understanding" of people's religious beliefs, and needed to win over 19 states to have a consensus for policy-making because a bare majority had the "propensity" to lead to division.[1134] Warner never evolved into a savvy foreign policy candidate, but he certainly stood his ground against Edwards' plea to liberalize the party.

Did Warner communicate well?

Republican and media pollster Frank Luntz looked at focus groups in Iowa and New Hampshire, and concluded the big winner was Mark Warner and stated the Governor "blew people away" with issues like education and red-state background; meanwhile Hillary Clinton came across "as too harsh and too negative and too in your face.[1135]

Both Warner and Feingold met party and labor leaders and elected officials (4.8.06) in Milwaukee, and the *Milwaukee Journal Sentinel* reported the contrast between the men.[1136] Warner did not support censure of the president, or timetables for troop withdrawal in Iraq; Warner supported the No Child Left Behind Act yet stated he was critical of the law's implementation.[1137] All of Warner's positions were different than Feingold's. Yet Warner's position on NCLB reflects the timidness of Warner's stance. As the *Milwaukee Journal Sentinel* reported:

> In interviews, Warner seems more comfortable discussing domestic policy than national security issues. And he still is polishing his communication skills. While displaying ease and humor, he can be disjointed, too, often starting new sentences before finishing his old ones. Asked in the interview whether he had an opinion about the legality of the government's wiretapping of Americans without warrants (a big issue for Feingold), Warner answered as follows:
> "Yes. I went to law school. I never practiced, so I'm not going to - I just came back. I was up at Harvard and got a couple of, spoke, there was kind of a fellow up there, had tried to bring in some of the law professor types. And boy, you know, after two or three hours of going around and around - net, probably yes. But there are arguments both ways, you know. And I hope, one of the things that absolutely - in my gut, it sure does seem wrong."[1138]

Warner said he thought the big lessons for Democrats from the 2004 election were the need to offer an agenda beyond criticizing Bush, and the necessity of competing in more than 16 or 17 states.[1139] Charlie Cook surmised (5.7.06) Warner "has even greater national security shortcomings than Edwards."[1140] He had been campaigning for a year but there was long way to go. James Carville said "I don't think Mark Warner is catching on out there, but Evan Bayh is raising a surprising amount of money."[1141] But Howard Fineman wrote, "Call me cynical, but this would indicate to me that Carville [who was close to the Clintons] is more worried about Warner" than Bayh.[1142]

The surprising end of Warner

Mark Warner abruptly announced he would not run for president on October 12, 2006.[1143] His kitchen cabinet advisors while governor "were shocked" to find out after a conference call (Oct.11), which they were told was convened to discuss "strategy."[1144] And when his PAC team found out at 9 a.m. on Oct. 12, they "burst into tears."[1145] The *Washington Post* said even Virginia Republicans "said they were surprised."[1146]

The *Washington Post*, on a front-page story, quoted Warner's "chief operative in New Jersey" that "Everyone's devastated [in the Warner camp]."[1147] And there was many stories that weighed average citizens thoughts and shocks. In a more in-depth citizen-orientated story, the *Washington Post* ("For Warner's Supporters It's a No-Win Situation") asked, then answered with citizens comments, "What about the stunned supporters and their wilting expectations? *But he raised so much money! He had such good buzz!*"[1148] Stunned supporters like Eddie Ratcliff of the Draft Mark Warner for President PAC had to cancel his order for 5000 Warner buttons, and told the *Post* he would return to catfishing.[1149] Charlottesville's *Daily Progress* quoted nearly a half dozen citizens in a report that "people in Charlottesville voiced surprise and some sadness" at Warner's decision.[1150]

The buzz like no other

The Hill said the White House field "lost a high-profile contender," and Warner's "pro-business and high approval ratings as a red-state governor vaulted him to the shortlist" for Democrats in 2008.[1151] The *Washington Post* reported "all signs pointed to a Warner candidacy" and his trips to early contested states were "largely successful."[1152] The *AP* said Warner "was seen as a viable Democratic alternative to Clinton."[1153] Time said "in the competition to be the un-Hillary, Warner had risen to the top."[1154] The *Richmond Times-Dispatch* said he had 'established himself as a national player."[1155]

Warner himself said he felt "we would have had as good a shot to be successful as any potential candidate in the field."[1156] But the *Washington Times* was particularly critical of Warner's statement of wanting a real life: "No matter that for nearly a decade, the political centrist demonstrated clearly that he seemed to want the presidency more than life itself."[1157] The same article quoted a University of Maryland political science professor who essentially bashed the candidate and said Warner "didn't have a snowball's chance of winning anything, except maybe being selected as" vice president.[1158] But the conservative *Washington Times* did not care for Warner to begin with.

In addition, Warner had a many more statewide appearances for Jim Webb's Senate campaign in Virginia, and although Forward Together PAC raised $400,000 for Webb's campaign the rate of case flow from Warner's aura would diminish.[1159] Indeed, Warner's optimism collapsed after the announcement. And by the time Warner left Virginia to go to Iowa for a state fundraiser "all the air had *pfffed* out of his balloon."[1160] Warner's spokeswoman said "We just shoved the governor onto a plane to fly off ignominiously to Iowa."[1161] That trip was Warner's seventh to Iowa since the 2004 election.[1162]

What was Warner's reasoning?

1) His family. He said in his statement he wanted to make a decision around Election Day 2006, "But there were hiring decisions and people who've put their lives on hold waiting to join this effort."[1163] His spokeswoman Ellen Qualls said if he told his friends not to quit their jobs for a campaign, according to the *Washington Post*, "they'd start to wonder why and news of his indecision might leak."[1164]

Warner put the bulk of his decision on family. He said he decided after Columbus Day weekend with his wife and daughters and his father in Connecticut.[1165] "This is the right time for me in my life to have a life for a little while," said Warner at the age of 51, with three daughters the age of 12, 15, and 16.[1166]

Slate ran a particularly favorable story (10.12.06) on a Warner trip to Iowa in which he was on his phone with his daughter who suffered from diabetes, and "there was a little more urgency in his voice as he tried to figure out if she was just being a grumpy teenager or if it was something more serious.....Running for office is a brutal, dehumanizing slog."[1167] *Time*'s subtitle of the story said "A potential Democratic candidate for President says he'd rather spend more time with his family. For once, it might be the truth."[1168] And Ryan Lizza wrote "No matter how well things seemed to be going for Warner, privately he was filled with self-doubt. He had built a machine that was hurling him forward toward a presidential race that he actually didn't want to enter."[1169]

2) Perhaps there was a skeleton in the closet. Warner insisted he was not running away from a scandal.[1170]

3) Warner would have had to play to the liberal base more than his liking, and if it had not already, an eventual campaign would have put him in a position to be something he was not. In Florida just days after dropping out, Warner said "We have to really get it right and getting it right will require big enough change that it can't be a Democrat-only answer or a Republican-only answer."[1171] The primary season would have made him more liberal.

4) Warner had other viable options: "It doesn't mean that I won't run for public office again."[1172] Perhaps John Warner would not seek reelection to the Senate in 2008, and then Gov. Kaine would have to step down in 2009 and leave Warner another option. Sen. Warner would be an octogenarian if he sought reelection.[1173] It was disappointing. Warner said "while the chance may never come again, I shouldn't move forward unless I'm willing to put everything else in my life on the back burner."[1174] But would he ever have the opportunity to run for president again? In addition, if he had made the decision five or six months earlier, he perhaps could have ran against George Allen—who was beatable after the Macaca moment of August 2006.

5) Was it Hillary? Having succeeded in wooing labor and given a favorable 2008 primary schedule, John Edwards was a solid candidate as he may have had the best year in 2006 on the Dems side, and though a different Democrat than Warner, both were arguably anti-Hillary.[1175] Warner had the money to take Clinton to the cleaners—if his success in his PAC was not enough evidence, his $200 million from NEXTEL would have sufficed.

Without a doubt, the economy of Warner's potential campaign was humming. Warner spent the $50,000 to get access to the Iowa Democrats voter information file in the summer of 2006.[1176] *The Hill* reported (7.12.06), "Since Warner began raising money after the 2005 November election, Forward Together [Warner's PAC] has raked in $8.2 million and contributed $860,500 to 108 candidates and political committees."[1177] Simultaneously, his One Virginia PAC to help Virginia candidates had $493,000 on hand.[1178] He campaigned for Iowa gubernatorial candidate Chet Culver,[1179] and gave him a check (July 2006) for $25,000.[1180] Forward Together allowed website visitors to choose 10 candidates to get Warner's PAC donations, and 9,000 visitors got the list of 50 down to 10, of which the top two received fundraisers with Warner in person.[1181] And unlike Romney, who was limiting himself to Utahans and Mormons, Warner used the $8 million he raised as evidence of his broad appeal, and commented

(July 2006) that at a recent fundraiser for his PAC, "Somebody looked around and said 25 percent of the people in the room are Republicans."[1182]

There were concerns for Warner. *The Hill* also said Clinton "widely projected status" as the frontrunner had "long dogged Warner's bid to keep his name recognition high and his coffers full."[1183] Even in Warner's own statement, he said his PAC "contributed more money this year to Democratic candidates and party organizations than any other federal leadership PAC. Our effort raised over $9 million. I headlined 86 events in 25 states to help raise or directly donate $7.3 million to Democrats this cycle."[1184] Warner took "67 trips to 28 states and five" countries.[1185] Would Warner have kept his coffers full?

Who benefited from Warner's departure?

Chris Cillizza said Bayh was "the most obvious winner."[1186] The *Fort Wayne Journal Gazette* reported, Bayh's "presidential campaign got good news," and quoted Charlie Cooks view that it was "inconceivable" that Warner's dropped bid "doesn't help Bayh some, and maybe a lot."[1187] And it was noteworthy that Bayh "made a nearly identical announcement five years ago when he said his twin sons were too young to weather a protracted presidential campaign."[1188] Like Warner, the dropping out still provided him the opportunity to appeal to family values. And Bayh was one of the few to give public praise, noting Warner was "an exceptional public servant, a great leader, and an influential voice in the Democratic Party. I know how tough a decision that this must have been."[1189] Bayh was the first presidential contender to give a statement.[1190] *Slate* reported (10.12.06) that Bayh and Kerry "made their praise public. The most likely beneficiary of Warner's departure may be Bayh, who was competing for a similar sphere of donors and activists as a representative of the centrist wing of the Democratic Party....[and] Bayh can claim executive experience, just as Warner could..."[1191] But Bayh still had the "charisma problem."[1192]

Tom Vilsack may have lost as well, seemingly because Evan Bayh received more hopeful news—even though national polls always showed Vilsack, Bayh, and Warner all beneath 5 percent, and usually closer to 1 or 2. What about Vilsack or Richardson being included in life-after-Warner articles? The *Slate* article suggesting Bayh's benefits did not mention Vilsack or Richardson.[1193] The *Des Moines Register* said Warner's drop out "could magnify Gov. Tom Vilsack's presence in the field as a centrist governor."[1194] But that was an Iowa paper. And even they mentioned "the first wave of national analysts suggested Warner's departure would benefit" Bayh the centrist and Edwards the southerner (yes, for some reason Edwards was still labeled one who would benefit because he was a 'southerner').[1195]

Bob Novak said Warner's decision "produced speculation at high levels of the Democratic Party" that Gore would perhaps run.[1196] But the opposition party may have benefited the most from Warner's departure? Republicans were excited, as the *Washington Post* reported Warner's decision "prompted a bit of quiet celebration among GOP leaders who had watched Warner capitalize on his state tenure to run for national office."[1197] Perhaps the main reason Mark Warner dropped out of the presidential race was because he could win the general election—but Republican support doesn't help in the Democratic primaries.

In the end, Mark Warner may have benefited the most (politically speaking) from his decision not to run for president. On August 31, 2007, Sen. John Warner (R-VA) decided not to seek re-election for 2008. In September, Mark Warner announced his decision to continue his political career, and he is a favorite to win the US Senate seat.

Part II: The Republicans

Allen
Brownback
Frist
Gilmore
Gingrich
Giuliani
Hagel
Huckabee
Hunter
McCain
Paul
Pataki
Romney
Tancredo
F. Thompson
T. Thompson
Santorum

Bloomberg (Ind.)

Senator George Allen

George F. Allen was born in Los Angeles County, California in 1952, and grew up on the west coast, and graduated from Palos Verdes High School.[1198] But in the 1960s he spent some time in Chicago while his father helped coach the Chicago Bears. When his father was named head coach of the LA Rams, the family moved back to California.

In the 1970s, when George H. Allen was named head coach of the Washington Redskins, George junior went east and graduated from the University of Virginia in 1974, and its Law School in 1977.[1199] The Allen family is still active in the National Football League and carrying on the tradition of their father; although George F. Allen went into politics, Bruce Allen has been the general manager for the Tampa Bay Buccaneers.[1200]

The future US Senator married Anne Patrice Rubel in 1979, but divorced in 1983.[1201] He married Susan Brown in 1986, and together had three children.[1202] Allen began his career in state politics in 1979, when he lost a bid for the Virginia House of Delegates, but won a seat two years later.[1203] In 1991, he was elected to the House of Representatives.[1204] When his Congressional seat disappeared after redistricting, Allen decided to run for governor in 1993.[1205]

Virginia was the only state to limit governors to one term, but his accomplishments as governor would showcase Allen as a conservative presidential prospect. As governor, he achieved a looser concealed weapons law, parental notification for abortions, the abolition of parole, and welfare reform.[1206]

Another Bush?

In 2000, he was elected to the U.S. Senate—an election that showed his votes tracking very similar to George W. Bush's,[1207] and from 2004 and beyond, Allen evolved into what some saw as a prototype of the President. Allen became a leader for Republicans when he succeeded Bill Frist to head the committee for GOP Senate elections for the 2004 cycle, and he was one of the first GOP leaders to tell then-Majority Leader Trent Lott to step down in December 2002 after comments Lott made at Strom Thurmond's birthday party.[1208] Allen urged Bill Frist to be the next Senate Majority Leader, and it worked. Allen was a partisan Republican who would have taken a leadership position in the Senate if it were available—a man who had done his duty for his party.

Boston Globe columnist Peter S. Canellos wrote (10.4.05) of the presidential candidates for 2008: only Jeb Bush and George Allen seemed "eager to adopt the Bush image of a President who is boldly aggressive overseas, committed to a steady run of tax cuts, and willing to pursue the social agenda of the religious right."[1209] Allen was vehemently against tax increases. In August 2005, George Allen was still repeating his famous line regarding his efforts to eliminate the federal estate tax: "We don't need IRS buzzards swarming around one of our loved one's funerals. There should be no taxation without respiration! [in reference to Patrick Henry's 'without representation]."[1210] Canellos said Allen was banking on the belief voters wanted more of the same, "He does not offer even a stylistic contrast with the president. He is blunt and direct, he pays homage to the wisdom of the common man, and he pursues a staunch conservative agenda."[1211]

Allen called Bush's strategist, Karl Rove (1.22.06) someone "who I admire a great deal. And he is a good friend," and "Karl Rove is trying to unite this country …."[1212] *US News* ran a story (6.29.05) how Republicans felt Allen was perhaps the next George W. Bush, quoting a 'GOP sage' who felt Allen had "that Bush quality."[1213]

Allen ardently supported the administration's efforts in Iraq. Allen didn't even rule out war with China, as he told the *Examiner* (Sept.2006) if Beijing tried to forcibly reunite Taiwan with mainland China, "Some Chinese leaders may miscalculate that the U.S. won't care, [that] the U.S. is not going to start a war over it."[1214] How many in the US would support a war with China given the war in Iraq? And if the Iraq War dragged on into 2005 and beyond, and if the President's approval rating continued to drop, would Allen want to be the next George W. Bush?

Allen split with Bush on education

There were exceptions to the view that Allen was like the President. Allen's support for Bush was weaker in the realm of education. Even as governor, Allen's reforms, including the Standards of Learning, were arguably "the toughest in the nation."[1215] But "Allen was regarded by his foes as an intellectual lightweight."[1216] Allen said (Jan.2006) he and former Virginia Gov. Mark Warner found "common ground" on education, and one of the "most important things" Warner did was resist calls to water down Virginia's Standards of Learning and instead "wholeheartedly" supported the education reforms Governor Allen began.[1217] Allen preferred Virginia's Standards of Learning, which he put in place as governor, over the Presidents No Child Left Behind Act passed in 2001.[1218] Allen defied the stereotype that Republicans were 'off' on the education issue by criticizing NCLB.

In August 2005, Allen said NCLB dumbed-down Virginias curriculum standards.[1219] "We've worked too hard to have the federales come in here and foul up what we've done down here," said Allen in a statement that drew "hoots and howls."[1220] Though the *Washington Post* did not clarify who in the audience gave the 'hoots and howls,' perhaps it was Rosco P. Coltrain or Cooter from the *Dukes of Hazard*.

In April 2006, he said Bush's policy was "the same thing we did" with the "same purpose, [but] not as comprehensive because it doesn't include science or writing or economics or history or technology but it's partially the same point of view. Unfortunately in the way this [NCLB] has actually been managed and implemented, it is harmful and counter productive for us in Virginia."[1221] NCLB did not fairly judge schools with minorities, as Allen said schools should have a grace period of three years to teach English to those not proficient in it: "If a kid comes in the fifth grade, make him take the test in eighth grade."[1222]

The GOP frontrunner for 2005

The *National Journal* published a survey of members of Congress, party officials, consultants and political activists to find out who had the best chance at getting the party nominations.[90] Democratic 'insiders' rated Clinton first, with Edwards second (but with only half the points as Clinton), then Mark Warner, Evan Bayh, and John Kerry.[1223] But it was the Republican poll that was worthy of attention. Republican insiders placed George Allen just ahead of John McCain; followed by Frist, Giuliani, and Romney.[1224] Was Allen a 'dark horse?

Having been ranked by GOP insiders as the most likely Republican to win the 2008 nomination, George Allen followed it with an invitation on *Meet the Press* (5.1.05). He stated "I'm for tax cuts for taxpayers. I want to make this country more conducive…"[1225] Shouldn't he have been more focused on Virginia? An interesting exchange between Tim Russert and Allen occurred over the number of Circuit Court judges confirmed by the Senate under President George W. Bush and Bill Clinton. Allen said, "I think you'll find on the Circuit Court judges that President Bush has the lowest percentage of Circuit Court judges…[confirmed]"; but Russert responded: "I just gave you the numbers. Clinton nominated 51; 35 were confirmed. Bush nominated 52; 35 were confirmed. Those are the numbers."[1226] "Well, I have different numbers than that," said Allen.[1227] Allen then appeared on *FOX News Sunday* on May 8 and ABC's *This Week* on May 15.

Republican strategist Mary Matalin appeared on *Meet the Press* and argued a candidate such as Allen was in a formidable position for the presidency. Why? A frontrunner like Sen. Clinton should be compared to dark horses in the polls. On one hand there was Clinton. With her, the

> …conventional wisdom presumes that she's positioned for a coronation. All the Democrats know she's only getting 40 percent. Front-runners, when they win on either side are in the 50, 60 ['s]. So there's lots of room for another Democrat here. And in both polls the other interesting thing is the strongest candidates are the asterisks at this point, the governors on the Democratic side and, I think, on our side. Governor Allen, for instance, the country doesn't know him. He's been in the House. He's been in the Senate. Highly successful at the Senate committee electing, or getting, more seats. He's been our governor… where he took the lead on education issues. He's a wonderful person, but my point is that people who the country doesn't know now tend to emerge as the strongest candidates.[1228]

Matalin was a Bush ally, Republican advisor to the first President Bush and Dick Cheney, and political commentator. She gave Allen $1,000.[1229] Matalin continued her public support of Allen, telling *Meet the Press* (1.23.06) he was the inside front-runner for 2008.[1230] Did Allen have Matalin on board as a strategist?

In October 2005, Sean Hannity of *FOX News* said, "As of today, I think you [Allen] will be the nominee of the Republican Party in 2008…"[1231]

Allen's unofficial campaign for president

The *Potomac News* reported (1.3.05) Allen was "being touted as a Reaganesque conservative with a sunny manner and a resume that includes stints in Congress, the U.S. Senate, and as Virginia's governor."[1232] The story went on to note that Allen gained recognition for leading the senatorial campaign committee in 2004—which picked up four GOP seats, including one at the price of Tom Daschle's (D-SD) career. In fact, Allen hired Dick Wadhams for his chief of staff.[1233] Wadhams ran the winning campaign for John Thune against Daschle in South Dakota.[1234]

Allen laid 2008 groundwork in 2005. After visiting New Hampshire in June, George Allen visited South Carolina in July.[1235] Allen raised $2.5 million between April and June 2005, and still did not have a challenger for 2006. George Will painted Allen as an iconic Republican. Allen, "as a University of Virginia graduate headed Young Virginians for Reagan in the 1976 nomination contest with President Ford, has Reagan's knack for expressing strong views in an unthreatening manner."[1236] And Will added that the ideal Republican candidate molds social conservatism and libertarianism together. "Social conservatives have no complaints with Allen, and libertarians vibrate like tuning forks to his invocations of 'Mister Jefferson,' as Virginians refer to their saint of minimal government."[1237]

As George Allen was becoming a more viable presidential candidate, he was also bringing faith into his politics. He told (April 2005) Pat Robertson that he had "been blessed by the Lord."[1238] The *Richmond Times-Dispatch* stated Allen's communication director, John Reid, was urging the Senator to talk more publicly about his faith.[1239] Reid stated Allen was just trying to "make sure people know how much he cares."[1240] Was Allen schmoozing to the Religious Right for the 2008 primaries? Despite the belief by the *Times-Dispatch* that Mark Warner would not run against Allen for Senate in '06, Allen sent out a mail solicitation stating Warner's could be "a very formidable opponent," and labeled Warner as a "multimillionaire."[1241] Allen wrote that he would need $20 million to beat the governor (Allen spent only $10 million in his first Senate campaign).[1242] Was Allen scaring money into his coffers?

When House Majority Leader John Boehner was asked about the next president, he said (3.6.06) "Well, there are a lot of good people out there contending…George Allen and I have been friends for 20 years. He's a good guy…."[1243] Boehner volunteered no one else's name. He hassled about John McCain: "…You know, some people look at him and begin to wonder, boy, is he one of us [Republicans]."[1244]

Allen's opponent for the other campaign

On March 7, 2006, it was official: George Allen had competition. The *Washington Post* wrote "…So all of a sudden, Virginia feels as if it has a Senate race."[1245] Former Navy Secretary (Reagan administration) James Webb announced his candidacy in the Virginia Democratic Senate primaries against a businessman from northern Virginia, Harold Miller.[1246] Webb's campaign staff was not from the Island of Misfits, he picked up Steve Jarding and David "Mudcat" Saunders, both who helped Mark Warner succeed in 2001.[1247] Former Sen. Bob Kerrey (D-NE) was Webb's finance chairman. By the end of March, Wes Clark officially endorsed Webb for the Democratic nomination (Clark received 9% in the Virginia presidential primary in 2004).[1248] Nine Senators endorsed Webb during the Democratic primary, including Harry Reid and Charles Schumer.[1249] Webb won the primary.

By June 29, Mark Warner had promised to campaign statewide for Webb and even held a fundraiser as he sold the candidate as a "progressive and independent voice" for the Senate.[1250] But Warner waited over two weeks to make public comments on Webb's primary victory.[1251] Warner said Webb would draw traditional Democrats, independents, and moderate Republicans.[1252] Even Webb said he had "nothing personally against George Allen at all. I just believe that we need independent thought right now."[1253] But even as Allen finally learned of his general election opponent for US Senate, Allen was still as high as second place for the 2008 Republican nomination in the *National Journal*'s poll (May 2006) of insiders—though Allen trailed McCain 3 to 1.[1254]

Allen was running for President as Webb challenged

In March 2006, on *Meet the Press*, Tim Russert pointed to Allen's travels in the past half year: New Hampshire, Georgia, Michigan, Nevada, Colorado, Arizona, North Carolina, Tennessee, India, China, Pakistan, and Taiwan.[1255] Still, Allen planned to spend St. Patrick's Day in Iowa; but Allen's consultant, Dick Waddams said most of Allen's out of state visits were aimed at raising money for his re-election.[1256] Mark Warner raised $2.5 million in one night in Virginia. The state was too dry for Allen? Allen told *Meet the Press* he would "look at [running for president] after" his reelection.[1257] He had spent the past two years solidifying a presidential run, now Allen had to act as though he never thought about it.

Webb's top advisor Steve Jarding asked in June 2006, "Does George Allen want to be senator or president? I think it's absolutely an issue this year, and it's something he is going to have to explain. It's pretty cynical to try to run for both and nod and wink at people."[1258]

Allen said (7.9.06) "There's a lot that will say, 'Oh, we want you to run for president, I hope you run, and so forth,' I said 'Fine, fine, but let's pay attention to the task at hand.'"[1259] He went to Iowa for two days in March and even noted then that he'd be back in June.[1260] In a different March 2006 trip, Allen spent a day each in Texas, South Carolina, then New Hampshire.[1261] *Knight Ridder* said (6.16.06) Allen "might be getting a little ahead of himself."[1262] He was running for Senate re-election even though he told the *New York Times* earlier in 2006 the Senate was "too slow for me."[1263]

ABC News reported (7.9.06) Allen "once thought his bid for re-election in relatively conservative Virginia might be a smooth path toward contending for the 2008 Republican presidential nomination. Now he's in a fight, although still favored, for his political life."[1264]

Webb's vulnerabilities

Webb said he would focus his campaign on national defense,[1265] which was a strong issue of his. But Webb still had many obstacles. The first was loyalty: He left the Democrats in 1976, but then supported Sen. Bob Kerrey (NE) for President in 1992 and former Democratic Senator Charles Robb (VA) in 1994, when Robb ran against Oliver North (of Iran-Contra fame).[1266] But in 2000, Webb supported President Bush and George Allen's campaign against Robb.[1267]

Webb also struggled with women voters. In the *Meet the Press* debate in September, Webb was asked to discuss his 1977 article, "Women Can't Fight" in which he said "No benefit can come to anyone from women serving in combat."[1268] Then a clip was shown of Commander Kathleen Murray at a press conference (9.13.06); she said Webb's attitude and philosophy "were major factors behind the unnecessary abuse and hazing received by me and my fellow women midshipmen."[1269] Tim Russert asked "When you say 'Being in the Naval Academy is a horny women's dream' you regret that."[1270] "Well, I do regret that…," said Webb, whose words would have better qualified as his apology had he not smirked when he said it.[1271] Webb also wrote a more recent article (1997) for the *Weekly Standard*, "The War on Military Culture," which questioned the policies of women in the military.[1272] But in 2006, Webb said he was "fully comfortable with women's ability to lead men," and his comments in the 70s was a time when "social experimentation was in place rather than allowing the military to make these decisions."[1273] But if Webb felt women could lead men in 2006, his belief was stunted when Russert pointed out "What happens now is that the Pentagon, rather than assigning women to combat, attaches them to combat."[1274] Was he sexist? *Washingtonian.com* kindly republished Webb's 1979 article.[1275]

In addition, the Allen campaign tried to pin Webb as a Hollywood liberal. Webb was an author, whose books include *Rules of Engagement*, which was turned into a movie.[1276] Already in June 2006, while referring to Webb's May fundraising trip to LA, Wadhams said "Have him tell you when he goes to Hollywood and what liberal, elitist actor's mansion he'll be raising money in next."[1277]

Finally, Webb's major problem was money. Allen had over $7.5 million while the *Washington Post* described Webb as "comparatively penniless."[1278] Webb had only $222,000 as of May 24.[1279] Two Zogby polls released in March 2006 had a double digit lead for Allen. An interactive survey had Allen ahead 52-41, and a telephone survey had Allen ahead 47-37, as John Zogby concluded "The bottom line—this is a competitive race because this is a competitive state, but Jim Webb has got to start getting some money in."[1280] Even by Labor Day, Webb was the only major Senate candidate in the country yet to air a television ad.[1281] But the money came flowing after Macaca.

Senator Macaca

George Allen's presidential hopes took a skid in August 2006. What was Allen's major mistake? The man's full name was Shekar Ramanuja Sidarth, but according to Indian custom he went by his surname and other friends called him 'Sid.'[1282] After August 11, he would forever be known as Macaca. Working for Jim Webb's campaign, Sidarth tracked Allen to Breaks, Virginia, near the Kentucky border.[1283] There, Allen looked into the camera Sidarth held and said, "This fellow here, over there with the yellow shirt, Macaca, or whatever his name

Karl McCarty: *The Last One Standing*

is, he's with my opponent."[1284] As Allen continued to talk, Sidarth kept filming.[1285] "He's following us around everywhere. And it's just great. We're going to places all over Virginia, and he's having it on film, and it's great to have you here, and you show it to your [sic] opponent because he's never been there and probably will never come so it's good for him to see what it's like out here in the real world [laughter from crowd, including "big whoops"]. So welcome, let's give a welcome to Macaca here! Welcome to America, and the real world of Virginia!"[1286] In a bit of irony, before speaking to Sidarth, Allen had said "My friends, we're going to run this campaign on positive, constructive ideas. And it's important that we motivate and inspire people for something."[1287] The speech was not positive and far from inspiring.

So what did Macaca mean? Context clues suggested it was a racial slur, or at the very least a word that had something to do with being foreign. In some European countries, "makak" is a derogatory term for North African immigrants.[1288] The word was also a genus of monkeys (with spelling variations).[1289] And Makaka is a South African town.[1290]

The bloggers killed Allen

The internet played a key role in the event, exacerbating Allen's embarrassment. A post on *Wonkette*, a sarcastic website, asked after four days, "and what hath Macacagate wrought? The end of George Allen's presidential ambitions, a week's worth of material for us (thanks, George!), [and] a shitload of bad internet art."[1291] Such material included a picture of Allen with "Dumbass" written across his forehead, a movie poster with Allen and a headdress in the famed movie *The Mysterious Macaca*; and lame jokes such as Richard Nixon's comments that "I am not Macaca," and Bill Clinton's belief that "Macaca did not have sexual relations with that women."[1292]

Then there was the *Wonkette* post titled "Big Pile of Macaca," which noted Allen's campaign manager, Dick Wadhams' comment that 'Macaca' came out of Sidarth's Mohawk like haircut… "Sounds reasonable. But, whoops, Sidarth doesn't have a Mohawk, so, can't be that. Maybe he meant to call him 'maraca,' after the Latin percussion instrument that the mambo kings utilized so well."[1293] The *AP* picture, posted on the *Washington Post*'s website posted Sidarth by his lonely self with an innocent face in front of a 'Jim Webb for Senate' background. He did not have a Mohawk.

Allen's incident was propelled with the video sharing website *YouTube*, and became "the grist for late-night talk shows."[1294] *Comedy Central* had a field day. Rob Corddry of *The Daily Show* said he was offended… "I'm from Macaca,"[1295] and asked "Where is Macaca? Right next to Yapipi."[1296] Corddry said "I don't know what 'macaque' means, but it sure as shit sounds racist. And…hear in Virginia, I'm still not sure if that helps or hurts the guy."[1297]

When Webb's campaign sent out a help-wanted email to shadow Allen on the campaign trail, *Wonkette* suggested the Webb campaign add another sentence to the job announcement: "Minority applicants are strongly encouraged, but should be prepared for weird abuse of some kind, because Allen's going to throw some incredibly obscure racial slur your way, which is totally going to lock up this race for us."[1298]

August was a slower political-news month, given the Congressional recess. Case in point was *Hotline On-Call*, which noted (8.24.06) in an article titled 'The Monkey is Not Dead. We Repeat. The Monkey Is Not Dead,' "It's Day 10 of our coverage of Macaca-iana or Macaca-gate or Liberal Washington Post-gate, or whatever you'd like to call it."[1299] On Sept. 26, *Slate* had the "George Allen Insult Generator," in which users could go under the category 'I am:' and click on a race, at which point an Allen cartoon would give an appropriate insult based on the color of the user's skin.[1300]

The consequences of a stupid joke

1) Team-Allen couldn't handle an internet crisis. The ordeal went on and on. George Allen apparently polled Virginians on whether he should have apologized.[1301] That is one of those factoids campaigns shouldn't let the public find out. And *Hotline* reported several Republicans close to the Allen campaign said he was frustrated with the response and ineffective crisis management.[1302] *Hotline* also suggested Allen's longtime strategist Chris LaCivita believed Allen's campaign did not sufficiently appreciate the role of bloggers.[1303] Conservative columnist Cal Thomas said "If the mockers, bloggers and columnists who jumped on George Allen don't jump with at least equal fervor on Andrew Young [a Wal-Mart supporter who made a racially insensitive comment], their political bias is showing."[1304] But Thomas' point could easily be evidence of the Republican's lack of ability to mobilize the netroots as opposed to a liberal bias. Thousands watched George Allen's demeaning comments to a 20 year-old Indian-American on *You Tube*. If a Republican Senator made the same comments twenty-five years ago before CNN and the internet's existence, the comment would have been forgotten about within a week, and certainly days. And when Allen was being ripped apart on the web, what past history did he have to succeed in damage control?

2) Allen burned a bridge with a growing voting block. There were over 80,000 adults with Indian ancestry in Virginia, and the community expanded heavily in the 1960s and '70s.[1305] Would they go overwhelmingly to the Webb camp? Over a quarter of Fairfax County's people were foreign born.[1306] Since 2000, whites in Loudoun County declined nine percent from the overall total; and Hispanics in Prince William County doubled.[1307] Gov. Kaine had already named an Indian business executive as secretary of technology.[1308] In 2004, Kerry was the first Democratic presidential candidate to win Fairfax County in four decades.[1309] A Mason-Dixon poll released Sept.10 had Allen ahead 46-42, but Webb led Northern Virginia by 13 points.[1310]

3) The whole Macaca incident added attention to the race, and the Webb coffers filled. In August, Webb raised over $1 million.[1311]

4) Allen added fuel to the fire. Tons of fuel. Allen also stereotyped in other events during the Macaca fallout. In the first week of September, he rode a horse in Buena Vista's annual Labor Day parade, as he had previous years, but this horse was named Bubba and Allen greeted onlookers with "Howdy! How y'all doing? Good to see y'all."[1312] The *Washington Post* quoted a Richmond Republican who said he cringed: "Seeing him with a horse called Bubba wearing cowboy boots, that doesn't resonate with us."[1313]

Let's have a party!

Then Allen held an ethnic rally (9.9.06). Allen himself was keeping Macaca in the news. Hmmm? Why would Sen. Allen have a rally for minorities? And why in Northern Virginia, where the minority population skyrocketed in recent years?[1314] Allen had suddenly become well versed in many languages through 'good mornings' and 'thank yous' to the crowd.[1315] Even his own website had links: "Watch Sen. Allen's Ethnic Rally" and "Click for Ethnic Rally Photos."[1316] He called it an *ethnic rally*, and showed he was not racist by having a separate rally for *those* people.

Stephen Colbert sarcastically supported the ethic rally, and apparently checked out Sen. Allen's pictures, as the *Colbert Report* showed what appeared to be a young Indian American, or what Stephen Colbert called a "minicaca."[1317] Allen put himself in a position that he deserved the ridicule. A *Wonkette* post noted Allen's website

> ...updated the old graphic with *video* of the ethics doing their rallying. We can only assume this is because Sen. Macaca is now totally embracing all sorts of archaic racialist terminology. Future campaign events will reportedly include a Darkie Promenade with the latest Race Music, next week's Pickaninny Jamboree and Rube Cotillion, the Chinaman's Cookout and Opium Fair.....and the Squarehead's Barn Dance featuring the Commonwealth Championship Jewboy Sack Races."[1318]

Even the conservative *Weekly Standard* seemingly turned on him, when a September edition put the Senator on the cover with a monkey on his back: "George Allen Monkeys Around."[1319] A *Hardball* link (9.25.06) on MSNBC.com asked "Is George Allen racist?"[1320] By then the question was not whether he was racist—a bad enough question to begin with, but "*How bad* was he racist?"

Allen even made comments that retracted original supporters: When Allen said he was slow to grasp the pain toward blacks in Old South symbols like the Confederate flag, the Sons of Confederate Veterans 'turned on Allen' as the immediate past state commander of the organization said such a "denunciation of the flag to score political points is anathema to our organization."[1321]

A closet Jew proud to eat pork chops

Following the likes of John Kerry, Wes Clark, and Madeline Albright, it became evident George Allen had an unknown Jewish past.[1322] Allen was a Presbyterian.[1323] But on Sept. 18, in a Fairfax Chamber of Commerce debate, *Channel 9* reporter Peggy Fox asked him about his family's Jewish lineage.[1324] Fox also asked if Allen learned about 'Macaca' from his mother, and the *AP* said Allen "glared at Fox for a moment, then said, 'I hope you're not trying to bring my mother into this matter.'"[1325] He accused the reporter of "making aspersions about people."[1326] The Macaca slayer had accused someone of slander.

But on Sept. 19, he acknowledged the ancestry, "a day after angrily ducking a question about possible Jewish forbears" in the debate.[1327] The answer came in a statement which he said his mother confirmed his Jewish blood after he read an August 25, 2006, article by *Forward*.[1328] Allen said he knew of his heritage when asked in the debate.[1329]

Allen's mother Henriette ("Etty") told the *Washington Post*'s Michael Shear (Sept.2006) she was raised Jewish in her native Tunisia.[1330] Allen claimed he had no insight on the Jewish past, and claimed he thought the Nazis imprisoned his grandfather because he strongly defended human freedoms.[1331] But in the summer of 2006, the Jewish paper *The Forward* reported he descended from a Sephardic Jewish Portuguese family that converted to Christianity in the 1400s; but when his lineage fled to Italy, they had reverted back to Jewish by the 1700s.[1332] Wadhams said Allen's maternal grandfather, Felix Lumbroso, was Jewish; and Allen said he did not know his maternal grandmothers religion.[1333]

The problem is Allen might have always known he was Jewish. Marc Fisher of the *Washington Post* noted (9.24.06) that in 2003, Bob Gibson of the *Charlottesville Daily Progress* asked the same question that Peggy Fox asked in the September 2006 debate. Gibson said, "It's funny, but the only time that George Allen ever wanted a correction from me in 27 years of covering his races was when I wrote about his mother's Jewish family origins. He insisted, through a press secretary, that his mother was raised a Christian."[1334] Not to mention he was callous on the issue, and told the *Times-Dispatch* it was "just an interesting nuance to my background…I still had a ham sandwich for lunch. And my mother made great pork chops."[1335] Compare this to Allen's comments on Sept.19: "I embrace and take great pride in every aspect of my diverse heritage, including the Lumbroso family line's Jewish heritage, which I learned of from a recent magazine article and my mother confirmed."[1336]

More, more, more

Macaca occurred when Congress was on recess, adding more time for the bloggers to focus on Allen. However, the vast majority of Americans may have seen other August 2006 news stories more pertinent than Macacagate, such as John Mark Karr's fake confession to Jon Benet Ramsey's 1996 murder, or Pluto's demotion as a planet. Then there was the shocking story of the Crocodile Hunter's death by a Sting Ray in early September. But just when the Macaca issue died down, some other 'Is-Allen-a-Racist?' story popped up again to rehash the whole incident.

For example, *The Nation* reported (8.29.06) in an article titled "Beyond Macaca: The Photograph That Haunts George Allen," in the summer of 1996, then-Gov. Allen "personally initiated" an association with a supremacist group known as the Council of Conservative Citizens (CCC), the successor group to the segregationists White Citizens Council.[1337] Allen suggested the photo-op with the CCC's founder and NRA spokesmen Charlton Heston, and the picture was put on the CCC's *Citizen Informer*.[1338] Allen's communications director said he was "unaware of the group you mention or their agenda and because we have no record of the Senator having involvement with them I cannot offer you any opinion on them."[1339] Though the Allen camp claimed ignorance, former Reagan speechwriter Peggy Noonan had previously stated that anyone connected to the CCC "does not deserve to be in a leadership position in America."[1340]

But there was more. Allen's defense on *Meet the Press* (9.17.06) was uninspiring. When Tim Russert said Macaca "must've been in your consciousness," Allen replied "Oh, it's just made up" and he "never heard it before."[1341]

He was asked about the Confederate flag in his living room, noose in his law office, and a Confederate troop picture in his governors' office.[1342] Allen said he wished he "had had these experiences earlier in life, because I would have made decisions differently…as a kid [in regard to the flag] I was rebellious, anti-establishment, I still am. And I looked at the flag as a symbol for that."[1343] Russert interjected "But you were governor."[1344] Allen said "that flag, to African-Americans, represents repression, segregation and violence against them. And I would never want to have anything to insult or offend someone, and so that's why I would not be utilizing that flag, because that's not who I am, and I would never want to have that image or, or harmful impact on fellow human beings who I want to make sure are part of team America, because we do need to compete much better against countries…."

First, what was *Team America*? Allen wasn't referring to the movie made by the creator's of Comedy Central's *South Park*. In addition, Allen used his apology for racial insensitivity as an excuse to distance himself from the establishment. "I still am" anti-establishment—this coming from the man many considered the prototype for Bush's replacement.[1345]

He was *that* racist?

On Sept. 24, *Salon* reported "Three former college football teammates" of Allen's said he "repeatedly used an inflammatory racial epithet and demonstrated racist attitudes towards blacks during the early 1970s."[1346] Allen said "this article is completely false in its allegations. I do not remember ever using that [N] word."[1347] Though the *Salon.com* article had some credibility problems (it had few sources, and Allen's blog had some well researched posts to respond to the charges by Sept.25),[1348] it was hard to believe Sen. Allen had never used the word.[1349] And the source for *Salon* was Ken Shelton, a radiologist in North Carolina who said Allen severed a deer head and put it into a black household's mailbox.[1350] By then the *Weekly Standard* cover was "George Allen Monkeys Around."[1351]

The problem is Larry Sabato entered the fray, as one of the most quoted political scientists for 2008 election news stories said "I'm going to stay with what I know is the case. And the fact is that he did use the N-word, whether he's denying it now or not. He did use it," (Sept. 25)[1352] Sabato went to college with Allen.[1353] Though Sabato too had credibility problems, saying the next day he himself never heard Allen say the word.[1354] *Wonkette* concluded "Larry Sabato Has an Almost Transparent Knowledge of George Allen's' Soul."[1355] Sabato eventually conceded "My conclusion is based on the very credible testimony I have heard for weeks, mainly from people I personally know and knew in the '70s."[1356]

Ed Gillespie defended Allen (9.26.06) not just on the N-word issue, but again, on Macaca. Chris Matthews told Gillespie, "Look, you are a great guy. I like this guy, Allen. I'm sad for him. I wish it hadn't happened, but that tape he's going to have to live with. It's a weird thing, to use a word you never heard of before in your life, he completely fabricated, and it just happens to be a word used against black people in North Africa where your mother came from. It just happens to be a word like that. That's hard to believe."[1357] The US Senate campaign in Virginia all came back to Macaca—six weeks after it was said. Not to mention the Jewish ordeal occurred in mid September, and days after the Larry Sabato comments on *Hardball*, the news organization had another racist story. Indeed, Patricia Waring, was the wife of the University of Virginia rugby club team who in 1978 apparently heard Allen say 'nigger' numerous times and asked him not to use the word.[1358]

On October 10, the Democratic Senatorial Campaign Committee released an ad in which the narrator said "George Allen: scandals, slurs and insults. Now after Allen's dark side is exposed he wants the race to be," and the voice switch to Allen's, "decided on the issues."[1359] The commercial, made by Squire Knapp Dunn, also said Allen voted against more body armor for troops, a minimum wage increase, but supported congressional raises; then tied him to oil and gas companies, and ended with a replay of the Macaca comment.[1360] The fact that Macaca was replayed nearly two months after it was said seemed to suggest that the campaign no longer was a debate on the issues, but rather a referendum on Allen's racism.[1361]

Macaca & Iraq: a losing combination

Allen's presidential ambitions were widely discussed during the ordeal, almost nailing the coffin on Allen '08. Even reports, not just editorials, hinted at a presidential demise. Bob Lewis's *AP* report's (8.23.06) opening sentence said the incident "clouds what has been a bright political career for Sen. George Allen, including any White House plans."[1362] Allen's worst card in this incident was that it was caught on tape. It showed him pointing to Sidarth and singling him out, Allen smiled as he did it—almost as if he was enjoying the whole ordeal.[1363] Show that Macaca clip a handful of times in Iowa and New Hampshire, and the Virginia Senator would be guaranteed to stay low in presidential polls. The fact that Allen looked (or was) 'un-presidential' may have been what propelled the slur's story just as much as the Webb-Allen race grew more competitive. How many Virginians voted against Allen because they did not want him to run for president?

However, Allen had a chance to win Virginia the whole time. A Zogby Interactive poll released in late August (and taken August 15-21: days after the Macaca incident) showed Webb ahead 47.9 to 46.6.[1364] But other polls had Allen slightly ahead. Webb had issues with women, notably his comments years earlier about women in the military. Jon Stewart joked in the winding days of the campaign, "Still in the tossup column, Virginia -- with Macaca Goldstein versus the He-man Woman Haters Club."[1365]

Allen's demise was twofold: Macaca and Iraq. His unwavering, and sometimes unfounded, support for the President on the war may have doomed his Senate campaign as much as his slur. The rising star of the GOP in 2005 had been completely obliterated.

The end

On November 8, there were reports a canvassing team found a change of 1,500 votes in Allen's favor in a heavily GOP precinct, a scenario which brought the difference from 7, 000 to 4,000.[1366] But Virginia voting was not punch card ballot, but rather all electronic machinery, so the final results after Election Day would likely hold to the same numbers even if there was a recount.[1367] They did. Allen was a gracious loser in his concession speech:

> ...My friends, sometimes winds, political or otherwise, can blow the leaves off branches and even break limbs. But a deep-rooted tree will stand, stay standing, it will regrow in the next season.
>
> In this season, the people of Virginia, who I always call the owners of the government, they have spoken, and I respect their decision. The Bible teaches us that there's a time and place for everything. And today, I've called and congratulated Jim Webb and his team for their victory. They had the prevailing winds.[1368]

An election that seemed a knock-out for Allen six months earlier guaranteed the Democrats control of the Senate for the 110th Congress. On December 10, 2006, Allen said he would not run for the nomination in 2008.[1369] For Allen fans, it was a sad ending. But with a little thinking, the demise would not have happened. When Allen left the Senate in January 2007, Romney, McCain, and Giuliani were about to announce their campaign for the presidency. Allen could have retired from the Senate and immediately launched a campaign.

Clearly from the above sources, he was going to Iowa as late as June of 2006. Allen could have said then, after further reflection, he would leave the Senate. Such a decision would have sent Virginia scrambling for a candidate (Jim Gilmore perhaps, considering he soon would set time aside to waste on a presidential campaign), but Allen's presidential bid would have been intact. Instead, his political career may be over, and at best he has an uphill climb: Mark Warner is the major player for the next US Senate seat up for grabs in Virginia.

Senator Sam Brownback

Sam Brownback once was the state president of the Future Farmers of America, and at the age of 30 he became Kansas's youngest agriculture secretary.[1370] When he entered the House in the Republican Revolution of 1994, he said the Departments of Commerce, Education, Energy, and Housing and Urban Development should be dismantled to downsize the federal government.[1371] Bob Dole announced he was leaving the Senate in the middle of 1996 to run for president, and Brownback ran for the open seat.

A social conservative

Sam Brownback won the special 1996 Republican primary with the help of William Bennett (former Reagan Education Secretary) and James Dobson (head of Focus on the Family).[1372] Pat Robertson helped him get elected as well. These three leaders' support is iconic of the support a Brownback presidential campaign expected as he would attempt to lead the social conservatives in 2008.

In July 2004, Brownback wrote an op-ed to the *National Review* titled "Defining Marriage Down" as a constitutional ban on gay marriage was debated. "Social science on this matter is conclusive: Children need both a mom and a dad. Study after study has shown that children do best in a home with a married, biological mother and father…There is *no* reliable social-scientific data demonstrating that children raised by same-sex coupled (or groups) do as well as children raised by married heterosexual parents."[1373] "Not least of the reasons heterosexual marriage is a positive social good is the fact that, in a married state, adults of both sexes are vastly healthier, happier, safer, and wealthier, and live longer lives."[1374]

He also previously presented the theory, according to the *Washington Post*, that abortion was a partial problem with Social Security because fewer children were growing up to become workers who could pay into the system."[1375]

Congressman Walter Jones (R-NC) had sought in the past to make pulpit endorsements legal, and in March 2005, Brownback backed the idea.[1376] Commenting on the pulpit bill, *The Kansas City Star* quoted Brownback, who was planning to introduce his own bill: "This bill will finally lift the fear and anxiety from houses of worship that seek to speak out on issues that affect … our nation."[1377] The article noted the current Internal Revenue Service code argued if a church advocates which candidates to vote for; the church could lose its tax-exempt status.

Harriet Miers for Supreme Court

President Bush announced Harriet Miers as the replacement for Sandra Day O'Conner on October 3, 2005. Miers was key in the selection of previous judicial nominees, and she spoke to many senators (before her own nomination) to get their thoughts on the vacancy left by Sandra Day O'Conner.[1378] Sen. John Cornyn (R-Texas) said, President Bush "picked the picker."[1379] The picker was immediately questioned on both sides of the political spectrum. She gave $1,000 to Al Gore's presidential bid in 1988 and $1,000 to Lloyd Bentsen's Senate bid for Texas.[1380] But she gave $5,000 for Bush's 2000 campaign and $5,000 for the Bush-Cheney Recount Fund.[1381]

Some Democrats were pleased with the pick. Harry Reid said he liked Miers, stating he was "happy" about the pick four times in the six minutes he discussed her (10.3.05)[1382]—and thus disturbed conservatives.

Brownback attacked Miers

Newt Gingrich said the White House needed "to finish out the Miers nomination and get her approved," on October 16.[1383] Though he was not entirely enthusiastic, his opinion differed much from George Allen and Brownback.

The *Richmond Times Dispatch* said Allen "reacted cautiously" to Bush's pick, with Allen himself stating that he "would surmise that most conservatives don't want to see another Souter."[1384] The comment was in reference to George H.W. Bush's pick to the court, David Souter, who turned out to be more liberal than expected. The *Washington Times* reported, Allen "stopped well short of endorsing" the nominee—and Sam Brownback did not even issue a press release and declined to discuss Miers.[1385] As a guest on *Meet the Press* (10.23.05), Allen said he did not think Miers was the most qualified candidate and was still "undecided" on whether to vote for her.[1386]

Brownback did release a statement on October 4: "I am not yet confident that Ms. Miers has a proven track record...we must trust but verify."[1387] When he met with Miers for an hour on October 6, he was still unconvinced and wanted "to see more information come forward."[1388]

Brownback received significant attention for his concerns. He appeared on *Good Morning America* on October 5, in which he expressed concern whether Miers was a "Souter-type candidate;" and if Miers considered Roe v. Wade "settled law" there would be a "good chance" he would vote against her.[1389] In his appearance on *Face the Nation* (10.9.05), Brownback denied *Newsweek*'s report that Brownback privately told some that the confirmation hearings would 'cut her up,' and said the President "probably did avoid a fight [by not nominating a clearer conservative], but I don't think that's necessarily good for the country or good for the court."[1390] He was asked on *FOX News Sunday* about the appropriateness of the Bush administration efforts to get allies in Iowa and New Hampshire to pressure Brownback to back Miers. "No, its not [appropriate]. And I don't know that anybody's actually doing that."[1391]

It was highly unlikely that Brownback did not know that anybody was 'actually doing that': The *New Hampshire Union-Leader* reported the White House's pressure through New Hampshire Republicans, the White House confirmed it, and the *AP* flat out reported that the White House was "seeking the help of Republican activists is Iowa and New Hampshire to pressure GOP senators with presidential hopes to support" Miers.[1392] In New Hampshire on October 11, Brownback was even handed a letter from RNC committeeman Tom Rath supporting Miers; the letter was handed to Brownback by GOP supporters and it asked for support for an up-or-down vote and fair process for the nominee.[1393]

Brownback's recognition was appropriate. As a judiciary committee member, he alone could prevent the nomination of Miers if all the panel's Democrats voted 'no' to take her nomination to the floor, and then he joined the Democrats. Of course, his reasons for voting against Miers would have had to have been different than the Democrats; still the nomination would not have gotten out of committee. This was the fight Brownback was likely looking for; George Stephanopoulos flat out said that Brownback really wanted to vote no.

Blocking Miers from the Senate floor vote could have immediately propelled him into the national spotlight (in some cases, his uneasiness about the nominee already did so). In so many years past, presidential contenders for the GOP nomination ran on socially conservative ideals. Whether it was Gary Bauer, Alan Keyes, Pat Buchanan or Pat Robertson—but these men never had the political power to prove their points. In 2005, a social conservative senator from Kansas had the power. Many times the right wing of the party could not understand why Roe v. Wade withstood a Supreme Court made up by a majority of Republican appointees. Brownback could tame the disappointment. Brownback could prevent another Souter, and prove—not just voice—his loyalty to the right.

The conservatives ripped her apart

Was the revolt against Miers premature? Sen. Lindsey Graham (R-SC) commented on his disgust at the early attacks on Miers. "Just shut up for a few minutes and just give the lady a chance to find out who she is…people want their 15 minutes of fame. This ain't about Harriet. It's about them."[1394] Suddenly, rightwing conservatives and political retreads were given prime television spots.

Pat Buchanan told *Good Morning America*, "There's no way this woman is qualified for the United States Supreme Court."[1395] He then appeared on *Meet the Press* on October 9. What constituted a presidential also-ran's appearance on *Meet the Press* just to clarify his opinion on Harriet Miers? Pat Buchanan was the voice of the Republican Party he had ditched in 2000. In addition, 2000 GOP presidential candidate Gary Bauer spoke on *Fox News Sunday* on October 9. Gary Bauer?

Nonetheless, conservative voices were disgusted: Rush Limbaugh said the pick "was made from weakness," Bill Kristol of the *Weekly Standard* was "demoralized," Charles Krauthammer asked for her withdrawal, and George Will said she should not be confirmed unless she "unexpectedly is found to have hitherto undisclosed interests and talents pertinent to the Court's role."[1396] Dick Cheney had to call Rush Limbaugh's program to calm the radio host's distaste for the pick.[1397] These conservatives might have been jealous that Focus on the Family founder James Dobson had the 'ins' with the Bush administration. Dobson said, "When you know some of the things I know—that I probably shouldn't know….you'll know why I've said with fear and trepidation (that) I believe Harriet Miers will be a good justice."[1398] How reassuring: a leader of an interest group had more knowledge of the nominee than most senators. Then Robert Bork—the famous (or infamous) blocked nominee of the 1980s—said the choice was a "disaster on every level."[1399]

But even Sen. Arlen Specter (R-PA), a moderate Republican who would have supported a moderate nominee (if that is what Miers would have been), said Miers needed a "crash course in constitutional law."[1400] Perhaps *Cliff Notes* could have given Miers a brief constitutional overview as the confirmation hearings were just weeks away.

Miers' poor defense

The President was confident of the pick: "I know her well enough to be able to say that she's not going to change, that 20 years from now she'll be the same person with the same philosophy that she is today."[1401] However, twenty five years earlier she was a Roman Catholic and a Democrat; in 2005 she was a Republican and a evangelical Christian.[1402] Bush emphasized that "part of Harriet Miers' life is her religion."[1403]

When Miers returned her 57 page questionnaire on her background and legal career to Sens. Arlen Specter (R-PA) and Patrick Leahy (D-VT), the Senators said the answers were insufficient and the information Miers provided about her background was "incomplete to insulting."[1404] "If you have a one-word answer and you've got a two-part question, that's not an answer," said Leahy.[1405] They sent the questionnaire back to Miers: "I think that's sort of an unprecedented thing to have to send a questionnaire back," said Leahy.[1406] Leahy discussed on *FOX News Sunday* how he and Specter asked Miers on conflicts of interests, given that the Supreme Court would be hearing cases on things she had worked on in the White House as White House Council. "She just sent back—quoted the ethics on—rules and recusal. We're [Specter and Leahy] both lawyers. We know what the rule says; we don't need to have that quoted back to us. We want to know how she's going to apply the rule."[1407] It was both Republicans and Democrats wanting more information from Miers. Even Sam Brownback pressed the administration for more documentation about Miers' White House Counsel work.[1408]

Brownback's finest hour

Miers withdrew her nomination, reasoning it was due to the call for documents. "While I believe that my lengthy career provides sufficient evidence for consideration of my nomination, I am convinced the efforts to obtain Executive Branch materials and information will continue."[1409] Bob Novak later wrote that those who managed Miers nomination "set the day of her demise as Oct. 18, when conservative Republican Senators Lindsey Graham ...and Brownback...called for the release of her work product as White House counsel to justify her confirmation."[1410]

What is most important, however, was that the Miers nomination left Brownback with notoriety. "Sen. Brownback emerges on the national scene," headlined a *Knight Ridder* article,[1411] an article which pointed out that Brownback was the only senator to get *New York Times* front page coverage for his meeting with Miers.[1412] In addition, *Rolling Stone* was working on a profile of Brownback, as was the *Washington Post*.[1413]

Who were the Snowflake babies?

Brownback was a staunch opponent of embryonic stem cell research. At a 2000 Senate Hearing, he told Arlen Specter (R-PA), "You had the Nazis in WWII saying, of these people, 'They're going to be killed, Why do we not experiment on them and find out what happens with these experiments? They are going to die anyway."[1414] Specter said the concentration camp prisoners "were living people;" Brownback said "These are living embryos."[1415]

In July 2006, the Senate revisited the stem cell debate. And Brownback played a role for the opposition towards the majority. Bush used his first veto to shoot down the legislation, and he also used children to bolster his argument.

Not to be confused with snowmen, snowflake babies was the name given to children who originated from frozen embryos.[1416] They did not have a corncob pipe, or a button nose. The President had them wear shirts ("This embryo was not discarded") in May 2005 during a House vote to expand federal funding for embryonic stem cell research.[1417] In 2006, Brownback appeared with (7.17.06) three snowflake babies born from donated frozen embryos, and reminded the public humans should not be grown "for spare parts."[1418] It was less clear who actually suggested humans should be grown for spare parts. But Brownback was willing to take the stance.

As of 2006, in the entire country, there was about 125 born from 'adopted' embryos, but there were 400,000 embryos in the country.[1419] White House Chief of Staff Josh Bolton said "that's very sad for this country."[1420]

Snowflakes appeared in the President's press conference. When Bush vetoed the bill, "in the crowd, too, were such familiar faces as" Karl Rove, Tony Snow, Rick Santorum, and Brownback.[1421] Sen. Santorum (R-PA) also held a snowflake on the day of the stem cell vote in the Senate.[1422] The *Milwaukee Journal Sentinel* reported two dozen snowflake babies—including Hailey and Jillian, Morgan and Maxwell, Ella and Noelle, all born from donated frozen embryos not needed for fertility treatments—were there for the eight words that "buttressed" Bush's entire speech: "These boys and girls are not spare parts."[1423] Okay, but their brothers and sisters were still in the freezer, or may have ended up in the trash can. The president would never use embryos for spare parts, just good photo-ops. A Bush aide said it "was a very moving ceremony."[1424]

Brownback's principal… or standup comedy tour?

Jon Stewart made "more tasteless jokes" of Brownback in a *Daily Show* bit called 'The stem cell prop comedy of Sam Brownback' in the Senate (7.19.06).[1425] Brownback was shown pointing between images of an eagle and an eagle egg, and said "The egg is the eagle because the eagle comes out of the egg."[1426] Stewart said "By that logic, Sen. Brownback is a vagina," and after laughs subsided, added, "I'm going to guess that sentence has never been uttered."[1427] On the Senate floor, Brownback showed drawings made by a child from an adopted embryo named Hannah, who made a chart of sad little embryos that asked "What, are you going to kill me?"[1428] Stewart said "...if you have a talking embryo who is cognizant enough to wonder if you're going to kill it, I say we don't do research on those ones. And if we find them and identify them, perhaps one of them will grant us three wishes."[1429]

Brownback's opposition to embryonic stem cells did not mean he was anti-science (or at least he tried to paint it that way): "We are getting increased positive results from using adult stem cells and umbilical cord stem cells."[1430] The Catholic lack of support on embryonic cells is noteworthy in its influence on Brownback and Santorum's positions. The US Conference of Catholic Bishops said, "Technical progress that makes humans themselves into mere raw material for research is in fact a regress in our humanity."[1431] But critics could suggest Brownback's presentation in the Senate and subsequent mocking by *The Daily Show* elevated Brownback to medieval times, instead of a noble stand for his principles.

Prison Reform

The *National Catholic Registry* asked "The Next Catholic President?— Sen. Sam Brownback, R-Kan., is looking into running for president—in part because of the state of the American family."[1432] He launched his presidential campaign with an overnight visit to the Angola, Louisiana prison were "incarceration was once considered a de facto death sentence."[1433] *World News*, a Christian news outlet, had Marvin Olasky join Brownback.[1434] The report noted Brownback's years spent speaking on prison reform and his actions on Sudan:

> … So he had the standing to visit the Angola prison and make it seem more than a campaign photo op. To meet the prisoners, Brownback changed from the proper business suit he wore for the fundraiser to blue jeans and a Kansas State sweatshirt. Instead of entering a dimly lit restaurant, he suddenly found himself in a light-filled and packed 700-seat prison chapel with cinderblock walls off which bounced the sound of a rollicking 30-member gospel choir singing a hymn about Jesus, 'He's on Time.'[1435]

Brownback was also featured in a *New York Times Magazine* article as a conservative who had come to "embrace prison reform."[1436] Brownback sponsored the Second Chance Act, which proposed the allocation of $100 million over two years for states to develop programs assisting offenders who were reentering society.[1437] About 700,000 ex-offenders would leave prison in 2007, and two-thirds were likely to be rearrested by 2010.[1438]

Compassionate Conservative

Despite Brownback's social conservatism, George Will argued that Brownback "has a mellow demeanor and mellifluous [smooth] voice—he briefly was a broadcaster—that softens his presentation of his social conservatism, which has a foreign-policy dimension involving support for human rights—especially opposing genocide in Darfur, and sex trafficking—and support for Israel."[1439] Brownback is Jerry Falwell without the vitriolic persona. The *AP* reported him (12.5.06) as one who "seeks to grab the 'compassionate conservative' title" Bush used in 2000, and "That means focusing on issues such as prison reform, cancer research and fighting AIDS in Africa not normally associated with conservatism."[1440]

As *U.S. News* reported (8.16.06) Brownback "made common cause with liberals by drawing attention to the genocide in Darfur and irked some conservatives by championing comprehensive immigration reform."[1441] Though with immigration reform, Brownback said "A lot of the future of the Republican Party will be appealing to Hispanic voters, a number of whom have very consistent values with the base of the party. But we've got to convince people that we want them…"[1442] Basically Brownback was going after what would hopefully be the future of the conservative base, but in the present-time he had alienated the current base.

A December 2006 *AP* report suggested, "Brownback's faith also leads him to tackle social injustice around the world. He's spearheaded legislation to fight genocide in Sudan, cut down human slave trafficking and prison recidivism."[1443] Brownback called himself a "full scale conservative" and used it in a November spot on *This Week*, and December stops in South Carolina, Kansas, and Iowa.[1444] Matt Browner Hamlin, of *The Right's Field* said the phrase, "conveys Brownback's commitment to movement conservatism and not some sort of watered-down, Johnny Come Lately conservatism that one might see in other GOP contenders. It conveys forcefulness and dedication -- themes that extend beyond ideology to suggest personal qualities that GOP voters want to see, particularly as it relates to how the next president carries on the Iraq war."[1445] He has talked about "compassionate conservatism."[1446] Brownback also got support from Cal Thomas, who wrote an op-ed in January 2007:

> The choice conservative Republicans must make is what to do for the next two years. They might consider following the example of Sen. Sam Brownback, R-Kan. In some ways Brownback… is trying to reinvent what it means to be a social conservative. To be more precise, he is trying to take the movement back to first principles, demonstrating what he is for, rather than what or whom he is against.[1447]

Thomas suggested the GOP-Christian voter should make the resolution like Glen Campbell's song, "You got to try a little kindness."[1448]

Could he win social conservatives 2008? Romney had once been favorable toward gays and abortion, Giuliani was a social moderate if not liberal, and McCain had bashed Falwell and Robertson. Would they go to Brownback? Or was he too compassionate?

Brownback is against state's rights

In January 2006, the Supreme Court upheld Oregon's assisted suicide law, and the first Senate Hearing after the decision was held in May, when Brownback asked for an exploration of the "unintended consequences and slippery slope of doctor assisted suicide," and went as far to suggest such laws "could actually create a financial incentive for insurance companies to encourage prematurely ending the lives of those who need long-term care."[1449] But the Oregon law required patients to give themselves the lethal dose.[1450] By mid 2006, about 250 patients used assisted suicide since Oregon had the bill in 1998, or about 30 a year in a state that had over 30,000 deaths annually.[1451] Nonetheless, the *AP* reported Brownback cited Netherlands as an example where such legalized suicides led to "involuntary euthanasia," and likewise Oregon's numbers would rise in the future.[1452]

Sen. Wyden said (May 2006) the law had not been abused, despite having publicly stated he voted against Oregon's two state-related iniatives and admitted it was "time for me to acknowledge that my fears concerning the poor elderly were, thankfully, never realized. The law has not been abused."[1453]

Some supporters of the assisted suicide bill said it brought greater discussion to quality of life issues, as Oregon's hospital death rate was the lowest in the country while the home death rate, with Utah, was one of the highest.[1454] In August 2006, Brownback introduced a bill to ban doctors from prescribing federally controlled drugs for use in assisted suicides.[1455] So after Labor Day, Sen. Ron Wyden (D-OR) announced he would block the bill through a hold, and with it Brownback's attack on Oregon's law allowing assisted suicide.[1456] Wyden was prepared to filibuster, so Brownback needed the support of 59 other Senators.[1457] Wyden said "What is ironic is that some who come to floor of [the] Senate to talk about state's rights are essentiallly saying they only believed in state's rights if they think the state is right...I do not belive a senator from another state should seek to overturn another state's law based on his personal beliefs."[1458] Brownback said assisted suicide was "a crucial topic for the country to address."[1459]

Brownback claims he did not evolve on pro-life stance

A *Kansas City-Star* article from 1996 quoted the executive director of Kansans for Life, who said when Brownback first ran, "he took a pro-choice position."[1460] The *Kansas Journal World* said the GOP chair of Kansas, Tim Schallenburger remembered conversing with Brownback in 1994 and surmised Brownback was not pro-life.[1461] Brownback's rebuttal on *FOX News Sunday* (1.28.07): "No, my position has become more clear, but it's not evolved. And you look at the record. Look at how I voted. Those votes are clear. I have a 100 percent pro-life record. And... too, look who's led on these issues. Who is the person that you interview about stem cell issues? Who is the person that you — that's been fighting on partial birth abortion issues? That record is consistently pro-life. I wasn't as clear in my statements at that point in time, but [t]he record is absolutely 100 percent."[1462]

Brownback's money problems

Besides name recognition, and actually raising money for 2008, Brownback has struggled with handling money. In 1997, the *Kansas City Star* reported his in-laws gave over $32,000 to seven PACs which then turned around and gave Brownback's campaign over $31,000; by the end of 2002 his relatives were fined $9,000 by the Federal Elections Commission and Brownback's campaign had to refund about $20,000 to the U.S. treasury.[1463]

But his bigger concern is his ties to the Jack Abramoff scandal. On January 3, 2006 Abramoff pleaded guilty in a U.S. District Court to honest services fraud, conspiracy and tax evasion with a plea amounting to almost 30 years in prison (though prosecutors were expected to ask for only a decade), $25 million in restitution, a layout of his finances/activities in a month and a half, and a payment of 1.7 million to the IRS.[1464]

In 2002, Brownback's Restore America PAC received the money from four tribes represented by Abramoff.[1465] Separate from the $42,000 related to Abramoff that Brownback re-donated elsewhere, Brownback also gave up a $5,000 donation from a California defense contractor (ADCS Inc.) which allegedly bribed Rep. Duke Cunningham.[1466] Brownback spokesman Brian Hart said the senator met with Abramoff once at a breakfast, but the two never met formally, according to Hart.[1467] "Sen. Brownback was never asked to do anything for or anything by Mr. Abramoff, his colleagues or his clients," said Hart.[1468]

As a presidential candidate treading the bottom of GOP polls, Brownback did not need the affiliation. Brownback's December 2005 returns came after the half dozen donation returns, but also before the mad dash of returns of Abramoff associated monies which occurred after the New Year.

Was Brownback hurt? The *Wichita Eagle* ran a political cartoon with the Senator on a pile of cash ($40,000 plus in Abramoff contributions) stating "We had no relationship at all, ok? I barely knew him [Abramoff], understand? Sheesh, get your mind out of the gutter."[1469] More irritating for Brownback was the cartoon's pile of cash was called Brownback Mountain—an indirect reference to the film *Brokeback Mountain*, a story about a homosexual relationship between cowboys. Brownback was dressed as a cowboy in the cartoon. Other re-direction of Abramoff related donations were not as lucky. When Sen. Conrad Burns (R-MT) donated $110,000 to an American Indian council, the council sent it back and said the money was tainted.[1470]

Brownback's friends

On December 4, 2006 Brownback formed an exploratory committee, and without much surprise, said he had decided "after much prayerful consideration," to consider running for the nomination.[1471] His exploratory advisory committee included 20 people, in what the *AP* called "an eclectic mix ranging from anti-abortion activists to business executives," including Tom Monaghan, Domino's Pizza founder; Bowie Kuhn, former MLB commissioner; and Rev. Frank Pavone, who headed pro-life Priests for Life; and Kevin McLaughlin, an Iowa investment banker.[1472] *McClatchy Newspapers*, too, reported how Monaghan was "putting his money and influence" to make Brownback the next president.[1473] Who was Monaghan? He sold the pizza business for $1 billion in 1998, to which *McClatchy* said since he had built, "his own utopia on 5,000 acres in southwest Florida: Ave Maria, a planned community of 11,000 homes, built around a massive church and a doctrinaire Catholic university also called Ave Maria."[1474] McLaughlin worked on the Forbes's presidential campaigns of 1996 and 2000, and founded Iowans for Discounted Taxes, which supported Forbes's flat tax plan.[1475] Brownback supports the flat tax.

How were his 2008 chances?

Name recognition is a concern for Brownback. *USA Today* noted (7.19.06) that in a picnic sponsored by Iowa's Republican Party, Brownback mingled with the crowd for two hours, "In contrast, [George] Pataki, the picnic's featured speaker," created "a stir" when he arrived "in a three-car motorcade. The next morning, *The Des Moines Register* runs three photos of Pataki. Brownback is relegated to a postage-stamp-sized head shot."[1476] And three quarters of the country never heard of him or didn't have enough of an opinion on him in a June 2006 Gallup poll.[1477]

Yet Brownback could do well in Iowa among social conservatives. Seventy-eight percent of white evangelical Protestants voted for Bush in 2004.[1478] Brownback used to be an evangelical protestant.[1479] He converted to Catholicism with Rick Santorum's support in 2002.[1480] But his message still appeals to evangelicals. One could legitimately argue a quarter of Republicans in the Iowa caucus were conservative Christians, as Pat Robertson received 25% in 1988, Pat Buchanan received 23% in 1996, and Alan Keyes and Gary Bauer combined for 23% in 2000.[1481]

As the *USA Today* pointed out in July 2006, Giuliani and Pataki supported abortion rights and were sympathetic to gay rights, Frist flipped his stance on embryonic stem cells, and Romney had not clearly articulated his past vs. present opinions on abortion.[1482] There is an opening for Brownback if Mike Huckabee doesn't fill it.

Brownback fights with losers

In July 2007, Brownback's campaign funded an phone call that said "Tom Tancredo has accepted tens of thousands of dollars from the founder of a Planned Parenthood network, the largest provider of abortion in the world," and despite calls by "pro life Republicans" to give the money back, he "stubbornly refuses to do so."[1483] Tancredo has often questioned Brownback's stance on immigration. John Tanton, the founder of a major Planned Parenthood network in Michigan, was the contributor to Tancredo called into question. The Eagle Forum's Phyllis Schlafly, a social conservative who earned her fame in the 1970s, defended Tancredo, and said if Tanton "thought he was going to change Tom Tancredo on abortion, he's a very foolish man."[1484] Does anybody pay attention when two losing candidates fight?

Brownback has tried to pick fights with the big guys, particularly Romney over (what else but) social issues. The *National Journal* noted (7.30.07) Romney ignored Brownback, "which is probably soul-crushing."[1485] *The Daily Show* joked (8.2.07) the way Brownback asked people to come to the Ames, Iowa Straw Poll was by promising good food from Famous Dave's.[1486]

So Brownback was ignored by the top tier candidates, and had to bribe supporters with food. Brownback placed third in the Ames, Iowa Straw Poll in August 2007, but his result was overshadowed by Mike Huckabee's second place finish to Romney.[1487] Brownback was close enough to second place Mike Huckabee that he should campaign up to the Iowa Caucus, yet critics see the Kansas Senator as nothing more than a second tier candidate.

Senator Bill Frist

Bill Frist graduated from Princeton in 1974, and a decade later he came to Vanderbilt University Medical Center and founded its transplant center, where "he performed over 150 heart and lung transplant procedures, including the first successful combined heart-lung transplant in the Southeast."[1488] Frist had 100 writings and abstracts on medical research, including his co-authorship of *Grand Rounds in Transplantation*.[1489] Other books included *Transplant: A Heart Surgeon's Account of the Life-and-Death Dramas of the New Medicine* (1989), which focused on the myths of transplantation; and as a Senator he wrote a book on Tennessee's senators in the twentieth century.[1490]

Frist had three sons with his wife Karyn.[1491] With little experience in politics before, Dr. Bill Frist was elected to the Senate in 1994. Frist was the only Senate candidate to defeat a full-term incumbent that year, when he became the first practicing physician elected to the Senate since 1928.[1492] In 2000, he was named chairman of the National Republican Senatorial Committee with the goal (at which he was successful) to win back a Senate majority of Republicans in 2002; an effort that outspent the Democratic senatorial committee by $66 million.[1493]

Frist called the 2004 Senate victories a "monumental victory," and had a 'victory tour' of the South (Florida, Georgia, and the Carolinas) on the Wednesday after Election Day.[1494] But Frist restated he would not seek reelection in the Senate for 2006, and the Majority Leader became a lame duck.[1495]

His website's biography noted (7.28.06), "Frist is also a strong supporter of President Bush's No Child Left Behind Act."[1496] He was 'a strong supporter' of Bush many times, perhaps too many for the sake of his presidential ambitions.

Terry Schiavo owed her life to Frist

By March 2005, Terry Schiavo had been in a persistent vegetative state for 15 years. Her biological family wanted her to live; her husband said it was time to take the tube out. Should the government intervene to reinstate her feeding tube? Republican staffers on Capital Hill circulated a memo hinting at political benefits for conservatives who took the issue up.[1497] *Fox News* reported that one of the talking points was that "this is an important moral issue and the pro-life base will be excited."[1498] Congress convened in special weekend session to address the Schiavo issue.[1499] The legislation that developed, according to Frist, "would provide Mrs. Schiavo a clear and appropriate avenue for appeal in federal court, and most importantly, we are confident this compromise will restore nutrition and hydration to Mrs. Schiavo as long as that appeal endures."[1500]

Frist stated that "we in the Senate recognize that it is extraordinary that we as a body act."[1501] The public didn't think so. An ABC poll showed legislative action was "distinctly unpopular" and not only did 60 percent oppose congressional intervention; but 70 percent actually called it "inappropriate for Congress to get involved" as they did.[1502] Would this later haunt Frist and the Republicans? Frist even used his status as a doctor, claiming "there seems to be insufficient information to conclude that Terri Schiavo is in a persistent vegetative state…I don't see any justification in removing hydration and nutrition."[1503] With their leadership positions, Frist and House Majority Leader Tom DeLay got significant attention, though Rick Santorum entered the fray as well. Santorum thanked the Democratic leadership for co-operating on a hurried process to consider the legislation.[1504]

Democrats surrendered

But what would the Democrats do anyway? As John Hardwood of the *Wall Street Journal* noted, the Democrats felt they were "behind the eight-ball. They don't want to be portrayed in this debate as people who are eager for that feeding tube to be removed."[1505] Sens. Clinton and Biden, among others were AWOL. Indeed, where were the Democrats? Richard Cohen of the *Washington Post* asked the same question, and conceded that "most of them seemed to be cowering in some bunker."[1506] After the 'values' problem in 2004, the last thing a Democratic candidate needed was the accusation that they actually "killed" Terry Schiavo. This explains muddied comments from Bill Richardson, who looked down open Congressional involvement and stated it was a states rights issue and the Congress and the President "shouldn't have gotten involved," but also stated if it was up to him "I would keep the tube in."[1507]

Frist overreacted

Still, a major concern was whether Frist went too far. Had he over justified his involvement in the Schiavo drama because he was a doctor? Said Frist from the Senate floor: "based on a review of the video footage, which I spent an hour or so looking at last night in my office…that footage to me, depicts something very different than persistent vegetative state."[1508] His spokesman later went back and argued Frist did not make a diagnosis and had "carefully reviewed" medical records and court documents.[1509] "But it was the video Frist mentioned on the Senate floor," chided Tim Cuprisin of the *Milwaukee Journal Sentinel*.[1510]

Frist had also stated from the senate floor that "Terri's husband will not divorce Terri and will not allow her parents to take care of her. Terri's husband, who I have not met, does have a girlfriend he lives with and they have children of their own."[1511] As EJ Dionne of the *Washington Post* wrote, "No accusation here, just a brisk walk through innuendo city."[1512]

Even more convincing of Frist incompetence was the release of Terri Schiavo's autopsy, which found Schiavo's brain had atrophied to about half its normal size and really had no hope of recovery.[1513] In defense of his remarks on the Senate floor in March, Frist stated that he had "never made a diagnosis."[1514] Frist had stated in March that "when the neurologist [in the video of Terri Schiavo] said, 'Look up,' there is no question in the video that she actually looks up."[1515] The autopsy found that Schiavo was blind.[1516] Some critics even went as far to say an autopsy of Bill Frist showed he himself had only half a brain.

Frist stated Schiavo "certainly seems to respond to visual stimuli."[1517] He was questioned on the *Today Show* (6.16.06) and declared, "I never said she responded" to stimulation.[1518] EJ Dionne wrote "We should not 'move on,' as

Senate Majority Leader Bill Frist suggested. No, we cannot move on until those politicians who felt entitled to make up facts and toss around unwarranted conclusions about Schiavo's condition take responsibility for what they said -- and apologize."[1519]

Critics were mad at Frist—they should have been irate at Santorum, who, according to *Newsweek*, had commented that "he would consider impeachment proceedings against the federal judges in the Terri Schiavo case; that he favors term limits for federal judges, and that he would consider redrawing the boundaries of judicial districts to break up the liberal Ninth Circuit. Frist, aides say, does not support any such ideas."[1520] New York Mayor Michael Bloomberg later asked of the Schiavo fiasco: "Was there anything more inappropriate?"[1521]

The courts system, not the Congress, won the Schiavo debate, and she died March 31, 2005.[1522] Did anything good come from the Schiavo ordeal? Visits to the U.S. Living Will Registry's internet site, where advanced directives could be stored for quick access by doctors and relatives, jumped from 500-daily to 50,000 when Schiavo was in the news; and though the visits leveled to 2,500 hits a day, the number of registered documents increased four times more than a year earlier. [1523]

The Gang of 14 shot down Frist

Another thorn in Frist's side in the spring of 2005 was the "nuclear option," also called the "constitutional option" by its Republican supporters. The goal was to prevent the Senate Democrats from continuing to filibuster some of President's Bush's judicial nominees. Frist wanted to abolish the fact only 40 votes could filibuster a judicial nominee. At the time, there were 44 Senate Democrats (45 with Independent Jim Jeffords of Vermont). Republicans were talking about changing Senate rules so that 51 Senators could cut off debate and force a vote.[1524] The *LA Times* quoted George Allen, stating "Senators ought to have the backbone and the gumption to get off their hind quarters and vote yes or vote no and be responsible for that vote with their constituents."[1525]

But the *Washington Times* reported (3.23.06) Republican Sens. Hagel and McCain were "undecided" and had "serious reservations."[1526] There was possibility that only 49 Republican Senators (including Frist) would support the rule change—that wasn't enough. As Gwen Ifill of PBS's *Washington Week* noted, "If Bill Frist is threatening the nuclear option and in the end has to pull back, he looks weak…Somehow the threats have to pay off."[1527]

The nuclear option or constitutional option to address judicial filibusters finally reached a result in May 2005 and had immense consequences. Frist argued that "I do not rise for party; I rise for principle,"[1528] Democrats felt much differently. Speaking on the Senate floor, Sen. Mark Dayton (D-MN) stated that "This isn't a 'constitutional option,' it's a campaign opportunity… [for Frist that]… will cut the Senate's heart out with this hatchet job. Why? To show the social conservatives he's heartless enough to be president. I respect the majority leader's right to run for president. I just wish he wouldn't use the institution of the Senate to do so."[1529]

There was no secret Frist was weighing his options about the presidency. But what were the consequences? If the vast majority of the Senate felt Frist would be gone by 2006, it inherently made the Majority Leader a lame duck. In the end, the question was whether Frist had the 50 votes (for then the Vice President could break the tie) of 55 Republican Senators to overturn the rule of filibustering judicial nominees and change it to an up-or-down vote. Frist did not. Was it Frist's fault because he had diminished his leadership capabilities in his decision not to seek re-election to the Senate?

The Majority Leader was overshadowed by Sen. McCain, who again walked a fine line. He teamed up with thirteen other centrist Senators (The Gang of 14, half of which were Democrats) to not change the Senate rule, but also let some conservative judges get an up-or-down vote on the Senate floor. In a May 15 appearance on ABC's *This Week*, McCain stated that "The Democrats never should have filibustered all those judges that they did. It was an abuse of the filibuster."[1530] So McCain preserved a Senate rule, and got more conservative judges an up-or-down vote. The majority leader wasn't Frist. Hence, no surprise McCain told the Lott's Leadership Institute at the University of Mississippi in November 2005, "I will tell anyone that of all the majority leaders we've had in the United States Senate, I believe that Trent Lott was the finest leader we've ever had."[1531]

HCA and 'not so blind' trusts

Bill Frist and his 'blind' trusts problems continued to drag on in the fall of 2005. The *ABC News* website ran an *AP* article titled "Frist: Stock Probe Will Affect 2008 Plans," but provide no direct quotes indicating Frist made such remarks.[1532] If Frist admitted the stock issues influenced his 2008 plans, it would have been one of the most asinine statements he could have made. In his visit to Iowa, he said "wait for the facts before passing judgment."[1533]

Facts were not in his favor. In January 2003, Frist so said, "I own no HCA stock," this despite one of his trustees wrote Frist two weeks earlier that one of his trusts received HCA stock.[1534] The *Washington Post* also found documentation showing those managing the trust regularly informed Frist when new HCA shares were put in his portfolio.[1535] And for the past four years, trustees wrote to Frist and the Senate 15 times regarding transactions in the trusts that Frist once described as "totally blind."[1536]

The *New York Times* questioned (10.24.05) the consequences of health care legislation as Frist sat with a cloud over his head. "Medical malpractice legislation, which Mr. Frist has called 'a majority priority' is stalled in the Senate and unlikely to be revived, in part because the bill would benefit a subsidiary of HCA."[1537] In the broader context, the health care crisis was growing in the nation and a Majority Leader—a transplant surgeon, in tune with medical issues—did not have the capacity to move the issue forward. Still, besides his visit to Iowa, the *Miami Herald* reported (11.2.05) Frist met with the cities "most powerful and controversial figures" in what was dubbed as an exploratory meeting on a run for president.[1538]

Frist's solution to gas prices: a problem

In the spring of 2006, gas prices were so high that politicians threw out solutions like candy at the Fourth of July parade. But of all these plans, Bill Frist's may have been the one to stir the most discussion, especially when he proposed a rebate. Bill Frist's was proud to tell *Hardball* "the Republicans…put out an eight point plan to look at supply, demand, make sure there's not price gouging as well."[1539] Adding more confusion, Frist's plan eventually became a 10-point plan.[1540] Let's have a ~~eight~~ ten point plan *after* prices skyrocket!

He defended his $100 gas rebate: "it will actually be a huge help and the whole idea is to get that relief to the American consumer today who really unexpectedly…has been hit by these skyrocketing gas prices."[1541] Why did Frist say 'unexpectedly'?

And so, through the Gas Price Relief and Rebate Act, single taxpayers earning up to $145,000 and married couples earning up to $218,000 would have received a rebate check in August 2006, and it was to be funded "by changing the way that businesses treat inventories for tax purposes, known as 'last in, first out' or LIFO, effectively causing them to pay more in tax."[1542] Frist himself wanted to expand the increased taxes beyond the five major oil companies to other industries.[1543] In an act of desperation or at the very least a calculated risk, Frist wanted to raise taxes and support a government handout—the antithesis of conservative principles.

Rex Tillerson, chairman of Exxon Mobil, called Frist's tax accounting change "nothing more than a backdoor windfall profits tax."[1544] And why did Frist propose to expand the tax on other industries? It was this demand which sparked the protest from the National Association of Manufacturers and Wal-Mart.[1545]

Frist was not the only one to support a rebate. Bill Richardson called (April 2006) on the oil and gas industry to contribute $50 million to create a rebate program to help consumers with high gas prices. "Americans are hurting and we need action now on high gas prices, not more task forces and studies. Talk is cheap but gas sure isn't," said Richardson, who could ask a lofty goal but was in no position to accomplish it.[1546] As one New York commentator lambasted Frist's proposal:

> This embarrassment recalled George McGovern's 1972 Presidential campaign pledge to hand every American a $1,000 "Demogrant." Frist's $100 checks lacked such sheer ambitiousness. They were small enough to enrage spend-happy Democrats and silly enough to embitter frugal Republicans. So, Frist slipped between the barstools and slammed flat on his fanny before abandoning this brainstorm. [And] Frist and House Speaker Dennis Hastert, R-Ill., the Laurel and Hardy of Capitol Hill, yanked a page from the playbook of Rep. Henry Waxman, D-Calif., when they demanded an inquisition into alleged oil-company profiteering.[1547]

On May 1, Frist abandoned the tax-increase-on-oil-companies-solution to pay for the rebate, yet the Senator said he would still push for the rebate, though "Frist gave no indication how the rebate, estimated to cost about $10 billion, would be paid for…"[1548] Then the *AP* reported (5.4.06) the rebate proposal "was all but abandoned Wednesday, ridiculed by Republicans as well as Democrats as insulting and inadequate."[1549] This, despite Frist's chief of staff's comment that "The political will is here [to get some relief passed]. The need is very real. And the urge to help constituents directly and quickly is omnipresent."[1550]

Time columnist, Joe Klein wrote, the "Republican's $100 rebate bribe" was "yet another indication" that "Frist has become the central clearinghouse for cheesy political ideas."[1551] The *New York Times* reported "The rise and fall of the Republican $100 rebate is a window into how Washington sometimes works in a slapdash way, featuring in this case congressional aides who misread the political climate and lawmakers desperate to hang onto their jobs in an election year. It is a story, as well, of how concepts and plans can get reduced to sound bites that make them seem absurd.[1552] Sen. Cornyn's (R-TX) aide said "The conservatives think it is socialist bunk, and the liberals think it is conservative trickery."[1553] Cornyn himself said Frist was hurt by the whole rebate ordeal.[1554]

Frist: Alaska could lower prices!

Another point to his plan was drilling in Alaska. Frist said his rebate would not "change supply and demand...And that's why it is important to increase exploration and domestic production" in the US..."We have to increase the supply here. The supply is here."[1555]

He told Iowans (4.24.06) "If the president 10 years ago had signed the Alaska drilling, we would have a million barrels of oil every day coming into the country. That increased supply would have affected prices."[1556] Frist sparred with Katie Couric when she inquired on the Arctic National Wildlife Refuge (ANWR) drilling: "That had repeatedly failed Congress. Some question the Republicans' sincerity because they know in the view of these critics that this won't pass."[1557] "We passed it last month in the United States Senate. It has overwhelming — maybe you don't support it — but it has overwhelming support. We passed it in the legislature back in 1996. President Clinton vetoed it. Unbelievable... And if President Clinton had not vetoed that, we would have more than a million barrels of oil coming here every single day. That's more oil than we import from Saudi Arabia right now. It's a matter [of] supply and demand. Right now we would have increase supply if it had not been vetoed by President Clinton."[1558]

Couric responded "I don't have a position on it."[1559] Was there overwhelming support for Alaska drilling? Pew found Americans were split on the issue, with about 10% undecided.[1560] Frist blamed high gas prices on a President who had not been in office for six years. Why couldn't the Republican-controlled government pass ANWR drilling? And did the Majority Leader of the Senate suggest Alaska would give us more oil than Saudi Arabia?

Frist told *Hardball* (4.28.06). "We're 60-percent dependent on foreign sources of oil, those sources being in unstable parts of the world right now -- Nigeria, the region of the Middle East, Iran, Saudi Arabia. We have to increase the supply here. The supply is here. We can drill for it, explore it in an environmentally friendly way, and that's why we are so convinced that we need to look at things like ANWR or the Alaska Wildlife Refuge."[1561] If 'the supply was here'—How much? Frist's notions of supply may very well have been exaggerated or dumbfounded, and his reliance on potential domestic oil misled. Indeed, an Energy Information Administration (EIA) analysis estimated,

> With respect to the world oil price impact, ANWR coastal plain oil production in 2025 is projected to constitute between 0.5 to 1.3 percent of total world oil consumption.[15] It is expected that the price impact of ANWR coastal plain production might reduce world oil prices by as much as 30 to 50 cents per barrel, relative to a projected 2025 world oil price of $27 per barrel (2002 dollars) in the *AEO2004* reference case. Assuming that world oil markets continue to work as they do today, the Organization of Petroleum Exporting Countries could countermand any potential price impact of ANWR coastal plain production by reducing its exports by an equal amount.[1562]

Thus, even if drilling began, OPEC could tighten the spigot to compensate the 'surplus' market. The EIA also said (July 2005): "Opening ANWR reduces import dependence by 4 percentage points, from 68 percent of petroleum product supplied in 2025 to 64 percent."[1563] Did Frist mention this meager decrease? It was the same old ANWR debate. But when a questioner at a news conference suggested some of the proposals in his plan were incorporated into the August 2005 energy bill, Frist replied (4.26.06) the Republican plan was "a bold package."[1564]

Other provisions in the Gas Price Relief and Rebate Act would have given the Federal Trade Commission the authority to prosecute any retailer unlawfully raising gas prices.[1565] This was not the case already? Frist's plan also asked for the Strategic Petroleum Reserve to suspend deposits until fall, which the President already said he would do days earlier.[1566] Frist's plan was attached as an amendment to the emergency supplemental for Iraq.[1567] Why did Frist's gas-price plan have to be attached to a defense bill to pass?

Frist dropped out of the presidential race before it began

Frist dropped out and took what he called a "sabbatical" from politics.[1568] Frist said (11.29.06):

> My dad in his later years wanted to impart some wisdom to his grandchildren and great grandchildren he would never meet. One thing he wrote that has stuck with me - in fact been a clarion call to me - was 'there is so much good to do in the world and so many ways to do it." Politics is a noble occupation. Medicine is a noble profession. Service to others underlies both. The people of Tennessee elected me twice to the U.S. Senate, and I was humbled and honored by their support and every day I did my best to serve them with integrity and common sense. Twelve years ago, I pledged to the people of Tennessee that I would serve two terms in the Senate – to serve as a true citizen legislator – and then return home. I said I'd come to the Senate with 20 years experience in healing, spend 12 years serving in Washington, then go right back to Tennessee to live where I grew up. I've never deviated from that commitment. And I will do just that. In the Bible, God tells us for everything there is a season, and for me, for now, this season of being an elected official has come to a close. I do not intend to run for president in 2008.[1569]

He stated he would "immediately resume" his regular medical mission trips as a doctor worldwide to serve those "in poverty, in famine, and in civil war. That is where my centeredness is fueled."[1570]

Why didn't he run?

His aides said, reported by the *New York Times*, that Frist "decided that he simply did not have the fire to run."[1571] His announcement to not run came in a released statement.[1572] But a *Washington Post/AP* report rehashed the HCA deal stock controversy dogging the senator, and of course—Terri Schiavo: "an act," by Frist, "widely seen as a sop to religious conservatives."[1573] The *LA Times* reported (12.1.06) Frist was "assailed" for his diagnosis on Terri Shiavo, and that "Frist's associates said his decision…had nothing to do with an ongoing" Securities Exchange Commission's "investigation of insider-trading charges in connection with his sale of shares in HCA., the hospital chain his father helped found."[1574] Joe Nichols wrote for *The Nation* (11.29.06):

> It is too bad that outgoing Senate Majority Leader Bill Frist… decided not to seek the Republican presidential nomination in 2006. It would have been entertaining to watch this sorry excuse for a senator try and explain a political journey that deadended when the physician-turned-legislator diagnosed brain-damaged Terry Schiavo via videotape -- producing an assessment of her condition that completely contradicted that of doctors who had actually examined her. The storm that followed his intervention in the Schiavo case represented the only instance in which most Americans actually noticed that Frist was one of the nation's most powerful political leaders.[1575]

Mother Jones exemplified the HCA critics:

> Some companies hire lobbyists to work Congress. Some have their executives lobby directly. But Tennessee's Frist family, the founders of Columbia/HCA Healthcare Corp., the nation's largest hospital conglomerate, has taken it a step further: They sent an heir to the Senate. And there, with disturbingly little controversy, Republican Sen. Bill Frist has co-sponsored bills that may allow his family's company to profit from the ongoing privatization of Medicare.[1576]

The *Washington Post* reported Frist was like George Allen, both "have landed there through their own mistakes, not the looming presence of the two early poll leaders."[1577]

Frist was too mechanical. As Joe Klein wrote already in the spring of 2006, "Frist will leave the Senate at the end of the year and start his presidential campaign. Quote, 'He'll disappear,' said a Republican consultant. 'He's not built for heavy weather. He's just not an instinctive politician. And when you're a light candidate, every maneuver seems naked and tactical. With Frist, it's been college Republican sort of stuff.'"[1578]

Frist's Majority Leader position in the Senate caused difficulty in waging a presidential campaign. Former Majority Leader Trent Lott had previously said (5.10.06) "I think that the prospect of being a candidate is a distraction and makes his job more difficult, but I don't think working with the White House is something that has been a problem for him… I say once again and it's been proven over and over again, majority leaders cannot be majority leader and run for president at the same time. It's an impossible job."[1579] Adding more injury to Frist's unsuccessful 2008 bid, Lott eventually became the GOP's Senate Leader after Frist left Congress.

Frist had little support from the social conservatives in his party—or at least not enough to run for president. In July 2005, he broke with the White House and supported the expansion of federal financing for embryonic stem cell research.[1580] So when the Doctor finally made a decision based on leadership, he was eventually punished for it by the loss of social conservative support. Dr. James Dobson of Focus on the Family was blunt at the time of Frist's switch: "The media have already begun speculating that Sen. Frist's announcement today is designed to improve his chances of winning the White House in 2008 ... If that is the case, he has gravely miscalculated."[1581]

What was the impact of Frist's departure?

An October 2006 CNN poll found 22 percent of respondents had "never heard of" Frist, with another 14 percent "unsure" to rate him; and when he was rated in the poll, more found him unfavorable (36) than favorable (28).[1582] Pat Buchanan stated, when asked on the impact of Frist departure,

> I think it's meaningless. I do think this: there's a vacuum on the conservative side for a real conservative candidate. I don't think Frist could fill that. He was wrong on the immigration issue. People feel he sold out, at least from my standpoint. I'll tell who's looking at that and who sees that vacuum, is Newt. Because Brownback—I don't know that Brownback's got the charisma or strength or money-raising ability there. Romney is trying to become that but it's tough to convert from a governor of Massachusetts into the Barry Goldwater of the Republican Party.[1583]

The *LA Times* was more favorable, reporting his decision "may boost support for other Republicans who have courted the party's social conservatives....with his withdrawal, several potential candidates in the GOP race will have less competition wooing these voters."[1584] Frist wasn't much of competition.

But it is hard to estimate who would have supported him. When Frist dropped out, the vice president of government affairs for the Family Research Council, Tom McClusky, praised Frist for the confirmation of Alito and Roberts, then added "But it is doubtful we would have supported him" because of the senator's stance on embryonic stem cell research.[1585] If any news developed the two-weeks after Frist's decision it was that he said he was open to running for governor of Tennessee in 2010. When Frist dropped out, he fell off a cliff and nobody asked about him.

Perhaps the greatest favor Bill Frist left for his party was leaving an opening for his fellow Tennessean, former Senator Fred Thompson, to enter the 2008 race.

Former Governor Jim Gilmore

ABC News reported former Virginia governor (1998-2002) and RNC chairman Jim Gilmore was considering a presidential run (11.28.06).[1586] The potential bid came out of nowhere, and was similar to former Oklahoma Gov. Frank Keating's consideration to run for president, except Gilmore, unfortunately, went through with the decision. Virginia had to be devastated. In 2005 the state was sitting with two ripe presidential candidates, Gov. Warner and Sen. Allen, and the one who ended up running was a dud from five years earlier. On January 9, 2007, Gilmore became the sixth Republican to form an exploratory committee.[1587]

Who was Jim Gilmore?

President Bush appointed him as chair of the Republican National Committee in 2001.[1588] Big deal. The *Richmond Times-Dispatch* quoted analyst Stuart Rothenberg who said, "There is no one in Iowa or New Hampshire who has ever heard of Jim Gilmore."[1589] The caption of Gilmore's picture for the *AP* (1.9.07) article [which said Gilmore was "little known outside his state"] on *ABCNews.com* said Gilmore "took the first step in a long-shot bid" with the filing of his papers.[1590] Gilmore began exploring his candidacy when Romney had just raised $6.5 million in one day.[1591] Money and name recognition were a problem. And Gilmore clearly lacked organization.

Another problem was his abortion stance. *Lifenews.com* covered his entry into the race and noted Gilmore said the field lacked a true conservative, "That's despite the possible candidacies of pro-life advocates like" Brownback "and others."[1592] The article noted when Gilmore ran for governor, he said abortion should be the decision of the mother and physician in the first 12 weeks, and after that he said they should be illegal except in cases of the mother's life.[1593] *LifeNews.com* went on to describe Romney as one "who recently converted to the pro-life position," Tommy Thompson as one "who opposed abortion but backs embryonic stem cell research," but called Brownback a "pro-life stalwart."[1594]

Gilmore's strengths

He was governor of Virginia when 9/11 occurred, though he was not remotely close to the Mayor of New York City in terms of stature from that day. But the commission he chaired from 1999-2003 was known as his ("Gilmore Commission") and assessed the country's terrorist response capabilities.[1595] So did he prepare Virginia for 9/11?

When Gilmore entered the nomination contest, he chaired the National Council on Readiness and Preparedness, a non-profit organization for homeland security grassroots discussion which provided forums developing national strategies for first responders, businesses, and community leaders nationwide.[1596] At the time of his candidacy, he was a partner in Kelley Drye Collier Shannon, where he chaired the Homeland Security Practice Group.[1597] So it appears his strength was national security. But make no mistake, his press release and *AP* coverage when he announced painted him as a tax-cutter first and foremost.

But was Gilmore a tax cutter?

The *AP* described him as "Virginia's former tax-slashing Republican governor."[1598] Gilmore said with the announcement of his exploratory committee that "Alone among those considering a candidacy for the Republican nomination, I have a record of real leadership as a tax cutter and job creator, as a leader on national security issues and a national leader in our party."[1599] And of course, he had to say he was "the type of mainstream Reagan conservative that has always kept his promises."[1600] Yes, Jim Gilmore was exactly what the Republican Party needed: another candidate looking at the past, rather being the future.

Gilmore, according to the *Times-Dispatch*, "disputed criticism, from Democrats and some Republicans, that he left the state's finances in disarray."[1601] The 9/11 attacks on the Pentagon did not help the economy, and the 2001 recession in Northern Virginia occurred in the technology community.[1602] The state's revenue's bottomed and some criticized Gilmore's car-tax relief which "ate up an increasing amount of state expenditures."[1603]

His 1997 campaign promised a property tax cut that local governments levied on cars and pick-up trucks.[1604] Early in his tenure, his car tax cut was passed in a Democratic-controlled legislature, and the "incremental phaseout" made Virginia reimburse local governments for every dollar in car tax revenues they lost.[1605] Critics said the reimbursements that were created were merely a huge state spending program that was bound to ruin Virginia's finances.[1606] Gilmore could not cut local car taxes, so the state funds he used to reimburse localities for the relief totaled about $700 million annually.[1607]

When the GOP-controlled General Assembly tried to diminish the car-tax cuts [after 9/11 and a troubled N. VA economy], Gilmore "rebuffed" them, and "for the first time a governor…crafted a state budget without legislative approval."[1608] This saga was reported in the *Richmond Times-Dispatch* the day after Gilmore launched his presidential bid. And the *AP* reported Gilmore's car tax in covering his announcement as well (1.9.07).[1609] In fact, the *AP* report concluded the stalemate from "GOP infighting left" Virginia "unable to reconcile its budget for the first time ever, and helped" Mark Warner "upset" Mark L. Early (R), "whom Gilmore supported."[1610]

Governing later commented (Feb.2005) Gilmore's tax cut was "politically popular but fiscally unsound," and he betrayed Virginia's culture of good management.[1611] The *National Review* (12.13.06) noted some blamed Gilmore for enabling Warner to win in 2001 as a fiscally responsible business man.[1612]

Gilmore 2008: R.I.P.

In late June, Gilmore underwent surgery for a detached retina, and cancelled a week's worth of campaign appearances.[1613] Then he canceled all appearances.

On July 14, 2007, Jim Gilmore dropped out of the presidential race,[1614] and the number of GOP presidential candidates fell to nine (with Fred Thompson pending).[1615] Gilmore didn't even have a press conference. In a written statement, he said the front-loaded schedule "made it impractical to continue."[1616] By

February 10, 2007, more than 30 states would have had their contests (Gilmore's home state was to be Feb. 12).[1617] In the second quarter of 2007, Gilmore raised $211,000, and "was a virtual unknown outside of Virginia."[1618]

Stephen Colbert said Gilmore's "departure strikes a severe blow to his party's diversity. Of the nine white Christian men running, Gilmore was the only one with a wife named Roxanne. We no longer have that choice."[1619] Colbert also took time in his show to pay tribute to Gilmore's campaign, and then went to a faded border for the tribute. The show replayed only what Colbert stated seconds earlier about taking a moment to pay tribute to Gilmore.

So how did Gilmore succeed?

The *Washington Post* noted his lack of success: "But he had his moments," such as the second debate when he "lashed out" at the three frontrunners for their lack of conservatism and labeled them "Rudy McRomney."[1620] And he broke with the President and asked to begin withdrawing US troops from Iraq, but "The letter received only a little attention."[1621] James Pindell of the *Boston Globe* wrote (7.14.07), "Practically speaking, his departure will have little effect on the race for president. Besides appearing in a June debate, he only campaigned once in New Hampshire."[1622]

However, Gilmore may have accomplished exactly what he wanted: the status as the top Republican in Virginia. The *Washington Post* reported (7.15.07) Gilmore held out the possibility "he might soon run for public office again in Virginia."[1623] He left open the option of running for Senate in 2008 if John Warner retired, or for governor in 2009.[1624] Gilmore said he would start a political action committee to influence Virginia's elections for 2007.[1625] In a December 2006 *National Review* article, Gilmore said "I'd love to run against Mark Warner."[1626] Gilmore was not a presidential candidate who wanted to be Secretary of State, Vice President, or some cabinet position.

Perhaps he just wanted to be Virginia's GOP nominee for whatever major nomination was available in the near future. That near future turned out to be August 31, 2007, when Sen. John Warner (R-VA) announced he was retiring from the US Senate.

Former House Speaker Newt Gingrich

In the 1980s' Gingrich took advantage of a House rule that allowed Representatives to read items into the record after Congressional sessions (and on C-SPAN), so he gave many speeches criticizing Democrats and separated the younger Congressional Republicans from the less aggressive, older GOP members.[1627] By 1984, Speaker of the House, Tip O'Neill, was so frustrated he ordered the cable TV camera to actually cover the whole House floor to show Gingrich's speeches addressed empty crowds.[1628] Gingrich provided a voice for conservative Republican's disgusted with the decades-long reign of Democratic rule in the House.

In 1990, he won his House seat in Georgia by only 983 votes.[1629] But he recuperated, and was the father of the "Contract with America" that became the 1994 anthem for Republicans. Gingrich is widely considered responsible for the GOP's regaining majority status of the House in 1994, and in 1995 he was named Speaker of the House and *Time*'s "Man of the Year."[1630]

His rising star faded. He was criticized for the budget showdown against the President which closed down the government temporarily.[1631] In 1997, he was fined $300,000 for ethics violations, and after the 1998 elections, Gingrich resigned as Speaker and from Congress.[1632]

After public office, he "staked out" a think-tank base at the American Enterprise Institute, gave speeches at $50,000 a piece, commentated on *FOX News*, and wrote two novels on what would have happened if the South won Gettysburg.[1633]

By 2005, he was touting his new book, *Winning the Future*.[1634] A January 2005 *AP* story by Ron Fournier claimed Gingrich was "taking steps toward a potential presidential bid in 2008 with a book criticizing President Bush's policies on Iraq and a tour of early campaign states [Iowa and New Hampshire]."[1635] He appeared on *FOX News Sunday* that same day (1.9.05) as the *AP* report. Since then, Gingrich had been a snake in the grass, waiting to run if the GOP candidates faltered.

Gingrich's weaknesses

1) He is polarizing. Pew found Nancy Pelosi had a higher favorability (54) in 2006 than Gingrich in 1994 (47).[1636] In 1994, he linked Democrats to Susan Smith, who killed two of her children in South Carolina three years earlier. Gingrich said the killing "reminds every American how sick the society is getting and how much we need to change things…The only way you get change is to vote Republican."[1637]

However, Gingrich has occasionally (especially in early 2005) been very complimentary of Hillary Clinton's chances for president. So much so, the *New York Times* said Gingrich's words came "to the chagrin of conservative loyalists."[1638] Yet it was Gingrich's strategic interest for Hillary Clinton to win the nomination, for she is seen as polarizing, and anti-Hillary sentiment in the

GOP would help the former Speaker if he entered the race. A uniting force such as Barack Obama on the Democratic side had no benefit to Gingrich '08.

2) Some ethical questions are glaring. In the late 1980s, Democrats accused him of "his management of a political action committee that raised $200,000-and gave $900 to candidates."[1639] And the Democratic Congressional Campaign Committee noted he received $13,000 from a group of friends to write a novel never published, during a time when he twice unsuccessfully ran for Congress.[1640]

But none of Gingrich's ethical concerns compared to his $300,000 ethics violation fine in the late 1990s. He had to do something wrong.

When he admitted his guilt in December 1996, Gingrich said he "brought down on the people's house a controversy which could weaken the faith people have in their government."[1641] In January 1997, the House ethics committee recommended a hefty fine "after concluding that his use of tax-deductible money for political purposes and inaccurate information supplied to investigators represented 'intentional or…reckless' disregard of House rules."[1642] Days later, the House voted "for the first time in history to discipline its speaker for ethical conduct" by a vote of 395-28 to impose a $300,000 fine.[1643] In May 1997, Gingrich said he would pay the $300,000 in four installments and borrow no more than half from Bob Dole to do it.[1644] By September 1998, Gingrich said he would not use any of Dole's money, as the *Washington Post* reported Gingrich's income "had been buoyed by book sales."[1645] In December 1998, Gingrich made his final payment of $150,000 to the ethics committee.[1646]

3) Gingrich appears woefully hypocritical on moral leadership. Newt Gingrich has the worst marriage past of all presidential candidates.[1647]

Gingrich ran for Congress in 1978 on the slogan of "Let Our Family Represent Your Family," even though he very well may have been cheating on his wife simultaneously.[1648] His first marriage was to his former high school geometry teacher.[1649] On that marriage, Gingrich has said (March 2007), "I was married very young and had my first daughter when I was very young, in fact at the end of my freshman year in college."[1650] His first marriage lasted 18 years, and Gingrich remarried months after his divorce in 1981.[1651] Gingrich first wife had, according to the *Washington Monthly*, "helped put him through graduate school," and they hassled "over the terms [of the divorce] while in the hospital, as she recovered from uterine cancer surgery."[1652] Anne Manning, a supposed Gingrich mistress in the late 1970's told *Vanity Fair* (1995), "We had oral sex. He prefers that modus operandi because then he can say, 'I never slept with her.'"[1653]

Remarried, Gingrich then had another affair during the Clinton impeachment proceedings, but claimed he was not a hypocrite because the President was impeached for lying about an affair, not having it.[1654] Already in January 2005, the *LA Times* reported "Many Republicans were furious when it was disclosed, in the course of a divorce from his second wife in 1999, that Gingrich had been conducting an extramarital relationship with a congressional aide even as Republicans were impeaching Clinton for lying about an affair…"[1655] He divorced his second wife in 2000, and remarried to "a former congressional aide who was in her 20s when she and Gingrich began their affair."[1656]

But Gingrich's dirty image is now clean. In December 2005, the *Church Report*'s editor-in-chief Jason Christy announced Newt Gingrich agreed to write a regular column for the magazine which was distributed to over 40,000 religious leaders nationwide.[1657] Christy said "For over 20 years Newt Gingrich has been on the cutting edge of conservative public policy and Christian issues in this nation."[1658] The *New York Times* reported (12.17.06) Gingrich set a goal of "what he calls the restoration of God to a central place in American government and culture."[1659] His ten-point Contract with America for the 21st Century included a call to "recenter America on the creator from whom all our liberties come" and judicial appointments for those understanding "the centrality of God in American history."[1660]

Mike Huckabee so aptly stated (April 2007), without naming names, particularly evangelical Christians, "talk as if, in this election cycle, Republican candidates aren't going to be held to a standard of personal accountability and responsibility for their personal lives. If that's true, there are going to be a lot of Republicans who will owe Bill Clinton a great big public apology."[1661]

Which GOP candidates did Gingrich like?

Gingrich did an automated phone call for George Allen's re-election campaign.[1662] The *National Journal* concluded Gingrich was holding out if Mitt Romney faltered (1.11.07);[1663] but Gingrich's op-ed with Giuliani on economic assistance to Iraqis in January 2007 only offered more questions to where and when Gingrich would enter the race. Why did Gingrich ally with Giuliani on Iraq?

Does Gingrich fill the void left by Santorum, Frist and Allen? Gingrich admitted there was "probably a vacuum" now that Santorum and Allen were out, "but you have to be fair. Governor Mitt Romney is working very hard to fill that vacuum, and may well succeed. Senator McCain would like to find a way to fill that vacuum and is working very hard at it."[1664] Gingrich wasn't shy when asked why conservatives doubt McCain:

> Well, I mean, look, I have a fundamental difference with Senator McCain on amnesty for illegal immigrants; on the tax policy, where he was very much against tax cuts; on the question of McCain-Feingold, … which I think is the first censorship bill since the Alien and Sedition Acts in the 1790s and I think is a profoundly bad bill and is part of why these last elections were so unendingly negative. So there are serious principle discussions, but Senator McCain is a relatively solid conservative. He's a very honest, hard-working man. He has a very patriotic record, both in the military and in the Congress. I served with him in the House. And you'd have to say, you know, either he or Giuliani is the frontrunner right now. And then McCain, in organizational terms, is the frontrunner. So he's a serious man. I do think on the movement right, in the areas that produced Ronald Reagan and produced Barry Goldwater, there's a yearning for a clearer voice of conservatism. And I think that Mitt Romney has an opportunity to fill that.[1665]

Gingrich had all but laughed in the face of McCain-Feingold campaign finance reform. He created a new political action committee, American Solutions for Winning the Future, which was organized as a 527 group, which could "raise and spend unlimited money with minimal disclosure."[1666] Gingrich said he would raise money for the committee to find bipartisan solutions to national problems, and any candidate of any party who wanted to share in the effort would be welcomed.[1667]

What looms for Gingrich

Gingrich was a snake in the grass, as his potential candidacy was to develop as the GOP nomination remained indecisive. Gingrich had to be amazed at the amount of social conservatives for 2008 that had dropped like flies. George Allen and Rick Santorum were kicked out of the Senate in 2006. Bill Frist's campaign went nowhere, so he did not officially start one. All three Senators could have held the mantel for conservatives. Then to Gingrich's ideological liking, the early frontrunner, McCain, collapsed by July 2007, and fell to fourth place for the nomination (according to polling). And after two years of campaigning, social conservative Sam Brownback had no momentum after the Ames, Iowa Straw Poll. In addition, Romney has completely flopped on social issues and Giuliani is a social liberal.

Gingrich needed the rise of Fred Thompson to fall on its face. Thompson did not exceed the high expectations the media placed on the former Tennessee Senator, who entered the race after Labor Day. Gingrich's plan was working. And if Thompson, Romney, and Giuliani could not solidify themselves as the frontrunner by late November, Gingrich would have pounced.

Unfortunately, Gingrich did not run for president. In late September, he announced he would run for president if $30 million could be pledged to his candidacy. A week later, Gingrich announced he would not run for president. He blamed his decision on the McCain-Feingold campaign finance reform bill, which he claimed "criminalizes" politicians.[1668]

Nonetheless, Newt Gingrich deserves much credit. Who would have thought a former Speaker tossed to the curb by his own party in the late 1990s would be welcomed back by Republicans? Gingrich is a very smart, articulate politician. Yet the rise of him as a presidential candidate was more evident of the slim pickings in his party, rather than the exceptional resume from the former Representative. At the very least, the former Speaker has benefited from media exposure towards his political organizations, and sold more of his books in the process. His decision on 2008, either way, was a win-win situation.

Former New York City Mayor Rudy Giuliani

Rudolph W. 'Rudy' Giuliani was born in Brooklyn in 1944.[1669] Giuliani ran unsuccessfully for New York City mayor in 1989, but won in 1993 and served after 9/11 then soon left office because of term limits. "So popular was the tough-on-crime mayor," according to the *AP*, "that there was rumblings of rescinding the city's term limits to let him serve on."[1670] He endorsed Mario Cuomo (over George Pataki) for New York Governor in 1994 and was not invited to the 1996 Republican convention.[1671] Giuliani dropped out of the US Senate race against Hillary Clinton in 2000 after the onset of prostate cancer and a highly public divorce.[1672] He hosted *Saturday Night Live* in 1997, and made a cameo in *Anger Management* in 2003.[1673]

When reminded that he supported John McCain in 2000, Giuliani said (August 2004) the *New York Times* made a mistake. "John McCain is a very good friend of mine, known him even longer than the President, but in 2000, I supported President Bush."[1674] Was this the case, or was Giuliani trying to negate his previous support for a 2008 contender?

The popular guy

Giuliani filed his paperwork for an exploratory committee on November 13, 2006.[1675] And he was still incredibly popular, as he was first of the country's most notable politicians when he scored a 64.2 "warming" rating in Quinnipiac's Thermometer poll released November 27. He bested second place Obama by six points.[1676] (The poll was before Obama-mania reached its height in early December 2006.) McCain was third (57.7), and those who finished fourth through sixth were not even presidential candidates (Condi Rice-56.1, Bill Clinton, 55.8; and Joe Lieberman 52.7).[1677]

By accounts of nationwide polls from December 2006, Giuliani was the frontrunner when he entered the 2008 campaign. The NBC/*Wall Street Journal* Poll had him ahead with 34, then McCain (29), Gingrich (10), Romney (8), among others; *ABC News/Washington Post* had Giuliani first with 34, followed by McCain (26), Gingrich (12), and Romney (5); and CNN had Giuliani at 29, followed by McCain (24), Gingrich (13), and Romney (6).[1678] These polls also indicate Romney, at the very least, was a credible second tier candidate.

But as he was the frontrunner, Giuliani seemed to lack organization power. *Time* reported (12.10.06) he "has yet to begin building much of a campaign operation."[1679]

Rudy's weaknesses

The *New York Times* noted (1.5.07) his JoinRudy2008.com website "liberally" featured Judith Nathan, but "nowhere" did it state his eighteen year marriage to Donna Hanover, his marriage to Regina Peruggi, his two children, or [Bernard] Kerik or Amadou Diallo.[1680] Or that "crime actually had begun to go down before he took office…"[1681] Giuliani had a long list of issues to address.

1) Giuliani had not endured an entire campaign since 1997. Giuliani raised $25 million during his brief Senate campaign in 2000, and $2 million remained and was transferable to a presidential account.[1682] Money was there. An *AP* article in February 2006 focused on Rudy's low profile. Rudy "...has flown under the media radar screen in recent months, building his businesses and enjoying a prosperous private life while assisting his chances in a crowded and conservative GOP primary field."[1683] He had Giuliani Partners, a security consulting and investment banking firm he founded in 2002; clients included Merrill Lynch and Nextel.[1684] This allowed him further contact with potential donors, but he really did not concentrate publicly with campaign issues (24/7) until January 2007.

2) Social issues are a thorn in his side. Michael Goodwin of the *New York Daily News* said, "...his pro-choice, pro-gun control, pro-gay rights stances" would be "a tough sell in some GOP primaries.[1685] Any credible media organization had been repeating that criticism since Giuliani was considered a possible presidential candidate.

Giuliani addressed the 2004 Republican Convention in New York City. Appearing *on Meet the Press* in August 2004, Giuliani reassured he was Republican. Republicans "have a better sense of how to give people more empowerment, how to reduce taxes...Socially, I'm a moderate.....but so is George Pataki, so is Arnold Schwarzenegger, so is Christie Whitman....when I started in politics back in '89-'90, we didn't have people like that."[1686] Giuliani downplayed the social issues. "...The largest part of this [2004 GOP] platform, however, is about the thing that I think is [the] most important thing in this country, which is defending America, carrying on the war against terrorism..."[1687]

The best way to overlook social liberalism was to emphasize national security. Giuliani was doing so even before the 2004 campaign was over. His gay rights stance would be a hurdle. He "once lived with two gay friends and their Shih Tzu, Bonnie."[1688] He once dressed in drag—which can easily be viewed on the internet.

Asked about the constitution amendment banning gay marriage in March 2004, Giuliani said "I certainly wouldn't support it at this time, but I don't think this is one of the critical issues."[1689] When asked about gay marriage in the 2004 GOP platform, Giuliani said (8.29.04):

> Well, I signed the law in New York City that created civil unions and I signed the second one that strengthened it, because I believe that we shouldn't discriminate against gays and lesbians. People have views of conscience, religion about this. We should respect all of them, but we shouldn't discriminate against people, and I think that's the right answer. Again, that's one part of the platform. The part of the platform that I agree with is the part that talks about tax reduction to fuel a private economy.[1690]

Has Giuliani succeeded with the moral conservatives? In 2005, Giuliani really wasn't hassled by the right. Cardinal William Keeler of Baltimore was disgusted by the potential of Rudy Giuliani addressing the Loyola college (a Jesuit school) commencement exercises in Maryland (May 2005). As supporter of gay rights and pro choice—would Giuliani be bombarded with hundreds of protesters at the graduation? The hype was overplayed. Indeed, "In the end, six whole people showed up [to protest] –and to make matters a little more comical, it turned out that Cardinal Keeler had *never* attended a commencement ceremony at Loyola."[1691] Was this a prelude to the conservative movement against the 'liberal' Giuliani?

In an interview that raised more questions than answers, Pat Robertson appeared on *This Week* (5.1.05). He did not endorse Rudy Giuliani for president, but conceded that he thought "he'd make a good president ...[however]…McCain I'd vote against under any circumstance."[1692] Robertson's attitude against McCain dated back to the 2000 campaign. But the compliment to Rudy was odd considering in the same interview Robertson stated that in regard to Bill Frist, "I just don't see him as a future president." So Rudy Giuliani, a pro-gay, pro-choice Republican would be a better choice? Robertson also favored Sam Brownback. In fact, Brownback had previously stated that "Pat got me elected" in referring to his 1996 Senate victory in Kansas.[1693] How could a religious conservative like Robertson put Giuliani and Brownback in the same category?

Giuliani has satisfied conservatives in the past. In 1999, he tried to halt public funding for the Brooklyn Museum of Art after a Virgin Mary portrait was decorated with elephant dung; and though he lost the court battle on First Amendment grounds, he helped form a 'decency commission' to set standards for museums to receive city monies.[1694] Though the exhibit stayed, Giuliani's handling of the situation appeased conservatives.

He told the Global Pastors Network in Orlando (Jan.2006) "I can't tell you from my heart how much I appreciate what you are doing—saving people, telling them about Jesus Christ and bringing them to God."[1695]

3) His marriages—all three of them. Giuliani's first marriage was to his second cousin, Regina Peruggi, and lasted nearly 14 years.[1696] The marriage was annulled by the Catholic Church because they did not get a church dispensation required when second cousins marry.[1697]

Giuliani then married Donna Hanover; they have two children, Andrew and Caroline.[1698] Hanover was extremely successful, and well known in New York media outlets. A Stanford and Columbia School of Journalism graduate, she became a local news anchorwoman.[1699] She occasionally acted, including a role as Ruth Carter Stapleton (Jimmy Carter's sister) in *The People vs. Larry Flynt*.[1700]

In the spring of 2000, the *New York Daily News'* Mitchell Fink wrote a column titled "Rudy & Friend Dine & Dine," and ended that "One restaurant staffer opined that the mayor was with his wife, but shown a picture of Donna Hanover, he said it wasn't her."[1701] *Salon* noted that "Playing a frantic game of catch-up, the next day's *New York Post* published a pair of undated surveillance-style photographs of Giuliani's female dining companion coming out yet another restaurant."[1702] This back and forth gossiping was documented on Salon.com, which noted when the *Daily News* published Fink's column, "it was open season on the mayor."[1703] Hanover was to appear in the adult-orientated "Vagina Monologues," but dropped out and cited "personal family circumstances,"[1704] which could have meant Rudy's prostate cancer, the breakup, or both.[1705]

In May 2000, in "separate, dramatic news conferences," Hanover and Giuliani announced their separation after 16 years of marriage.[1706] The announcement occurred after he marched with his mistress in the City's St. Patrick's Day parade, to which one *Daily News* columnist said was like "groping in the window at Macy's."[1707]

Giuliani extramarital speculation was nothing new. In 1997, a *Vanity Fair* article implied he had an affair with Cristyne Lategano, the mayor's communications director.[1708] In 1993, Lategano became the youngest person (age 28) to assume the New York City mayor's press secretary position.[1709] Oddly, Hanover implied Lategano at her press conference: "For several years, it was difficult to participate in Rudy's public life because of his relationship with one staff member."[1710] In the settlement Giuliani paid Hanover nearly $7 million.[1711]

Who is Judith Nathan? At the time of the Giuliani-Hanover split, Nathan, a certified nurse, was a drug company executive divorced and the mother of a teenager.[1712] She divorced Bruce Nathan, a wallpaper salesman, in 1992.[1713] Particularly audacious was Giuliani's cavalier attitude: it was Nathan who walked with Giuliani in the St. Patrick's Parade and a *CBS News* report in May 2000 noted Giuliani called her a "very good friend."[1714] Mayor Michael Bloomberg performed their marriage ceremony at Giuliani's old home, Gracie Mansion in May 2004.[1715] The wedding was Bloomberg's first, as he made exception to his belief in not to perform ceremonies.[1716]

4) Public education might be skeptical on Rudy. Giuliani once said, "My father used to threaten to put me in public school…and that was a really frightening thought."[1717]

Giuliani on crime fighting

According to the *Milwaukee Journal Sentinel* (August 2006), Giuliani "said…that success in New York came when more officers were added, when daily crime reports were used to hold everyone accountable and when officers stressed minor 'broken windows' violations that lead to a larger sense of disorder."[1718]

Steven Levitt and Stephan Dubner wrote in *Freakonomics* (p.129-130) that the mayor's 'broken window' strategy "probably had little effect" because he received credit for the decreased crime rate that had begun before he took office.[1719] Indeed:

> First, the drop in crime in New York began in 1990. By the end of 1993, the rate of property crime and violent crime, including homicides, had already fallen nearly 20 percent. Rudolph Giuliani, however, did not become mayor -- and install [police commissioner William] Bratton -- until early 1994. Crime was well on its way down before either man arrived...
> Second, the new police strategies were accompanied by a much more significant change within the police force: a hiring binge. Between 1991 and 2001, the NYPD grew by 45 percent, more than three times the national average. … an increase in the number of police, regardless of new strategies, *has* been proven to reduce crime... Many of these new police were in fact hired by David Dinkins, the mayor whom Giuliani defeated. Dinkins had been desperate to secure the law-and-order vote, having known all along that his opponent would be Giuliani, a former federal prosecutor...

> Most damaging to the claim that New York's police innovations radically lowered crime is one simple and often overlooked fact: crime went down *everywhere* in the 1990s, not only in New York.[1720]

However, coverage of Giuliani's tenor was in his favor. The *New York Times* reported (8.16.94) that in backing the president [Clinton] on crime, the mayor "has a strategy that for a Republican among Democrats may prove more successful than partisanship: pragmatism."[1721]

Giuliani said (1.13.00) home ownership would decrease crime because "people who own their own homes and have a real stake in the community" makes the city "better off."[1722] Between 1993 and 1997, New York City "accounted for 25% of the Nation's total crime decline" and the FBI called it the "Safest Large City in America."[1723] His theory was to focus on the little things. Giuliani noted in his farewell address how past administrations, "were too busy to pay attention to street level prostitution, panhandling, graffiti, street level drug dealing. [But] you can't be too busy to pay attention to those things, because those are the things that underlie the problems with crime you have in our society."[1724]

Who was Amadou Diallo?

Rudy could talk about crime; but when race, crime, and the NYPD mixed together, Giuliani's fan club thinned, especially after Amadou Diallo was shot 41 times by the NYPD in 1999.[1725]

> Of course, many prominent activists chastised the mayor for his aggressive policing policies. After African immigrant Amadou Diallo was wrongly gunned down by four white officers in 1999, for instance, Al Sharpton led thousands of protesters in a series of marches denouncing both Giuliani and the allegedly rampant police brutality over which he presided. With placards and chants, these protesters referred to Giuliani as, among other things, a "devil," a "murderer," a "monster," a "bloodsucker," and a "racist." Not to be outdone by Sharpton, Jesse Jackson condemned Giuliani for "having helped set a climate that seems to glorify police misbehavior and a callous disregard of the citizens." In a similar vein, Dr. Matthew Adams of Grace United Methodist Church lamented that under Giuliani's watch, "New York City has become the Mississippi of 1964" a blatant charge that the mayor and his police force were steeped in racism.[1726]

On the Amadou Diallo verdict, Giuliani said (March 2000), "If police officers act in the line of duty to protect a community against violent criminals and drug dealers, then …the community should stand up and support them when police officers' lives are put in jeopardy," though the *New York Times* said Giuliani was asked several times how he could answer concerns on police brutality and did not directly answer the questions.[1727]

Giuliani's critics fail to mention how the 1990s crime success was pro-minority, as John Perazzo wrote "Brooklyn's mostly black 75th Precinct, for instance, was the scene of 110 homicides in 1993, but only 37 in 1998. This trend was duplicated in precincts all over New York. It has been calculated that if citywide homicide rates had held steady at 1993 levels, rather than falling as they did, then 308 more whites, 2,299 more blacks, and 1,842 more Hispanics would have been murdered by the end of 1998."[1728]

Who is Bernard Kerik?

The nomination of Bernard Kerik to be the next secretary of the Homeland Security Department in December 2004 was viewed in a positive light initially. Kerik had been the police commissioner in New York City during 9/11. Two years into its creation, the department could have used a distinct leader to clean up, as the *Washington Post* wrote, after "two of the most ridiculed White House decisions of the first term: alerting the public to buy duct tape and plastic sheeting in case of a terrorist attack, and implementing a confusing color-coded terrorism alert system."[1729] The appointment was not a token cabinet position. In January 2003, the department was created when 22 government agencies were put into one new department.[1730]

Kerik was seen as a tough-talking street cop, and Bush felt the former police commissioner could guard America from future attacks.[1731] When unveiling the nomination, the President said Kerik was a "dedicated, innovative reformer" and "had great success in reducing crime in New York City."[1732] Kerik received compliments from Sens. Schumer and Clinton, who said "Bernard Kerik knows firsthand the challenges and needs of New York and other high-threat areas."[1733]

Giuliani's friend was a bad nominee

Those compliments continued, of course, until the President learned Kerik hired an illegal immigrant. Confirmation was on track for Kerik, despite "a host of questions about Kerik's quick riches after leaving public office and his responsibility for training the Iraqi police force on a mission for the administration."[1734]

White House Counsel Alberto Gonzales conducted the vetting process.[1735] Considering Kerik's botched nomination was a strike against the Bush administration, it is noteworthy that Gonzales became the Attorney General in Bush's second term.

What's most important, however, is that Kerik worked for Giuliani partners, became a security consultant and signed on to help start the Iraqi police force after the 2003 Iraq invasion.[1736] How mad was the Bush administration at America's Mayor? Was the incident a portrayal of Giuliani's incompetence?

CNN.com reported Giuliani "on at least two occasions," had "made a personal pitch to the White House" for Kerik to get the nomination.[1737] At the time of the nomination, Kerik was the senior vice president of Giuliani Partners,[1738] and when Kerik told reporters "What happened between me and the White House is my fault and nobody else's," he made the comments outside Giuliani Partners.[1739] New York's WNBC.com reported (12.14.04), "Giuliani still insisted Kerik would have been a 'very, very good choice,' for homeland security secretary if not for the nanny problem."[1740] There was more than just a nanny problem. David Keene, chairman of the American Conservative Union, told the *New York Times* the Kerik situation "really goes to the flip side of what people like about Rudy, which is that he is not seen as someone who is very careful about much of anything. It raises the question of what kind of people and what kind of checking would he do if he were in the position of making those kind of decisions."[1741]

Deborah Orin of the *New York Post* said (Dec.2004) "The exploding Bernard Kerik mess is raising questions about whether Rudy Giuliani Inc. is ready for the kind of prime time that he'd face in a 2008 presidential race. Even fans shake their heads at Giuliani's apparent ignorance of the tangle of skeletons trailing his pal and business partner. 'There is no way that he can run for president with Bernie Kerik as his business partner after this,' predicted a senior GOP strategist. 'It's going to be open season. It's takes away his halo.'"[1742] Giuliani himself said he did not know how the Kerik issue would play out if he went back into politics.[1743] John Hardwood of the *Wall Street Journal* said, "it's certainly an embarrassment for the White House. The president was very taken with the personality of Bernard Kerik, half Andy Sipowicz, half Dirty Harry. You know, a lot of tough, macho man of action about him."[1744]

But if there was a silver lining for Giuliani, it was how quickly Kerik moved out of the picture. Perhaps there was even a lack of outrage after the botched nomination. Joe Biden was questioned on the Kerik controversy on CNN's *Late Edition* (12.12.04). Biden said Kerik did the "absolutely" right thing in resigning: "Quite frankly, as Rudy Giuliani said, having a problem where you have maybe an undocumented alien, … having not paid properly withheld, we have been through this, you know, going all the way back to the attorney general's slot and the first administration of President Clinton. And this is a man who is going to be in charge of immigration."[1745] Kerik "did the graceful thing."[1746] Howard Dean said of the nomination (12.12.04), "it's a good thing he [Bush] pulled the plug very quickly and it's over and done with."[1747]

More than just a nanny problem

1) **Kerik previously had an arrest warrant on him.** Kerik did not mention in the vetting that a New Jersey judge issued a warrant for his arrest in 1998 for a civil dispute over unpaid bills.[1748] *Newsweek* was the organization which found the judge issued the arrest warrant "as part of a convoluted series of lawsuits relating to unpaid bills on his condo;" *Newsweek* faxed the evidence to the White House at six in the evening and within two hours Kerik gave a withdrawal letter to Bush.[1749]

2) **More than just an affair.** The nanny issue may have been convenient, as it was a similar reason Zoe Baird could not be Bill Clinton's attorney general in 1993.[1750] That alone may have been enough, given the jurisdiction of the department on immigration issues.

But the *New York Daily News* reported (12.13.04) Kerik "conducted two extramarital affairs simultaneously," including a decade long relationship with a city correction officer, Jeanette Pinero; and year long affair with publisher Judith Regan.[1751] Kerik's attorney said the "friendship" with Pinero ended in 1996.[1752] But it was in mid-1996 that Kerik met Hala Matli, and they married in 1998; at the time of the 2004 nomination, they were still married.[1753]

The *Daily News* said the affair with Pinero was "at the center of two lawsuits against the city, both brought by correction employees who claimed Kerik retaliated after they crossed her," and in 2003, the city settled one lawsuit for $250,000.[1754] The other involved a deputy warden who, having reprimanded Pinero, claimed Kerik stifled the warden's promotion.[1755]

3) Kickbacks from Taser. Kerik also received over $6 million in stock options from Taser International.[1756] *Newsweek* reported (12.19.04), he received the options

> ...without ever having invested any of his own money. Kerik joined the Taser board after leaving his police commissioner's job in 2002. New York City was a purchaser of the stun guns, as was the Department of Homeland Security. Kerik sold the stock in early November, shortly before an Amnesty International report charged that there had been more than 70 Taser-related deaths since 2001.[1757]

4) A diversion of funds. In August 2006, the *New York Daily News* reported the FBI was investigating what happened to over $1 million in rebates from cigarettes bought for sale to inmates and diverted to the Correction Foundation account.[1758] The rebates went into the city's budget, that was until Kerik became president of the foundation in 1995.[1759] The *Daily News* revealed already in 2003 that irregularies were in the foundation's records, and asked Kerik, who directed questions to his treasurer.[1760] The treasurer later pleaded guilty to stealing $137,000 from the foundation and went to prison.[1761]

5) Kerik's cops worked on what? In a different incident from 2002, Kerik paid a conflict of interest fine when he had three police officers research about Kerik's mother past for his book, which was published through Judith's Regan's company.[1762]

6) Kerik violated another conflict of interest law. In June 2006, he pled guilty to two misdemeanors in an agreement that allowed him to continue his new career as a security consultant in the Middle East.[1763] Kerik admitted as leader of New York City's Correction Department he received $165,000 in gifts from a company that attempted to do business with the city.[1764] Meanwhile Frank and Peter DiTommaso were charged with perjury, as the indictment said they denied their firms paid for most of Kerik's high class apartment renovation when Kerik headed the city's Department of Correction.[1765] Kerik admitted he took the gift even though he knew the company was attempting to do business with the city.[1766] The DiTommaso brothers were also under investigation by the city's Trade Waste Commission.[1767] Kerik admitted he violated the city's conflict of interest law, and agreed to pay $200,000 in retribution. As the *New York Daily News* pointed out, rank has its privileges:

> An ordinary cop who accepted a free cup of java would find himself under investigation by Internal Affairs and then hanged, drawn and quartered at high noon in front of City Hall. But, under a plea bargain that seems to have been worked out between Kerik's fast-talking lawyer and Bronx District Attorney Robert Johnson, Kerik will be set free after admitting that he accepted $200,000 in home renovations from a mob-connected company. If so, Johnson will make Kerik the envy of the run-of-street defendants who parade through the criminal courts every day.[1768]

Giuliani did not distance himself from Kerik, and instead issued a statement which argued the plea did not diminish Kerik's success: "Bernard Kerik has acknowledged his violations, but this should be evaluated in light of his service to the United States of America and the City of New York."[1769]

How close are Kerik and Giuliani?

In March 2004, Giuliani said,

> After the 2004 election, I'm going to sit down and think very seriously about what do I want to do? I'm very, very happy with what I'm doing right now. I have a business with the former police commissioner, Bernie Kerik. We do a lot of interesting things. We're getting involved now in trying to stop a lot of this spreading importation of illegal medicines where people think they're getting real medicines and they're getting animal medicines and other things. We do so many other--we work in Mexico City, we work all over the world. I'm very active. I enjoy it. And then, at some point, I'm going to probably want to get revolved in government, but I don't know yet when and it isn't on the table right now.[1770]

In 2005, Kerik still worked with Giuliani. *Newsday* reported (11.16.05) Kerik, while commentating on television, stated he had been working for Mobius Security Group Ltd. in which Kerik was a security adviser with the Jordanian government.[1771] Kerik resigned from Giuliani Partners after he withdrew his name for Homeland Security Secretary; but in March Giuliani Partners entered a joint venture with Sea Secure, which was actually a subsidiary of Mobius.[1772] In November, a Giuliani spokeswoman said Giuliani Partners was unaware of Kerik's job with Mobius.[1773]

Did Rudy have a pre-1993 mentality?

In October 2004, days before Election Day, Rudy continued to make known his support for President Bush by bashing John Kerry:

> John Kerry is still in a pre-9/11 mentality. He said that 9/11 didn't change him very much. He said he wants to go back to when terrorism was just a nuance, meaning pre-9/11. I don't know when the heck terrorism was just a nuisance. Was it just a nuisance when they attacked the World Trade Center in 1993 and killed people in my city in 1993? And John Kerry then proposed gutting our intelligence budget, and Teddy Kennedy had to oppose it? I mean, he has a pre-9/11 view, which is the reason why this country would be a lot safer in dealing with bin Laden and the other terrorists with George Bush sitting there. He understands the lessons of September 11. John Kerry has consistently indicated he does not understand what happened to this country. He's said it to the *New York Times*: "I wasn't changed very much by 9/11." Bob Kerrey said he was changed very much by 9/11. Different Kerrey, right?[1774]

John Kerry might have had a pre-9/11 view, but why did Giuliani say terrorism was more than a nuisance after the 1993 attack? It is likely that if the 1993 attack was seen as more than a nuisance in the 1990s, the effects of a second attack on the same building could have been limited. At least New York City's government would have spent the next eight years after 1993 preparing for the worst case scenario. Did they sufficiently prepare?

America's Mayor

In August 2006, came the release of Thomas Kean and Lee Hamilton's *Without Precedent:The Inside Story of the 9/11 Commission*. The 10-member commission was made by Congress in 2002 to investigate the government's response to 9/11,[1775] and the new book suggested the 20 month investigation might have suffered because of too-soft questioning on Giuliani, on May 19, 2004,[1776] in what was the second and final day of the hearing's examination of New York City's response.[1777] Kean and Hamilton wrote "It proved diffcult, if not impossible, to raise hard questions about 9/11 in New York without it being perceived as criticism of the individual police firefighters or…Giuliani…There were no questions posed to him about communication problems between policy and firefighters in the towers, or why New York City had its emergency response command center in World Trade Center 7 after the complex had been the target of the 1993 terrorist attack."[1778]

Indeed, Rudy was not that helpful. Kean and Hamilton's book also said, "…The questioning of Mayor Giuliani was a low point in terms of the commission's questioning of witnesses at our public hearings. We did not ask tough questions, nor did we get the information we needed to put on the public record."[1779] Giuliani's spokesman said it was news to them.[1780] Kean did say (8.13.06), "a lot of people said things outside of the public hearings which they felt they could not, for security reasons or some other reason, say in public."[1781] Hamilton said with Giuliani, "we simply let him off a little too easy. The bottom line, however, is that in the private testimony or conversations with the mayor, we really got the information we needed. In the public hearing, because of that environment that you've described, and I've commented on, I think we were a little easy on the mayor."[1782] Kean said "It was a criticism of ourselves," and Hamilton agreed.[1783]

So why wasn't Rudy hammered with questions?

Kean and Hamilton partially blamed their softness on one member of the commission, John F. Lehman, who said the response plans were "not worthy of the Boy Scouts, let alone this great city."[1784] Lehman's comments came the day prior to Giuliani's appearance before the commission.[1785] The chairs also suggested newspaper criticisms in editorials critical of their questioning of the city's fire and police officials at earlier hearings made them more soft.[1786]

Giuliani's spokeswoman, Sunny Mindel, replied in a statement that "It is surprising in as much as Rudy gave them all the time they wanted in his private testimony, which occurred before the public hearing…At the end of both sessions, Hamilton and Kean said they were pleased and grateful for Rudy's time and full cooperation. It really is confounding."[1787] But it begs the question if the 9/11 commision was as thorough as possible. They did, after all, let Cheney and Bush appear together, and Kean said "we didn't see any problem" with it.[1788] Indeed, Giuliani was asked in March 2004 about Bush, who said he would testify before the full commision for an hour. Giulani defended it: "But it would seem to me that why not start with an hour and see if it can't get done? I got to tell you one thing about President Bush, he's on time. Every time I've had a meeting with him. If it's 9:45, if you're one minute late, he's there at 9:45, and if it's 9:45 to 10:30, it's over at 10:30. It's a good discipline. I used to teach trial practice for a while, and if you get those questions in one hour, you can probably have a much better inquiry."[1789]

One hour sufficed the President to testify about all his knowledge on the worst attack in US history.

Was Giuliani forthright in public testimony?

He met with the Commission on April 20, 2004 in a three-hour closed session in a conference room at Giuliani Partners, in what was the first time he had been "extensively quizzed" before and during 9/11.[1790] That meeting focused on listening to Giuliani recall what he saw and the decisions he made.[1791]

The softness was accurate. In May 2004, the *New York Magazine* said 9/11 Commission member Bob Kerrey had a "high regard for Giuliani" and noted Giuliani's efforts "to go to all the funerals" of the victims—and compared him to the President, who had not yet attended a soldier's funeral.[1792] The magazine concluded Kerrey was "a hint" at how the Democratic commisioners would question Giuliani.[1793]

Indeed, coverage of the May 2004 hearing by *CBS* was titled "Venting at Rudy & 9/11 Panel" and *MSNBC.com* said "Giuliani says 9/11 families' anger misdirected." Indeed the *AP* noted three different relatives of 9/11 victims questioning Giuliani, as the article (5.20.04) concluded "Several relatives of victims said they were disgusted" the commission members given five minutes to question Giuliani "wasted time with redundant praise."[1794] Some in the crowd yelled "Talk about radios. Talk about the radios."[1795]

Giuliani addressed the criticism at the time. Relatives said the commision ineptly answered issues like malfunctioning radios, but the former mayor said the city was "unbelievably capable" and "terrificly effective."[1796]

He went on CBS's *Early Show* the next day and said "Their anger I understand, because they went through just terrible loss. But I think the anger is misplaced. The anger should not be at the people who tried very, very hard [and] did the best they could to try to save their loved ones."[1797] He repeated this the same day on the *Today Show*, "These people were doing the best they could. They were trying hard to save their loved ones. Some people did it right, some people made mistakes under pressure. And I don't know if you want to level blame and this tremendous kind of guilt on them."[1798] So it was inappropriate to question Giuliani. He also told *Today* "Here's the mistake. Nobody anticipated a catastrophic attack, planes being used as missiles, being driven into those buildings, and that's the reason for the losses....There was not a problem of coordination on Sept. 11. We got a story of heroism, we got a story of pride, and we got a story of support that helped get us through."[1799]

In addition, at the 2004 hearing, Giuliani, who the *AP* reported (5.20.04) as "one of the Bush Administration's most vocal supporters" did not get the warnings of a terrorist attack on his city within an August 6, 2001 White House briefing paper, and told the commission in all likelihood it would not have changed his city's precautions.[1800] Giuliani said "If that information had been given to us, or more warnings had been given in the summer of 2001, I can't honestly tell you we'd do anything differently. We were doing at the time everything we could think of....to protect the city."[1801] What did this email say?

Wayne Barrett and Dan Collins' *Grand Illusion: The Untold Story of Rudy Giuliani and 9/11* focused on breaking the mayor's reputation. A *New York Daily News* op-ed agreed with the book, noting (8.22.06) many failures: Giuliani's decision to put the city's command center on the 23rd floor of 7 WTC [World Trade Center] "over the objections of police and fire brass. The bunker went unused, and its 6,000 gallons of fuel my have destroyed the building."[1802] And Bernard Kerik was apparently serving as the mayor's body guard instead of running the police department on 9/11, as the book quoted the current police commissioner Raymond Kelly on 9/11: "I don't know who was directing. I literally don't."[1803]

Giuliani: radio communication problems should be expected

Of all people, the former mayor of New York seemingly thought the 9/11 Commission's recommendations were taken care of. Did he "concur" with the commission's findings and "their complaint that they haven't been listened to…"?[1804] Giuliani said (August 2006), "No. 1, most of the things they recommended I think made a great deal of sense. I think many of them have been implemented. I honestly can't tell you the ones that haven't been. Seems we've made a lot of changes."[1805] When asked about first responder communications, Giuliani legitimatized the lack of success: "They've been dealt with as much as they can be. Technology is technology. The radio issue is still being dealt with. It's still being dealt with four or five years later, because these technologies don't work 100 percent. You know, how many times has your cell phone gone down when you talked on the cell phone?"[1806] Worse yet, Alan Colmes affirmed the apathetic answer with a "Still happens;" Sean Hannity said "I have Cingular. Mine never goes down."[1807] Giuliani said "They all go down. So now multiply that under stress where thousands and thousands of people, including first responders trying to use their radios."[1808]

Nothing is more reassuring in protecting the country than hearing excuses.

Leader of the Pack

As of August 2007, Giuliani was still the nationwide frontrunner, as he finished first in the Gallup Poll (8.13-16.07) with 32 percent, followed by Fred Thompson (19), Romney (14), McCain (11), Huckabee (4), Paul (3), Hunter (2); and Hagel, Brownback, and Tancredo all with a percent each.[1809] Giuliani has fluctuated with 29 percent support to as high as 42 percent between April and August 2007; in that time frame he was always the GOP frontrunner.[1810] Likewise, *ABC News/Washington Post* polls have had Giuliani the GOP frontrunner from December 2006 to August 2007.[1811] But nationwide polls are different from individual states, and Romney has a hold on Iowa. Only more media scrutiny remains if Giuliani continues to lead in the national polls, and then loses the Iowa Caucus to Romney.

Senator Chuck Hagel

In 1962, Hagel's father died and left him as the father figure for his three younger brothers.[1812] Hagel was a newscaster in Omaha after returning from Vietnam, then staffed for a Nebraska Congressman, and was deputy administrator for the Veterans Administration under Ronald Reagan.[1813] He was also a lobbyist for Firestone in the 1980s, and founded Vanguard Cellular Systems, making him a cell phone pioneer who became a multi-millionaire.[1814]

Hagel's specialty was foreign policy, and elected in 1996, "he was the only newly elected Republican Senator willing to serve on the Foreign Relations Committee, a position he quickly turned into a pulpit."[1815] (No one else wanted the position.) On his spot on the Foreign Relations Committee, he later commented "I believed at the time, and believe as much today as I did then, that foreign policy was going to be the housing that framed all issues, that everything for the future of America would fall within that housing."[1816] Whether this was Hagel's exact perception when he received the Foreign Relations Committee membership is unclear, but there was no doubt after nearing a decade on the committee, the spot was advantageous to a presidential contender. By 2005, he had already visited 50 countries.[1817] But Hagel is not limited on domestic policy: Hagel has also presented major plans for Social Security and immigration reform.[1818]

Hagel the moderate

On the broad surface, Hagel could be considered a moderate Republican, particularly because of his criticism of the Iraq war. Hagel has argued a position on war should have nothing to do with politics.

In 2002, a Senate candidate in Georgia, Saxby Chambliss (R) ran an ad which linked bin Laden and Saddam Hussein to his opponent, Sen. Max Cleland (D).[1819] Cleland was a Vietnam veteran and triple-amputee. Bill Frist was the chair of the Republican Senatorial Campaign Committee. *Esquire* later stated Chuck Hagel threatened to endorse Cleland, and "chewed Frist's ass like it was steak."[1820] The ad came down.

He was also critical of the Pentagon and its civilian leadership over the commanders on the ground in Iraq. On August 15, 2004, he was asked if the US should put more troops in Iraq. "I think we have to rely on our commanders' analysis on the ground. I think we should be careful with that, that those commanders are not nuanced or compromised by the civilian leadership in the Pentagon saying, well, I've said we'll listen to the commanders, but, wink, wink, the commanders say we don't need more troops."[1821] The *National Review* called him "Senator Skeptic, R-France."[1822] Hagel did not rhetorically bash Sen. Kerry (like other Republicans) in the 2004 campaign.[1823] And when President Bush named Syria, North Korea, and Iraq as the Axis of Evil, Hagel labeled it "name calling."[1824]

Besides non-Iraq issues, Hagel voted against President Bush on three of the President's biggest domestic projects: the 2002 farm bill, the No Child Left

Behind education law passed in 2001, and Medicare Reform that included a drug benefit beginning in 2006.[1825] The 2002 farm bill was in a re-election year, but Hagel said "the future of agriculture in America is not continued subsidies."[1826] He said NCLB pushed "aside all the innovative, creative work" of educators and policymakers at the local level.[1827]

Other moderate actions include his resolution to open Cuba to all U.S. exports and to end every travel and credit restriction, which he offered in Bush's first month as President, saying the forty-year policy on Cuba was "senseless."[1828] He was only one of two senators who voted against extending trade sanctions on Iran and Libya.[1829]

Chuck Hagel avoids the partisan jargon. In April 2005, Hagel said, "The race to win the 24 hour news-cycle, to destroy the other party and win at any cost has squeezed out our ability to see beyond the immediate to the larger historically defining challenges of our time... Political leaders must stop this zero-sum game of political destruction. Institutions cannot function without the essential currencies of trust and confidence. We must work to build back that trust and confidence or we will be incapable of any bipartisan effort to provide solutions for America."[1830] He was a conservative, but without throwing the red meat. He stated before the 2006 midterms: "the Democrats have produced clear alternatives to some of these big problems," and "I would hope that after November 7....whatever happens....that this country can come back together with some consensus over the next two years, and deal with the big problems we face."[1831]

As David Broder of the *Washington Post* wrote in October 2005, "If you are looking for signs of the changing political environment in Washington and the Republican Party, Hagel's office is the place to begin."[1832] Broder believed if Hagel's public dissent had been combined with a popular President, "Hagel's views might well be regarded as heresy," but there was an increasing demand for what Hagel himself called "responsible governance."[1833] The opinion ended praising Hagel for sponsoring a bill with Rep. John Tanner (D-TN) to create a bipartisan commission to look at the challenge of entitlements' (Social Security, Medicare, and Medicaid) future.[1834]

Hagel the conservative

A closer look at Hagel's record indicates a conservative bend. In 2004, the *Washington Post* described him as an "anti-abortion, pro-school prayer, pro-school voucher conservative who voted to remove Bill Clinton from the White House..."[1835] He voted against the McCain-Feingold bill.[1836] He voted with his party 94 percent of the time in 2002, and 98 percent of Bush's legislation.[1837] David Broder noted (October 2005) the Bush loyalty Hagel showed on roll call votes in 2004, when he went with the President 94% of the time, even higher than Bill Frist.[1838]

"I don't think Hagel's voting record is at odds with social and economic conservatives. I think he's a very attractive candidate, especially if McCain did not run," said former Sen. Bob Kerry (D-NE) in November 2004.[1839]

How long has he been running?

He met with Iowa and New Hampshire delegates at the 2004 Republican convention; and stated in August 2004, "I will consider a race for the presidency."[1840] Hagel had the upside of being well-known in the western half of Iowa, where people read the *Omaha World-Herald* and watch Nebraska stations.[1841] The *Washington Post* reported on Hagel (11.15.04): "He Survived Vietnam and Won the Senate. Could Chuck Hagel Take the White House?"[1842] "Hagel, 58, is not your standard-issue politician. He is outspoken, does his own reading, thinking and even writing, and has the capacity to charm Nebraskans, foreigners, even Democrats."[1843] Even Hagel's brother told the *Post* that Hagel had "his mind made up that he is going to run for president in 2008."[1844] Hagel had three choices: run, return to private life, or seek a third term in the Senate in 2008 and perhaps become the chair of the Foreign Relations Committee.[1845]

By late fall 2006, it was unclear if he was considering running for president. In a rash of December 2006 nationwide polls for the Republican nomination, Hagel was not included in the *NBC News/Wall Street Journal* or CNN poll, and received nothing (-) in both the *ABC News/Washington Post* and *FOX News*/Opinion Dynamics poll.[1846]

Hagel's baggage? Not much.

In July 2004 *The Hill* reported Hagel used his official Senate website for political purposes at least five times between May 1998 and March 2004.[1847] *The Hill* reported "Hagel's brush with the Senate ethics rules may be the product of what political observers have described as political ambitions straining beyond the Senate."[1848] Little resulted from the issue.

Hagel is also tied to a major voting machine company, a connection well documented by *The Hill* in January 2003. By 2003, Election Systems & Software (ES&S) made half the voting machines in the nation, including all of Nebraska's.[1849] The company made optical scan and touch-screen vote-counting machines that were increasingly popular.[1850] *The Hill* reported, "An official at Nebraska's Election Administration estimated that ES&S machines tallied 85 percent of the votes cast in Hagel's 2002 and 1996 election races."[1851]

ES&S was actually American Information Systems, Inc (AIS) in 1996, until it merged with Business Records Corp. in 1997 and became ES&S.[1852] In a 1996 disclosure form that covered the previous year, Hagel, a Senate candidate, "did not report that he was still the chairman of AIS for the first 10 weeks of the year, as he was required to do."[1853] Indeed, Hagel was AIS chairman from the early 90's until March 1995, and also served as president of McCarthy & Co, from July 1992 until early 1996.[1854]

Why is McCarthy & Co important? ES&S was also a subsidiary of McCarthy Group, Inc, which was "jointly held by the holding firm and the Omaha World-Herald Co."[1855] The *Omaha World Herald* was Nebraska's largest newspaper. In the mid-1990s, Hagel had reported a financial stake of $1 million to $5 million in the McCarthy Group, a private merchant banking company headquartered in Omaha.[1856] Though in 2003, Michael R. McCarthy, the chairman of McCarthy Group, Inc. said Hagel's investment made Hagel a "minor shareholder."[1857] McCarthy was the treasurer for Hagel for Nebraska, then Hagel for Senate about three years until December 2002.[1858] And McCarthy's son Kevin worked for Hagel.[1859]

ES&S's competitors were Diebold Election Systems and Sequoia Voting Systems.[1860] So apparently Hagel has the inside ticket to electronic voting systems. But when explaining subsidiaries and acronyms (ES&S, AIS), the tree of connections takes too long for a voter to connect them, much less care.

Hagel v. Republican standard bearers

Besides Ron Paul, Chuck Hagel has been the most critical of President Bush over the Iraq war, so much so Hagel has not ruled out the possibility of running as an independent with Michael Bloomberg.

Hagel picked his battles with high profile figures the base could identify with. First, Hagel stabbed Lieberman with words. On *Meet the Press* (1.14.07), Sen. Joe Lieberman said, "With all respect, the other proposals represent the beginning of a retreat, of a defeat. And I think the consequences for the Middle East, which has been so important to our international stability over the years, and to the American people, who have been attacked on 9/11 by the same enemy that we're fighting in Iraq today, supported by a rising Islamist radical super-powered government in Iran, the consequences for us, for—I want to be personal—for my children and grandchildren, I fear will be disastrous. That's why I want to do everything I can to win in Iraq. … and I think that's what … my oath of office requires me to do."[1861]

Hagel said, "First, as I said before, I am not, nor any member of Congress that I'm aware of… is advocating defeat. That's ridiculous, and I'm offended that any responsible member of Congress or anyone else would even suggest such a thing. Senator Lieberman talks about his children and grandchildren. We all have children and grandchildren. He doesn't have a market on that, nor do any of my colleagues."[1862]

Then Hagel attacked Cheney. When Vice President Cheney said some don't have the stomach for the mission in Iraq, Hagel told Gwen Ifill (1.25.07), "Oh, I'm so sorry the vice president so underestimates the people of this country. He has so little faith in this country to say something like that. That's an astounding statement from the vice president of the United States. You're telling me — or maybe more directly, maybe the vice president should tell the families of those who have lost their lives, over 3,000, and over 23,000 wounded, some very seriously for life, that they don't have the stomach? Come on, let's get real here."[1863]

And there was more where that came from. Dick Cheney told *Newsweek* in January, "I believe firmly in Ronald Reagan's 11th Commandment: THOU SHALT NOT SPEAK ILL OF A FELLOW REPUBLICAN. But it's very hard sometimes to adhere to that where Chuck Hagel is involved."[1864] Hagel said (2.18.07), "I can't answer for the vice president's comments, but I do find that a bit puzzling, because I noted two weeks ago, *Congressional Quarterly* rated the

100 United States senators on their support of the Bush administration's policies in the Senate last year, 30 votes. The senior senator from Nebraska was the number one supporter of George Bush's policies in the Senate last year. Now, my friend [Sen.] Jack Reed [D-RI] will move further away from me hearing that. But I can't answer to the vice president. I certainly never said anything about him or anyone else, I don't get personal and that's the way I leave it."[1865]

Then it was Hagel vs. Rush. Conservative radio talk show host, Rush Limbaugh said, "If Chuck Hagel had been around during D-Day with the same kind of media we have today, he would have demanded that the invasion stop after the landing because there had been so many deaths. War is not something you put on a timetable."[1866] Limbaugh also called Hagel "Senator Betrayus" (a play on Gen. Petraeus, who led forces in Iraq).[1867] Hagel responded on *This Week* (2.4.07), "Well, listen, everybody has to be somewhere, everyone has to make a living. Rush has to make a living, and he has a right to say whatever, uh, he wants."

Then it was Hagel vs. McCain, finally. Hagel endorsed McCain 2000, but by 2007, McCain and Hagel's opinion on Iraq were starkly different. When allies divide on an issue that is the most pressing to the nation, a political union fades. Make no mistake: Hagel and McCain are friends. But Hagel's quest for a new direction in Iraq, and McCain's support for the surge, have nixed the idea of Hagel endorsing McCain a second time around.

The *Washington Post* reported (1.26.07), "Hagel has been eclipsed by Sen. John McCain …who has vigorously endorsed the president's war policies."[1868] And later in the article: "Earlier in their careers, McCain, 70, and Hagel, 60, were viewed as rising Republican stars, two plain-spoken outsiders with gritty military résumés. After losing to Bush in the 2000 GOP nomination battle, McCain greatly enhanced his stature inside the party by embracing Bush's Iraq policy. Meanwhile, Hagel, an early and persistent critic of the invasion, grew more estranged."[1869] McCain told the *Post*: "He's held his view for a long time and I've held mine for a long time, so it's not as if we suddenly find ourselves on the opposite side of the issue. I respect his views. I maintain my strong affection and respect for him."[1870] The allies may have been friends, but their differences were cemented.

In March 2007, McCain said Hagel let his Vietnam experiences dictate his Iraq views, and added "My views are not framed by events that happened 30 years ago," when asked about Hagel.[1871] "I don't think it would be fair to my constituents, intellectually, to have my views formed only by that one experience of my life. That's maybe where Chuck and I have some differences."[1872] However, on CNN (3.27.07), McCain said, "…And Chuck has honest, deep-seated, sincere feelings on this issue, as does Max Cleland and others. And, by the way, this strong difference of opinion we have has not impaired our friendship, which predates this and post-dates it."[1873]

Hagel the Independent

In May 2007 on *Face the Nation*, Hagel left open the possibility of running with Michael Bloomberg as an independent after dining with the New

York City Mayor: "We need some new, fresh, independent ideas to lead this country forward…We didn't make any deals, but I think Mayor Bloomberg is the kind of individual who should seriously think about this."[1874] Hagel maintains the respect of Democrats. In July 2007, Joe Biden said Hagel is a Republican he could have as his vice president.[1875]

In July 2007, Hagel said "I have no plans to change parties or run for president as an independent."[1876] Yet Hagel also did not completely rule out what could happen in the future. In September 2007, Hagel announced he would not run for re-election to the Senate, nor would he run for president.

His decision on the Senate was appropriate. There was early competition for the GOP primary in Nebraska for Hagel's job. Nebraska's Attorney General, Jon Bruning already was running to replace Hagel, and in July 2007, investment advisor Pat Flynn announced his attentions to run as well.[1877] And when Hagel announced his decision not to run, former Sen. Bob Kerrey (D-NE) announced he would consider running to fill the seat. One could argue Chuck Hagel would be content with Kerrey, a moderate Democrat who voted for the Iraq War authorization, replacing him.

Hagel's decision not to run for Senate or president does not mean Hagel is out of the 2008 picture. In fact, Hagel might be right on target to where he wants to be. His Senate and presidency announcement was not a surprise, as the only remaining option for Hagel is to run as Michael Bloomberg's vice president. Though Bloomberg and Hagel have hid from the spotlight in the fall of 2007, that does not mean they are out of the race for 2008. In fact, a strong potential independent campaign would recognize that an early entry would cause them to peak too early. Bloomberg-Hagel should keep quite until March or April 2008, after the Democratic and Republican nominations are set.

Former Governor Mike Huckabee

Like Bill Clinton, Mike Huckabee was born in Hope, Arkansas. The *Hotline* labeled him "an accidental governor."[1878] In July 1996, Arkansas was facing a constitutional crisis when Gov. Jim Guy Tucker had been convicted of federal charges and went back on his promise to resign quietly.[1879] But with the support of Democrats in the Legislature, Lieutenant Gov. Mike Huckabee—a Republican—threatened impeachment.[1880] Huckabee was minutes from taking the oath of office at the House chamber in Little Rock, when Tucker told Huckabee he decided to stay governor while appealing his conviction based on jury bias.[1881] But by the end of the day, July 15, 2004, Tucker decided to step down.[1882] When Tucker resigned, Huckabee became Arkansas's second Republican governor in 25 years, and only the third since reconstruction.[1883]

Huckabee is tied closely to religion. In 1989, he became the president of the Arkansas Baptist Convention, whose membership neared half a million.[1884] He was a Baptist minister for over a decade and his first book, *Character is the Issue*, talks of living a 'God-centered life.'[1885] As governor, Huckabee wrote to school superintendents reminding them students had a right to prayer.[1886]

Huckabee's record as governor

But was he the fervent right-wing moral conservative? Others argued he was a moderate. In his 2001 State of the State address he said he was pro life, "but I know not everyone agrees with me on that particular topic, and I respect that….in this day in which we talk about choice and the importance of it, surely we can agree that if under the Supreme Court choice is mandated, that choice should be as educated as is humanely possible."[1887] Huckabee is a Baptist minister, but not the 'fire and brimstone' preacher on the pulpit.

By 2004, he had significant bipartisan credibility on the Medicaid issue. Huckabee had touted his ARKids First plan in Arkansas, which provided health insurance for parents of children above Medicaid income limits (the state's working poor);[1888] but the plan required a small co-payment to avoid looking like a handout.[1889]

He was a successful governor and had a reputation of passing high profile legislation. In 1996, a conservation tax was passed to finance restoration of state parks.[1890] In 1997, came the ARKids First Program.[1891] In 1999, Huckabee "spearheaded a successful drive for public approval of a $1 billion reconstruction of hundreds of miles of interstate highways."[1892] The vote was just four years after a roads referendum endorsed by Jim Guy Tucker failed with only 20 percent support.[1893]

But there was a bump in the road when his wife, Janet, ran for Arkansas's Secretary of State in 2002 and lost 62-38.[1894]

The *Hotline* later said her ambitions were "responsible for his life-changing political bruises," and her run for Arkansas Sec. of State in 2002 "was savaged by Republicans in the state, and the relentless media coverage dragged down the governor's popularity and nearly threw his own re-election chances into jeopardy."[1895]

He recovered well, and stressed the obesity issue. He unveiled his "Healthy Arkansas" initiative in June 2004. His goal, as the *USA Today* reported a month later, was "to turn around a state that perennially ranks as one of the unhealthiest in the country by getting his citizens to exercise more, watch their weight and quit smoking. According to figures compiled by the Centers for Disease Control, nearly 8% of Arkansans suffer from diabetes; nearly 22% are considered obese and 26% smoke."[1896] In 2004, Arkansas became the first state to require schools to measure the body mass index (BMI) of students, and send the information (such as being overweight) to their parents.[1897] Huckabee even considered letting state employees use leftover sick days as vacation to improve healthy attitudes.[1898]

In considering a run in 2008, Huckabee did not seek re-election for governor in 2006, and launched his presidential campaign. Huckabee had a ripe situation looking into 2008. George Allen had imploded, Sam Brownback had little credibility beyond social issues, Romney was Mormon, Giuliani was far left on social issues, and McCain was still an unknown on whether he'd get the vote of the religious right.

Huckabee's conservative message is well thought out

He told *The Fix* (5.16.06) "Divorce is one of the key predictors of poverty for a child growing up in a home that's broken. Without making any judgments about the value or rightness or wrongness of it, it's an economic fact that when children are involved in a divorce they are more likely to end up spending part of their childhood in poverty than if they have a two-parent household."[1899]

Huckabee's logic in the public sphere was not based solely on religious pretexts or doctrine, in fact, what made Huckabee more moderate was that he used research and books to spark societal debate—not just his Baptist background. He talked about Robert Tubman's book *Bowling Alone,* a book marking societal shifts and the lack of community connections over time: "...there's a part of me that laments what we have lost, and that is a sense of community..."[1900] And he cited John Nesbit's book from a generation earlier, in *Mega Trends*: "...there really is a sense that he was very right, and that the more high tech we become, the more high touch we really need. Otherwise, we become very dehumanized."[1901] Though Huckabee did say people should not be politically forced to join civic clubs, but rather a matter of providing "the right sort of leadership and really create a climate in which people want to know their neighbors and want to feel a sense of responsibility and volunteerism."[1902]

He does, however, make it known religion is very important to his politics. "I would say that my faith has everything to do with my politics," said Huckabee (5.16.06), who also admitted "we've not been very good about depicting the Christian evangelical faith. We've done a lousy job, sometimes focusing more on what we seem to be against than what we're for. And I think that's our fault. I think we've done a lousy job of communicating warmth and heart. We've come across many times as being harsh and intolerant."[1903] Huckabee repeated similar comments in Iowa (July 2006), where he said "nothing would be more disingenuous for me to say than, 'I have faith, but I don't let it affect my politics.'"[1904]

But that faith is not limited to political issues of abortion. "I earn the right to push for a strong pro-life agenda only by making sure I'm concerned about poverty, hunger and homelessness. If I don't care about those issues, then my faith is incomplete."[1905] Huckabee continued, "At times people in my party scratch their heads and say, 'Why are you dealing with inadequate housing?' I say, 'How can you ignore that? Can you say as long as a kid didn't get aborted, heck, we don't care where he lives? Or as long as a kid didn't get aborted, we don't care if he gets an education? As long as we didn't abort the child, we don't care if he has access to health care?'"[1906]

Huckabee went after gay foster parents

The American Civil Liberties Union filed suit in 1999 challenging the Arkansas Child Welfare Review Board's regulation on behalf of four prospective foster parents.[1907] In late June 2006, the Arkansas Supreme Court unanimously struck down a ban on gay foster parents, and upheld a lower court's 2004 decision that threw out the ban.[1908] The Arkansas Child Welfare Board stopped the policy after the court defeat in 2004.[1909]

In Iowa, Huckabee was optimistic the Arkansas legislature would reinstate the ban on gay couples to foster parent, and equally upbeat that the court would uphold it.[1910] "Our attorneys read into that that if it was legislation it would likely stand, that we could in fact say that only married couples could be foster parents. We think that if we go back and codify that into law that probably takes care of it."[1911] Huckabee had legitimate hope in that the Court said officials went too far in imposing the ban, but, according to the *AP*, the court did not decide on the actual merit of such a ban.[1912] Still, the unanimous ruling said "the driving force behind the adoption of the regulations was not to promote the health, safety and welfare of foster children but rather based upon the board's view of morality and its bias against homosexuals."[1913] Huckabee said (July 2006) it would not have been struck down if it had been state law and not just a regulation, and the legislature would make it a law next year.[1914]

Huckabee's justification had concerns as well. "What I feared was going on was that the plaintiffs in this case were not as interested in foster children as they were in making the political point of homosexual activism....That's troubling that we would use children as a political tool to enact something that has nothing to do with the best interest of a foster child."[1915] So if the plaintiffs were not making a political issue of the case, then Huckabee would have sided with the plaintiffs? In addition, an equal argument would say Huckabee was using the children as a political tool. Was it better for a child to be in an orphanage all his childhood (for the sake of pandering to the religious right courtesy of Huckabee) or should children be allowed in a home of two caring adults? It was true,

Karl McCarty: *The Last One Standing* 173

however, that the four homosexuals who challenged the policy had not applied to be foster parents.[1916]

The court's ruling said the main force behind the regulation "was not to promote the health, safety and welfare of foster children."[1917]

An *AP* report quoted Huckabee in Iowa: "Marriage has historically never meant anything other than a man and a woman. It has never meant two men, two women, a man and his pet, or a man and a whole herd of pets," and activists "want to change rules that have been in place for thousands of years."[1918] So Huckabee equated homosexuality with bestiality?

But Huckabee did not support a constitutional amendment to ban gay marriage because "he'd rather see one affirm something [heterosexual marriage], rather than ban something else."[1919]

What were some of Huckabee's concerns?

Could Huckabee win the Republican nomination? He was nearing a decade as governor—one of the longest in the country as 2005 approached. Still, name recognition was a problem. But there are more pressing concerns for Huckabee '08.

1) He had trouble cracking the 'health' label. In 2005, he released *Quit Digging Your Grave With a Knife and Fork*, which focused on his 110 pound weight loss. Huckabee was very knowledgeable on health care, but the presidential candidate needed to have a broader appeal. The *Arkansas News Bureau* reported (7.16.07) if he ran for president, "it would be stoked in part by the national recognition he has received for his advocacy for healthy living after dropping 110 pounds to combat diseases."[1920]

Huckabee is much more than a 'health' candidate. He is a governor who can work with Democrats and whom independents can accept on social issues.

2) He has a weakness for accepting gifts. He reported $112,000 in gifts in 1999 (nearly 25% was clothes from one state appointee), and took $60,000 for speaking fees from a group he co-founded; he eventually responded with two lawsuits during an election year (one to receive more gifts, the other to halt the Ethics Commission from investigating himself).[1921] Still, lists of gifts were published in the media—even $70,000 of furniture from one political supporter, he then had to disown the furniture as his because of legal complications.[1922] A lawsuit "over Mansion practices" was settled without having to admit wrongdoing.[1923]

And the *Arkansas Times* reported over 50 out-of-state flights between January 1 and October 21, 2005 that appeared on the State Police Flight logs.[1924] Trips to Iowa were on the list, as well he and his wife's trip to Washington, D.C., in October 2005 to participate in the Marine Corps Marathon.[1925] This Marathon, of course, was a great benefit to Arkansas taxpayers.

3) His unique personality offers interesting quotes. The *Arkansas News Bureau* noted (July 2006) Huckabee had "been referred to as petty, egotistical, and thin-skinned, and questions have been raised about his ethics."[1926] Some in the Arkansas media referred to him as "The Huck."[1927]

What some saw as funny, others saw as tacky. The *Arkansas News Bureau* reported (7.16.06) critics had also accused "the governor of having an over-the-top sense of humor," noting the 7/11 quotes and a reference to Arkansas as a "banana republic in elections."[1928] In November 2005, Huckabee was asked about polls indicating Arkansans were split on the idea of Huckabee running for president and how serious he was about considering it. "Well...if I read that poll, I'd realize that what they'd like for me to do is lay down in the middle of the highway and they'd decide which side of me they'd run over, and I don't blame them."[1929] What? Then he added, "Democrats win when they talk and act like Republicans."[1930]

The jokes didn't stop there. Huckabee was a guest on *Late Edition* and was questioned about the 2005 elections. "...As bad a day as it may have appeared to be, I don't hear any Republican who's sitting in a tub of warm water with a handful of razor blades ready to say it's all over."[1931] In an online issue of *Washington Whispers* (June 2006), Huckabee was quoted with this line he had used elsewhere about his presidential ambitions: "I've got a map of 7-Elevens, a bunch of blue steel revolvers, and some ski masks. We're going to go all over the country and raise money in a very unique way."[1932]

At the Southern Republican Leadership Conference (Spring 2006), Huckabee said "The country was better off with Leave it to Beaver than Beavis and Butthead. We were better off when The Gideons gave Bibles to the fifth graders than when school nurses gave condoms to the sixth graders. We thought it was better for fathers to take their sons hunting than sons in urban areas hunting for their fathers."[1933]

In August 2007, Sen. Larry Craig (R-Idaho) troubles came to a boiling point and before it was over he said he would resign from the Senate by Sept. 30. Huckabee told *This Week* (9.2.07) Craig would have faced "a very, very challenging environment" if he had not decided to resign, then Huckabee quipped by an allusion to the toe-tapping signals Craig gave in airport restroom incident: "You might say we would be waiting until the other shoe dropped."[1934]

The Ames GOP Straw Poll

Republican only-straw polls had been held since 1979, and no candidate who skipped it won the caucus the next January.[1935] McCain and Giuliani skipped out, and Fred Thompson wasn't an official candidate yet when the Ames, Iowa Straw Poll was held August 11, 2007.

George W. Bush solidified his frontrunner status when he won with 7,418 votes in the 1999 straw poll, and defeated Steve Forbes.[1936] Huckabee likely had to place second in the 2007 straw poll to show he had some viable campaign organization.[1937] When Mitt Romney won the straw poll in August 2007, Huckabee, the second place finisher, was the candidate who came out on top. The final results: Romney placed first with 4,516 votes (31 percent), followed by Huckabee (18), Brownback (15), Tancredo (14), Paul (9), Tommy Thompson (7), then Fred Thompson, Giuliani, Hunter, and McCain rounded out the top 10.[1938]

Huckabee won Ames momentum

The media kindness after Huckabee's second place finish was obvious. Conservative columnist Bob Novak wrote: "Affable and sincere—and more important, seemingly harmless—Huckabee is treated well by the media that certainly don't share most of his views."[1939] David Gregory of *NBC News* said Romney won "as expected," "but Mike Huckabee is a big story…"[1940] Byron York of the *National Review* said "it was a really, really big win" for Huckabee.[1941] *NBC News* political director Chuck Todd said the "Huckabee story is amazing."[1942] Before Labor Day, Huckabee appeared on many news shows, including *Hannity & Colmes, The Colbert Report,* and *This Week*.

Huckabee's success was noteworthy. He had a negative ad run against him in the week before the straw poll by the Club for Growth, but didn't have any paid media for himself.[1943] While Brownback and Romney bused supporters in to the straw poll, Huckabee didn't buy a single bus.[1944] Margaret Carlson of *Bloomberg News* said Romney "was buying the Iowa straw poll," but Huckabee was winning the debates and "he got more votes than he bought tickets."[1945] Indeed, Romney spent $2 million to bus supporters in and paid $448 for each vote in the straw poll, while Huckabee spent $90,000 or $34 per person: "one dollar less than the $35 ticket price for the event."[1946]

Perhaps Huckabee is no longer a second tier GOP presidential candidate. At the very least, he is a credible vice presidential candidate.

Representative Duncan Hunter

Rep. Duncan Hunter announced his plans to run for president on October 30, 2006 on San Diego's Broadway Pier.[1947] Hunter was a Vietnam Veteran and Bronze Star recipient, and was strong advocate of border security, as "he played a leading role" in the 14-mile fence on the San Diego-Mexican border and co-authored the bill signed by President Bush in October 2006 to add 700 more miles of fencing on the Mexican border.[1948] He declared his candidacy at the age of 58, during his 13th term in the House; he represents the San Diego area.[1949] He first won his seat in 1980 with Ronald Reagan and upset a longtime Democratic incumbent, but has not faced a close race since.[1950] His declaration for an exploratory committee allowed him to raise money and organize right away.[1951] Hunter is leaving Congress. In March 2007, Duncan D. Hunter, 30, said he would run to replace his father.[1952]

Concerns with Hunter

1) Why did he announce his candidacy before the midterms? Hunter made his decision public eight days before the midterms.[1953] "This is going to be a long road, it's a challenging road, there's going to be some rough and tumble. But I think it's the right thing to do for our country."[1954] Mark Sandalow of the *San Francisco Chronicle*'s blog said, "Of course his timing can't be worse than" Dick Lugar's "carefully arranged presidential announcement" which came two hours after the Oklahoma City bombing.[1955] Both the Democratic and Republican national committees declined to comment on Hunter's candidacy because they were focusing on the midterms.[1956] But Hunter may have announced his bid in an effort to play a prominent role over Iraq, as he had become chairman of the House Armed Services Committee in 2003 and knew he was going to lose the spot—at least he could start raising money while still heading the committee.[1957] Hunter may have announced before the midterms so as not to appear he was running because he lost the chairmanship.

2) Name recognition was clearly an issue. The *AP* described him (10.30.06) as someone "known in the military's echelon for his congressional role but hardly a national name…" and "Analysts immediately characterized the quest as a long shot."[1958] *The Nation* posted the *AP*'s brief synopsis of a future announcement by Hunter and said "Who needs *The Onion* when you can find this report on the *AP* wire?"[1959] *Newsweek* too said "some analysts" were calling his announcement "ill timed and his bid a long shot."[1960] An *AP/ABC News* report (12.3.06) described him as a "long-shot candidate."[1961] *Reuters* said "His announcement took the Republican Party leadership by surprise."[1962] The *North County Times* (of San Diego and Riverside) caption said Hunter's intentions "left some political observers scratching their heads, others say it's far too early to say he won't be a factor in the presidential campaign..."[1963] Hunter himself said he made his decision just after traveling to Pennsylvania, New Hampshire, Connecticut, Arizona, and Oklahoma in October: "In typical Duncan Hunter fashion, I didn't consult with any Republican leaders."[1964] Perhaps he should have.

3) Hunter is the Republican Kucinich. Hunter was compared to Kucinich. In a *Washington Post* article titled, "Forget the Polls, Long Shot Says It's About the Message," the first sentence reported "For two people from opposing sides of the ideological spectrum," Kucinich and Hunter "have quite a bit in common."[1965] Both were presidential candidates, both believed their Iraq views were crucial to their campaigns, "And both are given virtually no chance to succeed."[1966] What drove them to run… "--ego? passion? something else?" asked the *Post*.[1967] They were teamed up with an "and" in six sentences…Kucinich *and* Hunter.[1968]

He is allied with the staunchest conservatives. His major endorsement is Ann Coulter, who has called Hunter her first choice for president.[1969] Coulter is a conservative author, who has suggested John and Elizabeth Edwards exploited their son's death (who died in a car wreck in 1996) for political gain. She also called John Edwards a faggot. Hunter has defended Coulter, stating "You know, I'm reminded of the debates between John Edwards and Dick Cheney in which John Edwards said some pretty personal things about Dick's family."[1970] So that legitimized Coulter's behavior?

4) Is Hunter a tax dodger? He hasn't paid all the taxes he should have. In October 2006 the *San Diego Union-Tribune* revealed Hunter's home was listed half its actual size, so he underpaid his taxes.[1971] Tax rolls listed the property as a two-bedroom, 2.5 bath house with 3,000 square feet of living space; but Hunter's insurance carrier said the house was actually 6,200 square feet of living space, it also included a 2,000 square foot guest house, pool, and tennis court.[1972] Hunter, who bought the house in 1994, said it was not his responsibility to make sure the records were correct: "All I know is what the county gives me."[1973] The house was destroyed in a 2003 wild fire, after which over two dozen homeowners told the county their properties were bigger than property records indicated.[1974]

5) Duncan Hunter loves broken jets. Duncan Hunter teamed up with Rep. Duke Cunningham in 1991 to write a letter to Defense Secretary Dick Cheney to end the "bureaucratic delays and get on with the DP-2 [plane] testing."[1975] Hunter has received over $35,000 in campaign donations from DuPont Aerospace, which started receiving government money for the DP-2 in 1988.[1976] DuPont said the plan would take off and land vertically, fly farther and faster, and have a higher capacity than comparable military aircraft; but *Copley News Service* noted, "For just as long, military officials have said it would never work as envisioned."[1977] Hunter defended the aircraft (6.12.07) and said the prototype represented "potential leap-ahead technology to support our Marines and Special forces," and asked for patience: "The idea around here that if the Pentagon doesn't come up with something, that if the services don't like it, you're not going to build it, is ridiculous."[1978] But at the very least, Hunter had supported this 'potential' for at least 16 years. At some point potential is no longer an excuse.

At the same subcommittee hearing in June 2007, Rep. Brad Miller (D-N.C) said the plan never received a positive technical review in over two decades.[1979] Hunter defended the use of earmarks (through the years the plane was given $63 million).[1980] DuPont gave Chris Cox, a former Congressman turned Securities Exchange Commission chair, $18,000 in donations, but even he had now conceded to *ABCNews.com* that the project should have been abandoned.[1981] Hunter defended himself by labeling the ABC report "a cheap shot."[1982]

Copley News Service reported (6.13.07), "The consensus of the expert witnesses [in 2003] was that the aircraft was nowhere near delivering on the promises cited by DuPont and its Congressional supporters," and included the quote from an aerospace engineer who called DP-2 "a pipe dream."[1983] The DP-2 had troubles in flight tests more than once, including a hard landing in 2003 and "engineering deficiencies" in 2004.[1984] A blogger commented on Signonsandiego.com:

> The most telling comment in the article was Hunter didn't understand the scientific principles that he was made aware of years ago that showed this jet was a joke. I guess when you don't 'believe' in evolution and you do believe that preemptive wars make us all safer, you probably don't have the mental capacity to understand the engineering of a jet, even if you tell them real slow.[1985]

The planes aren't the first instance of wasteful spending. Hunter also pushed the Navy to buy $27 million worth of Titan missiles that didn't fly correctly.[1986]

6) Hunter: Duke Cunningham's best friend. Duncan Hunter and Randy 'Duke' Cunningham were two California Congressmen who were very close friends in good times and bad.

Cunningham was sentenced March 3, 2006, in which the judge gave the defendant eight years and four months for bribery and tax evasion.[1987] Defense contactor Brent Wilkes was the one bribing Cunningham, and the CIA's No. 3 man (until the spring of 2006), Kyle Foggo, was also indicted in February 2007.[1988] Foggo and Wilkes were incredibly close: they attended the same high school, were roommates in college, best man in each other's weddings, and each named their sons after each other.[1989]

Wilkes, founder of defense contractor ADCS, contributed over $800,000 to 32 House members and candidates, and flew Republicans on his private jet.[1990] Founded in 1995, ADCS received over $90 million in government contracts.[1991] Wilkes' foundation gave Cunningham an award in 2002 (the event was called a 'Salute to Heroes') and Hunter in 2003.[1992] Wilkes spent more than $600,000 on Cunningham.[1993] Legally, Wilkes donated at least $35,000 to Hunter's campaign.[1994] According to *USA Today* (11.29.05), Wilkes and ADCS contributed $40,700 to Hunter since 1994.[1995] When the bribery scandal started unveiling in late 2005, Hunter gave a similar amount of money to a Marines charity.[1996]

In November 2005, *USA Today* reported Hunter "acknowledged that he joined with Cunningham in 1999 to contact Pentagon officials who reversed a decision and gave ADCS one of its first big contracts, for nearly $10 million. Hunter's spokesman, Joe Kasper, said the congressman was unavailable for

Karl McCarty: *The Last One Standing* 179

comment Tuesday."[1997] In late 2005, Hunter said, "Our job as San Diego congressmen is to do our best to make sure our guys get a fair shot, and Brent Wilkes and Tom Casey [the founder of Audre Inc., which specialized in automated document conversion systems] were aggressive and enthusiastic promoters of a breakthrough technology."[1998]

Where Wilkes made most of his money was through the Defense Department's purchase of his document conversion systems. Some argued the document conversion was a joke. In 1997, John McCain criticized the document conversion program pushed by Hunter and Cunningham: "…With military training exercises continuing to be cut, backlogs in aircraft and ship maintenance, flying hour shortfalls, military health care underfunded by $600 million, and 11,787 service members reportedly on food stamps," McCain questioned the funding of "a plethora of programs not requested by the Defense Department."[1999] *Copley News Service* concluded (12.4.05) "McCain was largely ignored."[2000] And before the end of 1997, Congress earmarked $20 million for document conversion systems, then even more in 1998, including an ADCS' project worth almost $10 million to digitize Panama Canal Zone documents to be handed to Panama in 1999.[2001]

How did Hunter and Cunningham sell the Panama project? They warned China might try to take over Panama once the US left, so the US needed to have blueprints of the buildings in Panama should the Chinese take over the tiny country.[2002] Even Wilkes argued ADCS used the most expensive technology to scan engineering drawings from the 1870s.[2003] These earmarks allowed Wilkes to live a life of luxury, including a $1.5 million home in his home state of California, and a second town house in the suburbs of Washington D.C.[2004] And then Wilkes used his corporate jet and took Cunningham for several out-of-state trips.[2005]

There were suggestions Hunter was going to be charged also in the scandal, but it did not happen.[2006] By early 2006, the Department of Justice was looking at information stretching back to 1997, and were looking at Hunter and Rep. Jerry Lewis (R-CA).[2007] All 28 Democrats on the House Armed Services Committee banded together to push Hunter, the chairman, to reinstate a special subcommittee dedicated to oversight and investigating the Pentagon, but Hunter resisted the idea.[2008]

Hunter has remained a friend until the end, as his spokesman, Joe Kasper, said, "Congressman Hunter does not condone Mr. Cunningham's actions, nor has he tried to defend them…Congressman Hunter is a close friend of Mr. Cunningham's, and friends don't abandon each other during times of difficulty."[2009] The *North County Times* also said Hunter "was the only elected official to appear at Cunningham's sentencing in March [2006] and continues to stay in touch with the convicted lawmaker, efforts he says he continues out of friendship and compassion for his former colleague."[2010]

Vote Duncan Hunter in 2008: the quintessential candidate for the military industrial complex.

Has Hunter opened his doors?
 Will Hunter continue to be associated with corruption? An *AP* report said (10.30.06) he was "a close ally" Rep. Randy 'Duke' Cunningham (D-CA), as Hunter accepted over $40,000 in donations from the same contractor of the Cunningham scandal.[2011] This was backed up by the *North County Times* (11.4.06): "Hunter, like Cunningham, took thousands of dollars in campaign contributions from defense contractors Mitchell Wade of Washington and Poway's Brent Wilkes, two men at the heart of the Cunningham influence-peddling case. Starting in the 1990s and continuing until last year, Hunter received a combined $46,000 from Wilkes, Wade and their associates."[2012]

 Hunter does not shy away from what others see as scandal. In some cases he invites it. In South Carolina (December 2006), three Democratic-affiliated students asked about ties to a defense contractor [Brent Wilkes] identified as a co-conspirator in Cunningham's bribery case, and suggested Hunter tried to cover up Abu Ghraib to avoid embarrassing the Titan-Corp (based in San Diego) which had interpreters at the prison.[2013] The students also said an Armed Services Committee staffer slipped a provision in a military authorizations bill that affronted an inspector general's uncovering of corruption in the reconstruction of Iraq.[2014] Hunter denied all three allegations, and said the Cunningham question was made by a staffer of a South Carolina congressman; and after the speech posed for pictures with the students.[2015] Hunter said of his knowledge of Wilkes: "When you open up the doors to a fundraiser and five or six or seven hundred folks come in, you don't have a crystal ball that tells which ones are going to have a problem five or 10 or 15 years off in the future."[2016]

 Hunter's 2008 campaign doesn't run away from Cunningham. In the news section of Hunter's presidential website, the coverage of the May GOP debate brought up the Cunningham scandal:

> Unfortunately, Hunter did not have the opportunity to respond [to] some questions. For example, he could have pointed out [in the debate] that the incidents of corruption among some Republican politicians—including his friend Duke Cunningham—were all investigated and prosecuted by a Republican Justice Department. Furthermore, political corruption is not unique to the Republicans and the very fact that the question was asked was indicative of the liberal bias of MSNBC, Politico.com, and Chris Matthews.[2017]

 So the fact that the Justice Department was controlled by Republicans meant Hunter was cleared? Wouldn't that suggest he might have gotten away with something?

Hunter's strengths
 1) Was there a job he wanted besides the presidency? The *North County Times* reported Hunter may have been using a presidential bid "to continue to put his own imprint on the debate over national security and the U.S. presence in Iraq and Afghanistan. Or he could be positioning himself for a 2008 vice presidency nomination or a Cabinet post such as defense secretary should the GOP retain the White House in 2008."[2018]

But Hunter's view of politics has been turned upside down. The *National Journal* noted (7.30.07) he "used to matter when he was a House chairman. This presidential campaign must be humbling."[2019]

2) Immigration remained a key issue, especially for the Republican base in the late spring of 2007. Hunter's announcement had to stifle Tom Tancredo supporters. Tancredo had an apparent immigration-based relationship with George Allen, and after the midterms Allen wouldn't carry the Tancredo beliefs in a presidential race. Hunter could. The *LA Times* described him (10.31.06) as "a hard-liner on illegal immigration."[2020] At his announcement, Hunter said "We are going to carry our message of a strong national defense and strong national borders…" to voters.[2021] *Reuters* reported Hunter's support for the 700 mile fence bill: "The legislation was popular with conservatives favoring a strong approach to illegal immigration. Another conservative activist who favors a tough approach to illegal immigration, Rep. Tom Tancredo of Colorado, is considering a presidential bid."[2022]

The *National Review*'s Jonah Goldberg said "If immigration weren't such a huge issue, it's inconceivable that the idea [of running for president] would have occurred to him. Hunter is dismissed by liberal critics, but a responsible political class would recognize the danger that the kindling of immigration could become a bonfire if ignored."[2023] In a visit to New Hampshire in January 2007, he asked the 700 mile fence be immediately constructed, as "Good fences make for good neighbors," and said the San Diego fence reduced drug trafficking over the border by 90 percent and cut the city's crime rate in half.[2024]

The problem is Tancredo and Hunter split the staunch anti-immigration vote. Hunter would be much more satisfied with his efforts if Tancredo stopped his campaign.

In a late June 2007 CNN nationwide poll, Hunter received less than one percent and scored as much as Jim Gilmore.[2025] His ninth place finish at the Iowa Straw Poll was embarrassing: he finished behind Fred Thompson and Giuliani, both did not enter the straw poll. But Tancredo, finished fourth with 14 percent.[2026] At this pace, Hunter will be out of the 2008 picture before Tancredo.

Senator John McCain

John S. McCain III was born in 1936 in the Panama Canal Zone.[2027] A Prisoner Of War (POW) for five years in Vietnam, he led a social-studies class for his fellow men in captivity.[2028]

He was elected to the House in 1982 and served two terms.[2029] First elected to the Senate in 1986, McCain was reelected overwhelmingly in the 2004 election. But the 2000 presidential campaign catapulted McCain to one of the elite Senators in the country. He gave George W. Bush a scare in the primaries with a victory (49-31) in New Hampshire. McCain was the anti-establishment candidate, but critics argued McCain became—and would remain—a media darling. McCain's consultant Mike Murphy, later called the press "our constituency."[2030] Only four Senate colleagues endorsed him in 2000: Jon Kyl (AZ), Mike DeWine (OH), Fred Thompson (TN) and Chuck Hagel (NE).[2031] With McCain struggling with religious conservatives, Bush won the South Carolina primary, after which McCain spoke in Virginia Beach, Virginia, attacking the Religious Right and labeled Bush "a Pat Robertson Republican who will lose to Al Gore."[2032]

Kerry-McCain '04

In 2000, Bush supporters spread rumors in South Carolina that McCain was insane, and he fathered a black child.[2033] He and his wife Cindy adopted a Bangladesh girl.[2034] To say 'animosity' split McCain and Bush in 2000 was an understatement. And McCain may have considered bolting the GOP when the Senate was divided 50-50, before Jim Jeffords (then R-VT) dodged the party and made the move first in 2001.[2035] Still, even up to 2004, McCain was a maverick, as seen by the possiblity he would be on the Kerry 2004 ticket. The *New York Times* reported (5.15.04) in an article titled "Undeterred by McCain Denials, Some See Him as Kerry's No. 2:"

> …. Despite weeks of steadfast rejections from Senator John McCain, some prominent Democrats are angling for him to run for vice president alongside Senator John Kerry, creating a bipartisan ticket that they say would instantly transform the presidential race. 'Senator McCain would not have to leave his party,' [former Democratic Senator Bob] Kerrey said. 'He could remain a Republican, would be given some authority for selection of Cabinet people. The only thing he would have to do is say, "I'm not going to appoint any judges who would overturn Roe v. Wade,"'….[2036]

Joe Biden supported the two party ticket on *Meet the Press* (5.16.04):

> I think John McCain would be a great candidate for vice president. I mean it. I know John doesn't like me saying it, but the truth of the matter is, it is. We need to heal the red and the blue here, man, the red states and the blue states. And John McCain is a loyal Republican. God, he drives me crazy how loyal he is as a Republican as much of a friend as he is. We disagree on a lot of things, but I'll tell you, the fact of the matter is that we've got to bring together the red and the blue here. This is a divided nation. And I think that--I would still urge John Kerry to pick up the phone and call John McCain. He'll say no probably. But I think John Kerry has an obligation to do that for the way he wants to heal. And I know John will listen. He'll say no, but I'm going to tell you, I'm counting on him being a more loyal American than he is a loyal Republican.
> And, John, I'm not so sure you're so happy about the Senate. I'd like to see you president instead of the guy we have now. So--but you're a great senator. But I think you'd also be

doing a great service. Do I think it's going to happen? No. But I think it is a reflection of the desire of this country, and the desire of people in both parties, to want to see this God-awful, vicious rift that exists in the nation healed, and John and John could go a long way to healing that rift.[2037]

McCain said, on the same program, "I will always take anyone's phone calls but I will not--I categorically will not do it. But I would like to add one additional quick comment. Joe's right, there's too much partisanship in America and there's too much partisanship in the Senate..."[2038]

McCain was cordial to John Kerry in the 2004 campaign, and Kerry even considered McCain to be his running mate. But McCain also made comments against the Massachusetts Senator. When asked if Kerry was accurate in claiming Osama bin Laden's video released in the last days of the campaign cost the Democrats a victory, McCain said "No. I believe that the Democrats at their convention failed to give a coherent message."[2039]

A loyal Bush supporter

McCain appeared on *Meet the Press* in November 2004. He said the U.S. needed "at least 40,000 or 50,000 more" troops in Iraq, and cited Gen. McCaffrey belief that the Army should be increased by 80,000 and the Marines by 20,000 to 30,000.[2040] He acknowledged "mistakes" were made at the beginning of the conflict, but "Every war, there are terrible mistakes made. The key is to fix them...and I believe that we've done a lot of things better."[2041] His stalwart support for the war had already been parlayed at the Republican Convention in August 2004, when he gave his support to the President's decision to go to war:

> Our choice wasn't between a benign status quo and the bloodshed of war. It was between war and a graver threat. Don't let anyone tell you otherwise. Not our critics abroad. Not our political opponents. And certainly not a disingenuous film maker who would have us believe that Saddam's Iraq was an oasis of peace when in fact it was a place of indescribable cruelty, torture chambers, mass graves and prisons that destroyed the lives of the small children held inside their walls. Whether or not Saddam possessed the terrible weapons he once had and used, freed from international pressure and the threat of military action, he would have acquired them again.[2042]

He then ended the speech with unequivocal support for the president: "Do not yield. Do not flinch. Stand up. Stand up with our President and fight. We're Americans. We're Americans, and we'll never surrender. They will."[2043]

In 2000, he was upset when Sam and Charles Wyly, a pair of pro-Bush Texas businessmen, spent $2.5 million "on a nominally independent advertising effort" against McCain.[2044] McCain at the time called them the "Wyly coyotes," and said to "tell them to keep their dirty money in the state of Texas."[2045] But by 2006, McCain accepted their money as they gave Straight Talk America PAC (political action committee) at least $20,000, and helped chair a Dallas fund-raiser for the PAC.[2046] The money was later returned because the brothers became part of a federal investigation,[2047] but it showed how accomodating McCain had become.

Why did McCain appear in *Wedding Crashers*?

John McCain appeared in the R-rated comedy *Wedding Crashers* which debuted July 15, 2005. The film included half-naked women, fondling under the kitchen table, and a grandma calling Eleanor Roosevelt a lesbian. McCain's scene was a cameo appearance with Democratic strategist James Carville, who both attend a Washington D.C. wedding. McCain's cameo was less than a minute and was neither funny nor pertinent to the plot. Having criticized the film industry in the past (though McCain's hearings focused more on violence—not sex),[2048] why did McCain appear in the film? In contrast, *Reuters* reported (7.14.05) how Hillary Clinton had recently "asked the U.S. Federal Trade Commission to investigate the origins of a downloadable modification that allows simulated sex in the personal computer version" of *Grand Theft Auto: San Andreas*.[2049]

He tried to joke off his connections in the movie, telling Jay Leno he "works with boobs every day."[2050] (Leno more than just interviewed McCain, and took him for a spin in a Corvette from his car collection.)[2051] Could McCain just push away this movie incident? On July 24, McCain said he was told the movie was going to be rated PG.[2052] McCain thought a movie called *Wedding Crashers* was going to be rated PG?

More ironic was his previous statement he gave on *Meet the Press* (11.21.04): "I think a lot of Americans are very uneasy…with some of the things they see on television, some of the fare that their children are exposed to…I do know that there's great discomfort out there amongst many people who want to raise their children in what they view as a healthy environment and they don't think that that's the case now with a lot of the stuff that's in the entertainment business."[2053]

McCain appeared on *Imus in the Morning* on July 20. He recognized that "some people that said that I shouldn't have been in the movie because it's R-rated and that I had been critical of R-rated movies. I've never been critical of the rating system or R-rated movies. A couple years ago, as I might remember, the— Hollywood was marketing R-rated movies to children, and, you know, that was a bad practice. We had hearings. They said they would stop, and as far as I know, they have stopped doing that. But look, you know, you can be attacked for most anything, and this is just another one.[2054] But just because McCain never had been critical of the rating system or R-rated movies, did that make it okay for him to be in an R-rated comedy? Don Imus told McCain "we want you to be president. Stop doing this stupid stuff, OK?"[2055]

McCain, Falwell & the Religious Right

McCain had long been an opponent to pork-fattened spending bills, a route that would continue to align McCain with fiscal conservatives. But some phrases were never forgotten, and whether McCain could heal the division between himself and the Jerry Falwell/Pat Robertson crowd (despite being consistently pro-life thru the years) remained to be seen.

His *Meet the Press* interview (4.2.06) was introduced by a 2000 quote from McCain: "Governor Bush is a Pat Robertson Republican who will lose to Al Gore."[2056] Later in the interview, another 2000 quote was shown: "Governor Bush swung far to the right and sought out the base support of Pat Robertson and Jerry Falwell…those aren't the ideas that I think are good for the Republican

Party."[2057] But when asked if he still believed Jerry Falwell was still an agent of intolerance, McCain said no.[2058] This was followed by a clip of Falwell comments on 9/11: "I really believe that the pagans, and the abortionists and the feminists, and the gays and lesbians who are actively trying to make that an alternative...I point the finger in their face and say, 'You helped this happen.'"[2059] McCain planned a trip to Falwell's Liberty College (5.13.06).[2060] Was McCain overreaching to his base?

In the summation of all of the above, McCain's stretch for the base support seemed a bit sappy. Jon Stewart asked McCain to appear on *The Daily Show* for the sole purpose to explain why he was visiting Jerry Falwell. McCain's interview was introduced to viewers with a picture of the Senator titled "Citizen McCain"—a direct reference to *Citizen Kane*.[2061] Stewart said he heard a "crazy story" that McCain was giving such a commencement. McCain said "Well, before I bring on my two lawyers....", Stewart said (smirking begrudgingly) "...don't make me love you."[2062] McCain said he also talked to Ivy League schools who don't allow military recruiters—i.e., he had spoken to a lot of schools "whose specific policies I may disagree with."[2063] Stewart asked if McCain was "going into crazy [political] base world."[2064] "I'm afraid so," said McCain while smirking.[2065] "When you see Falwell, do you feel nervous, do you have vomit in the back of your throat—what does if feel like?" asked Stewart.[2066] McCain had answered a serious question from his liberal and independent supporters by respectfully laughing off questions on Jerry Falwell. And how many social conservatives were watching *The Daily Show*?

Nor was it as if Falwell gave nothing in return. Falwell himself said he wanted no part of the 2000 anti-McCain offensive: "We weren't opposed to John McCain in 2000. We were more supporters of George Bush."[2067] and decided in the fall of 2005 it was time to reconcile.[2068] Bill Frist was scheduled to speak at Liberty in October 2006.[2069] Moreover, critics seemingly attacked McCain for uniting with Falwell while forgetting no reunion had occurred between McCain and Pat Robertson. In addition, McCain may have been pacifying the Religious Right's potential discontent than courting it. Why May 2006? McCain must have wanted his Falwell flip-flop sooner than later. But even Ted Kennedy said the idea of McCain "going down there" was "constructive and positive."[2070]

McCain's chief political advisor, Mike Weaver, said McCain was in between two story lines in the previous several months: "One is that he's not conservative enough to win the Republican nomination. The other is he's increasingly becoming too popular among conservatives and, gosh, we don't like that."[2071]

McCain still stated (4.2.06) "I don't have to agree with everything they [Christian Conservatives] stand for."[2072] The Falwell story was reported as a blatant strategy for moderate appeal: "in a hat trick designed to show both his political courage and wide appeal," McCain announced his scheduled commencement speeches not only for conservative Liberty University, but also former Sen. Bob Kerrey's (Democrat) New School University and Ohio State

University (Ohio being the battleground toss-up of 2004). Likewise, advisors said the Falwell controversy would fade by the summer when McCain would vote against a constitutional amendment barring same-sex marriage. For example, liberal columnist Paul Krugman ranted on McCain's ties to Falwell (a "kingmaker of today's Republican Party") but forgot to mention McCain had not repaired his relationship with Pat Robertson.[2073]

Concerns for McCain

1) **The moral conservatives still hate him.** McCain made up with Falwell, but the Baptist minister died in the spring of 2007. Leader of Focus on the Family, James Dobson said, "I would not vote for John McCain under any circumstances...and I pray that we won't get stuck with him."[2074] McCain said, "I'm obviously disappointed and I'd like to continue and have a dialogue with Dr. Dobson and other members of the community."[2075] On *Meet the Press* (1.21.07), he said "no" when asked if he would reach out to Dobson.[2076]

McCain's personal life included affair and divorce. According to Nicholas Kristof of the *New York Times*, McCain was married and living with his wife in 1979 when he "aggressively" courted a twenty-five year old who was quite wealthy.[2077] McCain divorced his wife and began his political career with his new wife's family fortune.[2078] Unlike Giuliani and Gingrich, McCain's offense occurred years before his pinnacle. In the 2000 campaign, Dr. James Dobson made a point of McCain's past that is was "reminiscent" of Bill Clinton's, and "The Senator is being touted by the media as a man of principle, yet he was involved with other women while married to his first wife."[2079] McCain had once said of his first marriage that "People wouldn't think so highly of me if they knew more about that."[2080] Dobson was more forgiving of Newt Gingrich for having an affair during Clinton's impeachment.

McCain has struggled with the gay marriage issue. On *Hardball* (10.18.06), McCain said "I think that gay marriage should be allowed, if there's a ceremony kind of thing, if you want to call it that. I don't have any problem with that, but I do believe in preserving the sanctity of a union between man and woman."[2081] Then, after a few minutes and multiple topics, McCain said "Could I just mention one other thing? On the issue of the gay marriage, I believe that people want to have private ceremonies, that's fine. I do not believe that gay marriages should be legal," to which boos came from the crowd at Iowa State University.[2082]

With Chris Matthews, Todd Purdum of *Vanity Fair* surmised the awkwardness of McCain's earlier appearance on *Hardball*:

> You [Chris Matthews] asked him a question, given the Mark Foley scandal, about the kind of prevalence of gay people in all walks of life and whether he thought there should be gay marriage. And he [McCain] began to answer, apparently quite openly, that he thought if people wanted to have a marriage ceremony, he was looking for a word, I had sensed, like commitment ceremony or civil union. He couldn't quite find it. But he basically said, "If people want to go off and have something they call a marriage, that's OK, but I believe in the sanctity of the union between a man and a woman." At the next commercial break, his adviser, John Weaver (ph), went up and talked to him. You guys

were making a move down on to the floor of the auditorium....And in his first answer after the break, which was about agriculture subsidies, he suddenly interrupted himself and said, "Could I just say one other thing about gay marriage? I don't think it should be legal." And the whole audience booed. These were kids, you know, from [Iowa]...[2083]

Purdum's *Vanity Fair* article noted McCain's second, later comments on gay marriage in the *Hardball* interview came "out of nowhere."[2084] And "Moments later, McCain remounts the stage for the program's final segment, and he bores into Weaver, standing quietly in the wings, with a cold look that seems to mingle irritation at Weaver's whispered advice with regret that he took it, and demands, almost hisses, 'Did I fix it? Did I fix it?'"[2085]

McCain has reaffirmed (11.19.06) "I'm not against civil Unions," and said, "no" when asked if homosexuality was a sin.[2086] In the 2006 midterms, Arizona became the first state ever to reject a ban on same-sex marriages.[2087] Chuck Todd, participating in a discussion with Purdum on *Hardball* concluded, "frankly, if he can't win Iowa, he probably can't win the nomination," and "He's got to be against" gay marriage.[2088]

So why does McCain appease the social conservatives? A former aide told *Vanity Fair* that "Yes, he's a social conservative, but his heart isn't in this stuff but he has to pretend [that it is], and he's not a good enough actor to pull it off. He just can't fake it well enough."[2089] And he was unwilling to impose his beliefs on religion, sexuality, and abortion on others .[2090]

Todd Purdum concluded, "McCain's own compromises in pursuit of the presidency may be necessary, even justified."[2091] McCain's ambitions was like Gov. Jack Stanton in *Primary Colors* talking to aide questioning the compromises of their campaign: "You don't think Abraham Lincoln was a whore before he was a president? He had to tell his little stories and smile his shit-eating, backcountry grin. He did it all just so he'd get the opportunity, one day, to stand in front of the nation and appeal to 'the better angels of our nature.' That's when the bullshit stops. And that's what this is all about."[2092]

2) McCain often speaks off the cuff. He also had his own sense of frankness—to make the unexpected, expected. In 2001, after discussing Rep. Tom Delay's opposition to McCain-Feingold, radio host Don Imus suggested he "wouldn't have been surprised to see Tom Delay" in Waco, Texas with David Koresh, a cult leader killed with 80 of his followers in 1993. [2093] "Well, you know," replied McCain laughing, "he's a previous – I think he was an exterminator in a previous life."[2094]

An August 2006 edition of *Esquire* said, "McCain has the peculiar habit of expressing affection with invectives, starting with jerk, rising on up through crazy bastard" and culminating with a word the *Arizona Daily Star* said "we can't print."[2095] Lindsey Graham told *Esquire* "If he's not calling you terrible names, he doesn't like you."[2096]

Vanity Fair (Feb.2007) quoted McCain with the liberal *New York Times* reporter: "This is Adam Nagourney, *New York Times*. They're a Communist paper, but he's O.K."[2097] He told the story of going to the Grand Canyon with his teenage son and a park ranger offered him some pills: "'It was—am I saying this right?—I.V. Propen. The stuff's a fucking miracle drug!' It doesn't seem fair to tell him the drug is nothing more miraculous than Advil. McCain will repeat the ibuprofen story a time or two over the course of 48 hours, and he brings it up again when I see him about a month later."[2098]

None of the above comments compares to his comment on Chelsea Clinton. In 1998, McCain told a Republican Senate fundraiser, "Why is Chelsea Clinton so ugly? Because her father is Janet Reno."[2099] The *Washington Post* said the joke "was too vicious to print."[2100] Maureen Dowd of the *New York Times* said McCain was "so revered by the press that his disgusting jape was largely nudged under the rug."[2101]

3) McCain is weathered. Age is still an issue, but he addressed naysayers, and said he would tell skeptics (11.19.06), that "I'm older than dirt and I have more scars than Frankenstein but I've learned a few things along the way and I'd like them to meet my 94 year old mother who just returned from France..."[2102] A *Vanity Fair* article, written by Todd Purdam in the beginning of 2007 also quoted McCain's line "as old as dirt, with more scars than Frankenstein."[2103] The article did a great job humanizing McCain, who was...

> ...visibly older, thinner, balder—and, yes, frailer—than he was just six years ago. Like his friend Bob Dole, he tries to minimize his disabilities, but they are serious. He suffered severe injuries when his plane was shot down over North Vietnam 40 years ago; his right knee was broken when his seat was ejected from the cockpit, and both arms were broken in the crash. These injuries were compounded by the profound abuse he endured during five and a half years in captivity.
> McCain seldom talks about the details of his torture by the North Vietnamese, but he has written about them in clinical depth. Despite the injuries he had already suffered, upon capture he was promptly bayoneted in the ankle and then beaten senseless. The North Vietnamese never set either of his broken arms. The only treatment of his broken knee involved cutting all the ligaments and cartilage, so that he never had more than 5 to 10 percent flexion during the entire time he was in prison. In 1968 he was offered early release, and when he refused, because others had been there longer, his captors went at him again; he suffered cracked ribs, teeth broken off at the gum line, and torture with ropes that lashed his arms behind his back and that were progressively tightened all through the night. Ultimately he taped a coerced confession. McCain's right knee still has limited flexibility. Most of the time this is not too noticeable...[2104]

President Bush once asked McCain if he wanted to work out with him; McCain said he physically could not work out; Bush said "What do you mean?"[2105] He also has to lather his face with sunblock.,[2106] because of his reoccurance of skin cancer.

Todd Purdam suggested McCain was repetitive behind the scenes and occasionally told the same stories.[2107] McCain told *Vanity Fair* how Reagan told him the same stories years apart at a similar White House function, though McCain said unlike Reagan, McCain shared "the same stories all the time" because he liked them.[2108] Nonetheless, in the two years before the midterms, McCain had 346 appearances around the country for Republicans.[2109]

4) Is McCain too harsh for international relations? In the summer of 2006, the *Washingtonian* ranked McCain second for "Hottest Temper" second only to Ted Stevens.[2110] Do his frustrations spill into issues of diplomacy?

In February 2005, McCain called for Russia to be excluded from the G8 summit (The Gathering of the 8 countries, in general the most economically powerful). McCain appeared on *FOX News Sunday* the following week and continued his criticisms of Russian President Vladimir Putin, and said he was "acting somewhat like a spoiled child," and that "every step he takes seems to be headed toward a restoration of the Russian empire."[2111] Does a strong president make those public comments on Russia?

McCain said "we should not include Russia in the G8" and he "would probably" boycott the meeting in July 2006 [if he was in the position to be invited]: "the repression of his own people; the recent elections in Belarus that he has been supporting the most Stalinistic dictator in Europe; interference in Ukraine; …the repression of…a free press and the autocracy; the restoration of the Russian empire; and, very seriously, the failure so far to really cooperate with us in addressing the threat of Iranian acquisition of nuclear weapons."[2112] It succinctly summarized his opinion on Russia and Putin, who McCain said was "certainly an autocrat who is seeking the consolidation of power with his old buddies from the KGB."[2113]

Dick Cheney accused (5.4.06) Russia of using energy reserves as "tools of intimidation or blackmail," and warned Russia it had "a choice to make. And there is no question that a return to democratic reform in Russia will generate future success for its people and greater respect among fellow nations."[2114]

McCain (5.7.06) said he was "very pleased with his [Cheney's] comments," as he listed the evidence of the Soviet restoration, including Belarus' "Stalinistic dictator named Lukashenko."[2115] McCain noted Lieberman and McCain's proposal for Bush to avoid the G-8 summit in St. Petersburg: "I believe it's important that he [Bush] tell Putin, 'Look, you are now making yourself ineligible for entry into the WTO [World Trade Organization]. But most of all, you've got responsibilities of a democracy, not just try[ing] to get all the benefit[s].' They've cut off the wine imports from Moldova and Georgia, and they want to be members of the WTO."[2116] McCain said he respected the President's decision, but said avoiding St. Petersburg for the G-8 is "what I would do."[2117] Yet even Colin Powell said (spring 2006) Bush told him of Vladimir Putin, 'I have looked in his eyes and I have seen his soul'; Powell said "I looked in his eyes and I still see the KGB."[2118]

When the G8 finally arrived, it was Putin's jab at Bush over Iraq that might have been the event of the meeting. Speaking to the audience from separate podiums, Bush said "I talked about my desire to promote institutional change in parts of the world, like Iraq, where there's a free press and free religion. And I told him [Putin] that a lot of people in our country would hope that Russia will do the same thing. I fully understand, however, that there will be a Russian-style democracy."[2119] Putin said "We certainly would not want to have [the] same kind of democracy as they have in Iraq, quite honestly."[2120] Caught off guard, Bush said "just wait."[2121]

Would McCain's rhetoric have changed the US relationship with Russia for the better? He is not different with other realms of the world. Campaigning in the midterms, McCain called Kim Jong Ill a "pip squeak in platform shoes."[2122]

5) McCain was slipping. *Time* said (12.10.06), "For McCain, the biggest potential threats at the moment (12.10.06) appear to be…Romney, who is getting good buzz on the right but is largely unknown even to Republicans," and…Giuliani, "who comes out ahead of McCain in many polls but has yet to begin building much of a campaign operation."[2123] By early 2007, his major threat was clearly his support for the president's surge on Iraq. Then by the spring, Fred Thompson, an endorser of McCain 2000, was slowly entering the race.

Before the massive exodus of members of Team McCain, McCain had already fallen in the polls. McCain was low on cash and momentum. In July 2007, Terry Nelson and John Weaver, McCain's top advisors, were fired. And more staffers kept jumping ship. *US News* said McCain was "broke, with less money than GOP presidential contender Ron Paul. Ridiculous."[2124] Here was the self-proclaimed fiscal conservative weary of earmarks and pork "who paid too little attention to his own bloated operation."[2125] Then a co-chair to John McCain's Florida campaign, state representative Bob Allen, was arrested for allegedly soliciting oral sex from a policeman in Florida (7.11.07). [2126]

Stephen Colbert said (7.19.07), "I believe the McCain Campaign now consists of the senator, his wife, and this guy they picked up hitch-hiking."[2127] Jay Leno said (7.18.07), "I don't want to say McCain's campaign is broke, but today he held a rally at the 99-cent store."[2128] A week later Leno suggested, "A cat in a nursing home in Providence, Rhode Island, can predict patient's deaths. They say the cat will walk through and curl up next to a patient, and within four hours the patient dies....Today, the cat curled up next to the John McCain campaign."[2129]

Hope remains for the old McCain

McCain said (4.25.07), "I'd remind you, in 1999, at this particular time, I was at 3 percent in the polls. With a 5 percent margin of error, we could have been at minus 2."[2130] Perhaps, Giuliani's lead in the polls was a good thing. For example, Hillary Clinton may have chased Obama (literally, in Selma Alabama for a civil rights march earlier in 2007), but McCain let Giuliani lead. As a sitting duck, social conservatives, in due time, could rip apart America's Mayor. Patience may be McCain's biggest asset.

In August 2007, McCain was the insurgent, a position he has run well as. And though Iowa is a mountain to climb for McCain, expectations are low enough for some success. McCain has already hit rock bottom; there is no way but up.

In addition, has McCain revived his old 'straight talk'? In August on the *Today Show*, he told Matt Lauer "As a baseball fan, yes," he felt Major League Baseball player Barry Bonds should have an asterisk by his all-time leading homerun record.[2131] And McCain said he would give Don Imus a second chance to have another radio show, despite Imus's racially insensitive remarks about the Rutgers University women's basketball team months earlier.[2132] When Lauer asked if McCain's would read his daughter *Facebook* diary if it were open on her computer, McCain said "Sure, I would and I'd tell her I read it." When Sen. Larry Craig (R-Idaho) apparently engaged in lewd behavior in a public bathroom, McCain was one of the first Senators to ask for Craig's resignation. (Ironically, Craig's actions were similar to the earlier charges against the co-chair of McCain's Florida campaign).

Perhaps the McCain of 2000 has returned. His success depends on New Hampshire, where independents pushed him to victory over Governor Bush in 2000. An American Research Group poll in July 2007 showed McCain had the support of eight percent of New Hampshire Republicans but 13 percent of the support from New Hampshire Independents likely to vote in a GOP primary.[2133]

The New Hampshire primary is on the same day for both political parties. Will independents vote for Obama the Democrat, or McCain the Republican?

Representative Ron Paul

Ron Paul's website described him as one who "never votes for legislation unless the proposed measure is expressly authorized by the Constitution."[2134] He often is called Dr. Paul, having been a specialist in obstetrics and gynecology.[2135] He voluntarily left the U.S. House in 1984 and went back to the medical field, but returned in 1997 representing the 14th Congressional district in Texas.[2136] He was the 1988 Libertarian presidential candidate and won 432,000 votes nationwide.[2137] On January 11, 2007 Paul filed papers for an exploratory committee.[2138]

McClatchy described him as (5.14.07), "Whippet-thin, with intense hang-dog eyes, the 71-year-old Paul comes across as a loopily enthusiastic professor, voice rising in pitch and pace, arms wavering, as he delves into pet issues, especially taking the country off the gold standard."[2139]

Dr. No

McClatchy said (5.14.07) with Paul: "It's a fine line between quixotic and committed, and just where Ron Paul falls is an open question..."[2140] Paul was, in some circles known as "Dr. No."[2141] He voted against the No Child Left Behind Act, the 2001 Patriot Act (and again in 2005), the authorization of force in Iraq, and had supported US withdrawal of the UN, and was a member of Tancredo's Immigration Reform Caucus.[2142] As one stated on PoliticalInsider.com, "Paul's anti-war, anti-Patriot Act, anti-big spending platform will get him some support, however, and he may do better than expected."[2143]

Paul has said he won't take a congressional pension, did not take Medicare or Medicaid from his patients, and did not allow his children to take student loans (because such loans were not from the government, but actually the taxpayer).[2144] Columnist Bob Novak said "He's a very engaging person...I'd like to see him as president. Can you imagine him at the United Nations?"[2145]

Paul is very skeptical of the Department of Homeland Security. Paul has stated (5.15.07), "We were spending $40 billion on security prior to 9/11, and they had all the information they needed there to deal with the threat, and it was inefficiency. So what do we do? We add a gigantic bureaucracy, which they're still working on trying to put it together, and a tremendous amount of increase in funds."[2146]

His libertarian stances have provided quotes many politicians would not dare to say. "Capitalism should not be condemned, since we haven't had capitalism."[2147] "When one gets in bed with government, one must expect the diseases it spreads."[2148] And "You wanna get rid of drug crime in this country? Fine, let's just get rid of all the drug laws."[2149]

The non-interventionist

Ron Paul voted against the Iraq war, and was particularly upset at President Bush's flop on nation building. At the first GOP presidential debate (5.3.07), Paul said,

> ... why are 70 percent of the American people now wanting us out of there, and why did the Republicans do so poorly last year? So I would suggest that we should look at foreign policy. I'm suggesting very strongly that we should have a foreign policy of non-

intervention, the traditional American foreign policy and the Republican foreign policy. Throughout the 20th century, the Republican Party benefited from a non-interventionist foreign policy. Think of how Eisenhower came in to stop the Korean War. Think of how Nixon was elected to stop the mess in Vietnam. How did we win the election in the year 2000? We talked about a humble foreign policy: No nation-building; don't police the world. That's conservative, it's Republican, it's pro-American -- it follows the founding fathers. And, besides, it follows the Constitution.[2150]

Later on in the debate, Paul said:
> If the goal of government is to be the policeman of the world, you lose liberty. And if the goal is to promote liberty, you can unify all segments. ... I believe that when we overdo our military aggressiveness, it actually weakens our national defense. I mean, we stood up to the Soviets. They had 40,000 nuclear weapons. Now we're fretting day in and day and night about third-world countries that have no army, navy or air force, and we're getting ready to go to war.[2151]

McClatchy reported (5.14.07), "Traceable to George Washington's warning against entangling foreign alliances, its post-World War II followers—including 'Mr. Republican' Sen. Robert Taft of Ohio—likely would share Paul's view of President Bush's adventures in democratic nation-building as muddleheaded folly."[2152] Paul continually associates with Robert Taft, as he did in the second presidential debate (5.15.07):
> I think the party has lost its way, because the conservative wing of the Republican Party always advocated a noninterventionist foreign policy.
> Senator Robert Taft didn't even want to be in NATO. George Bush won the election in the year 2000 campaigning on a humble foreign policy -- no nation-building, no policing of the world. Republicans were elected to end the Korean War. The Republicans were elected to end the Vietnam War. There's a strong tradition of being anti-war in the Republican party. It is the constitutional position. It is the advice of the Founders to follow a non-interventionist foreign policy, stay out of entangling alliances, be friends with countries, negotiate and talk with them and trade with them.
> Just think of the tremendous improvement -- relationships with Vietnam. We lost 60,000 men. We came home in defeat. Now we go over there and invest in Vietnam. So there's a lot of merit to the advice of the Founders and following the Constitution.
> And my argument is that we shouldn't go to war so carelessly. When we do, the wars don't end.[2153]

Giuliani vs. Paul

And it was that last excerpt above which caused the major fracas of the second GOP presidential debate. For the moderator asked if the belief of non-intervention changed with 9/11. Paul said actually [the move against],
> Non-intervention was a major contributing factor. Have you ever read the reasons they attacked us? They attack us because we've been over there; we've been bombing Iraq for 10 years. We've been in the Middle East -- I think Reagan was right. We don't understand the irrationality of Middle Eastern politics. So right now we're building an embassy in Iraq that's bigger than the Vatican. We're building 14 permanent bases. What would we say here if China was doing this in our country or in the Gulf of Mexico? We would be objecting. We need to look at what we do from the perspective of what would happen if somebody else did it to us.[2154]

For the record, there was an applause after Paul's remark.[2155] But then the quandary came for Paul: was he suggesting the US invited the 9/11 attacks? Paul responded:

> I'm suggesting that we listen to the people who attacked us and the reason they did it, and they are delighted that we're over there because Osama bin Laden has said, "I am glad you're over on our sand because we can target you so much easier." They have already now since that time have killed 3,400 of our men, and I don't think it was necessary.[2156]

Giuliani went in for the kill:

> ...may I comment on that? That's really an extraordinary statement. That's an extraordinary statement, as someone who lived through the attack of September 11, that we invited the attack because we were attacking Iraq. I don't think I've heard that before, and I've heard some pretty absurd explanations for September 11th. [there was an applause with cheers from the crowd] And I would ask the congressman to withdraw that comment and tell us that he didn't really mean that. [more applause followed][2157]

Paul's response:

> I believe very sincerely that the CIA is correct when they teach and talk about blowback. When we went into Iran in 1953 and installed the shah, yes, there was blowback. A reaction to that was the taking of our hostages and that persists. And if we ignore that, we ignore that at our own risk. If we think that we can do what we want around the world and not incite hatred, then we have a problem. They don't come here to attack us because we're rich and we're free. They come and they attack us because we're over there. I mean, what would we think if we were -- if other foreign countries were doing that to us?[2158]

Giuliani: Paul blamed the US for 9/11

What was most important was Giuliani's attempt to suggest Paul said the 9/11 attacks were caused by US attacks on Iraq. Paul meant US intervention in the Middle East, including Iraq, caused blowback. Even the *AP* failed to specify what Paul clarified, and reported (5.16.07) of Paul's "suggestion that U.S. bombing of Iraq had contributed to the terrorist attacks of 2001."[2159]

But if Giuliani said Paul's assertion that bombing Iraq caused 9/11 was absurd, did Giuliani suggest Iraq had nothing to do with 9/11? *That's an extraordinary statement, as someone who lived through the attack of September 11, that we invited the attack because we were attacking Iraq.* Hmmm. Giuliani always claimed Iraq was an extension of the war on terror, so now he unintentionally said Iraq was unrelated to 9/11. Giuliani was in the same branch of Republicans who claimed the US had to (in 2007) beat the terrorists in Iraq, or they would come to the US. Under that logic, the US had to have a reason to go into Iraq in 2003. What was it? To prevent another attack. If it was, why did Saddam and terrorists want to hurt the US? What was Giuliani's reason that Saddam and terrorists wanted to hurt the US? Because they were jihadists. Please. Giuliani, Romney, and others had such an easy time warning the public of jihadists, but a much difficult issue in explaining why they hated America. *Why were there jihadists?* That was the question Giuliani did not give a clear answer too. Ron Paul could tell voters why there were jihadists. Blowback.

Another point for Paul, was that he was consistent on Iraq being bombed as well. In October 2002, Paul said, "We are still in the Persian Gulf War. We have been bombing for 12 years..."[2160] Paul said (10.8.02), "While one can only condemn any country firing on our pilots, isn't the real argument whether we should continue to bomb Iraq relentlessly? Just since 1998, some 40,000 sorties have been flown over Iraq."[2161] Rudy: The US was bombing Iraq before the 2003 invasion.

Paul tried to clarify Rudy's attack. When told his critics felt he blamed the US for 9/11, Paul responded (after the debate), "No, I blamed bad policy over 50 years that leads to anti-Americanism. That's a little bit different from saying 'blame America.' Don't put words in my mouth."[2162] But media outlets put words in Paul's mouth. Chris Cillizza of the *Washington Post* said Paul "essentially insinuated that America invited the terrorist attacks."[2163] Byron York of the *National Review* wrote, "To many people, however, it did appear that Paul blamed the U.S. for the attacks," and included a quote from Ted Olson, a friend of Giuliani whose wife was killed during 9/11.[2164] Olson sided with his friend. York concluded by "cutting in" to Paul's comments, "Giuliani had scored some of the best, and perhaps easiest, points of the night."[2165] GOP strategist Charlie Black, a McCain ally, said of Giuliani: "I don't think it takes a lot of courage to use Ron Paul as a prop. But he got his 9/11 credential in there, so congratulations."[2166]

Paul initially lost the argument with Rudy

Others criticized Paul by asking why bin Laden should be listened to as the overriding view of Middle East opinion on the US. (Though in Paul' defense, he would never suggest to solely pay attention to bin Laden—because, as his critics overlooked, Paul was not that simplistic.) Jonah Goldberg continued to rip Paul apart online for the *National Review*: "The terrorists are 'delighted' we're in Iraq, he [Paul] claims, because Osama bin Laden says so. Maybe they are, maybe they aren't."[2167] Not to mention other Arabs (Kuwaitis, Saudis) were happy the US intervened in Kuwait in 1991.[2168] True, but why did their happiness factor in the US's decision. And if Paul implied the US did cause 9/11, there was a difference in saying it 'caused' rather than 'deserved' the attacks.

Nonetheless, The *National Review*'s Jonah Goldberg wrote, "Good for Rudy sticking it to Ron Paul on his blame America first isolationism."[2169] For the base of the GOP who thought America was innocent, Rudy scored some major points.

The *Washingtonpost.com* noted, "the audience's applause showed that Giuliani had struck a chord."[2170] *Reuters* said (5.16.07) Paul was "the longest of longshots," and said there was a "wild applause" when Giuliani called Paul's remark 'absurd.'[2171] The *AP* said Giuliani's "rebuke to Paul drew some of the loudest applause of the night from the partisan audience."[2172] Did the *AP* clarify the debate was sponsored by FOX? Fox's Brit Hume began the debate and told crowd to please, "limit applause during the question and answer portion of the debate so we can devote as much time as we can to the candidates themselves."[2173] That didn't happen, and at the very least, the popularity of Paul's comments were not evident in this hostile environment.

In addition, in the debate, Chris Wallace said to Paul, "…A recent poll found that 77 percent of Republicans disapprove of the idea of setting a timetable for withdrawal. Are you running for the nomination of the wrong party?"[2174] There was scattered laughter in the audience in the debate put on by FOX.[2175] Paul responded "you have to realize that the base of the Republican Party shrunk last year because of the war issue. So that percentage represents less people."[2176] Paul may not have represented the base of the party, but the true irony of those laughing at Paul: Who was the joke really on?

Ron Paul mania: Dr. No gets last laugh

Paul had some defenders. As one writer described sarcastically of Rudy in *Alternet*: "And that's when Ring Master Rudi Giuliani pulled the curtain back so the circus audience could be introduced to Blowback, the Great American Elephant," and "With a straight face," Rudy said how Paul's words were 'an extraordinary statement.'[2177] Rudy "was either lying or exhibiting a severe case of cognitive dissonance—denying the possibility of what the CIA (and 'wacko leftists') call 'blowback.'"[2178]

Thespoof.com reported (6.14.07) Rudy Giuliani talked to HBO's star mafia member, Tony Soprano: "That Ron Paul guy thinks I should read about foreign policy. I think it's about time he gets whacked."[2179] The website also had another 'report' in which President Bush praised Ron Paul: "Ron Paul is a livertarian. He likes liver."[2180]

Clearly, by mid June, the internet was on fire over Ron Paul searches, which was fueled in part by a good online team.[2181] Not to mention a Strategic Visions Poll (June) showed 57 percent of Iowa Republicans wanted the US to withdraw all its military forces from Iraq in a half year.[2182] His website said (6.13.07), "The first Ron Paul MeetUp group started with one person two months ago in Pasadena. Now there are 11,383 members in 269 cities who have held 293 events nationwide. Dr. Paul tops the charts among all presidential candidates on *Eventful.com*, *MySpace.com*, and *YouTube.com*…Interview requests from the national broadcast and print media are much more frequent now."[2183] Paul's MySpace page had 12,000 'friends' and, considering GOP hopefuls, was second only to Romney and McCain.[2184] He appeared on the *Colbert Report* in June, but before then had not even heard of the show.[2185] In the first quarter of 2007 he raised $640,000 and placed sixth out of ten candidates.[2186]

Rush Limbaugh tried to deflate Paul's popularity (5.16.07) and said, "He's got supporters, and they are spamming polls on the Internet…"[2187] Paul received no more than two percent of Republican support in CNN's and *USA Today* polls in early May.[2188] But Paul won the "Who won?" blog CNN.com posted the day after the debate, but the website took down the blog and redirected to a blog for the Democrats' debate days earlier, leaving Paul supporters to question whether CNN intervened on purpose.[2189]

When the CNN poll after the June Republican debate was up, Paul led in many categories. Including who respondents thought won the debate (53% said Paul), who knew the most about the issues (53% again), and who had the best one-liner (34% said Paul); Romney won as snappiest dresser (49%).[2190]

Ron Paul may not win the GOP nomination, but he has pulled his party to consider leaving Iraq. He has already exceeded expectations in this campaign. If he doesn't win the nomination, Paul could turn around and run as Libertarian later. Which was logical given Kent Snyder, a former staffer of the '88

Libertarian campaign was the chair of Paul's exploratory committee.[2191] Snyder said, "There's no question that it's an uphill battle, and that Dr. Paul is an underdog."[2192]

The Representative from Texas had already exceeded expectations before the Iowa Caucus. Who thought by the end of the second quarter of 2007, Ron Paul would have as much money as John McCain? He finished fifth in the Iowa Straw Poll in August 2007, and his nine percent finish showed he had a base of support,[2193] though Mike Huckabee was the GOP candidate who received all the attention for his second place finish to Romney.

Former Governor George Pataki

George Pataki was the underdog when he won the position of Peekskill mayor, New York Assembly and then State Senate, and swept into power in the 1994 elections knocking out Gov. Mario Cuomo.[2194]

Pataki was not Giuliani

Pataki was the governor of New York since 1995. As 2008 approached, he was the third person in the triangle of New York presidential contenders (the fourth if counting Mike Bloomberg), and the candidate with the largest uphill climb. Pataki never faced former New York's City Mayor Mario Cuomo's son Andrew in the 2002 general election for governor. But Andrew Cuomo placed second in the Democratic gubernatorial primary, partly because he made an off-the-cuff remark. In regard to George Pataki's role in 9/11: "He stood behind the leader [Giuliani]. He held the leader's coat. He was a great assistant to the leader. But he was not a leader," said Cuomo.[2195]

Many had not criticized Pataki for his leadership on 9/11, especially soon after the event. But how accurate was Andrew Cuomo's remarks? What would voters do in 2008? So much credit went to Rudy Giuliani—"America's Mayor." George Pataki was not "America's Governor." *New York Magazine* said (July 2004), "These days, if Rudy is Oprah, Pataki is Montel."[2196]

There also was past friction between Giuliani and Pataki. When Pataki won the governor's race, he did not take a congratulatory call from Giuliani, who endorsed Cuomo, for three weeks.[2197] There was an eventual thaw in the tension, as "It took six years and Giuliani's prostate cancer in 2000 for the chill to subside" and 9/11 brought them closer together.[2198] Could Pataki and Giuliani—two moderate Republicans—stay cordial in competitive White House bids?

Was Pataki running for president?

Pataki campaigned for Bush across the country in 2004, and introduced the President for his acceptance speech for the Republican nomination.[2199] He discussed a 2008 bid already in August of 2004, when he met with his chief of economic-development, Charles Gargano; and Arthur Finkelstein.[2200]

In July 2004, the *New York Magazine* wrote Pataki's "closest aides have cashed out of government, and two alpha Democrats are jockeying for his job. His poll numbers are mediocre, and the editorial pages have been unkind. On many weekends, he is not even in the state."[2201] In the fall of 2003, he spoke at the Iowa Republican Committee dinner, and traveled to New Hampshire in January and May 2004, then went to California in June 2004.[2202]

Was the Pataki bid anything serious? One of the governor's top fundraisers (Cathy Blaney) originated Pataki's donor base from Sen. Alfonse D'Amato and by the 2004 election had raised at least $9.5 million for the President's re-election.[2203] *New York Magazine* said (7.19.04) Pataki fundraisers had become "the go-to-guys" for the party regulars: "They have organized events for everyone from House Majority Leader Tom DeLay of Texas, the beneficiary of a $1,000-a-head cocktail hour at a Manhattan restaurant last September, to

House Speaker Dennis Hastert of Illinois, who collected campaign cash at the home of public-relations executive Howard Rubenstein last month."[2204] The money base kept Pataki in the field: "Pataki could raise at least $10 million, and maybe $30 million," Republican strategists suggested (July 2004).[2205] Two years later, clearly $10 million was not enough.

In the spring of 2005, invitations sent to lobbyists and donors to a $2,000-a-head golf outing in Westchester County directed the checks to be paid to George Pataki's 21st Century Freedom PAC, which was funding out of state expenses for the New York Governor.[2206] Lobbyists prone to the golf outing claimed the donation went to his governor's war chest in prior years.[2207]

Why didn't Pataki run for governor again?

The *New York Times* reported (7.15.05) Pataki's trip to Iowa for the National Governors Association meeting was a sign he was testing the waters. The paper quoted "associates" of Pataki, who stated if he sought the presidency, it would be "impossible" to run New York as governor.[2208] The "associates" also told the *New York Times* Pataki would make a decision on re-election for governor by September 2005.[2209] This September date was extended from Pataki's initially planned date to comment on whether to seek re-election.

Clearly Elliot Spitzer, New York's Attorney General seeking the Democratic Nomination for governor, was building a formidable campaign. Spitzer raised $6 million in the first half of 2005; Pataki raised less than $800,000 for the governor race in the same six months.[2210] In the same time frame, Pataki had raised over a million for his political action committee.[2211] Most signs showed Pataki was running for President. So why didn't he just let New York Republicans find his replacement?

On July 27, George Pataki announced that he would not seek reelection for governor, and on a future presidential run stated that "I'm not ruling anything in or out."[2212] Yet two days later, former New York Senator Alfonse D'Amato (R) had an op-ed for *Newsday* (7.29.07), giving a glowing endorsement for Pataki: "Note to Republican presidential primary candidates: Don't Underestimate George Pataki."[2213] Did Pataki know this was coming? And why did Pataki bow out—was it just to run for president? After all, as the *New York Daily News* argued (7.28.05), "the governor recognized that he was heading toward the end of an unbroken winning streak at the polls [to Eliot Spitzer]."[2214]

Pataki is simplsitic

Pataki's GOP Convention speech in 2004 exemplifies a lot of the governor: at times blatantly partisan, a dry sense of humor, and not the world's best speech giver. He was not the Obama version for the GOP convention in 2004:

> .... Senator Kerry, on the other hand
> Well, what can we say of Senator Kerry?
> He was for the war and then he was against the war.
> Then he was for it but he wouldn't fund it.
> Then he'd fund it but he wasn't for it.
> He was for the Patriot Act until he was against it.

Or was he against it until he was for it?
I forget. He probably does too.
This is a candidate who has to Google his own name to find out where he stands.
You saw their convention a few weeks ago. They had a slogan: "Hope is on the way." But with all their flip-flopping and zig-zagging their real slogan should be, "Hype is on the way."
You know, as Republicans we're lucky. This fall we're going to win one for the Gipper. But our opponents - they're going lose one with the Flipper.[2215]

He told South Carolinians (6.2.06), "We are two different parties with different points of view. We think every day is the Fourth of July and they think every day is April 15 tax day."[2216] He had to explain what he meant by April 15.

A Staged fight with Hillary (August 2006)

A "key advisor" to Sen. Clinton, Howard Wolfson, told the *AP* (Aug.2006) Pataki was "now thoroughly uninterested in being our governor even though he has several months left in his tenure," and stated he had "zero chance" of becoming President.[2217] But Pataki, in New Hampshire, actually answered back, stating "I think he's got me confused with his client, Hillary Clinton, who has talked a great deal about what she would do for New York, but in six years, it's always hard for me to point to anything other than her criticism of the national administration."[2218] Pataki's spokesman David Catalfamo said "One million fewer New Yorkers on welfare; the safest large state in America; a cleaner environment; and $140 billion in tax cuts—I guess if I were Hillary Clinton I wouldn't want to run against George Pataki's record either."[2219]

In August 2006, the *New York Daily News* ("Hil tops Dem poll, gov unimpressed") reported Pataki's criticism of Sen. Clinton as "one of the most polarizing personalities in American politics," as he justified his comments in that "she has focused more on the negative and on attacking, as opposed to coming up with any positive solutions."[2220] But after the comments, the *Daily News* added: "Clinton has made headlines since she was elected in 2000 by cozying up to Republicans" like Frist and Gingrich "on issues important to her."[2221] The paper did not include a Clinton response,[2222] though mentioned the *Time* magazine poll in which Clinton's approval rating remained at 53% and was the "the only Democrat" giving McCain "a run for his money," while "Pataki barely registers thus far in national presidential polls."[2223] But the *New York Post*'s article the same day (8.21.06) actually quoted a Clinton spokesman noting Pataki had once "praised Sen. Clinton for working in a bipartisan way and delivering for New York."[2224]

Pataki's remarks bashing Hillary was pure partisanship: he made his comments visiting New Hampshire.[2225] Pataki said "In fact, as I sit here I can't think of something where she's said, 'Let's do this together. Let's set this as a positive agenda.' It's been more from the outside criticizing," he told the *Concord Monitor*.[2226] This was completely false, according to Pataki's own words via *Media Matters*, he spoke at a rally to celebrate the Base Realignment and Closing Commision's decision to keep open the Niagra Falls Air Reserve Station in August 2005: "....I can tell you that Senator Clinton and her staff were there working there night and day helping us to get the message [to keep the base open]. And Senator, thank you."[2227]

Pataki's bureaucratic mess

Nearly four and half years after the 9/11 attacks, the 9/11 memorial site's future was still in question. Larry Silverstein was the private developer who leased the twin towers a month and a half before the attacks, and he was in disagreement over Pataki and Port Authority officials in New York and New Jersey (which owned the land) over the idea of building the Freedom Tower at Ground Zero.[2228] New York Attorney General and gubernatorial candidate Eliot Spitzer said "there's a very serious question about the economic viability" of the Freedom Tower.[2229] Spitzer later (3.27.06) called it an economic "white elephant."[2230]

The Port Authority walked out of talks with Silverstein on March 14, the deadline Pataki set to renegotiate Silverstein's multibillion dollar lease.[2231] Pataki's supporters accused Silverstein of wanting an extra $1 billion, and the Governor said Silverstein Properties "betrayed the public's trust and that of all New Yorkers."[2232] While both sides agreed to allow the Port Authority to build the Freedom Tower, a dispute focused on how to divide proceeds of a potential $3 billion in insurance, the follow through if insurers won a challenge in a federal appeals court, and also Silverstein's rent reductions in return for what he was giving back to the Port Authority.[2233]

The *AP* claimed (3.21.06), Pataki said "formal negotiations on development at ground zero will resume only when a private developer and the site's owners 'are prepared to act in good faith.'"[2234]

In May 2006, developer Frank Sciame was asked to cut cost from the plans that almost doubled the $500 million budget.[2235] His version preserved architect Michael Arad's belief that waterfalls would feed into reflecting pools.[2236] But it reduced exhibition galleries, limited the space for administrative offices, consolidated multiple entrances into one, put the names of victims on street level instead of underground, and ended up cutting costs to be just $10 million over budget ($510 million total).[2237] However, $100 million in costs to make the site buildable were transferred to the government agency owning the site.[2238]

For all the money Pataki had helped save, advocates for the families still insisted (6.26.06) the names of the dead should not be randomly arrayed.[2239] As the *New York Times* reported, "the names issue puts the families in conflict with Gov. George Pataki and Mayor Michael Bloomberg, who maintain that the names should be arranged randomly."[2240] Arad felt the names should be listed underground,[2241] and also supported the randomization of names.[2242] The director of the Cantor Fitzgerald Relief Fund said the victim's relatives wanted the nearly 3,000 names in order by where they worked and died, with affiliations, floor, and ages.[2243] Cantor Fitzgerald was a financial services company which lost 658 employees, and as of the spring of 2006, was yet to make a donation to the memorial.[2244]

There was even the debate on whether to charge admission for the WTC memorial. The New York Senate approved a bill that would bar any state monies from going to the memorial if the memorial had an admission fee.[2245] Mayor Bloomberg said he hoped Pataki "vetoes the bill because it's probably true that without being able to charge, we can't build the memorial."[2246] Oklahoma City's National Memorial Museum was $8 but it's Outdoor Symbolic Memorial was free and open 24 hours a day.[2247] But the Vietnam Veterans Memorial and the Holocaust Memorial Museum had free admission.[2248]

The memorial was planned to open by September 11, 2009,[2249] eight years after the attack. As *NY1* reported, "It's no secret the governor is considering a run for president and continuing delays at the site could tarnish his image as a leader, while signs of progress at the site—with George Pataki center stage—can only help."[2250] A Quinnipiac Poll (released 7.12.06) showed only 40% of New York City voters said the redevelopment at the WTC site was going "very well" or 'somewhat well," with 52% said it was going 'somewhat badly' or 'very badly' and was "the lowest grade in four years of polling on" the question and compared to a "44-47 percent split in an April [2006] Quinnipiac University poll."[2251]

The 1776 ft. Freedom Tower became a joke

The Freedom Tower was Pataki's baby: A 1776 foot tower that Pataki said was a symbol important to show "the country and the world that New York is not afraid to build tall, that we still stand strong."[2252] Even the Port Authority's vice chairman said the tower was a tough sell to future tenants after the 9/11 attacks, though admitted it was still important for Pataki.[2253] As Jon Stewart on *The Daily Show* mocked: "New York City was attacked 4 ½ years ago and since that time we have been locked in a vicious battle…over construction of the so-called Freedom Tower, set to stand in the former spot of the World Trade Center. In fact, it's been nearly two years since Gov. George Pataki announced New York would use the site to build the tallest, shiniest, terrorist-tauntiest skyscraper in the world: 1,776-foot-tall Freedom Tower! 1,776 feet—it's a stirring symbol of American subtlety. …By the way, the runner-up in the contest: The Apple Pie-Baseball-Eagle-Freedom-Flag-otarium."[2254] 'Reporter' Dan Bakkedahl talked of the possibility that a statue celebrating bureaucracy might be set up near the sight, which would be constructed of red tape and would be open only on Tuesdays and alternate Thursdays—except in May.[2255]

But nothing compared to the sarcasm of *The Onion* and the article titled "Five Years Later, NYC Unveils 9/11 Memorial Hole."[2256]

> From the wreckage and ashes of the World Trade Center, we have created a recess in the ground befitting the American spirit," said New York Governor George Pataki from a cinderblock-and-plastic-bucket-supported plywood platform near the Hole's precipice. "This vast chasm, dug at the very spot where the gleaming Twin Towers once rose to the sky, is a symbol of what we can accomplish if we work together.[2257]

The *Albany Times Union* blog headlined "Pataki Makes The Onion: George, They Are Not Laughing With You."[2258] *The Onion* described the Governor's cut of the ceremonial ribbon to release a "giant blue plastic tarpaulin, reportedly the largest of its kind, which fluttered and snapped while slowly settling into the detritus and mud at the bottom of the 70-foot Hole," and which drew a long sigh of "resignation" of 50,000 who gathered "to watch and shake their heads."[2259] In Pataki's supposed speech, he talked of the naysayers and invited them "to gaze down at this magnificent pit if they want proof of New Yorker's dedication to this project."[2260]

The Onion's analysis was a brilliant spoof on New Orleans Mayor Ray Nagin's comments on Ground Zero. When pressed about New Orleans recovery for a '60 Minutes' that aired in late August 2006 (but taped two months earlier), Nagin said "That's all right. You guys in New York City can't get a hole in the ground fixed. And it's five years later. So let's be fair."[2261]

A Sept. 11 Tribute Center opened just before the five year anniversary.[2262] But it was not the 9/11 memorial. At the center's ribbon cutting ceremoney (9.6.06), Pataki said "Tribute is a critical word, because for all the horror, for all the loss on Sept.11, we can never forget the courage with which New Yorkers responded."[2263] The Tribute WTC Visitor Center served as "a memorial space until the official memorial opens in 2009."[2264]

Pataki: 'He was the governor of New York during 9/11. Right?'

Pataki appeared on *Face the Nation* (9.10.06), but that was only because of the five year anniversary of 9/11. Talking about Homeland Security, Pataki added that there was "much more we need" to do, and tried to switch the topic, "…first of all, I think the borders. It is—when you're in a state of war, how can you be in a position where you have thousands of people crossing into the country illegally? Sure the vast majority of them want to be a part of America and the American dream, but we have to make sure that everybody [is] coming here legally and with good intentions. And…"[2265] And…that's when Bob Schieffer interrupted with "Well, let me—let me go…to to something closer to New York, and that is the trains [and safety]."[2266] Pataki had to stay on 9/11. The interview ended with Schieffer asking if Pataki was surprised that the rebuiding of ground zero "has been so slow?"[2267]

With little surprise, Pataki said no, and cited the issue of it being "hallowed ground, and we have to act very respectfully and prudently," and said there was 12,000 more residents in lower Manhatten today than "four or five years ago."[2268] And thirty million square feet of office space was damaged or destroyed, and Pataki said "Twenty million of that is back."[2269]

A month later, Pataki appeared on *Hardball* (10.11.06), but that was because the plane of Yankee pitcher Cory Lidle crashed into a high-rise building on the Upper East Side of Manhattan.[2270] Chris Matthews discussed how New Yorkers were so proud of their tall buidlings, but asked "How safe can you live at what height anymore?"[2271] Pataki responded:

> …I think that's the wrong question. We're New Yorkers, we're Americans. We've got to continue to build big and soar to new heights. We can't say, oh my god, since September 11th, we have to cower and think small and live in bunkers….We're going to build a Freedom Tower. It's going to be 1,776 feet tall. It's under construction right now, the tallest building ever built in America. And I'll tell you, I'd be comfortable working there.

I'd be comfortable having my kids work there. We cannot live in the shadow of fear simply because we are aware that we are in a different world since September 11th.[2272]

Later in the show, Pataki said "...we just have to make sure that we don't have people with limited flight experience just circling Manhattan and putting this great city at risk. And I certainly am going to be calling on the FAA to tighten up their rules and their restrictions on airspace over New York."[2273] Pataki already knew there was no terror link by the time he interviewed.[2274] It seemed as though he took advantage of his air time to play up his 9/11 card. Even MSNBC correspondent David Schuster said Mayor Bloomberg "was asked specifically at the news conference about security of New York. And unlike what you just heard with the governor, expressing some concerns about people flying around New York, the mayor seemed to have no concern, saying this was not a security issue, this was just a matter of a particular plane that for whatever reason went off-course and crashed."[2275]

Shuster's analysis was correct. Indeed, the *AP* reported (Oct.13) a similar disconnect between Bloomberg and Pataki. Pataki reportedly "said...the Federal Aviation Administration 'needs to take a much tougher line' about private, or general aviation, flights over the city...However...Bloomberg, a recreational pilot with decades of experience, said he believed the skies are safe under the current rules."[2276]

Pataki: leader of NY GOP

The *New York Times* concluded (12.5.05) Pataki was leaving a divided Republican party in New York. The state party was

> ...at war with itself, with some factions embracing a governor's race by Pataki's longtime nemesis, Tom Golisano, and others trying to force Mr. Pataki's pick for US Senate, Jeanine F. Pirro, out of the race. In New York City, Mayor Michael Bloomberg, a Republican, is trying to seize more control of the rebuilding of the World Trade Center site, one of Mr. Pataki's signature projects...Back at the fractious State Capital, where governors rule through a combination of rewards and retribution, his announcement in July that he would not seek a fourth term was considered by some as an act of disarmament, and an opportunity.[2277]

Jeanine Pirro dropped out of the US Senate race and switched to New York Attorney General race instead, as she "decided" her law enforcement background better qualified her for the AG race than the Senate.[2278] Pataki had endorsed Pirro in October 2005.[2279]

A campaign that never took off

In a November 2005 article titled "Clinton, Giuliani put 2008 presidential race in N.Y. state of mind," the *AP* completely focused on the two powerhouse candidates and New York presidential history. Then, near the end of the article, Pataki was finally mentioned: "Clinton and Giuliani are not the only New Yorkers who might make a White House bid in 2008. ... Pataki, is also considering a presidential run after ruling out a bid for a fourth term next year. Pataki, however, is barely a blip in national polls."[2280]

A year later, the *Des Moines Register* noted (12.2.06) "McCain isn't alone in his efforts to organize in Iowa. He is joined by other Republicans with similar motivations, including" Huckabee, Pataki and Romney. In September, Pataki opened an Urbandale, Iowa, office for his political action committee."[2281] Pataki was always clearly in the mix.

But the news he generated was entirely unrelated to the presidential campaign. As McCain called for 20,000 in Iraq, The *AP* reported Pataki had qualified for a $113,000 pension for his service to New York state.[2282] Pataki also agreed to let governor-elect Eliot Spitzer fill some vacant posts after the switch in eventual power; Pataki made numerous appointments in judgeships and for boards of public authorities, but he also left vacant positions such as the chairmanship of the Public Employment Relations Board which oversaw contract disputes with state unions.[2283] Spitzer, who had worried about having his hands tied with appointees Pataki could have chosen before the Spitzer era began, said "They listened to our concerns and in a number of areas gave us the ability to do what we want to do."[2284]

His spokeswoman told *ABC News* (12.4.06) Pataki was "weighing his options and making the decision with his family," as he visited New Hampshire and Iowa (for the tenth time of 2006) on December 5.[2285] He was still second fiddle to Rudy. The *AP* reported (11.7.06) that according to exit polls, "Less than half [of New Yorkers] said former New York Mayor Rudy Giuliani would make a good president, and just one in six said the same about Gov. George Pataki. In a head-to-head matchup, New York voters preferred Clinton over Giuliani for president by a 2-1 ratio."[2286] Considering Clinton was on the ballot the day these exit polls were taken, they were possibly inflated (three in five New Yorkers said Clinton would be a good president), but Pataki was still very low.[2287]

Conservatives: Pataki was not that conservative

He "suffered setbacks" when he lost three "prominent GOP activists," who decided they would not go with Pataki through 2008: Craig Shoenfeld, a lawyer/lobbyist who was the President's Iowa director in 2000, had resigned as Pataki's executive director of his Iowa office; and Ed Failor, the leader of Iowans for Tax Relief and Iowa Right to Life board member; and Loras Schulte, an Iowa Republican Party State Central Committee member.[2288]

Schulte and Failor worked for his 21st Century Freedom PAC, and Schulte told the *Register* she supported Pataki for other political issues, but now that Pataki was moving towards a presidential run it was time to step down from her position.[2289] Schulte said "In order to be true to myself, where I stood and what I believed, it was time to step away."[2290] Failor said he agreed with Pataki that states should decide abortion rather than the Supreme Court, but disagreed with Pataki that the states should keep it legal.[2291] In reporting the loss of Pataki team members, *Life News* noted:

> In July, Pataki vetoed a bill that would have authorized a group of new specialty license plates there, including one commemorating the September 11 terrorist attacks. The governor blamed the veto on a lawsuit supporters of the Choose Life license plate filed after they were denied a specialty plate.
> Last May, Pataki said he supported a bill in the legislature requiring taxpayers to spend $100 million annually on embryonic stem cell research, which requires the destruction of human life.

> He also signed legislation requiring hospitals -- including religious ones -- to distribute the morning after pill and signed another bill requiring health insurance plans to do the same thing.[2292]

His spokeswoman told *ABC News*, when asked about taking the Bill Frist-route of dropping out, that there was "always a possibility."[2293]

Pataki's spokeswoman said Failor and Schulte agreed to advise Pataki up to the midterms and "They fulfilled their commitment, and he is very thankful for that."[2294] That very well may have been the case, but why did Pataki curry Failor and Schulte's favor if they were going to leave anyway? So as presidential campaigns were about to be kicked off, Pataki reminded every conservative he was lukewarm at best on pro-life issues.

Pataki faded away

Pataki was the first presidential hopeful to open a NH office when he did so on Oct. 2, 2006.[2295] The *New Hampshire Union Leader* reported (1.31.07) though he did not "directly take himself out of presidential contention" Pataki told New Hampshire supporters he would not object if they endorsed other GOP presidential candidates.[2296] But for some reason Pataki is still given huge sums for his PAC. In April 2007, even after Pataki "was effectively out of the race," Pataki's Commonwealth PAC received $58,000 from one New Yorker.[2297] Bob Perry, the founder of the Swift Boat Veterans for Truth, gave Pataki's PAC $250,000 in the second quarter of 2007.[2298] Maybe Pataki 2008 isn't dead yet, but its revival will depend on the collapse of many other Republican presidential campaigns—if not all of them.

Former Governor Mitt Romney

Willard Mitt Romney married in 1969, and together he and Ann have five sons.[2299] Mitt Romney graduated with highest honors from Brigham Young University in 1971.[2300]

His dad was former Michigan Gov. George Romney, who ran unsuccessfully for the GOP nomination in 1968.[2301] Romney discussed his father on *Hardball* (12.12.05). When seeking the 1968 Republican nomination George Romney said he was brainwashed in regard to the Vietnam War. Were we brainwashed on the Iraq War? "Of course not," said Romney, who also stated his father "was right," and "[Defense Secretary] McNamara said that he lied to the American people."[2302]

Romney ran against Ted Kennedy for Senate in 1994 losing 58-41, but gave Kennedy his biggest competition since 1962.[2303] A major test of leadership was asked of Romney in February 1999. The Salt Lake City Winter Olympics Organizing Committee was in a deficit and suffering from misconduct charges; Romney took the committee's lead and undid what was almost a $400 million deficit, and the 2002 Olympic Games had a secure operation.[2304] Romney was so popular that many suspected Romney was seeking public office in Utah.[2305]

Instead, he ran for governor of Massachusetts and won the 2002 election. A Republican had won in the state that President Bush's campaign linked to liberalism in the 2004 presidential race. The popularity of Romney could be debated: the Democratic nominee who won the divisive primaries only had six weeks to size up Romney, who won by 5%.[2306] Could Romney be re-elected as governor in 2006? He decided not to run.

A businessman's candidate

During the November 2004 meeting at the Republican Governors Association annual meeting in New Orleans, Romney was officially made vice chairman, with a duty connected to fundraising. Romney eventually led the RGA in 2006.[2307]

Massachusetts companies already gave the RGA $1 million with Romney's help.[2308] For example, MassMutual Financial Group gave over $300,000 between 2003 and 2004, while Fidelity Investments gave $185,000.[2309] This money provided a sizable chunk of the $12 million spent on 11 governor races in 2004.[2310] The RGA had strong ties to the business sector. As the *Boston Globe* reported, its funds "are collected primarily from corporations and lobbying groups, which join the governors association as members."[2311] This membership allowed CEOs to mingle with governors. Thus, the RGA and Salt Lake City experiences were indicative of Romney's experience in bureaucracy and business. There should have been no surprise when Romney collected over $20 million for his presidential campaign in the first quarter of 2007.

But two issues had to be addressed. First, was his notoriety for flip-flopping on social issues. Second, his faith, Mormonism, was viewed with skepticism by some conservatives.

Flipping on Abortion

His 2002 gubernatorial platform stated "The choice to have an abortion is a deeply personal one. Women should be free to choose based on their own beliefs, not the government's."[2312]

Already on *FOX News Sunday* in February 2006, Chris Wallace brought up the abortion issue and showed Romney's 2002 comment in which he believed "women should have the right to make their own choice."[2313] The change, said Romney, "surrounded stem cell research...," he spent a lot of time with researchers and "came to the conclusion that ....when conception occurs that human life has begun. I'm not talking about religious definitions, but scientific definitions..."[2314] Wallace was confused on why a forty-year old issue was decided by Romney "in the last three years."[2315] Wallace's questioning was just the beginning.

The digs at Romney have been on and off. The end of 2006 was particularly rough. A *Washington Post/AP* report talked (12.23.06) of the "apparent gulf" between the 1994 version and the presidential candidate: "Is he the self-described moderate who unsuccessfully challenged Kennedy in the year of the Republican landslide, the self-described conservative now ready to bid for the Republican nomination in 2008, or merely an ambitious and adaptable politician?"[2316] This report noted the governor declined an interview request on his evolution of the thinking, aides said he did not have time for a telephone interview and Romney had answered questions on the topic numerous times.[2317] The article also said "questions" about Romney's "conservative credentials" could provide an opening for Brownback and Huckabee.[2318]

The *National Journal* called it "an awful December" for Romney.[2319] By the second week in January 2007, the *National Journal* ranked Brownback fourth out of 11 Republicans in the nomination hunt.[2320] The same day Romney raised $6.5 million, Brownback got the support of a half dozen conservatives in Massachusetts.[2321] Brownback's gains in Massachusetts was "mostly pro-life activists," such as Carol McKinley, the founder of Faithful Voice whose anti-Romney website had a "Pro-life Mitt Romney Watch."[2322] The *National Journal* said: "...notice how all of Brownback's digs seem to be at Romney's expense. He's staying away from McCain for a reason."[2323]

But Kris Mineau of Mass. Family Institute said that when people asked how Romney's switch on pro-life could be accepted, "I ask if they ever question Teddy Kennedy's or John Kerry's switches from pro-life to pro-choice."[2324] This *National Review Online* article (1.10.07) quoted Sen. Jim DeMint (R-SC) who said Romney "fells passionately that the value of human life begins at conception."[2325]

Flopping on gay rights

By Jan. 12, a longtime foe of Romney, Brain Camenker wrote a 28 page report that portrayed Romney as a gay rights sympathizer and it included five pages of footnotes.[2326] Camenker was a leader of MassResistance, which accused Romney as the "father of gay marriage."[2327] The *AP* quoted Camenker:

"...Romney is so clearly and blatantly faking this. He's a fraud,"[2328] such as a 1994 Senate debate in which Romney was asked about Boy Scouts and gays.[2329] The anti-gay Americans for Truth attacked Romney for criticizing Camenker, as a *Christian Newswire* press release by the group quoted President Peter LaBarbera, who said "Few people have demonstrated the courage that Brian has in fighting the self-styled 'queer' movement," as the release said "Romney uses liberal media stories to portray Camenker as an extremist troublemaker."[2330]

What are some of Romney's inconsistencies? In a letter to Log Cabin Republicans, Romney complimented "Don't Ask, Don't Tell" as a "step in the right direction," and the first steps toward gays serving "openly" in the military.[2331] Other sources, such as *EDGE Boston* (12.19.06) also quoted Romney in that 1994 letter: "we must make equality for gays and lesbians a mainstream concern."[2332] The Log Cabin head in 1994, Rich Tafel, "told the *New York Times* that he was surprised by Romney's 180-degree turn on gay rights."[2333] The Log Cabins had new leadership in December 2006 right at the height of the Romney spiel, and Patrick Sammon came to the post saying Romney needed "to explain what is clearly a shift" from 1994.[2334] The *New York Times/AP* reported the letter "now looms as a serious complication to Romney's presidential hopes."[2335] The Family Research Council president Tony Perkins called the incident "quite disturbing" and Paul Weyrich said "Unless he comes out with an abject repudiation of this, I think it makes him out to be a hypocrite."[2336]

And Romney opposed the Scouts policy that prohibited gays from being scoutmasters and did not allow the organization to publicly participate in the 2002 Olympics.[2337] He issued a 2003 proclamation declaring May 17 "Massachusetts Gay/Straight Youth Pride Day."[2338]

But Romney dug up a 1913 law in 2004 which said out-of-state couples could not marry if their marriage would be 'void' in their home state.[2339]

Romney's constitutional fight

Wire reports labeled him (11.25.06) "a fierce opponent of gay marriage."[2340] In November, Romney asked the Massachusetts Supreme Judicial Court to force a proposed anti-gay marriage amendment on the 2008 ballot if its legislature did not vote on it.[2341] Romney said the state's constitution required the Legislature to vote on whether the measure should be on the ballot, and if they did not vote upon their return to session after Jan. 2, 2007 (the last day of session) he said the secretary of state should be ordered by the court to put it on the ballot.[2342]

On Dec. 27, the Massachusetts Court said it had no authority to force the legislature to vote on a proposed constitutional amendment to ban gay marriage.[2343] Gay marriage opponents had collected 170,000 signatures in favor of such an amendment, but the measure needed the legislature approval to appear on the 2008 ballot, and lawmakers refused to vote on it in November.[2344] So Romney sued by trying to get lawmakers to make a decision; the amendment needed the approval of two consecutive two-year sessions to get on the 2008 ballot, and if lawmakers adjourned without taking a vote on the amendment the measure would die.[2345]

On Jan. 2, 2007, the legislature passed the amendment (62-134), and passed the mandatory 50 needed in favor.[2346] The amendment now had to pass the legislature in the next legislative session, then it would go to the voters in 2008. Kris Mineau of the Massachusetts Family Institute said "It was a miracle."[2347] Democratic Senate President Robert Travaglini was the presiding officer over the convention and supported the amendment, but incoming Democratic governor Deval Patrick urged the legislature to adjourn without voting.[2348]

By December 2006, Romney was on the defense for his reputation. But even Brownback endorser Dwight Duncan said the claim Romney is to blame for gay marriage in Massachusetts was "over the top."[2349] As the *National Review* quoted Mineau, who succinctly noted Romney's achievement: "…In 2005, he ardently supported a citizen petition for an amendment to end same-sex marriage that wound up gathering a record number of 170,000 signatures. Throughout 2006 he lobbied the state legislature that was refusing to vote on the amendment. His intense involvement culminated with the filing of a suit in the State Supreme Judicial Court in December [2006] to mandate the legislature to hold the votes as required by the state constitution."[2350]

The Real Romney

Then *You Tube* entered the fray, as a five-minute clip of an October 1994 debate with Ted Kennedy surfaced, and by the end of the day on January 10, 2006, over 12,000 had seen it.[2351] Titled "The Real Romney," the clip showed Romney saying the Boy Scouts should allow participation "regardless of their sexual orientation," (while also supporting the organization's right to make its own decision).[2352] This was the same debate he said "we should sustain and support" the Roe v. Wade decision.[2353] Ted Kennedy said Romney was "multiple choice."[2354] The 1994 version of Romney said, "You will not see me wavering on that matter, or be a multiple choice," and, as a cherry on top for conservative critics, the 1994 version of Romney said he "was an independent at the time of Reagan-Bush. I'm not trying to return to Reagan-Bush."[2355] The 2007 version of Romney went on the conservative internet broadcasts of *The Glenn and Helen Show* '…If you want to know where I stand…you don't just have to listen to my words; you can go look at my record as governor."[2356] Though one should not have looked at his gubernatorial campaign: in both his Senate AND governor race, he was endorsed by the Log Cabin Republicans.[2357]

What was so comical was Romney thought he was better than McCain. McCain said in November, that "I believe in the sanctity and unique role of marriage between man and woman, but I certainly don't believe in discriminating against any American," and "I believe that gay marriage should not be legal."[2358] Romney, "seeking to be seen as more conservative" than McCain, said "That's his position, and in my opinion, it's disingenuous."[2359] Romney also said, "Look, if somebody says they're in favor of gay marriage, I respect that view. If someone says, like I do, that I oppose same-sex marriage, I respect that view. But those who try and pretend to have it both ways, I find it to be disingenuous."[2360] As the *AP* reported: "Never mind that Romney's own position on gay marriage has been questioned in recent weeks - after a 1994 letter surfaced from his unsuccessful Senate challenge to Sen. Edward M. Kennedy, D-Mass. In it, Romney pledged to be more effective in promoting the gay agenda than the liberal senator."[2361]

The Mormon question: Romney will not answer doctrinal questions

Polygamy was outlawed by the Mormon faith in 1890,[2362] and soon Utah received statehood. But until 1978, African-Americans were denied full membership. In March 2006, Romney said "There ultimately will be a time when someone will go overboard, where someone will say something beyond the mark. And hopefully I will be able to rise to the occasion in a way that's memorable."[2363] When Judy Woodruff asked (June 2006) about specific questions on his religion, Romney said "If you have doctrines you want to talk about, go talk to the church. Because that's not my job."[2364]

Romney had done this before. Chris Wallace questioned Romney (2.26.06) about his specific religious beliefs, and concerns evangelicals have. "They say that you believe in books of scripture that are outside the bible….Do you believe in the Book of Mormons and do you follow the tenets of [Joseph's] Smith's religion?"[2365] Romney did not touch the question: "…I'm never going to get into a discussion about my personal beliefs and about particular doctrines of my church."[2366]

Mormonism is not a big deal

But Romney was not the only Mormon to be concerned. Chris Dodd, a Catholic, was married to Jackie Clegg, a Mormon from Utah.[2367] But Dodd was likely less worried about Mormonism than Romney. According to *The Hill*, at a BYU Management Society dinner at Georgetown University, Sen. Bob Bennett (R-Utah) "said a tongue-and-cheek Dodd told him, 'At Bob Jones University, we are now a two-cult family.' Bennett and Dodd's offices would not elaborate further."[2368] Sen. Harry Reid is also Mormon.[2369] Both of Utah's senators (Bennett and Hatch) were both Republicans and Mormon.[2370]

Albert Hunt of *Bloomberg News* said there was "no serious candidate" that had emerged from the ranks of the conservative right, and "After a few false starts the latest favorite to champion their agenda is Mitt Romney," (10.29.06).[2371] Romney was doing well in South Carolina, a state where a Romney might worry about evangelical backlash. *The State* reported (10.6.06) Romney was "emerging as a favorite of hard-core conservative Republicans" in South Carolina as "Their first pick" (George Allen) "lost standing when he made highly publicized racial slurs during a heated re-election campaign."[2372] The *Boston Globe* reported, (10.19.06), "By most accounts," Romney had "catapulted himself into the top tier of GOP hopefuls, in part by appealing to conservatives on immigration, national security, and other leading issues."[2373] Sen. Jim DeMint told South Carolina Republicans to hold off endorsement of candidates, as the pro-McCain Attorney General of the state said "I don't understand why anyone would want to dampen that early enthusiasm [toward McCain]."[2374] The Spartanburg County GOP Chairmen Rick Beltram said Romney "moved up the fastest."[2375] But not all South Carolinians are supportive of Romney's religion.

Yes, his faith will matter

According to a *Bloomberg/LA Times* poll in the spring of 2006, 53 percent of registered voters would not vote for a Muslim, followed by Mormon (37), evangelical Christian (22), Jew (14), then Catholic (9).[2376] Thirty-five percent of conservative Republicans said they would not vote a Mormon for president.[2377] In November 2006, Rasmussen found 43 percent of Americans say they would never vote for a Mormon, 38 percent said they would consider it, and 19 percent were unsure.[2378] The Rasmussen poll was slightly worse news for Romney than the *LA Times* poll taken months earlier. But that Rasmussen poll also showed "Currently, just 19% of Likely Voters" were "able to identify Romney as the Mormon candidate from a list of six potential presidential candidates."[2379]

The *Boston Globe* reported (Oct.2006), "some conservatives Christian voters view Mormonism as non-Christian, and the more Romney gains prominence, the more he confronts questions about his relationship with the Church."[2380]

Lee Brandy reported ("Romney Grilling in Bad Taste," 9.24.06) for *The State* that when traveling to South Carolina, Romney was grilled about his faith and "It was not a pretty sight, according to witnesses."[2381] The chairwoman of the Charleston County Republican Party, Cyndi Mosteller, an evangelical, "came armed with a bunch of material—and questions—about the Mormon Church" and said she was concerned about the Mormon view on polygamy and African-Americans.[2382] She wanted to asked the questions in an open state executive committee session, but Romney "nixed that idea" by ending a quick address with a 'thank you.'[2383] Romney was going to talk to the media for 15 minutes, at which point Mosteller continued to ask questions, and Romney's people ushered reporters out the door.[2384] What was the result? It seems as though Romney won the battle. *The State*'s headline was in Romney's favor, and the article quoted the embarrassment towards Mosteller from both a Charleston native/RNC member and the Spartanburg GOP chairman.[2385]

Brownback doesn't know if Romney is a true Christian

Was Romney a true Christian? Sam Brownback said, "Oh, I'm not going to get into theological issues, and we don't have religious tests for public office in this country, and we shouldn't have them. I think people bring their set of values into the public arena and they debate them based on the set of issues and ideas, not on their faith."[2386] That was a no. Brownback then said Romney's religion should not be an issue in the campaign.[2387]

Romney is a Mormon-backed candidate

As of June 2006, Romney's various PACs raised $1.6 million of which 45 percent came from Utahans, as Jon Huntsman Sr. (the father of Utah's governor) alone gave Romney nearly $130,000.[2388]

Then the *Boston Globe* reported (Oct. 2006) Romney's team had been "quietly" consulting with Mormon leaders for his presidential bid, as the President of the Church of Jesus Christ and Latter Day Saints, Gordon B. Hinkley, had "expressed no opposition" to Romney's grassroots efforts. (Despite Church officials saying they were neutral on politics.)[2389] One of the Church's 12 apostles leading the church worldwide met with Romney's son Josh (9.19.06) as the *Globe* reported BYU and the Church was tax-exempt and could not advocate on behalf of a candidate, but the Business School dean at Brigham Young University was clearly using his school email to ask 50 business school members to join the Romney presidential bid.[2390] The alumni of the BYU Management Society had 5,500 members in 40 US chapters and would serve as a great financial base.[2391]

The *Deseret Morning News* (Utah) reported weeks later that "Early media reports said leaders of the LDS [Latter Day Saints] Church had endorsed the effort, but the church denied that and Romney-backers quickly stepped away from it, saying church leaders really didn't even know about the alumni effort at BYU, which is owned and operated by the church."[2392] The *Berkshire-Eagle* opined (10.24.06), "We would urge him to abandon the political alliance he has struck with the hierarchy of the Mormon Church, as revealed in a series by the *Boston Globe*. Religion and politics don't mix, and in assisting Mr. Romney, the Mormon Church is jeopardizing the tax exempt status it receives in exchange for staying out of the political realm."[2393]

In November 2006 poll reported by the *Deseret Morning News* showed "Romney was by far the best liked" in Utah, as he led with 44 percent, followed McCain (15), Clinton (7), Giuliani (7), Rice (6), Obama (5) and Kerry (4).[2394]

A handful of mistakes

In April, Mike Huckabee claimed Romney was wrong to suggest he was a lifelong hunter despite never taking out a license.[2395] Huckabee said, "It would be like me saying I've been a lifelong golfer because I played putt-putt when I was 9 years old and I rode in a golf cart a couple of times."[2396] Despite saying he was a hunter nearly all his life, Romney had to respond to reporters inquiries, and the next day the campaign said he hunted twice in his life.[2397] "Officials in the four states where Romney" lived said he never took out a license.[2398] So Romney later explained his staff was incorrect, and said he actually hunted small game in Utah, where small game doesn't need a license.[2399] So not only has Romney reinvented himself on abortion and gay rights, he has also become a newly formed NRA machine.

Romney has erred, more than once, when he desperately grasped for the base of the party. He loves prisons with bad reputations. In a presidential debate in May, Romney said he wanted detainees on Guantanamo, "where they don't get the access to lawyers they get when they're on our soil. I don't want them in our prisons, I want them there. Some people have said we ought to close Guantanamo. My view is we ought to double Guantanamo."[2400] By June, senior Bush administration officials were already engaged in active discussions about closing the facility, and the President had publicly stated his desire to shut it down.[2401]

The *AP* reported in July 2007 of Romney's comments to South Florida Republicans that Venezuelan President Hugo Chavez "has tried to steal an inspiring phrase—'Patria o muerte, venceremos.' It does not belong to him. It belongs to a free Cuba." [2402] The *AP* clarified: "In truth, the phrase does not belong to free Cubans. It has been a trademark speech ending for Castro, their most despised opponent."[2403] The majority of Cuban-Americans in Florida vote Republican.

Success is on the horizon

After the second quarter of 2007, Romney had $44.4 million in receipts, but Romney gave his campaign nearly $9 million.[2404] Romney can give his campaign $40 to $60 million if needed.[2405] Despite polling strong in Iowa, he was "far weaker in South Carolina."[2406] Romney could spend more time campaigning, instead of worrying about dollars. A July 2007 CNN poll showed Romney in first place in Iowa with 25 percent, followed by Fred Thompson (14), Giuliani (13), McCain (10), Gingrich (6); Huckabee, Tancredo, Brownback and Tommy Thompson (2); and Hunter and Paul (1).[2407] In December 2006, Romney was only at nine percent in New Hampshire, but from April to late July 2007, he hovered around 25 percent in the state's GOP presidential preference polls.[2408]

He has also started to split from the Bush administration. Romney said (8.1.07) the Homeland Security Department was inefficient and needed major restructuring.[2409] And on expanded government healthcare: "The last thing I want is the guys managing the Katrina cleanup managing my health care system."[2410] This was the same Romney who supported President Bush's surge plan for Iraq in January 2007, and half a year later said it was "apparently" working.

Romney won the Iowa Straw Poll on August 11, 2007. But, as David Gregory of *NBC News* said, "as expected," Romney won the straw poll.[2411] Now Romney has to exceed expectations, not just reach them.

Representative Tom Tancredo

The 6th District Republican Congressman from Colorado first elected in 1998, Tancredo immediately raised eyebrows. He declined to go to a Clinton White House reception for freshmen Congressional members.[2412] In addition, Tancredo's district included Columbine High School, where the infamous shootings in the late 1990s shocked America. The school is just blocks from Tancredo's home.[2413] He was the only Colorado House member to vote for the National Rifle Association's bill in the House (despite the increased calls for gun control); and as a strong supporter of the Second Amendment, argued that Colorado's gun control laws were stronger than the federal governments.[2414] He voted against Bush's prescription drug entitlement because he felt it was too expensive, and against No Child Left Behind Act because he said it expanded federal government infringement on state responsibilities.[2415]

In a March 2006 report by *The Hill*, his wife Jackie discussed how she usually said, "Tom you can't say that," but he already had.[2416] According to Jackie, Tom stayed in Washington 10 days at a time to "justify a plane ticket," and wore a bullet-proof vest when delivering speeches.[2417]

Immigration, immigration, immigration

He already told the *Washington Times* editorial board in April of 2002 that the President was an obstacle to immigration reform and had an "open door" border policy that threatened national security.[2418] Immigration is Tancredo's main issue.

Tancredo was not a frontrunner; but he was gaining support for his immigration beliefs. *The Hill* described Tancredo (6.29.05) as an "outspoken critic of illegal immigration" who had pitted himself against [Congressional] … "conference centrists and a wide swath of economic concerns from agriculture to big business that have long been advocating for expanded guest-worker programs."[2419] Tancredo felt Bush's immigration beliefs constituted amnesty for illegal workers already in the country.

Sometimes he was articulate and respected. George Will released an op-ed on Tom Tancredo in October 2005, and discussed the mounting challenge of 11 million illegal immigrants: deporting the "equivalent of the population of Ohio" would be difficult.[2420] Tancredo's "silver bullet," wrote Will, "is to 'just enforce the law'—the law against hiring illegal immigrants. Give employers computerized means of checking the status of job applicants and, he says, illegals will go home."[2421]

Does Tancredo go over the top?

In 2002, the *Denver Post* reported of a high-school honor student who couldn't get financial aid for college because he was in the US illegally: Tancredo tried to have the family deported (unsuccessfully).[2422] This grandson of an Italian immigrant has decried "the cult of multiculturalism," and called the illegal aliens "a scourge that threatens the very future of our nation."[2423]

In late 2005, Utah Sen. Bob Bennett attached a provision to an agriculture department funding bill shielding religious groups (i.e. Mormons) from a federal law. Bennett's version allowed one to knowingly transport and harbor illegal immigrants as long as the illegal immigrant volunteered in a religious capacity.[2424] Not short on analogies, Tancredo released a statement saying the "...provision opens a hole in our immigration system so big, a terrorist could drive a truck bomb through it."[2425]

Tancredo visited New Hampshire in June 2006, it was his second trip there for the year, and it solidified him as a possible 2008 contender. In Nashua, he stated that although "I don't consider myself a candidate today....If no one will take this banner up [of immigration]—and I say this with great trepidation—yeah, I will [run for president]."[2426] Tancredo heavily emphasized his topic, immigration, and agreed many illegally entering the country were seeking employment, but others were "coming to kill you, and you, and me, and my children, and my grandchildren."[2427] And your neighbors, cats, dogs, mailmen, and billy goats. Thirty people came to see Tancredo in New Hampshire.[2428]

In November 2006, Tancredo said Miami "has become a Third World country. You just pick it up and take it and move it someplace. You would never know you're in the United States of America. You would certainly say you're in a Third World country."[2429] Two-thirds of Miami's population is Hispanic, according to the 2000 census.[2430] Florida Gov. Jeb Bush sent a letter to Tancredo citing the comments as "disappointing" and "naïve."[2431] Elsewhere, Jeb Bush was more steamed: "What a nut. I'm just disappointed. First of all, you know from a— he's from my own party. He's a Republican. He doesn't represent my views."[2432]

Tancredo has called for the abolition of Black and Hispanic congressional caucuses (Jan. 2007). "It is utterly hypocritical for Congress to extol the virtues of a colorblind society while officially sanctioning caucuses that are based solely on race."[2433] But Tancredo's requests came after suggestions that Rep. Stephen Cohen (D-TN), a Caucasian, was denied access to the Congressional Black Caucus.[2434]

There are many quotes from Tancredo on immigration: "...If we don't control immigration, legal and illegal, we will eventually reach the point where it won't be what kind of a nation we are, balkanized or united, we will actually have to face the fact that we are no longer a nation at all."[2435] MSNBC.com reported on Tancredo: "What other candidate is willing to voice concern about illegal immigrants bringing with them across the border diseases such as leprosy and tuberculosis?"[2436] Leprosy.

He may be inconsistent on playing the terrorism card with the immigration issue. He has said, "...the place where we have indicated more terrorists or potential terrorists, is our Northern border."[2437] But he has stated, "We have terrorists coming into the country both through our Northern and Southern borders."[2438] Is Tancredo's immigration efforts really about anti-terrorism?

Vote Tancredo 2008: Bomb Mecca

Pat Campbell of *WFLA* in Orlando asked Tom Tancredo in a radio interview how the U.S. should respond if several of its cities were attacked with nuclear weapons. "…If this happens in the United States, and we determine that it is the result of extremist, fundamentalist Muslims, you know, you could take out their holy sites."[2439] According to the *Rocky Mountain News*, Campbell then clarified: "You're talking about bombing Mecca."[2440] At which point Tancredo responded "Yeah." Tancredo later said "I do not advocate this," and his spokesman stated that Tancredo was a "free thinker" struggling with a hypothetical question.[2441] What a mentality: an attack by some Muslims deserves an attack on a holy site used by all. The *AP* report's title on FOXNews.com was "Tancredo: If They Nuke Us, Bomb Mecca."[2442]

After Tancredo suggested bombing Muslim holy sites in response to terrorist attacks, Tancredo and a group of Muslim, Christian, and Jewish representatives tried to write a peace statement. Instead, the group and Tancredo "disintegrated, with the two sides unable to agree on a joint statement about religion, terrorism, and retaliation," according to the *Denver Post*.[2443] The split came after Tancredo complained the 9/11 memorial for Flight 93 in Pennsylvania had a Muslim crescent because the terrorists were radical Muslims.[2444]

Tancredo has also said, "Radical Islam has been the foe of Christendom for centuries."[2445]

Other weaknesses

He is virtually unknown. A *Scripps Howard News Service* article on Tancredo's July 2005 trip to southeastern Iowa, said Tancredo had to repeatedly "explain that he was not Rep. Steve King, the local Republican congressman with who he shares a striking resemblance. When his small entourage finally arrived in Dubuque in the wee hours Saturday morning, Tancredo was met by a swarm of 'mayflies.'"[2446] Tom Tancredo visited South Carolina in August 2005, and raised some money for his Team America PAC that supported immigration reform-minded candidates, but was "greeted by smaller–than-expected audiences."[2447]

Scripps Howard News Service (July 2005) reported his childhood depression that led to a draft deferment for Vietnam; and that illegal immigrants worked for the contractor that installed Tancredo's home theater system.[2448]

The presidential candidate

By January 2007, it was clear in Tancredo's own words a presidential bid was "a distinct possibility."[2449] He was signing his book (*In Mortal Danger*) at the Barnes & Noble in Council Bluffs, Iowa on January 12.[2450] The campaign began despite having told the *Denver Post* in April 2006 that he "got the feeling" he would "not have to" run.[2451] But his spokesman Carlos Espinoza said (Jan.2007), "third place would be a huge victory" for Tancredo in Iowa, and "The reality is, McCain is not very popular guy in Iowa."[2452] *Media Matters* out of Colorado noted the *Denver Post* did not challenge the claim, and a December 2006 Research 2000 Iowa Poll had McCain leading 11 contestants with 27 percent followed by Giuliani (26), and Romney third with 9.[2453] Tancredo called McCain's plan for illegal immigrants "amnesty."

His expectations are low: Tancredo would like to finish third or fourth in the Iowa caucus.[2454] He is helped by Bay Buchanan, the sister of 1992 and 1996 presidential hopeful Pat Buchanan. But Tancredo 2008 may not end up being the remake of Pat Buchanan's insurgency of 1992. (Though Pat Buchanan has a similar view on illegal immigration as Tancredo.) In many cases, the crowds have been lower than expected. In 1992, the GOP nomination was between President George H.W. Bush and Pat Buchanan. In 2007, the GOP competition was often hovering around a total of ten candidates.

He has made his share of mistakes. He promised a package of gifts and all expenses trip to the nation's capitol to supporters if they brought 25 people to the GOP straw poll, but as the *AP* reported (7.31.07), "There was one problem with the pitch—a tour of the Capitol could be a violation of House ethics rules which prohibit the use of any buildings on the Capitol grounds for campaign purposes."[2455]

Tancredo campaigns on the hype that immigration (instead of Iraq) will be the major issue on the mind of caucus goers. But he has complimented Rep. Duncan Hunter (CA), who steals Tancredo's spotlight. Which of his GOP opponents had acceptable positions? Tancredo said (Jan.07), "Duncan Hunter is as close to anyone there. He's certainly been a consistent vote, the only consistent vote of the other members up there on the issue [of immigration].[2456] *MSNBC.com* reported (3.13.07) Hunter was "another anti-China, anti-illegal immigrant Republican hopeful," in an article about Tancredo's presidential campaign.[2457]

Tancredo finished third in the Iowa Straw Poll with 14 percent of the votes, and he will do better if Hunter drops out of the race (Hunter only scored one percent in the straw poll).

Former Senator Fred Thompson

Thompson was born in Alabama in 1942, but grew up near Lawrenceburg, Tennessee.[2458] He graduated from Memphis State University and received a law degree from Vanderbilt University Law School.[2459] In 1994, he won the special election for Vice President Al Gore's Senate seat.[2460] He was re-elected in 1996 and chose not to seek election in the 2002 elections.[2461] He considered running for president in 2000.[2462]

In 2002, his 38 year old daughter died of an accidental drug overdose and he decided not to run for Senate.[2463] He remarried in 2002 and as he was considering running in the spring of 2007, he had a 4-year-old daughter and a 6-month-old son.[2464] His current wife, Jeri, is a GOP strategist.[2465] Jeri was 29 when she married Fred.[2466] Joe Scarborough of MSNBC has asked whether Thompson's current wife "works the pole."[2467]

Time reported (5.24.07) Thompson had to overcome many hardships: "a marriage while in high school after conceiving a child with his teenage girlfriend, a subsequent divorce [after 26 years of marriage[2468]], a diagnosis of non-Hodgkin's lymphoma 2 ½ years ago and, perhaps most traumatic, the sudden death of his daughter Betsy in 2002 from an accidental overdose of prescription drugs."[2469]

He acted in over a dozen feature films, including *The Hunt for Red October*, *Cape Fear*, and *In the Line of Fire*.[2470] He also appeared in TV series such as *Matlock* and *Roseanne*.[2471] Thompson left (spring 2006) NBC's *Law & Order* after a five year stint playing Manhattan District Attorney Arthur Branch.[2472]

Freddie the Freeloader

USA Today brought up the issue whether he was is lazy.[2473] The *AP* said in his Senate tenure, "…he had few significant legislative achievements and established a reputation as a less-than-hard worker."[2474] Charlie Cook wrote (6.5.07), "Perhaps the biggest knock is the 'laziness' charge. There is no doubt that his slow-moving, ambling persona, [and] a lower metabolism rate that many think is systemic to being a Southerner, could be a problem…"[2475] *USA Today* said he has "a Southern drawl, a loping gait, a lined face and a balding pate."[2476]

The *New Republic* noted (4.13.07), "a long-standing reputation for lacking any passion, zeal, or vision for governing. Plus, he's said to be just the teensiest bit lazy."[2477] *Time* said (5.24.07) Thompson had "a reputation for resisting a demanding schedule."[2478] His high school football coach called him "smart, but he was lazy."[2479] One of Thompson's former advisors said the Senator "did the bare minimum to get by and then hightailed [it] to the Prime Rib or the Capital Grille."[2480]

Slate commented (5.31.07) "the laziness rap against Thompson is like the rap that former presidential hopeful Sen. George Allen isn't a genius. Or that John McCain is a hothead. It's an unresolved issue waiting for its moment to become a crisis for the campaign."[2481]

To all the girls Fred's loved before

Country music singer Lorrie Morgan said Thompson was "smart," and a good listener: "I think Fred Thompson is one of the best people I've ever met in my life, honestly."[2482] Morgan blamed herself for the end of their relationship.[2483] *The Sunday Times* (UK) was particularly detailed on Thompson's past girlfriends, but noted "he appears to have achieved the impossible and kept their friendship and respect," (6.24.07).[2484] Morgan told *The Sunday Times* Fred was "every woman's fantasy."[2485] After Morgan, Thompson dated a Republican fundraiser, Georgette Mosbacher, who said Thompson was "a really good listener."[2486] Margaret Carlson of *Bloomberg News* also praised Thompson.[2487]

Fred Thompson was pro-choice

According to *USA Today* (5.6.07), during his 1994 candidacy for US Senate, he answered a Project Vote Smart questionnaire and "indicated support for keeping abortion legal in the first trimester. His advisors note that he was endorsed by the anti-abortion community in that election and is an ardent opponent of abortion, although they do not claim past purity on the issue."[2488] *Gannett News Service* reported in another questionnaire during the 1994 campaign, Thompson provided a handwritten note stating "I do not believe abortion should be criminalized. This battle will be won in the hearts and souls of the American people."[2489] The *New Republic* said (4.13.07), "Thompson was, as recently as 1995, pro-choice."[2490]

In July 2007, billing records uncovered by the *New York Times* showed Thompson, in the early 1990s, was paid for 20 hours to lobby for a group to ease federal rules on abortion counseling.[2491] Thompson denied the charge, but records showed Thompson worked part-time for the National Family Planning and Reproductive Health Association from 1991-1994.[2492] The association, which provided board's minutes of September 1991 to the *LA Times*, said it hired Thompson "to lobby" the George H.W. Bush administration "to ease regulation that prevented clinics that received federal money from offering any abortion counseling."[2493] In fact, former Rep. Michael D. Barnes (D-MD) recommended Thompson for the lobbying job, and said the former Senator's denials were "absolutely bizarre."[2494]

To be perfectly clear, Thompson's spokesman initially said, "There's no documents to prove it, there's no billing records, and Thompson says he has no recollection of it, says it didn't happen."[2495]

Nixon & Thompson

Fred Thompson was the minority council for the Senate Watergate Committee in 1973 and 1974.[2496] But the *Boston Globe* reported (7.4.07) Thompson leaked information to the White House during the Watergate investigation.[2497] The *AP* said (7.7.07) Nixon viewed Thompson "as a willing, if not too bright, ally..."[2498] The *AP* noted how he "won fame in 1973" for revealing Nixon's installation of tapes in the White House, but "It was Thompson who tipped off the White House that the Senate committee knew about the tapes."[2499]

Nixon called Thompson "dumb as hell" and was worried Thompson would not be able to outsmart the committee's Democratic counsel.[2500] Tapes and transcripts showed that although Thompson presented himself publicly as one dedicated to the truth, he "worked cooperatively with the White House and accepted coaching from Nixon's lawyer."[2501] Thompson declined to comment for the *AP* story. Thompson wrote a book on his role in Watergate in 1975, *At That Point in Time*, in which he wrote he tried "to walk a fine line between a good-faith pursuit of the investigation and a good-faith attempt to insure balance and fairness."[2502]

In July 2007, Thompson official website of his anticipated 2008 campaign said he "gained national attention for leading the line of inquiry that revealed the audio-taping system in the White House Oval Office."[2503]

Will this bubble burst too?

Why did Fred Thompson enter so late? Bill Frist was supposed to run for president, when his hopes turned hopeless, Fred Thompson's ambitions found an opening.[2504] *FOX News* reported (4.19.07) Thompson was "registering well in national polls, as he flirts with a presidential run, [and] is the talk of this town's [Washington's] elite. It's a different story in early primary states where voters will choose the GOP nominee."[2505] In a May 2007 CNN poll of registered Republicans, Giuliani place first with 25 percent, followed by McCain (23), Thompson (13) and Romney (10).[2506]

He did not come to the first presidential debate in California, but the next day (5.4.07) he appeared at the Lincoln Day dinner for Orange County Republicans.[2507] But his speech given in California in early May "didn't live up to expectations."[2508] Conservative columnist Robert Novak called it "lackluster."[2509] *Time* said (5.9.07) he "began with some jokes that were well received but then abandoned his carefully written text and rambled through remarks that left many in the audience underwhelmed."[2510] *Slate* said (5.31.07) Thompson "tore up his speech and just ad-libbed."[2511] Was Thompson managing the expectations for his candidacy?

The *AP* reported (6.12.07), "If he runs it will be as a Washington outsider."[2512] He is not a Washington outsider. Thompson is "the celebrity who now lives in the tony Washington suburb of McLean, Va."[2513]

He is a McCain ally. As *USA Today* reported (5.9.07), some of the conservative's "fervor for Thompson cooled when they were reminded he was an original co-sponsor of the McCain-Feingold campaign finance bill."[2514] Fred Thompson was one of a handful of Senators to endorse McCain in 2000. How would that thrill the base? And what does Thompson offer new to the future of the GOP? He wrote an op-ed to the *Wall Street Journal* titled "Case Closed: Tax cuts mean growth," (April 2007).[2515] What GOP presidential candidate does not think *tax cuts mean growth*? Does Fred Thompson offer anything different than other Republican contenders?

The media's orchestrated expectation

In July 2007, *Washingtonpost.com* said Fred Thompson was "pulling double digits in every national and state poll we have seen."[2516] But the *New York*

Times reported (7.31.07) the money for June "was less than the $5 million that Mr. Thompson's supporters had hoped for and has met with some disappointment inside his camp, which has also been buffeted in recent days by staff defections and high-level disagreements."[2517] The headline: "Fred Thompson Came Up Short in June Money."[2518] The *New York Times* was less specific on which 'supporters' spread the benchmark $5 million. The *AP* reported (7.30.07) the $3 million Thompson raised "lags the original $5 million goal backers set for June, the first month in which he set out to raise money."[2519] Of course, the *AP* did not explain who those 'backers' were? Who is leaking in Fred Thompson's campaign? Why do news organizations release benchmarks that can't be proven to have existed?

In one of the most elongated announcements ever, Thompson finally broke the anticlimactic 'suspense' on September 5, 2007, and officially announced his candidacy on *The Tonight Show* with Jay Leno. The announcement came the same night Thompson's counterparts debated.

Former Governor Tommy Thompson

A four term governor of Wisconsin, Tommy Thompson surprised many when he announced his consideration for the presidency in November 2006, a month in which he turned 65.[2520] He had been active in the losing campaign of Mark Green against Gov. Jim Doyle in Wisconsin. In an ad against Doyle, Thompson claimed Doyle was "lying about Mark Green to cover" up failures.[2521] But Thompson was not helping GOP candidates nationwide in 2006, and his support for Mark Green was certainly not the midterm campaigning caliber of Barack Obama. At an Iowans for Wellness Prevention meeting in Des Moines a week after the midterms, Thompson said he intended to establish an exploratory committee after the first of the year.[2522] The November 2006 trip to Iowa was his fourth in six weeks.[2523] He said he hoped to run for president, "Why not? I'm from the Midwest. There should be a Midwestern candidate for president."[2524] In January he said "I'm the only farmer in the group. I'm the only one that rides motorcycles."[2525] In January 2007, he promised to spend at least one day a week in Iowa campaigning.[2526]

What were Tommy's issues?

Not Iraq. The *AP* reported, "He pushed for an overhaul of Wisconsin welfare laws, well before Congress and President Clinton took up the issue on the national level."[2527] The *Des Moines Register* reported (Jan.2007), "He cites his role in reforming welfare as governor and in running the nation's largest health-care programs as a federal administrator. After leaving office, he was chairman of the Global Fund to Fight AIDS, Tuberculosis and Malaria. He said that experience would help him lead on international matters."[2528]

Likewise, after the midterms, he predicted the two main issues of the race would be health care and energy; he said he did not think anybody had a "better handle" on health care than himself, and he cited his oversight of Medicare and told Iowans of his business partnership, which was planning to build an ethanol plant.[2529] Though the *AP* claimed Thompson said the top three issues would be Iraq, energy independence, and health care.[2530] The *AP* mentioned health care first.

Reuters too, quoted Thompson—in Iowa, but through a telephone interview—with "I believe the top issues for the presidential election are going to be energy and health care, and I think I have some of the best ideas in the country on both of them."[2531] He also said 'I'm in an enviable position because I'm an expert in most of those fields and can articulate a vision for America that is lacking right now," said the Governor who apparently did not mention Iraq to *Reuters*.[2532]

The not so funny Jewish comment

In April, he told a Jewish group, "I'm in the private sector and for the first time in my life I'm earning money. You know that's sort of part of the Jewish tradition and I do not find anything wrong with that."[2533] Then he came back to the podium: "I just want to clarify something because I didn't (by) any means want to infer or imply anything about Jews and finances and things. What I was referring to….is the accomplishments of the Jewish religion. You've been outstanding business people and I compliment you for that."[2534]

Thompson asked *Politico* reporters in an interview: "Have you ever made a mistake?"[2535] To which another blogger answered: "'Have you ever made a mistake?' You mean, a mistake where I make a Jewish joke in front of a Jewish audience? No. I never made a mistake like that."[2536] Thompson blamed the gaffe on fatigue:[2537] "I was tired, I made a mistake." The Israeli newspaper *Haaretz* first reported the flap.[2538] In fact, Shmuel Rosner, from *Haaretz*, also wrote how Thompson referred to "Israeli bonds" as "Jewish bonds."[2539] Thompson "came to woo but left behind a crowd of sophisticated adults giggling like teenagers at his expense," wrote Rosner.[2540]

Jay Leno said (4.19.07), "Presidential candidate Tommy Thompson, the former governor of Wisconsin, is speaking to a Jewish group ... and says to them, 'For the first time in my life I'm earning money, which is part of the Jewish tradition.' Then he apologized with, 'I'm sorry. ... I'm so sorry. That's the speech I was supposed to give in front of the Muslim group.'"[2541]

Thompson briefly supported the firing of homosexuals

In a May GOP debate, John Harris asked Thompson, "If a private employer finds homosexuality immoral, should he be allowed to fire a gay worker?"[2542] Thompson said, "I think that is left up to the individual business. I really sincerely believe that that is a issue that business people have got to make their own determination as to whether or not they should be."[2543] So the answer was yes? "Yes," Thompson replied.[2544]

Thompson later backtracked, and "said he thought he had been asked whether enough laws are on the books to protect gays, but his hearing aid went out during the debate."[2545] But in looking at the question which was asked him, Thompson gave an answer that was clearly on topic. If he had a hearing problem, why didn't he ask for the question to be repeated?[2546]

The non-debate version of Tommy Thompson said he wanted to imply employers should have as much control as possible in hiring and supervision, but should not be allowed to discriminate against homosexuals.[2547] Discrimination by employers, however, "is wrong. It's against the law, and I'm against it. And I made a mistake. I didn't hear the question properly."[2548] Thompson even linked gay prejudice to acts of racism.[2549]

Tommy Thompson's concerns to address

1) For a conservative, he had quite a bit of sick time conversion. A November 2006 report by the *Milwaukee Journal Sentinel* said Thompson racked up a $290,797 benefit from unused sick time for cash equivalent to pay for health care premiums, which ran "to about $9,900 a year for a retiree and his or her spouse in the Madison area, if they are eligible for Medicare."[2550]

2) Who were his donors? Darshan Dhaliwal, the Midwest gas mogul and owner of Bulk Petroleum, promised to raise $1,000,000 for Thompson: "Everybody has 500 friends."[2551] BP was one of the largest gas stations chains in the country, and made $2 billion annually.[2552] In 1999, Gov. Thompson proposed the state spend $2.5 million to open a University of Wisconsin campus in the Punjab region in India—based on Dhaliwal's asking.[2553] They traveled together on a trip to India, Dhaliwal promised scholarships to Indians who went to the campus, and by the end of the year there was a Dhaliwal hosted gathering raising $85,000 for Thompson.[2554] The foreign satellite campus never happened, but Dhaliwal gave $200,000 in 2001 for the Tommy G. Thompson Center at Marquette University in Milwaukee.[2555] And he promised Thompson 1,000 votes in Iowa.[2556] Also writing out an early check to Thompson was Gerald Boyle, infamous serial killer Jeffrey Dahmer's defense attorney.[2557]

3) The campaign hinged on Iowa. It became apparent it would all come down to Iowa, which was "central" to his strategy.[2558] Though this was not so much as winning the caucus, but more so getting supporters to the Ames Straw poll on August 11, 2007.[2559]

4) Did he have a chance? In an article headlined "McCain jumps in ring with Rudy," the *New York Daily News* wrote on the fight between the top two candidates and ended the report with Thompson, who "also announced plans" to go with a White House run.[2560] In the *AP* article on McCain's call for 'common-sense conservatism' in mid-November 2006, Duncan Hunter was described as another GOP contender, but neither Thompson nor Hagel were included.[2561] The *AP*'s report on Thompson's trip to Iowa opened with "He's far less known than some of his potential rivals…"[2562]

Tony Leys, not the first rate Thomas Beaumont, covered the *Des Moines Register* story on Thompson (11.16.06).[2563] The *National Journal*, ranking him eight out of eleven candidates (above Frank Keating, Jim Gilmore, and Duncan Hunter) said (1.11.07): "He became the first candidate to bash Bush (calling him a "good" but not "great" president). If that's the only way he gets attention, he'll have trouble convincing the rest of the field that's he's anything but a vanity candidate. He'll be able to raise a bit of early money, but most of his donors will be sympathetic friends and double-dippers."[2564] *Weekly Standard* executive director Fred Barnes advice to Thompson was "Run for governor, he was a great governor."[2565]

On December 8, the *Milwaukee Journal Sentinel*'s political cartoon had Thompson (holding a 2008 sign) in a form of a balloon leaking air.[2566] How was he received? The *Des Moines Register* said (Jan.4), he had a "relatively low profile compared" to his rivals.[2567] But he had hired two Iowa political organizers, Steve Grubbs and Brian Dumas.[2568] The *Milwaukee Journal Sentinel* reported (12.4.07) that in mid-November, the *AP* "promptly carried the news of Thompson's intentions—to form an exploratory committee early next year—as an 'urgent' dispatch, and CNN carried it as 'breaking news.' Since then, deafening silence."[2569]

Tommy Thompson had a lot of Iowa visits to make. He made half a dozen visits to Iowa in the fall of 2006.[2570] As of that late November 2006 tally, Romney led in Iowa visits (12), followed by Pataki (10), Brownback (8), Huckabee (7), and Gingrich (6).[2571]

Jay Leno said (4.9.07), "...[Tommy] Thompson has announced he is running for president of the United States. Experts are saying this announcement could have absolutely no affect on the race whatsoever."[2572] His bank was thin: Thompson loaned $75,000 to his campaign in the first quarter of 2007, an amount which was a fifth of his donations for the period.[2573] Thompson also loaned the campaign another $50,000 the next quarter.[2574] Of course—that was *Tommy* Thompson—not *Fred* Thompson.

This Thompson left the race

The day before the Iowa Straw Poll, the *Milwaukee Journal Sentinel* reported how Thompson saw the Wisconsin media as a road bump for his presidential ambitions.[2575] Then judgment day in Iowa occurred, and Tommy Thompson placed sixth at the Iowa Straw Poll,[2576] where he previously stated he needed a first or second place finish. When the *Milwaukee Journal Sentinel* reported Thompson's withdrawal from the 2008 race (8.13.07), the story about the former Wisconsin governor was pushed to page 3A.[2577]

Former Senator Rick Santorum

Rick Santorum was elected to the House in 1990, and was one of the 'Gang of Seven' freshman Republicans who helped expose the House bank scandal.[2578] He was elected to the Senate in 1994. When he campaigned for Senate, he favored raising the Social Security retirement age to 70 and even admitted that he would possibly "go even farther if I could."[2579] His support for creation of personal accounts dated back to 1999, even when George Bush was still governor of Texas.[2580] (After the 2004 election, President Bush began his effort to reform Social Security, and Santorum would be an ardent supporter.)

Santorum won reelection to the Senate in 2000 against Ron Klink, who opposed gun control and abortion.[2581] This is noteworthy because on paper, this moderate opponent (as opposed to a liberal Democrat) would seem to threaten the conservative Santorum. Instead, because gun control and pro-choice groups tend to cough up significant sums of money for Democrats, Klink had trouble raising money.[2582] In 2006, Santorum was up for election, and a pro-life Democrat would become his opponent. Would this hurt or help Santorum? And could he run for President in 2008 if he had to spend 2005 and 2006 focused on Pennsylvania?

After the 2000 elections, Santorum was elected the Republican Conference chairman, ranking him third in the Republican Senate leadership.[2583] When Majority Leader Trent Lott caught fire for his comments at Strom Thurmond's birthday party in December 2002, Santorum tried to get the spot, but it went to Bill Frist (though Santorum got an endorsement from Pennsylvania's other Senator, Arlen Specter).[2584]

Though conservative, Santorum supported minimum wage increases in his Congressional career. And he opposed President Bush's proposed $250,000 cap on pain and suffering damages in medical malpractice cases: Santorum's wife sued for $500,000 in 1999 because of back injuries and won $175,000.[2585]

Santorum was seen as a villain by the left, but a key event explained his conservative beliefs. In 1996, he and his wife found out their unborn child had a fatal defect and the baby died two hours after birth; and Santorum led a movement to ban partial-birth abortions.[2586]

Santorum was a loyal fit for the President. *Congressional Quarterly* said Santorum voted 95(%) of the time with the President in 2005, 100 in 2004, 99 in 2003, 96 in 2002, and 97 in 2001.[2587] If he could not run for President, his 2006 Senate race (in early 2005 at least) looked to be the best race of the midterm elections. His race against Bob Casey Jr. turned out to be overshadowed by George Allen's Senate campaign.

It Takes a Family to tick off Clinton

Rick Santorum's book *It Takes a Family: Conservatism and the Common Good*, went on sale the July 4th weekend in Washington bookstores (the official release date was 7.24.05). Santorum said his book was "not written to counter" Sen. Clinton's book, *It Takes a Village*, rather, it was "a book to counter her worldview, which in my opinion was not expressed in her book."[2588]

"In far too many families with young children, both parents are working...," wrote Santorum.[2589] A Greenberg, Quinlan, Rosner Research Inc. poll found only 30% of working moms would choose to stay at home full-time if money was not an object.[2590] He also wrote that overturning Roe v. Wade "can be done," and living together before marriage was "wrong."[2591]

Hillary Clinton declined to comment on Santorum's book thru her spokeswoman (7.5.05).[2592] No doubt Clinton disagreed with the book. Did she decline public battle against Santorum? She spoke up when she crossed Santorum in the basement of the Capital a week later. According to the *AP*, Clinton called out, "It takes a village, Rick, don't forget that."[2593] But Santorum came back: "It takes a family." [2594] Clinton then stated "Of course, a family is part of a village!"[2595] Santorum also told George Stephanopoulos that "yes," Hillary Clinton was a radical feminist, and did verify an encounter with Hillary on "It takes a Family" in passing.

Santorum has made some notable quotes

1) He said Boston liberalism was at heart of the Catholic Church priest abuse scandals. Santorum wrote to *Catholic Online* in 2002 that "while it is no excuse for this scandal, it is no surprise that Boston, a seat of academic, political, and cultural liberalism in America, lies at the center of the storm."[2596] In 2005, Santorum's quote was revived after the *Philadelphia News* columnist John Baer "raised them in print and prompted a political discourse in the blogosphere."[2597] Then the *Boston Globe* got involved. Mitt Romney came out against Santorum: "...I am going to suggest that he's wrong on the conclusion he's reached."[2598] Was Romney distancing himself from Santorum? Not exactly, indeed, Romney said, "people are entitled to their own viewpoints."[2599] John McCain said Santorum, "...has probably written off Massachusetts."[2600]

But Ted Kennedy "upbraided" Santorum in an "unusually personal attack" on the Senate floor (7.13.05).[2601] Was this necessary for a comment made three years earlier? John Kerry chimed in too. Kerry spokesman David Wade stated Santorum owed an apology.[2602] Did Santorum 'turn the other cheek'? "I don't think Ted Kennedy lecturing me on the teachings of the church and how the church should handle these problems is something I'm going to take particularly seriously."[2603] Yes, Santorum took the high road.

On ABC's *This Week* (7.31.05), Santorum agreed that he singled out Boston in 2002, noting that "In July of 2002, that was the epicenter."[2604] George Stephanopoulos interrupted (the *Globe* described it as cutting off) Santorum, "That simply is not true."[2605] The sex scandals were dispersed throughout the country, however, there were much national attention on Boston and Cardinal Bernard Law (who later resigned as Boston' handling of past abuse). In defense of Santorum, who told *This Week* that Kennedy and Kerry "did nothing" when the crisis occurred, the *Boston Globe* retrieved past articles showing Kennedy himself stated that "We're [the federal government] not the ones to do it."[2606]

So Santorum's quote from 2002, which seemed harsh and arbitrary, was rehashed at his expense three years later. But it brought up logical points in

Santorum's favor: Where was the government at the aid of the sexually abused? And was Boston the epicenter—and why? Most noteworthy of this episode was Kerry's inability to try to fix the abuse scandal. Had he been too concerned with his position on the political spectrum to fix the problems with his Church?

However, a grand jury (convened in April 2002) released a report in September 2005, alleging the Philadelphia archdiocese of a cover-up of 63 abusive priests during the reign of two archbishops between 1961-2003, with church officials themselves saying 44 priests had been credibly accused of sexual assaults since the 1950s but only one had been indicted.[2607] Apparently there was 'cultural liberalism' in Pennsylvania.

2) Santorum has made his share of Nazi analogies. In May 2006, Santorum blundered in his statements in support to end judicial filibusters and the possible rule change from Republicans. Santorum stated, "The audacity of some members to stand up and say, 'How dare you break this rule!'...It's the equivalent of Adolf Hitler in 1942 saying, 'I'm in Paris. How dare you invade me. How dare you bomb my city. It's mine.'"[2608] The Anti-Defamation League entered the fray, calling Santorum's comparison "outrageous."[2609] Perhaps Santorum's statements were out of line, but Jonathan Chait of the *Los Angeles Times* pointed out

> ...when Nazis are invoked, it's often not to make a moral comparison but to establish a logical principle. That's the main mistake made by those who decry Nazi allusions. They ignore, or fail to grasp, the distinction between comparing someone to Hitler and using a historical analogy that draws on the Nazi era. The latter is what Santorum did. He was trying to make the point that Democrats had broken the rules (by filibustering judges) and then were complaining when Republicans merely tried to restore them."[2610]

Few saw Santorum's comments in such a light.

Instead, the senator had to apologize. He stated that "Referencing Hitler was meant to dramatize the principle of an argument, not to characterize my Democratic colleagues."[2611] His apology might have meant something had he not criticized Sen. Robert Byrd in March. Byrd (D-WVA) was scolded two months earlier after he had compared Hitler's Nazis to the GOP's rule change on the filibuster, citing that it was similar to Hitler's success in winning dictatorial powers from the German Parliament: "Hitler never abandoned the cloak of legality."[2612] Santorum stated Byrd's Nazi references "lessen the credibility of the Senator and the decorum of the Senate."[2613]

The *Pittsburgh Tribune Review* noted (5.29.05) that after Santorum's own Hitler remarks, perhaps he tried to show off his "kinder, gentler side."[2614] Santorum followed his blunder by announcing he was co-sponsoring two bills: one to address more oversight in the pet industry and the other to add a bitter taste to engine coolants and antifreeze so children would be less likely to swallow the product. "As the father of six children and a dog owner, I understand the importance of protecting our loved ones from dangers that are found throughout our homes."[2615]

3) Gays loathe Santorum, and perhaps the opposite. In April 2003, Santorum said if "the Supreme Court says that you have the right to consensual sex within your home, then you have the right to bigamy," polygamy, incest, and adultery…"You have the right to anything."[2616] And in the same interview he said "In every society, the definition of marriage has not ever to my knowledge included homosexuality. That's not to pick on homosexuality. It's not, you know, man on child, man on dog, or whatever the case may be. It is one thing. And when you destroy that you have a dramatic impact on the quality…"[2617] At this point, the *AP* reporter, Lara Jakes Jordan, interrupted: "I'm sorry, I didn't think I was going to talk about 'man on dog' with a United States Senator; it's sort of freaking me out."[2618] Santorum has also said, "Isn't that the ultimate homeland security, standing up and defending marriage?"[2619]

Santorum considered running in 2008

In January 2005, Santorum said, "I'm not saying never," about running for president.[2620] Nor did Santorum rule out a 2008 run for President in his *Meet the Press* interview (Feb.2005), but instead stated he was focusing on re-election in 2006 to represent Pennsylvania in the Senate. If re-elected to the Senate he stated he would "be running for the whip's office,"[2621] which is a position that provides loyalty.

By May 2005, Sam Brownback doubted Santorum (who participated in Brownback's recent conversion to Catholicism) would seek the nomination in 2008.[2622] George Will was quite insistent, noting that Brownback had stated the Ames, Iowa straw poll would occur just nine months after Santorum's reelection bid, cutting in on Santorum's time needed to succeed in Iowa.[2623]

Then Santorum stated that his "intention is not to run" for president, then clarified his statement (7.27.05), saying that a little window should remain open because "I have no idea what's going to happen between now and 3 ½ years from now."[2624]

Santorum was okay in early 2005

Santorum sat behind the President in the first row at his second inauguration and opened up a rally for Bush's Social Security plan in Pennsylvania in early February 2005 (supporting private accounts). Santorum also had a Political Action Committee (PAC), America's Foundation, which had "been one of the 10 most active among lawmakers. Though it ended the year with only $12,451, it raised and contributed more than $2.6 million to help elect Republican candidates nationally in 2004."[2625]

In March 2005 pro-life Democrat, Robert P. Casey Jr., was "recruited"[2626] by national Democratic leaders to be Santorum's challenger. The Democratic Party had issues with Bob Casey Sr. in the 1990s—too conservative; but Casey Jr. was perfect for the Party in 2005. By the end of March, A *Daily News*/CN8 Keystone poll conducted at Franklin & Marshall College showed Pennsylvanians favored Casey with 44%, Santorum 1 point behind.[2627]

Rick Santorum had a fundraiser with the help of the President in June 2005. The cost was $250 for entrance and $10,000 for a picture with the President, and this early Bush fundraiser for 2006 candidates was expected to reign in about $750,000.[2628] The event brought in $1.5 million.[2629]

Santorum: "Who is this guy they call 'Bush'?"

A Survey USA poll in June 2005 found Rick Santorum had the highest disapproval rating of any US Senator: 44 percent.[2630]

President Bush came to Pennsylvania on Veterans Day 2005 and appeared with Arlen Specter; but Rick Santorum went to another event 116 miles away.[2631] Santorum raised over $1 million from a fundraiser with the president earlier in the year. Santorum citied a scheduling conflict as the reason for his absence. But the *Philadelphia Inquirer* was less sympathetic, reporting in the title that "Blaming schedule, Santorum will miss Bush's visit to PA."[2632] A *Daily News/CN8 Keystone* Poll released in November 2005 said he trailed Bob Casey 51 to 35.[2633]

When Bush came to Philadelphia for the World Affairs Council in December, Santorum actually participated in a picture, though the event provided cover for Santorum given the council's non-partisanship.[2634] The President needed Santorum to show party unity, and Santorum needed Bush for money. But Howard Fineman reported the reluctance: "So, as the door of Air Force One swung open, there was a smiling and waving president. A few steps behind him, smiling a little sheepishly: the junior senator from Pennsylvania. They didn't walk down the gangway to the tarmac arm-in-arm. But it was close enough to suit the political purpose at hand."[2635]

Santorum's attitude was different for John McCain when he appeared at a private Santorum fundraiser on December 2005.[2636] McCain raised $100,000 for Santorum,[2637] whose website posted a video link "Sen. McCain Supports Santorum."[2638] McCain praised Santorum: "He represents family values, he represents commitment to family and America, and he represents what—in my view—is the next generation of leadership of the Republican Party."[2639] Santorum needed a maverick GOP leader, not a president sinking in the polls; McCain needed exposure to GOP loyalists. And where else in the Republican leadership could he have asked for support? House Majority Leader Tom Delay and Senate Majority Leader Bill Frist were muddied in scandals. McCain was the logical choice for Santorum.

Santorum finally, officially left

Santorum lost his Senate reelection campaign, so much so that the race wasn't even much of a competition. Faced with an unpopular war and an unpopular president, and Santorum's support for both of them, his career was over. *McClatchy*'s story on presidential candidates (11.14.06) had Santorum under "Burnt Toast": as he "was the purest conservative in the pack. Then Democrats put a conservative up against him and he lost his seat in the Senate—and the presidential campaign table."[2640]

Although the writing on the wall seemed obvious, the *Philadelphia Inquirer* had to report "Santorum: No oval office run," (11.17.06).[2641] When asked if he would run for president, Santorum told the conservative *Michael Smerconish Show*, "Absolutely, positively not. Absolutely not…My wife would throw me out of the house if I do anything in '08."[2642]

The *Inquirer* went on to note that despite his 18 point loss to Casey, "some supporters hoped he would still fill the social conservative niche on the Republican ticket."

William J. Bennett, the former U.S. secretary of education and national drug czar, had predicted a "draft Rick Santorum" movement, citing a lack of conservatism on the part of the current GOP front-runners, Sen. John McCain of Arizona and former New York Mayor Rudy Giuliani. Bloggers hashed out the possibility over the last week, too, posting commentary under headlines like "Rick Santorum for President!" One online betting Web site listed his odds at 18-to-1, better than former Pennsylvania Gov. Tom Ridge, but longer than Giuliani, McCain, or Massachusetts Gov. Mitt Romney.[2643]

Mayor Michael Bloomberg

Who would have ever thought Rudy Giuliani's replacement as New York Mayor would be a presidential hopeful? The *New Yorker* wrote in December 2006,

> That Bloomberg got elected in the first place seems a historical accident. He had entered the race a political neophyte, and one whose switch from Democrat to Republican made him seem a naked opportunist. His gifts on the stump were minimal: He was brusque, infelicitous, maladroit, utterly unvisionary. But then, goes the conventional wisdom, came 9/11—and the mood of the electorate darkened. What voters wanted now was an equable hand to keep the economy afloat and the city from unraveling.[2644]

And Bloomberg did not confine himself to the city. He helped out Bloomberg-like candidates in the 2006 midterms: Arnold Schwarzenegger, Claire McCaskill, and Joe Lieberman.[2645] But he kept quiet about Iraq.[2646] Nor was it as though he had nothing to gain. As a Lieberman victory made the Senator head of the Homeland Security Committee—a victory for New York City, and the nod to McCaskill was seen as a chit to Sen. Schumer, who headed the Democratic Senatorial Campaign Committee.[2647]

Bloomberg was a Republican until 2007, when he switched to an Independent. The decision was not a surprise, more so an anointing of the existing status. The GOP mayor, on immigration, had leaned Democratic, and said (2006): "We're not going to deport 12 million people, so let's stop this fiction; let's give them permanent status."[2648] He called intelligent design (whose teaching was supported by many Republicans) "creationism by another name."[2649] And he questioned the Democratic and Republican hype over the Dubai Ports World debacle in the spring of 2006: "What I don't like is, all of a sudden it becomes the issue du jour and everybody's rushing up there waving a flag, beating their chests."[2650]

Bloomberg Hype

In June 2006, the *New Republic* reported New York City Mayor Michael Bloomberg was considering a third Party bid for the presidency.[2651] One source suggested Bloomberg said he would spend $500 million on a campaign if he wanted to.[2652] The strategy would be to garner signatures, after the two major parties' nominees were set, to get on the ballots of 50 states for the general election.[2653] A Quinnipiac poll released in June 2006 showed a 72% approval rating in New York City.[2654]

In Ireland, Bloomberg said (8.22.06) he would serve out his full mayoral term then leave politics to start a full time career in philanthropy: "I don't know how many times I have to say I am not going to run for president. But I'll say it one more time. I have no plans to run for president."[2655]

In September 2006, WCBS-TV of New York reported Bloomberg, who had "consistently denied" his interest in running, "held a secret strategy meeting" with DLC head Al From and Michael Steinhart, a Wall Street hedge fund manager, "and three deputy mayors."[2656] Steinhardt too, was a former chairman of the DLC and decade-long friend with Bloomberg.[2657] According to the sources,

Bloomberg was intrigued at running, but was quoted at the meeting as saying "How likely is a 5'7''-Jew-from-New-York billionaire who's divorced and running as an independent to become president of the United States."[2658]

According to *New York Magazine*, the origins date back to July 2006, and eventually "From found himself having supper at Steinhardt's apartment on the Upper East Side with Bloomberg and his senior political adjutants: deputy mayors Patti Harris, Kevin Sheekey, and Ed Skyler."[2659] From discussed DLC polling showing the alienation of voters from the two parties.[2660] Steinhardt's analysis was "They're serious about it."[2661]

Bloomberg's Strategy

The situation had to be right. Even in the favorable *New York Magazine* article, Bloomberg complimented McCain, but asked if McCain was "from the 'Straight-Talk-Express' or the guy that went to Liberty University."[2662] The 2008 race would have to evolve into a polarizing one. For example, if Giuliani or Romney passed by McCain for the GOP nomination, and the Republicans became anti-Hillary, Bloomberg would have an opening. If Obama won the nomination, Bloomberg would not run, given Obama's anti-polarization message.

1) Start late. If Bloomberg ran, he would likely delay until early 2008 for a surprise factor and/or to avoid the stagnation third party candidates can eventually attain. As Mark McKinnon stated, "In any third-party effort, you want to start late. You gotta catch lighting in a bottle, not let yourself get stale. If Perot had waited to start his campaign until after his daughter's wedding, he would probably have been president."[2663] And the triangulation of Clinton on the deficit issue pre-empted Perot's gains.

2) Unity '08? Would Bloomberg take advantage of Unity08, which was attempting to field a centrist candidate?[2664] As leftist as the liberal blogs may have been, Unity08 was quite different. In the Spring of 2006, a combination of Independents (former Maine Gov. Angus King), Republicans (Doug Bailey, President Ford's media advisor), and Democrats (Hamilton Jordon and Gerald Rafshoon, who worked with President Carter) had a goal to use the internet to offer an alternative to Democrats and Republicans and a system that they felt "polarized and alienated the American people."[2665] The goal was to form a voice for moderates, as they would "offer a split ticket, with one Democrat and one Republican or Independent."[2666]

Denver was made the organizational headquarters, primarily because Colorado was seen as a 'purple' state; but the functions of the movement was unclear. As the *Denver Post* reported (5.31.06), "Unity08 differs from previous third-party presidential bids that it does not have a presidential and vice presidential candidate attached to it. Rather, citizens will pick the ticket—made up of a candidate from each major party or an independent—through an online convention in the spring of 2008."[2667] How would it work?

A *FOX News*/Opinion Dynamics Poll (6.27-28.06) found a third party for federal and state offices was viewed as a "good idea" by half the population, while 37% said it was a 'bad idea.'[2668]

3) He has the money. Bloomberg spent $74 million in 2001, then had "wanton overkill" with $85 million in 2005.[2669] But he was also generous, and donated $144 million in 2005.[2670] *Forbes* estimated his worth at $5.3 billion, though his company might have been worth four times that.[2671]

4) Maybe just win a few states? Another scenario for Bloomberg would be to concentrate on just a few states. For example, if he wins New York and California (where he is a close friend of Arnold Schwarzenegger), he could throw the Electoral College totals for a loop so no candidate received the 270 necessary to win the presidency. But at that point, the House would choose the winner. Critics suggested that strategy could be pointless for Bloomberg to pursue, especially if the House remained controlled by Democrats. Then Bloomberg would have run for president only to get a Democrat elected. But maybe he would get a cabinet position. This strategy doesn't seem likely.

Did Bloomberg sexually harass?

Bloomberg settled a sexual harassment lawsuit in 2000; and before elected mayor in 2001, he "was the target of a sexual harassment lawsuit by a female executive who accused him of making repeated raunchy sexual comments while he was chief executive of his financial company, Bloomberg LP."[2672] The 2000 case dated back to 1997, and was settled without Bloomberg admitting any wrongdoing.[2673]

Is Bloomberg popular?

His approval numbers fell to 24 percent in 2003 but were above 70 percent by January 2006.[2674] In Quinnipiac's Thermometer Poll in 2006, Bloomberg finished with the seventh best warm rating in the country—and this poll was nationwide, not just in the college's home state.[2675] Though 44 percent of the public did not know enough to rate him.[2676] Frank Luntz, a Republican who advised Perot, apparently polled and found Bloomberg was in the mid-twenties versus Sen. Clinton and a non-McCain/Giuliani GOP candidate and was ahead of were Perot was at in the '92 campaign.[2677]

Bloomberg was great in New York. A June 2007 Siena College poll found Bloomberg lost in a hypothetical governors race (2010) to Gov. Elliot Spitzer by two points, despite that Spitzer won the 2006 election with a 70 percent landslide.[2678] In the poll, Bloomberg won New York City (49-37) and the downstate suburbs (53-37), but Spitzer did well upstate (55-24).[2679]

But nationwide, at least 40 percent of the public did not know who Bloomberg was. *A CBS/New York Times* poll from July 2007 said 62 percent had not heard of "Mike Bloomberg," but when a June 2007 *CNN*/Opinion Research poll asked about "New York City Mayor Michael Bloomberg," only 18 percent in the nationwide polls said they had "never heard of" Bloomberg (another 22 percent were "unsure" to give an opinion).[2680]

If many have not heard of Bloomberg, it could be an asset. Bloomberg's best interest is to lie low the next few months, and not peak too early. In the spring of 2008, he can announce his half billion dollar campaign for the presidency.

Afterword

This book was originally finished in August 2007. However, the process from final draft to publishing takes a while. Because the book is based almost entirely on historical facts, it was not necessary to continue adding numerous events to all the chapters. However, there are some important events which have occurred that aptly summarize the 2006-2007 phase of the 2008 campaign.

Who has caught the Fred '08 magic?

Fred Thompson appeared on *FOX News Sunday* in March 2007, and finally applied for his "Friends of Fred Thompson" committee on June 1.[2681] He had a spat with Michael Moore that ran on the internet in May.[2682] Speaking before the Virginia GOP (6.2.07) Thompson said he believed he might make a good president: "I'd do lots of things," but the *AP* noted Thompson said it "declining to elaborate."[2683] After Labor Day, he told Jay Leno he was running for president. Fred Thompson had been running for president for half a year. The same night Thompson chatted with Leno, the GOP held another presidential debate.

Thompson has disappointed many within the base of the Republican Party. Within days of his announcement, he told a Florida cable show "I don't remember the details of the" Terry Schiavo case.[2684] The base of the GOP remembers the details. He then topped off his impression to Florida. When he was asked about a catastrophic fund to help Floridians with skyrocketing homeowners insurance from recent hurricanes, Thompson said "I don't know enough about it yet."[2685]

On September 7, Thompson told Iowans, "Bin Laden being in the mountains of Pakistan or Afghanistan is not as important as there are probably al-Qaida operatives inside the United States of America."[2686] By the end of the day, after being criticized by Democrats, Thompson said bin Laden "ought to be caught and killed."[2687]

Thompson also has said the reason Iraqi citizens supported the US was because of al-Qaeda's ban on smoking.[2688] Ironically, those comments indicated political progress in Iraq were unrelated to the surge of US troops, even though Thompson favored the surge. Then Dr. James Dobson of Focus on the Family, a leader for social conservatives, said Fred Thompson was weak and had no passion (9.20.07).[2689]

Despite a rough start, Thompson is doing well in polls. Within a week of his official entry, a CNN nationwide poll had him in a statistical tie (29-28) with Giuliani for the nomination, with McCain in third (15) and Romney in fourth (11).[2690] The CBS/*New York Times* poll taken in early September had Giuliani first (27), followed by Thompson (22), McCain (18) and Romney (14).[2691] In a September Clemson University Palmetto Poll for South Carolina Giuliani led Thompson 19-18.[2692] Has the former Senator given a valid reason to vote for him?

Giuliani v. Clinton

In the second week of September, General Petraeus came to Congress to give his report on Iraq. On the first day of his testimony, the *New York Times* ran a one page advertisement paid for by liberal MoveOn.org. Titled "General Petraeus or General Betrayus," the ad set off a firestorm of criticism against Democrats for attacking a General who had been approved by the Senate in early 2007.

What ensued was not a debate on Iraq, but an all out battle between Clinton and Giuliani. Giuliani took out his own ad in the *New York Times* and attacked Clinton. In Giuliani's ad (9.14.07), he accused Clinton of participating in a "character attack" against the General, as she told Petraeus his progress report on Iraq required a "willing suspension of disbelief."[2693] If she made a mistake, that comment was the only one that made her 'guilty.' She did not defend MoveOn's ad. She did not immediately disavow the ad either.

However, Hillary Clinton voted for General Petraeus confirmation earlier in the year. Still, Giuliani's internet ad said Clinton "stood by silently" as the organization ran its ad.[2694] As Michael Kinsley of *Time* opined (9.19.07), "Another way of saying … she had nothing to do with the ad."[2695] But Giuliani accused Clinton of "joining with"[2696] MoveOn.org and "attacking" General Petraeus.[2697] In a radio ad aired in Iowa (9.18.07), Giuliani called himself MoveOn's "worst nightmare."[2698]

Giuliani was hypocritical. His *New York Times* ad ended with his quote that "These times call for statesmanship, not politicians spewing political venom."[2699] Yet the *AP* article after Giuliani's ad was titled "Giuliani attacks Clinton in ad."[2700] In addition, the ad asked, "Who should America listen to? A decorated soldier's commitment to defending America, or Hillary Clinton's commitment to defending MoveOn.org?"[2701] How was she defending MoveOn.org?

In Atlanta (9.13.07), Giuliani "blasted the *New York Times*" after a report suggested MoveOn.org was given a discounted rate ($64,000) to run their ad and asked the *New York Times* to give him the discounted rate for his own ad which he wanted on the day after President Bush addressed the nation on Iraq (9.14.07).[2702] So because the *Times* was wrong to give the liberal group an ad on the day they wanted (when General Petraeus addressed Congress), it would be ethical for the paper to give a Republican presidential candidate the ad on the day he wanted.

Giuliani's hypocrisy was like Rush Limbaugh, who was upset at the MoveOn ad,[2703] despite that Limbaugh had once called Sen. Hagel—a Vietnam Veteran—"Senator Betrayus." Why didn't Giuliani defend Hagel months earlier? Worse yet, Giuliani's campaign proudly explained "they reaped 'tens of thousands of dollars' in online donations" on the Friday of Giuliani's ad.[2704] Rudy Giuliani clearly profited from the staged fight with Hillary Clinton.

That is exactly what describes Giuliani's actions: staged. By the middle of September, in a matter of two weeks, he had met with former British Prime Minister Tony Blair, and his successor Gordon Brown.[2705] Giuliani then received an award from Margaret Thatcher, "who remains an iconic figure to American conservatives…"[2706] Dan Balz of the *Washington Post* noted (9.20.07), "Giuliani has relished the combat with Clinton, MoveOn and the *New York Times*—all three entities Republicans love to hate."[2707] Dan Balz asked, "What better way to shore up sagging support among Republicans than attacking Clinton?"[2708] The best way to get support was by attacking figure heads?

Appearances with foreign leaders does not make one a good president. Throwing bones to conservatives (posing with Thatcher, bashing Hillary, criticizing the New York Times) is symbolism, not substance. Did anybody stop to ask Rudy Giuliani what his plan for success in Iraq was? *Besides* supporting the president.

This was the shear brilliance of Giuliani: he had completely overshadowed John McCain's diligent—and public—support for the surge. In fact, in the presidential debate in early September 2007, it was McCain who won the debate. But within days, the public was focused on a *New York Times* ad.

6 months into surge, Romney concluded it was 'apparently working'

In that GOP debate (9.5.07), moderator Wendell Groler told Romney, "…you have suggested that U.S. troops in Iraq move to a support phase after the surge, which pretty much has to end in the spring, and a standby phase after that in Kuwait and Qatar. Correct me if I'm wrong, but it seems even Hillary Clinton is willing to commit troops to Iraq longer than that, sir."[2709] Romney said he didn't have a time frame he announced, then added, "the surge is apparently working. We're going to get a full report on that from General Petraeus and Ambassador Crocker very soon."[2710] So Romney's final opinion would depend on Petraeus's assessment, not Romney's judgment.

Clearly Romney did not give his blessing for the surge, for he continued: "If the surge is working, then we're going to be able to start bringing back our troop levels, slowly but surely, and play more of a support role over time."[2711] John McCain pounced on Romney: "Governor, the surge is working. The surge is working, sir. It is working."[2712] Romney relied, "That's just what I said."[2713] McCain stood firm: "No, not apparently -- it's working."[2714] McCain soon continued, "…But we are succeeding, and the great debate is not whether it's apparently working or not. The great debate is going to take place on the floor of the United States Senate, the middle of this month."[2715] McCain basically questioned what a former Massachusetts governor knew about foreign policy and Iraq. Good question.

Still, Romney brought up the issue minutes later: "we haven't heard from General Petraeus and Ambassador Crocker. I believe it's successful… but I'm going to hold out until we hear the report. I'm going to give them the benefit of hearing that. I know there are some early reports that they're going to say it's successful, and I certainly hope that's the case. But let's listen to their report."[2716]

So if Mitt Romney became president, he would not be commander in chief, but rather a delegator in chief. McCain has said, "We are winning."[2717]

'What is John McCain's stance on Iraq…?'

The problem with McCain's aggressive and logical attack on Romney is that it has been forgotten. Make no mistake, Romney may not be competitive as he once was. *Reuters* already reported "Romney saw little benefit from his win in last month's Iowa straw poll."[2718] Yet Giuliani is stealing the spotlight, and Fred Thompson is in second place for the nomination.

What is Thompson's solution to fix Iraq? The horserace for 2008—not the issues like Iraq, takes precedence.

The Democrats are no better. Who is Joe Biden? No doubt that is the question half of potential Democratic primary voters would ask today if they were asked about the Senator from Delaware. Biden is the only presidential candidate with a smart, realistic alternative to the president's surge, albeit not perfect. When he asked for a debate on the most pressing issue of this country, Dennis Kucinich and Mike Gravel showed up. Where were Clinton, Obama, and Edwards to give their in-depth plans for the future of Iraq?

That's right… they don't have one.

The purpose of this book

The presidential campaign has debased issues, and in the process the past becomes more important than the vision for the future. We can hold candidates responsible for their past actions and words, but the present system communication style blurs the truth. We need accountability, and I have tried to do so with over 2,700 endnotes in this book. When we start asking which presidential campaigns are running their operations on ideas and intelligence, rather than staged events, then we can fix the current problems. Otherwise, we continue them.

Endnotes for Part 1

[1] ABC News. Bayh Rules Out White House Bid in 2008. AP. Retrieved 1.13.06 from http://abcnews.go.com/Politics/print?id=2731217. Richard E. Cohen and Michael Barone. "The Almanac of American Politics—2004." The National Journal Group. 2003, page 594.

[2] Palladium-Item. "Bayh flirts with run for presidency." Pal-item.com Published July 15, 2005 and retrieved July 15, 2005 from http://www.pal-item.com/apps/pbcs.dll/article?AID=/20050715/NEWS03/507150327/1003/NEWS01.

[3] Richard E. Cohen and Michael Barone. "The Almanac of American Politics—2004." The National Journal Group. 2003, page 594

[4] ABC News. Bayh Rules Out White House Bid in 2008. AP. Retrieved 1.13.06 from http://abcnews.go.com/Politics/print?id=2731217.

[5] ABC News. Bayh Rules Out White House Bid in 2008. AP. Retrieved 1.13.06 from http://abcnews.go.com/Politics/print?id=2731217.

[6] ABC News. Bayh Rules Out White House Bid in 2008. AP. Retrieved 1.13.06 from http://abcnews.go.com/Politics/print?id=2731217

[7] ABC News. Bayh Rules Out White House Bid in 2008. AP. Retrieved 1.13.06 from http://abcnews.go.com/Politics/print?id=2731217.

[8] Terence Samuel. A cautious eye on the big prize. US News & World Report. February 26, 2001. page 26.

[9] Terence Samuel. A cautious eye on the big prize. US News & World Report. February 26, 2001. page 25.

[10] Terence Samuel. A cautious eye on the big prize. US News & World Report. February 26, 2001. page 25.

[11] Encyclopedia: Evan Bayh. Retrieved September 13, 2005 from http://www.nationmaster.com/encyclopedia/Evan-Bayh

[12] Mark Bennett. Indiana Sen. Evan Bayh offers his views on everything from the War in Iraq to family values. Terre Haute, Indiana News: TribStar.com. Posted August 23, 2005 and retrieved September 20, 2005 from http://www.tribstar.com/articles/2005/08/23/news/top_stories_yesterday/top03.txt.

[13] Mark Bennett. Indiana Sen. Evan Bayh offers his views on everything from the War in Iraq to family values. Terre Haute, Indiana News: TribStar.com. Posted August 23, 2005 and retrieved September 20, 2005 from http://www.tribstar.com/articles/2005/08/23/news/top_stories_yesterday/top03.txt.

[14] Terence Samuel. A cautious eye on the big prize. US New & World Report. February 26, 2001. page 26.

[15] Richard E. Cohen and Michael Barone. "The Almanac of American Politics—2004." The National Journal Group. 2003, page 594

[16] Third Way. "The Need For Third Way." Retrieved September 13, 2005 from http://www.third-way.com/need/.

[17] Third Way. "The Need For Third Way." Retrieved September 13, 2005 from http://www.third-way.com/need/.

[18] John F. Harris. "New Group to Tout Democrats' Centrist Values." Washingtonpost.com Published November 11, 2004 and retrieved September 13, 2005 from http://www.washingtonpost.com/wp-dyn/articles/A41113-2004Nov10.html.

[19] Retrieved 9.13.05 from http://www.third-way.com/cochairs/.

[20] John F. Harris. "New Group to Tout Democrats' Centrist Values." Washingtonpost.com Published November 11, 2004 and retrieved September 13, 2005 from http://www.washingtonpost.com/wp-dyn/articles/A41113-2004Nov10.html

[21] From the DLC. Retrieved August 25, 2007 at http://www.ndol.org/ndol_ci.cfm?kaid=85&subid=108&contentid=253426

[22] Evan Bayh. United States Senator. Retrieved 9.13.05 from http://www.third-way.com/cochairs/.

[23] Beth Fouhy. Clinton, Bayh Step Up Plans for 2008. AP. 12.3.06 and retrieved same day from http://abcnews.go.com/Poltiics/print?id=2697236.

[24] Reuters. Sen. Bayh to consider running for president. Dec.3, 2006. Retrieved 12.3.06 from http://abcnews.go.com/Politics/wireStory?id=2697147.

[25] Opening Arguments: Bayh: Now we must deliver. Posted Nov. 10 and retrieved Nov.17.06 from http://blogs.fortwayne.com/opening_arguments/2006/11/bayh_now_we_mus.html.

[26] Beth Fouhy. Clinton, Bayh Step Up Plans for 2008. AP. 12.3.06 and retrieved same day from http://abcnews.go.com/Poltiics/print?id=2697236.

[27] Taegan Goddard's Political Wire.Oct.19.2006. retrieved 10.31.06 from http://politicalwire.com/archives/2008_campaign/.

[28] Reuters. White House hopefuls lay ground in midterm. MSNBC.com. posted 10.27 and retrieved 10.31.2006 from http://www.msnbc.msn.com/id/15446725/print/1/displaymode/1098/.

[29] Thomas Beaumont. Bayh opts against run; Vilsack's benefit small. Des Moines Register. Dec. 17, 2006 and retrieved12.22.06from http://www.desmoinesregister.com/apps/pbcs.dll/article?AID=/20061217/NEWS09/612170335

[30] Beth Fouhy. Clinton, Bayh Step Up Plans for 2008. AP. Dec.3 and retrieved same day from http://abcnews.go.com/Poltiics/print?id=2697236.

[31] Reuters. Sen. Bayh to consider running for president. Dec.3, 2006. Retrieved 12.3.06 from http://abcnews.go.com/Politics/wireStory?id=2697147.

[32] Maureen Groppe. Will Bayh run? Stay tuned. Indy Star. Posted Dec. 2 and retrieved Dec.3 from http://www.indystar.com/apps/pbcs.dll/article?AID=20061202/LOCAL19/612020450/-1/ZONES04.

[33] AP. Indiana's Bayh to take first step toward '08 bid. Posted Dec.1 and retrieved 12.3.06 from http://www.msnbc.msn.com/id/15993662/.

[34] AP. Dec.16, 2006 and retrieved 1.13.07 from ABC News. Bayh Rules Out White House Bid in 2008. AP. Retrieved 1.13.06 from http://abcnews.go.com/Politics/print?id=2731217.

[35] Adam Nagourney. Evan Bayh withdraws from 2008 presidential field. International Herald Tribune. Published 12.17.06 @ http://www.iht.com/articles/2006/12/17/news/Bayh.php.

[36] Thomas Beaumont. Bayh opts against run; Vilsack's benefit small. Des Moines Register. Dec. 17, 2006 and retrieved 12.22.06 from http://www.desmoinesregister.com/apps/pbcs.dll/article?AID=/20061217/NEWS09/612170335.

[37] Thomas Beaumont. Bayh opts against run; Vilsack's benefit small. Des Moines Register. Dec. 17, 2006 and retrieved 12.22.06 from http://www.desmoinesregister.com/apps/pbcs.dll/article?AID=/20061217/NEWS09/612170335

[38] Carlos Torres. Bloomberg. Dec. 16. Indiana's Evan Bayh Won't Run for President in 2008 (update 3). Retrieved 12.19.06 from http://www.bloomberg.com/apps/news?pid=20601103&sid=aKRuvRDs0oc4&refer=us.

[39] Taegan Goddard's Political Wire Archives: 2008 Campaign. Retrieved December 15, 2004 from http://politicalwire.com/archives/2008_campaign/. See also Bayh get early look for '08 president race. Maureen Groppe of the Indianapolis Star, retrieved 7.27.07 from http://bayh2008.blogspot.com/.

[40] Carlos Torres. Bloomberg. Dec. 16. Indiana's Evan Bayh Won't Run for President in 2008 (update 3). Retrieved 12.19.06 from http://www.bloomberg.com/apps/news?pid=20601103&sid=aKRuvRDs0oc4&refer=us.

[41] Maureen Groppe. Bayh takes 1st step toward prez race. Indystar.com. Posted 12.3.06 and retrieved 12.14.06 from http://www.indystar.com/apps/pbcs.dll/article?AID=20061203/LOCAL19/61203001/1006/LOCAL.

[42] Devlin Barrett. Clinton says It Still 'Takes a Village'. Posted 12.10.06 and retrieved 12.14.06 from http://apnews.myway.com/article/20061210/D8LU8ON00.html.

[43] James Pindell. Obama events sold out. Thursday, December 7, 2006. Retrieved 12.14.06 from http://www.boston.com/news/local/poltics/primarysource/2006/12/obama_events_so.html.

[44] ABC News. Bayh Rules Out White House Bid in 2008. AP. Retrieved 1.13.06 from http://abcnews.go.com/Politics/print?id=2731217.

[45] Dan Balz. Clinton, Obama Clearing the Field. Dec.24, 2006. A01. Retrieved 1.13.07 from http://www.washingtonpost.com/wp-dyn/content/article/2006/12/23/AR2006122300970.html.

[46] WH2008 Democrats. Retrieved 12.14.06 from http://www.pollingreport.com.

[47] Scott Brooks. Obama fever grips NH. Dec. 11. 2006. Union Leader. Retrieved 12.14.06 from http://www.unionleader.com/article.aspx?headline=Obama+fever+grips+NH&articleId=96bb103b-6332-4304-ac8d-60da60b323e9.

[48] Adam Nagourney. Evan Bayh withdraws from 2008 presidential field. International Herald Tribune. Published 12.17.06 @ http://www.iht.com/articles/2006/12/17/news/Bayh.php.

[49] Thomas Beaumont. Bayh opts against run; Vilsack's benefit small. Des Moines Register. Dec. 17, 2006 and retrieved 12.22.06 from http://www.desmoinesregister.com/apps/pbcs.dll/article?AID=/20061217/NEWS09/612170335

[50] AP. Dec.16, 2006 and retrieved 1.13.07 from ABC News. Bayh Rules Out White House Bid in 2008. AP. Retrieved 1.13.06 from http://abcnews.go.com/Politics/print?id=2731217.

[51] Ken Bode. Bayh looks solid as running-mate material. Dec. 22 and retrieved same day from http://www.indystar.com/apps/pbcs.dll/article?AID=/20061222/OPINION/612220314/1002.

[52] Bob Schieffer. The Refreshing Honesty of Evan Bayh. CBS News. Retrieved 12.22.06 from http://www.cbsnews.com/stories/2006/12/17/opinion/schieffer/printable2274567.shtml.

[53] Thomas Beaumont. Bayh opts against run; Vilsack's benefit small. Des Moines Register. Dec. 17, 2006 and retrieved 12.22.06 from http://www.desmoinesregister.com/apps/pbcs.dll/article?AID=/20061217/NEWS09/612170335.

[54] Richard E. Cohen and Michael Barone. The Almanac of American Politics—2004. The National Journal Group. 2003, page 360

[55] Jim Davenport. Biden visits Edwards territory. AP. Posted 8.26.06 and retrieved 9.6.06 from http://www.newsobserver.com/114/story/479236.html.

[56] The newest political dynasty: Joe and Beau. Chris Barrish. The News Journal. Posted 11.12.06 and retrieved 11.17.06 from http://www.delawareonline.com/apps/pbcs.dll/article?AID=/20061112/NEWS/611120350.

[57] Richard E. Cohen and Michael Barone. The Almanac of American Politics—2004. The National Journal Group. 2003, page 360

[58] Richard E. Cohen and Michael Barone. The Almanac of American Politics—2004. The National Journal Group. 2003, page 360

[59] Jennifer Brooks. Carper, Biden named to key leadership posts. Nov. 15, 2006 and retrieved 11.17.06 from http://www.delawareonline.com/apps/pbcs.dll/article?AID=20061115/NEWS/611150353/-1/NEWS01.

[60] Richard E. Cohen and Michael Barone. The Almanac of American Politics—2004. The National Journal Group. 2003, page 361

[61] Richard E. Cohen and Michael Barone. The Almanac of American Politics—2004. The National Journal Group. 2003, page 361

[62] Jennifer Brooks. Biden learned lessons in '87 race. Delewareonline.com Posted July 17, 2005 and retrieved July 22, 2005 from http://www.delawareonline.com/apps/pbcs.dll/article?AID=/20050717/NEWS01/507170345/1006

[63] Bill Whalen (The Weekly Standard). CBS News. Joe Biden: Sleeper Candidate. Posted August 18, 2005 and retrieved August 20, 2005 from http://www.cbsnews.com/stories/2005/08/18/opinion/main786311.shtml. good web.

[64] Bill Whalen (The Weekly Standard). CBS News. Joe Biden: Sleeper Candidate. Posted August 18, 2005 and retrieved August 20, 2005 from http://www.cbsnews.com/stories/2005/08/18/opinion/main786311.shtml

[65] Bill Whalen (The Weekly Standard). CBS News. Joe Biden: Sleeper Candidate. Posted August 18, 2005 and retrieved August 20, 2005 from http://www.cbsnews.com/stories/2005/08/18/opinion/main786311.shtml

[66] Bill Whalen (The Weekly Standard). CBS News. Joe Biden: Sleeper Candidate. Posted August 18, 2005 and retrieved August 20, 2005 from http://www.cbsnews.com/stories/2005/08/18/opinion/main786311.shtml

[67] Bill Whalen (The Weekly Standard). CBS News. Joe Biden: Sleeper Candidate. Posted August 18, 2005 and retrieved August 20, 2005 from http://www.cbsnews.com/stories/2005/08/18/opinion/main786311.shtml

[68] Larry Sabato. Joseph Biden's Plagiarism; Michael Dukakis's 'Attack Video'—1988. Copyright 1988, retrieved August 11, 2006 from http://www.washingtonpost.com/wp-srv/politics/special/clinton/frenzy/biden.htm.

[69] Larry Sabato. Joseph Biden's Plagiarism; Michael Dukakis's 'Attack Video'—1988. Copyright 1988, retrieved August 11, 2006 from http://www.washingtonpost.com/wp-srv/politics/special/clinton/frenzy/biden.htm.

[70] Larry Sabato. Joseph Biden's Plagiarism; Michael Dukakis's 'Attack Video'—1988. Copyright 1988, retrieved August 11, 2006 from http://www.washingtonpost.com/wp-srv/politics/special/clinton/frenzy/biden.htm.

[71] Jennifer Brooks. Biden learned lessons in '87 race. Delewareonline.com Posted July 17, 2005 and retrieved July 22, 2005 from http://www.delawareonline.com/apps/pbcs.dll/article?AID/20050717/NEWS01/507170345/1006.

[72] Michael Nelson (ed). "The Elections of 1988." CQ Press, 1989. Rhodes Cook, Chapter 2, The Nominating Process. Page 46.

[73] Quote of the Day. Taegan Goddard's Political Wire. Retrieved 12.14.06 from http://www.politicalwire.com/archives/2008_campaign/.

[74] AP. In long shot 2008 presidential bid, Biden touts value of experience. Published 12.25.06 and retrieved 1.13.07 from http://www.iht.com/articles/ap/2006/12/26/america/NA_GEN_US_Biden_2008_Election.p...

[75] Jennifer Brooks. Biden learned lessons in '87 race. Delewareonline.com Posted July 17, 2005 and retrieved July 22, 2005 from http://www.delawareonline.com/apps/pbcs.dll/article?AID/20050717/NEWS01/507170345/1006

[76] John Distaso. Slamming Bush, Biden declares candidacy. Union Leader. July 2, 2006. Retrieved July 26, 2006 from http://www.unionleader.com/article.aspx?articleId=941b94e3-d381-4b23-906f-9b077b176483&headline=Slamming+Bush%2C+Biden+declares+candidacy"'%25%3C%3E%3A%24.

[77] Crooks and Liars. Posted 7.6.06 and retrieved 7.14.06 @ http://www.crooksandliars.com/posts/2006/07/06/biden-india-and-dunkin-doughnuts/.

[78] Liz Sidoti. Political Notebook. Biden Defends Remarks. AP. 7.6.06 and retrieved 7.14.06 from http://www.washingtonpost.com/wp-dyn/content/article/2006/07/07/AR2006070700924.html

[79] CBS/AP. Biden's Comments Ruffle Feathers. Posted July 7 and retrieved July 14, 2006 from http://www.cbsnews.com/stories/2006/07/07/politics/main1785303.shtml.

[80] Liz Sidoti. Political Notebook. Biden Defends Remarks. AP. July 7, 2006. Retrieved July 14, 2006 from http://www.washingtonpost.com/wp-dyn/content/article/2006/07/07/AR2006070700924.html.

[81] AP. Biden Forced to Explain comment About Indian-Americans. FOXNEWS.com. July 7 and retrieved July 14, 2006 from http://www.foxnews.com/printer_friendly_story/0,3566,202608,00.html.

[82] NewsMax.com. Hillary Clinton Regrets Gandhi Joke at Fund-Raiser. January 7, 2004 and retrieved July 28, 2006 from http://www.newsmax.com/archives/articles/2004/1/6/220449.shtml.

[83] NewsMax.com. Hillary Clinton Regrets Gandhi Joke at Fund-Raiser. January 7, 2004 and retrieved July 28, 2006 from http://www.newsmax.com/archives/articles/2004/1/6/220449.shtml.

[84] FOX News Sunday. Aired August 27. Retrieved September 6, 2006 from http://www.foxnews.com/story/0,2933,210668,00.html.

[85] Joe Biden's High Praise for Delaware. Delaware Watch. Retrieved 7.27.07 and posted 8.29.06 @ http://delawarewatch.blogspot.com/2006/08/joe-bidens-high-praise-for-delaware.html.

[86] Countdown with Keith Olbermann for Jan. 31. MSNBC.com. Retrieved 2.2.07 from http://www.msnbc.msn.com/id/16924881/.

[87] Countdown with Keith Olbermann for Jan. 31. MSNBC.com. Retrieved 2.2.07 from http://www.msnbc.msn.com/id/16924881/.

[88] Countdown with Keith Olbermann for Jan. 31. MSNBC.com. Retrieved 2.2.07 from http://www.msnbc.msn.com/id/16924881/.

[89] The Situation Room. Retrieved 2.2.07 from http://transcripts.cnn.com/TRANSCRIPTS/0701/31/sitroom.01.html.

[90] AP. Biden explains, apologizes for comments. Retrieved 2.1.07 from http://www.msnbc.msn.com/id/16923692/.

[91] AP. Biden explains, apologizes for comments. Retrieved 2.1.07 from http://www.msnbc.msn.com/id/16923692/.

[92] The situation Room, Feb.1, 2007. Retrieved 2.2.07 from http://transcripts.cnn.com/TRANSCRIPTS/0702/01/sitroom.03.html.

[93] The situation Room, Feb.1, 2007. Retrieved 2.2.07 from http://transcripts.cnn.com/TRANSCRIPTS/0702/01/sitroom.03.html.

[94] The Situation Room. Retrieved 2.2.07 from http://transcripts.cnn.com/TRANSCRIPTS/0701/31/sitroom.01.html.

[95] Hardball with Chris Matthews for Feb.1. MSNBC.com. Retrieved 2.2.07 from http://www.msnbc.msn.com/id/16943597/print/1/displaymode/1098/.

[96] Hardball with Chris Matthews for Feb.1. MSNBC.com. Retrieved 2.2.07 from http://www.msnbc.msn.com/id/16943597/print/1/displaymode/1098/.

[97] Countdown with Keith Olbermann' for Jan. 31. MSNBC.com. Retrieved 2.2.07 from http://www.msnbc.msn.com/id/16924881/.

[98] Hardball with Chris Matthews for Feb.1. MSNBC.com. Retrieved 2.2.07 from http://www.msnbc.msn.com/id/16943597/print/1/displaymode/1098/.

[99] Hardball with Chris Matthews for Feb.1. MSNBC.com. Retrieved 2.2.07 from http://www.msnbc.msn.com/id/16943597/print/1/displaymode/1098/.

[100] Hardball with Chris Matthews for Feb.1. MSNBC.com. Retrieved 2.2.07 from http://www.msnbc.msn.com/id/16943597/print/1/displaymode/1098/.

[101] Countdown with Keith Olbermann for Jan. 31. MSNBC.com. Retrieved 2.2.07 from http://www.msnbc.msn.com/id/16924881/.
[102] Hardball with Chris Matthews for Feb.1. MSNBC.com. Retrieved 2.2.07 from http://www.msnbc.msn.com/id/16943597/print/1/displaymode/1098/.
[103] Hardball with Chris Matthews for Feb.1. MSNBC.com. Retrieved 2.2.07 from http://www.msnbc.msn.com/id/16943597/print/1/displaymode/1098/.
[104] Countdown with Keith Olbermann for Jan. 31. MSNBC.com. Retrieved 2.2.07 from http://www.msnbc.msn.com/id/16924881/.
[105] Hardball with Chris Matthews for Feb.1. MSNBC.com. Retrieved 2.2.07 from http://www.msnbc.msn.com/id/16943597/print/1/displaymode/1098/.
[106] Perry Bacon. Why Joe Biden Isn't Being Coy About Running for President. Posted August 2, 2006 and retrieved August 25, 2006 from http://www.time.com/time/nation/printout/0,8816,1222255,00.html.
[107] AP. In long shot 2008 presidential bid, Biden touts value of experience. Published Dec.25, 2006 and retrieved 1.13.07 from http://www.iht.com/articles/ap/2006/12/26/america/NA_GEN_US_Biden_2008_Election.p...
[108] Jennifer Brooks. Carper, Biden named to key leadership posts. Nov. 15, 2006 and retrieved 11.17.06 from http://www.delawareonline.com/apps/pbcs.dll/article?AID=20061115/NEWS/611150353/-1/NEWS01.
[109] Jennifer Brooks. With trip to N.H., Biden begins 'second act'. Posted May 7, 2006 and retrieved June 30, 2006 from http://www.delawareonline.com/apps/pbcs.dll/article?AID=/20060507/NEWS/605070372.
[110] Washington beat by Jennifer Brooks. GOP pollster says Biden's delivery needs work. Posted April 9, 2006 and retrieved June 30, 2006 from http://www.delawareonline.com/apps/pbcs.dll/article?AID=/20060409/NEWS/604090359.
[111] Washington beat by Jennifer Brooks. GOP pollster says Biden's delivery needs work. Posted April 9, 2006 and retrieved June 30, 2006 from http://www.delawareonline.com/apps/pbcs.dll/article?AID=/20060409/NEWS/604090359
[112] Mark Preston. Hillary Clinton talks religion. CNN Political Editor. Posted June 29, 2006 and retrieved June 30, 2006 from http://www.cnn.com/2006/POLITICS/06/29/mg.thy/.
[113] Senator Joe Biden's Unite Our States: About Us: Speeches. Sept. 10, 2001. US Foreign Policy in the 21st Century: Defining Our Interests in a changing world. http://uniteourstates.com/about/speeches?id=0007 See also http://biden.senate.gov/newsroom/details.cfm?id=227895.
[114] Anne Saunders. AP. Biden in N.H.: 'I'm running for president'. Delaware Online. Posted June 18, 2006 and retrieved June 30, 2006 from http://www.delawareonline.com/apps/pbcs.dll/article?AID=/20060618/NEWS/606180348/-1/NEWS01.
[115] FOX News Sunday. Aired August 27. Retrieved September 6, 2006 from http://www.foxnews.com/story/0,2933,210668,00.html.
[116] Washington beat by Jennifer Brooks. GOP pollster says Biden's delivery needs work. Posted April 9, 2006 and retrieved June 30, 2006 from http://www.delawareonline.com/apps/pbcs.dll/article?AID=/20060409/NEWS/604090359.
[117] Washington beat by Jennifer Brooks. GOP pollster says Biden's delivery needs work. Posted April 9, 2006 and retrieved June 30, 2006 from http://www.delawareonline.com/apps/pbcs.dll/article?AID=/20060409/NEWS/604090359
[118] Ron Goldstein. The Case for Joe Biden. MSNBC.com. Newsweek. Posted 2.1.06 and retrieved 2.13.06 from http://www.msnbc.msn.com/id/11115989/site/newsweek/print/1/displaymode/1098/.
[119] Joe Biden for president. Get Informed. Speeches. Iraq's Future and America's Interests. Given 2.15.07 and retrieved 3.28.07 from http://www.joebiden.com/getinformed/speeches?id=0081.
[120] Post-Democratic Candidates' Debate Coverage. MSNBC.com. April 26, 2007. Retrieved May 3, 2006 from http://www.msnbc.msn.com/id/18351722/print/1/displaymode/1098/. 4/88.
[121] Biden calls on networks and DNC to sponsor Iraq debate. 5.17.07. Retrieved 5.26.07 from http://www.joebiden.com/newscenter/pressreleases?id=0065.
[122] Biden calls on networks and DNC to sponsor Iraq debate. 5.17.07. Retrieved 5.26.07 from http://www.joebiden.com/newscenter/pressreleases?id=0065.
[123] Biden calls on networks and DNC to sponsor Iraq debate. 5.17.07. Retrieved 5.26.07 from http://www.joebiden.com/newscenter/pressreleases?id=0065.
[124] Biden calls on networks and DNC to sponsor Iraq debate. 5.17.07. Retrieved 5.26.07 from http://www.joebiden.com/newscenter/pressreleases?id=0065.
[125] Brian Wheeler. Biden's Iraq-Only Debate Falls Largely on Deaf Ears. 6.8.07 and retrieved 6.15.07 from http://www.abcnews.go.com/print?id=3259615.
[126] Brian Wheeler. Biden's Iraq-Only Debate Falls Largely on Deaf Ears. 6.8.07 and retrieved 6.15.07 from http://www.abcnews.go.com/print?id=3259615.
[127] Brian Wheeler. Biden's Iraq-Only Debate Falls Largely on Deaf Ears. 6.8.07 and retrieved 6.15.07 from http://www.abcnews.go.com/print?id=3259615.
[128] Jennifer Brooks. "Biden Tests 2008 run for presidency." The Delaware News Journal. Posted June 20, 2005 and retrieved June 24, 2005 from http://www.delawareonline.com/apps/pbcs.dll/article?AID=/20050620/NEWS01/506200337/1006.
[129] Bill Shea. Fort Dodge, Iowa. The Messenger. Retrieved 10.31.2006 from http://www.messengernews.net/News/articles.asp?articleID=4680.
[130] NBC News. Meet the Press. Transcript for Jan.7, 2007 from MSNBC.com. Retrieved 1.13.07 from http://msnbc.msn.com/id/16456248/print/1/displaymode/1048/.
[131] Jennifer Brooks. With trip to N.H., Biden begins 'second act'. Posted May 7, 2006 and retrieved June 30, 2006 from http://www.delawareonline.com/apps/pbcs.dll/article?AID=/20060507/NEWS/605070372.

[132] Jennifer Brooks. With trip to N.H., Biden begins 'second act'. Posted May 7, 2006 and retrieved June 30, 2006 from http://www.delawareonline.com/apps/pbcs.dll/article?AID=/20060507/NEWS/605070372.

[133] POSTED TO Politics. New York's Premier Alternative Newspaper. Retrieved Jan.13 and posted 1.12.07 from http://www.nypress.com/blogx/display_blog.cfm?bid=43543282.

[134] POSTED TO Politics. New York's Premier Alternative Newspaper. Retrieved Jan.13 and posted 1.12.07 from http://www.nypress.com/blogx/display_blog.cfm?bid=43543282.

[135] NBC News. Meet the Press. Transcript for August 31. MSNBC.com. August 31, 2003 and retrieved Sept.25, 2006 from http://www.msnbc.msn.com/id/3080246/print/1/displaymode/1098/.

[136] AP. In long shot 2008 presidential bid, Biden touts value of experience. Published Dec.25, 2006 and retrieved 1.13.07 from http://www.iht.com/articles/ap/2006/12/26/america/NA_GEN_US_Biden_2008_Election.p...

[137] MSNBC.com. Hardball with Chris Matthews for January 10th. Updated January 11, 2006 and retrieved January 23, 2006 from http://www.msnbc.msn.com/id/10805375/.

[138] Richard Cohen. Loose Lips Sink. Washington Post. Published 1.12.06 and retrieved 7.27..07 from http://www.washingtonpost.com/wp-dyn/content/article/2006/01/11/AR2006/01/11/AR2006011102041.html.

[139] MSNBC.com. Hardball with Chris Matthews for January 10th. Updated January 11, 2006 and retrieved January 23, 2006 from http://www.msnbc.msn.com/id/10805375/

[140] MSNBC.com. Hardball with Chris Matthews for January 10th. Updated January 11, 2006 and retrieved January 23, 2006 from http://www.msnbc.msn.com/id/10805375/

[141] Susan Jones. Democrat Biden Calls Confirmation Hearings 'Broken'. CNSNews.com. Retrieved and Posted January 12, 2006 from http://www.cnsnews.com/ViewPolitics.asp?Page=/Politics/archive/200601/POL20060112c.html.

[142] MSNBC.com. Joe Biden: It's Time to Change the Conversation. Newsweek. Jonathan Darman. Retrieved January 30, 2006 from http://msnbc.msn.com/id/10857677/site/newsweek/.

[143] MSNBC.com. Joe Biden: It's Time to Change the Conversation. Newsweek. Jonathan Darman. Retrieved January 30, 2006 from http://msnbc.msn.com/id/10857677/site/newsweek/.

[144] MSNBC.com. Joe Biden: It's Time to Change the Conversation. Newsweek. Jonathan Darman. Retrieved January 30, 2006 from http://msnbc.msn.com/id/10857677/site/newsweek/.

[145] Harry F. Themal. Biden says he's on track for 2008 run. Delaware Online/The News Journal. Posted January 23, 2006 and retrieved same day from http://www.delawareonline.com/apps/pbcs.dll/article?AID=/20060123/OPINION03/601230323/1104.

[146] "In Praise of Joe Biden." Published January 15, 2006....See also Harry F. Themal. Biden says he's on track for 2008 run. Delaware Online/The News Journal. Posted January 23, 2006 and retrieved same day from http://www.delawareonline.com/apps/pbcs.dll/article?AID=/20060123/OPINION03/601230323/1104.

[147] Harry F. Themal. Biden says he's on track for 2008 run. Delaware Online/The News Journal. Posted January 23, 2006 and retrieved same day from http://www.delawareonline.com/apps/pbcs.dll/article?AID=/20060123/OPINION03/601230323/1104

[148] The Daily Show, January 2006, Comedy Central.

[149] MSNBC.com Hardball with Chris Matthews for Jan. 19th. MSNBC. Updated January 20, 2006 and retrieved January 23, 2006 from http://www.msnbc.msn.com/id/10945658/print/1/displaymode/1098/.

[150] Harry F. Themal. Biden says he's on track for 2008 run. Delaware Online/The News Journal. Posted January 23, 2006 and retrieved same day from http://www.delawareonline.com/apps/pbcs.dll/article?AID=/20060123/OPINION03/601230323/1104

[151] Jennifer Brooks. Biden Tests 2008 run for presidency. The Delaware News Journal. Posted June 20, 2005 and retrieved June 24, 2005 from http://www.delawareonline.com/apps/pbcs.dll/article?AID=/20050620/NEWS01/506200337/1006.

[152] AP. In long shot 2008 presidential bid, Biden touts value of experience. Published Dec.25, 2006 and retrieved 1.13.07 from http://www.iht.com/articles/ap/2006/12/26/america/NA_GEN_US_Biden_2008_Election.p...

[153] The Line: Debate Provides '08 Wake-up Call. Posted 7.27.07 and retrieved 8.1.07 from http://blog.washingtonpost.com/thefix/2007/07/friday_presidential_line_1.html.

[154] Campaign Race Rankings. Posted 7.23.07 and retrieved 8.1.07 from http://nationaljournal.com/racerankings/wh08/democrats/.

[155] Steve Kornacki. Also-Ran Biden Shows the Way at Debates. Retrieved 8.21.07 from http://www.observer.com/print/57052/full.

[156] Peter J. Boyer. General Clark's Battles. The New Yorker. Posted November 10, 2003 and retrieved November 9, 2005 from http://www.newyorker.com/printables/fact/031117fa_fact.

[157] Peter J. Boyer. General Clark's Battles. The New Yorker. Posted November 10, 2003 and retrieved November 9, 2005 from http://www.newyorker.com/printables/fact/031117fa_fact.

[158] FAIR. "Wesley Clark: The New Anti-War Candidate?" Fairness and Accuracy in Reporting. Posted September 16, 2003 and retrieved December 14, 2005 from http://www.fair.org/index.php?page=1839.

[159] Peter J. Boyer. "General Clark's Battles." The New Yorker. Posted November 10, 2003 and retrieved November 9, 2005 from http://www.newyorker.com/printables/fact/031117fa_fact

[160] Meet the Press. Jan.25, 2004. MSNBC.com. Retrieved 10.31.2006 from http://www.msnbc.msn.com/id/408066/print/1/displaymode/1098/.

[161] Meet the Press. Jan.25, 2004. MSNBC.com. Retrieved 10.31.2006 from http://www.msnbc.msn.com/id/408066/print/1/displaymode/1098/.

[162] Meet the Press. Jan.25, 2004. MSNBC.com. Retrieved 10.31.2006 from http://www.msnbc.msn.com/id/408066/print/1/displaymode/1098/.

[163] Meet the Press. Jan.25, 2004. MSNBC.com. Retrieved 10.31.2006 from http://www.msnbc.msn.com/id/408066/print/1/displaymode/1098/.
[164] Meet the Press. Jan.25, 2004. MSNBC.com. Retrieved 10.31.2006 from http://www.msnbc.msn.com/id/408066/print/1/displaymode/1098/.
[165] Peter J. Boyer. General Clark's Battles. The New Yorker. Posted November 10, 2003 and retrieved November 9, 2005 from http://www.newyorker.com/printables/fact/031117fa_fact
[166] Peter J. Boyer. General Clark's Battles. The New Yorker. Posted November 10, 2003 and retrieved November 9, 2005 from http://www.newyorker.com/printables/fact/031117fa_fact
[167] Peter J. Boyer. General Clark's Battles. The New Yorker. Posted November 10, 2003 and retrieved November 9, 2005 from http://www.newyorker.com/printables/fact/031117fa_fact
[168] Peter J. Boyer. General Clark's Battles. The New Yorker. Posted November 10, 2003 and retrieved November 9, 2005 from http://www.newyorker.com/printables/fact/031117fa_fact.
[169] NBC News. Meet the Press. Transcript for Nov. 16. MSNBC.com. November 16, 2003 and retrieved Sept.25, 2006 from http://www.msnbc.msn.com/id/3476052/print/1/displaymode/1098/.
[170] NBC News. Meet the Press. Transcript for Nov. 16. MSNBC.com. November 16, 2003 and retrieved Sept.25, 2006 from http://www.msnbc.msn.com/id/3476052/print/1/displaymode/1098/.
[171] NBC News. Meet the Press. Transcript for Nov. 16. MSNBC.com. November 16, 2003 and retrieved Sept.25, 2006 from http://www.msnbc.msn.com/id/3476052/print/1/displaymode/1098/.
[172] NBC News. Meet the Press. Transcript for Nov. 16. MSNBC.com. November 16, 2003 and retrieved Sept.25, 2006 from http://www.msnbc.msn.com/id/3476052/print/1/displaymode/1098/.
[173] John Nichols. The Nation. Which Side is Clark On? October 13, 2003 issue. Retrieved August 11, 2006 from http://www.thenation.com/docprint.mhtml?i=20031013&s=nichols.
[174] Meet the Press. Feb.1. 2004. MSNBC.com. Retrieved 10.31.2006 from http://www.msnbc.msn.com/id/4112959/print/1/displaymode/1098/.
[175] Meet the Press. Jan. 18. 2004. MSNBC.com. Retrieved 10.31.2006 from http://www.msnbc.msn.com/id/3979910/print/1/displaymode/1098/.
[176] Meet the Press. Jan 18, 2004. MSNBC.com. Transcript retrieved 10.31.2006 from http://www.msnbc.msn.com/id/3979910/print/1/displaymode/1098/.
[177] Edwards and Clark Still Have Outstanding Debt from 2004. Taegan Goddard's Political Wire. Retrieved 12.14.06 from http://politicalwire.com/archives/2008_campaign/.
[178] Alison Vekshin. Clark Replenishing political Fund. Arkansas News Bureau. Posted Aug. 9/Retrieved August 26, 2005 from http://www.arkansasnews.com/archive/2005/08/09/WashingtonDCBureau/325714.html.
[179] Tim Higgins. Clark tells Democrats speaking out is patriotic. The Des Moines Register. Posted September 1, 2005 and retrieved September 29, 2005 from http://www.desmoinesregister.com/apps/pbcs.dll/article?AID=/20050901/NEWS09/509010376/1056.
[180] KOTV—The News on 6. Wesley Clark Addresses Democrats At A Stillwater Gathering. AP. Retrieved November 3, 2005 from http://www.kotv.com/main/home/stories.asp?whichpage=1&id=91853.
[181] These appearances, as well as there corresponding transcripts, were found on Clark's WESPAC website, securingamerica.com on November 9, 2005.
[182] Steve Kornacki. I'd love to talk, Wes, but I've got Chris Dodd on hold… PoltiicsNH.com. Retrieved 9.25.06 from http://www.politicsnh.com?q=node/408.
[183] Steve Kornacki. I'd love to talk, Wes, but I've got Chris Dodd on hold… PoltiicsNH.com. Retrieved 9.25.06 from http://www.politicsnh.com?q=node/408.
[184] Clark Attends D.M. rally to campaign for Boswell. Abby Simons. Published October 9, 2006 and retrieved 10.31.06 from http://desmoinesregister.com/apps/pbcs.dll/article?AID=/20061009/NEWS09/610090323/1056.
[185] December 5. Teddy Davis reporting. New Clark Book on the Way. Retrieved 12.14.06 from http://blogs.abcnews.com/polticialradar/2006/12/new_clark_book_.html.
[186] Retrieved 11.15.06 @ http://securingamerica.com.
[187] WesPAC. Retrieved 10.31.06 from http://securingamerica.com/.
[188] Clark Bashes Bush. 10.21. Portsmouth Herald, Emily Anderson. Retrieved 10.31.2006 form http://securingamerica.com/
[189] WesPAC. Retrieved 10.31.06 from http://securingamerica.com/
[190] December 5. Teddy Davis reporting. New Clark Book on the Way. Retrieved 12.14.06 from http://blogs.abcnews.com/polticialradar/2006/12/new_clark_book_.html.
[191] TKS on National Review Online. I'll Bet You Never Guess What Wes Clark is Doing Today. 1.13.07 @ http://tks.nationalreview.com/post/?q=ZjkONzBhNmZjZTc1OGQ2ZTc1OWZmZjFiYzQxYmZmZDI=.
[192] TKS on National Review Online. I'll Bet You Never Guess What Wes Clark is Doing Today. 1.13.07 @ http://tks.nationalreview.com/post/?q=ZjkONzBhNmZjZTc1OGQ2ZTc1OWZmZjFiYzQxYmZmZDI=.
[193] Greg Giroux. DNC Meeting Provides Preview of 08 White House Primary. Yahoo! News. 2.5.07 and retrieved 5.3.07 from http://news.yahoo.com/s/cq/20070206/pl_cq_politics/dncmeetingprovidespreviewof08whitehouseprimary.
[194] Deborah Solomon. Generally Speaking. Published by the New York Times. 7.1.07 and retrieved 7.27.07 from http://securingamerica.com/.
[195] Richard E. Cohen and Michael Barone. "The Almanac of American Politics—2004." The National Journal Group. 2003, page 1101.
[196] Richard E. Cohen and Michael Barone. "The Almanac of American Politics—2004." The National Journal Group. 2003, page 1101.

[197] Richard E. Cohen and Michael Barone. "The Almanac of American Politics—2004." The National Journal Group. 2003, page 1101
[198] Richard E. Cohen and Michael Barone. "The Almanac of American Politics—2004." The National Journal Group. 2003, page 1101
[199] Judy Holland. "Moderate Clinton gains popularity." Hearst Newspapers. Lexington Herald-Leader. Posted November 12, 2004 and retrieved December 12, 2004 from http://www.kentucky.com/mld/heraldleader/news/nation/10161310.htm.
[200] George Lardner Jr. Hillary Clinton Starts PAC to Help Democrats. 2.7.01 and retrieved 12.15.04 from http://www.washingtonpost.com/ac2/wp-dyn/A35659-2001Feb6?language=printer.
[201] Richard E. Cohen and Michael Barone. "The Almanac of American Politics—2004." The National Journal Group. 2003, page 1101
[202] Opensecrets.org. HILLPAC-PAC contributions to Federal Candidates. 2002 Cycle. Retrieved December 15, 2004 from http://www.opensecrets.org/pacs/pacgot.asp?strID=C00363994&Cycle=2002.
[203] Opensecrets.org. HILLPAC-PAC Contributions to Federal Candidates. 2004 Cycle. Retrieved December 15, 2004 from http://www.opensecrets.org/pacs/pacgot.asp?strID=C00363994&Cycle=2004.
[204] WTNH.com Hillary Clinton in the Democratic spotlight: Will she or won't she? AP. Posted July 26, 2004 and retrieved October 5, 2005 from http://www.wtnh.com/Global/story.asp?S=2088562.
[205] MSNBC.com A web exclusive by Susannah Meadows. Hillary's Challenger—Jeanine Pirro on why she's running against the former First Lady. Posted Aug. 13, 2005 and retrieved Aug. 19, 2005 from http://msnbc.msn.com/id/8938354/side/newseek/print/1/displaymode/1098/.
[206] Noreen O'Donnell and Cara Matthews. Pirro ties up volatile week. The Journal News. Posted Aug. 13, 2005 and retrieved Aug. 19, 2005 from http://www.thejournalnews.com/apps/pbcs.dll/article?AID=/20050813/NEWS05/508130356/1021/NEWS05. See also http://www.nydems.org/html/videos/index.html.
[207] Alexander Bolton. Clinton digs deep, seeking landslide win. The Hill: http://www.hillnews.com/thehill/export/TheHill/News/Frontpage/102506/clinton.html.
[208] ABC News. FUNNIES: The Year's Best. Dec. 31, 2006 and retrieved 1.13.07 from http://abcnews.go.com/ThisWeek/print?id=2761572.
[209] Matt Bai. Mrs. Triangulation. The New York Times. Posted October 2, 2005 and retrieved October 4, 2005 from http://www.nytimes.com/2005/10/02/magazine/02hillary.html?8hpib=&pagewanted=print.
[210] NBC News: Meet the Press. Transcript for May 1. Posted and retrieved May 1, 2005 from http://www.msnbc.msn.com/id/7698687/.
[211] NBC News: Meet the Press. Transcript for May 1. Posted and retrieved May 1, 2005 from http://www.msnbc.msn.com/id/7698687/
[212] NBC News: Meet the Press. Transcript for May 1. Posted and retrieved May 1, 2005 from http://www.msnbc.msn.com/id/7698687/
[213] US intelligence 'dead wrong' on Iraq weapons: panel. Retrieved 6.17.05 from http://www.theallineed.com/news/0503/318164.htm.
[214] Charles Babington and Shailagh Murray. For Now, an Unofficial Rivalry. 12.8.06 and retrieved 12.14.06 from http://www.washingtonpost.com/wp-dyn/content/article/2006/12/07/AR2006120701755_pf.html.
[215] The Sunday Times. Friends of Hillary hint she may pull out of presidential race. Sarah Baxter. Posted Sept.3 and retrieved Sept.6, 2006 from http://www.timesonline.co.uk/article/0,,2089-2340352,00.html.
[216] The Sunday Times. Friends of Hillary hint she may pull out of presidential race. Sarah Baxter. Posted Sept.3 and retrieved Sept.6, 2006 from http://www.timesonline.co.uk/article/0,,2089-2340352,00.html.
[217] Hillary Rodham Clinton foresees female president. Milwaukee Journal Sentinel. September 1, 2006 12A.
[218] Jennifer Steinhauer. Pelosi is a woman on a mission: Democratic control of Congress. NY Times. MJS, 10.31.06, 4A.
[219] Michael Goodwin. Rudy vs. Hillary. New York Daily News. Milwaukee Journal Sentinel. Nov. 22, 2006 19A.
[220] AP. Sen. Clinton co-sponsors anti-flag burning law. Newsday.com. Posted December 5, 2005 and retrieved December 6, 2005 from http://www.newsday.com/news/local/wire/newyork/ny-bc-ny-brf--clinton-flag-1205dec05,0,7179096.story?coll=ny-region-apnewyork.
[221] AP. Sen. Clinton co-sponsors anti-flag burning law. Newsday.com. Posted December 5, 2005 and retrieved December 6, 2005 from http://www.newsday.com/news/local/wire/newyork/ny-bc-ny-brf--clinton-flag-1205dec05,0,7179096.story?coll=ny-region-apnewyork
[222] Katherine M. Skiba. Clinton promises dialogue with Iowa. MJS, Jan. 28, 2007, 3A.
[223] Katherine M. Skiba. Clinton promises dialogue with Iowa. MJS, Jan. 28, 2007, 3A.
[224] Katherine M. Skiba. Clinton promises dialogue with Iowa. MJS, Jan. 28, 2007, 3A
[225] WNBC/Marist Poll: National February 22, 2006. Retrieved February 27, 2006 from http://www.maristpoll.marist.edu/usapolls/HC060222.htm
[226] WNBC/Marist Poll: National February 22, 2006. Retrieved February 27, 2006 from http://www.maristpoll.marist.edu/usapolls/HC060222.htm
[227] CBS News/New York Times Poll. January 20-25, 2006. N=1229 adults nationwide. Retrieved February 17, 2006 from http://www.pollingreport.com/politics.htm
[228] CBS News/New York Times Poll. January 20-25, 2006. N=1229 adults nationwide. Retrieved February 17, 2006 from http://www.pollingreport.com/politics.htm
[229] Government and Politics. CNN Poll, Dec. 5-7. Retrieved 12.14.06 from http://www.pollingreport.com/politics.htm.

[230] ABC.com. Commander in Chief. Retrieved June 30, 2006 from http://abc.go.com/primetime/schedule/2005-06/commander.html.
[231] ABC.com. Commander in Chief. Retrieved June 30, 2006 from http://abc.go.com/primetime/schedule/2005-06/commander.html.
[232] ABC.com. Commander in Chief. Retrieved June 30, 2006 from http://abc.go.com/primetime/schedule/2005-06/commander.html.
[233] tv.com. Commander in Chief. Retrieved June 30, 2006 from http://www.tv.com/commander-in-chief/show/30463/summary.html.
[234] Retrieved 8.21.07 from http://www.presidentpolls2008.com/polls/abcnews_com-ABC-News-2008-Presidential-Opinion-Polls.html.
[235] Lynne Duke. Hillary's biggest issue? Yep, it's Bill. Milwaukee Journal Sentinel, Washington Post. Dec. 26, 2006, 13A.
[236] Hillary Clinton on Yahoo! News Photos. Retrieved 9.17.06 from http://news.yahoo.com/news?tmpl=story&u=/060820/ids_photos_en/r3174486097.jpg see picture
[237] Ana Marie Cox. Time.com. How Americans View Hillary: Popular but Polarizing. Posted Aug.19 and retrieved July 25, 2006 from http://www.time.com/time/magazine/article/0,9171,1229053,00.html.
[238] Ana Marie Cox. Time.com. How Americans View Hillary: Popular but Polarizing. Posted Aug.19 and retrieved July 25, 2006 from http://www.time.com/time/magazine/article/0,9171,1229053,00.html.
[239] Ana Marie Cox. Time.com. How Americans View Hillary: Popular but Polarizing. Posted Aug.19 and retrieved July 25, 2006 from http://www.time.com/time/magazine/article/0,9171,1229053,00.html.
[240] Brett Arends. Hatin' on Hillary: N.H. Dems lambaste Clinton. Posted Aug.7 and retrieved Aug.11, 2006 from http://news.bostonherald.com/columnists/view.bg?articleid=151737.
[241] AP. Falwell: Clinton comment 'tongue-in-cheek'. MSNBC.com. Sept. 25, 2006 and retrieved same day from http://www.msnbc.msn.com/id/14991714/print/1/displaymode/1098/.
[242] AP. Falwell: Clinton comment 'tongue-in-cheek'. MSNBC.com. Sept. 25, 2006 and retrieved same day from http://www.msnbc.msn.com/id/14991714/print/1/displaymode/1098/.
[243] LA Times/NY Times/AP. Warner decides against presidential bid. Milwaukee Journal Sentinel, Oct. 13, 2006, 3A.
[244] Maureen Dowd. A McCain-Clinton vodka contest? Yes. No. Um, maybe. NY Times. Milwaukee Journal Sentinel, Oct. 20, 2006 17A.
[245] Maureen Dowd. A McCain-Clinton vodka contest? Yes. No. Um, maybe. NY Times. Milwaukee Journal Sentinel, Oct. 20, 2006 17A.
[246] Maureen Dowd. A McCain-Clinton vodka contest? Yes. No. Um, maybe. NY Times. Milwaukee Journal Sentinel, Oct. 20, 2006 17A.
[247] Maureen Dowd. A McCain-Clinton vodka contest? Yes. No. Um, maybe. NY Times. Milwaukee Journal Sentinel, Oct. 20, 2006 17A.
[248] Maureen Dowd. A McCain-Clinton vodka contest? Yes. No. Um, maybe. NY Times. Milwaukee Journal Sentinel, Oct. 20, 2006 17A.
[249] Hardball's College Tour with John McCain. MSNBC.com. Oct. 18, retrieved 10.31.2006 from http://www.msnbc.msn.com/id/15330717/page/2/print/1/displaymode/1098/
[250] Hardball's College Tour with John McCain. MSNBC.com. Oct. 18, retrieved 10.31.2006 from http://www.msnbc.msn.com/id/15330717/page/2/print/1/displaymode/1098/
[251] AP. McCain: Alaska shows warming. Seattle Times. Posted Aug. 18/Retrieved Aug. 19, 2005 from http://seattletimes.nwsource.com/cgi-bin/PrintStory.pl?document_id=2002444083&zsection_id=2002111777&slug=climate18m&date=20050818.
[252] Tucson Citizen. Our Opinion: McCain taking lead role on global warming. Posted/Retrieved August 26, 2005 from http://www.tucsoncitizen.com/index.php?page=opinion&story_id=082605b4_edits.
[253] Liz Ruskin. Sens. McCain, Clinton probe melting Artic. Anchorage Daily News. Published 8.18.05 and retrieved 8.19.05 from http://www.adn.com/front/v-printer/story/6829476p-6724753c.html.
[254] Liz Ruskin. Sens. McCain, Clinton probe melting Artic. Anchorage Daily News. Published 8.18.05 and retrieved 8.19.05 from http://www.adn.com/front/v-printer/story/6829476p-6724753c.html
[255] AP. McCain: Alaska shows warming. Seattle Times. Posted Aug. 18/Retrieved Aug. 19, 2005 from http://seattletimes.nwsource.com/cgi-bin/PrintStory.pl?document_id=2002444083&zsection_id=2002111777&slug=climate18m&date=20050818
[256] Tucson Citizen. Our Opinion: McCain taking lead role on global warming. Posted/Retrieved August 26, 2005 from http://www.tucsoncitizen.com/index.php?page=opinion&story_id=082605b4_edits.
[257] Taegan Goddard's Political Wire. Quote of the Day. July 10, 2006 and retrieved July 14, 2006 from http://politicalwire.com/archives/2008_campaign/. From Esquire, posted on Hotline On Call.
[258] Todd Purdum. Prisoner of Conscience. Vanity Fair. For February 2007. Retrieved 1.13.07 from http://www.vanityfair.com/politics/features/2007/02/mccain200702?printable=true&currentPage=all.
[259] Herman Cain. Hezbocrats Attack Wal-Mart. Townhall.com Posted August 22, 2006 and retrieved September 6, 2006 from http://www.townhall.com/Common/Print.aspx.
[260] Beth Fouhy. Hillary Clinton Feels Heat Over Wal-Mart Ties. AP, March 12, 2006. Retrieved September 6, 2006 from http://www.commondreams.org/headlines06/0312-01.htm.
[261] Beth Fouhy. Hillary Clinton Feels Heat Over Wal-Mart Ties. AP, March 12, 2006. Retrieved September 6, 2006 from http://www.commondreams.org/headlines06/0312-01.htm.

[262] Glenn Thrush. Clinton: Cover Employees. Newsday. Posted January 26, 2006, and retrieved September 6, 2006 from http://www.newsday.com/news/nationworld/nation/ny-uswalm264601565jan26,0,3081473.story?coll=ny-top-headlines.
[263] Sebastian Mallaby. Anti-Wal-Mart Campaign. Doing Business with betrayal. Houston Chronicle. Posted September 3, 2006 and retrieved September 6, 2006 from http://www.chron.com/cs/CDA/printstory.mpl/editorial/outlook/4158741.
[264] Sebastian Mallaby. Anti-Wal-Mart Campaign. Doing Business with betrayal. Houston Chronicle. Posted September 3, 2006 and retrieved September 6, 2006 from http://www.chron.com/cs/CDA/printstory.mpl/editorial/outlook/4158741.
[265] Beth Fouhy. Hillary Clinton Feels Heat Over Wal-Mart Ties. AP, March 12, 2006. Retrieved September 6, 2006 from http://www.commondreams.org/headlines06/0312-01.htm.
[266] Devlin Barrett. Hillary Clinton Returns Wal-Mart Cash. ABC News. AP. Retrieved September 6, 2006 from http://www.abcnews.go.com/Politics/print?id=1578195.
[267] Devlin Barrett. Hillary Clinton Returns Wal-Mart Cash. ABC News. AP. Retrieved September 6, 2006 from http://www.abcnews.go.com/Politics/print?id=1578195.
[268] Adam Nagourney and Michael Barbaro. Eye on Election, Democrats Run as Wal-Mart Foe. Published August 17, 2006 and retrieved September 7, 2006 from http://www.nytimes.com/2006/08/17/washington/17dems.html?ex=1313467200&en=082dce1f1f00051b&ei=5090&partner=rssuserland&emc=rss.
[269] Devlin Barrett. February 3, 2006. Hillary Clinton Returns Wal-Mart Cash. ABC News. AP. Retrieved September 6, 2006 from http://www.abcnews.go.com/Politics/print?id=1578195.
[270] Glenn Thrush. Clinton: Cover Employees. Newsday. Posted January 26, 2006, and retrieved September 6, 2006 from http://www.newsday.com/news/nationworld/nation/ny-uswalm264601565jan26,0,3081473.story?coll=ny-top-headlines.
[271] Glenn Thrush. Clinton: Cover Employees. Newsday. Posted January 26, 2006, and retrieved September 6, 2006 from http://www.newsday.com/news/nationworld/nation/ny-uswalm264601565jan26,0,3081473.story?coll=ny-top-headlines.
[272] Glenn Thrush. Clinton: Cover Employees. Newsday. Posted January 26, 2006, and retrieved September 6, 2006 from http://www.newsday.com/news/nationworld/nation/ny-uswalm264601565jan26,0,3081473.story?coll=ny-top-headlines .
[273] Glenn Thrush. Clinton: Cover Employees. Newsday. Posted January 26, 2006, and retrieved September 6, 2006 from http://www.newsday.com/news/nationworld/nation/ny-uswalm264601565jan26,0,3081473.story?coll=ny-top-headlines.
[274] Glenn Thrush. Clinton: Cover Employees. Newsday. Posted January 26, 2006, and retrieved September 6, 2006 from http://www.newsday.com/news/nationworld/nation/ny-uswalm264601565jan26,0,3081473.story?coll=ny-top-headlines.
[275] Beth Fouhy. Hillary Clinton Feels Heat Over Wal-Mart Ties. AP, March 12, 2006. Retrieved September 6, 2006 from http://www.commondreams.org/headlines06/0312-01.htm.
[276] Richard Willing. USA Today. Nation. Lawsuits a volume business at Wal-Mart. Posted August 13, 2001 and retrieved September 6, 2006 from http://www.nfsi.org/walmart/Lawsuits%20a%20volume%20business%20at%20Wal-Mart.htm.
[277] Sebastian Mallaby. Anti-Wal-Mart Campaign. Doing Business with betrayal. Houston Chronicle. Posted September 3, 2006 and retrieved September 6, 2006 from http://www.chron.com/cs/CDA/printstory.mpl/editorial/outlook/4158741.
[278] New York Sun Editorial. Mrs. Clinton's Wal-Mart. February 6, 2006. Retrieved September 6, 2006 from http://www.nysun.com/article/27089.
[279] Beth Fouhy. Hillary Clinton Feels Heat Over Wal-Mart Ties. AP, March 12, 2006. Retrieved September 6, 2006 from http://www.commondreams.org/headlines06/0312-01.htm.
[280] Adam Nagourney and Michael Barbaro. Eye on Election, Democrats Run as Wal-Mart Foe. Published August 17, 2006 and retrieved September 7, 2006 from http://www.nytimes.com/2006/08/17/washington/17dems.html?ex=1313467200&en=082dce1f1f00051b&ei=5090&partner=rssuserland&emc=rss.
[281] Adam Nagourney and Michael Barbaro. Eye on Election, Democrats Run as Wal-Mart Foe. Published August 17, 2006 and retrieved September 7, 2006 from http://www.nytimes.com/2006/08/17/washington/17dems.html?ex=1313467200&en=082dce1f1f00051b&ei=5090&partner=rssuserland&emc=rss.
[282] Beth Fouhy. Hillary Clinton Feels Heat Over Wal-Mart Ties. AP, March 12, 2006. Retrieved September 6, 2006 from http://www.commondreams.org/headlines06/0312-01.htm.
[283] Beth Fouhy. Hillary Clinton Feels Heat Over Wal-Mart Ties. AP, March 12, 2006. Retrieved September 6, 2006 from http://www.commondreams.org/headlines06/0312-01.htm.
[284] AP. Sen. Clinton Faces Political Challenges with Ties to Wal-Mart. Posted March 10, 2006. FOXNEWS.com. Retrieved September 6, 2006 from http://www.foxnews.com/story/0,2933,187471,00.html.
[285] HillaryClinton.com Issues. Strengthening the Middle Class. Retrieved 8.1.07 from http://www.hillaryclinton.com/issues/middleclass/.
[286] The Onion. John Edwards Vows To End All Bad Things By 2011. Posted 7.16.07 and retrieved 8.1.07 from http://www.theonion.com/content/news/john_edwards_vows_to_end_all_bad.
[287] The Onion. John Edwards Vows To End All Bad Things By 2011. Posted 7.16.07 and retrieved 8.1.07 from http://www.theonion.com/content/news/john_edwards_vows_to_end_all_bad.
[288] Tom Daschle: Biography and Much More from Answers.com. Retrieved 7.11.07 from http://www.answers.com/topic/tom-daschle.
[289] Bipartisan Policy Center. Tom Daschle. Biography. Posted 2.26.07 and retrieved 7.11.07 from http://www.bipartisanpolicy.org/index.php/c/Tom_Daschle/d/Tom_Daschle_-_Biography.
[290] Tom Daschle: Biography and Much More from Answers.com. Retrieved 7.11.07 from http://www.answers.com/topic/tom-daschle.

[291] Bipartisan Policy Center. Tom Daschle. Biography. Posted 2.26.07 and retrieved 7.11.07 from http://www.bipartisanpolicy.org/index.php/c/Tom_Daschle/d/Tom_Daschle_-_Biography.

[292] Bipartisan Policy Center. Tom Daschle. Biography. Posted 2.26.07 and retrieved 7.11.07 from http://www.bipartisanpolicy.org/index.php/c/Tom_Daschle/d/Tom_Daschle_-_Biography.

[293] NBC NEWS. MTP transcript for August 22 (2004). Meet the Press. Retrieved 10.31.2006 and posted 10.31.2006 @ http://www.msnbc.msn.com/id/5772535/print/1/displaymode/1098/

[294] NBC NEWS. MTP transcript for Dec.26. (2004). Meet the Press. Retrieved 10.31.2006 and posted 10.31.2006 @ http://www.msnbc.msn.com/id/6755915/.

[295] NBC NEWS. MTP transcript for Dec.26. (2004). Meet the Press. Retrieved 10.31.2006 and posted 10.31.2006 @ http://www.msnbc.msn.com/id/6755915/.

[296] Tom Daschle Mulls White House Run. January 18, 2006 and retrieved February 13, 2006 from http://www.newsmax.com/archives/ic/2006/1/18/112020.shtml.

[297] The Fix by Chris Cillizza. Daschle to Iowa (Again). Washingtonpost.com. Retrieved February 17, 2006 from http://blogs.washingtonpost.com/thefix/2006/01/daschle_to_iowa.html.

[298] The Fix by Chris Cillizza. Daschle to Iowa (Again). Washingtonpost.com. Retrieved February 17, 2006 from http://blogs.washingtonpost.com/thefix/2006/01/daschle_to_iowa.html

[299] AP. Tom Daschle endorses Culver for governor. February 1, 2006 and retrieved February 13, 2006 from http://desmoinesregister.com/apps/pbcs.dll/article?AID=/20060201/NEWS09/60201010/1001/NEWS.

[300] Mary Clare Jalonick. AP. Ex-Senate leader tests support for White House bid. Posted May 17 and retrieved May 31, 2006 from http://www.suntimes.com/output/elect/daschle17.html.

[301] ABC News. Daschle Tests New Hampshire for Candidacy. Mary Clare Jalonick. Posted June 8, 2006 and retrieved June 16, 2006 from http://abcnews.go.com/Politics/wireStory?id=2055642.

[302] Hotline on Call. Is Tom Daschle for Real? Posted May 19, 2006 and retrieved June 16, 2006 from http://hotlineblog.nationaljournal.com/archives/2006/05/is_tom_daschle_.html.

[303] KELOLAND.COM: News for Sioux Falls, South Dakota, Minnesota and Iowa. President Tom Daschle? June 6, 2006, and retrieved June 16, 2006 from http://www.keloland.com/News/NewsDetail5440.cfm?Id=0,48573.

[304] ABC News. Daschle Tests New Hampshire for Candidacy. Mary Clare. Posted June 8, 2006 and retrieved June 16, 2006 from http://abcnews.go.com/Politics/wireStory?id=2055642.

[305] Tom Daschle mulls political comeback. Reuters. MSNBC.com. Posted July 3, 2006 and retrieved July 14, 2006 from http://www.msnbc.msn.com/id/13688450/print/1/displaymode/1098/.

[306] The Black Hills Pioneer, Newspapers, South Dakota, SD. Around South Dakota. Daschle says he is energized by campaign trip. Posted June 12, 2006 and retrieved June 16, 2006 from http://www.zwire.com/site/news.cfm?BRD=1300&dept_id=156931&newsid=16777652&PAG=461&rfi=9.

[307] Hotline on Call. Is Tom Daschle for Real? Posted May 19, 2006 and retrieved June 16, 2006 from http://hotlineblog.nationaljournal.com/archives/2006/05/is_tom_daschle_.html

[308] AP. Daschle Resigns From Apollo Board. Retrieved July 14, 2006 from http://news.moneycentral.msn.com/provider/providerarticle.asp?feed=AP&Date=20060707&ID=5851575.

[309] Daschle will not seek presidency. Posted 12.02.06 and retrieved Dec.14.06 from http://www.keloland.com/News/NewsDetail6371.cfm?Id=0,52869.

[310] Daschle will not seek presidency. Posted 12.02.06 and retrieved Dec.14.06 from http://www.keloland.com/News/NewsDetail6371.cfm?Id=0,52869.

[311] Daschle will Not Run for President. Retrieved 12.14.06 from http://politicalwire.com/archieves/2008_campaign/.

[312] Mark Leibovich. Just Ask: Kucinich Answers, 'Yes I Am'. 12.12.06 and retrieved from New York Times on 12.14.06 from http://www.nytimes.com/2006/12/12/us/politics/12dennis.html?ex=1323579600&en=ad2af566c2e42300&ei=5090&partner=rssuserland&emc=rss.

[313] Mark Leibovich. Just Ask: Kucinich Answers, 'Yes I Am'. 12.12.06 and retrieved from New York Times on 12.14.06 from http://www.nytimes.com/2006/12/12/us/politics/12dennis.html?ex=1323579600&en=ad2af566c2e42300&ei=5090&partner=rssuserland&emc=rss.

[314] Rachel Kapochunas. Sen. Dodd Becomes Fifth Democratic Candidate for 2008. The New York Times. Jan.12, 2007 and retrieved 1.13.07 from http://www.nytimes.com/cq/2007/01/12/cq_2119.html?pagewanted=print.

[315] Howard Fineman. Hillary's Challengers. May 31, 2006. Newsweek. MSNBC.com. retrieved June 30, 2006 from http://www.msnbc.msn.com/id/13065878/site/newsweek/page/2/print/1/displaymode/1098/, and http://en.wikipedia.org/wiki/Thomas_Dodd.

[316] Howard Fineman. Hillary's Challengers. May 31, 2006. Newsweek. MSNBC.com. retrieved June 30, 2006 from http://www.msnbc.msn.com/id/13065878/site/newsweek/page/2/print/1/displaymode/1098/.

[317] Rachel Kapochunas. Sen. Dodd Becomes Fifth Democratic Candidate for 2008. The New York Times. 1.12.07 and retrieved 1.13.07 from http://www.nytimes.com/cq/2007/01/12/cq_2119.html?pagewanted=print.

[318] David Lightman. Hartford Courant. Dodd To Test Waters. Posted 8.28.06 and retrieved 9.6.06 from http://www.courant.com/news/local/hc-dodd0828.artaug28,0,5975500,print.story

[319] Rachel Kapochunas. Sen. Dodd Becomes Fifth Democratic Candidate for 2008. The New York Times. Jan.12, 2007 and retrieved 1.13.07 from http://www.nytimes.com/cq/2007/01/12/cq_2119.html?pagewanted=print.

[320] Rachel Kapochunas. Sen. Dodd Becomes Fifth Democratic Candidate for 2008. The New York Times. Jan.12, 2007 and retrieved 1.13.07 from http://www.nytimes.com/cq/2007/01/12/cq_2119.html?pagewanted=print.

[321] Connecticut News from the Hartford Courant. David Lightman. Dodd Poised for Possible '08 Presidential Run. Posted May 22, 2006 and retrieved May 31, 2006 from http://www.courant.com/news/politics/hc-dodd-run-0522,0,1790154.story.

[322] Jason Horowitz. Can '08 Race Make Dodd Bedfellows? New York Observer. 12.4.06 and retrieved 12.14.06 from http://www.observer.com/printpage.asp?iid=13795&ic=News+Story+1.

[323] David Lightman. Iowa, 16 months and counting. The Swamp, Chicago Tribune blogs. Posted Sept. 10, 2006 and retrieved Sept. 25, 2006 from http://newsblogs.chicagotribune.com/news_com/news_theswamp/2006/09/iowa_16_months_.html.

[324] David Lightman. Democrats In Iowa Are Cool On Clinton. Courant.com. Posted 9.12.06 and retrieved 9.25.06 from http://www.courant.com/news/politics/hc-iowa0912.artsep12,0,5115593,print.story?coll=hc-headlines-politics.

[325] David Lightman. Dodd Enters. The '08 Race. Courant.com. Posted Jan.11 @ http://www.courant.com/news/local/hc-dodd0111.artjan11-updates,0,5577789,print.story?coll=hc-headlines-local.

[326] Connecticut News from the Hartford Courant. David Lightman. Dodd Poised for Possible '08 Presidential Run. Posted May 22, 2006 and retrieved May 31, 2006 from http://www.courant.com/news/politics/hc-dodd-run-0522,0,1790154.story.

[327] Beth Fouhy. Dodd declares '08 presidential candidacy. Jan.13, 2007 and posted Jan.12 @ http://www.localnewswatch.com/benton/stories/index.php?action=fullnews&id=43323. See also http://abcnews.go.com/print/?id=2786784.

[328] Andrew Miga. YAHOO!NEWS. Dodd well-positioned for White House bid. AP. 1.2.07 and retrieved 1.13.07 from http://www.boston.com/news/nation/articles/2007/01/02/dodd_well_positioned_for_white_house_bid/.

[329] Andrew Miga. YAHOO!NEWS. Dodd well-positioned for White House bid. AP. 1.2.07 and retrieved 1.13.07 from http://www.boston.com/news/nation/articles/2007/01/02/dodd_well_positioned_for_white_house_bid/.

[330] Jason Horowitz. Can '08 Race Make Dodd Bedfellows? New York Observer. 12.4.06 and retrieved 12.14.06 from http://www.observer.com/printpage.asp?iid=13795&ic=News+Story+1.

[331] Taegan Goddard's Political Wire. Quote of the Day. 10.31.06 from http://politicalwire.com/archives/2008_campaign/.

[332] Jackie Calmes. Selling an Insider's Experience for '08. 10.10.06 and retrieved 10.31.06 from http://online.wsj.com/public/article/SB116042220841387176-rMKcpkJvCJyAeMW8UDWw18cTDdI_20071010.html?mod=blogs.

[333] Howard Fineman. Hillary's Challengers. May 31, 2006. Newsweek. MSNBC.com. retrieved June 30, 2006 from http://www.msnbc.msn.com/id/13065878/site/newsweek/page/2/print/1/displaymode/1098/.

[334] David Lightman. Dodd to Announce Official Presidential Bid. Jan.10, 2007. Retrieved 1.13.07 from http://www.courant.com/news/politics/hce-dodd4prez.jan10,0,6751564.story?coll=hc-head....

[335] David Lightman. Dodd Enters The '08 Race. Courant.com. Posted Jan.11 @ http://www.courant.com/news/local/hc-dodd0111.artjan11-updates,0,5577789,print.story?coll=hc-headlines-local.

[336] Stan Simpson. Connecticut News from the Hartford Courant. Jan. 13. 2007 @ http://www.courant.com/news/local/hc-ctstan0113.artian13,0,6398454.column?coll=hc-utility-local.

[337] David Lightman. Dodd Enters. The '08 Race. Courant.com. Posted Jan.11 @ http://www.courant.com/news/local/hc-dodd0111.artjan11-updates,0,5577789,print.story?coll=hc-headlines-local.

[338] Rachel Kapochunas. Sen. Dodd Becomes Fifth Democratic Candidate for 2008. The New York Times. Jan.12, 2007 and retrieved 1.13.07 from http://www.nytimes.com/cq/2007/01/12/cq_2119.html?pagewanted=print

[339] Connecticut News from the Hartford Courant. David Lightman. Dodd Poised for Possible '08 Presidential Run. Posted May 22, 2006 and retrieved May 31, 2006 from http://www.courant.com/news/politics/hc-dodd-run-0522,0,1790154.story.

[340] Jason Horowitz. Can '08 Race Make Dodd Bedfellows? New York Observer. 12.4.06 and retrieved 12.14.06 from http://www.observer.com/printpage.asp?iid=13795&ic=News+Story+1.

[341] Jason Horowitz. Can '08 Race Make Dodd Bedfellows? New York Observer. 12.4.06 and retrieved 12.14.06 from http://www.observer.com/printpage.asp?iid=13795&ic=News+Story+1.

[342] Jason Horowitz. Can '08 Race Make Dodd Bedfellows? New York Observer. 12.4.06 and retrieved 12.14.06 from http://www.observer.com/printpage.asp?iid=13795&ic=News+Story+1.

[343] Connecticut News from the Hartford Courant. David Lightman. Dodd Poised for Possible '08 Presidential Run. Posted May 22, 2006 and retrieved May 31, 2006 from http://www.courant.com/news/politics/hc-dodd-run-0522,0,1790154.story.

[344] Don Imus. Chris Dodd: Jumps in 2008 Dem White House primary. Announces on Imus. 1.13.07 @ http://blogs.suntimes.com/sweet/2007/01/chris_dodd_jumps_in_2008_dem_w.html.

[345] FOXNews.com "Transcript: Sens. Dodd, McConnell on 'FNS'." Aired April 16, 2006 and retrieved April 24, 2006 from http://www.foxnews.com/printer_friendly_story/0,3566,191915,00.html.

[346] David Lightman. Iowa, 16 months and counting. The Swamp, Chicago Tribune blogs. Posted Sept. 10, 2006 and retrieved Sept. 25, 2006 from http://newsblogs.chicagotribune.com/news_com/news_theswamp/2006/09/iowa_16_months_.html.

[347] David Lightman. Democrats In Iowa Are Cool On Clinton. Courant.com. Posted 9.12.06 and retrieved 9.25.06 from http://www.courant.com/news/politics/hc-iowa0912.artsep12,0,5115593,print.story?coll=hc-headlines-politics.

[348] Jackie Calmes. Selling an Insider's Experience for '08. 10.10.06 and retrieved 10.31.06 from http://online.wsj.com/public/article/SB116042220841387176-rMKcpkJvCJyAeMW8UDWw18cTDdI_20071010.html?mod=blogs.

[349] David Lightman. Hartford Courant. Dodd To Test Waters. Posted August 28, and retrieved September 6, 2006 from http://www.courant.com/news/local/hc-dodd0828.artaug28,0,5975500,print.story.

[350] David Lightman. Hartford Courant. Dodd To Test Waters. Posted August 28, and retrieved September 6, 2006 from http://www.courant.com/news/local/hc-dodd0828.artaug28,0,5975500,print.story

[351] Jane Norman. Edwards leads in poll of likely caucus goers. Des Moines Register. Published and retrieved 12.14.06 from http://www.desmoinesregiter.com/apps/pbc.dll/article?AID=/20061214/NEWS09/612140397/1056.
[352] Jason Horowitz. Can '08 Race Make Dodd Bedfellows? New York Observer. 12.4.06 and retrieved 12.14.06 from http://www.observer.com/printpage.asp?iid=13795&ic=News+Story+1.
[353] Jason Horowitz. Can '08 Race Make Dodd Bedfellows? New York Observer. 12.4.06 and retrieved 12.14.06 from http://www.observer.com/printpage.asp?iid=13795&ic=News+Story+1.
[354] Beth Fouhy. Sen. Dodd to Decide on Joining 2008 Race. Dec. 12. 2006 and retrieved 12.14.06 form http://cbsnews.com/stories/2006/12/12/ap/politics/mainD8LVJ8380.shtml.
[355] David Lightman. Iowa, 16 months and counting. The Swamp, Chicago Tribune blogs. Posted 9.10.06 and retrieved 9.25.06 from http://newsblogs.chicagotribune.com/news_com/news_theswamp/2006/09/iowa_16_months_.html.
[356] The Bristol Press, 2007. Steve Collins. Local reaction to Dodd bid great choice, but no chance. 1.12.07 and retrieved next day @ http://www.bristolpress.com/site/news.cfm?newsid=17702717&BRD=1643&PAG=461&dept_id=571108&rfi=6.
[357] Chris Dodd is Taking Requests. Wonkette. 1.13.05 @ http://wonkette.com/politics/chris-dodd/chris-dodd-is-taking-requests-228048.php.
[358] CNN.com. Dodd runs to the beat of his own 'tunes'. Retrieved 1.13.07 from http://www.cnn.com/POLITICS/blogs/politicalticker/2007/01/dodd-runs-to-beat-of-his-own-tunes.
[359] Chris Dodd is Taking Requests. Wonkette. 1.13.05 @ http://wonkette.com/politics/chris-dodd/chris-dodd-is-taking-requests-228048.php.
[360] Amanda. Chris Dodd Got Crabs from John Doe, Still Not Cool. Retrieved Jan.13 @ http://wonkette.com/politics/chris-dodd/chris-dodd-got-crabs-from-john-doe-still-not-cool-228159.php.
[361] Amanda. Chris Dodd Got Crabs from John Doe, Still Not Cool. Retrieved Jan.13 @ http://wonkette.com/politics/chris-dodd/chris-dodd-got-crabs-from-john-doe-still-not-cool-228159.php.
[362] David Lightman. Courant.com. Dodd Gets Good Start. Posted June 24, 2006 and retrieved June 30, 2006 from http://www.courant.com/news/politics/hc-ctdodd0624.artjun24,0,4882048.story?coll=hc-headlines-politics.
[363] Tim Fernholz. Why is Chris Dodd Running for President?: Seriously, **why?**" Retrieved June 16, 2006 from http://www.tnr.com/blog/theplank?pid=18099.
[364] David Lightman. Dodd Enters. The '08 Race. Courant.com. Posted 1.11.07 @ http://www.courant.com/news/local/hc-dodd0111.artjan11-updates,0,5577789,print.story?coll=hc-headlines-local.
[365] David Lightman. Dodd Enters. The '08 Race. Courant.com. Posted Jan.11 @ http://www.courant.com/news/local/hc-dodd0111.artjan11-updates,0,5577789,print.story?coll=hc-headlines-local.
[366] David Lightman. Dodd Enters. The '08 Race. Courant.com. Posted Jan.11 @ http://www.courant.com/news/local/hc-dodd0111.artjan11-updates,0,5577789,print.story?coll=hc-headlines-local.
[367] Judie Jacobson. Jewish Ledger. Published 7.31.07 and retrieved 8.1.07 from http://www.jewishledger.com/articles/2007/07/31/enws/news04.txt.
[368] Judie Jacobson. Jewish Ledger. Published 7.31.07 and retrieved 8.1.07 from http://www.jewishledger.com/articles/2007/07/31/enws/news04.txt.
[369] Campaign Finance. At a Glance: Second Quarter 2007 Fundraising Summary. Retrieved 8.1.07 from http://projects.washingtonpost.com/2008-presidential-candidates/finance/2007q2/comparis...
[370] Richard E. Cohen and Michael Barone. "The Almanac of American Politics—2004." The National Journal Group. 2003, page 1191.
[371] Richard E. Cohen and Michael Barone. "The Almanac of American Politics—2004." The National Journal Group. 2003, page 1191
[372] Rob Christensen and Lynn Bonner. "Count on Edwards returning to the fray." Newsobserver.com. Published November 4, 2004 and retrieved October 4, 2005 from http://newsobserver.com/news/v-printer/story/1795976p-8095176c.html.
[373] Quote excerpted from Transcript for Jan. 2, 2005 Meet the Press. NBC News. Retrieved 10.31.2006 from http://www.msnbc.msn.com/id/6770575/print/1/displaymode/1098/
[374] Richard E. Cohen and Michael Barone. The Almanac of American Politics—2004. The National Journal Group. 2003, page 1192
[375] Adam Nagourney. The New York Times. Kerry Camp Sees Edwards Helping With Rural Vote. Published July 9, 2004 and retrieved July 28, 2006 from http://www.uselecitonatlas.org/INFORMATION/ARTICLES/20040709rural.html.
[376] Adam Nagourney. The New York Times. Kerry Camp Sees Edwards Helping With Rural Vote. Published July 9, 2004 and retrieved July 28, 2006 from http://www.uselecitonatlas.org/INFORMATION/ARTICLES/20040709rural.html
[377] Adam Nagourney. The New York Times. Kerry Camp Sees Edwards Helping With Rural Vote. Published July 9, 2004 and retrieved July 28, 2006 from http://www.uselecitonatlas.org/INFORMATION/ARTICLES/20040709rural.html
[378] Adam Nagourney. The New York Times. Kerry Camp Sees Edwards Helping With Rural Vote. Published July 9, 2004 and retrieved July 28, 2006 from http://www.uselecitonatlas.org/INFORMATION/ARTICLES/20040709rural.html
[379] Rob Christensen and Lynn Bonner. Count on Edwards returning to the fray. Newsobserver.com. Published November 4, 2004 and retrieved October 4, 2005 from http://newsobserver.com/news/v-printer/story/1795976p-8095176c.html
[380] Perry Bacon Jr. A Kickoff for John Edwards 2.0. Time. Dec.29, 2006 and retrieved 1.13.07 from http://www.time.com/time/nation/article/0,8599,1573215,00.html
[381] Tom Raum. Political junkies speculate on 2008 race. AP. The Arizona Daily Star. Retrieved December 15, 2004 from http://www.asstarnet.com/dailystar/relatedarticles/46526.php

[382] Perry Bacon Jr. A Kickoff for John Edwards 2.0. Time. Dec.29, 2006 and retrieved 1.13.07 from http://www.time.com/time/nation/article/0,8599,1573215,00.html
[383] ABC news. John and Elizabeth Edwards on 'This Week'. Aired 12.31.06 and retrieved Jan. 27, 2007 from http://abcnews.go.com/ThisWeek/print?id=2762463.
[384] Washington Post. Edwards' hair attracts costly attention. Posted 7.5.07 and retrieved 7.20.07 from http://www.chron.com/disp/story.mpl/politics/4946879.html.
[385] Washington Post. Edwards' hair attracts costly attention. Posted 7.5.07 and retrieved 7.20.07 from http://www.chron.com/disp/story.mpl/politics/4946879.html.
[386] Washington Post. Edwards' hair attracts costly attention. Posted 7.5.07 and retrieved 7.20.07 from http://www.chron.com/disp/story.mpl/politics/4946879.html.
[387] Washington Post. Edwards' hair attracts costly attention. Posted 7.5.07 and retrieved 7.20.07 from http://www.chron.com/disp/story.mpl/politics/4946879.html.
[388] The Funnies. Retrieved 8.1.07 from http://www.hillaryis44.org/?p=98.
[389] The Funnies. Retrieved 8.1.07 from http://www.hillaryis44.org/?p=98.
[390] Retrieved 7.20.07 from http://www.youtube.com/watch?v=2AE847UXu3Q.
[391] Richard E. Cohen and Michael Barone. "The Almanac of American Politics—2004." The National Journal Group. 2003, page 1190.
[392] Richard E. Cohen and Michael Barone. "The Almanac of American Politics—2004." The National Journal Group. 2003, page 1192.
[393] Thomas B. Edsall and John F. Harris. Bush aims to Forge a GOP Legacy. Washington Post, January 30, 2005, Page A01. Retrieved October 4, 2005 from http://www.washingtonpost.com/ac2/wp-dyn/A47559-2005Jan29?language=printer.
[394] Thomas B. Edsall and John F. Harris. Bush aims to Forge a GOP Legacy. Washington Post, January 30, 2005, Page A01. Retrieved October 4, 2005 from http://www.washingtonpost.com/ac2/wp-dyn/A47559-2005Jan29?language=printer
[395] Perry Bacon Jr. A Kickoff for John Edwards 2.0. Time. Dec.29, 2006 and retrieved 1.13.07 from http://www.time.com/time/nation/article/0,8599,1573215,00.html
[396] Nedra Pickler. AP. John Edwards shoots for White House again. December 29, 2006 and retrieved 1.13.06 from http://www.knoxnews.com/kns/election/article/0,1406,KNS_630_5243053,00.html.
[397] AP Interview: Edwards says Obama should run for president. Mike Baker. AP. Retrieved 12.14.06 from http://www.kansascity.com/mld/kansascity/news/poltiics/elections/16054364.htm
[398] AP. Edwards: I'm More Joyful Than Clinton. Retrieved 7.27.07 and posted 10.20.06 @ http://www.breihart.com/article.php?id=D8KSHGPO0&show_article=1.
[399] CNN. Elizabeth Edwards versus Hillary Clinton. 7.23.07 and retrieved 7.27.07 from http://politicalticker.blogs.cnn.com/2007/07/23/elizabeth-edwards-versus-hillary-clinton/.
[400] John Edwards' campaign: Dem version of McCain. Posted 7.19.07 and retrieved 7.20.07 from http://weblog.signonsandiego.com/weblogs/afb/archives/012832.html.
[401] CNN Political Ticker. Posted 8.8.07 and retrieved 8.21.07 from http://politicalticker.blogs.cnn.com/2007/08/08/elizabeth-edwards-cant-make-john-black-or-a-woman/.
[402] Alec MacGillis. Elizabeth Edwards Talks Tough. Posted 8.31.07 and retrieved September 3, 2007 from http://blog.washingtonpost.com/the-trail/2007/08/31/elizabeth_edwards_keeps_talkin.html.
[403] McClatchy. Edwards' poverty campaign brings criticism, comparisons. Posted 2007, and retrieved 8.1.07 from http://insurancenewsnet.com/article.asp?n=1&neID=200707191180.6.210_718400623162b08d.
[404] AP. Hagel: No 2008 Plans As Independent. Posted 7.8.07 and retrieved 8.1.07 from http://abcnews.go.com/Politics/wireStory?id=3356637.
[405] McClatchy. Edwards' poverty campaign brings criticism, comparisons. Posted 2007, and retrieved 8.1.07 from http://insurancenewsnet.com/article.asp?n=1&neID=200707191180.6.210_718400623162b08d.
[406] CentreDaily.com. Handicapping the '08 presidential race. Posted Nov.14.06 and retrieved 11.17.06 from http://www.centredaily.com/mld/centredaily/news/opinion/15998697.htm.
[407] Jackie Calmes. Edwards's Theme: U.S. Poverty. Wall Street Journal. Retrieved 1.13.07 and posted Dec.28, 2006 @ http://online.wsj.com/public/article/SB116725461738460888-Ups3_pA6nmNclAawkuv2dm4M_yw_20071228.html.
[408] AP. One Year After Defeat, Edwards Eyes White House Again. FOXNEWS.com Posted October 30, 2005 and retrieved November 8, 2005 from http://www.foxnews.com/printer_friendly_story/0,3566,173940,00.html.
[409] AP. One Year After Defeat, Edwards Eyes White House Again. FOXNEWS.com Posted October 30, 2005 and retrieved November 8, 2005 from http://www.foxnews.com/printer_friendly_story/0,3566,173940,00.html
[410] Hardball with Chris Matthews for Dec. 12. Retrieved 12.14.06 from http://www.msnbc.msn.com/id/16186985/print/1/displaymode/1098/
[411] Hardball with Chris Matthews for Dec. 12. Retrieved 12.14.06 from http://www.msnbc.msn.com/id/16186985/print/1/displaymode/1098/
[412] Hardball with Chris Matthews for Dec. 12. Retrieved 12.14.06 from http://www.msnbc.msn.com/id/16186985/print/1/displaymode/1098/
[413] Hardball with Chris Matthews for Dec. 12. Retrieved 12.14.06 from http://www.msnbc.msn.com/id/16186985/print/1/displaymode/1098/
[414] ABC Good Morning America, December 28, 2006.
[415] Roll Call quoted at Taegan Goddard's Political Wire for March 30, 2006 and retrieved on April 10, 2006 from http://politicalwire.com/archives/2008_campaign/

[416] Perry Bacon Jr. DNC, State Leaders, Weigh in on Primary Schedule Scramble. Posted 8.31.07 and retrieved September 3, 2007 from http://blog.washingtonpost.com/the-trail/2007/08/31/post_53.html.

[417] Meet the Press. September 30, 2007.

[418] Jonathan Roos. Iowa: Poll. Giuliani, McCain stand out in mock matchups. Published Sept. 24, 2006 and retrieved next day @ http://desmoinesregister.com/apps/pbcs/dll/article?AID=/20060924/NEWS09/609240335/1056.

[419] Jonathan Roos. Iowa: Poll. Giuliani, McCain stand out in mock matchups. Published Sept. 24, 2006 and retrieved next day @ http://desmoinesregister.com/apps/pbcs/dll/article?AID=/20060924/NEWS09/609240335/1056.

[420] Jane Norman. Edwards leads in poll of likely caucus goers. Des Moines Register. Published and retrieved 12.14.06 from http://www.desmoinesregister.com/apps/pbc.dll/article?AID=/20061214/NEWS09/612140397/1056.

[421] Jane Norman. Edwards leads in poll of likely caucus goers. Des Moines Register. Published and retrieved 12.14.06 from http://www.desmoinesregister.com/apps/pbc.dll/article?AID=/20061214/NEWS09/612140397/1056.

[422] Thomas Beaumont. Edwards to enter race, visit Iowa. Des Moines Register, Published December 22, 2006. Retrieved same Day @ http://www.desmoinesregister.com/apps/pbcs.dll/article?AID=/20061222/NEWS09/612220369/1001/NEWS.

[423] Dec. 11, 2006 on Nightly News.

[424] CNN.com. CNN Political Ticker Edwards, Romney lead in Iowa Polls. Posted 7.27.07 and retrieved 8.1.07 from http://politicalticker.blogs.cnn.com/2007/07/27/edwards-romney-lead-in-iowa-poll/.

[425] The Washington Post. Feingold's censure motion roils both parties. MSNBC.com Posted March 15, 2006 and retrieved March 17, 2006 from http://www.msnbc.msn.com/id/11817221/print/1/displaymode/1098/.

[426] Chris Cillizza. Russ Feingold: Bucking Convention All The Way to White House? Posted June 5, 2006 and retrieved July 14, 2006 from http://blog.washingtonpost.com/thefix/2006/06/insider_interveiw_russ_feingold.html.

[427] The Washington Post. Feingold's censure motion roils both parties. MSNBC.com Posted March 15, 2006 and retrieved March 17, 2006 from http://www.msnbc.msn.com/id/11817221/print/1/displaymode/1098/

[428] Chris Cillizza. Russ Feingold: Bucking Convention All The Way to White House? Posted June 5, 2006 and retrieved July 14, 2006 from http://blog.washingtonpost.com/thefix/2006/06/insider_interveiw_russ_feingold.html

[429] Chris Cillizza. Russ Feingold: Bucking Convention All The Way to White House? Posted June 5, 2006 and retrieved July 14, 2006 from http://blog.washingtonpost.com/thefix/2006/06/insider_interveiw_russ_feingold.html

[430] John Brummett. "Anti-war versus pro-Hillary." Arkansas News Bureau. Posted November 24, 2005 and retrieved November 29, 2005 from http://www.arkansasnews.com/archive/2005/11/24/JohnBrummett/331137.html.

[431] Russ Feingold. "On Opposing The USA Patriot Act." Retrieved November 10, 2005 from http://www.archipelago.org/vol6-2/feingold.htm.

[432] Russ Feingold. "On Opposing The USA Patriot Act." Retrieved November 10, 2005 from http://www.archipelago.org/vol6-2/feingold.htm

[433] Russ Feingold. "On Opposing The USA Patriot Act." Retrieved November 10, 2005 from http://www.archipelago.org/vol6-2/feingold.htm

[434] Katherine M. Skiba, The Milwaukee Journal Sentinel. Analyst says planned divorce hurts Feingold's presidential hopes for '08. For the St. Paul Pioneer Press. Posted April 13, 2005 and retrieved April 14, 2005 from http://www.twincities.com/mld/pioneerpress/news/local/11377205.htm.

[435] Katherine M. Skiba. Feingold answers questions online. Milwaukee Journal Sentinel, 6A. August 12, 2006.

[436] Ed O'Keefe. Feingold Calls for Bush's Censure. ABC News. Posted March 12, 2006 and retrieved March 17, 2006 from http://abcnews.go.com/ThisWeek/print?id=1715495.

[437] The Washington Post. Feingold's censure motion roils both parties. MSNBC.com Posted March 15, 2006 and retrieved March 17, 2006 from http://www.msnbc.msn.com/id/11817221/print/1/displaymode/1098/.

[438] Ed O'Keefe. Feingold Calls for Bush's Censure. ABC News. Posted March 12, 2006 and retrieved March 17, 2006 from http://abcnews.go.com/ThisWeek/print?id=1715495

[439] Ed O'Keefe. Feingold Calls for Bush's Censure. ABC News. Posted March 12, 2006 and retrieved March 17, 2006 from http://abcnews.go.com/ThisWeek/print?id=1715495

[440] Press Releases. Frist Dismisses Feingold's stunt, calls on Democrats to confront Genuine threats to national security. Bill Frist, M.D. Posted March 14, 2006 and retrieved March 17, 2006 from http://frist.senate.gov/index.cfm?FuseAction=PressReleases.Detail&PressRelease_id=2301.

[441] The Washington Post. Feingold's censure motion roils both parties. MSNBC.com Posted March 15, 2006 and retrieved March 17, 2006 from http://www.msnbc.msn.com/id/11817221/print/1/displaymode/1098/.

[442] Dana Milbank. Democrats mum on call for censure. Washington Post. The Milwaukee Journal Sentinel, March 15, 2006, 1A.

[443] Dana Milbank. Democrats mum on call for censure. Washington Post. The Milwaukee Journal Sentinel, March 15, 2006, 1A.

[444] Dana Milbank. Democrats mum on call for censure. Washington Post. The Milwaukee Journal Sentinel, March 15, 2006, 1A.

[445] Craig Gilbert. Public divide on Bush Censure, polls indicate. Milwaukee Journal Sentinel, March 16, 2006, 21A.

[446] Craig Gilbert. Heroic or out of line, Feingold gets noticed. Milwaukee Journals Sentinel, March 16, 2006, 11A.

[447] TV Squad. The Daily Show: March 15, 2006. Posted Mar.16, 2006 and retrieved March 17, 2006 from http://www.tvsquad.com/2006/03/16/the-daily-show-march-15-2006/.

[448] TV Squad. The Daily Show: March 15, 2006. Posted Mar.16, 2006 and retrieved March 17, 2006 from http://www.tvsquad.com/2006/03/16/the-daily-show-march-15-2006/.

[449] Dotty Lynch. Will Russ Feingold Stand Alone Again? CBS News. Posted March 13, 2006 and retrieved March 27, 2006 from http://www.cbsnews.com/stories/2006/03/13/opinion/lynch/main1397694.shtml.

[450] FOXNews.com. Transcript: Sen. Carl Levin on 'FNS'. Aired March 26, 2006 and retrieved March 27, 2006 from http://www.foxnews.com/story/0,2933,189140,00.html.

[451] Craig Gilbert. Even Democrats leery of Feingold resolution. The Milwaukee Journal Sentinel, March 14, 2006, 1A.

[452] Craig Gilbert. Even Democrats leery of Feingold resolution. The Milwaukee Journal Sentinel, March 14, 2006, 1A.

[453] Dana Milbank. Democrats mum on call for censure. Washington Post. The Milwaukee Journal Sentinel, March 15, 2006, 1A.

[454] Shailagh Murray. A Senate Maverick Acts to Force an Issue. Washington Post. Published March 15, A01, and retrieved July 14, 2006 from http://www.washingtonpost.com/wp-dyn/content/article/2006/03/14/AR2006031401752.html.

[455] Thomas J. Dodd. Wikipedia. Retrieved July 14, 2006 from http://en.wikipedia.org/wiki/Thomas_Dodd.

[456] The Washington Post. Feingold's censure motion roils both parties. MSNBC.com Posted March 15, 2006 and retrieved March 17, 2006 from http://www.msnbc.msn.com/id/11817221/print/1/displaymode/1098/

[457] AP. Censure Resolution could pay dividends for Feingold. The Fond du Lac Reporter, March 26, 2006.

[458] Jill Zuckman. Once again, Feingold takes unpopular stance on Patriot Act. Chicago Tribune. Posted Feb. 28, 2006 and retrieved March 17, 2006 from http://www.mercurynews.com/mld/mercurynews/news/politics/13984927.htm

[459] Craig Gilbert and Katherine M. Skiba. Feingold ranks at the bottom of one list of 2008 hopefuls. Sunday March 26, 2006, Milwaukee Journal Sentinel, 11A.

[460] Craig Gilbert and Katherine M. Skiba. Feingold ranks at the bottom of one list of 2008 hopefuls. Sunday March 26, 2006, Milwaukee Journal Sentinel, 11A.

[461] Craig Gilbert and Katherine M. Skiba. Feingold ranks at the bottom of one list of 2008 hopefuls. Sunday March 26, 2006, Milwaukee Journal Sentinel, 11A.

[462] Russ Feingold. Censure of Bush appropriate. The Milwaukee Journal Sentinel. March 18, 2006, 11A.

[463] Editorial board. Milwaukee journal Sentinel. Censure is premature, unfair. March 16, 2006, 16A.

[464] Bill Glauber. Feingold connects at home. Milwaukee Journal Sentinel, March 21, 2006, 3A.

[465] Jill Zuckman. Once again, Feingold takes unpopular stance on Patriot Act. Chicago Tribune. Posted Feb. 28, 2006 and retrieved March 17, 2006 from http://www.mercurynews.com/mld/mercurynews/news/politics/13984927.htm.

[466] The Washington Post. Feingold's censure motion roils both parties. MSNBC.com Posted March 15, 2006 and retrieved March 17, 2006 from http://www.msnbc.msn.com/id/11817221/print/1/displaymode/1098/

[467] The Washington Post. Feingold's censure motion roils both parties. MSNBC.com Posted March 15, 2006 and retrieved March 17, 2006 from http://www.msnbc.msn.com/id/11817221/print/1/displaymode/1098/

[468] Rasmussen Reports. 38% favor censure of President Bush. Survey of 1,000 Adults, March 15-16, 2006, retrieved March 17, 2006 from http://www.rasmussenreports.com/2006/March%20Dailies/Censure.htm.

[469] Craig Gilbert. GOP to air ad criticizing Feingold for censure proposal. Milwaukee Journal Sentinel, March 21, 2006 3A.

[470] Craig Gilbert. President fires back on Feingold censure effort. Milwaukee Journal Sentinel, March 22, 2006, 1A.

[471] Political figures. Sen. Russell D. Feingold (D-Wisconsin). Retrieved 5.31.06 from http:///www.pollingreport.com/E-F.htm.

[472] FOX News. Transcript: Sen. Russ Feingold on 'FNS'. Posted and retrieved April 3, 2006 from http://www.foxnews.com/story/0,2933,190226,00.html.

[473] Craig Gilbert. Like Nixon, Bush is defying Congress, Dean testifies. The Milwaukee Journal Sentinel, April 1, 2006, 11A.

[474] Craig Gilbert. Like Nixon, Bush is defying Congress, Dean testifies. The Milwaukee Journal Sentinel, April 1, 2006, 11A.

[475] Craig Gilbert. Like Nixon, Bush is defying Congress, Dean testifies. The Milwaukee Journal Sentinel, April 1, 2006, 11A.

[476] Craig Gilbert. Like Nixon, Bush is defying Congress, Dean testifies. The Milwaukee Journal Sentinel, April 1, 2006, 11A.

[477] Craig Gilbert. Like Nixon, Bush is defying Congress, Dean testifies. The Milwaukee Journal Sentinel, April 1, 2006, 11A.

[478] FOX News. Transcript: Sen. Russ Feingold on 'FNS'. Posted and retrieved April 3, 2006 from http://www.foxnews.com/story/0,2933,190226,00.html.

[479] FOX News. Transcript: Sen. Russ Feingold on 'FNS'. Posted and retrieved April 3, 2006 from http://www.foxnews.com/story/0,2933,190226,00.html.

[480] FOX News. Transcript: Sen. Russ Feingold on 'FNS'. Posted and retrieved April 3, 2006 from http://www.foxnews.com/story/0,2933,190226,00.html.

[481] FOX News. Transcript: Sen. Russ Feingold on 'FNS'. Posted and retrieved April 3, 2006 from http://www.foxnews.com/story/0,2933,190226,00.html.

[482] FOX News. Transcript: Sen. Lindsey Graham on 'FNS'. Posted/Retrieved April 3, 2006 from http://www.foxnews.com/story/0,2922,190226,00.html.

[483] Conklin: Russ for virtual president in 2008. Melanie Conklin. The Wisconsin State Journal. Posted and retrieved March 21, 2005 at http://www.madison.com/wsj/home/features/index.php?ntid=32422&ntpid=1.

[484] Feingold in Dixie on mission of diplomacy. Craig Gilbert. The Milwaukee Journal Sentinel. March 29, 2005 1A.

[485] Southern Strategy for Feingold. Craig Gilbert. The Milwaukee Journal Sentinel. March 31, 2005 1A.

[486] A Democratic dark horse poised to emerge. Tom Curry. MSNBC posted and retrieved March 30, 2005 from http://msnbc.msn.com/id/7326869/.

[487] A Democratic dark horse poised to emerge. Tom Curry. MSNBC posted and retrieved March 30, 2005 from http://msnbc.msn.com/id/7326869/.
[488] Frederic J. Frommer. AP. Feingold using leadership PAC to raise profile. Posted April 4, 2005. Retrieved May 1, 2005 from http://www.signonsandiego.com/news/politics/20050404-2317-feingold-leadershippac.html.
[489] Craig Gilbert and Katherine M. Skiba. Feingold is running in the middle. Milwaukee Journal Sentinel, April 23, 2006, 7A.
[490] Craig Gilbert and Katherine M. Skiba. Feingold is running in the middle. Milwaukee Journal Sentinel, April 23, 2006, 7A.
[491] AP. Feingold looks to '08, heartens Iowa activists. The Fond du Lac Reporter. April 30, 2006, 1A.
[492] Media Matters For America. Newsweek's Meacham called Sen. Feingold "a sane Howard Dean." Retrieved January 6, 2006 from http://mediamatters.org/items/printable/200601030001.
[493] The Democratic Party of Wisconsin. " Retrieved January 6, 2006 from http://www.wisdems.org/ht/redisplay/1/printerfreindly/1.
[494] FOX NEWS. Cheney Defends Electronic Surveillance of Suspected Al Qaeda. Posted January 5, 2005 and retrieved next day from http://www.foxnews.com/printer_friendly_story/0,3566,180638,00.html.
[495] Craig Gilbert. Feingold clicks with blog fans. Milwaukee Journal Sentinel, February 27, 2006, 12A.
[496] Craig Gilbert. Feingold clicks with blog fans. Milwaukee Journal Sentinel, February 27, 2006, 12A.
[497] The Washington Post. Feingold's censure motion roils both parties. MSNBC.com Posted March 15, 2006 and retrieved March 17, 2006 from http://www.msnbc.msn.com/id/11817221/print/1/displaymode/1098/
[498] Craig Gilbert. Feingold clicks with blog fans. Milwaukee Journal Sentinel, February 27, 2006, 12A.
[499] Are Town Hall Meetings Obsolete? Taegan Goddard's Political Wire. Retrieved 3.8.06 from http://www.politicalwire.com/.
[500] Chris Cillizza. Feingold Makes and Iowa Move. Washingtonpost.com, the Fix. Posted and retrieved March 8, 2006 from http://blog.washingtonpost.com/thefix/.
[501] Chris Cillizza. Feingold Makes and Iowa Move. Washingtonpost.com, the Fix. Posted and retrieved March 8, 2006 from http://blog.washingtonpost.com/thefix/
[502] Craig Gilbert. Feingold Emerging as alternative to Clinton. MSJ. July 9, 2006, 3A.
[503] Craig Gilbert. Feingold Emerging as alternative to Clinton. MSJ. July 9, 2006, 3A.
[504] Salon.com. Walter Shapiro. Which way to the White House? Retrieved June 16, 2006 from http://www.salon.com/new/feature/2006/06/05/democrats/index_np.html.
[505] Salon.com. Walter Shapiro. Which way to the White House? Retrieved June 16, 2006 from http://www.salon.com/new/feature/2006/06/05/democrats/index_np.html.
[506] Sarah Liebowitz. Feingold and Warner have their day with the Dems. Concord Monitor. June 4 , 2006 and retrieved June 16, 2006 from http://www.concordmonitor.com/apps/pbcs.dll/article?AID=/20060604/REPOSITORY/606040374
[507] Sarah Liebowitz. Feingold and Warner have their day with the Dems. Concord Monitor. June 4 , 2006 and retrieved June 16, 2006 from http://www.concordmonitor.com/apps/pbcs.dll/article?AID=/20060604/REPOSITORY/606040374.
[508] Sarah Liebowitz. Feingold and Warner have their day with the Dems. Concord Monitor. June 4 , 2006 and retrieved June 16, 2006 from http://www.concordmonitor.com/apps/pbcs.dll/article?AID=/20060604/REPOSITORY/606040374
[509] Craig Gilbert. Milwaukee Journal Sentinel. Feingold rules out 2008 run for president. 1A/19A.
[510] CentreDaily.com. Handicapping the '08 presidential race. Posted Nov.14.06 and retrieved 11.17.06 from http://www.centredaily.com/mld/centredaily/news/opinion/15998697.htm.
[511] AP. McCain considers running for U.S. presidency in 2008 Biden [sic]. 11.14. Retrieved 11.17.06 from http://www.chinapost.com/tw/p_detail.asp?id=95130&GRP=D&onNews=.
[512] Craig Gilbert. Milwaukee Journal-Sentinel. Feingold to sift election results before deciding on big run. Nov.4. 2006,
[513] AP. McCain considers running for U.S. presidency in 2008 Biden [sic]. 11.14. Retrieved 11.17.06 from http://www.chinapost.com/tw/p_detail.asp?id=95130&GRP=D&onNews=.
[514] Craig Gilbert. Milwaukee Journal Sentinel. Feingold rules out 2008 run for president. 1A/19A.
[515] Craig Gilbert. Milwaukee Journal Sentinel. Feingold rules out 2008 run for president. 1A/19A.
[516] Craig Gilbert. Milwaukee Journal Sentinel. Feingold rules out 2008 run for president. 1A/19A.
[517] Brian C. Mooney. Kerry's barnstorming sparks talk of run. Boston Globe. Oct. 9, 2006 and retrieved 10.31.06 from http://www.boston.com/news/nation/articles/2006/10/09/kerrys_barnstorming_sparks_talk_of_a_run?mode=PF..
[518] Replayed on This Week , Nov. 19, 2006.
[519] Craig Gilbert. Milwaukee Journal Sentinel. Feingold rules out 2008 run for president. 1A/19A.
[520] Adam Nagourney. Evan Bayh withdraws from 2008 presidential field. International Herald Tribune. Published 12.17.06 @ http://www.iht.com/articles/2006/12/17/news/Bayh.php.
[521] Craig Gilbert. Milwaukee Journal-Sentinel. Feingold to sift election results before deciding on big run. Nov.4. 2006,
[522] Craig Gilbert. Milwaukee Journal-Sentinel. Feingold to sift election results before deciding on big run. Nov.4. 2006,
[523] Craig Gilbert. Milwaukee Journal Sentinel. Feingold rules out 2008 run for president. 1A/19A.
[524] Craig Gilbert. Feingold alters the calculus in presidential race. Milwaukee Journal Sentinel. Nov. 13, 2006, 3A.
[525] Craig Gilbert. Feingold alters the calculus in presidential race. Milwaukee Journal Sentinel. Nov. 13, 2006, 3A.
[526] David Edwards. Feingold: Censure Bush, Cheney for 'their repeated assaults on the rule of law.' 7.22.07 and retrieved 8.1.07 from http://rawstory.com/news/2007/Feingold_Censure_Bush_Cheney_for_their_0722.html.
[527] Chris Baltimore. Senate Democrat calls to censure Bush over Iraq. Posted 7.22.07 and retrieved 8.1.07 from http://www.reuters.com/article/politicsNews/idUSN22295196200707022.

[528] Progressive Patriots Fund. Russ Feingold. Censure Resolutions. Retrieved 8.1.07 from http://www.progressivepatriotsfund.com/issues/censure/.
[529] Mike Gravel Biography. Gravel 2008. Retrieved 6.15.07 from http://www.gravel2008.us/bio.
[530] Alex Koppelman. Salon.com. Don't worry, be Mike Gravel. 5.7.07 and retrieved 7.20.07 from http://www.salon.com/news/feature/2007/05/07/mike_gravel/print.html.
[531] Alex Koppelman. Salon.com. Don't worry, be Mike Gravel. 5.7.07 and retrieved 7.20.07 from http://www.salon.com/news/feature/2007/05/07/mike_gravel/print.html.
[532] Alex Koppelman. Salon.com. Don't worry, be Mike Gravel. 5.7.07 and retrieved 7.20.07 from http://www.salon.com/news/feature/2007/05/07/mike_gravel/print.html.
[533] Alex Koppelman. Salon.com. Don't worry, be Mike Gravel. 5.7.07 and retrieved 7.20.07 from http://www.salon.com/news/feature/2007/05/07/mike_gravel/print.html.
[534] Alex Koppelman. Salon.com. Don't worry, be Mike Gravel. 5.7.07 and retrieved 7.20.07 from http://www.salon.com/news/feature/2007/05/07/mike_gravel/print.html.
[535] Alex Koppelman. Salon.com. Don't worry, be Mike Gravel. 5.7.07 and retrieved 7.20.07 from http://www.salon.com/news/feature/2007/05/07/mike_gravel/print.html.
[536] Alex Koppelman. Salon.com. Don't worry, be Mike Gravel. 5.7.07 and retrieved 7.20.07 from http://www.salon.com/news/feature/2007/05/07/mike_gravel/print.html.
[537] Philip Elliott. Ex-Alaska Sen. Gravel Runs for President. ABC News. AP. Retrieved April 24, 2006 from http://abcnews.go.com/Politics/print?id=1851783.
[538] Philip Elliott. Ex-Alaska Sen. Gravel Runs for President. ABC News. AP. Retrieved April 24, 2006 from http://abcnews.go.com/Politics/print?id=1851783.
[539] Alex Koppelman. Salon.com. Don't worry, be Mike Gravel. 5.7.07 and retrieved 7.20.07 from http://www.salon.com/news/feature/2007/05/07/mike_gravel/print.html.
[540] Alex Koppelman. Salon.com. Don't worry, be Mike Gravel. 5.7.07 and retrieved 7.20.07 from http://www.salon.com/news/feature/2007/05/07/mike_gravel/print.html.
[541] Kyle Hopkins. Debate propels former Alaska senator Gravel into limelight. 5.3.07, retrieved same day from http://www.adn.com/news/politics/story/8850141p-8750780c.html.
[542] Philip Elliott. "Ex-Alaska Sen. Gravel Runs for President." ABC News. AP. Retrieved April 24, 2006 from http://abcnews.go.com/Politics/print?id=1851783.
[543] Philip Elliott. "Ex-Alaska Sen. Gravel Runs for President." ABC News. AP. Retrieved April 24, 2006 from http://abcnews.go.com/Politics/print?id=1851783.
[544] U.S. Newswire. Sen. Mike Gravel Announces Run for President. Posted April 17, 2006 and retrieved April 24, 2006 from http://releases.usnewswire.com/printing.asp?id=64065.
[545] U.S. Newswire. Sen. Mike Gravel Announces Run for President. Posted April 17, 2006 and retrieved April 24, 2006 from http://releases.usnewswire.com/printing.asp?id=64065.
[546] Philip Elliott. "Ex-Alaska Sen. Gravel Runs for President." ABC News. AP. Retrieved April 24, 2006 from http://abcnews.go.com/Politics/print?id=1851783.
[547] The Democracy Foundation. Senator Mike Gravel. Retrieved April 28, 2006 from http://ni4d.us/democracyfoundation/people/gravel.htm.
[548] Need the Poll results for this. Pollingreport.com. Iraq-8 in Table of Contents. Washington Post Poll. August 7-11, 2003. N=1,003 adults nationwide. MoE= +/-3. Retrieved May 5, 2006 from http://www.pollingreport.com/iraq8.htm.
[549] Felice Belman. The White House is a speck in Mike Gravel's big picture. May 29, 2006 and retrieved July 28, 2006 from http://www.concordmonitor.com/apps/pbcs.dll/article?AID=/20060529/REPOSITORY/605290306/1043/NEWS01
[550] Kenneth Partridge. Gravel: 'Let the people decide'. Greenwich Post. Posted July 27, 2006 and retrieved July 28, 2006 from http://www.acorn-online.com/news/publish/article_8225.shtml.
[551] Philip Elliott. "Ex-Alaska Sen. Gravel Runs for President." ABC News. AP. Retrieved April 24, 2006 from http://abcnews.go.com/Politics/print?id=1851783.
[552] U.S. Newswire. Sen. Mike Gravel Announces Run for President. Posted April 17, 2006 and retrieved April 24, 2006 from http://releases.usnewswire.com/printing.asp?id=64065
[553] Oval Office 2008. Mike Gravel-You'd have to be quite old to remember him, I suspect. And probably Alaskan. Retrieved April 24, 2006 from http://www.ovaloffice2008.com/2006/04/mike-gravel-youd-have-to-be-quite-old.html.
[554] Dana Milbank. A Democratic Dark Horse Who Isn't Afraid to Take the Lead. Published April 18, 2006 page A02, and retrieved April 28, 2006 from http://www.washingtonpost.com/wp-dyn/content/article/2006/04/17/AR2006041701297.html.
[555] Kenneth Partridge. Gravel: 'Let the people decide'. Greenwich Post. Posted July 27, 2006 and retrieved July 28, 2006 from http://www.acorn-online.com/news/publish/article_8225.shtml
[556] Democratic Candidates' Debate for April 26. MSNBC.com. Retrieved 5.3.07 from http://www.msnbc.msn.com/id/18351716/print/1/displaymode/1098/. 17/32.
[557] Felice Belman. The White House is a speck in Mike Gravel's big picture. May 29, 2006 and retrieved July 28, 2006 from http://www.concordmonitor.com/apps/pbcs.dll/article?AID=/20060529/REPOSITORY/605290306/1043/NEWS01.
[558] Oval Office 2008. Mike Gravel-You'd have to be quite old to remember him, I suspect. And probably Alaskan. Retrieved 4.24.06 from http://www.ovaloffice2008.com/2006/04/mike-gravel-youd-have-to-be-quite-old.html.
[559] Philip Elliott. Ex-Alaska Sen. Gravel Runs for President. ABC News. AP. Retrieved April 24, 2006 from http://abcnews.go.com/Politics/print?id=1851783.

[560] James W. Pindell. Gravel makes first foray into New Hampshire. Posted May 26, 2006 and retrieved July 28, 2006 from http://www.politicsnh.com/?q=node/262.
[561] Alex Koppelman. Salon.com. Don't worry, be Mike Gravel. 5.7.07 and retrieved 7.20.07 from http://www.salon.com/news/feature/2007/05/07/mike_gravel/print.html.
[562] Alex Koppelman. Salon.com. Don't worry, be Mike Gravel. 5.7.07 and retrieved 7.20.07 from http://www.salon.com/news/feature/2007/05/07/mike_gravel/print.html.
[563] Susan Page. USA Today. Long-shot candidates have much to gain in consolation prizes. Posted/retrieved 6.15.07 from http://www.usatoday.com/news/politics/election2008/2007-06-14-campaign-consolation_N.htm.
[564] Dana Milbank. A Democratic Dark Horse Who Isn't Afraid to Take the Lead. Published April 18, 2006 page A02, and retrieved April 28, 2006 from http://www.washingtonpost.com/wp-dyn/content/article/2006/04/17/AR2006041701297.html.
[565] Dana Milbank. A Democratic Dark Horse Who Isn't Afraid to Take the Lead. Published April 18, 2006 page A02, and retrieved April 28, 2006 from http://www.washingtonpost.com/wp-dyn/content/article/2006/04/17/AR2006041701297.html
[566] Dana Milbank. A Democratic Dark Horse Who Isn't Afraid to Take the Lead. Published April 18, 2006 page A02, and retrieved April 28, 2006 from http://www.washingtonpost.com/wp-dyn/content/article/2006/04/17/AR2006041701297.html
[567] Dana Milbank. A Democratic Dark Horse Who Isn't Afraid to Take the Lead. Published April 18, 2006 page A02, and retrieved April 28, 2006 from http://www.washingtonpost.com/wp-dyn/content/article/2006/04/17/AR2006041701297.html
[568] Keach Hagey. Presidential hopeful slams 'politics as usual.' Local News. Greenwich Time. Posted July 27, 2006 and retrieved July 28, 2006 from http://www.greenwichtime.com/news/local/scn-gt-gravel5jul27,0,926849.story?coll=green-news-local-headl...
[569] Political Radar. Kucinich to Announce Candidacy at Noon. Dec. 12.2006. Retrieved 12.14.06 from http://blogs.abcnews.com/politicalradar/2006/12/kucinich_to_ann.html.
[570] Thomas Beaumont. Vilsack gives duck to TV host. Thomas Beaumont. Published December 19,2006 and retrieved 12.22.06 from http://www.desmoinesregister.com/apps/pbcs.dll/article?AID=/20061219/NEWS09/612190384.
[571] CNN.com. the Situation Room. For 12.12.06 and retrieved 12.14.06 from http://transcripts.cnn.com/TRANSCRIPTS/0612/12/sitroom.01.html
[572] Irregular Times. Journalists Ignore Democratic Pack for 2008. Retrieved 12.14.06 from http://www.irregulartimes.com/index.php/archives/2006/12/02/whole-pack-2008-dems/.
[573] Mike in the News. Gravel 2008. Let the People Decide. Retrieved 12.14.06 from http://www.gravel2008.us/.
[574] Mike in the News. Gravel 2008. Let the People Decide. Retrieved 12.14.06 from http://www.gravel2008.us/.
[575] AP. 'Granny D' endorses longshot hopeful. Portsmouth Herald Local News. Retrieved 12.14.06 from http://www.seacoastonline.com/news/12092006/nhnews-ph-nh-gravel.granny.html.
[576] AP. 'Granny D' endorses longshot hopeful. Portsmouth Herald Local News. Retrieved 12.14.06 from http://www.seacoastonline.com/news/12092006/nhnews-ph-nh-gravel.granny.html.
[577] AP. 'Granny D' endorses longshot hopeful. Portsmouth Herald Local News. Retrieved 12.14.06 from http://www.seacoastonline.com/news/12092006/nhnews-ph-nh-gravel.granny.html.
[578] Philip Elliott. Ex-Alaska Sen. Gravel Runs for President. ABC News. AP. Retrieved April 24, 2006 from http://abcnews.go.com/Politics/print?id=1851783
[579] Kenneth Partridge. Gravel: 'Let the people decide'. Greenwich Post. Posted July 27, 2006 and retrieved July 28, 2006 from http://www.acorn-online.com/news/publish/article_8225.shtml.
[580] Jen Keefe. Alaskan eyes White House. Portsmouth Herald Local News. Retrieved July 28, 2006 from http://www.seacoastonline.com/news/06242006/news/108774.htm.
[581] Post-Democratic Candidates' Debate Coverage. MSNBC.com. April 26, 2007. Retrieved May 3, 2006 from http://www.msnbc.msn.com/id/18351722/print/1/displaymode/1098/. 13/88
[582] Mike Gravel. The New York Times. Retrieved 7.27.07 from http://topics.nytimes.com/top/reference/timestopics/people/g/mike_gravel/index.html.
[583] Felice Belman. The White House is a speck in Mike Gravel's big picture. May 29, 2006 and retrieved July 28, 2006 from http://www.concordmonitor.com/apps/pbcs.dll/article?AID=/20060529/REPOSITORY/605290306/1043/NEWS01
[584] Emil Steiner. Mike Gravel: Presidential Candidate Gets Metaphorical. Posted 6.19.07 and retrieved 8.1.07 from http://www.blog.washingtonpost.com/offbeat/2007/06/mike_gravel_metaphore_of_a_pre.html.
[585] Mary Lu Carnevale. Mike Gravel Meets YouTube. Washington Wire. WSJ.com. Posted 6.19.07 and retrieved 8.1.07 from http://blogs.wsj.com/washwire/2007/06/19/mike-gravel-meets-youtube/.
[586] Joel Connelly: Presidential candidates off but running. 4.30.07 and retrieved 5.3.07 from http://blog.seattlepi.nwsource.com/seattlepolitics/archives/114708.asp.
[587] Democratic Candidates' Debate for April 26. MSNBC.com. Retrieved 5.3.07 from http://www.msnbc.msn.com/id/18351716/print/1/displaymode/1098/. 9/32.
[588] Democratic Candidates' Debate for April 26. MSNBC.com. Retrieved 5.3.07 from http://www.msnbc.msn.com/id/18351716/print/1/displaymode/1098/. 9/32; Laughing, personally observed.
[589] Democratic Candidates' Debate for April 26. MSNBC.com. Retrieved 5.3.07 from http://www.msnbc.msn.com/id/18351716/print/1/displaymode/1098/. 26/32.
[590] Democratic Candidates' Debate for April 26. MSNBC.com. Retrieved 5.3.07 from http://www.msnbc.msn.com/id/18351716/print/1/displaymode/1098/. 29/32.

[591] Democratic Candidates' Debate for April 26. MSNBC.com. Retrieved 5.3.07 from http://www.msnbc.msn.com/id/18351716/print/1/displaymode/1098/. 29/32.
[592] Democratic Candidates' Debate for April 26. MSNBC.com. Retrieved 5.3.07 from http://www.msnbc.msn.com/id/18351716/print/1/displaymode/1098/. 29/32.
[593] CNN.com. Transcripts. Situation Room. Aired 4.30.07. Retrieved 5.3.07 from http://transcripts.cnn.com/TRANSCRIPTS/0704/30/sitroom.01.html. 8/19
[594] John Heilemann. The Comeback Kid. New York Magazine. Retrieved May 31, 2006 from http://www.nymetro.com/news/politics/17065/.
[595] Karen Breslau. The Resurrection of Al Gore. Issue 14.05—May 2006. Retrieved May 22, 2006 from http://www.wired.com/archive/14.05/gore.html.
[596] Karen Breslau. The Resurrection of Al Gore. Wired. Issue 14.05—May 2006. Retrieved May 22, 2006 from http://www.wired.com/archive/14.05/gore.html.
[597] Karen Breslau. The Resurrection of Al Gore. Issue 14.05—May 2006. Retrieved May 22, 2006 from http://www.wired.com/archive/14.05/gore.html.
[598] Al Gore and David Blood Graft Sustainability Research into Traditional Investing Analysis. William Baue. Posted November 9, 2004 and retrieved from http://www.socialfunds.com/news/article.cgi/article1568.html.
[599] Al Gore and David Blood Graft Sustainability Research into Traditional Investing Analysis. William Baue. Posted November 9, 2004 and retrieved from http://www.socialfunds.com/news/article.cgi/article1568.html
[600] Sundeep Tucker. 11.4.04 and retrieved 6.10.06 from http://www.asria.org/news/press/1102909264/print? Blood and Gore Launch Firm With a Difference. www.generationim.com.
[601] Karen Breslau. The Resurrection of Al Gore. Issue 14.05—May 2006. Retrieved May 22, 2006 from http://www.wired.com/archive/14.05/gore.html.
[602] Ezra Klein. "The New New Gore." American Prospect Online. Issue Date April 8, 2006, retrieved April 10, 2006 from http://www.prospect.org/web/printerfriendly-view.ww?id=11299.
[603] Ezra Klein. "The New New Gore." American Prospect Online. Issue Date April 8, 2006, retrieved April 10, 2006 from http://www.prospect.org/web/printerfriendly-view.ww?id=11299.
[604] Ezra Klein. The New New Gore. American Prospect Online. Issue Date April 8, 2006, retrieved April 10, 2006 from http://www.prospect.org/web/printerfriendly-view.ww?id=11299.
[605] Ezra Klein. The New New Gore. American Prospect Online. Issue Date April 8, 2006, retrieved April 10, 2006 from http://www.prospect.org/web/printerfriendly-view.ww?id=11299.
[606] Ezra Klein. The New New Gore. American Prospect Online. Issue Date April 8, 2006, retrieved April 10, 2006 from http://www.prospect.org/web/printerfriendly-view.ww?id=11299.
[607] AP. Al Gore Unveils Cable TV Channel. Posted and retrieved April 5, 2005 from http://www.cbsnews.com/stories/2005/04/05/entertainment/main685563.shtml.
[608] AP. Al Gore Unveils Cable TV Channel. Posted and retrieved April 5, 2005 from http://www.cbsnews.com/stories/2005/04/05/entertainment/main685563.shtml. And from Jennifer Harper. The Washington Times. Gore cable channel to debut with news youths can use. Retrieved 4.14.05 from http://washingtontimes.com/national/20050404-112512-9752r.htm.
[609] John Heilemann. The Comeback Kid. New York Magazine. Retrieved May 31, 2006 from http://www.nymetro.com/news/politics/17065/
[610] David Remnick. Ozone Man. The New Yorker. Issue for April 24, 2006 and retrieved same day from http://www.newyorker.com/talk/content/articles/060424ta_talk_remnick.
[611] David Remnick. Ozone Man. The New Yorker. Issue for April 24, 2006 and retrieved same day from http://www.newyorker.com/talk/content/articles/060424ta_talk_remnick.
[612] David Remnick. Ozone Man. The New Yorker. Issue for April 24, 2006 and retrieved same day from http://www.newyorker.com/talk/content/articles/060424ta_talk_remnick
[613] John Heilemann. The Comeback Kid. New York Magazine. Retrieved May 31, 2006 from http://www.nymetro.com/news/politics/17065/
[614] David Remnick. "Ozone Man." The New Yorker. Issue for April 24, 2006 and retrieved same day from http://www.newyorker.com/talk/content/articles/060424ta_talk_remnick.
[615] David Remnick. "Ozone Man." The New Yorker. Issue for April 24, 2006 and retrieved same day from http://www.newyorker.com/talk/content/articles/060424ta_talk_remnick.
[616] Amazon.com. An Inconvenient Truth. Says the film was to be released November 21, 2006.
[617] David Germain. 'Truth' makes short list for Oscar nod. AP. Posted Nov. 16, 2006 and retrieved 11.17.06 from http://www.mercurynews.com/mld/mercurynews/entertainment/movies/16028813.htm.
[618] David Germain. 'Truth' makes short list for Oscar nod. AP. Posted Nov. 16, 2006 and retrieved 11.17.06 from http://www.mercurynews.com/mld/mercurynews/entertainment/movies/16028813.htm.
[619] CNN.com. the Situation Room. For 12.12.06 and retrieved 12.14.06 from http://transcripts.cnn.com/TRANSCRIPTS/0612/12/sitroom.01.html
[620] CNN.com. the Situation Room. For 12.12.06 and retrieved 12.14.06 from http://transcripts.cnn.com/TRANSCRIPTS/0612/12/sitroom.01.html
[621] Clinton Speaks. Taegan Goddard's Political Wire. 9.21.06 and retrieved 9.25.06 from http://politicalwire.com/archies/2008_campaign/.
[622] MSNBC News Services. UK issues warming warning, hires Gore. 10.30.06 and retrieved 12.14.06 from http://www.msnbc.msn..com/id/15480912/print/1/displaymode/1098/.

[623] AP. Gore chases Oscar nod, possible 2008 bid. Posted Dec.11 and retrieved 12.14.06 from http://www.msnbc.msn.com/id/16156972/print/1/displaymode/1098/.
[624] ABC Good Morning America, December 28, 2006.
[625] Peter Schweizer. Gore isn't quite as green as he's led the world to believe. USA Today. Aug. 10, 2006, Retrieved 9.25.2006 from http://www.usatoday.com/news/opinion/editorials/2006-08-09-gore-green.htm.
[626] Peter Schweizer. Gore isn't quite as green as he's led the world to believe. USA Today. Aug. 10, 2006, Retrieved 9.25.2006 from http://www.usatoday.com/news/opinion/editorials/2006-08-09-gore-green.htm.
[627] Peter Schweizer. Gore isn't quite as green as he's led the world to believe. USA Today. Aug. 10, 2006, Retrieved 9.25.2006 from http://www.usatoday.com/news/opinion/editorials/2006-08-09-gore-green.htm.
[628] Peter Schweizer. Gore isn't quite as green as he's led the world to believe. USA Today. Aug. 10, 2006, Retrieved 9.25.2006 from http://www.usatoday.com/news/opinion/editorials/2006-08-09-gore-green.htm.
[629] Peter Schweizer. Gore isn't quite as green as he's led the world to believe. USA Today. Aug. 10, 2006, Retrieved 9.25.2006 from http://www.usatoday.com/news/opinion/editorials/2006-08-09-gore-green.htm.
[630] Peter Schweizer. Gore isn't quite as green as he's led the world to believe. USA Today. Aug. 10, 2006, Retrieved 9.25.2006 from http://www.usatoday.com/news/opinion/editorials/2006-08-09-gore-green.htm.
[631] Carolina A. Miranda. 10 Questions for Al Gore. Time. Nov.27, 2006. Retrieved 12.14.06 from http://www.time.com/time/magazine/printout/0,8816,1562957,00.html.
[632] NBC News. Meet the Press. Transcript for Nov.26. Retrieved 12.3. 2006 from http://msnbc.msn.com/id/15850729/print/1/displaymode/1098/
[633] NBC News. Meet the Press. Transcript for Nov.26. Retrieved 12.3. 2006 from http://msnbc.msn.com/id/15850729/print/1/displaymode/1098/.
[634] NBC News. Meet the Press. Transcript for Nov.26. Retrieved 12.3. 2006 from http://msnbc.msn.com/id/15850729/print/1/displaymode/1098/.
[635] NBC News. Meet the Press. Transcript for Nov.26. Retrieved 12.3. 2006 from http://msnbc.msn.com/id/15850729/print/1/displaymode/1098/.
[636] Carolina A. Miranda. 10 Questions for Al Gore. Time. Nov.27, 2006. Retrieved 12.14.06 from http://www.time.com/time/magazine/printout/0,8816,1562957,00.html.
[637] Ralph Z. Hallow. Huckabee 'serious' about presidency. May 17, 2006. Retrieved May 31, 2006 from http://www.washingtontimes.com/national/20060516-101743-7524r.htm.
[638] AP. Gore's high profile gathers some buzz. Milwaukee Journal Sentinel. Dec.12, 2006, 5A.
[639] CNN.com. Transcripts. Situation Room for 11.30.06 and retrieved 12.3.06 from http://transcripts.com/TRANSCRIPTS/0611/30/sitroom.01.html.
[640] The Tonight Show with Jay Leno, 11.29.06.
[641] Hardball with Chris Matthew's for Nov.30. MSNBC.com. Retrieved 12.3.06 from http://www.msnbc.msn.com/id/15988680/.
[642] Hardball with Chris Matthew's for Nov.30. MSNBC.com. Retrieved 12.3.06 from http://www.msnbc.msn.com/id/15988680/.
[643] CNN.com. The Situation Room. Nov. 29, 2006 and retrieved 12.3.06 from http://transcripts.cnn.com/TRANSCRIPTS/0611/29/sitroom.03.html.
[644] AP. Gore chases Oscar nod, possible 2008 bid. Posted Dec.11 and retrieved 12.14.06 from http://www.msnbc.msn.com/id/16156972/print/1/displaymode/1098/.
[645] CNN.com. The Situation Room. Nov. 29, 2006 and retrieved 12.3.06 from http://transcripts.cnn.com/TRANSCRIPTS/0611/29/sitroom.03.html.
[646] AP. Gore chases Oscar nod, possible 2008 bid. Posted Dec.11 and retrieved 12.14.06 from http://www.msnbc.msn.com/id/16156972/print/1/displaymode/1098/.
[647] CNN.com. Transcripts. Situation Room for 11.29. Retrieved 12.3.06 from http://transcripts.cnn.com/TRANSCRIPTS/0611/29/sitroom.01.html.
[648] AP. Gore chases Oscar nod, possible 2008 bid. Posted Dec.11 and retrieved 12.14.06 from http://www.msnbc.msn.com/id/16156972/print/1/displaymode/1098/.
[649] CNN.com. Transcripts. Situation Room for 11.30.06 and retrieved 12.3.06 from http://transcripts.com/TRANSCRIPTS/0611/30/sitroom.01.html.
[650] ABC's This Week for Nov.26, 2006.
[651] Hardball with Chris Matthew's for Nov.30. MSNBC.com. Retrieved 12.3.06 from http://www.msnbc.msn.com/id/15988680/.
[652] Taegan Goddard's Political Wire. Carter Backs Gore for 2008. Retrieved 12.14.06 from http://politicalwire.com/archives/2008_campaign/.
[653] Hardball with Chris Matthew's for Nov.30. MSNBC.com. Retrieved 12.3.06 from http://www.msnbc.msn.com/id/15988680/.
[654] AP. Gore chases Oscar nod, possible 2008 bid. Posted Dec.11 and retrieved 12.14.06 from http://www.msnbc.msn.com/id/16156972/print/1/displaymode/1098/.
[655] AP. Gore chases Oscar nod, possible 2008 bid. Posted Dec.11 and retrieved 12.14.06 from http://www.msnbc.msn.com/id/16156972/print/1/displaymode/1098/.
[656] AP. Gore's high profile gathers some buzz. Milwaukee Journal Sentinel. Dec.12, 2006, 5A.
[657] AP. MSNBC.com. Gore reflects on Live Earth, '08 bid. Posted 7.7.07 and retrieved 8.1.07 from http://www.msnbc.msn.com/id/19652185/print/1/displaymode/1098/.

[658] Boston Herald. Gore's kid: No way dad's running for White House. Posted 7.23.07 and retrieved 8.1.07 from http://news.bostonherald.com/politics/view.bg?articleid=1012868.
[659] NBC News. Meet the Press. Transcript for Oct.31. MSNBC.com. October 31, 2004 and retrieved Sept.25, 2006 from http://www.msnbc.msn.com/id/6200928/print/1/displaymode/1098/.
[660] New York Daily News. I wasn't Swift enough—Kerry. AP Posted/Retrieved April 10, 2006 from http://www.nydailynews.com/news/politics/story/405714p-345003c.html.
[661] New York Daily News. I wasn't Swift enough—Kerry. AP. Posted/Retrieved April 10, 2006 from http://www.nydailynews.com/news/politics/story/405714p-345003c.html
[662] ABCNEWS: Kerry: Taking Federal Money a Mistake. Posted 4.9.06 and retrieved 4.10.06 from http://abcnews.go.com/Politics/print?id=1823175.
[663] ABCNEWS: Kerry: Taking Federal Money a Mistake. Posted 4.9.06 and retrieved 4.10.06 from http://abcnews.go.com/Politics/print?id=1823175.
[664] MSNBC.com. Transcript for April 9. NBC News, Meet the Press. Aired April 9, 2006 and retrieved April 10, 2006 from http://www.msnbc.msn.com/id/12169680/print/1/displaymode/1098/
[665] MSNBC.com. Transcript for April 9. NBC News, Meet the Press. Aired April 9, 2006 and retrieved April 10, 2006 from http://www.msnbc.msn.com/id/12169680/print/1/displaymode/1098/
[666] Ellen Goodman. Don't Run, John Kerry. Boston Globe. Posted April 28, 2006 and retrieved May 8, 2006 from http://www.boston.com/news/globe/editiorial_opinion/oped/articles/2006/04/28/dont_run_john_kerry/
[667] MSNBC. Transcript for January 22. NBC NEWS/Meet the Press. Retrieved January 23, 2006 from http://www.msnbc.msn.com/id/10909406/print/1/displaymode/1098/.
[668] MSNBC. Transcript for January 22. NBC NEWS/Meet the Press. Retrieved January 23, 2006 from http://www.msnbc.msn.com/id/10909406/print/1/displaymode/1098/.
[669] MSNBC. Transcript for January 22. NBC NEWS/Meet the Press. Retrieved January 23, 2006 from http://www.msnbc.msn.com/id/10909406/print/1/displaymode/1098/.
[670] Joel Connelly. In the Northwest: Teresa Heinz Kerry hasn't lost her outspoken way. Posted 3.7.05 and retrieved 8.1.07 from http://seattlepi.nwsource.com/connelly/214744_joel07.html
[671] Kerry Defends Wife's 'Shove It' Comment. WTAE from Pittsburgh. Posted 7.25.04 and retrieved 7.27.07 from http://www.thepittsburghchannel.com/news/3576476/detail.html. See also Joel Connelly. In the Northwest: Teresa Heinz Kerry hasn't lost her outspoken way. Posted 3.7.05 and retrieved 8.1.07 from http://seattlepi.nwsource.com/connelly/214744_joel07.html.
[672] Joel Connelly. In the Northwest: Teresa Heinz Kerry hasn't lost her outspoken way. Posted 3.7.05 and retrieved 8.1.07 from http://seattlepi.nwsource.com/connelly/214744_joel07.html
[673] CNN.com. Kerry's wife to journalist: 'Shove it'. Posted 7.26.04 and retrieved 7.27.07 from http://www.cnn.com/2004/ALLPOLITICS/07/26/dems.heinz.remark/index.html.
[674] Kerry Defends Wife's 'Shove It' Comment. WTAE from Pittsburgh. Posted 7.25.04 and retrieved 7.27.07 from http://www.thepittsburghchannel.com/news/3576476/detail.html.
[675] Kerry Defends Wife's 'Shove It' Comment. WTAE from Pittsburgh. Posted 7.25.04 and retrieved 7.27.07 from http://www.thepittsburghchannel.com/news/3576476/detail.html.
[676] Kerry Defends Wife's 'Shove It' Comment. WTAE from Pittsburgh. Posted 7.25.04 and retrieved 7.27.07 from http://www.thepittsburghchannel.com/news/3576476/detail.html.
[677] Kerry Defends Wife's 'Shove It' Comment. WTAE from Pittsburgh. Posted 7.25.04 and retrieved 7.27.07 from http://www.thepittsburghchannel.com/news/3576476/detail.html.
[678] CNN.com. Kerry's wife to journalist: 'Shove it'. Posted 7.26.04 and retrieved 7.27.07 from http://www.cnn.com/2004/ALLPOLITICS/07/26/dems.heinz.remark/index.html.
[679] CNN.com. Kerry's wife to journalist: 'Shove it'. Posted 7.26.04 and retrieved 7.27.07 from http://www.cnn.com/2004/ALLPOLITICS/07/26/dems.heinz.remark/index.html.
[680] Kerry Defends Wife's 'Shove It' Comment. WTAE from Pittsburgh. Posted 7.25.04 and retrieved 7.27.07 from http://www.thepittsburghchannel.com/news/3576476/detail.html.
[681] Geraldine Sealey. My name is Teresa Heinz Kerry. Posted 7.28.04 and retrieved 8.1.07 from http://dir.salon.com/story/news/feature/2004/07/28/heinz_kerry/index.html.
[682] Transcript for August 1, 2004. Meet the Press. NBC News. MSNBC.com. Retrieved 10.31.2006 from http://www.msnbc.msn.com/id/5574180/1/displaymode/1098/.
[683] NBC News. Meet the Press. Transcript for August 8, 2004. Retrieved 10.31.06 from http://www.msnbc.msn.com/id/5640412/print/1/displaymode/1098/.
[684] Teresa Heinz Kerry quotes. Retrieved 7.27.07 from http://thinkexist.com/quotes/teresa_heinz_kerry/.
[685] Teresa Heinz Kerry quotes. Retrieved 7.27.07 from http://thinkexist.com/quotes/teresa_heinz_kerry/.
[686] Joel Connelly. In the Northwest: Teresa Heinz Kerry hasn't lost her outspoken way. Posted 3.7.05 and retrieved 8.1.07 from http://seattlepi.nwsource.com/connelly/214744_joel07.html
[687] NBC News. Meet the Press. Aired Aug. 1, 2004 and retrieved 10.31.06 from http://www.msnbc.msn.com/id/5574180/print/1/diplaymode/1098/. MSNBC.com.
[688] Kate Zernicke. The Swift boat battle is not over. NY Times/ Milwaukee Journal Sentinel. May 28, 2006, 10A.
[689] Kate Zernicke. The Swift boat battle is not over. NY Times/ Milwaukee Journal Sentinel. May 28, 2006, 10A.
[690] Kate Zernicke. The Swift boat battle is not over. NY Times/ Milwaukee Journal Sentinel. May 28, 2006, 10A.
[691] Thomas Lipscomb. John Kerry's Skimmer Scam. Posted 6.12.06 and retrieved 6.16.06 from http://news.yahoo.com/s/realclearpolitics/20060612/cm_rcp/john_kerrys_skimmer_scam.

[692] Joan Vennochi. Kerry's military records. The Boston Globe. The Milwaukee Journal Sentinel, May 27, 2005 26A.
[693] Joan Vennochi. Kerry's military records. The Boston Globe. The Milwaukee Journal Sentinel, May 27, 2005 26A.
[694] Joan Vennochi. Kerry's military records. The Boston Globe. The Milwaukee Journal Sentinel, May 27, 2005 26A.
[695] Joan Vennochi. Kerry's military records. The Boston Globe. The Milwaukee Journal Sentinel, May 27, 2005 26A.
[696] NBC News. Meet the Press. February 15, 2004. Retrieved MSNBC.com. on 10.31.2006 @ http://www.msnbc.msn.com/id/4265280/print/1/displaymode/1098/.
[697] Marie Cocco. Character lessons from the Kerry smear. Newsday.com. Posted June 14, 2005 and retrieved June 17, 2005 from http://www.newsday.com/news/opinion/ny-opcoc144303282jun14,0,4052819.column?coll=ny-viewpoints-headlines.
[698] Transcript shows John Kerry's Yale grades similar to President Bush's. AP. Retrieved June 7, 2005 from http://www.wric.com/Global.asp?S=3440177.
[699] Michael Kranish of the Boston Globe. "Kerry, Bush had similar grad average while at Yale." Published June 7, 2005 ; Chicago Tribune. Retrieved June 17, 2005 from http://www.chicagotribune.com/news/nationworld/chi-0506070195jun07,1,3555006.story?coll=chi-newsnationworld-hed.
[700] Fox News. Fox Poll: a look toward 2008 Election and quick glance back at 2004. Dana Blanton. Posted June 16, 2005 and retrieved June 17, 2008 from http://www.foxnews.com/story/0,2933,159796,00.html.
[701] Michael Kranish. Kerry releases full records. Boston Globe. The Milwaukee Journal Sentinel, June 7, 2005 8A.
[702] The Democratic Daily. John Kerry on CNN's Late Edition (Sept.10.06) Retrieved 10.31.06 from http://blog.thedemocraticdaily.com/?p=4143.
[703] The Democratic Daily. John Kerry on CNN's Late Edition (Sept.10.06) Retrieved 10.31.06 from http://blog.thedemocraticdaily.com/?p=4143.
[704] Sandy Berger Investigation: What Did Kerry Know? Washington Dispatch. Posted by Nasty McPhilthy. 7.21.04 and retrieved 10.31.06 from http://www.freerepublic.com/focus/f-news/1175555/posts.
[705] Free Republic. Berger Quits as An Advisor to Kerry, removed files with highest security level. Posted 7/21/04 and retrieved 10.31.2006 from http://www.freerepublic.com/focus/f-news/1175329/posts.
[706] The Washington Dispatch. CK Rairden. Sandy Berger Investigation: What Did Kerry Now? Posted July 21, 2004 and retrieved 10.31.2006 from http://www.washingtondispatch.com/opionion/article_9605.shtml.
[707] The Washington Dispatch. CK Rairden. Sandy Berger Investigation: What Did Kerry Now? Posted July 21, 2004 and retrieved 10.31.2006 from http://www.washingtondispatch.com/opionion/article_9605.shtml.
[708] The Washington Dispatch. CK Rairden. Sandy Berger Investigation: What Did Kerry Now? Posted July 21, 2004 and retrieved 10.31.2006 from http://www.washingtondispatch.com/opionion/article_9605.shtml.
[709] FOXNews.com. Berger: 'I Deeply Regret' and 'Honest Mistake' Posted July 22, 2004 and retrieved 10.31.2006 from http://www.foxnews.com/printer_friendly_story/0,3566,126428,00.html
[710] FOXNews.com. Berger: 'I Deeply Regret' and 'Honest Mistake' Posted July 22, 2004 and retrieved 10.31.2006 from http://www.foxnews.com/printer_friendly_story/0,3566,126428,00.html
[711] FOXNews.com. Berger: 'I Deeply Regret' and 'Honest Mistake' Posted July 22, 2004 and retrieved 10.31.2006 from http://www.foxnews.com/printer_friendly_story/0,3566,126428,00.html
[712] Dan Balz. Kerry Urges Democrats to Fight Values 'Assault. Washington Post. Published November 20, 2004 and retrieved September 21, 2005 from http://www.washingtonpost.com/ac2/wp-dyn/A63697-2004Nov19?language=printer.
[713] Peter S. Canellos. In '08, familiar faces could aid Democrats. Boston.com/The Boston Globe. Posted 11.16.04 and retrieved 10.4.05 from http://www.boston.com/news/nation/washington/articles/2004/11/16/in_08_familiar_faces_could_aid_democrats?mode=PF.
[714] Glen Johnson. Kerry run in '08 called conceivable. Boston.com. Posted 11.9.04 and retrieved 10.4.05 from http://www.boston.com/news/nation/articles/2004/11/09/kerry_run_in_08_called_conceivable/.
[715] Mark Leibovich. After the Race, John Kerry Climbs Back Up the Hill. The Washington Post, Published November 17, 2004 on page C01, and retrieved September 21, 2005 from http://www.washingtonpost.com/ac2/wp-dyn/A55424-2004Nov16?language=printer.
[716] Maeve Reston. Analysis: Kerry sees place for a big role in future. Post-gazette.com. Posted November 15, 2004 and retrieved September 21, 2005 from http://www.post-gazette.com/pg/pp/04320/412080.stm.
[717] Dan Balz. Kerry Urges Democrats to Fight Values 'Assault. Washington Post. Published November 20, 2004 and retrieved September 21, 2005 from http://www.washingtonpost.com/ac2/wp-dyn/A63697-2004Nov19?language=printer
[718] Mark Leibovich. After the Race, John Kerry Climbs Back Up the Hill. The Washington Post, Published November 17, 2004 on page C01, and retrieved September 21, 2005 from http://www.washingtonpost.com/ac2/wp-dyn/A55424-2004Nov16?language=printer.
[719] Mike Allen. 'Fired Up' Kerry Returning to Senate. The Washington Post Published November 9, 2004 page A02, and retrieved September 21, 2005 from http://www.washingtonpost.com/ac2/wp-dyn/A35224-2004Nov8?language=printer.
[720] Mike Allen. 'Fired Up' Kerry Returning to Senate.' The Washington Post Published November 9, 2004 page A02, and retrieved September 21, 2005 from http://www.washingtonpost.com/ac2/wp-dyn/A35224-2004Nov8?language=printer
[721] Political Figures: K. John Kerry. CBS News/NY Times Poll. Nov.18-21. N=795 reg. voters nationwide. Retrieved February 13, 2006 from http://pollingreport.com/k.htm.
[722] Political Figures: K. Fox News/Opinion Dynamics Poll. February 7-8, 2006. Retrieved February 13, 2006 from http://pollingreport/k.htm.
[723] Carl P. Leubsdorf. Kerry the sequel? Some are wary. The Dallas Morning News. The Milwaukee Journal Sentinel, May 13, 2005, 21A.

[724] Carl P. Leubsdorf. Kerry the sequel? Some are wary. The Dallas Morning News. The Milwaukee Journal Sentinel, May 13, 2005, 21A.
[725] Andrew Miga. Sen. John Kerry Keeps 2008 Options Open. AP. Retrieved January 6, 2006 from http://abcnews.go.com/Politics/print?id=1462247.
[726] Andrew Miga. Sen. John Kerry Keeps 2008 Options Open. AP. Retrieved January 6, 2006 from http://abcnews.go.com/Politics/print?id=1462247.
[727] Chris Cillizza. All signs Point to a 2nd Kerry Presidential Bid. Posted 10.9.06 and retrieved 10.13.2006 from http://blog.washingtonpost.com/thefix/.
[728] Chris Cillizza. All signs Point to a 2nd Kerry Presidential Bid. Posted 10.9.06 and retrieved 10.13.2006 from http://blog.washingtonpost.com/thefix/.
[729] Chris Cillizza. All signs Point to a 2nd Kerry Presidential Bid. Posted 10.9.06 and retrieved 10.13.2006 from http://blog.washingtonpost.com/thefix/.
[730] Reuters. White House hopefuls lay ground in midterm. MSNBC.com. posted 10.27 and retrieved 10.31.2006 from http://www.msnbc.msn.com/id/15446725/print/1/displaymode/1098/.
[731] Brian C. Mooney. Kerry's barnstorming sparks talk of run. Boston Globe. Oct. 9, 2006 and retrieved 10.31.06 from http://www.boston.com/news/nation/articles/2006/10/09/kerrys_barnstorming_sparks_talk_of_a_run?mode=PF.
[732] Brian C. Mooney. Kerry's barnstorming sparks talk of run. Boston Globe. Oct. 9, 2006 and retrieved 10.31.06 from http://www.boston.com/news/nation/articles/2006/10/09/kerrys_barnstorming_sparks_talk_of_a_run?mode=PF.
[733] Brian C. Mooney. Kerry's barnstorming sparks talk of run. Boston Globe. Oct. 9, 2006 and retrieved 10.31.06 from http://www.boston.com/news/nation/articles/2006/10/09/kerrys_barnstorming_sparks_talk_of_a_run?mode=PF.
[734] JohnKerry.com. 'This Week' with quest Senator John Kerry. Aired 10.22 and retrieved 10.31.06 from http://www.johnkerry.com/news/articles/newsarticle.html?id=49.
[735] JohnKerry.com. 'This Week' with quest Senator John Kerry. Aired 10.22 and retrieved 10.31.06 from http://www.johnkerry.com/news/articles/newsarticle.html?id=49.
[736] Taegan Goddard's Political Wire. Oct.19.2006. retrieved 10.31.06 from http://politicalwire.com/archives/2008_campaign/.
[737] JohnKerry.com. 'This Week' with quest Senator John Kerry. Aired 10.22 and retrieved 10.31.06 from http://www.johnkerry.com/news/articles/newsarticle.html?id=49.
[738] Hardball with Chris Matthews for Nov. 1. MSNBC.com. Transcript retrieved 11.17.06 from http://www.msnbc.msn.com/id/15530499/..
[739] Mark Kilmer. Redstate.org. John Kerry makes Joe Biden seem smart. Retrieved 11.17.06 from http://breakingnews.redstate.com/blogs/mark_kilmer/2006/nov/02/johny_kerry_makes_joe_biden_seem_smart.
[740] AP. White House slams Kerry for Iraq remarks. Oct. 31, 2006 @ http://msnbc.msn.com/id/15499174/print/1/displaymode/1098/.
[741] Hardball with Chris Matthews. MSNBC.com. Oct.31, 7p.m. Retrieved 11.17.06 from http://msnbc.msn.com/id/15514343/.
[742] Hardball with Chris Matthews. MSNBC.com. Oct.31, 7p.m. Retrieved 11.17.06 from http://msnbc.msn.com/id/15514343/.
[743] Jonah Goldberg. Kerry, Kerry, quite contrary. National Review. MJS, Nov.2,2006.
[744] ABC News. Funnies: Kerry Carnage. Nov.5, 2006. Retrieved 1.13.07 from http://abcnews.go.com/ThisWeek/print?id=2629990.
[745] ABC News. Funnies: Kerry Carnage. Nov.5, 2006. Retrieved 1.13.07 from http://abcnews.go.com/ThisWeek/print?id=2629990
[746] Hardball with Chris Matthews for Nov. 1. MSNBC.com. Transcript retrieved 11.17.06 from http://www.msnbc.msn.com/id/15530499/.
[747] Personal Notes, NBC Nightly News, Nov.1.2006.
[748] Hardball with Chris Matthews for Nov. 1. MSNBC.com. Transcript retrieved 11.17.06 from http://www.msnbc.msn.com/id/15530499/.
[749] Jennifer Loven. Kerry, Bush trade jabs. Nov. 1, 2006 3A. AP. MJS. SB8 p 35.
[750] Personal Notes, NBC Nightly News, Nov.1.2006.
[751] Craig Gilbert. Milwaukee Journal-Sentinel. Feingold to sift election results before deciding on big run. Nov.4. 2006, SB 8 p 36.
[752] Hardball with Chris Matthews for Nov. 1. MSNBC.com. Transcript retrieved 11.17.06 from http://www.msnbc.msn.com/id/15530499/.
[753] Personal Notes, NBC Nightly News, Nov.1.2006.
[754] Personal Notes. NBC Nightly News. Nov. 1. 2006.
[755] O. Kay Henderson. Vilsack: Iraq no joking matter. Posted Nov. 1. 2006 and retrieved 11.17.06 from http://www.radioiowa.com/gestalt/go.cfm?objectid=8EE4E9A3-45D2-4F31-83237D1EE9E99112.
[756] Z. Byron Wolf. What on Earth Did Schumer Say to Kerry? Political Radar. Posted Nov.14, and retrieved 11.17.06 from http://blogs.abcnews.com/politicalradar/2006/11/what_on_earth_d.html.
[757] Thomas Ferraro. Kerry draws Republican fire for Iraq comment. Oct. 31, 2006. http://wwww.washingtonpost.com/wp-dyn/content/article/2006/10/31/AR2006103100829_pf.html.
[758] Hardball with Chris Matthews for Nov. 1. MSNBC.com. Transcript retrieved 11.17.06 from http://www.msnbc.msn.com/id/15530499/.

[759] Hardball with Chris Matthews for Nov. 1. MSNBC.com. Transcript retrieved 11.17.06 from http://www.msnbc.msn.com/id/15530499/.
[760] SB 8 p 35. Carlson cartoon.
[761] Thomas Ferraro. Kerry slip-up not seen hurting Democrats at polls. Nov. 2 and retrieved 11.17.06 from http://elections.us.reuters.com/top/news/usnN02400192.html.
[762] "Kennedy supports another Kerry presidential bid." James Gordon Meek. New York Daily News. Posted March 7, 2005 and retrieved March 10, 2004 from http://www.grandforks.com/mld/mercurynews/news/politics/11070820.htm.
[763] AP. "Ted Kennedy Will Run for Another Term." NBC 10 News. Posted October 12, 2005 and retrieved October 20, 2005 from http://www.turnto10.com/politics/5091560/detail.html.
[764] Glen Johnson. "Kennedy: I'll support Kerry in 2008 Race." AP. Posted October 12, 2005 and retrieved October 20, 2005 from http://news.yahoo.com/s/ap/20051013/ap_on_el_pr_kennedy2008&printer=1.
[765] Reuters. "Kennedy says he'd again back Kerry for president." Washingtonpost.com. Posted April 23, 2006 and retrieved April 24, 2006 from http://www.washingtonpost.com/wp-dyn/content/article/2006/04/23/AR2006042300354.html.
[766] Rick Klein. Kerry to postpone decision on '08 run. Dec. 2, 2006 and retrieved 12.14.06 from http://www.boston.com/news/nation/articles/2006/12/02/kerry_to_postpone_decision_on_08_run/.
[767] Rick Klein. Kerry to postpone decision on '08 run. Dec. 2, 2006 and retrieved 12.14.06 from http://www.boston.com/news/nation/articles/2006/12/02/kerry_to_postpone_decision_on_08_run/.
[768] Rick Klein. Kerry to postpone decision on '08 run. Dec. 2, 2006 and retrieved 12.14.06 from http://www.boston.com/news/nation/articles/2006/12/02/kerry_to_postpone_decision_on_08_run/.
[769] Scot Lehigh. Giving Kerry a helpful push. Posted Dec. 14, 2006 and retrieved 12.14.06 from http://www.boston.com/news/globe/editorial_opinion/oped/articles/2006/12/14/giving_kerry_a_helpful_push/.
[770] Scot Lehigh. Giving Kerry a helpful push. Posted Dec. 14, 2006 and retrieved 12.14.06 from http://www.boston.com/news/globe/editorial_opinion/oped/articles/2006/12/14/giving_kerry_a_helpful_push/.
[771] Scot Lehigh. Giving Kerry a helpful push. Posted Dec. 14, 2006 and retrieved 12.14.06 from http://www.boston.com/news/globe/editorial_opinion/oped/articles/2006/12/14/giving_kerry_a_helpful_push/.
[772] Scot Lehigh. Giving Kerry a helpful push. Posted Dec. 14, 2006 and retrieved 12.14.06 from http://www.boston.com/news/globe/editorial_opinion/oped/articles/2006/12/14/giving_kerry_a_helpful_push/.
[773] ABC News. Kennedy Support for Kerry Contingent on Timeline. Posted 12.12. and retrieved 12.14.06 from http://blogs.abcnews.com/polticalradar/2006/12/kennedy_support.html.
[774] ABC News. Kennedy Support for Kerry Contingent on Timeline. Posted 12.12. and retrieved 12.14.06 from http://blogs.abcnews.com/polticalradar/2006/12/kennedy_support.html.
[775] Rick Klein. Kennedy rethinks support for a Kerry presidential run in '08. Globe. Posted Dec.11 and retrieved 12.14.06 from http://www.boston.com/news/nation/washington/articles/2006/12/11/kennedy_drops_support_for_a_kerry_presidential_run_in_08/.
[776] Rick Klein. Kennedy rethinks support for a Kerry presidential run in '08. Globe. Posted Dec.11 and retrieved 12.14.06 from http://www.boston.com/news/nation/washington/articles/2006/12/11/kennedy_drops_support_for_a_kerry_presidential_run_in_08/
[777] Rick Klein. Kennedy rethinks support for a Kerry presidential run in '08. Globe. Posted Dec.11 and retrieved 12.14.06 from http://www.boston.com/news/nation/washington/articles/2006/12/11/kennedy_drops_support_for_a_kerry_presidential_run_in_08/
[778] Hardball with Chris Matthews for Dec. 5.MSNBC.com. Retrieved 12.14.06 from http://www.msnbc.msn.com/id/16075305/.
[779] Joel Connelly. A fuming Kerry goes on the offensive. MSJ/Seattle Post Intelligencer. Nov. 2, 2006, 17A. SB 10.34.
[780] Personal notes. This Week for Nov. 26, 2006 Sunday Funnies.
[781] Taegan Goddard' Political Wire. Kerry Acting Like a Candidate. Dec. 1, 2006. and retrieved 12.14.06 from http://politicalwire.com/archives/2008_campaign/.
[782] Taegan Goddard' Political Wire. Kerry Acting Like a Candidate. Dec. 1, 2006. and retrieved 12.14.06 from http://politicalwire.com/archives/2008_campaign/.
[783] CentreDaily.com. Handicapping the '08 presidential race. Posted Nov.14.06 and retrieved 11.17.06 from http://www.centredaily.com/mld/centredaily/news/opinion/15998697.htm. Good web, see Midterms.
[784] FOX News. Transcript: Sen. John Kerry on 'FNS'. Chris Wallace. Aired 11.19 and retrieved 12.3.06 from http://www.foxnews.com/story/0,2933,230589,00.html.
[785] FOX News. Transcript: Sen. John Kerry on 'FNS'. Chris Wallace. Aired 11.19 and retrieved 12.3.06 from http://www.foxnews.com/story/0,2933,230589,00.html.
[786] FOX News. Transcript: Sen. John Kerry on 'FNS'. Chris Wallace. Aired 11.19 and retrieved 12.3.06 from http://www.foxnews.com/story/0,2933,230589,00.html
[787] FOX News. Transcript: Sen. John Kerry on 'FNS'. Chris Wallace. Aired 11.19 and retrieved 12.3.06 from http://www.foxnews.com/story/0,2933,230589,00.html
[788] Quinnipiac University. November 27, 2006—More Americans Think Well of Speaker Pelosi, Quinnipiac University National Thermometer Finds; President is low on List, But Kerry is Last. Retrieved 12.14.06 from http://www.quinnipiac.edu/x1284.xml?ReleaseId=990&ss=print.

[789] Rick Klein. Kennedy rethinks support for a Kerry presidential run in '08. Globe. Posted Dec.11 and retrieved 12.14.06 from http://www.boston.com/news/nation/washington/articles/2006/12/11/kennedy_drops_support_for_a_kerry_presidential_run_in_08/

[790] Taegan Goddard' Political Wire. Kerry Acting Like a Candidate. Dec. 1, 2006. and retrieved 12.14.06 from http://politicalwire.com/archives/2008_campaign/.

[791] Clinton, McCain top NH Poll. The AP. Union Leader. Retrieved 10.31. 2006 and posted at http://www.unionleader.com/article.aspx?headline=Clinton%2C+McCain+top+NH+'08+poll&articleId=7b63b9fd-2034-4b26-90d6-3246d1f679fa. Linked to "complete results of UNH"s presidential poll" @ http://www.unh.edu/survey-center/primary101206.pdf

[792] Retrieved 12.14.06 from http://www.pollingreport.com.

[793] Retrieved 12.14.06 from http://www.pollingreport.com.

[794] Hardball with Chris Matthews for Dec.5. MSNBC.com. Retrieved 12.14.06 from http://www.msnbc.msn.com/id/16075305/.

[795] Hardball with Chris Matthews for Dec. 5.MSNBC.com. Retrieved 12.14.06 from http://www.msnbc.msn.com/id/16075305/.

[796] Hardball with Chris Matthews for Dec. 5.MSNBC.com. Retrieved 12.14.06 from http://www.msnbc.msn.com/id/16075305/.

[797] Hardball with Chris Matthews for Jan.24. MSNBC.com. Retrieved 1.25.07 from http://www.msnbc.msn.com/id/16809939/print/1/displaymode/1098/.

[798] Senator Joe Biden. Senator Biden Issues Statement on Senator John Kerry's Decision to Not Seek the Presidency and Remain in the U.S. Senate. Posted 1.24.07 and retrieved next day from http://www.allamericanpartiots.com/m-news+article+storyid-18049.html.

[799] Reuters. Kerry says he will not seek White House in 2008. Posted 1.25.07 from http://www.abs.cbnnews.com/storypage.aspx?StoryId=64528.

[800] Reuters. Kerry says he will not seek White House in 2008. Posted 1.25.07 from http://www.abs.cbnnews.com/storypage.aspx?StoryId=64528.

[801] Reuters. Kerry says he will not seek White House in 2008. Posted 1.25.07 from http://www.abs.cbnnews.com/storypage.aspx?StoryId=64528.

[802] Reuters. Kerry says he will not seek White House in 2008. Posted 1.25.07 from http://www.abs.cbnnews.com/storypage.aspx?StoryId=64528.

[803] Joe Milicia. Kucinich Launches Presidential Bid. Tuesday, 12.12.06 and retrieved 12.14.06 from http://www.washingtonpost.com/wp-dyn/content/article/2006/12/12/AR2006121200349.html.

[804] Political Radar. Kucinich to Announce Candidacy at Noon. 12.12.06 and retrieved 12.14.06 from http://blogs.abcnews.com/politicalradar/2006/12/kucinich_to_ann.html.

[805] Joe Milicia. Kucinich Launches Presidential Bid. Tuesday, Dec.12.06 and retrieved 12.14.06 from http://www.washingtonpost.com/wp-dyn/content/article/2006/12/12/AR2006121200349.html.

[806] Union Leader. Kucinich will enter the race tomorrow. Dec. 11, 2006 and retrieved 12.1.406 from http://www.unionleader.com/article.aspx?headline=Kucinich+will+enter+the+race+tomorrow&articleId=4e5e7a5c-2c94-453d-ae6c-24f31fbf751f.

[807] Kansas City.com. A look at presidential candidate Dennis Kucinich. AP. Posted Dec.12 and retrieved Dec.14, 2006 from http://www.kansascity.com/mld/kansascity/news/politics/elections/16222868.htm.

[808] Union Leader. Kucinich will enter the race tomorrow. Dec. 11, 2006 and retrieved 12.1.406 from http://www.unionleader.com/article.aspx?headline=Kucinich+will+enter+the+race+tomorrow&articleId=4e5e7a5c-2c94-453d-ae6c-24f31fbf751f.

[809] Political Radar. Kucinich to Announce Candidacy at Noon. Dec. 12.2006. Retrieved 12.14.06 from http://blogs.abcnews.com/politicalradar/2006/12/kucinich_to_ann.html.

[810] Kansas City.com. A look at presidential candidate Dennis Kucinich. AP. Posted Dec.12 and retrieved Dec.14, 2006 from http://www.kansascity.com/mld/kansascity/news/politics/elections/16222868.htm.

[811] Union Leader. Kucinich will enter the race tomorrow. Dec. 11, 2006 and retrieved 12.1.406 from http://www.unionleader.com/article.aspx?headline=Kucinich+will+enter+the+race+tomorrow&articleId=4e5e7a5c-2c94-453d-ae6c-24f31fbf751f.

[812] Union Leader. Kucinich will enter the race tomorrow. Dec. 11, 2006 and retrieved 12.1.406 from http://www.unionleader.com/article.aspx?headline=Kucinich+will+enter+the+race+tomorrow&articleId=4e5e7a5c-2c94-453d-ae6c-24f31fbf751f.

[813] Dennis J. Kucinich. Rep. Dennis Kucinich: Out of Iraq and Back to the American City. Given Jan.8, 2007 and retrieved 1.11.07 from http://www.politicalaffairs.net/article/article/articleview.4666/1/32/.

[814] Compiled by Daniel Kurtzman. Dennis Kucinich Jokes. Retrieved 7.27.07 from http://politicalhumor.about.com/library/blkucinichjokes.htm.

[815] Compiled by Daniel Kurtzman. Dennis Kucinich Jokes. Retrieved 7.27.07 from http://politicalhumor.about.com/library/blkucinichjokes.htm.

[816] Compiled by Daniel Kurtzman. Dennis Kucinich Jokes. Retrieved 7.27.07 from http://politicalhumor.about.com/library/blkucinichjokes.htm.

[817] Joe Milicia. Kucinich Launches Presidential Bid. Tuesday, 12.12.06 and retrieved 12.14.06 from http://www.washingtonpost.com/wp-dyn/content/article/2006/12/12/AR2006121200349.html.

[818] Mark Leibovich. Just Ask: Kucinich Answers, 'Yes I Am'. 12.12.06 and retrieved from New York Times on 12.14. 06 from http://www.nytimes.com/2006/12/12/us/politics/12dennis.html?ex=1323579600&en=ad2af566c2e42300&ei=5090&partner=rssuserland&emc=rss.
[819] Mark Leibovich. Just Ask: Kucinich Answers, 'Yes I Am'. 12.12.06 and retrieved from New York Times on 12.14. 06 from http://www.nytimes.com/2006/12/12/us/politics/12dennis.html?ex=1323579600&en=ad2af566c2e42300&ei=5090&partner=rssuserland&emc=rss.
[820] Mark Leibovich. Just Ask: Kucinich Answers, 'Yes I Am'. 12.12.06 and retrieved from New York Times on 12.14. 06 from http://www.nytimes.com/2006/12/12/us/politics/12dennis.html?ex=1323579600&en=ad2af566c2e42300&ei=5090&partner=rssuserland&emc=rss.
[821] Mark Leibovich. Just Ask: Kucinich Answers, 'Yes I Am'. 12.12.06 and retrieved from New York Times on 12.14. 06 from http://www.nytimes.com/2006/12/12/us/politics/12dennis.html?ex=1323579600&en=ad2af566c2e42300&ei=5090&partner=rssuserland&emc=rss.
[822] Mark Leibovich. Just Ask: Kucinich Answers, 'Yes I Am'. 12.12.06 and retrieved from New York Times on 12.14. 06 from http://www.nytimes.com/2006/12/12/us/politics/12dennis.html?ex=1323579600&en=ad2af566c2e42300&ei=5090&partner=rssuserland&emc=rss.
[823] By Qshio. The Kucinich Niche. Qshio's Blog. Retrieved 12.14.06 from http://houseoflabor.tpmcafe.com/blog/qshio/2006/dec/14/the_kucinich_niche.
[824] Late Night Political Jokes. April 30, 2007. Retrieved 5.3.07 from http://politicalhumor.about.com/library/bldailyfeed3.htm.
[825] The Funnies. Retrieved 8.1.07 from http://www.hillaryis44.org/?p=98.
[826] The Funnies. Retrieved 8.1.07 from http://www.hillaryis44.org/?p=98.
[827] Joe Milicia. Kucinich Launches Presidential Bid. Tuesday, Dec.12.06 and retrieved 12.14.06 from http://www.washingtonpost.com/wp-dyn/content/article/2006/12/12/AR2006121200349.html.
[828] Robert Paul Reyes. Dennis Kucinich Enters 2008 Presidential Race. Dec.14.06 and retrieved same day from http://www.americanchronicle.com/articles/viewArticle.asp?articleID=17923.
[829] By Qshio. The Kucinich Niche. Qshio's Blog. Retrieved 12.14.06 from http://houseoflabor.tpmcafe.com/blog/qshio/2006/dec/14/the_kucinich_niche.
[830] By Qshio. The Kucinich Niche. Qshio's Blog. Retrieved 12.14.06 from http://houseoflabor.tpmcafe.com/blog/qshio/2006/dec/14/the_kucinich_niche.
[831] CNN.com. the Situation Room. For Dec.12. Retrieved 12.14.06 from http://transcripts.cnn.com/TRANSCRIPTS/0612/12/sitroom.01.html.
[832] Joe Milicia. Kucinich Launches Presidential Bid. Tuesday, Dec.12.06 and retrieved 12.14.06 from http://www.washingtonpost.com/wp-dyn/content/article/2006/12/12/AR2006121200349.html.
[833] Joe Milicia. Kucinich Launches Presidential Bid. Tuesday, Dec.12.06 and retrieved 12.14.06 from http://www.washingtonpost.com/wp-dyn/content/article/2006/12/12/AR2006121200349.html.
[834] Joe Milicia. Kucinich Launches Presidential Bid. Tuesday, Dec.12.06 and retrieved 12.14.06 from http://www.washingtonpost.com/wp-dyn/content/article/2006/12/12/AR2006121200349.html.
[835] Union Leader. Kucinich will enter the race tomorrow. Dec. 11, 2006 and retrieved 12.1.406 from http://www.unionleader.com/article.aspx?headline=Kucinich+will+enter+the+race+tomorrow&articleId=4e5e7a5c-2c94-453d-ae6c-24f31fbf751f.
[836] CNN.com. the Situation Room. For Dec.12. Retrieved 12.14.06 from http://transcripts.cnn.com/TRANSCRIPTS/0612/12/sitroom.01.html
[837] CNN.com. the Situation Room. For Dec.12. Retrieved 12.14.06 from http://transcripts.cnn.com/TRANSCRIPTS/0612/12/sitroom.01.html
[838] Susan Page. USA Today. Long-shot candidates have much to gain in consolation prizes. Posted/retrieved 6.15.07 from http://www.usatoday.com/news/politics/election2008/2007-06-14-campaign-consolation_N.htm.
[839] Kucinich in singing role off Broadway. Stephan Koff. The Plain Dealer. Jan.9, 2007 and retrieved 1.13.07 from http://www.cleveland.com/printer/printer.ssf?/base/ispol/1168343901112520.xml&coll=2.
[840] Infoplease.com. Barack Obama. Retrieved August 11, 2006 from http://www.infoplease.com/ipa/A0930136.html.
[841] St. Louis Post-Dispatch. AP. Senator blasts political corruption in Kenya. MJS, August 26, 2006, 3A.
[842] St. Louis Post-Dispatch. AP. Senator blasts political corruption in Kenya. MJS, August 26, 2006, 3A.
[843] NBC News. Meet the Press. July 25, 2004. MSNBC.com. Retrieved 10.31.2006 from http://www.msnbc.msn.com/id/5488345/print/1/displaymode/1098/.
[844] Joe Klein. The Fresh Face. Time. Oct. 15, 2006 and retrieved Oct. 31, 2006 form http://www.time.com/magazine/printout/0,8816,1546362,00.html.
[845] Joe Klein. The Fresh Face. Time. Oct. 15, 2006 and retrieved Oct. 31, 2006 form http://www.time.com/magazine/printout/0,8816,1546362,00.html.
[846] Infoplease.com. Barack Obama. Retrieved August 11, 2006 from http://www.infoplease.com/ipa/A0930136.html.
[847] William Finnegan. The Candidate. The New Yorker. Posted May 24, 2004 and retrieved August 11, 2006 from http://www.newyorker.com/printables/fact/040531fa_fact1.

[848] Garret M. Graff. Barack Obama. Washingtonian.com. Retrieved Oct. 31.2006 from http://www.washingtonian.com/articles/mediapolitics/1836.html.
[849] David Weigel. Great Barack Hope. The American Spectator. Published June 27, 2004 and retrieved August 11, 2006 from http://www.spectator.org/util/print.asp?art_id=6880.
[850] David Weigel. Great Barack Hope. The American Spectator. Published June 27, 2004 and retrieved August 11, 2006 from http://www.spectator.org/util/print.asp?art_id=6880
[851] David Weigel. Great Barack Hope. The American Spectator. Published June 27, 2004 and retrieved August 11, 2006 from http://www.spectator.org/util/print.asp?art_id=6880
[852] Chris Cillizza. 2008: The Case Against Barack Obama. Washingtonpost.com. The Fix. Retrieved July 28, 2006 from http://blog.washingtonpost.com/thefix/2006/07/2008_the_case_against_barack_o.html.
[853] Patrick O'Conner. The Hill.com. Mike Ditka emerges as possible Senate candidate. Posted July 8, 2004 and retrieved August 11, 2006 from http://www.hillnews.com/news/070804/ditka.aspx.
[854] Patrick O'Conner. The Hill.com. Mike Ditka emerges as possible Senate candidate. Posted July 8, 2004 and retrieved August 11, 2006 from http://www.hillnews.com/news/070804/ditka.aspx.
[855] Garret M. Graff. Barack Obama. Washingtonian.com. Retrieved Oct. 31.2006 from http://www.washingtonian.com/articles/mediapolitics/1836.html.
[856] Chris Cillizza. 2008: The Case Against Barack Obama. Washingtonpost.com. The Fix. Retrieved July 28, 2006 from http://blog.washingtonpost.com/thefix/2006/07/2008_the_case_against_barack_o.html.
[857] NBC NEWS. MTP transcript for August 22 (2004). Meet the Press. Retrieved 10.31.2006 and posted 10.31.2006 @ http://www.msnbc.msn.com/id/5772535/print/1/displaymode/1098/
[858] Rising Star: Senate Candidate Barack Obama Delivers Rousing Keynote at DNC. Democracy Now!. Retrieved August 11, 2006 from http://www.democracynow.org/article.pl?sid=04/07/28/1313225.
[859] Amanda Reavy. Durbin: Obama should run for president. Published May 29, 2006 and retrieved June 5, 2006 from http://www.sj-r.com/Sections/News/Stories/87160.asp.
[860] Charles Babington. Obama's Profile Has Democrats Taking Notice. Published June 18, 2006, A01. Retrieved June 30, 2006 from http://www.washingtonpost.com/wp-dyn/content/article/2006/06/17/AR2006061700736_pf.html.
[861] Taegan Goddard's Political Wire. Report from the Steak Fry. September 18, 2006 and retrieved 9.25.06 from http://polticalwire.com/archives/2008_campaign. Contributed by Dan Conley.
[862] Garret M. Graff. Barack Obama. Washingtonian.com. Retrieved Oct. 31.2006 from http://www.washingtonian.com/articles/mediapolitics/1836.html.
[863] Dan Balz. Obama Says He'll Consider A 2008 Bid for The Presidency." Oct. 23, 2006, pg. A01. Retrieved 10.31.06 from http://www.washingtonpost.com/wp-dyn/content/article/2006/10/22/AR2006102200220_pf.html.
[864] Obama Planned to Make News Last Week. Oct. 29, 2006. Taegan Goddard's Political Wire. Retrieved 10.31.2006 from http://politicalwire.com/archives/2008_campaign/.
[865] Dan Balz. Obama Says He'll Consider A 2008 Bid for The Presidency." Oct. 23, 2006, pg. A01. Retrieved 10.31.06 from http://www.washingtonpost.com/wp-dyn/content/article/2006/10/22/AR2006102200220_pf.html.
[866] Garret M. Graff. Barack Obama. Washingtonian.com. Retrieved Oct. 31.2006 from http://www.washingtonian.com/articles/mediapolitics/1836.html.
[867] Garret M. Graff. Barack Obama. Washingtonian.com. Retrieved Oct. 31.2006 from http://www.washingtonian.com/articles/mediapolitics/1836.html.
[868] 'Hardball with Chris Mathews' for Oct. 23. MSNBC.com. Retrieved 10.31.06 from http://www.msnbc.msn.com/id/15400205/.
[869] Taegan Goddard's' Political Wire. Obama mania. 10.16.06 and retrieved 12.14.06 from http://www.politicalwire.com/archives/10/16/obama_mania.html.
[870] Taegan Goddard's' Political Wire. Obama mania. 10.16.06 and retrieved 12.14.06 from http://www.politicalwire.com/archives/10/16/obama_mania.html.
[871] Dan Balz. Obama Says He'll Consider A 2008 Bid for The Presidency." Oct. 23, 2006, pg. A01. Retrieved 10.31.06 from http://www.washingtonpost.com/wp-dyn/content/article/2006/10/22/AR2006102200220_pf.html
[872] Linda Feldman. Two years till election day, and the race is on. The Christian Science Monitor. Posted Nov. 15, 2006 and retrieved 11.17.06 from http://www.csmonitor.com/2006/1115/p01s01-uspo.htm.
[873] CentreDaily.com. Handicapping the '08 presidential race. Posted 11.14.06 and retrieved 11.17.06 from http://www.centredaily.com/mld/centredaily/news/opinion/15998697.htm.
[874] Thomas Beaumont. Obama talks with top advisors in Iowa. Des Moines Register. Pub. 11.26 and retrieved 12.3.06 from http://desmoinesregister.com/apps/pbcs.dll/article?AID=/20061126/NEWS09/611260332&template=printart.
[875] Helen Kennedy. Obama's Prez-zence felt in Hil territory. New York Daily News. Retrieved 12.14.06 from http://www.nydailynews.com/front/story/477358p-401517c.html.
[876] The Sunday Times. Obama mania. Posted Nov.5. 2006, 12.14.06 Sarah Baxter. http://www.timesonline.co.uk/printFriendly/0,,1-531-2432130-531,00.html.
[877] Gail Russell Chaddock. What's driving Obama-mania? CSmonitor.com. Posted 12.12.06 and retrieved 12.14.06 from http://csmonitor.com/2006/1212/p01s01-uspo.html.
[878] Gail Russell Chaddock. What's driving Obama-mania? CSmonitor.com. Posted 12.12.06 and retrieved 12.14.06 from http://csmonitor.com/2006/1212/p01s01-uspo.html.
[879] Gail Russell Chaddock. What's driving Obama-mania? CSmonitor.com. Posted 12.12.06 and retrieved 12.14.06 from http://csmonitor.com/2006/1212/p01s01-uspo.html.

[880] Scott Brooks. Obama fever grips NH. Dec. 11. 2006. Union Leader. Retrieved 12.14.06 from http://www.unionleader.com/article.aspx?headline=Obama+fever+grips+NH&articleId=96bb103b-6332-4304-ac8d-60da60b323e9

[881] Lynn Sweet. Obama: will not 'dilly dally' on white House decision. Retrieved 11.17.06 from http://blogs.suntimes/sweet/2006/11/obama_will_not_dilly_dally_on.html.

[882] AP. MSNBC.com Famed Pastor defends invitation to Obama. Posted Nov.30, 2006 and retrieved Dec.3.06 from http://www.msnbc.msn.com/id/15966732/print/1/displaymode/1098/.

[883] Tom Curry. Will Obama force Clinton early entry? Posted Nov.30 and retrieved 12.3.06 from http://www.msnbc.msn.com/id/15969751/.

[884] Scott Brooks. Obama fever grips NH. Dec. 11. 2006. Union Leader. Retrieved 12.14.06 from http://www.unionleader.com/article.aspx?headline=Obama+fever+grips+NH&articleId=96bb103b-6332-4304-ac8d-60da60b323e9.

[885] Adam Nagourney. Dec.11, 2006. Obama Offers Flavor of Potential campaign. Retrieved 12.14.06 from http://www.nytimes.com/2006/12/11/us/11obama.html?ex=1323493200&en=e9213d6383f8297c&ei=5088&partner=rssnyt&emc=rss.

[886] Adam Nagourney. Dec.11, 2006. Obama Offers Flavor of Potential campaign. Retrieved 12.14.06 from http://www.nytimes.com/2006/12/11/us/11obama.html?ex=1323493200&en=e9213d6383f8297c&ei=5088&partner=rssnyt&emc=rss

[887] Adam Nagourney. Dec.11, 2006. Obama Offers Flavor of Potential campaign. Retrieved 12.14.06 from http://www.nytimes.com/2006/12/11/us/11obama.html?ex=1323493200&en=e9213d6383f8297c&ei=5088&partner=rssnyt&emc=rss

[888] Craig Gilbert. Obama dips his toe deeper into presidential waters. Milwaukee Journal Sentinel. 1A/9A. Dec.11, 2006.

[889] Gail Russell Chaddock. What's driving Obama-mania? CSmonitor.com. Posted 12.12.06 and retrieved 12.14.06 from http://csmonitor.com/2006/1212/p01s01-uspo.html.

[890] Adam Nagourney. Dec.11, 2006. Obama Offers Flavor of Potential campaign. Retrieved 12.14.06 from http://www.nytimes.com/2006/12/11/us/11obama.html?ex=1323493200&en=e9213d6383f8297c&ei=5088&partner=rssnyt&emc=rss

[891] CNN.com. Obama heads to New Hampshire to celebrate Dem' victories. Nov.28, 2006. Retrieved 12.14.06 from http://www.cnn.com/POLITICS/blogs/politicalticker/2006/11/obama-heads-to-new-hampshire-to.html.

[892] Political Radar. Grassroots Group Pushes Obama to Go in '08. Dec. 13, 2006. retrieved next day from http://blogs.abcnews.com/politicalradar/2006/12/grassroots_grou.html.

[893] Political Radar. Grassroots Group Pushes Obama to Go in '08. Dec. 13, 2006. retrieved next day from http://blogs.abcnews.com/politicalradar/2006/12/grassroots_grou.html.

[894] Adam Nagourney. Evan Bayh withdraws from 2008 presidential field. International Herald Tribune. Published 12.17.06 @ http://www.iht.com/articles/2006/12/17/news/Bayh.php.

[895] Dan Balz. Clinton, Obama Clearing the Field. Dec.24, 2006 and retrieved 1.13.06 from http://www.washingtonpost.com/wp-dyn/content/article/2006/12/23/AR2006122300970_pf.html.

[896] Beth Fouhy. Obama, Clinton Making 2008 Moves. AP. Retrieved 1.13.06and posted 1.12 @ http://abcnews.go.com/Politics/wireStory?id=2791797.

[897] Dan Balz. Clinton, Obama Clearing the Field. Dec.24, 2006 and retrieved 1.13.06 from http://www.washingtonpost.com/wp-dyn/content/article/2006/12/23/AR2006122300970_pf.html.

[898] Gail Russell Chaddock. What's driving Obama-mania? CSmonitor.com. Posted 12.12.06 and retrieved 12.14.06 from http://csmonitor.com/2006/1212/p01s01-uspo.html.

[899] Charles Babington and Shailagh Murray. For Now, an Unofficial Rivalry. Dec. 8 and retrieved 12.14.06 from http://www.washingtonpost.com/wp-dyn/content/article/2006/12/07/AR2006120701755_pf.html.

[900] Hotline on Call. Oprah Endorses Obama? September 25, 2006. Retrieved 1.13.07 from http://hotlineblog.nationaljournal.com/archives/2006/09/oprah_endorses.html.

[901] Matthew Borghese. Oprah Supports Barack Obama for President. All Headline News. 9.25.06 and retrieved 1.13.07 from http://www.allheadlinenews.com/articles/7004974435.

[902] Oprah's Cut with Barack Obama. Retrieved 1.13.07 from http://www2.oprah.com/omagazine/200411/omag_200411_ocut.jhtml.

[903] Lynn Sweet. Oprah's mansion bash for Obama sold out. Posted 7.31.07 and retrieved 8.1.07 from http://www.suntimes.com/news/sweet/490395,CST-NWS-sweet31.article.

[904] George Will. Run Now, Obama. Washington Post. Published Dec. 14.2006 and retrieved same day from http://www.washingtonpost.com/wp-dyn/content/article/2006/12/13/AR2006121301901_pf.html.

[905] 2008: The Case for Barack Obama. The Fix. Chris Cillizza. Posted July 25, 2006 and retrieved July 28, 2006 from http://blog.washingtonpost.com/thefix/2006/07/2008_the_case_for_barack_obama_1.html

[906] 2008: The Case for Barack Obama. The Fix. Chris Cillizza. Posted July 25, 2006 and retrieved July 28, 2006 from http://blog.washingtonpost.com/thefix/2006/07/2008_the_case_for_barack_obama_1.html

[907] 2008: The Case for Barack Obama. The Fix. Chris Cillizza. Posted July 25, 2006 and retrieved July 28, 2006 from http://blog.washingtonpost.com/thefix/2006/07/2008_the_case_for_barack_obama_1.html

[908] George Will. Run Now, Obama. Washington Post. Published Dec. 14.2006 and retrieved same day from http://www.washingtonpost.com/wp-dyn/content/article/2006/12/13/AR2006121301901_pf.html.

[909] Kenneth T. Walsh. Obama: Ready for Prime Time? 12. 13.06 and retrieved 12.14 from http://www.usnews.com/usnews/news/articles/061213/13obama.htm. See also p 9/11 of http://transcripts.cnn.com/TRANSCRIPTS/0612/12/sitroom.02/html.
[910] George Will. Run Now, Obama. Washington Post. Published Dec. 14.2006 and retrieved same day from http://www.washingtonpost.com/wp-dyn/content/article/2006/12/13/AR2006121301901_pf.html.
[911] Dan Balz. Obama Says He'll Consider A 2008 Bid for The Presidency." Oct. 23, 2006, pg. A01. Retrieved 10.31.06 from http://www.washingtonpost.com/wp-dyn/content/article/2006/10/22/AR2006102200220_pf.html
[912] Joe Klein. The Fresh Face. Time. Oct. 15, 2006 and retrieved Oct. 31, 2006 form http://www.time.com/magazine/printout/0,8816,1546362,00.html.
[913] Garret M. Graff. Barack Obama. Washingtonian.com. Retrieved Oct. 31.2006 from http://www.washingtonian.com/articles/mediapolitics/1836.html.
[914] Joe Klein. The Fresh Face. Time. Oct. 15, 2006 and retrieved Oct. 31, 2006 form http://www.time.com/magazine/printout/0,8816,1546362,00.html.
[915] Garret M. Graff. Barack Obama. Washingtonian.com. Retrieved Oct. 31.2006 from http://www.washingtonian.com/articles/mediapolitics/1836.html.
[916] Joe Klein. The Fresh Face. Time. Oct. 15, 2006 and retrieved Oct. 31, 2006 form http://www.time.com/magazine/printout/0,8816,1546362,00.html.
[917] Garret M. Graff. Barack Obama. Washingtonian.com. Retrieved Oct. 31.2006 from http://www.washingtonian.com/articles/mediapolitics/1836.html.
[918] 'Hardball with Chris Mathews' for Oct. 23. MSNBC.com. Retrieved 10.31.06 from http://www.msnbc.msn.com/id/15400205/.
[919] JohnKerry.com. 'This Week' with quest Senator John Kerry. Aired 10.22 and retrieved 10.31.06 from http://www.johnkerry.com/news/articles/newsarticle.html?id=49.
[920] The Economist. Man versus machine. Posted 1.18.07 and retrieved 8.1.07 from http://www.economist.com/world/na/displaystory.cmf?story_id=8561999.
[921] Dan Balz. Obama Says He'll Consider A 2008 Bid for The Presidency." Oct. 23, 2006, pg. A01. Retrieved 10.31.06 from http://www.washingtonpost.com/wp-dyn/content/article/2006/10/22/AR2006102200220_pf.html.
[922] Garret M. Graff. Barack Obama. Washingtonian.com. Retrieved Oct. 31.2006 from http://www.washingtonian.com/articles/mediapolitics/1836.html.
[923] Bob Herbert. Let's not rush Obama. NY Times. MJS, Oct. 24, 2006, 11A.
[924] Garret M. Graff. Barack Obama. Washingtonian.com. Retrieved Oct. 31.2006 from http://www.washingtonian.com/articles/mediapolitics/1836.html.
[925] Garret M. Graff. Barack Obama. Washingtonian.com. Retrieved Oct. 31.2006 from http://www.washingtonian.com/articles/mediapolitics/1836.html.
[926] NBC News. Meet the Press. Oct. 22, 2006 MSNBC.com. Retrieved 10.31.2006 from http://www.msnbc.msn.com/id/15304689/print/1/displaymode/1098/.
[927] Chris Cillizza. 2008: The Case Against Barack Obama. Washingtonpost.com. The Fix. Retrieved July 28, 2006 from http://blog.washingtonpost.com/thefix/2006/07/2008_the_case_against_barack_o.html.
[928] Government and Politics. USA Today/Gallup Poll. Nov.2-5, 2006. Retrieved 12.14.06 from http://www.pollingreport.com/politics.htm.
[929] David Espo. Obama: Democrats Must Court Evangelicals. Posted June 28, 2006 and retrieved July 14, 2006 from http://www.washingtonpost.com/wp-dyn/content/article/2006/06/28/AR2006062800281.html.
[930] David Espo. Obama: Democrats Must Court Evangelicals. Posted June 28, 2006 and retrieved July 14, 2006 from http://www.washingtonpost.com/wp-dyn/content/article/2006/06/28/AR2006062800281.html
[931] NBC News. Meet the Press. July 25, 2004. MSNBC.com. Retrieved 10.31.2006 from http://www.msnbc.msn.com/id/5488345/print/1/displaymode/1098/.
[932] Ron Fournier. MSNBC.com. GOP chair urges party to refocus on core. Politics-MSNBC.com. retrieved 12.3 and posted 12.1.06 from http://www.msnbc.msn.com/id/15984548/.
[933] Ron Fournier. MSNBC.com. GOP chair urges party to refocus on core. Politics-MSNBC.com. retrieved 12.3 and posted 12.1.06 from http://www.msnbc.msn.com/id/15984548/.
[934] Ron Fournier. MSNBC.com. GOP chair urges party to refocus on core. Politics-MSNBC.com. retrieved 12.3 and posted 12.1.06 from http://www.msnbc.msn.com/id/15984548/.
[935] CNN.com. Situation Room 12.03.06. Retrieved same day @ http://transcripts.cnn.com/TRANSCRIPTS/0612/03/le.01.html.
[936] CNN.com. Situation Room 12.03.06. Retrieved same day @ http://transcripts.cnn.com/TRANSCRIPTS/0612/03/le.01.html.
[937] AP. MSNBC.com Famed Pastor defends invitation to Obama. Posted Nov.30, 2006 and retrieved Dec.3.06 from http://www.msnbc.msn.com/id/15966732/print/1/displaymode/1098/.
[938] Retrieved 12.3.06 from http://www.msnbc.msn.com/id/3036697/.
[939] AP. MSNBC.com Famed Pastor defends invitation to Obama. Posted Nov.30, 2006 and retrieved Dec.3.06 from http://www.msnbc.msn.com/id/15966732/print/1/displaymode/1098/.
[940] MSNBC.com. MTP Transcript for Dec.24. Meet the Press, online at MSNBC.com. Retrieved 1.13.07 from http://www.msnbc.msn.com/id/16202841/.
[941] MSNBC.com. MTP Transcript for Dec.24. Meet the Press, online at MSNBC.com. Retrieved 1.13.07 from http://www.msnbc.msn.com/id/16202841/.

[942] MSNBC.com. MTP Transcript for Dec.24. Meet the Press, online at MSNBC.com. Retrieved 1.13.07 from http://www.msnbc.msn.com/id/16202841/.
[943] MSNBC.com. MTP Transcript for Dec.24. Meet the Press, online at MSNBC.com. Retrieved 1.13.07 from http://www.msnbc.msn.com/id/16202841/.
[944] Gillian Flaccus. Obama discusses sexuality, spirituality at AIDS conference. AP. Posted Dec. 1, 2006 and retrieved 12.14.06 from http://www.mercurynews.com/mld/mercurynews/news/breaking_news/16138985.htm.
[945] Gillian Flaccus. Obama discusses sexuality, spirituality at AIDS conference. AP. Posted Dec. 1, 2006 and retrieved 12.14.06 from http://www.mercurynews.com/mld/mercurynews/news/breaking_news/16138985.htm.
[946] Gillian Flaccus. Obama discusses sexuality, spirituality at AIDS conference. AP. Posted Dec. 1, 2006 and retrieved 12.14.06 from http://www.mercurynews.com/mld/mercurynews/news/breaking_news/16138985.htm.
[947] Gillian Flaccus. Obama discusses sexuality, spirituality at AIDS conference. AP. Posted Dec. 1, 2006 and retrieved 12.14.06 from http://www.mercurynews.com/mld/mercurynews/news/breaking_news/16138985.htm.
[948] MSNBC.com. MTP Transcript for Dec.24. Meet the Press, online at MSNBC.com. Retrieved 1.13.07 from http://www.msnbc.msn.com/id/16202841/.
[949] Barack Obama. Playing the Faith Card. Excerpt from The Audacity of Hope. The Sunday Times Magazine. Retrieved 12.14.06 from http://www.timesonline.co.uk/article/0,,2099-2432130_2,00.html.
[950] Douglas Burns. News Analysis: Why Barack Obama can win the Iowa Caucus. 12.26.06 and retrieved 1.13.07 from http://www.carrollspaper.com/main.asp?SectionID=29&SubSectionID=137&ArticleID=3132.
[951] Infoplease.com. Barack Obama. Retrieved August 11, 2006 from http://www.infoplease.com/ipa/A0930136.html.
[952] Joe Klein. The Fresh Face. Time. Oct. 15, 2006 and retrieved Oct. 31, 2006 form http://www.time.com/magazine/printout/0,8816,1546362,00.html.
[953] The Sunday Times. Obama Mania. Sarah Baxter Nov.5, 2006. Retrieved12.14.06 from http://www.timesonline.co.uk/article/0,,2099-2432120,00.html.
[954] The Milwaukee Journal-Sentinel. Midterms surpass presidential race spending. Nov. 4, 2006. 1A.
[955] The Sunday Times. Obama Mania. Sarah Baxter Nov.5, 2006. Retrieved12.14.06 from http://www.timesonline.co.uk/article/0,,2099-2432120,00.html.
[956] AP. Sen. Obama, rapper Ludacris meet for a chat. Nov.30, 2006 and retrieved 12.3.06 from http://www.msnbc.msn.com/id/15972471/.
[957] AP. Sen. Obama, rapper Ludacris meet for a chat. Nov.30, 2006 and retrieved 12.3.06 from http://www.msnbc.msn.com/id/15972471/.
[958] AP. Sen. Obama, rapper Ludacris meet for a chat. Nov.30, 2006 and retrieved 12.3.06 from http://www.msnbc.msn.com/id/15972471/.
[959] AP. Sen. Obama, rapper Ludacris meet for a chat. Nov.30, 2006 and retrieved 12.3.06 from http://www.msnbc.msn.com/id/15972471/.
[960] Tom Raum. AP. My Way News. Obama Debate Comments Set Off Firestorm. Posted 7.24.07 and retrieved 8.1.07 from http://apnews.myway.com/article/20070724/D8QJ7P100.html.
[961] Tom Raum. AP. My Way News. Obama Debate Comments Set Off Firestorm. Posted 7.24.07 and retrieved 8.1.07 from http://apnews.myway.com/article/20070724/D8QJ7P100.html.
[962] Tom Raum. AP. My Way News. Obama Debate Comments Set Off Firestorm. Posted 7.24.07 and retrieved 8.1.07 from http://apnews.myway.com/article/20070724/D8QJ7P100.html.
[963] Tom Raum. AP. My Way News. Obama Debate Comments Set Off Firestorm. Posted 7.24.07 and retrieved 8.1.07 from http://apnews.myway.com/article/20070724/D8QJ7P100.html.
[964] Tom Raum. AP. Clinton slaps Obama foreign-policy overture. Retrieved 8.1.07 from http://www.deseretnews.com/dn/view/0,1249,695194748,00.html.
[965] The Daily Show. August 2, 2007. Comedy Central.
[966] Obama says he might send troops to Pakistan. 8.1.07 @ http://demediacraticnation.wordpress.com/tag/democraps/.
[967] The Daily Show. August 2, 2007. Comedy Central.
[968] CNN.com. CNN Political Ticker Powell dispenses foreign policy advice to Obama. Posted 6.10.07 and retrieved 8.1.07 from http://politicalticker.blogs.cnn.com/2007/06/10/powell-dispenses-foreign-policy-advice-to-obama/.
[969] Michael Riley. Richardson's political shape turning Oval. Denver Post. Posted April 16, 2006 and retrieved June 30, 2006 from http://www.denverpost.com/portlet/article/html/fragments/print_article.jsp?article=3715416
[970] Richard E. Cohen and Michael Barone. The Almanac of American Politics—2004. The National Journal Group. 2003, page 1069
[971] AP. Richardson to Kerry: Don't pick me. MSNBC.com. Posted July 1, 2004 and retrieved November 10, 2005 from http://msnbc.msn.com/id/5345707/.
[972] AP. Richardson to Kerry: Don't pick me. MSNBC.com. Posted July 1, 2004 and retrieved November 10, 2005 from http://msnbc.msn.com/id/5345707/.
[973] Mark Z. Barabek. For Richardson, time to run. FortWayne.com. Posted August 19, 2005 and retrieved same day from http://origin.miami.com/mld/journalgazette/news/nation/politics/12424235.htm.
[974] Michael Riley. Richardson's political shape turning Oval. Denver Post. Posted April 16, 2006 and retrieved June 30, 2006 from http://www.denverpost.com/portlet/article/html/fragments/print_article.jsp?article=3715416.
[975] Deborah Baker. New Mexico Governor Says He'll Slow Down. AP. Posted and retrieved June 24, 2005 from http://www.guardian.co.uk/uslatest/story/0,1282,-5095085,00.html.
[976] Deborah Baker. New Mexico Governor Says He'll Slow Down. AP. Posted and retrieved June 24, 2005 from http://www.guardian.co.uk/uslatest/story/0,1282,-5095085,00.html.

[977] Michael Riley. Richardson's political shape turning Oval. Denver Post. Posted April 16, 2006 and retrieved June 30, 2006 from http://www.denverpost.com/portlet/article/html/fragments/print_article.jsp?article=3715416.

[978] Richard E. Cohen and Michael Barone. The Almanac of American Politics—2004. The National Journal Group. 2003, page 1068.

[979] Mark Z. Barabek. For Richardson, time to run. FortWayne.com. Posted August 19, 2005 and retrieved same day from http://origin.miami.com/mld/journalgazette/news/nation/politics/12424235.htm.

[980] Richard E. Cohen and Michael Barone. The Almanac of American Politics—2004. The National Journal Group. 2003, page 1068

[981] Richard E. Cohen and Michael Barone. The Almanac of American Politics—2004. The National Journal Group. 2003, page 1068

[982] Steve Terrell. Richardson on Richardson. The New Mexican. Posted September 25, 2005 and retrieved October 5, 2005 from http://www.freenewmexican.com/news/32919.html.

[983] Steve Terrell. Richardson on Richardson. The New Mexican. Posted September 25, 2005 and retrieved October 5, 2005 from http://www.freenewmexican.com/news/32919.html

[984] Margot Roosevelt. Bill Richardson. Time. Posted 8.13.05 and retrieved 8.19.05 from http://www.time.com/time/nation/printout/0,8816,1093647,00.html.

[985] Steve Terrell. Richardson on Richardson. The New Mexican. Posted September 25, 2005 and retrieved October 5, 2005 from http://www.freenewmexican.com/news/32919.html

[986] Penguin Group USA. Between Worlds. Retrieved November 10, 2005 from http://www.penguinputnam.com/nf/Book/BookDisplay/0,,0_0399153241,00.html.

[987] Richardson's life and times. The Washington Times. Published November 7, 2005 and retrieved November 10, 2005 from http://www.washingtontimes.com/fuctions/print.php?StoryID=20051106-103221-1958r.

[988] Richardson's life and times. The Washington Times. Published November 7, 2005 and retrieved November 10, 2005 from http://www.washingtontimes.com/fuctions/print.php?StoryID=20051106-103221-1958r

[989] Hardball with Chris Matthews for Feb. 26. Retrieved 3.8.07 from http://www.msnbc.msn.com/id/17365816/print/1/displaymode/1098/.

[990] AP. N.M. governor admits he wasn't drafted by baseball team. The Milwaukee Journal Sentinel, November 25, 2005, 11A.

[991] AP. N.M. governor admits he wasn't drafted by baseball team. The Milwaukee Journal Sentinel, November 25, 2005, 11A.

[992] AP. N.M. governor admits he wasn't drafted by baseball team. The Milwaukee Journal Sentinel, November 25, 2005, 11A.

[993] Hardball with Chris Matthews for Jan.22. MSNBC.com. Retrieved 1.13.06 from http://www.msnbc.msn.com/id/16771748/.

[994] Chicago Tribune. U.S. Reporter Heads Home, Freed by Sudan in Espionage Case. Sept. 10, 2006 and retrieved 9.25.2006 from http://www.latimes.com/news/printedition/aection/la-fg-journalist10sep10,1,3313996.story?coll=la-news-a...

[995] Chicago Tribune. U.S. Reporter Heads Home, Freed by Sudan in Espionage Case. Sept. 10, 2006 and retrieved 9.25.2006 from http://www.latimes.com/news/printedition/aection/la-fg-journalist10sep10,1,3313996.story?coll=la-news-a...

[996] Chicago Tribune. U.S. Reporter Heads Home, Freed by Sudan in Espionage Case. Sept. 10, 2006 and retrieved 9.25.2006 from http://www.latimes.com/news/printedition/aection/la-fg-journalist10sep10,1,3313996.story?coll=la-news-a...

[997] AP. New Mexico Governor to serve as diplomatic troubleshooter in Sudan. Sept.6, 2006 and retrieved same day from http://www.iht.com/articles/ap/2006/09/06/america/NA_GEN_US_Sudan_Richardson.php

[998] Barry Massey. North Korea Invites Gov. Richardson to visit. AP. Posted July 6, 2005 and retrieved July 8, 2005 from http://www.abqjorunal.com/news/state/apkorea07-06-05.htm.

[999] Barry Massey. North Korea Invites Gov. Richardson to visit. AP. Posted July 6, 2005 and retrieved July 8, 2005 from http://www.abqjorunal.com/news/state/apkorea07-06-05.htm

[1000] Barry Massey. Governor signs bill to provide tax relief. AP. The Albuquerque Tribune. Posted 4.5.05 and retrieved 4.15.05 from http://www.abqtrib.com/albq/nw_local_state_government/article/0,2564,ALBQ_19859_3676574,00.html.

[1001] Bill Richardson: Tax Breaks for Military. Oct. 17, 2006 and retrieved 11.17.2006 from http://www.newmax.com/archives/ic/2006/10/17/170907.shtml. NewsMax.com.

[1002] Alan Greenblatt. A Governor in Overdrive. Governing.com. New Mexico's Governor's Race. Retrieved May 31, 2006 from http://www.governing.com/news/5nm.htm.

[1003] ABC News. Richardson to Dem Majority: Listen to the Guvs. Dec. 6, 2006 and retrieved 12.14.06 from http://blogs.abcnews.com/politicalradar/2006/12/richardson_to_d.html.

[1004] ABC News. Richardson to Dem Majority: Listen to the Guvs. Dec. 6, 2006 and retrieved 12.14.06 from http://blogs.abcnews.com/politicalradar/2006/12/richardson_to_d.html.

[1005] John F. Harris.'04 Voting: Realignment—Or a Tilt? Washington Post. Published November 28, 2004 on page A01, and retrieved September 21, 2005 from http://www.washingtonpost.com/ac2/wp-dyn/A16756-2004Nov27?language=printer.

[1006] Richard Satran. Reuters. Richardson urges Democrats not to ignore Hispanics. Posted November 4, 2005 and retrieved November 10, 2005 from http://abcnews.go.com/Politics/wireStory?id=1283050.

[1007] Richard Satran. Reuters. Richardson urges Democrats not to ignore Hispanics. Posted November 4, 2005 and retrieved November 10, 2005 from http://abcnews.go.com/Politics/wireStory?id=1283050.

[1008] Carl Sullivan. The Right Candidate? Web Exclusive from Newsweek. Posted November 4, 2005 and retrieved November 10, 2005 from http://msnbc.msn.com/id/9929185/site/newseek/.
[1009] Carl Sullivan. The Right Candidate? Web Exclusive from Newsweek. Posted November 4, 2005 and retrieved November 10, 2005 from http://msnbc.msn.com/id/9929185/site/newseek/.
[1010] NBC News. Meet the Press. MTP Transcript for Dec.31. MSNBC.com. Retrieved 1.13.07 from http://www.msnbc.msn.com/id/16311173/print/1/displaymode/1098/.
[1011] Michael Riley. Richardson's political shape turning Oval. Denver Post. Posted April 16, 2006 and retrieved June 30, 2006 from http://www.denverpost.com/portlet/article/html/fragments/print_article.jsp?article=3715416
[1012] WGA Policy Resolution 04-13. "Western States Presidential Caucus/Primary." June 22, 2004 in Sante Fe New Mexico. Retrieved December 14, 2005 from http://www.westgov.org/wga/policy/04/caucus.pdf, and http://www.gwu.edu/~action/2008/wgares062204.html.
[1013] Kate Nash. National Guard Help Proposed. The Albuquerque Journal Posted January 5, 2005 and retrieved January 10, 2005 from http://www.abjjournal.com/paperboy/ia/news/state/283179nm01-05-05.htm?rrc.
[1014] NBC News: Meet The Press. Transcript for Jan. 9. Posted January 9, 2005 and retrieved May 10, 2005 from http://www.msnbc.msn.com/id/6805000/.
[1015] Leonard David. Virgin Galactic Partners With New Mexico On Spaceport. Posted 12.14.05 and retrieved 6.30.06 from http://www.space.com/news/051214_spaceport_newmexico.html.
[1016] David Miles of The New Mexican. Going long to land an NFL team. Posted 3.16.06 and retrieved 6.30.06 from http://www.freenewmexican.com/news/40861.html.
[1017] Campaign Finance. At a Glance: Second Quarter 2007 Fundraising Summary. Retrieved 8.1.07 from http://projects.washingtonpost.com/2008-presidential-candidates/finance/2007q2/comparis...
[1018] The Line: Debate Provides '08 Wake-up Call. Posted 7.27.07 and retrieved 8.1.07 from http://blog.washingtonpost.com/thefix/2007/07/friday_presidential_line_1.html.
[1019] Exclusive Poll Shows Candidate Standings Shuffle. Posted 7.26.07 and retrieved 8.1.07 from http://www.kcci.com/politics/13763159/detail.html.
[1020] Judie Jacobson. Jewish Ledger. Published 7.31.07 and retrieved 8.1.07 from http://www.jewishledger.com/articles/2007/07/31/enws/news04.txt.
[1021] Lynn Campbell. Vilsack known as serious, intense, studious, stubborn. Des Moines Register. 11.9.06 and retrieved 11.17.06 from http://desmoinesregister.com/apps/pbcs.dll/article?AID=20061109/NEWS09/61109041&template=print
[1022] Lynn Campbell. Vilsack known as serious, intense, studious, stubborn. Des Moines Register. 11.9.06 and retrieved 11.17.06 from http://desmoinesregister.com/apps/pbcs.dll/article?AID=20061109/NEWS09/61109041&template=print.
[1023] AP. Vilsack officially seeks 2008 nomination. MSNBC.com. 11.30.06 retrieved 12.3.06 from http://www.msnbc.msn.com/id/15969341/print/1/displaymode/1098/.
[1024] Lynn Campbell. Vilsack known as serious, intense, studious, stubborn. Des Moines Register. 11.9.06 and retrieved 11.17.06 from http://desmoinesregister.com/apps/pbcs.dll/article?AID=20061109/NEWS09/61109041&template=print.
[1025] Lynn Campbell. Vilsack known as serious, intense, studious, stubborn. Des Moines Register. 11.9.06 and retrieved 11.17.06 from http://desmoinesregister.com/apps/pbcs.dll/article?AID=20061109/NEWS09/61109041&template=print.
[1026] AP. Vilsack officially seeks 2008 nomination. MSNBC.com. Nov.30, 2006. Retrieved 12.3.06 from http://www.msnbc.msn.com/id/15969341/print/1/displaymode/1098/.
[1027] Thomas Beaumont. Vilsack to make White House run. Des Moines Register. . Published 11.9.06 and retrieved 11.17.06 from http://desomoinesregister.com/apps/pbcs.dll/article?AID=/20061109/NEWS09/611090409&lead=1&template.
[1028] Richard E. Cohen and Michael Barone. The Almanac of American Politics—2004. The National Journal Group. 2003, page 624.
[1029] Richard E. Cohen and Michael Barone. The Almanac of American Politics—2004. The National Journal Group. 2003, page 624.
[1030] Thomas Beaumont. Vilsack raises centrist profile. The Des Moines Register. Published December 5, 2004 and retrieved October 5, 2005 from http://desmoinesregister.com/apps/pbcs.dll/article?AID=/20041205/NEWS10/412050335/1001. good web
[1031] Thomas Beaumont. Vilsack raises centrist profile. The Des Moines Register. Published December 5, 2004 and retrieved October 5, 2005 from http://desmoinesregister.com/apps/pbcs.dll/article?AID=/20041205/NEWS10/412050335/1001
[1032] From the DLC. Retrieved August 25, 2007 at http://www.ndol.org/ndol_ci.cfm?kaid=85&subid=108&contentid=253426.
[1033] David Yepsen. Yes, governor-er, Mr. President. The Des Moines Register. Posted April 6, 2003 and retrieved December 15, 2004 from http://www.desmoinesregister.com/opinion/stories/c5917686/20901167.html.
[1034] David Yepsen. Yes, governor-er, Mr. President. The Des Moines Register. Posted April 6, 2003 and retrieved December 15, 2004 from http://www.desmoinesregister.com/opinion/stories/c5917686/20901167.html.
[1035] AP. Vilsack not odds-on favorite to be 2008 presidential nominee. WCFCourier.com. Posted June 13, 2005 and retrieved July 8, 2005 from http://www.wcfcourier.com/articles/2005/06/13/news/breaking_news/doc42ad5ac1cf5c9476150690.txt.
[1036] Kate Zernike. Iowa Governor Will Give Felons the Right to Vote. The New York Times. Published June 18, 2005 and retrieved June 24, 2005 from http://www.nytimes.com/2005/06/18/national/18iowa.html.
[1037] Kate Zernike. Iowa Governor Will Give Felons the Right to Vote. The New York Times. Published June 18, 2005 and retrieved June 24, 2005 from http://www.nytimes.com/2005/06/18/national/18iowa.html.

[1038] David Yepsen. Yepsen: Why restore voting rights to felons? To win elections The Des Moines Register. Posted June 21, 2005 and retrieved June 24, 2005 from http://desmoinesregister.com/apps/pbcs.dll/article?AID=/20050621/OPINION01/506210345/1035.

[1039] Thomas Beaumont. Vilsack to make White House run. Des Moines Register. . Published Nov. 9 and retrieved 11.17.06 from http://desomoinesregister.com/apps/pbcs.dll/article?AID=/20061109/NEWS09/611090409&lead=1&template.

[1040] Cnn.com. Democrat Vilsack launches run for White House. Posted 11.9.06 and retrieved 11.17.06 from http://www.cnn.com/2006/POLITICS/11/09/vilsack.president.ap.

[1041] Zachary Goldfarb. Vilsack Faces Hurdles in 2008 Run. Washingtonpost.com. Retrieved 11.10.06, A13. Retrieved 11.17.06 from http://www.washingtonpost.com/wp-dyn/content/article/2006/11/09/AR2006110901861_pf.html.

[1042] Zachary Goldfarb. Vilsack Faces Hurdles in 2008 Run. Washingtonpost.com. Retrieved Nov.10, 2006 A13. Retrieved 11.17.06 from http://www.washingtonpost.com/wp-dyn/content/article/2006/11/09/AR2006110901861_pf.html

[1043] Quoted in Thomas Beaumont. Underdog Vilsack open's '08 campaign. Des Moines Register. Published 11.10.06 and retrieved 11.17.06 from http://desmoinesregister.com/apps/pbcs.dll/article?AID=/20061110/NEWS09/611100389

[1044] Oval Office 2008. Tom Vilsack—how long can a long-shot shoot? Nov. 30 and retrieved 12.14.06 from http://www.ovaloffice.com/.

[1045] Comedy Central's The Colbert Report.

[1046] Comedy Central's The Colbert Report.

[1047] Dec. 11, 2006. Nightly News.

[1048] Thomas Beaumont. Vilsack gives duck to TV host. Thomas Beaumont. Published 11.19.06 and retrieved 12.22.06 from http://www.desmoinesregister.com/apps/pbcs.dll/article?AID=/20061219/NEWS09/612190384.

[1049] Thomas Beaumont. Vilsack gives duck to TV host. Thomas Beaumont. Published 11.19.06 and retrieved 12.22.06 from http://www.desmoinesregister.com/apps/pbcs.dll/article?AID=/20061219/NEWS09/612190384.

[1050] TPM Café. Eric Kleefeld. Breaking: Vilsack Can be Funny! Really! http://auctionhouse.tpmcafe.com/blog/electioncentral/2006/dec/19/vilsack_shows_some_wit_on_i_the_daily_show_i

[1051] Thomas Beaumont. Vilsack gives duck to TV host. Thomas Beaumont. Published December 19,2006 and retrieved 12.22.06 from http://www.desmoinesregister.com/apps/pbcs.dll/article?AID=/20061219/NEWS09/612190384.

[1052] Thomas Beaumont. Vilsack gives duck to TV host. Thomas Beaumont. Published December 19,2006 and retrieved 12.22.06 from http://www.desmoinesregister.com/apps/pbcs.dll/article?AID=/20061219/NEWS09/612190384.

[1053] Thomas Beaumont. Underdog Vilsack open's ''08 campaign. Des Moines Register. Published 11.10.06 and retrieved 11.17.06 from http://desmoinesregister.com/apps/pbcs.dll/article?AID=/20061110/NEWS09/611100389

[1054] Thomas Beaumont. Underdog Vilsack open's ''08 campaign. Des Moines Register. Published 11.10.06 and retrieved 11.17.06 from http://desmoinesregister.com/apps/pbcs.dll/article?AID=/20061110/NEWS09/611100389

[1055] Charlotte Ebby. Democratic officials say caucuses will be fair field. 11.29.06. Retrieved 12.14.06 from http://qctimes.net/articles/2006/11/29/news/state/doc456dla4db9906493379775.txt.

[1056] Mike Glover. 12.2.06. AP. Iowa Dems Declare Neutrality in Caucuses. 12.3.06 @ http://abcnews.go.com/Politics/print?id=2695807.

[1057] Mike Glover. 12.2.06. AP. Iowa Dems Declare Neutrality in Caucuses. 12.3.06 @ http://abcnews.go.com/Politics/print?id=2695807.

[1058] Jane Norman. Edwards leads in poll of likely caucus goers. Des Moines Register. Published and retrieved 12.14.06 from http://www.desmoinesregister.com/apps/pbc.dll/article?AID=/20061214/NEWS09/612140397/1056.

[1059] Tim Higgins. Scandals in Iowa unlikely to hurt Vilsack at caucuses. Des Moines Register. Published December 2, 2006 and retrieved 12.3.06 from http://desmoinesregister.com/apps/pbcs.dll/article?AID=/20061202/NEWS10/612020325&template=printart.

[1060] Tim Higgins. Scandals in Iowa unlikely to hurt Vilsack at caucuses. Des Moines Register. Published December 2, 2006 and retrieved 12.3.06 from http://desmoinesregister.com/apps/pbcs.dll/article?AID=/20061202/NEWS10/612020325&template=printart

[1061] Thomas Beaumont. Bayh opts against run; Vilsack's benefit small. Des Moines Register. Dec. 17, 2006 and retrieved12.22.06from http://www.desmoinesregister.com/apps/pbcs.dll/article?AID=/20061217/NEWS09/612170335.

[1062] Jonathan Roos. Iowa: Poll. Giuliani, McCain stand out in mock matchups. Published Sept. 24, 2006 and retrieved next day @ http://desmoinesregister.com/apps/pbcs/dll/article?AID=/20060924/NEWS09/609240335/1056. see Edwards/Iowa success in midterms.

[1063] Craig Gilbert. Democratic candidates vow to end war.. Milwaukee Journal Sentinel, Feb.4, 2007, 1A.

[1064] Craig Gilbert. Democratic candidates vow to end war.. Milwaukee Journal Sentinel, Feb.4, 2007, 1A.

[1065] Adam Nagourney. War handicaps Senators in '08 White House Race. Published June 2, 2006 and retrieved June 30, 2006 from Common Dreams (published in NY Times). @ http://www.commondreams.org/cgi-bin/print.cgi?file=/headlines06/0602-02.htm.

[1066] Adam Nagourney. War handicaps Senators in '08 White House Race. Published June 2, 2006 and retrieved June 30, 2006 from Common Dreams (published in NY Times). @ http://www.commondreams.org/cgi-bin/print.cgi?file=/headlines06/0602-02.htm.

[1067] Daniel Barrick. Iowa's Governor drops in. Concord Monitor. Posted June 15, 2006 and retrieved July 14, 2006 from http://www.concordmoniter.com/apps/pbcs.dll/article?AID=/20060615/REPOSITORY/606150326.

[1068] Vilsack doesn't see message in Lieberman loss. WHOtv.com Des Moines. Retrieved September 6, 2006 from http://www.whotv.com/global/story.asp?s=5263173&ClientType=Printable,

[1069] Vilsack on FOX News Sunday. December 2006

[1070] O'Donnell, Hannity baselessly report that Bush called for 'timetable. Posted Jan11 and retrieved 1.13.07 from http://mediamatters.org/items/200701110011.
[1071] O'Donnell, Hannity baselessly report that Bush called for 'timetable. Posted Jan11 and retrieved 1.13.07 from http://mediamatters.org/items/200701110011.
[1072] Vilsack on Hannity & Colmes. Jan.11.2007 and retrieved Jan.12, 2007 from http://www.whotv.com/Global/story.asp?S=5924959.
[1073] Des Moines Register. Jan. 21, 2007. Where they stand on Iraq. Retrieved 2.8.07 from http://www.desmoinesregister.com/apps/pbcs.dll/article?AID=/20070121/NEWS09/701210348/1056/NEWS09.
[1074] Jane Norman. Vilsack calls for immediate end to Iraq war financing. Feb. 4, 2007, retrieved 2.8.07 @ http://desmoinesregister.com/apps/pbcs.dll/article?AID=20070204/NEWS09/70204340&template=printart.
[1075] Jane Norman. Vilsack calls for immediate end to Iraq war financing. Feb. 4, 2007, retrieved 2.8.07 @ http://desmoinesregister.com/apps/pbcs.dll/article?AID=20070204/NEWS09/70204340&template=printart
[1076] Jane Norman. Get troops out Vilsack says on CNN. Des Moines Register. Published Feb.5 and retrieved 2.8.08 from http://desmoinesregister.com/apps/pbcs.dll/article?AID=/20070205/NEWS/702050324&template=printart.
[1077] Jane Norman. Get troops out Vilsack says on CNN. Des Moines Register. Published Feb.5 and retrieved 2.8.08 from http://desmoinesregister.com/apps/pbcs.dll/article?AID=/20070205/NEWS/702050324&template=printart.
[1078] Jane Norman. Get troops out Vilsack says on CNN. Des Moines Register. Published Feb.5 and retrieved 2.8.08 from http://desmoinesregister.com/apps/pbcs.dll/article?AID=/20070205/NEWS/702050324&template=printart.
[1079] CNN.com. Late Edition aired 2.4.07. Retrieved 3.8.07 from http://transcipts.cnn.com/TRANSCRIPTS/0702/04/le.01.html. 9/20
[1080] Jane Norman. Get troops out Vilsack says on CNN. Des Moines Register. Published Feb.5 and retrieved 2.8.08 from http://desmoinesregister.com/apps/pbcs.dll/article?AID=/20070205/NEWS/702050324&template=printart.
[1081] Jane Norman. Get troops out Vilsack says on CNN. Des Moines Register. Published Feb.5 and retrieved 2.8.08 from http://desmoinesregister.com/apps/pbcs.dll/article?AID=/20070205/NEWS/702050324&template=printart.
[1082] Jane Norman. Get troops out Vilsack says on CNN. Des Moines Register. Published Feb.5 and retrieved 2.8.08 from http://desmoinesregister.com/apps/pbcs.dll/article?AID=/20070205/NEWS/702050324&template=printart.
[1083] Jane Norman. Get troops out Vilsack says on CNN. Des Moines Register. Published Feb.5 and retrieved 2.8.08 from http://desmoinesregister.com/apps/pbcs.dll/article?AID=/20070205/NEWS/702050324&template=printart.
[1084] Hardball with Chris Matthews' for March 26. MSNBC.com. Retrieved 3.28.07 from http://www.msnbc.msn.com/id/17814560/print/1/displaymode/1098/. 19/23.
[1085] Hardball with Chris Matthews' for March 26. MSNBC.com. Retrieved 3.28.07 from http://www.msnbc.msn.com/id/17814560/print/1/displaymode/1098/. 20/23.
[1086] Hardball with Chris Matthews' for Feb. 23. MSNBC.com. Retrieved 3.8.07 from http://www.msnbc.msn.com/id/17349457/print/1/displaymode/1098/. 12/15
[1087] Hardball with Chris Matthews' for March 26. MSNBC.com. Retrieved 3.28.07 from http://www.msnbc.msn.com/id/17814560/print/1/displaymode/1098/. 21/23.
[1088] ABC news. Funnies: Vilsack Shaves His Head. 2.25.07 and retrieved 3.8.07 from http://abcnews.go.com/ThisWeek/print?id=2921307.
[1089] Richard E. Cohen and Michael Barone. "The Almanac of American Politics—2004." The National Journal Group. 2003.
[1090] Richard E. Cohen and Michael Barone. "The Almanac of American Politics—2004." The National Journal Group. 2003.
[1091] Paul Starobin. "The Man With the Golden Phone." The Atlantic Monthly. Page 42. May 2006.
[1092] Paul Starobin. "The Man With the Golden Phone." The Atlantic Monthly. Page 42. May 2006.
[1093] Paul Starobin. "The Man With the Golden Phone." The Atlantic Monthly. Page 42. May 2006.
[1094] Paul Starobin. "The Man With the Golden Phone." The Atlantic Monthly. Page 42. May 2006.
[1095] Richard E. Cohen and Michael Barone. "The Almanac of American Politics—2004." The National Journal Group. 2003.
[1096] Style Weekly in Richmond, Virginia. Chasing Bubba. By Scott Bass. Published October 12, 2005 and retrieved 10/25/05 from http://www.styleweekly.com/article.asp?idarticle=11175
[1097] Richard E. Cohen and Michael Barone. "The Almanac of American Politics—2004." The National Journal Group. 2003.
[1098] Style Weekly in Richmond, Virginia. Chasing Bubba. By Scott Bass. Published October 12, 2005 and retrieved 10/25/05 from http://www.styleweekly.com/article.asp?idarticle=11175
[1099] Style Weekly in Richmond, Virginia. Chasing Bubba. By Scott Bass. Published October 12, 2005 and retrieved 10/25/05 from http://www.styleweekly.com/article.asp?idarticle=11175
[1100] Richard E. Cohen and Michael Barone. "The Almanac of American Politics—2004." The National Journal Group. 2003
[1101] Style Weekly in Richmond, Virginia. Chasing Bubba. By Scott Bass. Published October 12, 2005 and retrieved 10/25/05 from http://www.styleweekly.com/article.asp?idarticle=11175
[1102] Style Weekly in Richmond, Virginia. Chasing Bubba. By Scott Bass. Published October 12, 2005 and retrieved 10/25/05 from http://www.styleweekly.com/article.asp?idarticle=11175.
[1103] Paul Starobin. "The Man With the Golden Phone." The Atlantic Monthly. Page 44. May 2006.
[1104] Style Weekly in Richmond, Virginia. Chasing Bubba. By Scott Bass. Published October 12, 2005 and retrieved 10/25/05 from http://www.styleweekly.com/article.asp?idarticle=11175

[1105] Style Weekly in Richmond, Virginia. Chasing Bubba. By Scott Bass. Published October 12, 2005 and retrieved 10/25/05 from http://www.styleweekly.com/article.asp?idarticle=11175
[1106] Style Weekly in Richmond, Virginia. Chasing Bubba. By Scott Bass. Published October 12, 2005 and retrieved 10/25/05 from http://www.styleweekly.com/article.asp?idarticle=11175
[1107] Michael D. Shear. Speculation Grows On Presidential Bid for Warner in 2008. Washington Post. Published November 14, 2004, C01 and retrieved December 14, 2004 from http://www.washingtonpost.com/ac2/wp-dyn/A48211-2004Nov13?lanuguage=printer.
[1108] Michael D. Shear. Speculation Grows On Presidential Bid for Warner in 2008. Washington Post. Published November 14, 2004, C01 and retrieved December 14, 2004 from http://www.washingtonpost.com/ac2/wp-dyn/A48211-2004Nov13?lanuguage=printer
[1109] Michael D. Shear. Speculation Grows On Presidential Bid for Warner in 2008. Washington Post. Published November 14, 2004, C01 and retrieved December 14, 2004 from http://www.washingtonpost.com/ac2/wp-dyn/A48211-2004Nov13?lanuguage=printer
[1110] Michael D. Shear. Speculation Grows On Presidential Bid for Warner in 2008. Washington Post. Published November 14, 2004, C01 and retrieved December 14, 2004 from http://www.washingtonpost.com/ac2/wp-dyn/A48211-2004Nov13?lanuguage=printer
[1111] Governing. "A- Virginia." February 2005, page 90. Retrieved 10/27/05 from http://results.gpponline.org/StateOVerview.aspx?id=138.
[1112] Governing. "A- Virginia." February 2005, page 90. Retrieved 10/27/05 from http://results.gpponline.org/StateOVerview.aspx?id=138.
[1113] Governing. "A- Virginia." February 2005, page 90. Retrieved 10/27/05 from http://results.gpponline.org/StateOVerview.aspx?id=138.
[1114] Editorials. "Warner and Pals." The Roanoke Times. Posted April 8, 2005 and retrieved April 14, 2005 from http://www.roanoke.com/editorials\21505.html.
[1115] Michael D. Shear. "Warner's Prospects Keep Va. Guessing." Washingtonpost.com. Published January 9, 2005 and retrieved October 1, 2005 from http://www.washingtonpost.com/ac2/wp-dyn/A59350-2005Jan8?language=printer.
[1116] Michael D. Shear. "Warner's Prospects Keep Va. Guessing." Washingtonpost.com. Published January 9, 2005 and retrieved October 1, 2005 from http://www.washingtonpost.com/ac2/wp-dyn/A59350-2005Jan8?language=printer
[1117] Michael D. Shear. "Warner's Prospects Keep Va. Guessing." Washingtonpost.com. Published January 9, 2005 and retrieved October 1, 2005 from http://www.washingtonpost.com/ac2/wp-dyn/A59350-2005Jan8?language=printer
[1118] Amanda Ripley and Karen Tumulty. America's 5 Best Governors. Time.com. Posted November 13, 2005 and retrieved November 17, 2005 from http://www.time.com/time/magazine/printout/0,8816,1129494,00.html.
[1119] Interview Transcripts. Newt discusses new terror attacks and rioting on Hannity & Colmes. November 9, 2005 and retrieved November 22, 2005 from http://www.newt.org/index.php?src=news&prid=1283&category=Interview%20Transcripts
[1120] Mark Leibovich and Michael D. Shear. Warner Visits N.H. Amid Much Speculation. The Washington Post. Published November 19, 2005 and retrieved November 22, 2005 from http://www.washingtonpost.com/wp-dyn/content/article/2005/11/18/AR2005111802660.html.
[1121] ABC 7 News. Warner: Education, Close Ties with Asia Key to Winning 'Race for Future.' Posted and retrieved November 29, 2005 from http://www.wjla.com/news/stories/1105/281464.html.
[1122] CBS News. Face the Nation-November 13, 2005. Transcript courtesy of Burrelle's information services. Retrieved November 15, 2005 from http://www.cbsnews.com/htdocs/pdf/face_111305.pdf.
[1123] CBS News. Face the Nation-November 13, 2005. Transcript courtesy of Burrelle's information services. Retrieved November 15, 2005 from http://www.cbsnews.com/htdocs/pdf/face_111305.pdf.
[1124] CBS News. Face the Nation-November 13, 2005. Transcript courtesy of Burrelle's information services. Retrieved November 15, 2005 from http://www.cbsnews.com/htdocs/pdf/face_111305.pdf.
[1125] CBS News. Face the Nation-November 13, 2005. Transcript courtesy of Burrelle's information services. Retrieved November 15, 2005 from http://www.cbsnews.com/htdocs/pdf/face_111305.pdf
[1126] Kurt Badenhausen. Virginia: The Best State for Business. Posted August 16, 2006 and retrieved Sept.6, 2006 from http://www.forbes.com/business/2006/08/15/virginia-business-climate_cz_kb_0815virginia.html.
[1127] Kurt Badenhausen. Virginia: The Best State for Business. Posted August 16, 2006 and retrieved Sept.6, 2006 from http://www.forbes.com/business/2006/08/15/virginia-business-climate_cz_kb_0815virginia.html
[1128] Kurt Badenhausen. Virginia: The Best State for Business. Posted August 16, 2006 and retrieved Sept.6, 2006 from http://www.forbes.com/business/2006/08/15/virginia-business-climate_cz_kb_0815virginia.html
[1129] Thomas Beaumont. Warner: Fundraising shows appeal. Des Moines Register.com Published July 12 and retrieved July 14, 2006 from http://www.desmoinesregister.com/apps/pbcs.dll/article?AID=/20060712/NEWS09/607120371
[1130] Thomas Beaumont. Traveling Iowa, Edwards rakes moderate Democrats. July 8, 2006 and retrieved August 11, 2006 from http://desmoinesregister.com/apps/pbcs.dll/article?AID=/20060708/NEWS09/607080342/1001/NEWS. good web.
[1131] Thomas Beaumont. Warner: Fundraising shows appeal. Des Moines Register.com Published July 12 and retrieved July 14, 2006 from http://www.desmoinesregister.com/apps/pbcs.dll/article?AID=/20060712/NEWS09/607120371
[1132] Chris Cillizza. Evan Bayh's Pitch Down the Middle. The Fix. Washington Post. Posted July 18 and retrieved July 28, 2006 from http://blog.washingtonpost.com/thefix/2006/07/evan_bayh_pitch_down_the_midd.html.
[1133] Chris Cillizza. Evan Bayh's Pitch Down the Middle. The Fix. Washington Post. Posted July 18 and retrieved July 28, 2006 from http://blog.washingtonpost.com/thefix/2006/07/evan_bayh_pitch_down_the_midd.html

[1134] Michael W. Lenz. Biden visit backs Hassan's run. Exeter News. Posted July 7, 2006 and retrieved http://www.seacoastonline.com/news/exeter/07072006/nhnews-e-ex-biden0707.html.
[1135] Craig Gilbert, Katherine M. Skiba, and Daniel W. Reilly. Feingold divides Democrats, pollster says. The Milwaukee Journal Sentinel, March 31, 2006, 4A.
[1136] Craig Gilbert. Feingold, Warner: A study in Democratic contrasts. The Milwaukee Journal Sentinel. Posted and retrieved April 24, 2006 from http://www.macon.com/mld/macon/news/nation/14416028.htm.
[1137] Craig Gilbert. Feingold, Warner: A study in Democratic contrasts. The Milwaukee Journal Sentinel. Posted and retrieved April 24, 2006 from http://www.macon.com/mld/macon/news/nation/14416028.htm
[1138] Craig Gilbert. Feingold, Warner: A study in Democratic contrasts. The Milwaukee Journal Sentinel. Posted and retrieved April 24, 2006 from http://www.macon.com/mld/macon/news/nation/14416028.htm
[1139] Craig Gilbert. Feingold, Warner: A study in Democratic contrasts. The Milwaukee Journal Sentinel. Posted and retrieved April 24, 2006 from http://www.macon.com/mld/macon/news/nation/14416028.htm
[1140] Charlie Cook. Circling the White House. Washington Post. Published May 7, 2006, B05, and retrieved May 8, 2006 from http://www.washingtonpost.com/wp-dyn/content/article/2006/05/05/AR2006050501720.html.
[1141] Howard Fineman. Test Marketing Hillary. MSNBC.com Posted May 3, 2006 and retrieved May 8, 2006 from http://www.msnbc.msn.com/id/12613279/site/newsweek/print/1/displaymode/1098/.
[1142] Howard Fineman. Test Marketing Hillary. MSNBC.com Posted May 3, 2006 and retrieved May 8, 2006 from http://www.msnbc.msn.com/id/12613279/site/newsweek/print/1/displaymode/1098/.
[1143] Michael D. Shear. Warner Won't Make 2008 Run For President. Washington Post Oct. 13, 2001, A01. Retrieved Oct.13, 2006 from http://www.washingtonpost.com/wp-dyn/content/article/2006/10/12/AR2006101200510_pf.html.
[1144] Michael D. Shear. Warner Won't Make 2008 Run For President. Washington Post Oct. 13, 2001, A01. Retrieved Oct.13, 2006 from http://www.washingtonpost.com/wp-dyn/content/article/2006/10/12/AR2006101200510_pf.html.
[1145] Michael D. Shear. Warner Won't Make 2008 Run For President. Washington Post Oct. 13, 2001, A01. Retrieved Oct.13, 2006 from http://www.washingtonpost.com/wp-dyn/content/article/2006/10/12/AR2006101200510_pf.html.
[1146] Michael D. Shear. Warner Won't Make 2008 Run For President. Washington Post Oct. 13, 2001, A01. Retrieved Oct.13, 2006 from http://www.washingtonpost.com/wp-dyn/content/article/2006/10/12/AR2006101200510_pf.html.
[1147] Michael D. Shear. Warner Won't Make 2008 Run For President. Washington Post Oct. 13, 2001, A01. Retrieved Oct.13, 2006 from http://www.washingtonpost.com/wp-dyn/content/article/2006/10/12/AR2006101200510_pf.html.
[1148] Libby Copeland. For Warner's Supporters It's a No-Win Situation. Wash. Post. Oct. 13, 2006 retrieved same day from http://www.washingtonpost.com/wp-dyn/content/article/2006/10/12/AR2006101201968_pf.html.
[1149] Libby Copeland. For Warner's Supporters It's a No-Win Situation. Wash. Post. Oct. 13, 2006 retrieved same day from http://www.washingtonpost.com/wp-dyn/content/article/2006/10/12/AR2006101201968_pf.html.
[1150] Bob Gibson. Daily Progress. Warner's Decision. Oct. 13, 2006 and retrieved same day from http://www.dailyprogress.com/servlet/Satellite?pagename=CDP%2FMGArticle%2FCDP_BasicArticle....
[1151] Elana Schor. Warner drops out of '08 race. The Hill. Posted October 11, and retrieved October 13, 2006 from http://www.thehill.com/thehill/export/TheHill/News/Frontpage/101106/warner.html.
[1152] Michael D. Shear. Warner Won't Make 2008 Run For President. Washington Post Oct. 13, 2001, A01. Retrieved Oct.13, 2006 from http://www.washingtonpost.com/wp-dyn/content/article/2006/10/12/AR2006101200510_pf.html.
[1153] Bob Lewis. AP. Warner Decides Not to Run for President. Oct. 12, retrieved Oct. 13, 2006 from http://www.washingtonpost.com/wp-dyn/content/article/2006/10/12/AR2006101200529.html.
[1154] James Carney. Why did Mark Warner Quit? Oct. 12. 2006 and retrieved Oct. 13, 2006 from http://www.time.com/time/nation/article/0,8599,1545871,00.html.
[1155] Warner says no. Richmond Times Dispatch. Oct.13 and retrieved Oct.31.06 from http://timesdipatch.com/servlet/Satellite?pagename=RTD%2FMGArticle%2FRTD_BasicArti...
[1156] Statement of Governor Mark Warner. Oct. 12, 2006. Published Oct. 12, 2006. and Retrieved October 13, 2006 from http://www.nytimes.com/2006/10/12/us/politics/12text-warner.html.
[1157] Adrienne Washington. Virginia misses chance for White House duel. Washington Times. Published/Retrieved Oct. 13, 2006 from http://washingtontimes.com/functions/print.php?StoryID=20061012-105325-8147r.
[1158] Adrienne Washington. Virginia misses chance for White House duel. Washington Times. Published/Retrieved Oct. 13, 2006 from http://washingtontimes.com/functions/print.php?StoryID=20061012-105325-8147r
[1159] Elana Schor. Warner drops out of '08 race. The Hill. Posted October 11, and retrieved October 13, 2006 from http://www.thehill.com/thehill/export/TheHill/News/Frontpage/101106/warner.html.
[1160] Libby Copeland. For Warner's Supporters It's a No-Win Situation. Wash. Post. Oct. 13, 2006 retrieved same day from http://www.washingtonpost.com/wp-dyn/content/article/2006/10/12/AR2006101201968_pf.html
[1161] Libby Copeland. For Warner's Supporters It's a No-Win Situation. Wash. Post. Oct. 13, 2006 retrieved same day from http://www.washingtonpost.com/wp-dyn/content/article/2006/10/12/AR2006101201968_pf.html.
[1162] Tim Higgins and Thomas Beaumont. Ex-Virginia governor drops presidential bid. Posted and retrieved Oct. 13, 2006 from http://desmoinesregister.com/apps/pbcs.dll/article?AID=20061013/NEWS09/610130366/1001/NEWS.
[1163] Statement of Governor Mark Warner. Oct. 12, 2006. Published Oct. 12, 2006. and Retrieved October 13, 2006 from http://www.nytimes.com/2006/10/12/us/politics/12text-warner.html.
[1164] Libby Copeland. For Warner's Supporters It's a No-Win Situation. Wash. Post. Oct. 13, 2006 retrieved same day from http://www.washingtonpost.com/wp-dyn/content/article/2006/10/12/AR2006101201968_pf.html.
[1165] Michael D. Shear. Warner Won't Make 2008 Run for President. Oct. 13, 2006 and retrieved Oct. 3 from http://www.washingtonpost.com/wp-dyn/content/article/2006/10/12/AR2006101200510.html.

[1166] Bob Lewis. AP. Warner Decides Not to Run for President. Oct. 12, retrieved Oct. 13, 2006 from http://www.washingtonpost.com/wp-dyn/content/article/2006/10/12/AR2006101200529.html.
[1167] John Dickerson. The Book of Mark. Posted Oct. 12, and retrieved Oct. 13, 2006 from http://www.slate.com/id/2151423/.
[1168] James Carney. Why did Mark Warner Quit? Oct. 12. 2006 and retrieved Oct. 13, 2006 from http://www.time.com/time/nation/article/0,8599,1545871,00.html.
[1169] With Warner Out, Will Gore Run. Taegan Goddard's Political Wire. Oct.23, 2006, 10.31.2006 and retrieved 10.31.2006 from http://politicalwire.com/archives/2008_campaign/.
[1170] Michael D. Shear. Warner Won't Make 2008 Run for President. Oct. 13, 2006 and retrieved Oct. 3 from http://www.washingtonpost.com/wp-dyn/content/article/2006/10/12/AR2006/10/12/AR2006101200510.html.
[1171] Bob Lewis. AP. Warner Decides Not to Run for President. Oct. 12, retrieved Oct. 13, 2006 from http://www.washingtonpost.com/wp-dyn/content/article/2006/10/12/AR2006101200529.html.
[1172] Statement of Governor Mark Warner. Oct. 12, 2006. Published Oct. 12, 2006. and Retrieved October 13, 2006 from http://www.nytimes.com/2006/10/12/us/politics/12text-warner.html.
[1173] Bob Lewis. AP. Warner Decides Not to Run for President. Oct. 12, retrieved Oct. 13, 2006 from http://www.washingtonpost.com/wp-dyn/content/article/2006/10/12/AR2006101200529.html.
[1174] Statement of Governor Mark Warner. Oct. 12, 2006. Published Oct. 12, 2006. and Retrieved October 13, 2006 from http://www.nytimes.com/2006/10/12/us/politics/12text-warner.html.
[1175] Chris Cillizza. Warner's Out: Winners and Losers. Posted 10.12.06 and retrieved 10.13.06 from http://blog.washingtonpost.com/thefix/.
[1176] Tim Higgins and Thomas Beaumont. Ex-Virginia governor drops presidential bid. Posted and retrieved Oct. 13, 2006 from http://desmoinesregister.com/apps/pbcs.dll/article?AID=20061013/NEWS09/610130366/1001/NEWS.
[1177] Jonathan E. Kaplan. Eyeing '08, Warner woos his party with $860,500. The Hill . Posted 7.12.06 and retrieved July 14, 2006 from http://www.thehill.com/thehill/export/TheHill/News/Frontpage/071206/news3.html.
[1178] Jonathan E. Kaplan. Eyeing '08, Warner woos his party with $860,500. The Hill . Posted 7.12.06 and retrieved July 14, 2006 from http://www.thehill.com/thehill/export/TheHill/News/Frontpage/071206/news3.html
[1179] Jonathan E. Kaplan. Eyeing '08, Warner woos his party with $860,500. The Hill . Posted 7.12.06 and retrieved July 14, 2006 from http://www.thehill.com/thehill/export/TheHill/News/Frontpage/071206/news3.html
[1180] Thomas Beaumont. Warner: Fundraising shows appeal. Des Moines Register.com Published July 12 and retrieved July 14, 2006 from http://www.desmoinesregister.com/apps/pbcs.dll/article?AID=/20060712/NEWS09/607120371.
[1181] Jonathan E. Kaplan. Eyeing '08, Warner woos his party with $860,500. The Hill . Posted 7.12.06 and retrieved July 14, 2006 from http://www.thehill.com/thehill/export/TheHill/News/Frontpage/071206/news3.html
[1182] Thomas Beaumont. Warner: Fundraising shows appeal. Des Moines Register.com Published July 12 and retrieved July 14, 2006 from http://www.desmoinesregister.com/apps/pbcs.dll/article?AID=/20060712/NEWS09/607120371.
[1183] Elana Schor. Warner drops out of '08 race. The Hill. Posted October 11, and retrieved October 13, 2006 from http://www.thehill.com/thehill/export/TheHill/News/Frontpage/101106/warner.html.
[1184] Statement of Governor Mark Warner. Oct. 12, 2006. Published Oct. 12, 2006. and Retrieved October 13, 2006 from http://www.nytimes.com/2006/10/12/us/politics/12text-warner.html.
[1185] Statement of Governor Mark Warner. Oct. 12, 2006. Published Oct. 12, 2006. and Retrieved October 13, 2006 from http://www.nytimes.com/2006/10/12/us/politics/12text-warner.html.
[1186] Chris Cillizza. Warner's Out: Winners and Losers. Posted 10.12.06 and retrieved 10.13.06 from http://blog.washingtonpost.com/thefix/.
[1187] Sylvia Smith. Washington editor. Ex-Va. Gov. Warner won't seek Democratic presidential nomination. Oct. 12, 2006 and retrieved Oct. 13, 2006 from http://www.fortwayne.com/mld/journalgazette/news/nation/15742274.htm.
[1188] Sylvia Smith. Washington editor. Ex-Va. Gov. Warner won't seek Democratic presidential nomination. Oct. 12, 2006 and retrieved Oct. 13, 2006 from http://www.fortwayne.com/mld/journalgazette/news/nation/15742274.htm.
[1189] Sylvia Smith. Washington editor. Ex-Va. Gov. Warner won't seek Democratic presidential nomination. Oct. 12, 2006 and retrieved Oct. 13, 2006 from http://www.fortwayne.com/mld/journalgazette/news/nation/15742274.htm.
[1190] Chris Cillizza. Warner's Out: Winners and Losers. Posted 10.12.06 and retrieved 10.13.06 from http://blog.washingtonpost.com/thefix/.
[1191] John Dickerson. The Book of Mark. Posted Oct. 12, and retrieved Oct. 13, 2006 from http://www.slate.com/id/2151423/.
[1192] Chris Cillizza. Warner's Out: Winners and Losers. Posted 10.12.06 and retrieved 10.13.06 from http://blog.washingtonpost.com/thefix/.
[1193] John Dickerson. The Book of Mark. Posted Oct. 12, and retrieved Oct. 13, 2006 from http://www.slate.com/id/2151423/.
[1194] Tim Higgins and Thomas Beaumont. Ex-Virginia governor drops presidential bid. Posted and retrieved Oct. 13, 2006 from http://desmoinesregister.com/apps/pbcs.dll/article?AID=20061013/NEWS09/610130366/1001/NEWS.
[1195] Tim Higgins and Thomas Beaumont. Ex-Virginia governor drops presidential bid. Posted and retrieved Oct. 13, 2006 from http://desmoinesregister.com/apps/pbcs.dll/article?AID=20061013/NEWS09/610130366/1001/NEWS.
[1196] With Warner Out, Will Gore Run. Taegan Goddard's Political Wire. Oct.23, 2006, 10.31.2006 and retrieved 10.31.2006 from http://politicalwire.com/archives/2008_campaign/.
[1197] Michael D. Shear. Warner Won't Make 2008 Run For President. Washington Post Oct. 13, 2001, A01. Retrieved Oct.13, 2006 from http://www.washingtonpost.com/wp-dyn/content/article/2006/10/12/AR2006101200510_pf.html.

Endnotes for Part II

[1198] The Examiner. Meet the Next President: George Allen stays the course. Bill Sammon. Posted Sept. 19.2006 and retrieved 10.13.2006 from http://www.examiner.com/a-295550~Meet_the_Next_President__George_Allen_stays_the_couse.html.

[1199] The Examiner. Meet the Next President: George Allen stays the course. Bill Sammon. Posted Sept. 19.2006 and retrieved 10.13.2006 from http://www.examiner.com/a-295550~Meet_the_Next_President__George_Allen_stays_the_couse.html.

[1200] Bruce Allen. General Manager. Retrieved 8.1.07 from http://www.buccaneers.com

[1201] The Examiner. Meet the Next President: George Allen stays the course. Bill Sammon. Posted Sept. 19.2006 and retrieved 10.13.2006 from http://www.examiner.com/a-295550~Meet_the_Next_President__George_Allen_stays_the_couse.html.

[1202] The Examiner. Meet the Next President: George Allen stays the course. Bill Sammon. Posted Sept. 19.2006 and retrieved 10.13.2006 from http://www.examiner.com/a-295550~Meet_the_Next_President__George_Allen_stays_the_couse.html.

[1203] The Examiner. Meet the Next President: George Allen stays the course. Bill Sammon. Posted Sept. 19.2006 and retrieved 10.13.2006 from http://www.examiner.com/a-295550~Meet_the_Next_President__George_Allen_stays_the_couse.html.

[1204] The Examiner. Meet the Next President: George Allen stays the course. Bill Sammon. Posted Sept. 19.2006 and retrieved 10.13.2006 from http://www.examiner.com/a-295550~Meet_the_Next_President__George_Allen_stays_the_couse.html.

[1205] Richard E. Cohen and Michael Barone. The Almanac of American Politics—2004. The National Journal Group. 2003, page 1642.

[1206] Richard E. Cohen and Michael Barone. The Almanac of American Politics—2004. The National Journal Group. 2003, page 1642.

[1207] Richard E. Cohen and Michael Barone. The Almanac of American Politics—2004. The National Journal Group. 2003, page 1642.

[1208] Richard E. Cohen and Michael Barone. "The Almanac of American Politics—2004." The National Journal Group. 2003, page 1643.

[1209] Peter S. Canellos. Succeeding Bush: A GOP shortlist. Boston.com/Boston Globe. Posted and retrieved October 4, 2005 from http://www.boston.com/news/nation/articles/2005/10/04/succeeding_bush_a_gop_short_list/.

[1210] Michael Shear. As Allen Listens, the Curious Watch. The Washington Post. Posted Aug. 16, 2005/Retrieved Aug. 19 2005 from http://www.washingtonpost.com/wp-dyn/content/article/2005/08/15/AR2005081501334.html.

[1211] Peter S. Canellos. Succeeding Bush: A GOP shortlist. Boston.com/Boston Globe. Posted and retrieved October 4, 2005 from http://www.boston.com/news/nation/articles/2005/10/04/succeeding_bush_a_gop_short_list/.

[1212] CNN.com. CNN Late Edition with Wolf Blitzer. Aired January 22, 2006, transcript retrieved January 23, 2006 from http://transcripts.cnn.com/TRANSCRIPTS/0601/22/le.01.html.

[1213] USNews.com. White House Week (8/29/05). Retrieved Aug. 26, 2005 from http://www.usnews.com/usnews/news/articles/050829/29whitehouse.htm.

[1214] The Examiner. Meet the Next President: George Allen stays the course. Bill Sammon. Posted Sept. 19.2006 and retrieved 10.13.2006 from http://www.examiner.com/a-295550~Meet_the_Next_President__George_Allen_stays_the_couse.html.

[1215] Richard E. Cohen and Michael Barone. "The Almanac of American Politics—2004." The National Journal Group. 2003, page 1642.

[1216] Richard E. Cohen and Michael Barone. "The Almanac of American Politics—2004." The National Journal Group. 2003, page 1642.

[1217] NH INSIDER. Your Source for NH Politics—Senator George Allen. Posted January 25, 2006 and retrieved February 6, 2006 from http://www.nhinsider.com/senator-george-allen/.

[1218] Fred Barnes. The Virginian. Opinion Journal. April 22, 2006 and retrieved 10.13.2006 from http://www.opinionjournal.com/editorial/feature/html?id=110008274.

[1219] Michael Shear. As Allen Listens, the Curious Watch. The Washington Post. Posted Aug. 16, 2005/Retrieved Aug. 19 2005 from http://www.washingtonpost.com/wp-dyn/content/article/2005/08/15/AR2005081501334.html

[1220] Michael Shear. As Allen Listens, the Curious Watch. The Washington Post. Posted Aug. 16, 2005/Retrieved Aug. 19 2005 from http://www.washingtonpost.com/wp-dyn/content/article/2005/08/15/AR2005081501334.html

[1221] Fred Barnes. The Virginian. Opinion Journal. April 22, 2006 and retrieved 10.13.2006 from http://www.opinionjournal.com/editorial/feature/html?id=110008274.

[1222] Fred Barnes. The Virginian. Opinion Journal. April 22, 2006 and retrieved 10.13.2006 from http://www.opinionjournal.com/editorial/feature/html?id=110008274.

[1223] Glen Yoder. Romney, Kerry make top 5 of presidential poll. The Boston Globe. Posted April 29, 2005 and retrieved May 5, 2005 from http://www.boston.com/news/local/massachusetts/articles/2005/04/29/romney_kerry_make_top_5_of_presidential_poll/.
[1224] Tyler Whitley. "Allen's presidential chances rated high." Richmond-Times Dispatch." Posted April 29, 2005 and retrieved May 5, 2005 from http://www.timesdispatch.com/servlet/Satellite?pagename=RTD%2FMGArticle%2FRTD_BasicArticle&c=MGArticle&cid=1031782425167&path=!news&s=1045855934842.
[1225] NBC News: Meet the Press. Transcript for May 1. Posted and retrieved May 1, 2005 from http://www.msnbc.msn.com/id/7698687/.
[1226] NBC News: Meet the Press. Transcript for May 1. Posted and retrieved May 1, 2005 from http://www.msnbc.msn.com/id/7698687/.
[1227] NBC News: Meet the Press. Transcript for May 1. Posted and retrieved May 1, 2005 from http://www.msnbc.msn.com/id/7698687/.
[1228] NBC News. Transcript for May 8. Meet the Press. Posted May 8, 2005 and retrieved June 7, 2005 from http://www.msnbc.msn.com/id/7761272/.
[1229] Peter Hardin. "GOP groups are being generous to Allen." The Richmond Times-Dispatch. Posted Aug. 7, Retrieved August 26, 2005 from http://www.timesdispatch.com/servlet/Satellite?pagename=RTD%2FMGArticle%2FRTD_BasicArticle&c=MGArticle&cid=1031784292047&path=!news!politics&s=1045855935264.
[1230] MSNBC. Transcript for January 22. NBC NEWS/Meet the Press. Retrieved January 23, 2006 from http://www.msnbc.msn.com/id/10909406/print/1/displaymode/1098/.
[1231] Hannity Calls Allen The '08 Frontrunner. 10.24.05. Retrieved 6.29.07 from http://hotlineblog.nationaljournal.com/archives/2005/10/hannity_calls_a.html.
[1232] Virginia looks to 2008 (George Allen and Mark Warner). Tyler Whitley. Potomac News. January 3, 2005. Retrieved March 31, 2005 from http://www.freerepublic.com/focus/f-news/1313850/posts.
[1233] Virginia looks to 2008 (George Allen and Mark Warner). Tyler Whitley. Potomac News. January 3, 2005. Retrieved March 31, 2005 from http://www.freerepublic.com/focus/f-news/1313850/posts.
[1234] Virginia looks to 2008 (George Allen and Mark Warner). Tyler Whitley. Potomac News. January 3, 2005. Retrieved March 31, 2005 from http://www.freerepublic.com/focus/f-news/1313850/posts.
[1235] Allen to headline events in South Carolina. Richmond Times-Dispatch. 6.29.05 and retrieved 7.22.05 from TimesDispatch.com.
[1236] George Will. First and 10 in New Hampshire. The Washington Post. Posted/retrieved July 8, 2005 from http://www.dfw.com/mld/dfw/news/opinion/12083995.htm.
[1237] George Will. First and 10 in New Hampshire. The Washington Post. Posted/retrieved July 8, 2005 from http://www.dfw.com/mld/dfw/news/opinion/12083995.htm
[1238] Peter Hardin. Allen Bringing faith into view. Richmond Times-Dispatch. Posted April 11, 2005 and retrieved April 14, 2005 from http://www.timesdispatch.com/servlet/Satellite?pagename=RTD/MGArticle/RTD_BasicArticle&c=MGArticle&cid=1031782073782.
[1239] Peter Hardin. Allen Bringing faith into view. Richmond Times-Dispatch. Posted April 11, 2005 and retrieved April 14, 2005 from http://www.timesdispatch.com/servlet/Satellite?pagename=RTD/MGArticle/RTD_BasicArticle&c=MGArticle&cid=1031782073782.
[1240] Peter Hardin. Allen Bringing faith into view. Richmond Times-Dispatch. Posted April 11, 2005 and retrieved April 14, 2005 from http://www.timesdispatch.com/servlet/Satellite?pagename=RTD/MGArticle/RTD_BasicArticle&c=MGArticle&cid=1031782073782
[1241] Jeff E. Schapiro. Allen says potential foe has edge. Richmond Times-Dispatch. Posted April 5, 2005 and retrieved April 14, 2005 from http://www.timesdispatch.com/servlet/Satellite?pagename=RTD%2FMGArticle%2FRTD_BasicArticle&c=MGArticle&cid=1031781970075&path=!news&s=1045855934842.
[1242] Jeff E. Schapiro. Allen says potential foe has edge. Richmond Times-Dispatch. Posted April 5, 2005 and retrieved April 14, 2005 from http://www.timesdispatch.com/servlet/Satellite?pagename=RTD%2FMGArticle%2FRTD_BasicArticle&c=MGArticle&cid=1031781970075&path=!news&s=1045855934842.
[1243] MSNBC.com. Hardball with Chris Matthews for March 6. Retrieved March 8, 2006 from http://www.msnbc.msn.com/id/11711647/print/1/displaymode/1098/.
[1244] MSNBC.com. Hardball with Chris Matthews for March 6. Retrieved March 8, 2006 from http://www.msnbc.msn.com/id/11711647/print/1/displaymode/1098/
[1245] Robert Barnes. Democrat's See Allen's Invincibility Cloak Loosening. Washington Post. Published and Retrieved March 8, 2006 from http://www.washingtonpost.com/wp-dyn/content/article/2006/03/07/AR200603071587.html.
[1246] Warren Fiske. Democratic Challenger to Allen joins election fray. The Virginian-Pilot. Posted and retrieved March 8, 2005 from http://home.hamptonroads.com/stories/story/cfm?story=100760&ran=170754.
[1247] Warren Fiske. Democratic Challenger to Allen joins election fray. The Virginian-Pilot. Posted and retrieved March 8, 2005 from http://home.hamptonroads.com/stories/story/cfm?story=100760&ran=170754.

[1248] Chris Graham. Clark Endorses Webb for Senate nomination. Augusta Free Press. Posted March 30, 2006 and retrieved April 3, 2006 from http://www.augustafreepress.com/stories/story/Reader$39359.
[1249] Warren Fiske. The Virginia-Pilot. Allen defends plans for Iowa appearance. June 15, 2006. Retrieved July 14, 2006 from http://home.hamptonroads.com/stories/story.cfm?story=106100&ran=76274.
[1250] Chris L. Jenkins. Warner Promises Webb Support Of United Party. Published June 30, 2006 B01. Retrieved July 14, 2006 from http://www.washingtonpost.com/wp-dyn/content/article/2006/06/29/AR2006062902196.html.
[1251] Chris L. Jenkins. Warner Promises Webb Support Of United Party. Published June 30, 2006 B01. Retrieved July 14, 2006 from http://www.washingtonpost.com/wp-dyn/content/article/2006/06/29/AR2006062902196.html
[1252] Chris L. Jenkins. Warner Promises Webb Support Of United Party. Published June 30, 2006 B01. Retrieved July 14, 2006 from http://www.washingtonpost.com/wp-dyn/content/article/2006/06/29/AR2006062902196.html
[1253] Edward O'Keefe. On the trail: Cowboy Boots vs. Combat Boots. ABC News. July 9, 2006 and retrieved July 14, 2006 from http://abcnews.go.com/ThisWeek/print?id=2170020
[1254] George Allen. Wikipedia. 2008 Presidential Election Speculation @ http://en.wikipedia.org/wiki/George_Allen (U.S. politician) See footnote 60: McCain Roars Past Allen In New NJ Insiders Poll.
[1255] NBC News. Meet the Press. Transcript for March 12. Retrieved March 8, 2006 from http://www.msnbc.msn.com/id/11711506/print/1/displaymode/1098/
[1256] Chris Cillizza. Will Dem Challengers Keep Allen at Home? The Fix. Washingtonpost.com Politics Blog. Posted March 3 and retrieved March 8, 2006 from http://www.washingtonpost.com/thefix/2006/03/george_allen_heads_to_iowa.html.
[1257] NBC News. Meet the Press. Transcript for March 12. Retrieved March 17, 2006 from http://www.msnbc.msn.com/id/11711506/print/1/displaymode/1098/.
[1258] Warren Fiske. The Virginia-Pilot. Allen defends plans for Iowa appearance. June 15, 2006. Retrieved July 14, 2006 from http://home.hamptonroads.com/stories/story.cfm?story=106100&ran=76274.
[1259] Edward O'Keefe. On the trail: Cowboy Boots vs. Combat Boots. ABC News. July 9, 2006 and retrieved July 14, 2006 from http://abcnews.go.com/ThisWeek/print?id=2170020.
[1260] Warren Fiske. The Virginia-Pilot. Allen defends plans for Iowa appearance. June 15, 2006. Retrieved July 14, 2006 from http://home.hamptonroads.com/stories/story.cfm?story=106100&ran=76274.
[1261] Tyler Whitley. Iowa, say hello to George Allen. Times-Dispatch. Posted March 19, 2006 and retrieved July 14, 2006 from http://www.timesdispatch.com/servlet/Satellite?pagename=RTD/MGArticle/RTD_BasicArticle&c=MGArticle&cid=1137834807104.
[1262] Steven Thomma. Va. Republican George Allen facing tough fight for his Senate seat. Knight Ridder Newspapers. Posted June 18, 2006 and retrieved July 14, 2006 from http://www.belleville.com/mld/belleville/news/nation/14836742.htm.
[1263] Steven Thomma. Va. Republican George Allen facing tough fight for his Senate seat. Knight Ridder Newspapers. Posted June 18, 2006 and retrieved July 14, 2006 from http://www.belleville.com/mld/belleville/news/nation/14836742.htm
[1264] Edward O'Keefe. On the trail: Cowboy Boots vs. Combat Boots. ABC News. July 9, 2006 and retrieved July 14, 2006 from http://abcnews.go.com/ThisWeek/print?id=2170020
[1265] Chris Jenkins. Reagan Navy Secretary Enters Race to Challenge Sen. Allen. Washington Post. Posted and retrieved March 8, 2005 from http://www.washingtonpost.com/wp-dyn/content/article/2006/03/07/AR2006030701503.html
[1266] Chris Jenkins. Reagan Navy Secretary Enters Race to Challenge Sen. Allen. Washington Post. Posted and retrieved March 8, 2005 from http://www.washingtonpost.com/wp-dyn/content/article/2006/03/07/AR2006030701503.html.
[1267] Chris Jenkins. Reagan Navy Secretary Enters Race to Challenge Sen. Allen. Washington Post. Posted and retrieved March 8, 2005 from http://www.washingtonpost.com/wp-dyn/content/article/2006/03/07/AR2006030701503.html
[1268] MSNBC.com. Transcript for Sept.17, 206. NBC News/Meet the press. Retrieved Sept. 25, 2006 from http://www.msnbc.msn.com/id/14815993/pint/1/displaymode/1098/.
[1269] MSNBC.com. Transcript for Sept.17, 206. NBC News/Meet the press. Retrieved Sept. 25, 2006 from http://www.msnbc.msn.com/id/14815993/pint/1/displaymode/1098/.
[1270] MSNBC.com. Transcript for Sept.17, 206. NBC News/Meet the press. Retrieved Sept. 25, 2006 from http://www.msnbc.msn.com/id/14815993/pint/1/displaymode/1098/.
[1271] MSNBC.com. Transcript for Sept.17, 206. NBC News/Meet the press. Retrieved Sept. 25, 2006 from http://www.msnbc.msn.com/id/14815993/pint/1/displaymode/1098/. Smirk personally observed.
[1272] MSNBC.com. Transcript for Sept.17, 206. NBC News/Meet the press. Retrieved Sept. 25, 2006 from http://www.msnbc.msn.com/id/14815993/pint/1/displaymode/1098/.
[1273] MSNBC.com. Transcript for Sept.17, 206. NBC News/Meet the press. Retrieved Sept. 25, 2006 from http://www.msnbc.msn.com/id/14815993/pint/1/displaymode/1098/.
[1274] MSNBC.com. Transcript for Sept.17, 206. NBC News/Meet the press. Retrieved Sept. 25, 2006 from http://www.msnbc.msn.com/id/14815993/pint/1/displaymode/1098/.
[1275] James Webb (1979). Why Women Can't Fight. Retrieved 10.31.06 from http://www.washingtonian.com/aricles/mediapolitics/2182.html.
[1276] Chris L. Jenkins. Warner Promises Webb Support Of United Party. Published June 30, 2006 B01. Retrieved July 14, 2006 from http://www.washingtonpost.com/wp-dyn/content/article/2006/06/29/AR2006062902196.html
[1277] Warren Fiske. The Virginia-Pilot. Allen defends plans for Iowa appearance. June 15, 2006. Retrieved July 14, 2006 from http://home.hamptonroads.com/stories/story.cfm?story=106100&ran=76274.

[1278] Chris L. Jenkins. Warner Promises Webb Support Of United Party. Published June 30, 2006 B01. Retrieved July 14, 2006 from http://www.washingtonpost.com/wp-dyn/content/article/2006/06/29/AR2006062902196.html

[1279] Warren Fiske. The Virginia-Pilot. Allen defends plans for Iowa appearance. June 15, 2006. Retrieved July 14, 2006 from http://home.hamptonroads.com/stories/story.cfm?story=106100&ran=76274.

[1280] Zogby International. VA-Allen Builds Lead Over Webb. Released July 27, 2006 and retrieved July 28, 2006 from http://www.zogby.com/news/ReadNews.dbm?ID=1151.

[1281] Paul West. Baltimore Sun. Va. Senator aims to repel Democrats. Posted September 4 and retrieved September 6, 2006 from http://www.baltimoresun.com/news/nationworld/bal-te.midterm04sep04,0,1979034.story?coll=bal-home-headlines.

[1282] Fredrick Kunkle. Fairfax Native Says Allen's Words Stung. Published B01, August 25, 2006 and retrieved same day from http://www.washingtonpost.com/wp-dyn/content/article/2006/08/24/AR2006082401639_pf.html.

[1283] Fredrick Kunkle. Fairfax Native Says Allen's Words Stung. Published B01, August 25, 2006 and retrieved same day from http://www.washingtonpost.com/wp-dyn/content/article/2006/08/24/AR2006082401639_pf.html

[1284] Fredrick Kunkle. Fairfax Native Says Allen's Words Stung. Published B01, August 25, 2006 and retrieved same day from http://www.washingtonpost.com/wp-dyn/content/article/2006/08/24/AR2006082401639_pf.html.

[1285] Fredrick Kunkle. Fairfax Native Says Allen's Words Stung. Published B01, August 25, 2006 and retrieved same day from http://www.washingtonpost.com/wp-dyn/content/article/2006/08/24/AR2006082401639_pf.html

[1286] Fredrick Kunkle. Fairfax Native Says Allen's Words Stung. Published B01, August 25, 2006 and retrieved same day from http://www.washingtonpost.com/wp-dyn/content/article/2006/08/24/AR2006082401639_pf.html

[1287] Washington Post Editorial. George Allen's America. Posted August 15, 2006 and retrieved August 25, 2006 from http://www.washingtonpost.com/wp-dyn/content/article/2006/08/14/AR2006081401114_pf.html.

[1288] Eugene Robinson. George Allen's macaca moment. Posted August 22 and retrieved August 26, 2006 from http://www.theroyalgazette.com/apps/pbcs.dll/article?AID=/20060822/OPINION/108220163.

[1289] Tim Graham. Washington Post Pounds George Allen with Supposedly Racist Gaffe. Posted August 15 and retrieved August 25, 2006 from http://newsbusters.org/node/6991

[1290] The Roanoke Times. Webb campaign says Allen used slur. August 15, 2006. Retrieved Sept.6, 2006 from http://www.roanoke.com/news/roanoke/wb/wb/xp-78224.

[1291] Along with George Allen's Presidential Ambitions, Taste and Humor Are also casualties of Macacagate. Wonketter.com. Retrieved August 25, 2006 from http://www.wonkette.com/politics/macaca/along-with-george-allens-presidential-ambitions-taste-and-humor-are-also-causalties-of-macacagate-194968.php/.

[1292] Along with George Allen's Presidential Ambitions, Taste and Humor Are also casualties of Macacagate. Wonketter.com. Retrieved August 25, 2006 from http://www.wonkette.com/politics/macaca/along-with-george-allens-presidential-ambitions-taste-and-humor-are-also-causalties-of-macacagate-194968.php/.

[1293] Wonkette. Big Pile of Macaca. Retrieved August 25, 2006 from http://wonkette.com/politics/george-allen/a-big-pile-of-macaca-194151.php.

[1294] Bob Lewis. AP. Sen. George Allen Gives Direct Apology. ABC News. Posted August 23, 2006 and Retrieved August 25, 2006 from http://abcnews.go.com/Politics/print?id=2348430.

[1295] The Daily Show on Comedy Central.

[1296] The Daily Show; Eugene Robinson. George Allen's macaca moment. Posted August 22 and retrieved August 26, 2006 from http://www.theroyalgazette.com/apps/pbcs.dll/article?AID=/20060822/OPINION/108220163.

[1297] Truthdig. Corddry: Unsure if Allen's Racism Helps or Hurts Him. Posted August 16, 2006, and retrieved August 25, 2006 from http://www.truthdig.com/avbooth/print/20060816_corddry_george_allen/.

[1298] Be George Allen's New Monkey. Wonkette.com. Ken Layne. Posted http://wonkette.com/politics/george-allen/be-georgeallens-new-monkey_19625. Retrieved 8.25.06.

[1299] Hotline On Call. The Monkey Is Not Dead. We Repeat. The Monkey Is Not Dead. Posted August 24, and retrieved August 26, 2006 from http://hotlineblog.nationaljournal.com/archives/2006/08/.

[1300] Slate, through Wonkette. The George Allen Insult Generator. Retrieved October 13, 2006 from http://www.wonkette.com/politics/george%20allen/.

[1301] Hardball with Chris Matthews' for August 25. MSNBC.com. Retrieved September 6, 2006 from http://www.msnbc.msn.com/id/1455886/print/1/displaymode/1098/ 5/18.

[1302] Allen's campaign Shifts Gears, Seeks Help. Posted August 22, 2006 and retrieved August 25, 2006 from http://hotlineblog.nationaljournal.com/archives/2006/08/allens_campaign.html.

[1303] Allen's campaign Shifts Gears, Seeks Help. Posted August 22, 2006 and retrieved August 25, 2006 from http://hotlineblog.nationaljournal.com/archives/2006/08/allens_campaign.html.

[1304] Cal Thomas. Will Allen's denouncers be equal-opportunity critics? August 23, and retrieved August 25, 2006 from http://www.baltimoresun.com/news/opinion/oped/bal-op.thomas23aug23,0,7412728.story

[1305] Washington Post. Michael D. Shear and Leef Smith. For One Group, 'Macaca' Recalls slurs After 9/11. Page C01. Published August 20 and retrieved August 25, 2006t from http://www.washingtonpost.com/wp-dyn/content/article/2006/08/19/AR2006081900626.html.

[1306] Tim Craig. Minorities in GOP rally for Allen in N.Va. Washington Post. Published September 10, 2006, C06. Retrieved Sept 25, 2006 from http://www.washingtonpost.com/wp-dyn/content/article/2006/09/09/AR2006090900944_pf.html.

[1307] Tim Craig. Minorities in GOP rally for Allen in N.Va. Washington Post. Published September 10, 2006, C06. Retrieved Sept 25, 2006 from http://www.washingtonpost.com/wp-dyn/content/article/2006/09/09/AR2006090900944_pf.html

[1308] Washington Post. Michael D. Shear and Leef Smith. For One Group, 'Macaca' Recalls slurs After 9/11. Page C01. Published August 20 and retrieved August 25, 2006t from http://www.washingtonpost.com/wp-dyn/content/article/2006/08/19/AR2006081900626.html

[1309] Tim Craig. Minorities in GOP rally for Allen in N.Va. Washington Post. Published September 10, 2006, C06. Retrieved Sept 25, 2006 from http://www.washingtonpost.com/wp-dyn/content/article/2006/09/09/AR2006090900944_pf.html.

[1310] Tim Craig. Minorities in GOP rally for Allen in N.Va. Washington Post. Published September 10, 2006, C06. Retrieved Sept 25, 2006 from http://www.washingtonpost.com/wp-dyn/content/article/2006/09/09/AR2006090900944_pf.html

[1311] Hardball with Chris Matthews for Sept. 26, 2006. MSNBC.com. Retrieved 10.13.2006 from http://www.msnbc.msn.com/id/15029661/print/1/displaymode/1098/. P 2/19.

[1312] Tim Craig. Minorities in GOP rally for Allen in N.Va. Washington Post. Published September 10, 2006, C06. Retrieved Sept 25, 2006 from http://www.washingtonpost.com/wp-dyn/content/article/2006/09/09/AR2006090900944_pf.html

[1313] Tim Craig. Minorities in GOP rally for Allen in N.Va. Washington Post. Published September 10, 2006, C06. Retrieved Sept 25, 2006 from http://www.washingtonpost.com/wp-dyn/content/article/2006/09/09/AR2006090900944_pf.html

[1314] Tim Craig. Minorities in GOP rally for Allen in N.Va. Washington Post. Published September 10, 2006, C06. Retrieved Sept 25, 2006 from http://www.washingtonpost.com/wp-dyn/content/article/2006/09/09/AR2006090900944_pf.html

[1315] Tim Craig. Minorities in GOP rally for Allen in N.Va. Washington Post. Published September 10, 2006, C06. Retrieved Sept 25, 2006 from http://www.washingtonpost.com/wp-dyn/content/article/2006/09/09/AR2006090900944_pf.html

[1316] John Amato. Crooks and Liars. Macaca Allen's Ethnic Rally. Retrieved September 25, 2006 from http://www.crooksandliars.com/2006/09/13/macaca-allens-ethic-rally/.

[1317] Colbert Mocks Allen's 'Ethnic Rally'. Truthdig. Posted 9.15.06 and retrieved 9.25.06 from htt://www.truthdig.com/avbooth/item/20060915_colbert_mocks_allens_ethnic_rally/.

[1318] George Allen's Ethnic Rally, Day Two. Wonkette. Retrieved September 25, 2006 from http://www.wonkette.com/politics/george-allen/george-allens-ethnic-rally-day-two-200166.php.

[1319] Icon in Bad Days for Big Dig. The Weekly Standard. Retrieved Sept. 25, 2006 from http://www.weeklystandard.com/Content/Public/Articles/000/000/012/555ivsyw.asp.

[1320] More from Hardball with Chris Matthews. Retrieved September 25, 2006f @ http://www.msnbc.msn.com/id/14906529/.

[1321] Allen's remarks irk Sons of Confederate Veterans. Milwaukee Journal Sentinel. 11A 9.29.06..

[1322] Peter Hardin and Jeff E. Schapiro. Allen tells of his Jewish heritage. Richmond Times-Dispatch. Posted Sept. 20 and retrieved 10.13.06 from http://www.timesdispatch.com/servelet/Satellite?c=MGArticle&cid=1149190712778&pagename=RTD/...

[1323] Marc Fisher. Sen. Allen's Diet of Pork Chops, Ham Sandwiches and Crow. Posted Sept. 24 and retrieved 10.13.06 from http://www.washigntonpost.com/wp-dyn/content/article/2006/09/23/AR2006092300958.html.

[1324] Marc Fisher. Sen. Allen's Diet of Pork Chops, Ham Sandwiches and Crow. Posted Sept. 24 and retrieved 10.13.06 from http://www.washingtonpost.com/wp-dyn/content/article/2006/09/23/AR2006092300958.html.

[1325] Bob Lewis. Senator fumes over questioned heritage. AP. Milwaukee Journal Sentinel. Nation and World. Sept. 20, 2006, 9A.

[1326] Slate. Christopher Beam, Torie Bosch, and Josh Levin. The George Allen Insult Generator. Retrieved 10.13.06 from http://www.slate.com/toolbar.aspx?action=print&id=2150347. Posted Sept. 26.

[1327] Peter Hardin and Jeff E. Schapiro. Allen tells of his Jewish heritage. Richmond Times-Dispatch. Posted Sept. 20 and retrieved 10.13.06 from http://www.timesdispatch.com/servelet/Satellite?c=MGArticle&cid=1149190712778&pagename=RTD/...

[1328] Peter Hardin and Jeff E. Schapiro. Allen tells of his Jewish heritage. Richmond Times-Dispatch. Posted Sept. 20 and retrieved 10.13.06 from http://www.timesdispatch.com/servelet/Satellite?c=MGArticle&cid=1149190712778&pagename=RTD/...

[1329] Peter Hardin and Jeff E. Schapiro. Allen tells of his Jewish heritage. Richmond Times-Dispatch. Posted Sept. 20 and retrieved 10.13.06 from http://www.timesdispatch.com/servelet/Satellite?c=MGArticle&cid=1149190712778&pagename=RTD/...

[1330] Marc Fisher. Sen. Allen's Diet of Pork Chops, Ham Sandwiches and Crow. Posted Sept. 24 and retrieved 10.13.06 from http://www.washigntonpost.com/wp-dyn/content/article/2006/09/23/AR2006092300958.html.

[1331] Marc Fisher. Sen. Allen's Diet of Pork Chops, Ham Sandwiches and Crow. Posted Sept. 24 and retrieved 10.13.06 from http://www.washingtonpost.com/wp-dyn/content/article/2006/09/23/AR2006092300958.html.

[1332] Marc Fisher. Sen. Allen's Diet of Pork Chops, Ham Sandwiches and Crow. Posted Sept. 24 and retrieved 10.13.06 from http://www.washingtonpost.com/wp-dyn/content/article/2006/09/23/AR2006092300958.html.

[1333] Peter Hardin and Jeff E. Schapiro. Allen tells of his Jewish heritage. Richmond Times-Dispatch. Posted Sept. 20 and retrieved 10.13.06 from http://www.timesdispatch.com/servelet/Satellite?c=MGArticle&cid=1149190712778&pagename=RTD/...

[1334] Marc Fisher. Sen. Allen's Diet of Pork Chops, Ham Sandwiches and Crow. Posted Sept. 24 and retrieved 10.13.06 from http://www.washigntonpost.com/wp-dyn/content/article/2006/09/23/AR2006092300958.html.

[1335] Peter Hardin and Jeff E. Schapiro. Allen tells of his Jewish heritage. Richmond Times-Dispatch. Posted Sept. 20 and retrieved 10.13.06 from http://www.timesdispatch.com/servelet/Satellite?c=MGArticle&cid=1149190712778&pagename=RTD/...

[1336] Bob Lewis. Senator fumes over questioned heritage. AP. Milwaukee Journal Sentinel. Nation and World. Sept. 20, 2006, 9A.

[1337] Max Blumenthal. Beyond Macaca: The Photograph That Haunts George Allen. THE Nation. Posted August 29 and retrieved September 6, 2006 from http://www.thenation.com/doc/20060911/george_allen.

[1338] Max Blumenthal. Beyond Macaca: The Photograph That Haunts George Allen. THE Nation. Posted August 29 and retrieved September 6, 2006 from http://www.thenation.com/doc/20060911/george_allen.

[1339] Max Blumenthal. Beyond Macaca: The Photograph That Haunts George Allen. THE Nation. Posted August 29 and retrieved September 6, 2006 from http://www.thenation.com/doc/20060911/george_allen.

[1340] Max Blumenthal. Beyond Macaca: The Photograph That Haunts George Allen. THE Nation. Posted August 29 and retrieved September 6, 2006 from http://www.thenation.com/doc/20060911/george_allen

[1341] MSNBC.com. Transcript for Sept.17, 206. NBC News/Meet the press. Retrieved Sept. 25, 2006 from http://www.msnbc.msn.com/id/14815993/pint/1/displaymode/1098/.

[1342] MSNBC.com. Transcript for Sept.17, 206. NBC News/Meet the press. Retrieved Sept. 25, 2006 from http://www.msnbc.msn.com/id/14815993/pint/1/displaymode/1098/.

[1343] MSNBC.com. Transcript for Sept.17, 206. NBC News/Meet the press. Retrieved Sept. 25, 2006 from http://www.msnbc.msn.com/id/14815993/pint/1/displaymode/1098/.

[1344] MSNBC.com. Transcript for Sept.17, 206. NBC News/Meet the press. Retrieved Sept. 25, 2006 from http://www.msnbc.msn.com/id/14815993/pint/1/displaymode/1098/.

[1345] MSNBC.com. Transcript for Sept.17, 206. NBC News/Meet the press. Retrieved Sept. 25, 2006 from http://www.msnbc.msn.com/id/14815993/pint/1/displaymode/1098/.

[1346] Allen's Racist Past Probed. Sept. 24, 2006. Retrieved 10.31.06 from http://politicalwire.com/archives/2008_campaign/.

[1347] Hardball with Chris Matthews for Sept. 26, 2006. MSNBC.com. Retrieved 10.13.2006 from http://www.msnbc.msn.com/id/15029661/print/1/displaymode/1098/. 1/19.

[1348] Larry Sabato Has an Almost Transparent Knowledge of George Allen's Soul. Posted Sept. 26, Retrieved 10.13. 2006 from Wonkette.

[1349] George Allen in Using Non-Hilarious Slur Shocker. Wonkette. Retrieved 10.13. 2006 from http://wonkette.com/politics/george-allen-in-using-nonhillarious-slur-schocker-202948.php.

[1350] AP. Virginia Senator denies use of racial slur; ex-teammate made accusation. Milwaukee Journal Sentinel. 9.25.06, 4A.

[1351] Hardball with Chris Matthews for Sept. 26, 2006. MSNBC.com. Retrieved 10.13.2006 from http://www.msnbc.msn.com/id/15029661/print/1/displaymode/1098/. 2/19.

[1352] Hardball with Chris Matthews for Sept. 26, 2006. MSNBC.com. Retrieved 10.13.2006 from http://www.msnbc.msn.com/id/15029661/print/1/displaymode/1098/. 1/19.

[1353] Hardball with Chris Matthews for Sept. 26, 2006. MSNBC.com. Retrieved 10.13.2006 from http://www.msnbc.msn.com/id/15029661/print/1/displaymode/1098/. 2/19.

[1354] Hardball with Chris Matthews for Sept. 26, 2006. MSNBC.com. Retrieved 10.13.2006 from http://www.msnbc.msn.com/id/15029661/print/1/displaymode/1098/. 5/19.

[1355] George Allen. Wonkette. The George Allen Insult Generator. Link on Wonkette. Retrieved 10.13.06 from http://www.wonkette.com/politics/george%20allen/.

[1356] Pundit says he didn't hear Allen use racist slur. Political Briefing. Milwaukee Journal Sentinel. 9.28.06, 8A.

[1357] Hardball with Chris Matthews for Sept. 26, 2006. MSNBC.com. Retrieved 10.13.2006 from http://www.msnbc.msn.com/id/15029661/print/1/displaymode/1098/. 9/19.

[1358] Mark Finkelstein. Chris Matthews/NewsBusters.org. Hardball: 27 minutes for Allegations Against Allen, 0 For Those Against Webb. Posted 9.28 and retrieved 10.13.06 from http://newsusters.org/taxonomy/term/206.

[1359] Chris Cillizza. Senate Dems Take to Virginia Airwaves. 10.10.26, and retrieved 10.13.06 from http://blog.washingtonpost.com/thefix/.

[1360] Chris Cillizza. Senate Dems Take to Virginia Airwaves. 10.10.26, and retrieved 10.13.06 from http://blog.washingtonpost.com/thefix/.

[1361] Chris Cillizza. Senate Dems Take to Virginia Airwaves. 10.10.26, and retrieved 10.13.06 from http://blog.washingtonpost.com/thefix/.

[1362] Bob Lewis. AP. Sen. George Allen Gives Direct Apology. ABC News. Posted August 23, 2006 and Retrieved August 25, 2006 from http://abcnews.go.com/Politics/print?id=2348430.

[1363] Bob Lewis. AP. Sen. George Allen Gives Direct Apology. ABC News. Posted August 23, 2006 and Retrieved August 25, 2006 from http://abcnews.go.com/Politics/print?id=2348430.

[1364] Bob Gibson. Daily Progress (Charlottesville). Novelists to stump for Webb. August 30, 2006 and retrieved Sept.6, 2006 from http://www.dailyprogress.com/servlet/Satellite?pagename=CDP%2FMGArticle%2FCDP_BasicArticle&c=MGArticle&cid=1149190293046&path=!news.

[1365] ABC News. Funnies: Kerry Carnage. Nov.5, 2006. Retrieved 1.13.07 from http://abcnews.go.com/ThisWeek/print?id=2629990

[1366] Hardball with Chris Matthews for Nov. 8, 7p.m. MSNBC.com. Retrieved 11.17.06 from http://www.msnbc.msn.com/id/15939296/.

[1367] Hardball with Chris Matthews for Nov. 8, 7p.m. MSNBC.com. Retrieved 11.17.06 from http://www.msnbc.msn.com/id/15939296/.
[1368] Hardball with Chris Matthews for Nov. 9. MSNBC.com. Retrieved 11.17.06 from http://www.msnbc.msn.com/id/15655160/.
[1369] George Allen. Wikipedia. 2008 Presidential Election Speculation @ http://en.wikipedia.org/wiki/George_Allen (U.S. politician) See footnote 65: Article from mercurynews.com.
[1370] Libby Copeland. Faith Based Initiative. Washington Post. Published June 7, 2006, C01. Retrieved June 16, 2006 from http://www.washingtonpost.com/wp-dyn/content/article/2006/06/06/AR2006060601616.html.
[1371] Libby Copeland. Faith Based Initiative. Washington Post. Published June 7, 2006, C01. Retrieved June 16, 2006 from http://www.washingtonpost.com/wp-dyn/content/article/2006/06/06/AR2006060601616.html.
[1372] Richard E. Cohen and Michael Barone. The Almanac of American Politics—2004. The National Journal Group. 2003, page 650
[1373] Sam Brownback. "Defining Marriage Down." National Review Online. Posted July 9, 2004 and retrieved November 10, 2005 from http://www.nationalreview.com/comment/brownback200407090921.asp.
[1374] Sam Brownback. "Defining Marriage Down." National Review Online. Posted July 9, 2004 and retrieved November 10, 2005 from http://www.nationalreview.com/comment/brownback200407090921.asp
[1375] Libby Copeland. Faith Based Initiative. Washington Post. Published June 7, 2006, C01. Retrieved June 16, 2006 from http://www.washingtonpost.com/wp-dyn/content/article/2006/06/06/AR2006060601616.html.
[1376] "Thou shalt not endorse...for now." Steve Kraske. The Kansas City Star. Posted March 27, 2005 and retrieved April 6, 2005 from http://www.kansascity.com/mld/kansascity/news/politics/11239846.htm.
[1377] Congressman Walter B. Jones. Releases by Dexteranet. Posted 3.2.05 and retrieved from http://jones.house.gov/release.cfm?id=284.
[1378] Craig Gilbert. Bush turns to ally. The Milwaukee Journal Sentinel. October 4, 2005, 1A.
[1379] Craig Gilbert. Bush turns to ally. The Milwaukee Journal Sentinel. October 4, 2005, 1A
[1380] ABC News. Miers Gave to GOP Candidates, Democrats. AP. Posted and retrieved October 4, 2005 from http://www.abcnews.go.com/Politics/print?id=1181492.
[1381] ABC News. Miers Gave to GOP Candidates, Democrats." AP. Posted and retrieved October 4, 2005 from http://www.abcnews.go.com/Politics/print?id=1181492.
[1382] Charles Hurt. "Some Republicans balk, but confirmation expected." The Washington Times. Published October 4, 2005 and retrieved same day from http://www.washingtontimes.com/functions/print.php?StoryID=20051004-121731-5934r.
[1383] CBS News. "Face the Nation—October 16, 2005." Transcript courtesy of Burrelle's Information Services. Retrieved October 28, 2005 from http://www.cbsnews.com/htdocs/pdf/face_101605.pdf.
[1384] Peter Hardin. "Allen cautious on Miers pick." Richmond Times-Dispatch. Posted and retrieved October 4, 2005 from http://www.timesdispatch.com/servlet/Satellite?pagename=RTD%2FMGArticle%2FRTD_BasicArticle&c=MGArticle&cid=1031785432229&path=%21news%21politics&s=1045855935264.
[1385] Charles Hurt. "Some Republicans balk, but confirmation expected." The Washington Times. Published October 4, 2005 and retrieved same day from http://www.washingtontimes.com/functions/print.php?StoryID=20051004-121731-5934r.
[1386] MSNBC.com. "Transcript for October 23". NBC News/Meet the Press. Posted October 23, 2005 and retrieved October 25, 2005 from http://www.msnbc.com/id/9764239/
[1387] Sam Brownback. "Brownback Comments on Miers Nomination." Posted October 4, 2005 and retrieved October 27, 2005 from http://brownback.senate.gove/pressapp/record.cfm?id=246818.
[1388] Shailagh Murray and Charles Babbington. "Miers Makes Rounds on Hill." Washington Post. Published October 7, 2005 and retrieved October 27, 2005 from www.washingtonpost.com/wp-dyn/content/article/2005/10/06/AR2005100601713.html.
[1389] ABC News. "GOP Senator Concerned About Miers' Abortion Views." Posted October 5, 2005 and retrieved October 11, 2005 from http://abcnews.go.com/GMA/print?id=1184984.
[1390] CBS News. "Face the Nation-October 9, 2005." Transcript courtesy of Burrelle's Information Services. Retrieved October 20, 2005 from http://www.cbsnews.com/htdocs/pdf/face_10905.pdf.
[1391] FOXNEWS.com "Transcript: Judiciary Panelists Debate Miers." Fox News Sunday. Posted October 23, 2004 and retrieved October 25, 2005 from http://www.foxnews.com/pinter_friendly_story/0,3566,173186,00.html.
[1392] Nedra Pickler. "Bush staff rallies support for Miers." AP. The Milwaukee Journal Sentinel. October 14, 2005, 13A.
[1393] Nedra Pickler. Bush staff rallies support for Miers. AP. The Milwaukee Journal Sentinel. October 14, 2005, 13A.
[1394] FOXNEWS.com. "Transcript: Conservatives Debate Miers' Nomination." Fox News Sunday. Posted October 10, 2005 and retrieved October 27, 2005 from http://www.foxnews.com/printer_friendly_story/0,3566,171680,00.html.
[1395] Finlay Lewis. "Bush: Miers 'shares my philosophy'." Copley News Service. Posted and Retrieved October 5, 2005 from http://www.signonsandiego.com/news/politics/20051005-9999-1n5bush.html.
[1396] MSNBC.com. "Transcript for October 9." NBC News/Meet the Press. Posted October 9, 2005 and retrieved October 27, 2005 from http://www.msnbc.msn.com/id/9579343/.
[1397] Charles Hurt. "Some Republicans balk, but confirmation expected." The Washington Times. Published October 4, 2005 and retrieved same day from http://www.washingtontimes.com/functions/print.php?StoryID=20051004-121731-5934r.
[1398] M.E. Sprengelmeyer. "Dobson to clarify info." Rocky Mountain News. Posted October 11, 2005 and retrieved October 11, 2005 from http://www.rockymountainnews.com/drmn/state/article/0,1299,DRMN_21_4149655,00.html.

[1399] Jennifer Loven. "Bork says Miers nomination is 'a disaster on every level.'" AP. The Milwaukee Journal Sentinel., October 8, 2005, 7A.
[1400] Sheryl Gay Stolberg. "Bush touts Miers pick again, but tide of grumbling rises." New York Times/ The Milwaukee Journal Sentinel. October 9, 2005, 8A.
[1401] FOXNEWS.com. "Transcript: Conservatives Debate Miers' Nomination." Fox News Sunday. Posted October 10, 2005 and retrieved October 27, 2005 from http://www.foxnews.com/printer_friendly_story/0,3566,171680,00.html
[1402] MSNBC.com. "Transcript for October 9." NBC News/Meet the Press. Posted October 9, 2005 and retrieved October 27, 2005 from http://www.msnbc.msn.com/id/9579343/
[1403] Tom Raum. "Bush administration pleasing very few with shifting Miers strategy." AP. The Milwaukee Journal Sentinel. October 21, 2005, 16A.
[1404] Editorial. "Harriet Miers' rough road to confirmation." Lafayetter Journal and Courier Online. Published October 24, 2005 and retrieved October 25, 2005 from http://www.lafayettejc.com/apps/pbcs.dll/article?AID=/20051024/OPINION01/510240302.
[1405] Cox News Service, AP. "Senators demand details from Miers." The Milwaukee Journal Sentinel. October 20, 2005, 3A.
[1406] FOXNEWS.com "Transcript: Judiciary Panelists Debate Miers." Fox News Sunday. Posted October 23, 2004 and retrieved October 25, 2005 from http://www.foxnews.com/pinter_friendly_story/0,3566,173186,00.html. Or http://www.foxnews.com/story/0,2933,173186,00.html.
[1407] FOXNEWS.com "Transcript: Judiciary Panelists Debate Miers." Fox News Sunday. Posted October 23, 2004 and retrieved October 25, 2005 from http://www.foxnews.com/pinter_friendly_story/0,3566,173186,00.html
[1408] Matt Stearns. "Sen. Brownback emerges on the national scene." Knight Ridder Newspapers. Posted October 23, 2005 and retrieved November 1, 2005 from http://www.fortwayne.com/mld/newssentinel/news/editorial/12977807.htm
[1409] Terrence. " Miers Withdrawals Supreme Court Nomination." AP/ABC News. Posted and retrieved October 27, 2005 from http://abcnews.go.com/Politics/print?id=1255208.
[1410] Robert Novak. "Miers' staff knew senators demanded files." The Chicago Sun-Times. Posted October 30, 2005 and retrieved November 3, 2005 from http://www.suntimes.com/output/novak/cst-edt-novak30.html.
[1411] Matt Stearns. "Sen. Brownback emerges on the national scene." Knight Ridder Newspapers. Posted October 23, 2005 and retrieved November 1, 2005 from http://www.fortwayne.com/mld/newssentinel/news/editorial/12977807.htm.
[1412] Matt Stearns. "Sen. Brownback emerges on the national scene." Knight Ridder Newspapers. Posted October 23, 2005 and retrieved November 1, 2005 from http://www.fortwayne.com/mld/newssentinel/news/editorial/12977807.htm
[1413] Matt Stearns. "Sen. Brownback emerges on the national scene." Knight Ridder Newspapers. Posted October 23, 2005 and retrieved November 1, 2005 from http://www.fortwayne.com/mld/newssentinel/news/editorial/12977807.htm
[1414] Libby Copeland. Faith Based Initiative. Washington Post. Published June 7, 2006, C01. Retrieved June 16, 2006 from http://www.washingtonpost.com/wp-dyn/content/article/2006/06/06/AR2006060601616.html.
[1415] Libby Copeland. Faith Based Initiative. Washington Post. Published June 7, 2006, C01. Retrieved June 16, 2006 from http://www.washingtonpost.com/wp-dyn/content/article/2006/06/06/AR2006060601616.html.
[1416] Margaret Carlson of Bloomberg. Bush unrealistic about stem cells. Seattle Post-Intelligencer. Posted July 21, and retrieved July 28, 2006 from http://seattlepi.nwsource.com/opinion/278308_carlson21.html.
[1417] Margaret Carlson of Bloomberg. Bush unrealistic about stem cells. Seattle Post-Intelligencer. Posted July 21, and retrieved July 28, 2006 from http://seattlepi.nwsource.com/opinion/278308_carlson21.html.
[1418] Katherine M. Skiba. White House blasts stem cell bill. Milwaukee Journal Sentinel. 7.17.06. 1 A/9A.
[1419] Margaret Carlson of Bloomberg. Bush unrealistic about stem cells. Seattle Post-Intelligencer. Posted July 21, and retrieved July 28, 2006 from http://seattlepi.nwsource.com/opinion/278308_carlson21.html.
[1420] MTP Transcript for July 23. MSNBC.com. Meet the Press, NBC News. Retrieved July 28, 2006 from http://www.msnbc.msn.com/id/13904922/print/1/displaymode/1098/.
[1421] Katherine M. Skiba. July 20, 2006. Bush's first veto rejects stem cell research bill. Milwaukee Journal Sentinel. July 20, 2006. 1A.
[1422] Margaret Carlson of Bloomberg. Bush unrealistic about stem cells. Seattle Post-Intelligencer. Posted July 21, and retrieved July 28, 2006 from http://seattlepi.nwsource.com/opinion/278308_carlson21.html.
[1423] Katherine M. Skiba. July 20, 2006. Bush's first veto rejects stem cell research bill. Milwaukee Journal Sentinel. July 20, 2006. 1A.
[1424] MTP Transcript for July 23. MSNBC.com. Meet the Press, NBC News. Retrieved July 28, 2006 from http://www.msnbc.msn.com/id/13904922/print/1/displaymode/1098/. 10/16.
[1425] WE Blog: 'The stem cell prop comedy of Sam Brownback'. Retrieved July 28, 2006 from http://blogs.kansas.com/weblog/2006/07/the_stem_cell_p.html.
[1426] WE Blog: "The stem cell prop comedy of Sam Brownback'. Retrieved July 28, 2006 from http://blogs.kansas.com/weblog/2006/07/the_stem_cell_p.html
[1427] WE Blog: 'The stem cell prop comedy of Sam Brownback'. Retrieved July 28, 2006 from http://blogs.kansas.com/weblog/2006/07/the_stem_cell_p.html
[1428] The Daily Show: July 19, 2006 and retrieved July 28, 2006 from http://www.tvsquad.com/2006/07/20/the-daily-show-july-19-2006/. WE Blog: 'The stem cell prop comedy of Sam Brownback'. Retrieved July 28, 2006 from http://blogs.kansas.com/weblog/2006/07/the_stem_cell_p.html
[1429] WE Blog: 'The stem cell prop comedy of Sam Brownback'. Retrieved July 28, 2006 from http://blogs.kansas.com/weblog/2006/07/the_stem_cell_p.html

[1430] Julie Anderson. Senator supports president's veto. The Derby Reporter. Published July 24, and retrieved July 28 from http://www.derbydailyrep.com/articles/2006/07/24/news/news3.txt.
[1431] Katherine M. Skiba. Showdown set on stem cells. Milwaukee Journal Sentinel. July 15, 2006. 15A.
[1432] Tim Drake. The Next Catholic President? Posed 1.2.07 and retrieved 1.13.06 from http://ncegister.com/site/article/1678/
[1433] Vincent. World News. Dec.15, 2006 and retrieved 1.13.07 from http://www.worldmagblog.com/blog/archives/028108.html.
[1434] Vincent. World News. Dec.15, 2006 and retrieved 1.13.07 from http://www.worldmagblog.com/blog/archives/028108.html.
[1435] Vincent. World News. Dec.15, 2006 and retrieved 1.13.07 from http://www.worldmagblog.com/blog/archives/028108.html.
[1436] Bill Berkowitz. Brownback brands himself 'Full scale conservative' Media Transparency. Posted 1.4.07 and retrieved 1.13.07 from http://www.mediatransparency.org/storyprinterfriendly.php?storyID=170
[1437] Bill Berkowitz. Brownback brands himself 'Full scale conservative' Media Transparency. Posted 1.4.07 and retrieved 1.13.07 from http://www.mediatransparency.org/storyprinterfriendly.php?storyID=170
[1438] Bill Berkowitz. Brownback brands himself 'Full scale conservative' Media Transparency. Posted 1.4.07 and retrieved 1.13.07 from http://www.mediatransparency.org/storyprinterfriendly.php?storyID=170.
[1439] George Will, Washington Post.
[1440] Mike Glover. AP. Brownback: energize GOP base. Posted Dec.5 and retrieved 12.14 from http://seattlepi.nwsource.com/national/1131AP_Brownback_2008.html.
[1441] Dan Gilgoff. Q& A with Sen. Sam Brownback. U.S. News & World Report. Posted Aug.16 and retrieved Sept.6, 2006 from http://www.usnews.com/usnews/news/articles/060816/16brownback.htm.
[1442] Dan Gilgoff. Q& A with Sen. Sam Brownback. U.S. News & World Report. Posted Aug.16 and retrieved Sept.6, 2006 from http://www.usnews.com/usnews/news/articles/060816/16brownback.htm.
[1443] Bill Berkowitz. Brownback brands himself 'Full scale conservative' Media Transparency. Posted 1.4.07 and retrieved 1.13.07 from http://www.mediatransparency.org/storyprinterfriendly.php?storyID=170
[1444] Bill Berkowitz. Brownback brands himself 'Full scale conservative' Media Transparency. Posted 1.4.07 and retrieved 1.13.07 from http://www.mediatransparency.org/storyprinterfriendly.php?storyID=170
[1445] Bill Berkowitz. Brownback brands himself 'Full scale conservative' Media Transparency. Posted 1.4.07 and retrieved 1.13.07 from http://www.mediatransparency.org/storyprinterfriendly.php?storyID=170
[1446] Bill Berkowitz. Brownback brands himself 'Full scale conservative' Media Transparency. Posted 1.4.07 and retrieved 1.13.07 from http://www.mediatransparency.org/storyprinterfriendly.php?storyID=170
[1447] Cal Thomas. New resolution for the right. Posted Jan2 and retrieved 1.13.07 from http://www.charlotte.com/mld/observer/news/opinion/16364321.htm.
[1448] Cal Thomas. New resolution for the right. Posted Jan2 and retrieved 1.13.07 from http://www.charlotte.com/mld/observer/news/opinion/16364321.htm.
[1449] Matthew Daly. Oregon's assisted suicide law scrutinized in Senate hearing. AP. 5.25.06 and retrieved September 6, 2006 from http://www.gtconnect.com/articles/2006/05/26/news/oregon/frista03.txt
[1450] Matthew Daly. Oregon's assisted suicide law scrutinized in Senate hearing. AP. 5.25.06 and retrieved September 6, 2006 from http://www.gtconnect.com/articles/2006/05/26/news/oregon/frista03.txt
[1451] Matthew Daly. Oregon's assisted suicide law scrutinized in Senate hearing. AP. 5.25.06 and retrieved September 6, 2006 from http://www.gtconnect.com/articles/2006/05/26/news/oregon/frista03.txt
[1452] Matthew Daly. Oregon's assisted suicide law scrutinized in Senate hearing. AP. 5.25.06 and retrieved September 6, 2006 from http://www.gtconnect.com/articles/2006/05/26/news/oregon/frista03.txt
[1453] Matthew Daly. Oregon's assisted suicide law scrutinized in Senate hearing. AP. 5.25.06 and retrieved September 6, 2006 from http://www.gtconnect.com/articles/2006/05/26/news/oregon/frista03.txt
[1454] Matthew Daly. Oregon's assisted suicide law scrutinized in Senate hearing. 5.25.06 and retrieved September 6, 2006 from http://www.gtconnect.com/articles/2006/05/26/news/oregon/frista03.txt
[1455] AP. Wyden blocks bill seeking to derail Oregon assisted suicide law. September 6 (retrieved and posted) @ http://www.newsreview/info/article/20060906/NEWS/109060076.
[1456] AP. Wyden blocks bill seeking to derail Oregon assisted suicide law. September 6 (retrieved and posted) @ http://www.newsreview/info/article/20060906/NEWS/109060076.
[1457] AP. Wyden blocks bill seeking to derail Oregon assisted suicide law. September 6 (retrieved and posted) @ http://www.newsreview/info/article/20060906/NEWS/109060076.
[1458] AP. Wyden blocks bill seeking to derail Oregon assisted suicide law. May 26, 2006. September 6 (retrieved and posted) @ http://www.newsreview/info/article/20060906/NEWS/109060076.
[1459] AP. Wyden blocks bill seeking to derail Oregon assisted suicide law. September 6 (retrieved and posted) @ http://www.newsreview/info/article/20060906/NEWS/109060076.
[1460] Transcript: Sen. Sam Brownback on 'FOX News Sunday'. Aired Jan. 28, 2007 and retrieved 2.8.07 from http://www.foxnews.com/story/0,2933,247842,00.html. 4/5
[1461] Transcript: Sen. Sam Brownback on 'FOX News Sunday'. Aired Jan. 28, 2007 and retrieved 2.8.07 from http://www.foxnews.com/story/0,2933,247842,00.html. 4/5
[1462] Transcript: Sen. Sam Brownback on 'FOX News Sunday'. Aired Jan. 28, 2007 and retrieved 2.8.07 from http://www.foxnews.com/story/0,2933,247842,00.html. 5/5

[1463] Richard E. Cohen and Michael Barone. "The Almanac of American Politics—2004." The National Journal Group. 2003, page 651.
[1464] FOX NEWS. "Abramoff Pleads Guilty to Federal Fraud Charges. FOXNews.com. Posted January 4, 2006 and retrieved January 6, 2006 from http://www.foxnews.com/printer_friendly_story/0,3566,180409,00.html.
[1465] San Hananel. "Brownback to give away funds linked to lobbyist." AP. Wichita Eagle. Posted December 22, 2005 and retrieved January 6, 2006 from http://www.kansas.com/mld/kansas/news/state/13462829.htm.
[1466] San Hananel. "Brownback to give away funds linked to lobbyist." AP. Wichita Eagle. Posted December 22, 2005 and retrieved January 6, 2006 from http://www.kansas.com/mld/kansas/news/state/13462829.htm.
[1467] Alan Bjerga. "Kansas delegates return Abramoff's money. Wichita Eagle. Posted January 6, 2006 and retrieved same day from http://www.kansas.com/mld/kansas/news/13561955.htm.
[1468] Alan Bjerga. "Kansas delegates return Abramoff's money. Wichita Eagle. Posted January 6, 2006 and retrieved same day from http://www.kansas.com/mld/kansas/news/13561955.htm.
[1469] Posted January 8, 2006 on The Wichita Eagle's website, and retrieved January 10, 2006 from http://www.kansas.com/mld/eagle/13579504.htm. Cartoon by Richard Crowson of The Wichita Eagle.
[1470] AP. "Sen. Burns Faces Tough Re-Election Bid With Abramoff Ties." FOXNEWS.com Posted Friday January 20, 2006 and retrieved January 30, 2006 from http://www.foxnews.com/printer_friendly_story/0,3566,182373,00.html.
[1471] AP. Brownback takes step towards White House bid. 7Online.com. U.S. and World News from WABC-TV. Retrieved 12.14 and posted Dec. 4 @ http://abclocal.go.com/wabc/story?section=nation_world&id=4821440.
[1472] Bill Berkowitz. Brownback brands himself 'Full scale conservative' Media Transparency. Posted 1.4.07 and retrieved 1.13.07 from http://www.mediatransparency.org/storyprinterfriendly.php?storyID=170
[1473] Bill Berkowitz. Brownback brands himself 'Full scale conservative' Media Transparency. Posted 1.4.07 and retrieved 1.13.07 from http://www.mediatransparency.org/storyprinterfriendly.php?storyID=170
[1474] Bill Berkowitz. Brownback brands himself 'Full scale conservative' Media Transparency. Posted 1.4.07 and retrieved 1.13.07 from http://www.mediatransparency.org/storyprinterfriendly.php?storyID=170
[1475] Bill Berkowitz. Brownback brands himself 'Full scale conservative' Media Transparency. Posted 1.4.07 and retrieved 1.13.07 from http://www.mediatransparency.org/storyprinterfriendly.php?storyID=170
[1476] Susan Page. USA Today. Will Christian right embrace—and support—one of its own? Posted 7.19.06 and retrieved 7.28.06 from http://www.usatoday.com/news/washington/2006-07-18-christian-right-vote_x.htm.
[1477] Susan Page. USA Today. Will Christian right embrace—and support—one of its own? Posted July 19, 2006 and retrieved July 28, 2006 from http://www.usatoday.com/news/washington/2006-07-18-christian-right-vote_x.htm.
[1478] Susan Page. USA Today. Will Christian right embrace—and support—one of its own? Posted July 19, 2006 and retrieved July 28, 2006 from http://www.usatoday.com/news/washington/2006-07-18-christian-right-vote_x.htm.
[1479] Susan Page. USA Today. Will Christian right embrace—and support—one of its own? Posted July 19, 2006 and retrieved July 28, 2006 from http://www.usatoday.com/news/washington/2006-07-18-christian-right-vote_x.htm.
[1480] Bill Berkowitz. Brownback brands himself 'Full scale conservative' Media Transparency. Posted 1.4.07 and retrieved 1.13.07 from http://www.mediatransparency.org/storyprinterfriendly.php?storyID=170
[1481] Susan Page. USA Today. Will Christian right embrace—and support—one of its own? Posted July 19, 2006 and retrieved July 28, 2006 from http://www.usatoday.com/news/washington/2006-07-18-christian-right-vote_x.htm.
[1482] Susan Page. USA Today. Will Christian right embrace—and support—one of its own? Posted July 19, 2006 and retrieved July 28, 2006 from http://www.usatoday.com/news/washington/2006-07-18-christian-right-vote_x.htm.
[1483] Tancredo Demands Brownback Apologize. Posted 7.23.07 and retrieved 8.1.07 from http://teamtancredo.typepad.com/team_tancredo/2007/07/tancredo-demand.html.
[1484] M.E. Sprengelmeyer. Back roads to the White House. Posted 7.23.07 and retrieved 8.1.07 from http://blogs.rockymountainnews.com/denver/Sprengelmeyer/archives/2007/07/brownback_a...
[1485] National Journal Rankings. The Republicans. 7.30.07 and retrieved 8.1.07 from http://nationaljournal.com/racerankings/wh08/republicans/.
[1486] The Daily Show, August 2, 2007.
[1487] RJ Elliott. Iowa Straw Poll Results. Published 8.12.07 and retrieved 8.21.07 from http://blogcritics.org/archives/2007/08/12/023738.php.
[1488] Biography. Bill Frist, M.D. Retrieved July 28, 2006 from http://frist.senate.gov/index.cfm?FuseAction=AboutSenatorFrist.Biography.
[1489] Biography of Majority Leader Bill Frist, M.D. PDF file was obtained through http://frist.senate.gov/index.cfm?FuseAction=AboutSenatorFrist.Biography, retrieved July 28, 2006.
[1490] Biography of Majority Leader Bill Frist, M.D. PDF file was obtained through http://frist.senate.gov/index.cfm?FuseAction=AboutSenatorFrist.Biography, retrieved July 28, 2006.
[1491] Biography. Bill Frist, M.D. Retrieved July 28, 2006 from http://frist.senate.gov/index.cfm?FuseAction=AboutSenatorFrist.Biography.
[1492] Biography. Bill Frist, M.D. Retrieved July 28, 2006 from http://frist.senate.gov/index.cfm?FuseAction=AboutSenatorFrist.Biography.
[1493] Richard E. Cohen and Michael Barone. "The Almanac of American Politics—2004." Bill Frist. The National Journal Group. 2003, page 1480.
[1494] Tom Raum. Political junkies speculate on 2008 race. AP. The Arizona Daily Star. Retrieved December 15, 2004 from http://www.asstarnet.com/dailystar/relatedarticles/46526.php
[1495] Tom Raum. Political junkies speculate on 2008 race. AP. The Arizona Daily Star. Retrieved December 15, 2004 from http://www.asstarnet.com/dailystar/relatedarticles/46526.php

[1496] Biography of Majority Leader Bill Frist, M.D. PDF file was obtained 7.28.06 through http://frist.senate.gov/index.cfm?FuseAction=AboutSenatorFrist.Biography.
[1497] Fox News Sunday. "Transcript: Sen. Martinez on 'FNS'." Posted and retrieved March 20, 2005, from http://www.foxnews.com_printer_friendly_story/0,3566,150959,00.html.
[1498] Fox News Sunday. "Transcript: Sen. Martinez on 'FNS'." Posted and retrieved March 20, 2005, from http://www.foxnews.com_printer_friendly_story/0,3566,150959,00.html.
[1499] Fox News Sunday. "Transcript: Sen. Martinez on 'FNS'." Posted and retrieved March 20, 2005, from http://www.foxnews.com_printer_friendly_story/0,3566,150959,00.html.
[1500] Congress prepares to intervene in feeding tube case. Knight Ridder News Service and AP, the Milwaukee Journal Sentinel, March 20, 2005 1A.
[1501] Bush enters fray in right-to-die case dividing the US. David Teather and Richard Luscombe. The Guardian. Posted and retrieved March 21, 2005 from http://www.guardian.co.uk/usa/story/0,12271,1442416,00.html.
[1502] "Poll: No Role for Government in Schiavo Case." Analyzed by Gary Langer. ABC News. Posted March 21, 2005 and retrieved March 31 from http://abcnews.go.com/Politics/PollVault/story?id=599622&page=1.
[1503] Bill Frist's balancing Act. U.S. News and World Report for the week of 4/4/05. Retrieved 3.28.05 from http://www.usnews.com/usnews/news/articles/050404/4culture.b.htm.
[1504] Congress prepares to intervene in feeding tube case. Knight Ridder News Service and AP, the Milwaukee Journal Sentinel, March 20, 2005 1A.
[1505] NBC News: Meet the Press. "Transcript: March 20." Posted and retrieved March 20, 2005 from http://www.msnbc.msn.com/id/7231263/. 6/15.
[1506] Where were key Democrats in Schiavo Debate? Richard Cohen. Washington Post. The Milwaukee Journal Sentinel. March 25, 2005. 19A.
[1507] Fox News Sunday. "Transcript: Immigration Laws on 'Fox News Sunday'." Posted and retrieved March 27, 2005 on http://www.foxnews.com/story/0,2933,151631,00.html.
[1508] Out of context, videos showed only one side of Schiavo story. Tim Cuprisin. The Milwaukee Journal Sentinel. April 1, 2005.
[1509] Out of context, videos showed only one side of Schiavo story. Tim Cuprisin. The Milwaukee Journal Sentinel. April 1, 2005.
[1510] Out of context, videos showed only one side of Schiavo story. Tim Cuprisin. The Milwaukee Journal Sentinel. April 1, 2005.
[1511] EJ Dionne Jr. "Where's the Apology?" The Washington Post. Posted and retrieved June 17, 2005 from http://www.washingtonpost.com/wp-dyn/content/article/2005/06/16/AR2005061601375.html
[1512] EJ Dionne Jr. "Where's the Apology?" The Washington Post. Posted and retrieved June 17, 2005 from http://www.washingtonpost.com/wp-dyn/content/article/2005/06/16/AR2005061601375.html
[1513] Joanne Kenen. Sen. Frist defends role in Schiavo case. Reuters. Posted June 16, 2005 and retrieved June 24, 2005 from http://www.alertnet.org/thenews/newsdesk/N1636368.htm.
[1514] Joanne Kenen. Sen. Frist defends role in Schiavo case. Reuters. Posted June 16, 2005 and retrieved June 24, 2005 from http://www.alertnet.org/thenews/newsdesk/N1636368.htm.
[1515] Joanne Kenen. Sen. Frist defends role in Schiavo case. Reuters. Posted June 16, 2005 and retrieved June 24, 2005 from http://www.alertnet.org/thenews/newsdesk/N1636368.htm.
[1516] Joanne Kenen. Sen. Frist defends role in Schiavo case. Reuters. Posted June 16, 2005 and retrieved June 24, 2005 from http://www.alertnet.org/thenews/newsdesk/N1636368.htm.
[1517] Janet Hook. Frist Plagued again by comments on Schiavo. LA Times. Posted June 17, 2005 and retrieved June 24 from http://www.latimes.com/news/nationworld/nation/la-na-frist17jun17,0,1567488.story?coll=la-home-nation.
[1518] Janet Hook. Frist Plagued again by comments on Schiavo. LA Times. Posted June 17, 2005 and retrieved June 24 from http://www.latimes.com/news/nationworld/nation/la-na-frist17jun17,0,1567488.story?coll=la-home-nation
[1519] EJ Dionne Jr. "Where's the Apology?" The Washington Post. Posted and retrieved June 17, 2005 from http://www.washingtonpost.com/wp-dyn/content/article/2005/06/16/AR2005061601375.html.
[1520] Newsweek. Lindsay Graham Expresses Concern over Bill Frist's Involvement in Prayer Service About easing Senate Filibuster Debate rule. Posted April 17, 2005 and retrieved April 18, 2005 from http://www.finance.lycos.com/qc/news/story.aspx?story=200504171422_PRN__NYSU013&symbols=QCNEWS:0.
[1521] His American Dream. John Heilemann. New York Magazine. Posted 12.11 and retrieved 12.14.06 from http://nymag.com/news/politics/25015/. 4 /11.
[1522] Mitch Stacy. A legacy emerges after death of Schiavo. The Milwaukee Journal Sentinel, March 31, 2006, 7A.
[1523] Mitch Stacy. A legacy emerges after death of Schiavo. The Milwaukee Journal Sentinel, March 31, 2006, 7A.
[1524] Senate Democrats erect shield to obstruct 'nuclear option'. Edwin Chen. Los Angeles Times. Posted March 16, 2005 and retrieved March 31 2005 from http://www.latimes.com/news/politics/la-na-reid16mar16,1,4751988.story?coll=la-headlines-politics&ctrack=1&cset=true.
[1525] Senate Democrats erect shield to obstruct 'nuclear option'. Edwin Chen. Los Angeles Times. Posted March 16, 2005 and retrieved March 31 2005 from http://www.latimes.com/news/politics/la-na-reid16mar16,1,4751988.story?coll=la-headlines-politics&ctrack=1&cset=true.
[1526] Support falters for the 'nuclear option'. Charles Hurt. The Washington Times. Published March 23, 2005 and retrieved March 31, 2005 from http://www.washtimes.com/national/20050323-121608-8533r.htm.
[1527] NBC News: Meet the Press. Transcript: March 20. Posted and retrieved March 20, 2005 from http://www.msnbc.msn.com/id/7231263/.

[1528] Margaret Talev. Frist's political skills being tested. McClatchy Newspapers. Posted May 23, 2005 and retrieved June 5, 2005 from http://www.sitnews.us/0505news/052305/052305_shns_frist.html.
[1529] Margaret Talev. Frist's political skills being tested. McClatchy Newspapers. Posted May 23, 2005 and retrieved June 5, 2005 from http://www.sitnews.us/0505news/052305/052305_shns_frist.html.
[1530] ABC News, This Week. May 15 show. Transcript provided by sundaymorningtalk.com. Retrieved June 2, 2005 from http://www.sundaymorningtalk.com/smt/smt_transcripts/tw_2005_05_15.html.
[1531] The Hill, 11/22/05; NY Times 11,27/05. Retrieved from Research from the DNC for the 2008 candidates, Retrieved February 13, 2006 from http://www.washingtonpost.com/wp-srv/politics/documents/dnc_McCain08Watch12-05.pdf
[1532] James Beltran. Frist: Stock Probe Will Affect 2008 Plans. AP. Retrieved November 3, 2005 from http://abcnews.go.com/Politics/print?id=1242683.
[1533] CBS/AP. "New Questions On Frist Stock Sales." CBS NEWS. Posted October 24, 2005 and retrieved November 1, 2005 from http://www.cbsnews.com/stories/2005/10/24/politics/printable966981.shtml.
[1534] CBS/AP. "New Questions On Frist Stock Sales." CBS NEWS. Posted October 24, 2005 and retrieved November 1, 2005 from http://www.cbsnews.com/stories/2005/10/24/politics/printable966981.shtml
[1535] CBS/AP. "New Questions On Frist Stock Sales." CBS NEWS. Posted October 24, 2005 and retrieved November 1, 2005 from http://www.cbsnews.com/stories/2005/10/24/politics/printable966981.shtml
[1536] CBS/AP. "New Questions On Frist Stock Sales." CBS NEWS. Posted October 24, 2005 and retrieved November 1, 2005 from http://www.cbsnews.com/stories/2005/10/24/politics/printable966981.shtml
[1537] Sheryl Gay Stolberg. For Frist, A Political Fortune May be Inextricably Linked to a Financial One. The New York Times. Posted October 25, 2005 and retrieved November 1, 2005 from http://www.nytimes.com/2005/10/25/politics/25frist.html?pagewanted=print.
[1538] Oscar Corral. Frist meeting in Coral Gables hints at run for White House. Miami Herald. Posted October 12, 2005 and retrieved November 2, 2005 from http://www.miami.com/mld/miamiherald/news/12878423.htm.
[1539] Hardball with Chris Matthews for April 27. MSNBC.com. Retrieved April 28, 2006 from http://www.msnbc.msn.com/id/12531719/.
[1540] FOX News. Senate Republicans Seek Taxpayer Rebate Checks for Gas Price Relief. Posted April 27, 2006 and retrieved May 8, 2006 from http://www.foxnews.com/story/0,2933,193327,00.html.
[1541] Hardball with Chris Matthews for April 27. MSNBC.com. Retrieved April 28, 2006 from http://www.msnbc.msn.com/id/12531719/.
[1542] Tax-News.com. Frist Drops Gas Rebate Plan Amid Outcry From Business Lobby. Leroy Baker. Posted May 3, 2006 and retrieved May 8, 2006 from http://tax-news.com/asp/story/story_open.asp?storyname=23496.
[1543] Tax-News.com. Frist Drops Gas Rebate Plan Amid Outcry From Business Lobby. Leroy Baker. Posted May 3, 2006 and retrieved May 8, 2006 from http://tax-news.com/asp/story/story_open.asp?storyname=23496
[1544] H. Josef Hebert. First ends tax push in gas plan. AP. Milwaukee Journal Sentinel. May 2, 2006, 1A.
[1545] H . Josef Hebert. First ends tax push in gas plan. AP. Milwaukee Journal Sentinel. May 2, 2006, 1A.
[1546] Melanie Hunter. Do Something Now, Democratic Governors Tell Bush. CNSNews.com. Posted April 26, 2006 and retrieved April 28, 2006 from http://www.cnsnews.com/ViewNation.asp?Page=/Nation/archive/200604/NAT20060426b.html.
[1547] Deroy Murdock: Today's GOP looks more and more like the party of LBJ. Union Leader. Retrieved May 8, 2006 from http://www.unionleader.com/article.aspx?articleId=7e488162-8b36-4e55-9aff-650f8c704f06&headline=Deroy+Murdock%3a+Today%27s+GOP+looks+more+and+more+like+the+party+of+LBJ%22%27%25%3c%3e%3a%24,
[1548] H. Josef Hebert. First ends tax push in gas plan. AP. Milwaukee Journal Sentinel. May 2, 2006, 1A.
[1549] H. Josef Herbert. AP. House Panel Questions Exxon Mobil Payment. Chron.com. Posted May 4, 2006 and retrieved May 8, 2006 from http://www.chron.com/disp/story.mpl/ap/politics/3841815.html.
[1550] Carl Hulse. New York Times. $3 gas and $100 rebates? Milwaukee Journal Sentinel, April 28, 2006, 1A.
[1551] Joe Klein. A Fair Trade for Lower Gas Prices. TIME.com. Posted May 7, 2006 and retrieved May 8, 2006 from http://www.time.com/time/nation/printout/0,8816,1191805,00.html.
[1552] Sheryl Gay Stolberg and Carl Hulse. Frist gas rebate plan shows ideas don't always become law. New York Times. Retrieved from the Tenneessean.com on May 20, 2006 and posted May 5, 2006 at http://tennessean.com/apps/pbcs.dll/article?AID=/20060505/NEWS02/605050416/1009/NEWS.
[1553] Socialist Bunk and Conservative Trickery. Posted May 1, 2006 and retrieved May 8, 2006 from http://rightofftheshore.blogspot.com/2006/05/socialist-bunk-and-conservative.html.
[1554] Sheryl Gay Stolberg and Carl Hulse. Frist gas rebate plan shows ideas don't always become law. New York Times. Retrieved from the Tenneessean.com on May 20, 2006 and posted May 5, 2006 at http://tennessean.com/apps/pbcs.dll/article?AID=/20060505/NEWS02/605050416/1009/NEWS.
[1555] Hardball with Chris Matthews for April 27. MSNBC.com. Retrieved April 28, 2006 from http://www.msnbc.msn.com/id/12531719/.
[1556] Sioux City Journal. Frist says Congress should protect ethanol competitor. Posted April 24, 2006 and retrieved April 24, 2006 from http://www.siouxcityjournal.com/articles/2006/04/24/news/latest_news/6452382c4bb7bfb68625715a00679b37.txt.
[1557] Think Progress. Frist on High Gas Prices: It's Clinton's Fault. Retrieved May 8, 2006 from http://thinkprogress.org/2006/05/02/frist-gas-prices/
[1558] Think Progress. Frist on High Gas Prices: It's Clinton's Fault. Retrieved May 8, 2006 from http://thinkprogress.org/2006/05/02/frist-gas-prices/

[1559] Think Progress. Frist on High Gas Prices: It's Clinton's Fault. Retrieved May 8, 2006 from http://thinkprogress.org/2006/05/02/frist-gas-prices/

[1560] Summary of Findings: Public Worried about Iran but Wary of Military Action. Pew. Released May 26, 2006 and retrieved May 31, 2006 from http://people-press.org/reports/display.php3?ReportID=277.

[1561] Media Matters. O'Donnell let Frist mislead on ANWR drilling, Exxon Mobil profits. Posted May 1 and retrieved May 31, 2006 from http://mediamatters.org/items/200605010003.

[1562] http://www.eia.doe.gov/oiaf/servicerpt/ogp/results.html. See also Media Matters. O'Donnell let Frist mislead on ANWR drilling, Exxon Mobil profits. Posted May 1 and retrieved May 31, 2006 from http://mediamatters.org/items/200605010003.

[1563] Media Matters. O'Donnell let Frist mislead on ANWR drilling, Exxon Mobil profits. Posted May 1 and retrieved May 31, 2006 from http://mediamatters.org/items/200605010003.

[1564] David Stout. Republicans Offer Plan on Gas Prices. New York Times. Posted April 27, 2006 and retrieved May 8, 2006 from http://www.nytimes.com/2006/04/27/washington/27cnd-gas.html?ex=1303790400&en=514daad1caa852cb&ei=5089&partner=rssyahoo&emc=rss.

[1565] FOX News. Senate Republicans Seek Taxpayer Rebate Checks for Gas Price Relief. Posted April 27, 2006 and retrieved May 8, 2006 from http://www.foxnews.com/story/0,2933,193327,00.html.

[1566] FOX News. Senate Republicans Seek Taxpayer Rebate Checks for Gas Price Relief. Posted April 27, 2006 and retrieved May 8, 2006 from http://www.foxnews.com/story/0,2933,193327,00.html.

[1567] FOX News. Senate Republicans Seek Taxpayer Rebate Checks for Gas Price Relief. Posted April 27, 2006 and retrieved May 8, 2006 from http://www.foxnews.com/story/0,2933,193327,00.html.

[1568] Bill Frist. Chattanoogan. Bill Frist Will Not Run for President in 2008. Breaking News. Posted 11.29.06 and retrieved 12.3.06 from http://www.chattanoogan.com/articles/article_97469.asp/.

[1569] Bill Frist. Chattanoogan. Bill Frist Will Not Run for President in 2008. Breaking News. Posted 11.29.06 and retrieved 12.3.06 from http://www.chattanoogan.com/articles/article_97469.asp/.

[1570] Bill Frist. Chattanoogan. Bill Frist Will Not Run for President in 2008. Breaking News. Posted 11.29.06 and retrieved 12.3.06 from http://www.chattanoogan.com/articles/article_97469.asp/.

[1571] Kate Zerniki. Frist Announces He'll Forgo a Run for the White House. Published Nov.30, 2006 in the New York Times, and retrieved 12.3.06 from http://ww.nytimes.com/2006/11/30/us/politics/30frist.html?...

[1572] Kate Zerniki. Frist Announces He'll Forgo a Run for the White House. Published Nov.30, 2006 in the New York Times, and retrieved 12.3.06 from http://ww.nytimes.com/2006/11/30/us/politics/30frist.html? ...

[1573] Washington Post/AP. Senator will not seek White House. Washington Post/AP. Milwaukee Journal Sentinel. 11.30.06. 3A.

[1574] LA Times. Frist won't run for President in 2008, small boost for McCain and others. The China Post. Posted 12.1.06 and retrieved 12.3.06 from http://www.chinapost.com.tw/p_detail.asp?id=96520&GRP=D&onNews=.

[1575] John Nichols. Farewell to Senator Bill Frist, R-Frist Family. Posted 11.29 and retrieved 12.3.06 from http://www.thenation.com/blogs/thebeat?bid=1&pid=144105. 1/4.

[1576] John Nichols. Farewell to Senator Bill Frist, R-Frist Family. Posted 11.29.06 and retrieved 12.3.06 from http://www.thenation.com/blogs/thebeat?bid=1&pid=144105. 2/4.

[1577] Dan Balz. Clinton, Obama Clearing the Field. 12.24,06. A01. Retrieved 1.13.07 from http://www.washingtonpost.com/wp-dyn/content/article/2006/12/23/AR2006122300970.html.

[1578] CNN.com. Late Edition with Wolf Blitzer, aired April 2, 2006. Retrieved April 3, 2006 from http://transcripts.cnn.com/TRANSCRIPTS/0604/02/le.01.html 14/20.

[1579] Hardball with Chris Matthews for May 10. MSNBC.com. Retrieved May 22, 2006 from http://www.msnbc.msn..com/id/12756628/

[1580] H. Josef Hebert. Frist Breaks With Bush on Stem-Cell Bill. Posted 7.29.05 and retrieved 7.29.05 from http://abcnews.go.com/Health/pint?id=990152.

[1581] Meet the Press. NBC News. Transcript for July 31 (2005). Retrieved 8.2.05 from http://www.msnbc.msn.com/id/8714260/print/1/displaymode/1098/.

[1582] Political Figures: E-F. Bill Frist (R-Tennessee). Retrieved 7.27.07 from http://pollingreport.com/E-F.htm.

[1583] Hardball with Chris Matthew's for Nov.30. MSNBC.com. Retrieved 12.3.06 from http://www.msnbc.msn.com/id/15988680/. 3/21.

[1584] LA Times. Frist won't run for President in 2008, small boost for McCain and others. The China Post. Posted 12.1.06 and retrieved 12.3.06 from http://www.chinapost.com.tw/p_detail.asp?id=96520&GRP=D&onNews=.

[1585] LA Times. Frist won't run for President in 2008, small boost for McCain and others. The China Post. Posted 12.1.06 and retrieved 12.3.06 from http://www.chinapost.com.tw/p_detail.asp?id=96520&GRP=D&onNews=.

[1586] Gilmore Still Mulling options. Nov.28. Retrieved 12.14.06 from http://blogs.abcnews.com/politicalradar/2006/11/gilmore_still_m.html.

[1587] Bob Lewis. Ex-Gov. Gilmore Eyes GOP White House Bid. ABC News. AP. Posted Jan.9, 2007 and retrieved 1.13.2007 from http://www.abcnews.go.com/Politics/wireStory?id=2781393.

[1588] Gilmore 1st major candidate to drop out. Dionne Walker. AP. 7.15.07 and retrieved 7.20.07 from http://www.leadingthecharge.com/ViewArticle.aspx?id=133665&source=2.; And Mike Glover. AP. Former Va. Governor Jim Gilmore running for president. 4.28.07 and retrieved 5.3.07 from http://www.unionleader.com.

[1589] Tyler Whitley. Gilmore a step closer. Richmond-Times Dispatch. Posted Jan.10, 2007 and retrieved 1.13.06 from http://www.timesdispatch.com/servlet/Satellite?pagename=RTD%2FMGAriticle%2FRTD_BasicArticle&%0...

[1590] Bob Lewis. Ex-Gov. Gilmore Eyes GOP White House Bid. ABC News. AP. Posted Jan.9, 2007 and retrieved 1.13.2007 from http://www.abcnews.go.com/Politics/wireStory?id=2781393.
[1591] Tyler Whitley. Gilmore a step closer. Richmond-Times Dispatch. Posted Jan.10, 2007 and retrieved 1.13.06 from http://www.timesdispatch.com/servlet/Satellite?pagename=RTD%2FMGAriticle%2FRTD_BasicArticle&%0...
[1592] Steven Ertelt. Former Virginia Gov. Jim Gilmore Considers 2008 Republican Prez Bid. Jan.10.2007. Retrieved 1.13.06 from http://www.lifenews.com/nat2858.html.
[1593] Steven Ertelt. Former Virginia Gov. Jim Gilmore Considers 2008 Republican Prez Bid. Jan.10.2007. Retrieved 1.13.06 from http://www.lifenews.com/nat2858.html.
[1594] Steven Ertelt. Former Virginia Gov. Jim Gilmore Considers 2008 Republican Prez Bid. Jan.10.2007. Retrieved 1.13.06 from http://www.lifenews.com/nat2858.html.
[1595] Hotline on Call: Gilmore's Announcement. Posted Jan.9, 2007 and retrieved 1.13.07 from http://hotlineblog.nationaljournal.com/archives.com/archives/2007/01/gilmores_announ.html.
[1596] Hotline on Call: Gilmore's Announcement. Posted Jan.9, 2007 and retrieved 1.13.07 from http://hotlineblog.nationaljournal.com/archives.com/archives/2007/01/gilmores_announ.html.
[1597] Hotline on Call: Gilmore's Announcement. Posted Jan.9, 2007 and retrieved 1.13.07 from http://hotlineblog.nationaljournal.com/archives.com/archives/2007/01/gilmores_announ.html.
[1598] Bob Lewis. Ex-Gov. Gilmore eyes GOP White House bid. Posted Jan.9 and retrieved 1.13.07 from http://www.leadingthecharge.com/ViewArticle.aspx?id=43150&source=2.
[1599] Tyler Whitley. Gilmore a step closer. Richmond-Times Dispatch. Posted Jan.10, 2007 and retrieved 1.13.06 from http://www.timesdispatch.com/servlet/Satellite?pagename=RTD%2FMGAriticle%2FRTD_BasicArticle&%0...
[1600] Bob Lewis. Ex-Gov. Gilmore Eyes GOP White House Bid. ABC News. AP. Posted Jan.9, 2007 and retrieved 1.13.2007 from http://www.abcnews.go.com/Politics/wireStory?id=2781393.
[1601] Tyler Whitley. Gilmore a step closer. Richmond-Times Dispatch. Posted Jan.10, 2007 and retrieved 1.13.06 from http://www.timesdispatch.com/servlet/Satellite?pagename=RTD%2FMGAriticle%2FRTD_BasicArticle&%0...
[1602] Tyler Whitley. Gilmore a step closer. Richmond-Times Dispatch. Posted Jan.10, 2007 and retrieved 1.13.06 from http://www.timesdispatch.com/servlet/Satellite?pagename=RTD%2FMGAriticle%2FRTD_BasicArticle&%0...
[1603] Tyler Whitley. Gilmore a step closer. Richmond-Times Dispatch. Posted Jan.10, 2007 and retrieved 1.13.06 from http://www.timesdispatch.com/servlet/Satellite?pagename=RTD%2FMGAriticle%2FRTD_BasicArticle&%0...
[1604] Bob Lewis. Ex-Gov. Gilmore Eyes GOP White House Bid. ABC News. AP. Posted Jan.9, 2007 and retrieved 1.13.2007 from http://www.abcnews.go.com/Politics/wireStory?id=2781393.
[1605] Bob Lewis. Ex-Gov. Gilmore Eyes GOP White House Bid. ABC News. AP. Posted Jan.9, 2007 and retrieved 1.13.2007 from http://www.abcnews.go.com/Politics/wireStory?id=2781393.
[1606] Bob Lewis. Ex-Gov. Gilmore Eyes GOP White House Bid. ABC News. AP. Posted Jan.9, 2007 and retrieved 1.13.2007 from http://www.abcnews.go.com/Politics/wireStory?id=2781393.
[1607] Tyler Whitley. Gilmore a step closer. Richmond-Times Dispatch. Posted Jan.10, 2007 and retrieved 1.13.06 from http://www.timesdispatch.com/servlet/Satellite?pagename=RTD%2FMGAriticle%2FRTD_BasicArticle&%0...
[1608] Tyler Whitley. Gilmore a step closer. Richmond-Times Dispatch. Posted Jan.10, 2007 and retrieved 1.13.06 from http://www.timesdispatch.com/servlet/Satellite?pagename=RTD%2FMGAriticle%2FRTD_BasicArticle&%0...
[1609] Bob Lewis. Ex-Gov. Gilmore Eyes GOP White House Bid. ABC News. AP. Posted Jan.9, 2007 and retrieved 1.13.2007 from http://www.abcnews.go.com/Politics/wireStory?id=2781393.
[1610] Bob Lewis. Ex-Gov. Gilmore Eyes GOP White House Bid. ABC News. AP. Posted Jan.9, 2007 and retrieved 1.13.2007 from http://www.abcnews.go.com/Politics/wireStory?id=2781393
[1611] Governing. "A- Virginia." February 2005, page 90. Retrieved 10/27/05 from http://results.gpponline.org/StateOVerview.aspx?id=138.
[1612] Jonathan Martin. Virginia Republican for President. National Review Online. 12.13.06 and retrieved 5.3.07 from http://article.nationalreview.com/?q=ZTE1YjkzNzgzMjkyMDdjYTBkYTJmNDU4Y2M4Mjg3MmE=.
[1613] Bob Lewis. Gilmore Recovers, Suspends Campaign. AP. Retrieved 7.20.07 from http://www.abcnews.go.com/print?id=3339622.
[1614] Gilmore 1st major candidate to drop out. Dionne Walker. AP. 7.15.07 and retrieved 7.20.07 from http://www.leadingthecharge.com/ViewArticle.aspx?id=133665&source=2.
[1615] AP. Former Virginia Governor Jim Gilmore Exits Presidential Race. Posted 7.15.07 and retrieved 7.20.07 from http://www.foxnews.com/story/0,2933,289326,00.html.
[1616] Gilmore 1st major candidate to drop out. Dionne Walker. AP. 7.15.07 and retrieved 7.20.07 from http://www.leadingthecharge.com/ViewArticle.aspx?id=133665&source=2.
[1617] Gilmore 1st major candidate to drop out. Dionne Walker. AP. 7.15.07 and retrieved 7.20.07 from http://www.leadingthecharge.com/ViewArticle.aspx?id=133665&source=2. See also http://www.washingtonpost.com/wp-dyn/content/article/2007/07/15/Ar2007071500202_pf.html.
[1618] Michael D. Shear. Gilmore Ends Bid For White House. Washingtonpost.com. Posted 7.15.07 and retrieved 7.20.07 from http://www.washingtonpost.com/wp-dyn/content/article/2007/07/14/AR2007071400805_pf.html.
[1619] The Funnies. Retrieved 8.1.07 from http://www.hillaryis44.org/?p=98.
[1620] Michael D. Shear. Gilmore Ends Bid For White House. Washingtonpost.com. Posted 7.15.07 and retrieved 7.20.07 from http://www.washingtonpost.com/wp-dyn/content/article/2007/07/14/AR2007071400805_pf.html.
[1621] Michael D. Shear. Gilmore Ends Bid For White House. Washingtonpost.com. Posted 7.15.07 and retrieved 7.20.07 from http://www.washingtonpost.com/wp-dyn/content/article/2007/07/14/AR2007071400805_pf.html.

[1622] James Pindell. Gilmore leaves Republican presidential race. 7.14.07 and retrieved 7.20.07 from http://www.boston.com/news/local/politics/primarysource/2007/07/gilmore_leaves.html.
[1623] Michael D. Shear. Gilmore Ends Bid For White House. Washingtonpost.com. Posted 7.15.07 and retrieved 7.20.07 from http://www.washingtonpost.com/wp-dyn/content/article/2007/07/14/AR2007071400805_pf.html.
[1624] Michael D. Shear. Gilmore Ends Bid For White House. Washingtonpost.com. Posted 7.15.07 and retrieved 7.20.07 from http://www.washingtonpost.com/wp-dyn/content/article/2007/07/14/AR2007071400805_pf.html.
[1625] Michael D. Shear. Gilmore Ends Bid For White House. Washingtonpost.com. Posted 7.15.07 and retrieved 7.20.07 from http://www.washingtonpost.com/wp-dyn/content/article/2007/07/14/AR2007071400805_pf.html.
[1626] Jonathan Martin. Virginia Republican for President. National Review Online. 12.13.06 and retrieved 5.3.07 from http://article.nationalreview.com/?q=ZTE1YjkzNzgzMjkyMDdjYTBkYTJmNDU4Y2M4Mjg3MmE=.
[1627] Newt Gingrich. Biography and Much More from Answers.com. Retrieved 7.20.07 from http://www.answers.com/topic/newt-gingrich.
[1628] Newt Gingrich. Biography and Much More from Answers.com. Retrieved 7.20.07 from http://www.answers.com/topic/newt-gingrich.
[1629] Newt Gingrich. Biography and Much More from Answers.com . Retrieved 7.20.07 from http://www.answers.com/topic/newt-gingrich
[1630] Newt Gingrich. Biography and Much More from Answers.com. Retrieved 7.20.07 from http://www.answers.com/topic/newt-gingrich.
[1631] Janet Hook. LA Times. Gingrich Writes Act 2 of his Political Life. Posted 1.16.05 and retrieved 7.20.07 from http://www.newt.org/backpage.sp?art=1463.
[1632] Newt Gingrich. Biography and Much More from Answers.com . Retrieved 7.20.07 from http://www.answers.com/topic/newt-gingrich
[1633] Janet Hook. LA Times. Gingrich Writes Act 2 of his Political Life. Posted 1.16.05 and retrieved 7.20.07 from http://www.newt.org/backpage.sp?art=1463.
[1634] Janet Hook. LA Times. Gingrich Writes Act 2 of his Political Life. Posted 1.16.05 and retrieved 7.20.07 from http://www.newt.org/backpage.sp?art=1463.
[1635] Ron Fournier. Gingrich doesn't rule out presidential run. AP, Posted January 9, 2005 and retrieved January 12, 2005 from http://edition.cnn.com/2005/ALLPOLITICS/01/09/gingrich.ap/.
[1636] Pew Research. Public to '08 Contenders—It's Too Early. Released and retrieved 12.14.06 from http://people-press-org/reports/print.php3?PageID=1106. See also http://people-press.org/reports/display.php3?ReportID=298.
[1637] Jake Tapper. Gingrich Admits to Affair During Clinton Impeachment. ABC News. 3.9.07 and retrieved 6.29.07 from http://abcnews.go.com/print?id=2937633.
[1638] NBC News. Meet the Press. Transcript for May 15 (2005). Retrieved @ http://www.msnbc.msn.com/id/7862265/.
[1639] Newt Gingrich. Biography and Much More from Answers.com . Retrieved 7.20.07 from http://www.answers.com/topic/newt-gingrich.
[1640] Newt Gingrich. Biography and Much More from Answers.com . Retrieved 7.20.07 from http://www.answers.com/topic/newt-gingrich.
[1641] AP. Arizona Daily Wildcat. Ethics vote in: Gingrich keeps speaker's job, loses $300,000. January 22, 1997 and retrieved 8.1.07 from http://wc.arizona.edu/~wildcat/papers/90/80/01_3_m.html.
[1642] John E. Yang and Helen Dewar. Ethics Panel Supports Reprimand of Gingrich. 1.18.97 and retrieved 8.1.07 from http://www.washingtonpost.com/wp-srv/politics/govt/leadership/stories/011897.htm.
[1643] AP. Arizona Daily Wildcat. Ethics vote in: Gingrich keeps speaker's job, loses $300,000. January 22, 1997 and retrieved 8.1.07 from http://wc.arizona.edu/~wildcat/papers/90/80/01_3_m.html.
[1644] John E. Yang. Speaker Sets $150,000 Limit on Borrowing From Dole. A01. May 16, 1997. Retrieved 8.1.07 from http://www.washingtonpost.com/wp-srv/politics/govt'leadership/stories/051697.htm.
[1645] Bill McAllister. Gingrich to Pay Penalty With His Own Money. A19. Published 9.15.98 and retrieved 8.1.07 from http://www.washingtonpost.com/wp-srv/politics/govt/leadership/stories/091598.htm.
[1646] Gingrich pays off ethic penalty. 12.30.98 and retrieved 8.1.07 from http://www.washingtonpost.com/wp-srv/politics/govt/leadership/stories/gingrich123198.htm.
[1647] High Infidelity. Steve Benen. Washington Monthly. July/August 2006. Retrieved June 30, 2006 from http://www.washingtonmonthly.com/features/2006/0607.benen.html.
[1648] High Infidelity. Steve Benen. Washington Monthly. July/August 2006. Retrieved June 30, 2006 from http://www.washingtonmonthly.com/features/2006/0607.benen.html. 2/4.
[1649] Jake Tapper. Gingrich Admits to Affair During Clinton Impeachment. ABC News. 3.9.07 and retrieved 6.29.07 from http://abcnews.go.com/print?id=2937633.
[1650] Jake Tapper. Gingrich Admits to Affair During Clinton Impeachment. ABC News. 3.9.07 and retrieved 6.29.07 from http://abcnews.go.com/print?id=2937633.
[1651] Jake Tapper. Gingrich Admits to Affair During Clinton Impeachment. ABC News. 3.9.07 and retrieved 6.29.07 from http://abcnews.go.com/print?id=2937633.
[1652] High Infidelity. Steve Benen. Washington Monthly. July/August 2006. Retrieved June 30, 2006 from http://www.washingtonmonthly.com/features/2006/0607.benen.html. 2/4.
[1653] High Infidelity. Steve Benen. Washington Monthly. July/August 2006. Retrieved June 30, 2006 from http://www.washingtonmonthly.com/features/2006/0607.benen.html. 2/4.
[1654] Bill Schneider. CNN Senior Political Analyst. Gingrich confession: Clearing the way for a 2008 run? CNN.com. Posted 3.9.07 and retrieved 6.29.07 from http://www.cnn.com/2007/POLITICS/03/09/gingrich.schneider/index.html.

[1655] Janet Hook. LA Times. Gingrich Writes Act 2 of his Political Life. Posted 1.16.05 and retrieved 7.20.07 from http://www.newt.org/backpage.sp?art=1463.
[1656] Jake Tapper. Gingrich Admits to Affair During Clinton Impeachment. ABC News. 3.9.07 and retrieved 6.29.07 from http://abcnews.go.com/print?id=2937633.
[1657] Dave Bohon. WDC MEDIA. "Newt Gingrich Signs as Columnist for Church Report. Posted December 13, 2005 and retrieved December 15, 2005 form http://www.michnews.com/artman/publish/article_10805.shtml See also http://www.newt.org/backpage.asp?art=2567.
[1658] Dave Bohon. WDC MEDIA. Newt Gingrich Signs as Columnist for Church Report. Posted December 13, 2005 and retrieved December 15, 2005 form http://www.michnews.com/artman/publish/article_10805.shtml
[1659] John M. Broder. Gingrich sees a higher calling. New York Times. Milwaukee Journal Sentinel. Dec.17, 2006, 5A.
[1660] John M. Broder. Gingrich sees a higher calling. New York Times. Milwaukee Journal Sentinel. Dec.17, 2006, 5A.
[1661] AP. Huckabee: Character issues apply to GOP, too. MSNBC.com. Posted 4.6.07 and retrieved 8.1.07 from http://www.msnbc.msn.com/id/17980177/print/1/displaymode/1098/.
[1662] NBC Nightly News, Nov.6.2006.
[1663] National Journal Group Inc. White House 2008 Rankings. Jan. 11. 2007. Retrieved 1.13.07 from http://nationaljournal.com/racerankings/wh08/republicans/.
[1664] FOX News. Transcript: Newt Gingrich on 'FNS'. Chris Wallace. Aired 11.19 and retrieved 12.3.06 from http://www.foxnews.com/story/0,2933,230591,00.html. 4/5.
[1665] FOX News. Transcript: Newt Gingrich on 'FNS'. Chris Wallace. Aired 11.19 and retrieved 12.3.06 from http://www.foxnews.com/story/0,2933,230591,00.html. 4/5.
[1666] John M. Broder. Gingrich sees a higher calling. New York Times. Milwaukee Journal Sentinel. Dec.17, 2006, 5A.
[1667] John M. Broder. Gingrich sees a higher calling. New York Times. Milwaukee Journal Sentinel. Dec.17, 2006, 5A.
[1668] ABC This Week. September 30, 2007.
[1669] McCain vs. Giuliani: Tale of the Tape. Nov. 17.2006. Retrieved same day @ http://www.cbsnews.com/stories/2006/11/15/politics/printable2184018.shtml.
[1670] AP. "Clinton, Giuliani put 2008 presidential race in N.Y. state of mind." USA TODAY. Posted November 19, 2005 and retrieved December 14, 2005 from http://www.usatoday.com/news/washington/2005-11-19-hillary-versus-rudy_x.htm?csp=34.
[1671] MSNBC.com. Transcript for August 29. NBC News/Meet the Press. Posted August 29, 2004 and retrieved September 29, 2005 from http://www.msnbc.msn.com/id/5858461/.
[1672] McCain vs. Giuliani: Tale of the Tape. Nov. 17.2006. Retrieved same day @ http://www.cbsnews.com/stories/2006/11/15/politics/printable2184018.shtml.
[1673] McCain vs. Giuliani: Tale of the Tape. Nov. 17.2006. Retrieved same day @ http://www.cbsnews.com/stories/2006/11/15/politics/printable2184018.shtml
[1674] MSNBC.com. Transcript for August 29. NBC News/Meet the Press. Posted August 29, 2004 and retrieved September 29, 2005 from http://www.msnbc.msn.com/id/5858461/. 7/16.
[1675] Chris Cillizza. The Fix. McCain Files Prez Paperwork, Thompson Mulling a Run. Retrieved 11.17.06 from http//blog.washingtonpost.com/thefix/2006/11/mccain_makes_it_official.html. Posted 11.15.06.
[1676] Quinnipiac University. November 27, 2006—More Americans Think Well of Speaker Pelosi, Quinnipiac University National Thermometer Finds; President is low on List, But Kerry is Last. Retrieved 12.14.06 from http://www.quinnipiac.edu/x1284.xml?ReleaseId=990&ss=print. P 1/28.
[1677] Quinnipiac University. November 27, 2006—More Americans Think Well of Speaker Pelosi, Quinnipiac University National Thermometer Finds; President is low on List, But Kerry is Last. Retrieved 12.14.06 from http://www.quinnipiac.edu/x1284.xml?ReleaseId=990&ss=print. 2/28
[1678] WH2008: Republican Nomination. Retrieved 12.14.06 from http://pollingreport.com/WH08rep.htm.
[1679] Karen Tumulty. Why it's Dangerous For the Maverick To be The…Frontrunner. Time. Posted Dec.10 and retrieved 12.14.06 from http://www.time.com/time/magazine/printout/0,8816,1568457,00.html. Title later changed.
[1680] Joyce Purnick. Giuliani's Strategy Is All on His Web Site. New York Times. Posted Jan.5, 2007 and retrieved 1.13.07 from http://www.nytimes.com/2007/01/05/nyregion/05cnd-rudy.html?ex=1325653200&en=52b...
[1681] Joyce Purnick. Giuliani's Strategy Is All on His Web Site. New York Times. Posted Jan.5, 2007 and retrieved 1.13.07 from http://www.nytimes.com/2007/01/05/nyregion/05cnd-rudy.html?ex=1325653200&en=52b...
[1682] Chris Cillizza. 2008: The Case for Rudy Giuliani. Washington Post. Posted March 15, 2006 and retrieved August 25, 2006 from http://blog.washingtonpost.com/thefix/2006/03/2008_the_case_for_rudy_giuliani.html.
[1683] Beth Fouhy. AP Giuliani maintaining a low profile about '08. Posted February 12, 2006 and retrieved February 17, 2006 from http://www.contracostatimes.com/mld/cctimes/news/local/state/california/13854427.htm.
[1684] Chris Cillizza. 2008: The Case Against Rudy Giuliani. Washington Post. Posted March 16, 2006 and retrieved August 25, 2006 from http://blog.washingtonpost.com/thefix/2006/03/2008_the_case_against_rudy_giu.html
[1685] Michael Goodwin. New York Daily News. Milwaukee Journal Sentinel, Nov.22, 2006. 19A.
[1686] MSNBC.com. Transcript for August 29. NBC News/Meet the Press. Posted August 29, 2004 and retrieved September 29, 2005 from http://www.msnbc.msn.com/id/5858461/. 3/16.
[1687] MSNBC.com. Transcript for August 29. NBC News/Meet the Press. Posted August 29, 2004 and retrieved September 29, 2005 from http://www.msnbc.msn.com/id/5858461/. 3/16.
[1688] David Saltonstall. Corn on Rudy's Plate. NY Daily News. Posted April 30, 2006 and retrieved May 22, 2006 from http://www.nydailynews.com/news/politics/v-pfriendly/story/413386p-349548c.html

[1689] Meet the Press. NBC News. Posted 10.31.2004 and aired March 7 2004 and Retrieved @ http://www.msnbc.msn.com/id/4456277/print/1/displaymode/1098/.

[1690] Meet the Press. NBC News. Aug 29, 2004. and Retrieved @ http://www.msnbc.msn.com/id/5858461/print/1/displaymode/1098/.

[1691] John Podhoretz. Rudy & the Right. The New York Post. Posted and retrieved May 24, 2005 from http://www.nypost.com/postopinion/opedcolumnists/47054.htm.

[1692] ABC News: This Week. May 1 interview with Pat Robertson. Transcript provided by sundingmorningtalk.com. Retrieved June 2, 2005 from http://www.sundaymorningtalk.com/smt/2005/05/pat_robertson_e.html.

[1693] George F. Will. Brownback's Plans for 2008. MSNBC.com & Newsweek. Posted May 29, 2005 and retrieved June 2, 2005 from http://www.msnbc.msn.com/id/8017004/site/newsweek/.

[1694] Tom Bevan. RealClearPolitics. Deconstructing Giuliani. August 13 and retrieved August 25, 2006 from http://www.foxnews.com/story/0,2933,208161,00.html.

[1695] Hilary Hylton. "Rudy Heads South." Time.com. Posted January 31, 2006 and retrieved February 6, 2006 from http://www.time.com/time/nation/article/0,8599,1154798,00.html.

[1696] AP. Giuliani to Wed At Gracie Mansion. April 25, 2003. Retrieved from CBS NEWS on Sept.6, 2006 from http://www.cbsnews.com/stories/2003/04/25/national/main551053.shtml

[1697] AP. Giuliani to Wed At Gracie Mansion. April 25, 2003. Retrieved from CBS NEWS on Sept.6, 2006 from http://www.cbsnews.com/stories/2003/04/25/national/main551053.shtml

[1698] AP. Giuliani to Wed At Gracie Mansion. April 25, 2003. Retrieved from CBS NEWS on Sept.6, 2006 from http://www.cbsnews.com/stories/2003/04/25/national/main551053.shtml

[1699] CBS. The Women in Giuliani's Life. Posted May 11, 2000 and retrieved Sept.6, 2006 from http://www.cbsnews.com/stories/2000/05/11/politics/prinatable194350.shtml

[1700] CBS. The Women in Giuliani's Life. Posted May 11, 2000 and retrieved Sept.6, 2006 from http://www.cbsnews.com/stories/2000/05/11/politics/prinatable194350.shtml

[1701] Salon Politics 2000. Rudy's 'very good friend'. Posted May 4, 2000 and retrieved September 6, 2006 from http://archive.salon.com/politics2000/feature/2000/05/04/giuliani/index.html.

[1702] Salon Politics 2000. Rudy's 'very good friend'. Posted May 4, 2000 and retrieved September 6, 2006 from http://archive.salon.com/politics2000/feature/2000/05/04/giuliani/index.html.

[1703] Salon Politics 2000. Rudy's 'very good friend'. Posted May 4, 2000 and retrieved September 6, 2006 from http://archive.salon.com/politics2000/feature/2000/05/04/giuliani/index.html.

[1704] Salon Politics 2000. Rudy's 'very good friend'. Posted May 4, 2000 and retrieved September 6, 2006 from http://archive.salon.com/politics2000/feature/2000/05/04/giuliani/index.html.

[1705] CBS. The Women in Giuliani's Life. Posted May 11, 2000 and retrieved Sept.6, 2006 from http://www.cbsnews.com/stories/2000/05/11/politics/prinatable194350.shtml

[1706] CBS. The Women in Giuliani's Life. Posted May 11, 2000 and retrieved Sept.6, 2006 from http://www.cbsnews.com/stories/2000/05/11/politics/prinatable194350.shtml

[1707] High Infidelity. Steve Benen. Washington Monthly. July/August 2006. Retrieved June 30, 2006 from http://www.washingtonmonthly.com/features/2006/0607.benen.html. 2/4.

[1708] Salon Politics 2000. Jesse Drucker. Rudy's 'very good friend'. Posted May 4, 2000 and retrieved September 6, 2006 from http://archive.salon.com/politics2000/feature/2000/05/04/giuliani/index.html.

[1709] CBS. The Women in Giuliani's Life. Posted May 11, 2000 and retrieved Sept.6, 2006 from http://www.cbsnews.com/stories/2000/05/11/politics/prinatable194350.shtml

[1710] CBS. The Women in Giuliani's Life. Posted May 11, 2000 and retrieved Sept.6, 2006 from http://www.cbsnews.com/stories/2000/05/11/politics/prinatable194350.shtml

[1711] AP. Giuliani to Wed At Gracie Mansion. April 25, 2003. Retrieved from CBS NEWS on Sept.6, 2006 from http://www.cbsnews.com/stories/2003/04/25/national/main551053.shtml

[1712] CBS. The Women in Giuliani's Life. Posted May 11, 2000 and retrieved Sept.6, 2006 from http://www.cbsnews.com/stories/2000/05/11/politics/prinatable194350.shtml

[1713] AP. Giuliani to Wed At Gracie Mansion. April 25, 2003. Retrieved from CBS NEWS on Sept.6, 2006 from http://www.cbsnews.com/stories/2003/04/25/national/main551053.shtml

[1714] CBS. The Women in Giuliani's Life. Posted May 11, 2000 and retrieved Sept.6, 2006 from http://www.cbsnews.com/stories/2000/05/11/politics/prinatable194350.shtml

[1715] AP. Giuliani to Wed At Gracie Mansion. April 25, 2003. Retrieved from CBS NEWS on Sept.6, 2006 from http://www.cbsnews.com/stories/2003/04/25/national/main551053.shtml

[1716] AP. Giuliani to Wed At Gracie Mansion. April 25, 2003. Retrieved from CBS NEWS on Sept.6, 2006 from http://www.cbsnews.com/stories/2003/04/25/national/main551053.shtml

[1717] Michael Powell. 'Giuliani Time' Recalls Ex-Mayor's Less Heroic Deeds. Washington Post. Published May 26, 2006, Page C05 and retrieved May 31, 2006 from http://www.washingtonpost.com/wp-dyn/content/article/2006/05/25/AR2006052502136.html.

[1718] Greg J. Borowski. Green team taps Giuliani. Milwaukee Journal Sentinel. August 24, 2006, 1B/5B.

[1719] The myth of Giuliani's crime-fighting. July 21, 2006. Retrieved 9.6.06 from http://www.brendan-nyhan.com/blog/2006/07/the_myth_of_giu.html.

[1720] The myth of Giuliani's crime-fighting. July 21, 2006. Retrieved 9.6.06 from http://www.brendan-nyhan.com/blog/2006/07/the_myth_of_giu.html. As quoted by Brendan Nyhan.

[1721] Giuliani's Crime Strategy. New York Times. Published August 16, 1994. and Retrieved 9.6.06 from http://query.nytimes.com/gst/fullpage.html?res=9C07E1DF1130F935A2575BC0A962958260.
[1722] Rudy Giuliani on Crime. Retrieved 9.6.2006 from http://ontheissues.org/Domestic/Rudy_Giuliani_Crime.htm. From Giuliani's State of the City Address: Jan.13.2000.
[1723] Rudy Giuliani on Crime. Retrieved 9.6.2006 from http://ontheissues.org/Domestic/Rudy_Giuliani_Crime.htm. From RudyYes.com on Dec.9.1999.
[1724] John Perazzo. Front Page Magazine. January 3, 2002. Retrieved 9.6.2006 from http://frontpagemag.com/Articles/ReadArticle.asp?ID=1380.
[1725] Joyce Purnick. Giuliani's Strategy Is All on His Web Site. New York Times. Posted Jan.5, 2007 and retrieved 1.13.07 from http://www.nytimes.com/2007/01/05/nyregion/05cnd-rudy.html?ex=1325653200&en=52b...
[1726] John Perazzo. Front Page Magazine. January 3, 2002. Retrieved 9.6.2006 from http://frontpagemag.com/Articles/ReadArticle.asp?ID=1380.
[1727] Rudy Giuliani on Crime. Retrieved 9.6.2006 from http://ontheissues.org/Domestic/Rudy_Giuliani_Crime.htm. New York Times. A-23, March 3, 2000.
[1728] John Perazzo. Front Page Magazine. January 3, 2002. Retrieved 9.6.2006 from http://frontpagemag.com/Articles/ReadArticle.asp?ID=1380.
[1729] Jim VandeiHei and Mike Allen. White House Puts Blame on Kerik. The Washington Post. December 12, 2004, Page A01. Retrieved September 21, 2005 from http://www.washingtonpost.com/ac2/wp-dyn/A57960-2004Dec11?language=printer
[1730] CNN. Bush nominates Kerik for Homeland Security. 12.3.04 and retrieved 7.28.06 from http://www.cnn.com/2004/ALLPOLITICS/12/03/homeland.security
[1731] Jim VandeiHei and Mike Allen. "White House Puts Blame on Kerik." The Washington Post. December 12, 2004, Page A01. Retrieved September 21, 2005 from http://www.washingtonpost.com/ac2/wp-dyn/A57960-2004Dec11?language=printer
[1732] CNN. Bush nominates Kerik for Homeland Security. December 3, 2004 and retrieved July 28, 2006 from http://www.cnn.com/2004/ALLPOLITICS/12/03/homeland.security.
[1733] CNN. Bush nominates Kerik for Homeland Security. December 3, 2004 and retrieved July 28, 2006 from http://www.cnn.com/2004/ALLPOLITICS/12/03/homeland.security
[1734] Jim VandeiHei and Mike Allen. White House Puts Blame on Kerik. The Washington Post. December 12, 2004, Page A01. Retrieved September 21, 2005 from http://www.washingtonpost.com/ac2/wp-dyn/A57960-2004Dec11?language=printer
[1735] Jim VandeiHei and Mike Allen. White House Puts Blame on Kerik. The Washington Post. December 12, 2004, Page A01. Retrieved September 21, 2005 from http://www.washingtonpost.com/ac2/wp-dyn/A57960-2004Dec11?language=printer.
[1736] AP. "Profile: Bernard Kerik." FOXNews.com. Posted December 2, 2004 and retrieved September 21, 2005 from http://www.foxnews.com/printer_freindly_story/0,3566,140351,00.html.
[1737] CNN. Bush nominates Kerik for Homeland Security. December 3, 2004 and retrieved July 28, 2006 from http://www.cnn.com/2004/ALLPOLITICS/12/03/homeland.security
[1738] CNN. Bush nominates Kerik for Homeland Security. December 3, 2004 and retrieved July 28, 2006 from http://www.cnn.com/2004/ALLPOLITICS/12/03/homeland.security
[1739] WNBC.com. Kerik's Nanny Least of Ex-Nominee's Problems. Posted December 14, 2004 and retrieved July 28, 2006 form http://www.wnbc.com/news/3991421/detail.html.
[1740] WNBC.com. Kerik's Nanny Least of Ex-Nominee's Problems. Posted December 14, 2004 and retrieved July 28, 2006 form http://www.wnbc.com/news/3991421/detail.html
[1741] Geoff Earle. "GOP Centrists promote Giuliani." The Hill. Posted June 23, 2005 and retrieved June 24, 2005 from http://www.thehill.com/thehill/export/TheHill/News/Frontpage/062305/giuliani.html.
[1742] NBC News. Meet the Press. Transcript for Dec. 19. MSNBC.com. Retrieved 10.3. 2006 from http://www.msnbc.msn.com/id/6734557/print/1/displaymode/1098/. 11/13.
[1743] NBC News. Meet the Press. Transcript for Dec. 19. MSNBC.com. Retrieved 10.3. 2006 from http://www.msnbc.msn.com/id/6734557/print/1/displaymode/1098/. 11/13.
[1744] NBC News. Meet the Press. Transcript for Dec. 19. MSNBC.com. Retrieved 10.3. 2006 from http://www.msnbc.msn.com/id/6734557/print/1/displaymode/1098/. 11/13.
[1745] CNN.com. "CNN Late Edition with Wolf Blitzer." Aired December 12, 2004. Retrieved November 17, 2005 from http://transcripts.cnn.com/TRANSCRIPTS/0412/12/le.01.html. 6/27
[1746] CNN.com. "CNN Late Edition with Wolf Blitzer." Aired December 12, 2004. Retrieved November 17, 2005 from http://transcripts.cnn.com/TRANSCRIPTS/0412/12/le.01.html 6/27.
[1747] NBC News. Meet the Press. Transcript for Dec. 12, 2004 MSNBC.com. Retrieved 10.3. 2006 from http://www.msnbc.msn.com/id/6702005/print/1/displaymode/1098/.
[1748] Jim VandeiHei and Mike Allen. White House Puts Blame on Kerik. The Washington Post. December 12, 2004, Page A01. Retrieved September 21, 2005 from http://www.washingtonpost.com/ac2/wp-dyn/A57960-2004Dec11?language=printer.
[1749] Mark Hosenball. Newsweek. Withdrawn. Why Did Bernard Kerik Really Bow out? MSNBC.com. Posted December 19, 2004 and retrieved July 28, 2006 from http://www.msnbc.msn.com/id/6697161/site/newsweek/print/1/displaymode/1098/.

[1750] Mark Hosenball. Newsweek. Withdrawn. Why Did Bernard Kerik Really Bow out? MSNBC.com. Posted December 19, 2004 and retrieved July 28, 2006 from http://www.msnbc.msn.com/id/6697161/site/newsweek/print/1/displaymode/1098/.

[1751] Russ Buettner. Now his double affair laid bare. New York Daily News. Posted December 14, 2004 and retrieved July 28, 2006 from http://www.nydailynews.com/front/story/261625p-224000c.html. See also http://stevegilliard.blogspot.com/2004/12/shenanigans.html.

[1752] Russ Buettner. Now his double affair laid bare. New York Daily News. Posted December 14, 2004 and retrieved July 28, 2006 from http://www.nydailynews.com/front/story/261625p-224000c.html.

[1753] Russ Buettner. Now his double affair laid bare. New York Daily News. Posted December 14, 2004 and retrieved July 28, 2006 from http://www.nydailynews.com/front/story/261625p-224000c.html. WNBC.com. Kerik's Nanny Least of Ex-Nominee's Problems. Posted December 14, 2004 and retrieved July 28, 2006 form http://www.wnbc.com/news/3991421/detail.html

[1754] Russ Buettner. Now his double affair laid bare. New York Daily News. Posted December 14, 2004 and retrieved July 28, 2006 from http://www.nydailynews.com/front/story/261625p-224000c.html.

[1755] Russ Buettner. Now his double affair laid bare. New York Daily News. Posted December 14, 2004 and retrieved July 28, 2006 from http://www.nydailynews.com/front/story/261625p-224000c.html.

[1756] WNBC.com. Kerik's Nanny Least of Ex-Nominee's Problems. Posted December 14, 2004 and retrieved July 28, 2006 form http://www.wnbc.com/news/3991421/detail.html

[1757] Mark Hosenball. Newsweek. Withdrawn. Why Did Bernard Kerik Really Bow out? MSNBC.com. Posted December 19, 2004 and retrieved July 28, 2006 from http://www.msnbc.msn.com/id/6697161/site/newsweek/print/1/displaymode/1098/.

[1758] Greg B. Smith and Russ Buettner. Bernie faces FBI probe of charity's missing 1M. New York Daily News. Posed August 4 and retrieved September 6, 2006 from http://www.nydailynews.com/front/story/440760p-371293c.html. See also http://z14.invisionfree.com/GangstersInc/index.php?showtopic=68.

[1759] Greg B. Smith and Russ Buettner. Bernie faces FBI probe of charity's missing 1M. New York Daily News. Posed August 4 and retrieved September 6, 2006 from http://www.nydailynews.com/front/story/440760p-371293c.html

[1760] Greg B. Smith and Russ Buettner. Bernie faces FBI probe of charity's missing 1M. New York Daily News. Posed August 4 and retrieved September 6, 2006 from http://www.nydailynews.com/front/story/440760p-371293c.html

[1761] Greg B. Smith and Russ Buettner. Bernie faces FBI probe of charity's missing 1M. New York Daily News. Posed August 4 and retrieved September 6, 2006 from http://www.nydailynews.com/front/story/440760p-371293c.html

[1762] WNBC.com. Kerik's Nanny Least of Ex-Nominee's Problems. Posted December 14, 2004 and retrieved July 28, 2006 form http://www.wnbc.com/news/3991421/detail.html

[1763] AP. Kerik pleads guilty to pair of misdemeanors. MJS. July 1, 2006, 3A.

[1764] AP. Kerik pleads guilty to pair of misdemeanors. MJS. July 1, 2006, 3A.

[1765] Newsday. Anthony M. Destefano. Two charged with perjury in Bernard Kerik case. Posted July 20, 2006 and retrieved July 28, 2006 from http://www.newsday.com/news/local/newyork/am-keri0720,0,5684367.story?coll=ny-nycnews-headlines.

[1766] Newsday. Anthony M. Destefano. Two charged with perjury in Bernard Kerik case. Posted July 20, 2006 and retrieved July 28, 2006 from http://www.newsday.com/news/local/newyork/am-keri0720,0,5684367.story?coll=ny-nycnews-headlines.

[1767] Newsday. Anthony M. Destefano. Two charged with perjury in Bernard Kerik case. Posted July 20, 2006 and retrieved July 28, 2006 from http://www.newsday.com/news/local/newyork/am-keri0720,0,5684367.story?coll=ny-nycnews-headlines.

[1768] Editorials. Supreme Court Goes Overboard. RHIP. Retrieved June 30, 2006 from http://www.dailynews.com/news/ideas_opinions/story/4310092p-363360c.html.

[1769] AP. Kerik pleads guilty to pair of misdemeanors. MJS. July 1, 2006, 3A.

[1770] NBC News. Meet the Press. Aired March 7, 2004. MSNBC.com. Retrieved 10.31.2006 form http://www.msnbc.msn.com/id/1/displaymode/1098/.

[1771] Graham Rayman and Dan Janison. "New questions about alleged Kerik ethical violations." Newsday. Posted November 16, 2005 and retrieved November 17, 2005 from http://www.nynewsday.com/news/local/manhattan/nyc-keri1117,0,1294748.story?coll=nyc-moreny-headlines.

[1772] Graham Rayman and Dan Janison. "New questions about alleged Kerik ethical violations." Newsday. Posted November 16, 2005 and retrieved November 17, 2005 from http://www.nynewsday.com/news/local/manhattan/nyc-keri1117,0,1294748.story?coll=nyc-moreny-headlines.

[1773] Graham Rayman and Dan Janison. "New questions about alleged Kerik ethical violations." Newsday. Posted November 16, 2005 and retrieved November 17, 2005 from http://www.nynewsday.com/news/local/manhattan/nyc-keri1117,0,1294748.story?coll=nyc-moreny-headlines.

[1774] NBC News. MTP transcript for October 31, 2004. Retrieved 10.31.06 from http://msnbc.msn.com/id/6362470/print/1/displaymode/1098/.

[1775] Detnews.com. 9/11 panel leaders say Giuliani got off easy. Posted August 7, 2006 and retrieved September 6, 2006 from http://detnews.com/apps/pbcs.dll/article?AID=/20060807/NATION/608070375&template=printart.

[1776] New York Times. 9/11 panel leaders say Giuliani got off easy. August 7, 2006 and retrieved September 6, 2006 from http://detnews.com/apps/pbcs.dll/article?AID=/20060807/NATION/608070375.

[1777] CBS/AP. Venting at Rudy & 9/11 Panel. Posted May 20, 2004 and retrieved September 6, 2006 from http://www.cbsnews.com/stories/2004/04/21/terror/main612959.shtml.

[1778] Adam Nichols. 9/11 panel heads say Rudy got off easy. New York Daily News. Posted August 5, 2006 and retrieved September 6, 2006 from http://www.nydailynews.com/front/story/440950p-371428c.html.
[1779] Kean and Hamilton. Without Precedent: The Inside Story of The 9/11 Commission. Page 230/231. MTP Transcript for Aug. 13. Meet the Press. NBC News. Retrieved August 25, 2006 from http://www.msnbc.msn.com/id/14273400/print/1/displaymode/1098/. Page 10/16.
[1780] MTP Transcript for Aug. 13. Meet the Press. NBC News. Retrieved August 25, 2006 from http://www.msnbc.msn.com/id/14273400/print/1/displaymode/1098/. Page 10/16
[1781] MTP Transcript for Aug. 13. Meet the Press. NBC News. Retrieved August 25, 2006 from http://www.msnbc.msn.com/id/14273400/print/1/displaymode/1098/. Page 9/16.
[1782] MTP Transcript for Aug. 13. Meet the Press. NBC News. Retrieved August 25, 2006 from http://www.msnbc.msn.com/id/14273400/print/1/displaymode/1098/. Page 9/16.
[1783] MTP Transcript for Aug. 13. Meet the Press. NBC News. Retrieved August 25, 2006 from http://www.msnbc.msn.com/id/14273400/print/1/displaymode/1098/. Page 10/16.
[1784] New York Times. 9/11 panel leaders say Giuliani got off easy. August 7, 2006 and retrieved September 6, 2006 from http://detnews.com/apps/pbcs.dll/article?AID=/20060807/NATION/608070375.
[1785] New York Times. 9/11 panel leaders say Giuliani got off easy. August 7, 2006 and retrieved September 6, 2006 from http://detnews.com/apps/pbcs.dll/article?AID=/20060807/NATION/608070375.
[1786] AP. 9/11 Commissioners Expose Obstructions. Posted August 5, 2006. Retrieved September 6, 2006 from http://www.cbsnews.com/stories/2006/08/05/terror/main/1868087.shtml.
[1787] New York Times. 9/11 panel leaders say Giuliani got off easy. August 7, 2006 and retrieved September 6, 2006 from http://detnews.com/apps/pbcs.dll/article?AID=/20060807/NATION/608070375.
[1788] Meet the Press. NBC News. 10.31.2006. and aired April 4, 2004 and Retrieved @ http://www.msnbc.msn.com/id/4663767/print/1/displaymode/1098/. 2/15.
[1789] Meet the Press. NBC News. 10.31.06 and aired Marcy 7, 2004 and retrieved @ http://www.msnbc.msn.com/id/4456277/print/1/displaymode/1098/.
[1790] Chris Smith. A Test for Rudy. Rudy Giuliani faces 9/11 Commission. Posted May 10, 2004 and retrieved September 6, 2006 from http://newyorkmetro.com/nymetro/news/trends/columns/cityside/n-10336/.
[1791] Chris Smith. A Test for Rudy. Rudy Giuliani faces 9/11 Commission. Posted May 10, 2004 and retrieved September 6, 2006 from http://newyorkmetro.com/nymetro/news/trends/columns/cityside/n-10336/.
[1792] Chris Smith. A Test for Rudy. Rudy Giuliani faces 9/11 Commission. Posted May 10, 2004 and retrieved September 6, 2006 from http://newyorkmetro.com/nymetro/news/trends/columns/cityside/n-10336/.
[1793] Chris Smith. A Test for Rudy. Rudy Giuliani faces 9/11 Commission. Posted May 10, 2004 and retrieved September 6, 2006 from http://newyorkmetro.com/nymetro/news/trends/columns/cityside/n-10336/.
[1794] CBS/AP. Venting AT Rudy & 9/11 panel. Posted May 20, 2004 and retrieved September 6, 2006 from http://www.cbsnews.com/stories/2004/04/21/terror/main612959.shtml.
[1795] CBS/AP. Venting AT Rudy & 9/11 panel. Posted May 20, 2004 and retrieved September 6, 2006 from http://www.cbsnews.com/stories/2004/04/21/terror/main612959.shtml.
[1796] MSNBC staff and news service reports. Giuliani says 9/11 families anger misdirected. Posted May 20, 2004 and retrieved September 6, 2006 from http://www.msnbc.msn.com/id/5012645/.
[1797] CBS/AP. Venting AT Rudy & 9/11 panel. Posted May 20, 2004 and retrieved September 6, 2006 from http://www.cbsnews.com/stories/2004/04/21/terror/main612959.shtml.
[1798] MSNBC staff and news service reports. Giuliani says 9/11 families anger misdirected. Posted May 20, 2004 and retrieved September 6, 2006 from http://www.msnbc.msn.com/id/5012645/.
[1799] MSNBC staff and news service reports. Giuliani says 9/11 families anger misdirected. Posted May 20, 2004 and retrieved September 6, 2006 from http://www.msnbc.msn.com/id/5012645/.
[1800] CBS/AP. Venting AT Rudy & 9/11 panel. Posted May 20, 2004 and retrieved September 6, 2006 from http://www.cbsnews.com/stories/2004/04/21/terror/main612959.shtml.
[1801] MSNBC staff and news service reports. Giuliani says 9/11 families anger misdirected. Posted May 20, 2004 and retrieved September 6, 2006 from http://www.msnbc.msn.com/id/5012645/.
[1802] New York Daily News. Time to downsize Rudy 9/11 myth. Posted August 22, 2006 and retrieved September 6, 2006 from http://www.nydailynews.com/front/story/445698p-375131c.html.
[1803] New York Daily News. Time to downsize Rudy 9/11 myth. Posted August 22, 2006 and retrieved September 6, 2006 from http://www.nydailynews.com/front/story/445698p-375131c.html.
[1804] Giuliani: We Are Going to Be Attacked Again. August 11, 2006. Retrieved 11.17.06 from http://www.foxnews.com/story/0,2933,207934,00.html. 3/5
[1805] Giuliani: We Are Going to Be Attacked Again. August 11, 2006. Retrieved 11.17.06 from http://www.foxnews.com/story/0,2933,207934,00.html. 3/5
[1806] Giuliani: We Are Going to Be Attacked Again. August 11, 2006. Retrieved 11.17.06 from http://www.foxnews.com/story/0,2933,207934,00.html. 3/5
[1807] Giuliani: We Are Going to Be Attacked Again. August 11, 2006. Retrieved 11.17.06 from http://www.foxnews.com/story/0,2933,207934,00.html. 3/5
[1808] Giuliani: We Are Going to Be Attacked Again. August 11, 2006. Retrieved 11.17.06 from http://www.foxnews.com/story/0,2933,207934,00.html. 3/5
[1809] WH2008: Republicans. Gallup Poll. August 13-16, 2007. Retrieved 8.21.07 from http://www.pollingreport.com/wh08.htm.

[1810] WH2008: Republicans. Gallup Poll. August 13-16, 2007. Retrieved 8.21.07 from http://www.pollingreport.com/wh08.htm.
[1811] ABC-News-National-Polls, 2008 Primary Presidential Election Polls. Retrieved 8.21.07 from http://www.usaelectionpolls.com/2008/abc-news-national-polls.html.
[1812] Jake Thompson. Sen. Chuck Hagel is Midlander of the Year. Omaha.com/Omaha World-Herald. Published Jan.1, 2006 and retrieved March 17, 2006 from http://www.omaha.com/index.php?u_pg=1638&u_sid=2091386. See also http://www.negop.org/newsdetails.asp?id=126.
[1813] McCook Daily Gazette. Hagel puts Nebraska in the spotlight. Posted July 6, 2005 and retrieved July 8, 2005 from http://www.mccookgazette.com/story/1108629.html.
[1814] Robert G. Kaiser. The Political Veteran. The Washington Post. Posted November 15, 2004 and retrieved September 21, 2005 from http://www.washingtonpost.com/ac2/wp-dyn/A50063-2004Nov14?language=printer
[1815] Robert G. Kaiser. The Political Veteran. The Washington Post. Posted November 15, 2004 and retrieved September 21, 2005 from http://www.washingtonpost.com/ac2/wp-dyn/A50063-2004Nov14?language=printer
[1816] Jake Thompson. Sen. Chuck Hagel is Midlander of the Year. Omaha.com/Omaha World-Herald. Published Jan.1, 2006 and retrieved March 17, 2006 from http://www.omaha.com/index.php?u_pg=1638&u_sid=2091386.
[1817] Don Walton. Hagel poised for presidential bid in 2008. Lincoln Journal Star. Posted November 22, 2004 and retrieved December 15, 2004 from http://www.journalstar.com/articles/2004/11/22/local/doc419fc655a69d7648118098.txt
[1818] Don Walton. Hagel poised for presidential bid in 2008. Lincoln Journal Star. Posted November 22, 2004 and retrieved December 15, 2004 from http://www.journalstar.com/articles/2004/11/22/local/doc419fc655a69d7648118098.txt.
[1819] Esquire. Before this is over, you might see calls for his impeachment. Retrieved 3.8.07 from http://www.esquire.com/print-this/chuckhagel10407.
[1820] Esquire. Before this is over, you might see calls for his impeachment. Retrieved 3.8.07 from http://www.esquire.com/print-this/chuckhagel10407.
[1821] Joseph R. Biden Jr. "ABC This Week with George Stephanopoulos." Posted August 15, 2005 and retrieved November 8, 2005 from http://biden.senate.gov/newsroom/details/cfm?id=225326&&.
[1822] Don Walton. Hagel poised for presidential bid in 2008. Lincoln Journal Star. Posted November 22, 2004 and retrieved December 15, 2004 from http://www.journalstar.com/articles/2004/11/22/local/doc419fc655a69d7648118098.txt
[1823] Robert G. Kaiser. "The Political Veteran." The Washington Post. Posted November 15, 2004 and retrieved September 21, 2005 from http://www.washingtonpost.com/ac2/wp-dyn/A50063-2004Nov14?language=printer
[1824] Richard E. Cohen and Michael Barone. "The Almanac of American Politics—2004." The National Journal Group. 2003, page 967.
[1825] Robert G. Kaiser. The Political Veteran. The Washington Post. Posted November 15, 2004 and retrieved September 21, 2005 from http://www.washingtonpost.com/ac2/wp-dyn/A50063-2004Nov14?language=printer
[1826] Don Walton. "Hagel poised for presidential bid in 2008." Lincoln Journal Star. Posted November 22, 2004 and retrieved December 15, 2004 from http://www.journalstar.com/articles/2004/11/22/local/doc419fc655a69d7648118098.txt
[1827] Don Walton. Sen. Chuck Hagel will consider presidential race in 2008. Lincoln Journal Star. Posted August 15, 2004 and retrieved October 5, 2005 from http://www.journalstar.com/articles/2004/08/15/top_story/10053731.txt
[1828] Richard E. Cohen and Michael Barone. "The Almanac of American Politics—2004." The National Journal Group. 2003, page 967.
[1829] Richard E. Cohen and Michael Barone. "The Almanac of American Politics—2004." The National Journal Group. 2003, page 967.
[1830] Chuck Hagel. 21st Century American Challenges. Southwest Nebraska News. Posted April 29, 2005 and retrieved May 5, 2005 from http://www.swnebr.net/newspaper/cgi-bin/articles/articlearchiver.pl?157341.
[1831] CNN. Late Edition. Aired 10.15.06 and retrieved 10.31.06 form http://transcripts.cnn.com/TRANSCRIPTS/0610/15/le.01.html.
[1832] David Broder. A different mood in the GOP. The Washington Post. Published October 28, 2005 and retrieved November 11, 2005 from http://www.ocala.com/apps/pbcs.dll/article?AID=/20051028/OPINION/51028003/1030/news08.
[1833] David Broder. A different mood in the GOP. The Washington Post. Published October 28, 2005 and retrieved November 11, 2005 from http://www.ocala.com/apps/pbcs.dll/article?AID=/20051028/OPINION/51028003/1030/news08
[1834] David Broder. A different mood in the GOP. The Washington Post. Published October 28, 2005 and retrieved November 11, 2005 from http://www.ocala.com/apps/pbcs.dll/article?AID=/20051028/OPINION/51028003/1030/news08
[1835] Robert G. Kaiser. "The Political Veteran." The Washington Post. Posted November 15, 2004 and retrieved September 21, 2005 from http://www.washingtonpost.com/ac2/wp-dyn/A50063-2004Nov14?language=printer
[1836] Don Walton. "Hagel poised for presidential bid in 2008." Lincoln Journal Star. Posted November 22, 2004 and retrieved December 15, 2004 from http://www.journalstar.com/articles/2004/11/22/local/doc419fc655a69d7648118098.txt
[1837] Don Walton. "Hagel poised for presidential bid in 2008." Lincoln Journal Star. Posted November 22, 2004 and retrieved December 15, 2004 from http://www.journalstar.com/articles/2004/11/22/local/doc419fc655a69d7648118098.txt
[1838] David Broder. A different mood in the GOP. The Washington Post. Published October 28, 2005 and retrieved November 11, 2005 from http://www.ocala.com/apps/pbcs.dll/article?AID=/20051028/OPINION/51028003/1030/news08
[1839] Don Walton. "Hagel poised for presidential bid in 2008." Lincoln Journal Star. Posted November 22, 2004 and retrieved December 15, 2004 from http://www.journalstar.com/articles/2004/11/22/local/doc419fc655a69d7648118098.txt
[1840] Don Walton. Sen. Chuck Hagel will consider presidential race in 2008. Lincoln Journal Star. Posted August 15, 2004 and retrieved October 5, 2005 from http://www.journalstar.com/articles/2004/08/15/top_story/10053731.txt.
[1841] Geoff Earle. In McCain's shadow, Hagel prepares for '08. The Hill. Posted June 9, 2005 and retrieved June 24, 2005 from http://www.thehill.com/thehill/export/TheHill/News/Frontpage/060905/hagel.html.

[1842] Robert G. Kaiser. "The Political Veteran." The Washington Post. Posted November 15, 2004 and retrieved September 21, 2005 from http://www.washingtonpost.com/ac2/wp-dyn/A50063-2004Nov14?language=printer.
[1843] Robert G. Kaiser. "The Political Veteran." The Washington Post. Posted November 15, 2004 and retrieved September 21, 2005 from http://www.washingtonpost.com/ac2/wp-dyn/A50063-2004Nov14?language=printer
[1844] Robert G. Kaiser. "The Political Veteran." The Washington Post. Posted November 15, 2004 and retrieved September 21, 2005 from http://www.washingtonpost.com/ac2/wp-dyn/A50063-2004Nov14?language=printer
[1845] Don Walton. "Hagel poised for presidential bid in 2008." Lincoln Journal Star. Posted November 22, 2004 and retrieved December 15, 2004 from http://www.journalstar.com/articles/2004/11/22/local/doc419fc655a69d7648118098.txt
[1846] WH2008: Republican Nomination. Retreived12.14.06 from http://pollingreport.com/WH08rep.htm.
[1847] Alexander Bolton. Hagel '08 stumbles at outset. The Hill. Posted August 8, 2004 and retrieved October 5, 2005 from http://hillnews.com/news/070804/hagel.aspx.
[1848] Alexander Bolton. Hagel '08 stumbles at outset. The Hill. Posted August 8, 2004 and retrieved October 5, 2005 from http://hillnews.com/news/070804/hagel.aspx.
[1849] Alexander Bolton. Hagel's ethics filings pose disclosure issue. January 29, 2003. The Hill. Retrieved July 14, 2006 from http://www.hillnews/news/012903/hagel.aspx.
[1850] Alexander Bolton. Hagel's ethics filings pose disclosure issue. January 29, 2003. The Hill. Retrieved July 14, 2006 from http://www.hillnews/news/012903/hagel.aspx.
[1851] Alexander Bolton. Hagel's ethics filings pose disclosure issue. January 29, 2003. The Hill. Retrieved July 14, 2006 from http://www.hillnews/news/012903/hagel.aspx.
[1852] Alexander Bolton. Hagel's ethics filings pose disclosure issue. January 29, 2003. The Hill. Retrieved July 14, 2006 from http://www.hillnews/news/012903/hagel.aspx.
[1853] Alexander Bolton. Hagel's ethics filings pose disclosure issue. January 29, 2003. The Hill. Retrieved July 14, 2006 from http://www.hillnews/news/012903/hagel.aspx.
[1854] Alexander Bolton. Hagel's ethics filings pose disclosure issue. January 29, 2003. The Hill. Retrieved July 14, 2006 from http://www.hillnews/news/012903/hagel.aspx
[1855] Alexander Bolton. Hagel's ethics filings pose disclosure issue. January 29, 2003. The Hill. Retrieved July 14, 2006 from http://www.hillnews/news/012903/hagel.aspx.
[1856] Alexander Bolton. Hagel's ethics filings pose disclosure issue. January 29, 2003. The Hill. Retrieved July 14, 2006 from http://www.hillnews/news/012903/hagel.aspx.
[1857] Alexander Bolton. Hagel's ethics filings pose disclosure issue. January 29, 2003. The Hill. Retrieved July 14, 2006 from http://www.hillnews/news/012903/hagel.aspx
[1858] Alexander Bolton. Hagel's ethics filings pose disclosure issue. January 29, 2003. The Hill. Retrieved July 14, 2006 from http://www.hillnews/news/012903/hagel.aspx
[1859] Alexander Bolton. Hagel's ethics filings pose disclosure issue. January 29, 2003. The Hill. Retrieved July 14, 2006 from http://www.hillnews/news/012903/hagel.aspx
[1860] Alexander Bolton. Hagel's ethics filings pose disclosure issue. January 29, 2003. The Hill. Retrieved July 14, 2006 from http://www.hillnews/news/012903/hagel.aspx
[1861] MTP Transcript for Jan.14, 2007. Meet the Press. MSNBC.com. NBC News. Retrieved 2.8.07 from http://www.msnbc.msn.com/id/16577874/print/1/displaymode/1098/.
[1862] MTP Transcript for Jan.14, 2007. Meet the Press. MSNBC.com. NBC News. Retrieved 2.8.07 from http://www.msnbc.msn.com/id/16577874/print/1/displaymode/1098/.
[1863] Archive for the "Chuck Hagel" Category. 2.8.07. , posted 2.4.07 @ http://www.crooksandliars.com/category/the-senate/chuck-hagel/
[1864] Jonathan Darman. Rebel Chuck Hagel: A President in the Making? Newsweek. MSNBC.com. Feb.5, 2007. Retrieved 2.8.07 from http://www.msnbc.msn.com/id/16841355/site/newsweek/print/1/displaymode/1098/. .
[1865] MTP Transcript for Feb. 18, 2007. Meet the Press. MSNBC.com. NBC News. Retrieved 3.5.07 from http://www.msnbc.msn.com/id/17168627/print/1/displaymode/1098/.
[1866] Rush Limbaugh is the foremost advocate for freedom and democracy in. Posted 2.6.07 and retrieved 2.8.07 from http://newyork.craigslist.org/jsy/pol/274138442.html.
[1867] Rush Limbaugh is the foremost advocate for freedom and democracy in. Posted 2.6.07 and retrieved 2.8.07 from http://newyork.craigslist.org/jsy/pol/274138442.html.
[1868] Shailagh Murray. Hagel Ponders White House Run As War Criticism Raises His Profile. Jan. 26, 2007. A01. Retrieved 2.8.07 from http://www.washingtonpost.com/wp-dyn/content/article/2007/01/25/AR2007012502086_pf.html.
[1869] Shailagh Murray. Hagel Ponders White House Run As War Criticism Raises His Profile. Jan. 26, 2007. A01. Retrieved 2.8.07 from http://www.washingtonpost.com/wp-dyn/content/article/2007/01/25/AR2007012502086_pf.html.
[1870] Shailagh Murray. Hagel Ponders White House Run As War Criticism Raises His Profile. Jan. 26, 2007. A01. Retrieved 2.8.07 from http://www.washingtonpost.com/wp-dyn/content/article/2007/01/25/AR2007012502086_pf.html.
[1871] McCain on Hagel, ETC. New York Sun Politics Blog. Retrieved 3.28.07 from http://www.nysunpolitics.com/blog/2007/03/mccain-on-hagel-etc.html. Posted 3.28.07 by Ryan Sager.
[1872] McCain on Hagel, ETC. New York Sun Politics Blog. Retrieved 3.28.07 from http://www.nysunpolitics.com/blog/2007/03/mccain-on-hagel-etc.html. Posted 3.28.07 by Ryan Sager.
[1873] CNN.com. Situation Room with Wolf Blitzer. Aired 3.27.07 from http://transcripts.cnn.com/TRANSCRIPTS/0703/27/sitroom.01.html.
[1874] CBS News. Hagel-Bloomberg In '08? You Never Know. Posted 5.13.07 and retrieved 8.24.07 from http://www.cbsnews.com/stories/2007/05/13/ftn/printable2795705.shtml.

[1875] Hagel as Lieberman? Chuck Todd. Retrieved 8.1.07 from http://firstread.msnbc.msn.com/archive/2007/07/23/285608.aspx.
[1876] AP. Hagel: No 2008 Plans As Independent. Posted 7.8.07 and retrieved 8.1.07 from http://abcnews.go.com/Politics/wireStory?id=3356637.
[1877] KOTA Television. Second Candidate for Hagel's Senate seat. Posted 7.31.07 and retrieved 8.1.07 from http://www.kduhtv.com/viewStory.php?id=5676.
[1878] H-MRI: Mike Huckabee, The Sam's Club Candidate? Posted August 25, 2006 and retrieved 11.17.06 http://hotlineblog.nationaljournal.com/archives/2006/08/hmri_mike_hucka.html.
[1879] James Jefferson. A decade after the madness, Mike Huckabee reflects. Arkansas News Bureau. July 16, and retrieved August 25, 2006 from http://www.arkansasnews.com/archive/2006/07/16/News/336891.html.
[1880] James Jefferson. A decade after the madness, Mike Huckabee reflects. Arkansas News Bureau. July 16, and retrieved August 25, 2006 from http://www.arkansasnews.com/archive/2006/07/16/News/336891.html
[1881] James Jefferson. A decade after the madness, Mike Huckabee reflects. Arkansas News Bureau. July 16, and retrieved August 25, 2006 from http://www.arkansasnews.com/archive/2006/07/16/News/336891.html
[1882] James Jefferson. A decade after the madness, Mike Huckabee reflects. Arkansas News Bureau. July 16, and retrieved August 25, 2006 from http://www.arkansasnews.com/archive/2006/07/16/News/336891.html
[1883] James Jefferson. A decade after the madness, Mike Huckabee reflects. Arkansas News Bureau. July 16, and retrieved August 25, 2006 from http://www.arkansasnews.com/archive/2006/07/16/News/336891.html
[1884] Richard E. Cohen and Michael Barone. The Almanac of American Politics—2004. The National Journal Group. 2003, page 130.
[1885] Fergus Cullen. "Will Mike Huckabee follow the same path as Bill Clinton?" The Union Leader and New Hampshire Sunday News. Posted August 31, 2005 and retrieved September 8, 2005 from http://www.theunionleader.com/articles_showfast.html?article=59781.
[1886] Fergus Cullen. "Will Mike Huckabee follow the same path as Bill Clinton?" The Union Leader and New Hampshire Sunday News. Posted August 31, 2005 and retrieved September 8, 2005 from http://www.theunionleader.com/articles_showfast.html?article=59781
[1887] Mike Huckabee on Abortion. On the Issues. Retrieved 11.29.05 from http://www.ontheissues.org/Governor/Mike_Huckabee_Abortion.htm.
[1888] James Jefferson. A decade after the madness, Mike Huckabee reflects. Arkansas News Bureau. July 16, and retrieved August 25, 2006 from http://www.arkansasnews.com/archive/2006/07/16/News/336891.html
[1889] Richard E. Cohen and Michael Barone. "The Almanac of American Politics—2004." The National Journal Group. 2003, page 130
[1890] James Jefferson. A decade after the madness, Mike Huckabee reflects. Arkansas News Bureau. July 16, and retrieved August 25, 2006 from http://www.arkansasnews.com/archive/2006/07/16/News/336891.html
[1891] James Jefferson. A decade after the madness, Mike Huckabee reflects. Arkansas News Bureau. July 16, and retrieved August 25, 2006 from http://www.arkansasnews.com/archive/2006/07/16/News/336891.html
[1892] James Jefferson. A decade after the madness, Mike Huckabee reflects. Arkansas News Bureau. July 16, and retrieved August 25, 2006 from http://www.arkansasnews.com/archive/2006/07/16/News/336891.html
[1893] Governing.com. Public Officials of the Year 2005. Mike Huckabee, Trim Waist, Hefty Record. From the November 2005 issue. Retrieved May 31, 2006 from http://governing.com/poy/2005/huckabee.htm.
[1894] Warwick Sabin. "Huckabee for president?" The Arkansas Times. Posted September 22, 2005 and retrieved same day from http://www.arktimes.com/Articles/ArticleViewer.aspx?ArticleID=c3641402-8f22-4daa-b89b-4fdb68f887aa.
[1895] [fixed sic] H-MRI: Mike Huckabee, The Sam's Club Candidate? Posted August 25, 2006 and retrieved 11.17.06 http://hotlineblog.nationaljournal.com/archives/2006/08/hmri_mike_hucka.html.
[1896] Kathy Kiely. Governor's healthy state. USA TODAY. Posted July 11, 2004 and retrieved 11.29.05 from http://www.usatoday.com/news/health/2004-07-11-arkansas-governor_x.htm.
[1897] Kathy Kiely. Governor's healthy state. USA TODAY. Posted July 11, 2004 and retrieved 11.29.05 from http://www.usatoday.com/news/health/2004-07-11-arkansas-governor_x.htm.
[1898] Kathy Kiely. Governor's healthy state. USA TODAY. Posted July 11, 2004 and retrieved 11.29.05 from http://www.usatoday.com/news/health/2004-07-11-arkansas-governor_x.htm.
[1899] The Fix. Interview with Arkansas Gov. Mike Huckabee. Interviewed May 16, 2006 and retrieved July 14, 2006 from http://www.washingtonpost.com/wp-dyn/content/article/2006/05/22/AR2006052201237_pf.html.
[1900] The Fix. Interview with Arkansas Gov. Mike Huckabee. Interviewed May 16, 2006 and retrieved July 14, 2006 from http://www.washingtonpost.com/wp-dyn/content/article/2006/05/22/AR2006052201237_pf.html.
[1901] The Fix. Interview with Arkansas Gov. Mike Huckabee. Interviewed May 16, 2006 and retrieved July 14, 2006 from http://www.washingtonpost.com/wp-dyn/content/article/2006/05/22/AR2006052201237_pf.html.
[1902] The Fix. Interview with Arkansas Gov. Mike Huckabee. Interviewed May 16, 2006 and retrieved July 14, 2006 from http://www.washingtonpost.com/wp-dyn/content/article/2006/05/22/AR2006052201237_pf.html.
[1903] The Fix. Interview with Arkansas Gov. Mike Huckabee. Interviewed May 16, 2006 and retrieved July 14, 2006 from http://www.washingtonpost.com/wp-dyn/content/article/2006/05/22/AR2006052201237_pf.html.
[1904] David Yepsen. Yepsen: Huckabee courts right religiously. Des Moines Register. Published July 16, 2006 and retrieved July 28, 2006 from http://desmoinesregister.com/apps/pbcs.dll/article?AID=/20060716/OPINION01/60715074/1001/NEWS.

[1905] David Yepsen. Yepsen: Huckabee courts right religiously. Des Moines Register. Published July 16, 2006 and retrieved July 28, 2006 from http://desmoinesregister.com/apps/pbcs.dll/article?AID=/20060716/OPINION01/60715074/1001/NEWS
[1906] David Yepsen. Yepsen: Huckabee courts right religiously. Des Moines Register. Published July 16, 2006 and retrieved July 28, 2006 from http://desmoinesregister.com/apps/pbcs.dll/article?AID=/20060716/OPINION01/60715074/1001/NEWS
[1907] Rob Moritz. Huckabee supports legislation to ban gay foster parenting. Posted July 1, 2006 and retrieved July 28, 2006 from http://www.arkansasnews.com/archive/2006/07/01/News/336804.html.
[1908] Arkansas Gov. Mike Huckabee: Ban Gay Foster Parents. Newsmax.com. June 30, 2006 and retrieved July 28, 2006 from http://newsmax.com/archives/ic/2006/6/30/131101.shtml.
[1909] Arkansas Gov. Mike Huckabee: Ban Gay Foster Parents. Newsmax.com. June 30, 2006 and retrieved July 28, 2006 from http://newsmax.com/archives/ic/2006/6/30/131101.shtml.
[1910] Mike Glover. Huckabee Optimistic of Gay Parents Ban. AP. Posted July 8, 2006 and retrieved July 28, 2006 from http://www.examiner.com/a-170906~Huckabee_Optimistic_of_Gay_Parents_Ban.html.
[1911] Mike Glover. Huckabee Optimistic of Gay Parents Ban. AP. Posted July 8, 2006 and retrieved July 28, 2006 from http://www.examiner.com/a-170906~Huckabee_Optimistic_of_Gay_Parents_Ban.html
[1912] Mike Glover. Huckabee Optimistic of Gay Parents Ban. AP. Posted July 8, 2006 and retrieved July 28, 2006 from http://www.examiner.com/a-170906~Huckabee_Optimistic_of_Gay_Parents_Ban.html.
[1913] Arkansas Gov. Mike Huckabee: Ban Gay Foster Parents. Newsmax.com. June 30, 2006 and retrieved July 28, 2006 from http://newsmax.com/archives/ic/2006/6/30/131101.shtml.
[1914] FOX 16 of Little Rock. Gay Foster Parent Ban. Posted July 9, 2006 and retrieved July 28, 2006 from http://www.fox16.com/news/story.aspx?content_id=09302117-4F41-4125-9367-AE2F674E99D3.
[1915] Mike Glover. Huckabee Optimistic of Gay Parents Ban. AP. Posted July 8, 2006 and retrieved July 28, 2006 from http://www.examiner.com/a-170906~Huckabee_Optimistic_of_Gay_Parents_Ban.html
[1916] Arkansas Gov. Mike Huckabee: Ban Gay Foster Parents. Newsmax.com. June 30, 2006 and retrieved July 28, 2006 from http://newsmax.com/archives/ic/2006/6/30/131101.shtml.
[1917] Arkansas Gov. Mike Huckabee: Ban Gay Foster Parents. Newsmax.com. June 30, 2006 and retrieved July 28, 2006 from http://newsmax.com/archives/ic/2006/6/30/131101.shtml.
[1918] Mike Glover. Huckabee Optimistic of Gay Parents Ban. AP. Posted July 8, 2006 and retrieved July 28, 2006 from http://www.examiner.com/a-170906~Huckabee_Optimistic_of_Gay_Parents_Ban.html
[1919] H-MRI: Mike Huckabee, The Sam's Club Candidate? Posted August 25, 2006 and retrieved 11.17.06 http://hotlineblog.nationaljournal.com/archives/2006/08/hmri_mike_hucka.html
[1920] James Jefferson. A decade after the madness, Mike Huckabee reflects. Arkansas News Bureau. July 16, and retrieved August 25, 2006 from http://www.arkansasnews.com/archive/2006/07/16/News/336891.html.
[1921] Richard E. Cohen and Michael Barone. The Almanac of American Politics—2004. The National Journal Group. 2003, page 131.
[1922] Warwick Sabin. Huckabee for president? The Arkansas Times. Posted September 22, 2005 and retrieved same day from http://www.arktimes.com/Articles/ArticleViewer.aspx?ArticleID=c3641402-8f22-4daa-b89b-4fdb68f887aa.
[1923] Warwick Sabin. Huckabee for president? The Arkansas Times. Posted September 22, 2005 and retrieved same day from http://www.arktimes.com/Articles/ArticleViewer.aspx?ArticleID=c3641402-8f22-4daa-b89b-4fdb68f887aa.
[1924] Arkansas Times Staff. The governor's flight log. The Arkansas Times. Posted November 3, 2005 and retrieved November 29, 2005 from http://arktimes.com/Articles/ArticleViewer.aspx?ArticleID=d79947ac-759b-46f0-9d16-405d6881b708.
[1925] Warwick Sabin. Have plane, will travel. Updated 11.3.05 and retrieved 12.14.05 from http://mikehuckabee.com/.
[1926] James Jefferson. A decade after the madness, Mike Huckabee reflects. Arkansas News Bureau. July 16, and retrieved August 25, 2006 from http://www.arkansasnews.com/archive/2006/07/16/News/336891.html
[1927] H-MRI: Mike Huckabee, The Sam's Club Candidate? Posted August 25, 2006 and retrieved 11.17.06 http://hotlineblog.nationaljournal.com/archives/2006/08/hmri_mike_hucka.html.
[1928] James Jefferson. A decade after the madness, Mike Huckabee reflects. Arkansas News Bureau. July 16, and retrieved August 25, 2006 from http://www.arkansasnews.com/archive/2006/07/16/News/336891.html
[1929] FOXNews.com. Transcript: Governors Evaluate 2005 Election. Fox News Sunday. Posted November 14, 2005 and retrieved November 15, 2005 from http://www.foxnews.com/printer_friendly_story/0,3566,175477,00.html.
[1930] FOXNews.com. Transcript: Governors Evaluate 2005 Election. Fox News Sunday. Posted November 14, 2005 and retrieved November 15, 2005 from http://www.foxnews.com/printer_friendly_story/0,3566,175477,00.html
[1931] CNN. CNN Late Edition with Wolf Blitzer—Aired November 13, 2005. CNN. Retrieved November 18, 2005 from http://transcripts.cnn.com/TRANSCRIPTS/0511/13/le.01.html.
[1932] US News.com. Washington Whispers. Unique Fundraising: Masks and Guns? Retrieved June 16, 2006 from http://www.usnews.com/usnews/politics/whispers/articles/060619/19whisplead_2.htm.
[1933] The Fix. Interview with Arkansas Gov. Mike Huckabee. Interviewed May 16, 2006 and retrieved July 14, 2006 from http://www.washingtonpost.com/wp-dyn/content/article/2006/05/22/AR2006052201237_pf.html.
[1934] Brain Knowlton. Sunday Sampler Platter 2, Sept. 2. Retrieved September 2, 2007 from http://thecaucus.blogs.nytimes.com/2007/09/02/sunday-sampler-platter-sept-2/.
[1935] AP. Romney scales down plans for Iowa straw poll. Posted 7.22.07 and retrieved 8.1.07 from http://www.boston.com/news/nation/articles/2007/07/22/romney_scales_down_plans_for_iowa_straw_poll/.

[1936] Michael Luo. Romney Hopes to Win Straw Poll in Iowa. The New York Times. 7.30.07 and retrieved 8.1.07 from http://www.nytimes.com/2007/07/30/us/politics/30romney.html?ie...
[1937] The Line: Debate Provides '08 Wake-up Call. Posted 7.27.07 and retrieved 8.1.07 from http://blog.washingtonpost.com/thefix/2007/07/friday_presidential_line_1.html.
[1938] McCain plays down 10th place finish in Iowa straw poll. CNN.com. Retrieved 8.14.07 from http://www.cnn.com/2007/POLITICS/08/14/mccain.straw.poll.ap/index.html.
[1939] Marc Ambinder. Why the Media Likes Huckabee. Posted 8.15.07 and retrieved 8.21.07 from http://marcambinder.theatlantic.com/archives/2007/08/why_the_media_likes_huckabee.php.
[1940] Meet the Press. Aug.12, 2007 and retrieved 8.14.07 from http://www.msnbc.msn.com/id/20214115/print/1/displaymode/1098/
[1941] Meet the Press. Aug.12, 2007 and retrieved 8.14.07 from http://www.msnbc.msn.com/id/20214115/print/1/displaymode/1098/.
[1942] Meet the Press. Aug.12, 2007 and retrieved 8.14.07 from http://www.msnbc.msn.com/id/20214115/print/1/displaymode/1098/.
[1943] Meet the Press. Aug.12, 2007 and retrieved 8.14.07 from http://www.msnbc.msn.com/id/20214115/print/1/displaymode/1098/.
[1944] Meet the Press. Aug.12, 2007 and retrieved 8.14.07 from http://www.msnbc.msn.com/id/20214115/print/1/displaymode/1098/.
[1945] Meet the Press. Aug.12, 2007 and retrieved 8.14.07 from http://www.msnbc.msn.com/id/20214115/print/1/displaymode/1098/.
[1946] Huckabee Coming to S.C. Campaigns & Elections. Retrieved 8.14.07 from http://campaignsandelections.com/sc/releases/index.cfm?ID=3025.
[1947] San Diego Business Journal Online. Duncan Hunter Mulls Run for President. Posted 10.31.06 from http://www.sdbj.com.
[1948] CNN.com. GOP chairman takes first steps toward /08 bid. Posted 10.30 and retrieved 11.17.06 from http://www.cnn.com/2006/POLITICS/10/30/hunter.2008.ap/.
[1949] FOX 6 San Diego. Rep Duncan Hunter to Run for President in 08. Published 10.30.06 from http://www.fox6.com/news/local/story.
[1950] Tony Perry. San Diego's Rep Duncan Hunter to make presidential bid. LA Times. Posted 10.31. and retrieved 11.17.06 from http://www.latimes.com/news/politics/la-me-duncan31oc31,1,43823.story?coll=la-headlines-politics.
[1951] Milwaukee Journal Sentinel. 6A. 10.31.06. California Congressman plans bid for White House.
[1952] SignOnSanDiego.com. Duncan Hunter's son looking to replace him in House. 3.21.07 and retrieved 6.15.07 from http://www.signonsandiego.com/news/politics/20070321-1248-ca-hunter-2008.html.
[1953] Marc Sandalow: Duncan Hunter's curious timing. SF Gate. Posted Oct. 30, 2006 and retrieved 11.17.06 from http://www.sfgate.com/cgi-bin/blogs/sfgate/detail?blogid=14&entry_id=10370.
[1954] Marc Sandalow: Duncan Hunter's curious timing. SF Gate. Posted Oct. 30, 2006 and retrieved 11.17.06 from http://www.sfgate.com/cgi-bin/blogs/sfgate/detail?blogid=14&entry_id=10370.
[1955] Marc Sandalow: Duncan Hunter's curious timing. SF Gate. Posted Oct. 30, 2006 and retrieved 11.17.06 from http://www.sfgate.com/cgi-bin/blogs/sfgate/detail?blogid=14&entry_id=10370.
[1956] Mark Walker. NCTimes.com. Posted Nov. 4 and retrieved 11.17.06 from http://www.nctimes.com/articles/2006/11/05/news/top_stories/21_51_5611_4_06.prt.
[1957] CNN.com. GOP chairman takes first steps toward /08 bid. Posted 10.30 and retrieved 11.17.06 from http://www.cnn.com/2006/POLITICS/10/30/hunter.2008.ap/.
[1958] CNN.com. GOP chairman takes first steps toward /08 bid. Posted 10.30 and retrieved 11.17.06 from http://www.cnn.com/2006/POLITICS/10/30/hunter.2008.ap/.
[1959] YAHOO! News. The Nation. Oct. 30, 2006 and retrieved 11.17.06 from http://news.yahoo.com/s/thenation/20061030/cm_thenation/151344405&printer=1.
[1960] Jamie Reno. Rep. Duncan Hunter explains why he's decided to run for the White house and how he' his [sic] '08 campaign message. Posted 10.31 from MSNBC.com. and retrieved 11.17.06.
[1961] Beth Fouhy. Clinton, Bayh Step Up Plans for 2008. AP. Dec.3 and retrieved same day from http://abcnews.go.com/Poltiics/print?id=2697236. See also http://www.chinadaily.com/cn/world/2006-12/04/content_749275.htm.
[1962] Marty Graham. Rep. Duncan Hunter to run for president. Oct. 30, 2006 and retrieved 11.17.06 from http://elections.us.reuters.com/top/news/usnN30410376.html.
[1963] Mark Walker. NCTimes.com. Posted 11.4.06 and retrieved 11.17.06 from http://www.nctimes.com/articles/2006/11/05/news/top_stories/21_51_5611_4_06.prt.
[1964] Marty Graham. Rep. Duncan Hunter to run for president. Oct. 30, 2006 and retrieved 11.17.06 from http://elections.us.reuters.com/top/news/usnN30410376.html.
[1965] Zachary A. Goldfarb. Washingtonpost.com. Forget Polls, Long Shots Say It's About the Message. Special to the Washington Post. Dec.26, 2006 A2. Retrieved 1.13.07 from http://www.washingtonpost.com/wp-dyn/content/article/2006/12/25/AR2006122500458_pf.html.
[1966] Zachary A. Goldfarb. Washingtonpost.com. Forget Polls, Long Shots Say It's About the Message. Special to the Washington Post. Dec.26, 2006 A2. Retrieved 1.13.07 from http://www.washingtonpost.com/wp-dyn/content/article/2006/12/25/AR2006122500458_pf.html.

Karl McCarty: *The Last One Standing* 302

[1967] Zachary A. Goldfarb. Washingtonpost.com. Forget Polls, Long Shots Say It's About the Message. Special to the Washington Post. Dec.26, 2006 A2. Retrieved 1.13.07 from http://www.washingtonpost.com/wp-dyn/content/article/2006/12/25/AR2006122500458_pf.html.

[1968] Zachary A. Goldfarb. Washingtonpost.com. Forget Polls, Long Shots Say It's About the Message. Special to the Washington Post. Dec.26, 2006 A2. Retrieved 1.13.07 from http://www.washingtonpost.com/wp-dyn/content/article/2006/12/25/AR2006122500458_pf.html.

[1969] MSNBC.com. Hunter defends Ann Coulter against critics. Posted 7.2.07 and retrieved 8.1.07 from http://www.msnbc.msn.com/id/19570266/.

[1970] MSNBC.com. Hunter defends Ann Coulter against critics. Posted 7.2.07 and retrieved 8.1.07 from http://www.msnbc.msn.com/id/19570266/.

[1971] The Richmond Democrat. Is Duncan Hunter a tax dodger? 4.12.07. Retrieved 6.15.07 from http://richmonddemocrat.blogspot.com/search/label/Duke%20Cunningham.

[1972] Jeff McDonald. Hunter got break on taxes for home. 10.8.06 and retrieved 6.15.07 from http://www.signonsandiego.com/news/metro/20061008-9999-1n8duncan.html.

[1973] Jeff McDonald. Hunter got break on taxes for home. 10.8.06 and retrieved 6.15.07 from http://www.signonsandiego.com/news/metro/20061008-9999-1n8duncan.html.

[1974] Jeff McDonald. Hunter got break on taxes for home. 10.8.06 and retrieved 6.15.07 from http://www.signonsandiego.com/news/metro/20061008-9999-1n8duncan.html.

[1975] 1991 Cunningham/Hunter DP-2 Letter. Retrieved from POGO (The Project On Government Oversight on 6.15.07 and posted the day before @ http://pogoblog.typepad.com/pogo/2007/06/1991_cunningham.html.

[1976] Jerry Kammer and Paul M. Krawzak. Hunter defends support for jet. 6.13.07 and retrieved 6.15.07 from http://www.signonsandiego.com/news/politics/20070613-9999-1n13airmark.html.

[1977] Jerry Kammer and Paul M. Krawzak. Hunter defends support for jet. 6.13.07 and retrieved 6.15.07 from http://www.signonsandiego.com/news/politics/20070613-9999-1n13airmark.html.

[1978] Jerry Kammer and Paul M. Krawzak. Hunter defends support for jet. 6.13.07 and retrieved 6.15.07 from http://www.signonsandiego.com/news/politics/20070613-9999-1n13airmark.html.

[1979] Jerry Kammer and Paul M. Krawzak. Hunter defends support for jet. 6.13.07 and retrieved 6.15.07 from http://www.signonsandiego.com/news/politics/20070613-9999-1n13airmark.html.

[1980] Jerry Kammer and Paul M. Krawzak. Hunter defends support for jet. 6.13.07 and retrieved 6.15.07 from http://www.signonsandiego.com/news/politics/20070613-9999-1n13airmark.html.

[1981] Jerry Kammer and Paul M. Krawzak. Hunter defends support for jet. 6.13.07 and retrieved 6.15.07 from http://www.signonsandiego.com/news/politics/20070613-9999-1n13airmark.html.

[1982] Jerry Kammer and Paul M. Krawzak. Hunter defends support for jet. 6.13.07 and retrieved 6.15.07 from http://www.signonsandiego.com/news/politics/20070613-9999-1n13airmark.html.

[1983] Jerry Kammer and Paul M. Krawzak. Hunter defends support for jet. 6.13.07 and retrieved 6.15.07 from http://www.signonsandiego.com/news/politics/20070613-9999-1n13airmark.html.

[1984] Jerry Kammer and Paul M. Krawzak. Hunter defends support for jet. 6.13.07 and retrieved 6.15.07 from http://www.signonsandiego.com/news/politics/20070613-9999-1n13airmark.html.

[1985] By 92036 on 6.13.07 and retrieved 6.15.07 posted at the end of: Jerry Kammer and Paul M. Krawzak. Hunter defends support for jet. 6.13.07 and retrieved 6.15.07 from http://www.signonsandiego.com/news/politics/20070613-9999-1n13airmark.html.

[1986] Justin Rood. Hunter Pushed Earmarks for Scandal Firm's Client. Posted 6.8.06 and retrieved 6.15.07 from http://www.tpmmuckraker.com/archives/cats/duncan_hunter/.

[1987] Dan Anderson. Randy 'Duke' Cunningham Forum. 3.3.06 and retrieved 6.15.07 from http://www.dukecunningham.org/forum/read.php?f=1&i=1262&t=1262.

[1988] Elana Schor. Wilkes and Foggo indicted. The Hill. Leading The News. Posted 2.14.07 and retrieved 6.15.07 from http://thehill.com/leading-the-news/wilkes-and-foggo-indicted-2007-02-14.html.

[1989] Dean Calbreath and Jerry Kammer. Contractor 'knew how to grease the wheels.' Copley News Service. Posted 12.4.05 and retrieved 6.15.07 from http://www.signonsandiego.com/uniontrib/20051204/news_1n4adcs.html.

[1990] Matt Kelley and Jim Drinkard. USA Today. Contractor spends big on key lawmakers. Posted 11.29.05 and retrieved 6.15.07 from http://www.usatoday.com/news/washington/2005-11-29-cunningham-case_x.htm.

[1991] Matt Kelley and Jim Drinkard. USA Today. Contractor spends big on key lawmakers. Posted 11.29.05 and retrieved 6.15.07 from http://www.usatoday.com/news/washington/2005-11-29-cunningham-case_x.htm.

[1992] Matt Kelley and Jim Drinkard. USA Today. Contractor spends big on key lawmakers. Posted 11.29.05 and retrieved 6.15.07 from http://www.usatoday.com/news/washington/2005-11-29-cunningham-case_x.htm.

[1993] Matt Kelley and Jim Drinkard. USA Today. Contractor spends big on key lawmakers. Posted 11.29.05 and retrieved 6.15.07 from http://www.usatoday.com/news/washington/2005-11-29-cunningham-case_x.htm.

[1994] Dean Calbreath and Jerry Kammer. Contractor 'knew how to grease the wheels.' Copley News Service. Posted 12.4.05 and retrieved 6.15.07 from http://www.signonsandiego.com/uniontrib/20051204/news_1n4adcs.html.

[1995] Matt Kelley and Jim Drinkard. USA Today. Contractor spends big on key lawmakers. Posted 11.29.05 and retrieved 6.15.07 from http://www.usatoday.com/news/washington/2005-11-29-cunningham-case_x.htm.

[1996] Hunter is Duke's Friend 'til the end. The Hill. Posted 3.7.06 @ http://www.hillnews.com/thehill/export/ThHill/News/Frontpage/030706/duke.thml, and retrieved 6.15.07 from http://en.wikipedia.org/wiki/Duncan_Hunter.

[1997] Matt Kelley and Jim Drinkard. USA Today. Contractor spends big on key lawmakers. Posted 11.29.05 and retrieved 6.15.07 from http://www.usatoday.com/news/washington/2005-11-29-cunningham-case_x.htm.

[1998] Dean Calbreath and Jerry Kammer. Contractor 'knew how to grease the wheels.' Copley News Service. Posted 12.4.05 and retrieved 6.15.07 from http://www.signonsandiego.com/uniontrib/20051204/news_1n4adcs.html.

[1999] Dean Calbreath and Jerry Kammer. Contractor 'knew how to grease the wheels.' Copley News Service. Posted 12.4.05 and retrieved 6.15.07 from http://www.signonsandiego.com/uniontrib/20051204/news_1n4adcs.html.

[2000] Dean Calbreath and Jerry Kammer. Contractor 'knew how to grease the wheels.' Copley News Service. Posted 12.4.05 and retrieved 6.15.07 from http://www.signonsandiego.com/uniontrib/20051204/news_1n4adcs.html. Dean Calbreath and Jerry Kammer. Contractor 'knew how to grease the wheels.' Copley News Service. Posted 12.4.05 and retrieved 6.15.07 from http://www.signonsandiego.com/uniontrib/20051204/news_1n4adcs.html.

[2001] Dean Calbreath and Jerry Kammer. Contractor 'knew how to grease the wheels.' Copley News Service. Posted 12.4.05 and retrieved 6.15.07 from http://www.signonsandiego.com/uniontrib/20051204/news_1n4adcs.html.

[2002] Dean Calbreath and Jerry Kammer. Contractor 'knew how to grease the wheels.' Copley News Service. Posted 12.4.05 and retrieved 6.15.07 from http://www.signonsandiego.com/uniontrib/20051204/news_1n4adcs.html.

[2003] Dean Calbreath and Jerry Kammer. Contractor 'knew how to grease the wheels.' Copley News Service. Posted 12.4.05 and retrieved 6.15.07 from http://www.signonsandiego.com/uniontrib/20051204/news_1n4adcs.html.

[2004] Dean Calbreath and Jerry Kammer. Contractor 'knew how to grease the wheels.' Copley News Service. Posted 12.4.05 and retrieved 6.15.07 from http://www.signonsandiego.com/uniontrib/20051204/news_1n4adcs.html.

[2005] Dean Calbreath and Jerry Kammer. Contractor 'knew how to grease the wheels.' Copley News Service. Posted 12.4.05 and retrieved 6.15.07 from http://www.signonsandiego.com/uniontrib/20051204/news_1n4adcs.html.

[2006] Duke Cunningham's briber about to roll over? 3.3.06. Retrieved 6.15.07 from http://www.preemptivekarma.com/archives/2006/03/duke_cunningham_1.html.

[2007] Justin Rood. Congress Drags Feet, Impedes Cunningham Probe. 7.26.06 and retrieved 6.15.07 from http://www.tpmmuckraker.com/archives/cats/duncan_hunter/.

[2008] Justin Rood. Pentagon Watchdog Owns Cabin With Rumsfeld Pal. Posted 6.12.06 and retrieved 6.15.07 from http://www.tpmmuckraker.com/archives/cats/duncan_hunter/.

[2009] Hunter is Duke's Friend 'til the end. The Hill. Posted 3.7.06 @ http://www.hillnews.com/thehill/export/ThHill/News/Frontpage/030706/duke.thml, and retrieved 6.15.07 from http://en.wikepedia.org/wiki/Duncan_Hunter.

[2010] Mark Walker. NCTimes.com. Posted 11.4.06 and retrieved 11.17.06 from http://www.nctimes.com/articles/2006/11/05/news/top_stories/21_51_5611_4_06.prt.

[2011] CNN.com. GOP chairman takes first steps toward '08 bid. Posted 10.30.06 and retrieved 11.17.06 from http://www.cnn.com/2006/POLITICS/10/30/hunter.2008.ap. See Elliot Spagat's AP report for 10.30.06 @ http://www.washingtonpost.com/wp-dyn/content/article/2006/10/30/AR2006103000121.html.

[2012] Mark Walker. NCTimes.com. Posted 11.4.06 and retrieved 11.17.06 from http://www.nctimes.com/articles/2006/11/05/news/top_stories/21_51_5611_4_06.prt.

[2013] Finlay Lewis. Copley News Service. Signonsandiego.com. Posted 12.2.06 and retrieved 1.13.07 from http://www.signonsandiego.com/news/politics/20061202-9999-1n2hunter.html.

[2014] Finlay Lewis. Copley News Service. Signonsandiego.com. Posted 12.2.06 and retrieved 1.13.07 from http://www.signonsandiego.com/news/politics/20061202-9999-1n2hunter.html.

[2015] Finlay Lewis. Copley News Service. Signonsandiego.com. Posted Dec.2 and retrieved 1.13.07 from http://www.signonsandiego.com/news/politics/20061202-9999-1n2hunter.html.

[2016] Finlay Lewis. Copley News Service. Signonsandiego.com. Posted Dec.2 and retrieved 1.13.07 from http://www.signonsandiego.com/news/politics/20061202-9999-1n2hunter.html.

[2017] The GOP Debate. In the News. The Official Site of Duncan Hunter for US President in 2008. Posted 5.5.06 and retrieved 6.15.07 from http://www.gohunter08.com/shownews.asp?artid=39.

[2018] Mark Walker. NCTimes.com. Posted Nov. 4 and retrieved 11.17.06 from http://www.nctimes.com/articles/2006/11/05/news/top_stories/21_51_5611_4_06.prt.

[2019] National Journal Rankings. The Republicans. 7.30.07 and retrieved 8.1.07 from http://nationaljournal.com/racerankings/wh08/republicans/.

[2020] Tony Perry. San Diego's Rep Duncan Hunter to make presidential bid. LA Times. Posted 10.31. and retrieved 11.17.06 from http://www.latimes.com/news/politics/la-me-duncan31oc31,1,43823.story?coll=la-headlines-politics.

[2021] Tony Perry. San Diego's Rep Duncan Hunter to make presidential bid. LA Times. Posted 10.31. and retrieved 11.17.06 from http://www.latimes.com/news/politics/la-me-duncan31oc31,1,43823.story?coll=la-headlines-politics.

[2022] Marty Graham. Rep. Duncan Hunter to run for president. 10.30.06 and retrieved 11.17.06 from http://elections.us.reuters.com/top/news/usnN30410376.html.

[2023] Jonah Goldberg on Immigration on National Review Online. http://article.nationalreview.com/?q=NDAxOTczYTRjZTA3NWI2NDcyMGUwY2ZlYjU4MzJlOGE= Posted 11.3.06 and retrieved 11.17.06.

[2024] Victoria Guay. California's Hunter campaigns. Citizen.com. The Citizen of Laconia. New Hampshire. Retrieved 1.13. and posted 1.7.07 from http://www.citizen.com/apps/pbcs.dll/article?AID=/20070107/CITIZEN_01/101070162/-1/CITIZEN.

[2025] Election Center 2008. CNN.com. Duncan Hunter. Retrieved 8.21.07 from http://www.cnn.com/ELECTION/2008/candidates/duncan.hunter.html.

[2026] RJ Elliott. Iowa Straw Poll Results. Published 8.12.07 and retrieved 8.21.07 from http://blogcritics.org/archives/2007/08/12/023738.php.
[2027] McCain vs. Giuliani: Tale of the Tape. Nov. 17.2006. Retrieved 7.11.07 @ http://www.cbsnews.com/stories/2006/11/15/politics/printable2184018.shtml.
[2028] Todd Purdum. Prisoner of Conscience. Vanity Fair. For February 2007. Retrieved 1.13.07 from http://www.vanityfair.com/politics/features/2007/02/mccain200702?printable=true&currentPage=all.
[2029] McCain vs. Giuliani: Tale of the Tape. Nov. 17.2006. Retrieved 7.11.06 @ http://www.cbsnews.com/stories/2006/11/15/politics/printable2184018.shtml.
[2030] Richard E. Cohen and Michael Barone. The Almanac of American Politics—2004. The National Journal Group. 2003, page 103.
[2031] Richard E. Cohen and Michael Barone. "The Almanac of American Politics—2004." The National Journal Group. 2003, page 103.
[2032] Joel Connelly and Ed Offley. "McCain and Bush clash over Revs. Robertson, Falwell." The Seattle Post-Intelligencer. Posted February 29, 2000 and retrieved December 14, 2005 from http://seattlepi.nwsource.com/national/gops29.shtml.
[2033] Todd Purdum. Prisoner of Conscience. Vanity Fair. For February 2007. Retrieved 1.13.07 from http://www.vanityfair.com/politics/features/2007/02/mccain200702?printable=true&currentPage=all.
[2034] Todd Purdum. Prisoner of Conscience. Vanity Fair. For February 2007. Retrieved 1.13.07 from http://www.vanityfair.com/politics/features/2007/02/mccain200702?printable=true&currentPage=all.
[2035] Todd Purdum. Prisoner of Conscience. Vanity Fair. For February 2007. Retrieved 1.13.07 from http://www.vanityfair.com/politics/features/2007/02/mccain200702?printable=true&currentPage=all.
[2036] Meet the Press. May 16. 2004. MSNBC.com. Retrieved 10.31.2006 from http://www.msnbc.msn.com/id/4992558/print/1/displaymode/1098/.
[2037] Meet the Press. May 16. 2004. MSNBC.com. Retrieved 10.31.2006 from http://www.msnbc.msn.com/id/4992558/print/1/displaymode/1098/.
[2038] Meet the Press. May 16. 2004. MSNBC.com. Retrieved 10.31.2006 from http://www.msnbc.msn.com/id/4992558/print/1/displaymode/1098/.
[2039] NBC News. "Transcript for Nov. 21." Meet the Press. Posted November 21, 2004 and retrieved August 26, 2005 from http://www.msnbc.msn.com/id/6531547/
[2040] NBC News. "Transcript for Nov. 21." Meet the Press. Posted November 21, 2004 and retrieved August 26, 2005 from http://www.msnbc.msn.com/id/6531547/.
[2041] NBC News. "Transcript for Nov. 21." Meet the Press. Posted November 21, 2004 and retrieved August 26, 2005 from http://www.msnbc.msn.com/id/6531547/
[2042] CBS News. "Text of McCain's RNC Speech." Posted August 30, 2004 and retrieved November 10, 2005 from http://www.cbsnews.com/stories/2004/08/30/politics/main639572.shtml.
[2043] CBS News. "Text of McCain's RNC Speech." Posted August 30, 2004 and retrieved November 10, 2005 from http://www.cbsnews.com/stories/2004/08/30/politics/main639572.shtml
[2044] Todd Purdum. Prisoner of Conscience. Vanity Fair. For February 2007. Retrieved 1.13.07 from http://www.vanityfair.com/politics/features/2007/02/mccain200702?printable=true&currentPage=all.
[2045] Todd Purdum. Prisoner of Conscience. Vanity Fair. For February 2007. Retrieved 1.13.07 from http://www.vanityfair.com/politics/features/2007/02/mccain200702?printable=true&currentPage=all.
[2046] Todd Purdum. Prisoner of Conscience. Vanity Fair. For February 2007. Retrieved 1.13.07 from http://www.vanityfair.com/politics/features/2007/02/mccain200702?printable=true&currentPage=all.
[2047] Todd Purdum. Prisoner of Conscience. Vanity Fair. For February 2007. Retrieved 1.13.07 from http://www.vanityfair.com/politics/features/2007/02/mccain200702?printable=true&currentPage=all.
[2048] Kathleen Parker. Clinton leads decency effort while McCain appears in bawdy movie. 7.22.05 and retrieved same day from http://www.gwinnettdailypost.com.
[2049] Reuters. Peter Kaplan. Sen. Clinton seeks 'Grand Theft' sex scene probe. Posted 7.14.05 and retrieved 7.22.05 from http://today.reuters.co.uk.
[2050] AP. McCain Confused over Criticism for "Crashers" cameo. TheNewOrleansChannel.com. Posted July 19, 2005 and retrieved July 22, 2005 from http://www.theneworleanschannel.com/entertainment/4741743/detail.html.
[2051] MSNBC. Sen. John McCain on Imus. Posted July 20, 2005 and retrieved September 14, 2005 from http://www.msnbc.msn.com/id/8642797/print/1/displaymode/1098/
[2052] ABC's This Week, July 24, 2005
[2053] NBC News. Transcript for Nov. 21. Meet the Press. Posted November 21, 2004 and retrieved August 26, 2005 from http://www.msnbc.msn.com/id/6531547/
[2054] MSNBC. Sen. John McCain on Imus. Posted July 20, 2005 and retrieved September 14, 2005 from http://www.msnbc.msn.com/id/8642797/print/1/displaymode/1098/.
[2055] MSNBC. Sen. John McCain on Imus. Posted July 20, 2005 and retrieved September 14, 2005 from http://www.msnbc.msn.com/id/8642797/print/1/displaymode/1098/
[2056] MSNBC.com. Transcript for April 2. NBC News/Meet the Press. Posted April 2, 2006 and retrieved next day from http://www.msnbc.msn.com/id/12067487/print/1/displaymode/1098/.
[2057] MSNBC.com. Transcript for April 2. NBC News/Meet the Press. Posted April 2, 2006 and retrieved next day from http://www.msnbc.msn.com/id/12067487/print/1/displaymode/1098/
[2058] MSNBC.com. Transcript for April 2. NBC News/Meet the Press. Posted April 2, 2006 and retrieved next day from http://www.msnbc.msn.com/id/12067487/print/1/displaymode/1098/

[2059] MSNBC.com. Transcript for April 2. NBC News/Meet the Press. Posted April 2, 2006 and retrieved next day from http://www.msnbc.msn.com/id/12067487/print/1/displaymode/1098/
[2060] Ron. Brown. McCain to speak at Liberty graduation. The Lynchburg News & Advance. Posted March 28, 2006 and retrieved April 10, 2006 from http://www.newsadvance.com/servlet/Satellite?pagename=LNA/MGArticle/LNA_BasicArticle&c=MGArticle&cid=1137834984968&path.
[2061] TV Squad. The Daily Show: April 4, 2006. Posted April 5, 2006, and retrieved April 10, 2006 from http://www.tvsquad.com/2006/04/05/the-daily-show-april-4-2006/.
[2062] The Third Path. John McCain on The Daily Show. Aired Tuesday, April 4, 2006 and retrieved April 10, 2006 from http://lincmad.blogspot.com/2006/04/john-mccain-on-daily-show.html.
[2063] The Third Path. John McCain on The Daily Show. Aired Tuesday, April 4, 2006 and retrieved April 10, 2006 from http://lincmad.blogspot.com/2006/04/john-mccain-on-daily-show.htmlv
[2064] The Third Path. John McCain on The Daily Show. Aired Tuesday, April 4, 2006 and retrieved April 10, 2006 from http://lincmad.blogspot.com/2006/04/john-mccain-on-daily-show.html
[2065] The Third Path. John McCain on The Daily Show. Aired Tuesday, April 4, 2006 and retrieved April 10, 2006 from http://lincmad.blogspot.com/2006/04/john-mccain-on-daily-show.html
[2066] The Third Path. John McCain on The Daily Show. Aired Tuesday, April 4, 2006 and retrieved April 10, 2006 from http://lincmad.blogspot.com/2006/04/john-mccain-on-daily-show.html
[2067] Ron. Brown. McCain to speak at Liberty graduation. The Lynchburg News & Advance. Posted March 28, 2006 and retrieved April 10, 2006 from http://www.newsadvance.com/servlet/Satellite?pagename=LNA/MGArticle/LNA_BasicArticle&c=MGArticle&cid=1137834984968&path.
[2068] Jill Lawrence. Once-foe McCain makes a friend of Bush dynasty. USA TODAY. Posted/retrieved April 10, 2006 from http://www.usatoday.com/news/washington/2006-04-09-mccain_x.htm?POE=NEWISVA
[2069] Jill Lawrence. Once-foe McCain makes a friend of Bush dynasty. USA TODAY. Posted/retrieved April 10, 2006 from http://www.usatoday.com/news/washington/2006-04-09-mccain_x.htm?POE=NEWISVA
[2070] Douglas K. Daniel. Kerry Dismisses idea whites run nomination. Seattle Post-Intelligencer. Retrieved April 24, 2006 from http://seattlepi.nwsource.com/national/1153AP_Kerry_Democrats.html
[2071] Dan Balz. McCain's Rhetoric Goes Back to the Future. Washington Post, Published April 9, 2006 page A07, retrieved April 10, 2005 from http://www.washingtonpost.com/wp-dyn/content/article/2006/04/08/AR2006040801012.html.
[2072] AP. McCain Softens Language on Jerry Falwell. Washington Post. Posted April 2, 2006 and retrieved April 10, 2006 from http://www.washingtonpost.com/wp-dyn/content/article/2006/04/02/AR2006040200391.html.
[2073] Paul Krugman. Moderate McCain courts religious right. The New York Times. The Milwaukee Journal Sentinel, April 4, 2006, 9A.
[2074] NBC News. Meet the Press. MTP Transcript for Jan.21, 2007. Retrieved 2.8.07 from http://www.msnbc.msn.com/id/16634747/print/1/displaymode/1098/.
[2075] NBC News. Meet the Press. MTP Transcript for Jan.21, 2007. Retrieved 2.8.07 from http://www.msnbc.msn.com/id/16634747/print/1/displaymode/1098/.
[2076] NBC News. Meet the Press. MTP Transcript for Jan.21, 2007. Retrieved 2.8.07 from http://www.msnbc.msn.com/id/16634747/print/1/displaymode/1098/.
[2077] High Infidelity. Steve Benen. Washington Monthly. July/August 2006. Retrieved June 30, 2006 from http://www.washingtonmonthly.com/features/2006/0607.benen.html.
[2078] High Infidelity. Steve Benen. Washington Monthly. July/August 2006. Retrieved June 30, 2006 from http://www.washingtonmonthly.com/features/2006/0607.benen.html.
[2079] High Infidelity. Steve Benen. Washington Monthly. July/August 2006. Retrieved June 30, 2006 from http://www.washingtonmonthly.com/features/2006/0607.benen.html.
[2080] Joe Klein. The Fresh Face. Time. Oct. 15, 2006 and retrieved Oct. 31, 2006 form http://www.time.com/magazine/printout/0,8816,1546362,00.html.
[2081] Hardball's College Tour with John McCain. MSNBC.com. Oct. 18, retrieved 10.31.2006 from http://www.msnbc.msn.com/id/15330717/page/2/print/1/displaymode/1098/.
[2082] Hardball's College Tour with John McCain. MSNBC.com. Oct. 18, retrieved 10.31.2006 from http://www.msnbc.msn.com/id/15330717/page/2/print/1/displaymode/1098/
[2083] Hardball with Chris Matthews for Jan.3. MSNBC.com. Retrieved 1.13.07 from http://www.msnbc.msn.com/id/16469533/print/1/displaymode/1098/.
[2084] Todd Purdum. Prisoner of Conscience. Vanity Fair. For February 2007. Retrieved 1.13.07 from http://www.vanityfair.com/politics/features/2007/02/mccain200702?printable=true&currentPage=all.
[2085] Todd Purdum. Prisoner of Conscience. Vanity Fair. For February 2007. Retrieved 1.13.07 from http://www.vanityfair.com/politics/features/2007/02/mccain200702?printable=true&currentPage=all.
[2086] John McCain on ABC's This Week, Nov. 19, 2006.
[2087] USA TODAY staff. Democratic wins trigger Rumsfeld resignation; Senate control still unclear. Posted 11.8.06 and retrieved 7.20.07 from http://www.usatoday.com/news/politicalselections/vote2006/2006-11-07-election-main_x.htm.
[2088] Hardball with Chris Matthews for Jan.3. MSNBC.com. Retrieved 1.13.07 from http://www.msnbc.msn.com/id/16469533/print/1/displaymode/1098/.
[2089] Todd Purdum. Prisoner of Conscience. Vanity Fair. For February 2007. Retrieved 1.13.07 from http://www.vanityfair.com/politics/features/2007/02/mccain200702?printable=true&currentPage=all.

[2090] Todd Purdum. Prisoner of Conscience. Vanity Fair. For February 2007. Retrieved 1.13.07 from http://www.vanityfair.com/politics/features/2007/02/mccain200702?printable=true&currentPage=all.
[2091] Todd Purdum. Prisoner of Conscience. Vanity Fair. For February 2007. Retrieved 1.13.07 from http://www.vanityfair.com/politics/features/2007/02/mccain200702?printable=true&currentPage=all.
[2092] Todd Purdum. Prisoner of Conscience. Vanity Fair. For February 2007. Retrieved 1.13.07 from http://www.vanityfair.com/politics/features/2007/02/mccain200702?printable=true&currentPage=all.
[2093] CNSNews.com. McCain and Imus Joke About Waco, Delay. March 28, 2001 and retrieved May 31, 2006 from http://www.newsmax.com/archives/articles/2001/3/27/203356.shtml.
[2094] CNSNews.com. McCain and Imus Joke About Waco, Delay. March 28, 2001 and retrieved May 31, 2006 from http://www.newsmax.com/archives/articles/2001/3/27/203356.shtml.
[2095] Daniel Scarpinato. Salty-tongued McCain darling of Men's mags. Arizona Daily Star. Published July 15, 2006, and retrieved Sept.6, 2006 from http://www.azstarnet.com/metro/137992.
[2096] Daniel Scarpinato. Salty-tongued McCain darling of Men's mags. Arizona Daily Star. Published July 15, 2006, and retrieved Sept.6, 2006 from http://www.azstarnet.com/metro/137992.
[2097] Todd Purdum. Prisoner of Conscience. Vanity Fair. For February 2007. Retrieved 1.13.07 from http://www.vanityfair.com/politics/features/2007/02/mccain200702?printable=true&currentPage=all.
[2098] Todd Purdum. Prisoner of Conscience. Vanity Fair. For February 2007. Retrieved 1.13.07 from http://www.vanityfair.com/politics/features/2007/02/mccain200702?printable=true&currentPage=all.
[2099] David Corn. A joke too bad to print? Salon Newsreal. From 1998. Retrieved 7.11.07 from http://www.salon.com/news/1998/06/25newsb.html.
[2100] David Corn. A joke too bad to print? Salon Newsreal. From 1998. Retrieved 7.11.07 from http://www.salon.com/news/1998/06/25newsb.html.
[2101] David Corn. A joke too bad to print? Salon Newsreal. From 1998. Retrieved 7.11.07 from http://www.salon.com/news/1998/06/25newsb.html.
[2102] Nov. 19, 2006 . ABC's This Week.
[2103] Todd Purdum. Prisoner of Conscience. Vanity Fair. For February 2007. Retrieved 1.13.07 from http://www.vanityfair.com/politics/features/2007/02/mccain200702?printable=true&currentPage=all.
[2104] Todd Purdum. Prisoner of Conscience. Vanity Fair. For February 2007. Retrieved 1.13.07 from http://www.vanityfair.com/politics/features/2007/02/mccain200702?printable=true&currentPage=all.
[2105] Todd Purdum. Prisoner of Conscience. Vanity Fair. For February 2007. Retrieved 1.13.07 from http://www.vanityfair.com/politics/features/2007/02/mccain200702?printable=true&currentPage=all.
[2106] Todd Purdum. Prisoner of Conscience. Vanity Fair. For February 2007. Retrieved 1.13.07 from http://www.vanityfair.com/politics/features/2007/02/mccain200702?printable=true&currentPage=all.
[2107] Todd Purdum. Prisoner of Conscience. Vanity Fair. For February 2007. Retrieved 1.13.07 from http://www.vanityfair.com/politics/features/2007/02/mccain200702?printable=true&currentPage=all.
[2108] Todd Purdum. Prisoner of Conscience. Vanity Fair. For February 2007. Retrieved 1.13.07 from http://www.vanityfair.com/politics/features/2007/02/mccain200702?printable=true&currentPage=all.
[2109] Todd Purdum. Prisoner of Conscience. Vanity Fair. For February 2007. Retrieved 1.13.07 from http://www.vanityfair.com/politics/features/2007/02/mccain200702?printable=true&currentPage=all.
[2110] Todd Purdum. Prisoner of Conscience. Vanity Fair. For February 2007. Retrieved 1.13.07 from http://www.vanityfair.com/politics/features/2007/02/mccain200702?printable=true&currentPage=all.
[2111] Fox News Sunday. Transcript: Sen. John McCain on Fox. Posted February 28, 2005 and retrieved March 3, 2005 from http://www.foxnews.com/story/0,2933,148875,00.html.
[2112] MSNBC.com. Transcript for April 2. NBC News/Meet the Press. Posted April 2, 2006 and retrieved next day from http://www.msnbc.msn.com/id/12067487/print/1/displaymode/1098/.
[2113] MSNBC.com. Transcript for April 2. NBC News/Meet the Press. Posted April 2, 2006 and retrieved next day from http://www.msnbc.msn.com/id/12067487/print/1/displaymode/1098/.
[2114] David Espo. Russia interfering with rights, Cheney says. AP. Milwaukee Journal Sentinel. May 5, 2006, 3A.
[2115] A CBS News. Face the Nation. Sunday, May 7, 2006. Transcript courtesy of Burrelle's information services. Retrieved May 8, 2006 from http://www.cbsnews.com/htdocs/pdf/face_050706.pdf.
[2116] A CBS News. Face the Nation. Sunday, May 7, 2006. Transcript courtesy of Burrelle's information services. Retrieved May 8, 2006 from http://www.cbsnews.com/htdocs/pdf/face_050706.pdf.
[2117] A CBS News. Face the Nation. Sunday, May 7, 2006. Transcript courtesy of Burrelle's information services. Retrieved May 8, 2006 from http://www.cbsnews.com/htdocs/pdf/face_050706.pdf.
[2118] Roger Simon. Giuliani Says He Wouldn't Run for President as an Independent. Posed June 8, 2006 and retrieved June 16, 2006 from http://www.bloomberg.com/apps/news?pid=washingtonstory&sid=abmN1G45wcSA.
[2119] Think Progress. Putin Jabs Bush: 'We Certainly would not want…the same kind of democracy as they have in Iraq. Retrieved July 28, 2006 from http://thinkprogress.org/2006/07/15/putin-jab/.
[2120] Think Progress. Putin Jabs Bush: 'We Certainly would not want…the same kind of democracy as they have in Iraq. Retrieved July 28, 2006 from http://thinkprogress.org/2006/07/15/putin-jab/.
[2121] Think Progress. Putin Jabs Bush: 'We Certainly would not want…the same kind of democracy as they have in Iraq. Retrieved July 28, 2006 from http://thinkprogress.org/2006/07/15/putin-jab/.
[2122] Todd Purdum. Prisoner of Conscience. Vanity Fair. For February 2007. Retrieved 1.13.07 from http://www.vanityfair.com/politics/features/2007/02/mccain200702?printable=true&currentPage=all.

[2123] Karen Tumulty. Why it's Dangerous For the Maverick To be The…Frontrunner. Time. Posted 12.10.06 and retrieved 12.14.06 from http://www.time.com/time/magazine/printout/0,8816,1568457,00.html.
[2124] Gloria Borger. Where's The Real McCain? Posted 7.18.07 and retrieved 7.20.07 from http://www.cbsnews.com/stories/2007/07/15/politics/main2062879.shtml.
[2125] Gloria Borger. Where's The Real McCain? Posted 7.18.07 and retrieved 7.20.07 from http://www.cbsnews.com/stories/2007/07/15/politics/main2062879.shtml.
[2126] The Blotter. McCain Official Busted on Sex Charge. 7.12.07 and retrieved 8.21.07 from http://blogs.abcnews.com/theblotter/2007/07/mccain-official.html.
[2127] The Funnies. Retrieved 8.1.07 from http://www.hillaryis44.org/?p=98.
[2128] The Funnies. Retrieved 8.1.07 from http://www.hillaryis44.org/?p=98.
[2129] The Funnies. Retrieved 8.1.07 from http://www.hillaryis44.org/?p=98.
[2130] CNN.com. Transcripts. Larry King Live. Aired April 25. Retrieved 5.3.07 from http://transcripts.cnn.com/TRANSCRIPTS/0704/25/lkl.01.html. 7/13.
[2131] Mike Celizic. McCain answers Lauer's off-beat questions. MSNBC.com. Posted August 9, 2007 and retrieved 8.21.07 from http://www.msnbc.com/id/2019303/print/1/displaymode/1098/.
[2132] Mike Celizic. McCain answers Lauer's off-beat questions. MSNBC.com. Posted August 9, 2007 and retrieved 8.21.07 from http://www.msnbc.com/id/2019303/print/1/displaymode/1098/
[2133] American Research Group, Inc. Retrieved 8.21.07 from http://www.americanresearchgroup.com/pres08/nhrep8-708.html.
[2134] Congressman Ron Paul. Who is Ron Paul? Retrieved 6.15.07 from http://www.house.gov/paul/bio.shtml.
[2135] Congressman Ron Paul. Who is Ron Paul? Retrieved 6.15.07 from http://www.house.gov/paul/bio.shtml.
[2136] Congressman Ron Paul. Who is Ron Paul? Retrieved 6.15.07 from http://www.house.gov/paul/bio.shtml.
[2137] Jan.13, 2007. Ron Paul's Second Try. 1.13.07 from Political Insider. http://politicalinsider.com/.
[2138] Ron Paul Files Papers to Run for President Potentially Opening up Texas Congressional Seat. 1.13. and posted 1.11.07 @ http://www.quorumreport.com/buzz.buzz.cfm.
[2139] Matt Sterns. Rep. Ron Paul cast himself as alternative candidate in GOP race. 5.14.07 and retrieved 5.16.07 from http://www.fortwayne.com/mld/newssentinel/news/editorial/17225285.htm.
[2140] Matt Sterns. Rep. Ron Paul cast himself as alternative candidate in GOP race. 5.14.07 and retrieved 5.16.07 from http://www.fortwayne.com/mld/newssentinel/news/editorial/17225285.htm.
[2141] TX 14: The First Open '08 House Seat? The Hotline Political Network. Jan.11 and retrieved 1.13.07 from http://hotlineblog.nationaljournal.com/archives/2007/01/tx_14_the_first.html.
[2142] Ron Paul Explores Presidentian [sic] run in 2008 Retrieved1.13.07 from http://newsblaze.com/story/20070112212526nnn.nb/newsblaze/OPINIONS/Opinions.html.
[2143] Jan.13, 2007. Ron Paul's Second Try. 1.13.07 from Political Insider. http://politicalinsider.com/.
[2144] ABC host tells Paul, Gravel they have no chance to win. The Raw Story. Posted 7.9.07 and retrieved 7.11.07 from http://rawstory.com/printstory.php?story=6778.
[2145] Robert Novak Wants Ron Paul Presidency? Justin Gardner. Retrieved 8.1.07 from http://donklephant.com/2007/08/01/robert-novak-wants-ron-paul-presidency/.
[2146] The New York Times. Republican Presidential Debate in South Carolina. May 15, 2007. Retrieved 5.16.07 from http://www.nytimes.com/2007/05/15/us/politics/16repubs-text.html?_r=1&bl=&ei=5087%0A&en=849e3ad2470dcca4&ex=1179633600&pagewanted=print&oref=slogin/ 10/31.
[2147] Brainy Quote. Ron Paul Quotes. Retrieved 7.27.07 from http://www.brainyqoute.com/quotes/authors/r/ron_paul.html.
[2148] Brainy Quote. Ron Paul Quotes. Retrieved 7.27.07 from http://www.brainyqoute.com/quotes/authors/r/ron_paul.html.
[2149] Brainy Quote. Ron Paul Quotes. Retrieved 7.27.07 from http://www.brainyqoute.com/quotes/authors/r/ron_paul.html.
[2150] GOP Presidential Candidates Debate for May 3. MSNBC.com. Aired May 3, retrieved 5.4.07 from http://www.msnbc.msn.com/id/18488970/print/1/displaymode/1098/. 5/43.
[2151] GOP Presidential Candidates Debate for May 3. MSNBC.com. Aired May 3, retrieved 5.4.07 from http://www.msnbc.msn.com/id/18488970/print/1/displaymode/1098/. 16/43.
[2152] Matt Sterns. McClatchy Newspapers. Rep. Ron Paul cast himself as alternative candidate in GOP race. 5.14.07 and retrieved 5.16.07 from http://www.fortwayne.com/mld/newssentinel/news/editorial/17225285.htm.
[2153] The New York Times. Republican Presidential Debate in South Carolina. May 15, 2007. Retrieved 5.16.07 from http://www.nytimes.com/2007/05/15/us/politics/16repubs-text.html?_r=1&bl=&ei=5087%0A&en=849e3ad2470dcca4&ex=1179633600&pagewanted=print&oref=slogin/ 21/31.
[2154] The New York Times. Republican Presidential Debate in South Carolina. May 15, 2007. Retrieved 5.16.07 from http://www.nytimes.com/2007/05/15/us/politics/16repubs-text.html?_r=1&bl=&ei=5087%0A&en=849e3ad2470dcca4&ex=1179633600&pagewanted=print&oref=slogin/ 22/31.
[2155] The New York Times. Republican Presidential Debate in South Carolina. May 15, 2007. Retrieved 5.16.07 from http://www.nytimes.com/2007/05/15/us/politics/16repubs-text.html?_r=1&bl=&ei=5087%0A&en=849e3ad2470dcca4&ex=1179633600&pagewanted=print&oref=slogin/ 22/31.
[2156] The New York Times. Republican Presidential Debate in South Carolina. May 15, 2007. Retrieved 5.16.07 from http://www.nytimes.com/2007/05/15/us/politics/16repubs-text.html?_r=1&bl=&ei=5087%0A&en=849e3ad2470dcca4&ex=1179633600&pagewanted=print&oref=slogin/ 22/31.
[2157] The New York Times. Republican Presidential Debate in South Carolina. May 15, 2007. Retrieved 5.16.07 from http://www.nytimes.com/2007/05/15/us/politics/16repubs-text.html?_r=1&bl=&ei=5087%0A&en=849e3ad2470dcca4&ex=1179633600&pagewanted=print&oref=slogin/ 22/31.

[2158] The New York Times. Republican Presidential Debate in South Carolina. May 15, 2007. Retrieved 5.16.07 from http://www.nytimes.com/2007/05/15/us/politics/16repubs-text.html?_r=1&bl=&ei=5087%0A&en=849e3ad2470dcca4&ex=1179633600&pagewanted=print&oref=slogin/ 22/31.

[2159] AP. Liz Sodoti. Analysis: Second GOP Debate Contentious. 5.16.07 and retrieved same day @ http://www.washingtonpost.com/wp-dyn/content/article/2007/05/16/AR2007051600140.html.

[2160] AntiWar.com. Opposing the Use of Military Forces Against Iraq. Rep. Ron Paul (R-TX). 10.10.02. Retrieved 6.15.07 from http://www.antiwar.com/paul/paul51.html.

[2161] LewRockwell.com. Iraq: Claim vs. Reality. Ron Paul. October 8, 2002. Retrieved 6.18.07 from http://www.lewrockwell.com/paul/paul58.html. 2/4.

[2162] Byron York. The National Review Online. Giuliani Up, McCain Up, Romney Down, and Ron Paul Out—Way Out. 5.16.07 and retrieved same day from http://article.nationalreview.com.

[2163] Chris Cillizza. The Fix. At Second Debate, a Few Sparks Fly. The Fix. Retrieved 5.16.07 from http://blog.washingtonpost.com/thefix/2007/05/the_debate_that_was.html?nav=rss_blog.

[2164] Byron York. The National Review Online. Giuliani Up, McCain Up, Romney Down, and Ron Paul Out—Way Out. 5.16.07 and retrieved same day from http://article.nationalreview.com.

[2165] Byron York. The National Review Online. Giuliani Up, McCain Up, Romney Down, and Ron Paul Out—Way Out. 5.16.07 and retrieved same day from http://article.nationalreview.com.

[2166] Byron York. The National Review Online. Giuliani Up, McCain Up, Romney Down, and Ron Paul Out—Way Out. 5.16.07 and retrieved same day from http://article.nationalreview.com.

[2167] Jonah Goldberg. WWTD? Who Cares? 5.16.07 and retrieved 6.15.07 from http://article.nationalreview.com/?q=MDVlM2M0ODVhNzIxNzk5ODRhNjY4YWE0MDY4ZmJjMGU=.

[2168] Jonah Goldberg. WWTD? Who Cares? 5.16.07 and retrieved 6.15.07 from http://article.nationalreview.com/?q=MDVlM2M0ODVhNzIxNzk5ODRhNjY4YWE0MDY4ZmJjMGU=.

[2169] Michael Brendan Dougherty. Ron Paul's isolationism is a foreign concept. See caption. Posted 6.13.07 and retrieved 6.15.07 from http://www.politico.com/news/stories/0607/4477.html.

[2170] Chris Cillizza. The Fix. At Second Debate, a Few Sparks Fly. The Fix. Retrieved 5.16.07 from http://blog.washingtonpost.com/thefix/2007/05/the_debate_that_was.html?nav=rss_blog.

[2171] Reuters. Giuliani Calls Ron Paul 'Absurd' on 9/11. NewsMax.com. Posted and retrieved 5.16.07 from http://www.newsmax.com/archives/ic/2007/5/15/224151.shtml.

[2172] AP. Liz Sodoti. Analysis: Second GOP Debate Contentious. 5.16.07 and retrieved same day @ http://www.washingtonpost.com/wp-dyn/content/article/2007/05/16/AR2007051600140.html.

[2173] The New York Times. Republican Presidential Debate in South Carolina. May 15, 2007. Retrieved 5.16.07 from http://www.nytimes.com/2007/05/15/us/politics/16repubs-text.html?_r=1&bl=&ei=5087%0A&en=849e3ad2470dcca4&ex=1179633600&pagewanted=print&oref=slogin/ 1/31.

[2174] The New York Times. Republican Presidential Debate in South Carolina. May 15, 2007. Retrieved 5.16.07 from http://www.nytimes.com/2007/05/15/us/politics/16repubs-text.html?_r=1&bl=&ei=5087%0A&en=849e3ad2470dcca4&ex=1179633600&pagewanted=print&oref=slogin/ 4/31.

[2175] The New York Times. Republican Presidential Debate in South Carolina. May 15, 2007. Retrieved 5.16.07 from http://www.nytimes.com/2007/05/15/us/politics/16repubs-text.html?_r=1&bl=&ei=5087%0A&en=849e3ad2470dcca4&ex=1179633600&pagewanted=print&oref=slogin/ 4/31.

[2176] The New York Times. Republican Presidential Debate in South Carolina. May 15, 2007. Retrieved 5.16.07 from http://www.nytimes.com/2007/05/15/us/politics/16repubs-text.html?_r=1&bl=&ei=5087%0A&en=849e3ad2470dcca4&ex=1179633600&pagewanted=print&oref=slogin/ 4/31.

[2177] Sean Gonsalves. Pulse of the Twin Cities. Locally Grown Alternative Newspaper. Retrieved 6.15.07 from http://www.pulsetc.com/article.php?sic=3323.

[2178] Sean Gonsalves. Pulse of the Twin Cities. Locally Grown Alternative Newspaper. Retrieved 6.15.07 from http://www.pulsetc.com/article.php?sic=3323.

[2179] Rudy Giuliani Threatens to Whack Ron Paul. Posted 6.14.07 and retrieved next day @ http://www.thespoof.com/news/spoof.cfm?headline=s2i20340.

[2180] TheSpoof.com. Bush praises Ron Paul funny satire story. Posted 6.12.07 and retrieved 6.15.07 from http://www.thespoof.com/news/spoof.cfm?headline=s2i20216.

[2181] Michael Kraft. Ron Paul On Colbert. Posted 6.14.07 and retrieved next day @ http://www.charlotteconservative.com/index.php/2007/06ron-paul-on-colbert.

[2182] Michael Brendan Dougherty. Ron Paul's isolationism is a foreign concept. See caption. Posted 6.13.07 and retrieved 6.15.07 from http://www.politico.com/news/stories/0607/4477.html.

[2183] New Video: Enthusiasm Keeps Building. 6.13.07 and retrieved 6.15.07 from http://www.ronpaul2008.com/.

[2184] Matt Sterns. Rep. Ron Paul cast himself as alternative candidate in GOP race. 5.14.07 and retrieved 5.16.07 from http://www.fortwayne.com/mld/newssentinel/news/editorial/17225285.htm.

[2185] Susan Page. USA Today. Long-shot candidates have much to gain in consolation prizes. Posted/retrieved 6.15.07 from http://www.usatoday.com/news/politics/election2008/2007-06-14-campaign-consolation_N.htm.

[2186] Matt Sterns. Rep. Ron Paul cast himself as alternative candidate in GOP race. 5.14.07 and retrieved 5.16.07 from http://www.fortwayne.com/mld/newssentinel/news/editorial/17225285.htm.

[2187] Rush Limbaugh. Analysis: Is Ron Paul Internet Buzz Real or Spam? C.M. Paulson. Posted 6.1.07 and retrieved 6.15.07 from http://www.associatedcontent.com/article/266436/analysis_is_ron_paul_internet_buzz.html.

[2188] Rush Limbaugh. Analysis: Is Ron Paul Internet Buzz Real or Spam? C.M. Paulson. Posted 6.1.07 and retrieved 6.15.07 from http://www.associatedcontent.com/article/266436/analysis_is_ron_paul_internet_buzz.html.
[2189] Silencing Ron Paul's Supporters—Commentary USA. Retrieved 6.11.07 from http://www.commentary.usa.com/commentary/politics/silencing-ron-pauls-supporters.html.
[2190] Stafford 'Doc' Williamson. Republican Debate: Surprising CNN Winner, Nuclear vs. BioMass and Ethanol. 6.10.07 and retrieved 6.15.07 from http://www.americanchronicle.com/articles/viewArticle.asp?aticleID=29205.
[2191] Ron Paul for President. Off the Kuff. Jan.12, 2007 and retrieved next day @ http://www.offthekuff.com/mt.archives/008649.html.
[2192] Ron Paul for President. Off the Kuff. Jan.12, 2007 and retrieved next day @ http://www.offthekuff.com/mt.archives/008649.html
[2193] RJ Elliott. Iowa Straw Poll Results. Published 8.12.07 and retrieved 8.21.07 from http://blogcritics.org/archives/2007/08/12/023738.php.
[2194] Joel Siegel. The Pataki Puzzle. New York Magazine. Posted July 19, 2004 and retrieved 12.14.06 from http://nymag.com/nymetro/news/politics/newyork/features/9494/index.html.
[2195] Richard E. Cohen and Michael Barone. The Almanac of American Politics—2004. The National Journal Group. 2003, page 1092
[2196] Joel Siegel. The Pataki Puzzle. New York Magazine. Posted July 19, 2004 and retrieved 12.14.06 from http://nymag.com/nymetro/news/politics/newyork/features/9494/index.html.
[2197] Richard E. Cohen and Michael Barone. The Almanac of American Politics—2004. The National Journal Group. 2003, page 1092.
[2198] Joel Siegel. The Pataki Puzzle. New York Magazine. Posted July 19, 2004 and retrieved 12.14.06 from http://nymag.com/nymetro/news/politics/newyork/features/9494/index.html.
[2199] Charles Gasparino. "Politics: Next, President Pataki?" MSNBC.com/Newsweek, Inc. Posted in August 2004 and retrieved October 5, 2005 from http://www.msnbc.msn.com/id/5782747/site/newsweek/.
[2200] Charles Gasparino. "Politics: Next, President Pataki?" MSNBC.com/Newsweek, Inc. Posted in August 2004 and retrieved October 5, 2005 from http://www.msnbc.msn.com/id/5782747/site/newsweek/
[2201] Joel Siegel. The Pataki Puzzle. New York Magazine. Posted July 19, 2004 and retrieved 12.14.06 from http://nymag.com/nymetro/news/politics/newyork/features/9494/index.html.
[2202] Joel Siegel. The Pataki Puzzle. New York Magazine. Posted July 19, 2004 and retrieved 12.14.06 from http://nymag.com/nymetro/news/politics/newyork/features/9494/index.html.
[2203] Joel Siegel. The Pataki Puzzle. New York Magazine. Posted July 19, 2004 and retrieved 12.14.06 from http://nymag.com/nymetro/news/politics/newyork/features/9494/index.html.
[2204] Joel Siegel. The Pataki Puzzle. New York Magazine. Posted July 19, 2004 and retrieved 12.14.06 from http://nymag.com/nymetro/news/politics/newyork/features/9494/index.html.
[2205] Joel Siegel. The Pataki Puzzle. New York Magazine. Posted July 19, 2004 and retrieved 12.14.06 from http://nymag.com/nymetro/news/politics/newyork/features/9494/index.html.
[2206] Jay Gallagher. Pataki fundraiser spurs talk of national run. Rochester Democrat and Chronicle. Posted June 16, 2005 and retrieved July 1, 2005 from http://www.democratandchronicle.com/apps/pbcs.dll/article?AID=/20050616/NEWS01/506160369/1002/NEWS
[2207] Jay Gallagher. Pataki fundraiser spurs talk of national run. Rochester Democrat and Chronicle. Posted June 16, 2005 and retrieved July 1, 2005 from http://www.democratandchronicle.com/apps/pbcs.dll/article?AID=/20050616/NEWS01/506160369/1002/NEWS.
[2208] Adam Nagourney. Pataki will test '08 winds in Iowa. The New York Times. Published July 15, 2005 and retrieved July 15, 2005 from http://www.nytimes.com/2005/07/15/politics/15pataki/html
[2209] Adam Nagourney. Pataki will test '08 winds in Iowa. The New York Times. Published July 15, 2005 and retrieved July 15, 2005 from http://www.nytimes.com/2005/07/15/politics/15pataki/html.
[2210] Marc Humbert. Pataki off to Iowa as New York Fundraising Lags. AP. Posted July 15, 2005 and retrieved July 15, 2005 from http://www.newsday.com/news/local/wire/newyork/ny-bc-ny--pataki0715jul15,0,4664776.story?coll=ny-region-apnewyork.
[2211] Marc Humbert. Pataki off to Iowa as New York Fundraising Lags. AP. Posted July 15, 2005 and retrieved July 15, 2005 from http://www.newsday.com/news/local/wire/newyork/ny-bc-ny--pataki0715jul15,0,4664776.story?coll=ny-region-apnewyork.
[2212] Gov. Pataki rules out run for 4th term in New York. The Milwaukee Journal Sentinel, July 28, 2005, 10A.
[2213] Alfonse M. D'Amato. Never underestimate George Pataki. Newsday. Posted/Retrieved July 29, 2005 from http://www.newsday.com/news/opinion/ny-opdam294362011jul29,0,4249429.story?coll=ny-viewpoints-headlines.
[2214] George Pataki bows out. New York Daily News. Posted July 28, 2005 and retrieved July 29, 2005 from http://www.nydailynews.com/news/ideas_opinions/story/332160p-283824c.html.
[2215] Online Newshour: New York Gov. George Pataki Addresses GOP Convention. Sept. 2, 2004. Retrieved 11.17.2006 from http://www.pbs.org/newshour/vote2004/repconvention/speeches/pataki.html.
[2216] AP. New York governor visits Grand Strand. June 3, 2006 and retrieved June 30, 2006 from http://www.thestate.com/mld/thestate/news/local/14730631.htm.
[2217] Marc Humbert. Critics: Pataki running for President full time. Aug.5 and retrieved Sept. 21, 2006 from http://www.unionleader.com/article.aspx?articleId=896471eb-ede1-451e-9a65-127e28fcdf0d&headline=Critics%3a+Pataki+running+for+President+full+time.

[2218] Marc Humbert. Critics: Pataki running for President full time. Aug.5 and retrieved Sept. 21, 2006 from http://www.unionleader.com/article.aspx?articleId=896471eb-ede1-451e-9a65-127e28fcdf0d&headline=Critics%3a+Pataki+running+for+President+full+time.

[2219] Marc Humbert. Critics: Pataki running for President full time. Aug.5 and retrieved Sept. 21, 2006 from http://www.unionleader.com/article.aspx?articleId=896471eb-ede1-451e-9a65-127e28fcdf0d&headline=Critics%3a+Pataki+running+for+President+full+time.

[2220] Media Matters for America. NY Daily News reported Pataki's attack on Clinton, omitted Dem response. Posted 8.21.06 and retrieved 11.17.06 from http://mediamatters.org/items/printable/200608210002.

[2221] Michael McAuliff. Hil tops Dem poll, gov unimpressed. Posted Aug.21, 2006 and retrieved 11.17.06 from http://www.nydailynews.com/08-21-2006/news/v-pfreindly/story/445313p-374997c.html.

[2222] Media Matters for America. NY Daily News reported Pataki's attack on Clinton, omitted Dem response. Posted 8.21.06 and retrieved 11.17.06 from http://mediamatters.org/items/printable/200608210002.

[2223] Michael McAuliff. Hil tops Dem poll, gov unimpressed. Posted Aug.21, 2006 and retrieved 11.17.06 from http://www.nydailynews.com/08-21-2006/news/v-pfreindly/story/445313p-374997c.html.

[2224] Media Matters for America. NY Daily News reported Pataki's attack on Clinton, omitted Dem response. Posted 8.21.06 and retrieved 11.17.06 from http://mediamatters.org/items/printable/200608210002.

[2225] Media Matters for America. NY Daily News reported Pataki's attack on Clinton, omitted Dem response. Posted 8.21.06 and retrieved 11.17.06 from http://mediamatters.org/items/printable/200608210002.

[2226] Media Matters for America. NY Daily News reported Pataki's attack on Clinton, omitted Dem response. Posted 8.21.06 and retrieved 11.17.06 from http://mediamatters.org/items/printable/200608210002.

[2227] Media Matters for America. NY Daily News reported Pataki's attack on Clinton, omitted Dem response. Posted 8.21.06 and retrieved 11.17.06 from http://mediamatters.org/items/printable/200608210002.

[2228] AP. Spitzer raises concerns about viability of Freedom Tower plans. Posted March 25, 2006 and retrieved March 27, 2006 from newsday.com and also http://www.voicesofsept11.org/artman/publish/news/article_002778.php.

[2229] AP. Spitzer raises concerns about viability of Freedom Tower plans. Posted March 25, 2006 and retrieved March 27, 2006 from newsday.com and also http://www.voicesofsept11.org/artman/publish/news/article_002778.php

[2230] AP. Pataki: Freedom Tower is economically viable. Posted March 27, 2006 and retrieved same day from http://www.newsday.com/news/local/wire/newyork/ny-bc-ny--pataki-groundzero0327mar...

[2231] AP. Newsday. Pataki urges 'good faith' negotiations on ground zero.' Posted March 21, 2006 and retrieved March 27, 2006 from http://www.wstm.com/Global/story.asp?S=4665231 and Newsday.com.

[2232] Paul D. Colford. Pataki says Ground Zero developer 'has betrayed the public's trust'. New York Daily News. Posted March 16, 2006 and retrieved March 27, 2006 from http://www.belleville.com/mld/belleville/news/nation/14111274.htm.

[2233] Paul D. Colford. Pataki says Ground Zero developer 'has betrayed the public's trust'. New York Daily News. Posted March 16, 2006 and retrieved March 27, 2006 from http://www.belleville.com/mld/belleville/news/nation/14111274.htm.

[2234] AP. Newsday. Pataki urges 'good faith' negotiations on ground zero.' Posted March 21, 2006 and retrieved March 27, 2006 from http://www.wstm.com/Global/story.asp?S=4665231. And newsday.com.

[2235] BBC News. 9/11 Memorial plans scaled down. Posted June 21, 2006 and retrieved June 30, 2006 from http://news.bbc.co.uk/2/hi/amercicas/5101048.stm.

[2236] BBC News. 9/11 Memorial plans scaled down. Posted June 21, 2006 and retrieved June 30, 2006 from http://news.bbc.co.uk/2/hi/amercicas/5101048.stm.

[2237] BBC News. 9/11 Memorial plans scaled down. Posted June 21, 2006 and retrieved June 30, 2006 from http://news.bbc.co.uk/2/hi/amercicas/5101048.stm.

[2238] Amy Westfeldt. State Agency Goes Ahead With 9/11 Memorial. AP. Posted June 30, 2006 and retrieved same day from http://www.washingtonpost.com/wp-dyn/content/article/2006/06/30/AR2006063000441.html.

[2239] David W. Dunlap. 9/11 Memorial Faces Setback Over Names. Published June 27 and retrieved June 30, 2006 from http://www.nytimes.com/2006/06/27/nyregion/27names.html.

[2240] David W. Dunlap. 9/11 Memorial Faces Setback Over Names. Published June 27 and retrieved June 30, 2006 from http://www.nytimes.com/2006/06/27/nyregion/27names.html.

[2241] Amy Westfeldt. State Agency Goes Ahead With 9/11 Memorial. AP. Posted June 30, 2006 and retrieved same day from http://www.washingtonpost.com/wp-dyn/content/article/2006/06/30/AR2006063000441.html

[2242] Amy Westfeldt. State Agency Goes Ahead With 9/11 Memorial. AP. Posted June 30, 2006 and retrieved same day from http://www.washingtonpost.com/wp-dyn/content/article/2006/06/30/AR2006063000441.html

[2243] David W. Dunlap. 9/11 Memorial Faces Setback Over Names. Published June 27 and retrieved June 30, 2006 from http://www.nytimes.com/2006/06/27/nyregion/27names.html.

[2244] David W. Dunlap. 9/11 Memorial Faces Setback Over Names. Published June 27 and retrieved June 30, 2006 from http://www.nytimes.com/2006/06/27/nyregion/27names.html.

[2245] Verena Dobnik. Admission Fee for 9/11 Museum Debated. AP. June 24, 2006, Page A07 of Washington Post, and retrieved June 30, 2006 from http://www.washingtonpost.com/wp-dyn/content/article/2006/06/23/AR2006062301545.html.

[2246] Verena Dobnik. Admission Fee for 9/11 Museum Debated. AP. June 24, 2006, Page A07 of Washington Post, and retrieved June 30, 2006 from http://www.washingtonpost.com/wp-dyn/content/article/2006/06/23/AR2006062301545.html.

[2247] Verena Dobnik. Admission Fee for 9/11 Museum Debated. AP. June 24, 2006, Page A07 of Washington Post, and retrieved June 30, 2006 from http://www.washingtonpost.com/wp-dyn/content/article/2006/06/23/AR2006062301545.html.

[2248] Verena Dobnik. Admission Fee for 9/11 Museum Debated. AP. June 24, 2006, Page A07 of Washington Post, and retrieved June 30, 2006 from http://www.washingtonpost.com/wp-dyn/content/article/2006/06/23/AR2006062301545.html.

[2249] Amy Westfeldt. State Agency Goes Ahead With 9/11 Memorial. AP. Posted June 30, 2006 and retrieved same day from http://www.washingtonpost.com/wp-dyn/content/article/2006/06/30/AR2006063000441.html

[2250] Rebecca Spitz. NY1: Top Stories. Governor Pataki Outlines Progress Downtown. Posted June 29, 2006 and retrieved June 30, 2006 from http://www.ny1.com/ny1/content/index.jsp?stid=1&aid=60623.

[2251] Quinnipiac University. July 12, 2006, New Yorkers Like Mayor's Big Talk, Quinnipiac Poll Finds; But Most Don't Think He'll Run For President. Retrieved July 14, 2006 from http://www.quinnipiac.edu/x11385.xml?ReleaseID=935.

[2252] AP. Pataki: Freedom Tower is economically viable. Posted March 27, 2006 and retrieved same day from http://www.newsday.com/news/local/wire/newyork/ny-bc-ny--pataki-groundzero0327mar...

[2253] Paul D. Colford. Pataki says Ground Zero developer 'has betrayed the public's trust'. New York Daily News. Posted March 16, 2006 and retrieved March 27, 2006 from http://www.belleville.com/mld/belleville/news/nation/14111274.htm.

[2254] London Free Press. Today Entertainment. Posted March 26, 2006 and retrieved March 27, 2006 from http://www.lfpress.ca/newsstand/Today/Entertainment/2006/03/26/1505855-sun.html.

[2255] TV Squad. The Daily Show: March 22, 2006. Posted March 23, 2006 and retrieved March 27, 2006 from http://www.tvsqaud.com/2006/03/23/the-daily-show-march-22-2206/.

[2256] The Onion. NYC Unveils 9/11 Memorial Hole. Posted and retrieved September 6, 2006 form http://www.theonion.com/content/node/52325.

[2257] The Onion. NYC Unveils 9/11 Memorial Hole. Posted and retrieved September 6, 2006 form http://www.theonion.com/content/node/52325.

[2258] Rick Karlin. Pataki Makes the Onion: George, They Are Not Laughing With You. Posted and retrieved September 6, 2006 from http://blogs.timesunion.com/capitol/?p=2066.

[2259] The Onion. NYC Unveils 9/11 Memorial Hole. Posted and retrieved September 6, 2006 form http://www.theonion.com/content/node/52325.

[2260] The Onion. NYC Unveils 9/11 Memorial Hole. Posted and retrieved September 6, 2006 form http://www.theonion.com/content/node/52325.

[2261] NBC News. Meet the Press. MTP Transcript for Aug.27. MSNBC.com. Retrieved Sept.6, 2006 from http://www.msnbc.msn.com/id/14452115/print/1/displaymode/1098/.

[2262] Deepti Hajela. AP. Sept. 11 Tribute Center opens. Posted September 6 and retrieved same day from http://seattlepi.nwsource.com/national/1110AP_Attacks_Tribute_Center.html.

[2263] Deepti Hajela. AP. Sept. 11 Tribute Center opens. Posted September 6 and retrieved same day from http://seattlepi.nwsource.com/national/1110AP_Attacks_Tribute_Center.html.

[2264] Deepti Hajela. AP. Sept. 11 Tribute Center opens. Posted September 6 and retrieved same day from http://seattlepi.nwsource.com/national/1110AP_Attacks_Tribute_Center.html.

[2265] CBS News. Face the Nation for Sept. 10, 2006. Retrieved Sept. 25, 2006. Transcript courtesy of Burrelle's Information Services. http://www.cbsnews.com/htdocs/pdf/face_091006.pdf.

[2266] CBS News. Face the Nation for Sept. 10, 2006. Retrieved Sept. 25, 2006. Transcript courtesy of Burrelle's Information Services. http://www.cbsnews.com/htdocs/pdf/face_091006.pdf.

[2267] CBS News. Face the Nation for Sept. 10, 2006. Retrieved Sept. 25, 2006. Transcript courtesy of Burrelle's Information Services. http://www.cbsnews.com/htdocs/pdf/face_091006.pdf.

[2268] CBS News. Face the Nation for Sept. 10, 2006. Retrieved Sept. 25, 2006. Transcript courtesy of Burrelle's Information Services. http://www.cbsnews.com/htdocs/pdf/face_091006.pdf.

[2269] CBS News. Face the Nation for Sept. 10, 2006. Retrieved Sept. 25, 2006. Transcript courtesy of Burrelle's Information Services. http://www.cbsnews.com/htdocs/pdf/face_091006.pdf.

[2270] Hardball with Chris Matthews for Oct. 11. MSNBC.com. Posted Oct. 12, retrieved Oct. 13 from http://www.msnbc.msn.com/id/15240123/print/1/displaymode/1098/.

[2271] Hardball with Chris Matthews for Oct. 11. MSNBC.com. Posted Oct. 12, retrieved Oct. 13 from http://www.msnbc.msn.com/id/15240123/print/1/displaymode/1098/.

[2272] Hardball with Chris Matthews for Oct. 11. MSNBC.com. Posted Oct. 12, retrieved Oct. 13 from http://www.msnbc.msn.com/id/15240123/print/1/displaymode/1098/.

[2273] Hardball with Chris Matthews for Oct. 11. MSNBC.com. Posted Oct. 12, retrieved Oct. 13 from http://www.msnbc.msn.com/id/15240123/print/1/displaymode/1098/.

[2274] Hardball with Chris Matthews for Oct. 11. MSNBC.com. Posted Oct. 12, retrieved Oct. 13 from http://www.msnbc.msn.com/id/15240123/print/1/displaymode/1098/.

[2275] Hardball with Chris Matthews for Oct. 11. MSNBC.com. Posted Oct. 12, retrieved Oct. 13 from http://www.msnbc.msn.com/id/15240123/print/1/displaymode/1098/.

[2276] AP. Crash makes politicians worry about safety of New York's skies. Milwaukee Journal Sentinel. Oct. 13, 2006. 16A. SB 8 p 20.

[2277] The New York Times, 12/05/2005. Retrieved from Research from the DNC for the 2008 candidates, Retrieved February 13, 2006 from http://www.washingtonpost.com/wp-srv/politics/documents/dnc_Pataki08Watch12-05.pdf.

[2278] AP. Clinton rival drops out of Senate race. The Milwaukee Journal Sentinel, December 22,2005, 13A.

[2279] AP. Clinton rival drops out of Senate race. The Milwaukee Journal Sentinel, December 22,2005, 13A.

[2280] AP. Clinton, Giuliani put 2008 presidential race in N.Y. state of mind. USATODAY.com. Posted November 19, 2005 and retrieved November 30, 2005 from http://usatoday.com/news/washington/2005-11-19-hillary-versus-rudy_x.htm.

[2281] Des Moines Register. McCain to open office in Iowa. Tim Higgins. Dec. 2, 2006. Retrieved next day @ http://desmoinesregister.com/apps/pbcs.dll/article?AID=/20061202/NEWS10/612020338&template=printart.

[2282] AP New York. Pataki qualified for more than $113,000-a-year pension. Dec. 14, and retrieved same day from http://www.newsday.com/news/local/wire/newyork/ny-bc-ny--patkai-pension1214dec14,0,7850667.story...

[2283] Danny Hakim and Michael Cooper. Pataki Agrees to Let Spitzer Fill Some Vacant Posts. Dec. 13, 2006. Retrieved 12.14.06 from http://travel.nytimes.com/2006/12/13/nyregion/13appoint.html?

[2284] Danny Hakim and Michael Cooper. Pataki Agrees to Let Spitzer Fill Some Vacant Posts. Dec. 13, 2006. Retrieved 12.14.06 from http://travel.nytimes.com/2006/12/13/nyregion/13appoint.html?

[2285] ABC news. Teddy Davis reporting. Nearing '08 Decision, Pataki Heads to New Hampshire and Iowa. Posted 12.4.06 and retrieved 12.14.06 from http://blogs.abcnews.go.com/politicalradar/2006/12/nearing_08_deci.html.

[2286] Karen Matthews. Highlights from New York exit poll. Nov.7, 2006 and retrieved 11.17.06 from http://www.newsday.com/news/local/wire/newyork/ny-bc/ny-eln--exitpoll-glan1107no07,0,1750064.stor...

[2287] Karen Matthews. Highlights from New York exit poll. Nov.7, 2006 and retrieved 11.17.06 from http://www.newsday.com/news/local/wire/newyork/ny-bc/ny-eln--exitpoll-glan1107no07,0,1750064.stor...

[2288] ABC news. Teddy Davis reporting. Nearing /08 Decision, Pataki Heads to New Hampshire and Iowa. Posted Dec.4 and retrieved 12.14.06 from http://blogs.abcnews.go.com/politicalradar/2006/12/nearing_08_deci.html.

[2289] Steven Ertelt. LifeNews.com. George Pataki Loses Iowa Supporters Over His Pro-Abortion Position. Posted Nov.22 and retrieved 12.14.06 from http://www.lifenews.com/nat2779.hml.

[2290] Thomas Beaumont. Iowans withdraw support for Pataki. Nov.22. Retrieved 12.14.06 from http://desmoinesregister.com/apps/pbcs.dll/article?AID=/20061122/NEWS09/611220377/-1/SPORTS06.

[2291] Steven Ertelt. LifeNews.com. George Pataki Loses Iowa Supporters Over His Pro-Abortion Position. Posted Nov.22 and retrieved 12.14.06 from http://www.lifenews.com/nat2779.hml.

[2292] Steven Ertelt. LifeNews.com. George Pataki Loses Iowa Supporters Over His Pro-Abortion Position. Posted Nov.22 and retrieved 12.14.06 from http://www.lifenews.com/nat2779.hml.

[2293] ABC news. Teddy Davis reporting. Nearing '08 Decision, Pataki Heads to New Hampshire and Iowa. Posted Dec.4 and retrieved 12.14.06 from http://blogs.abcnews.go.com/politicalradar/2006/12/nearing_08_deci.html.

[2294] Thomas Beaumont. Iowans withdraw support for Pataki. Nov.22. Retrieved 12.14.06 from http://desmoinesregister.com/apps/pbcs.dll/article?AID=/20061122/NEWS09/611220377/-1/SPORTS06.

[2295] Holly Kramer. Pataki, potential presidential hopeful, opens NH office. Oct.3, 2006. AP/Union Leader. Retrieved from http://www.unionleader.com.

[2296] John Distaso. Pataki isn't ready to join the race. Jan. 31, 2007. Union Leader. Retrieved 2.8.07.

[2297] Michelle Breidenbach. Donors still put money on Pataki. Posted 7.18.07 and retrieved 7.20.07 from http://www.syracuse.com/articles/news/index.ssf?/base/news-0/1184750379300360.xml&c...

[2298] Michelle Breidenbach. Donors still put money on Pataki. Posted 7.18.07 and retrieved 7.20.07 from http://www.syracuse.com/articles/news/index.ssf?/base/news-0/1184750379300360.xml&c...

[2299] AP. "Biographic information on Gov. Mitt Romney." Boston.com. Posted December 14, 2005 and retrieved December 15, 2005 from http://www.boston.com/news/local/massachusetts/articles/2005/12/14/biographic_information_on_gov_mitt_romney/.

[2300] AP. "Biographic information on Gov. Mitt Romney." Boston.com. Posted December 14, 2005 and retrieved December 15, 2005 from http://www.boston.com/news/local/massachusetts/articles/2005/12/14/biographic_information_on_gov_mitt_romney/

[2301] Glen Johnson. Mass. Gov. Romney to Skip Re-election Bid. AP. Retrieved 12.15.05 from http://abcnews.go.com/US/print?id=1408226.

[2302] MSNBC. Hardball with Chris Mathews for Dec. 12th. MSNBC Retrieved December 15, 2005 from http://msnbc.msn.com/id/10451500/.

[2303] Richard E. Cohen and Michael Barone. The Almanac of American Politics—2004. The National Journal Group. 2003, page 772.

[2304] Richard E. Cohen and Michael Barone. The Almanac of American Politics—2004. The National Journal Group. 2003, page 772.

[2305] Richard E. Cohen and Michael Barone. The Almanac of American Politics—2004. The National Journal Group. 2003, page 772.

[2306] Richard E. Cohen and Michael Barone. The Almanac of American Politics—2004. The National Journal Group. 2003, page 771,772.

[2307] Thomas Beaumont. "Governors conference in Iowa offers look at potential 2008 field." The Des Moines Register. Posted July 14, 2005 and retrieved July 15, 2005 from http://www.desmoinesregister.com/apps/pbcs.dll/article?AID=/20050714/NEWS09/507140374/1056.

[2308] Yvonne Abraham. "Romney says new post won't hinder duties." Boston Globe. Posted November 20, 2005 and retrieved September 21, 2005 from http://www.boston.com/news/politics/governors/articles/2004/11/20/romney_says_post_wont_hinder_duties/.

[2309] Frank Phillips and Yvonne Abraham. "GOP governors eye Romney for post." Boston.com. Posted November 1, 2005 and retrieved September 21, 2005 from http://www.boston.com/news/local/articles/2004/11/16/gop_governors_eye_romney_for_post?mode=PF

[2310] Frank Phillips and Yvonne Abraham. "GOP governors eye Romney for post." Boston.com. Posted November 1, 2005 and retrieved September 21, 2005 from http://www.boston.com/news/local/articles/2004/11/16/gop_governors_eye_romney_for_post?mode=PF

[2311] Frank Phillips and Yvonne Abraham. "GOP governors eye Romney for post." Boston.com. Posted November 1, 2005 and retrieved September 21, 2005 from http://www.boston.com/news/local/articles/2004/11/16/gop_governors_eye_romney_for_post?mode=PF

[2312] Selwyn Duke. American Chronicle. Mitt Romney: A Massachusetts Liberal for President. Posted 1.11 and retrieved 1.13 from http://www.americanchronicle.com/articles/viewArticle.asp?articleID=189980.

[2313] FOXNews.com. Transcript: Mass. Gov. Mitt Romney on 'FNS'. FOX News. Posted/Retrieved February 27, 2006 from http://www.foxnews.com/printer_friendly_story/0,3566,186080,00.html

[2314] FOXNews.com. Transcript: Mass. Gov. Mitt Romney on 'FNS'. FOX News. Posted/Retrieved February 27, 2006 from http://www.foxnews.com/printer_friendly_story/0,3566,186080,00.html

[2315] FOXNews.com. "Transcript: Mass. Gov. Mitt Romney on 'FNS'. FOX News. Posted/Retrieved February 27, 2006 from http://www.foxnews.com/printer_friendly_story/0,3566,186080,00.html

[2316] Washington Post/AP. Which Romney will Run? MJS, Dec.23, 2006, 3A.

[2317] Washington Post/AP. Which Romney will Run? MJS, Dec.23, 2006, 3A.

[2318] Washington Post/AP. Which Romney will Run? MJS, Dec.23, 2006, 3A.

[2319] National Journal Group Inc. White House 2008 Rankings. Jan. 11. 2007. Retrieved 1.13.07 from http://nationaljournal.com/racerankings/wh08/republicans/.

[2320] National Journal Group Inc. White House 2008 Rankings. Jan. 11. 2007. Retrieved 1.13.07 from http://nationaljournal.com/racerankings/wh08/republicans/.

[2321] National Journal Group Inc. White House 2008 Rankings. Jan. 11. 2007. Retrieved 1.13.07 from http://nationaljournal.com/racerankings/wh08/republicans/.

[2322] Kathryn Jean Lopez. National Review Online. 1.13.07 and posted 1.10.07 @ http://article.nationalreview.com/?q=YTUxMTViMDAxZGNhYiO0NiA0ODBlZiRhMWVmOGIwNWU=/.

[2323] National Journal Group Inc. White House 2008 Rankings. Jan. 11. 2007. Retrieved 1.13.07 from http://nationaljournal.com/racerankings/wh08/republicans/.

[2324] Kathryn Jean Lopez. National Review Online. 1.13.07 and posted 1.10.07 @ http://article.nationalreview.com/?q=YTUxMTViMDAxZGNhYiO0NiA0ODBlZiRhMWVmOGIwNWU=/.

[2325] Kathryn Jean Lopez. National Review Online. 1.13.07 and posted 1.10.07 @ http://article.nationalreview.com/?q=YTUxMTViMDAxZGNhYiO0NiA0ODBlZiRhMWVmOGIwNWU=/.

[2326] Steve LeBlanc. Report blasts Romney's political record. 1.12.07 and retrieved 1.13.07 from http://www.newsone.ca/westfallweeklynews/ViewArticle.aspx?id=43392&source=2.

[2327] Kathryn Jean Lopez. National Review Online. 1.13.07 and posted 1.10.07 @ http://article.nationalreview.com/?q=YTUxMTViMDAxZGNhYiO0NiA0ODBlZiRhMWVmOGIwNWU=/.

[2328] Steve LeBlanc. Report blasts Romney's political record. 1.12.07 and retrieved 1.13.07 from http://www.newsone.ca/westfallweeklynews/ViewArticle.aspx?id=43392&source=2.

[2329] Steve LeBlanc. Report blasts Romney's political record. 1.12.07 and retrieved 1.13.07 from http://www.newsone.ca/westfallweeklynews/ViewArticle.aspx?id=43392&source=2.

[2330] Peter LaBarbera. Americans for Truth Calls on Mitt Romney to Apologize for Attacking Pro-Family Hero Brian Camenker. Posted and Retrieved 1.13.07 from http://www.christiannewswire.com/news/201361936.html.

[2331] Selwyn Duke. American Chronicle. Mitt Romney: A Massachusetts Liberal for President. Posted 1.11 and retrieved 1.13 from http://www.americanchronicle.com/articles/viewArticle.asp?articleID=189980.

[2332] Peter Cassels. Log Cabin President Seeks Explanation from Romney. Dec.19, 2006 and Retrieved 1.13.07 from http://www.edgeboston.com/index.php?ci=108&ch=news&sc=glbt&sc2=news&sc3_id=circumstance.

[2333] Peter Cassels. Log Cabin President Seeks Explanation from Romney. Dec.19, 2006 and Retrieved 1.13.07 from http://www.edgeboston.com/index.php?ci=108&ch=news&sc=glbt&sc2=news&sc3_id=circumstance.

[2334] Andy Humm. Log Cabin Promotes From Within. Posted 12.21.06 and retrieved 1.13.07 from http://www.gaycitynews.com/site/news.cfm?newsid=17621528&BRD=2729&PAG=461&...

[2335] NY Times. Letter may hurt Romney in '08. Milwaukee Journal Sentinel. Dec. 10, 2006 17A.

[2336] NY Times. Letter may hurt Romney in '08. Milwaukee Journal Sentinel. Dec. 10, 2006 17A.

[2337] Selwyn Duke. American Chronicle. Mitt Romney: A Massachusetts Liberal for President. Posted 1.11 and retrieved 1.13 from http://www.americanchronicle.com/articles/viewArticle.asp?articleID=189980.

[2338] James Kirchick: Mitt Romney's pomp and circumstance. Posted 1.11.07 and retrieve d1.13.07 from http://www.examiner.com/a-522561~James_Kirchick__Mitt_Romney_s_pomp_and_circumstance.

[2339] Yvonne Abraham. Romney: gay outsiders can't marry in Mass. Posted April 25, 2006. and retrieved 1.13.07 from http://www.boston.com/news/local/articles/2004/04/25/romney_gay_outsiders_can't_marry_in_mass?.

[2340] Wire reports. Milwaukee Journal Sentinel. November 25, 2006 11A. Governor asks court for gay marriage referendum.

[2341] Wire reports. Milwaukee Journal Sentinel. November 25, 2006 11A. Governor asks court for gay marriage referendum.

[2342] Wire reports. Milwaukee Journal Sentinel. November 25, 2006 11A. Governor asks court for gay marriage referendum.

[2343] Jay Lindsay. Top court can't force vote on gay marriage. AP. Milwaukee Journal Sentinel. December 28, 2006, 3A.

[2344] Jay Lindsay. Top court can't force vote on gay marriage. AP. Milwaukee Journal Sentinel. December 28, 2006, 3A.

[2345] Jay Lindsay. Top court can't force vote on gay marriage. AP. Milwaukee Journal Sentinel. December 28, 2006, 3A.

[2346] Massachusetts marriage amendment overcomes opposition, passes. Published Jan.11, 2007 and retrieved 1.13.07 from http://www.floridabaptistwitnes.com/6840.article.

[2347] Massachusetts marriage amendment overcomes opposition, passes. Published Jan.11, 2007 and retrieved 1.13.07 from http://www.floridabaptistwitnes.com/6840.article.

[2348] Massachusetts marriage amendment overcomes opposition, passes. Published Jan.11, 2007 and retrieved 1.13.07 from http://www.floridabaptistwitnes.com/6840.article.
[2349] Kathryn Jean Lopez. National Review Online. 1.13.07 and posted 1.10.07 @ http://article.nationalreview.com/?q=YTUxMTViMDAxZGNhYiO0NiA0ODBlZiRhMWVmOGIwNWU=/.
[2350] Kathryn Jean Lopez. National Review Online. 1.13.07 and posted 1.10.07 @ http://article.nationalreview.com/?q=YTUxMTViMDAxZGNhYiO0NiA0ODBlZiRhMWVmOGIwNWU=/.
[2351] Rick Klein. Old Romney debate clip is now a hit on the Web. Posted Jan.11, 2007 and retrieved 1.13.07 from http://www.boston.com/news/local/articles/2007/01/11/old_romney_debate_clip_is_now_a_hit_on_the_web.
[2352] Rick Klein. Old Romney debate clip is now a hit on the Web. Posted Jan.11, 2007 and retrieved 1.13.07 from http://www.boston.com/news/local/articles/2007/01/11/old_romney_debate_clip_is_now_a_hit_on_the_web
[2353] Rick Klein. Old Romney debate clip is now a hit on the Web. Posted Jan.11, 2007 and retrieved 1.13.07 from http://www.boston.com/news/local/articles/2007/01/11/old_romney_debate_clip_is_now_a_hit_on_the_web
[2354] Rick Klein. Old Romney debate clip is now a hit on the Web. Posted Jan.11, 2007 and retrieved 1.13.07 from http://www.boston.com/news/local/articles/2007/01/11/old_romney_debate_clip_is_now_a_hit_on_the_web
[2355] Rick Klein. Old Romney debate clip is now a hit on the Web. Posted Jan.11, 2007 and retrieved 1.13.07 from http://www.boston.com/news/local/articles/2007/01/11/old_romney_debate_clip_is_now_a_hit_on_the_web
[2356] Rick Klein. Old Romney debate clip is now a hit on the Web. Posted Jan.11, 2007 and retrieved 1.13.07 from http://www.boston.com/news/local/articles/2007/01/11/old_romney_debate_clip_is_now_a_hit_on_the_web
[2357] James Kirchick: Mitt Romney's pomp and circumstance. Posted 1.11.07 and retrieved 1.13.07 from http://www.examiner.com/a-522561~James_Kirchick__Mitt_Romney_s_pomp_and_circumstance.
[2358] Liz Sidoti. John McCain a Target for All Sides. Examiner.com. AP. Posted Jan. 4, 2007 and retrieved 1.13.07 from http://www.examiner.com/a-489685~John_McCain_a_Target_for_All_Sides.html.
[2359] Liz Sidoti. John McCain a Target for All Sides. Examiner.com. AP. Posted Jan. 4, 2007 and retrieved 1.13.07 from http://www.examiner.com/a-489685~John_McCain_a_Target_for_All_Sides.html.
[2360] Liz Sidoti. John McCain a Target for All Sides. Examiner.com. AP. Posted Jan. 4, 2007 and retrieved 1.13.07 from http://www.examiner.com/a-489685~John_McCain_a_Target_for_All_Sides.html.
[2361] Liz Sidoti. John McCain a Target for All Sides. Examiner.com. AP. Posted Jan. 4, 2007 and retrieved 1.13.07 from http://www.examiner.com/a-489685~John_McCain_a_Target_for_All_Sides.html.
[2362] Kimberly Winston. Mormon Faith Seen as a Guide for Mitt Romney. Religion News Service. Published July 15, 2006 and retrieved August 11, 2006 from http://www.theledger.com/apps/pbcs.dll/article?AID=/20060715/NEWS/607150321/1326.
[2363] Heidi Przbyla. Romney's Religion May be Hurdle in Presidential Bid, Poll Shows. Bloomberg. 7.3.06 and retrieved 7.14.06 from http://www.bloomberg.com/apps/news?pid=washgingtonstory&sid=awU0UNxmMDDM
[2364] Kimberly Winston. Mormon Faith Seen as a Guide for Mitt Romney. Religion News Service. Published July 15, 2006 and retrieved August 11, 2006 from http://www.theledger.com/apps/pbcs.dll/article?AID=/20060715/NEWS/607150321/1326.
[2365] FOXNews.com. Transcript: Mass. Gov. Mitt Romney on 'FNS'. FOX News. Posted/Retrieved February 27, 2006 from http://www.foxnews.com/printer_friendly_story/0,3566,186080,00.html.
[2366] FOXNews.com. Transcript: Mass. Gov. Mitt Romney on 'FNS'. FOX News. Posted/Retrieved February 27, 2006 from http://www.foxnews.com/printer_friendly_story/0,3566,186080,00.html
[2367] Under the Dome. A Mormon First Lady? Posted July 25, 2006 and retrieved July 28, 2006 from http://thehill.com/thehill/export/TheHill/News/UndertheDome/072506.html.
[2368] Under the Dome. A Mormon First Lady? Posted July 25, 2006 and retrieved July 28, 2006 from http://thehill.com/thehill/export/TheHill/News/UndertheDome/072506.html
[2369] NBC NEWS. MTP transcript for Dec. 5. (2004). Meet the Press. Retrieved 10.31.2006 and posted 10.31.2006 @ http://www.msnbc.msn.com/id/6646457/.
[2370] Bob Bernick Jr. Poll: Mitt is top Utah choice. Deseret Morning News. Retrieved 12.14.06 from http://deseretnews.com/dn/view/0,1249,650208389,00.html
[2371] Albert R. Hunt. Letter from Washington: For anti-McCain right, it's 'Mitt Romney in 'O8' Posted Oct. 29, 2006 and retrieved 10.312006 from http://www.iht.com/articles/200610/29/news/letter.php.
[2372] Lee Brandy. Romney gets boost in S.C. The State. Posted Oct. 7, 2006 and retrieved 10.31.2006 from http://www.thestate.com/mld/state/news/politics/15705299.htm.
[2373] Scott Helman and Michael Levenson. Romney camp consulted with Mormon leaders. Globe Staff. Oct. 19, 2006. 10.31.06 from http://www.boston.com/news/nation/articles/2006/10/19/romney_camp_consulted_with_mormon_leaders.
[2374] Lee Brandy. Romney gets boost in S.C. The State. Posted Oct. 7, 2006 and retrieved 10.31.2006 from http://www.thestate.com/mld/state/news/politics/15705299.htm.
[2375] Lee Brandy. Romney gets boost in S.C. The State. Posted Oct. 7, 2006 and retrieved 10.31.2006 from http://www.thestate.com/mld/state/news/politics/15705299.htm.
[2376] Heidi Przbyla. Romney's Religion May be Hurdle in Presidential Bid, Poll Shows. Bloomberg. 7.3.06 and retrieved 7.14.06 from http://www.bloomberg.com/apps/news?pid=washgingtonstory&sid=awU0UNxmMDDM.
[2377] Heidi Przbyla. Romney's Religion May be Hurdle in Presidential Bid, Poll Shows. Bloomberg. 7.3.06 and retrieved 7.14.06 from http://www.bloomberg.com/apps/news?pid=washgingtonstory&sid=awU0UNxmMDDM.
[2378] Rasmussen Reports. Election 2008: 43% would never vote for Mormon candidate. Posted Nov.20 and retrieved 12.14.06 from http://www.rasmussenreports.com/Political%20Tracking/Dailies/MormanMittRomney.htm.

[2379] Rasmussen Reports. Election 2008: 43% would never vote for Mormon candidate. Posted Nov.20 and retrieved 12.14.06 from http://www.rasmussenreports.com/Political%20Tracking/Dailies/MormanMittRomney.htm.
[2380] Scott Helman and Michael Levenson. Support of Mormons sought. Milwaukee Journal Sentinel. Oct. 22, 2006, 6A.
[2381] Lee Brandy. Romney grilling 'in bad taste'. Posted Sept. 24, 2006 and retrieved 9.25.2006 from http://www.thestate.com/mld/thestate/news.local/15594211.htm.
[2382] Lee Brandy. Romney grilling 'in bad taste'. Posted Sept. 24, 2006 and retrieved 9.25.2006 from http://www.thestate.com/mld/thestate/news.local/15594211.htm.
[2383] Lee Brandy. Romney grilling 'in bad taste'. Posted Sept. 24, 2006 and retrieved 9.25.2006 from http://www.thestate.com/mld/thestate/news.local/15594211.htm.
[2384] Lee Brandy. Romney grilling 'in bad taste'. Posted Sept. 24, 2006 and retrieved 9.25.2006 from http://www.thestate.com/mld/thestate/news.local/15594211.htm.
[2385] Lee Brandy. Romney grilling 'in bad taste'. Posted Sept. 24, 2006 and retrieved 9.25.2006 from http://www.thestate.com/mld/thestate/news.local/15594211.htm.
[2386] Transcript: Sen. Sam Brownback on 'FOX News Sunday'. Aired Jan. 28, 2007 and retrieved 2.8.07 from http://www.foxnews.com/story/0,2933,247842,00.html.
[2387] Transcript: Sen. Sam Brownback on 'FOX News Sunday'. Aired Jan. 28, 2007 and retrieved 2.8.07 from http://www.foxnews.com/story/0,2933,247842,00.html.
[2388] Bob Bernick Jr. Poll: Mitt is top Utah choice. Deseret Morning News. Retrieved 12.14.06 from http://deseretnews.com/dn/view/0,1249,650208389,00.html
[2389] Scott Helman and Michael Levenson. Support of Mormons sought. Milwaukee Journal Sentinel, Oct. 22, 2006, 6A.
[2390] Scott Helman and Michael Levenson. Support of Mormons sought. Milwaukee Journal Sentinel. Oct. 22, 2006, 6A.
[2391] Scott Helman and Michael Levenson. Romney camp consulted with Mormon leaders. Globe Staff. Oct. 19, 2006. 10.31.06 from http://www.boston.com/news/nation/articles/2006/10/19/romney_camp_consulted_with_mormon_leaders.
[2392] Bob Bernick Jr. Poll: Mitt is top Utah choice. Deseret Morning News. Retrieved 12.14.06 from http://deseretnews.com/dn/view/0,1249,650208389,00.html
[2393] Berkshire Eagle. Kerry, Romney and 2008. Posted 10.24.06 and retrieved 10.31.2006 from http://www.berkshireeagle.com/editorials/ci_4540431.
[2394] Bob Bernick Jr. Poll: Mitt is top Utah choice. Deseret Morning News. Retrieved 12.14.06 from http://deseretnews.com/dn/view/0,1249,650208389,00.html .
[2395] AP. Huckabee questions Romney hunting claim. Posted 4.9.07 and retrieved 8.1.07 from http://www.msnbc.msn.com/id/18020502/print/1/displaymode/1098/.
[2396] AP. Huckabee questions Romney hunting claim. Posted 4.9.07 and retrieved 8.1.07 from http://www.msnbc.msn.com/id/18020502/print/1/displaymode/1098/.
[2397] AP. Huckabee questions Romney hunting claim. Posted 4.9.07 and retrieved 8.1.07 from http://www.msnbc.msn.com/id/18020502/print/1/displaymode/1098/.
[2398] AP. Huckabee questions Romney hunting claim. Posted 4.9.07 and retrieved 8.1.07 from http://www.msnbc.msn.com/id/18020502/print/1/displaymode/1098/.
[2399] AP. Huckabee questions Romney hunting claim. Posted 4.9.07 and retrieved 8.1.07 from http://www.msnbc.msn.com/id/18020502/print/1/displaymode/1098/.
[2400] Crooks and Liars; Think Progress. Romney: 'We Ought to Double Guantanamo.' Posted 5.16.07 and retrieved 6.29.07 from http://thinkprogress.org/2007/05/16/romney-guantanamo/.
[2401] Josh White and Robin Wright. Washington Post Staff Writers. Guantanamo Splits Administration. Posted 6.22.07 and retrieved 6.29.07 from http://www.washingtonpost.com/wp-dyn/content/article/2007/06/21/AR2007062102341_pf.html.
[2402] Tom Raum. AP. Clinton slaps Obama foreign-policy overture. Retrieved 8.1.07 from http://www.deseretnews.com/dn/view/0,1249,695194748,00.html.
[2403] Tom Raum. AP. Clinton slaps Obama foreign-policy overture. Retrieved 8.1.07 from http://www.deseretnews.com/dn/view/0,1249,695194748,00.html.
[2404] Glen Johnson. Latest Romney Ad Hones in on Immigration. AP. Posted 7.31.07 and retrieved 8.1.07 from http://www.forbes.com/feeds/ap/2007/07/31/ap3974198.html.
[2405] The Line: Debate Provides '08 Wake-up Call. Posted 7.27.07 and retrieved 8.1.07 from http://blog.washingtonpost.com/thefix/2007/07/friday_presidential_line_1.html.
[2406] The Line: Debate Provides '08 Wake-up Call. Posted 7.27.07 and retrieved 8.1.07 from http://blog.washingtonpost.com/thefix/2007/07/friday_presidential_line_1.html.
[2407] CNN.com. CNN Political Ticker Edwards, Romney lead in Iowa Polls. Posted 7.27.07 and retrieved 8.1.07 from http://politicalticker.blogs.cnn.com/2007/07/27/edwards-romney-lead-in-iowa-poll/.
[2408] American Research Group. New Hampshire. Retrieved 8.21.07 http://www.americanresearchgroup.com/pres/08/nhrep8-708.html.
[2409] AP. Glen Johnson. Forbes.com. Posted/Retrieved 8.1.07 from http://www.forbes.com/feeds/ap/2007/08/01/ap3976388.html.
[2410] AP. Glen Johnson. Forbes.com. Posted/Retrieved 8.1.07 from http://www.forbes.com/feeds/ap/2007/08/01/ap3976388.html.
[2411] Meet the Press. Aug.12, 2007 and retrieved 8.14.07 from http://www.msnbc.msn.com/id/20214115/print/1/displaymode/1098/.
[2412] Richard E. Cohen and Michael Barone. "The Almanac of American Politics—2004." The National Journal Group. 2003, page 325.

[2413] Richard E. Cohen and Michael Barone. "The Almanac of American Politics—2004." The National Journal Group. 2003, page 325.
[2414] Richard E. Cohen and Michael Barone. "The Almanac of American Politics—2004." The National Journal Group. 2003, page 325.
[2415] George F. Will. "Tom Tancredo puts a jolt in GOP." The New Hampshire Union Leader. Posted October 9, 2005 and retrieved October 11, 2005 from http://www.theunionleader.com/articles_showfast.html?article=61522
[2416] Betsy Rothstein. I say, 'Tom, you can't say that'—but he usually already has. Capital Living, The Hill. Posted March 7 and retrieved March 8, 2006 from http://www.hillnews.com/thehill/export/TheHill/Features/CapitalLiving/030706.html.
[2417] Betsy Rothstein. I say, 'Tom, you can't say that'—but he usually already has. Capital Living, The Hill. Posted March 7 and retrieved March 8, 2006 from http://www.hillnews.com/thehill/export/TheHill/Features/CapitalLiving/030706.html
[2418] Richard E. Cohen and Michael Barone. "The Almanac of American Politics—2004." The National Journal Group. 2003, page 326.
[2419] Patrick O'Conner. Tancredo bashes Bush on migrant 'amnesty.' The Hill. Posted June 29, 2005 and retrieved July 8, 2005 from http://www.thehill.com/thehill/export/TheHill/News/Frontpage/062905/Tancredo.html .
[2420] George F. Will. "Tom Tancredo puts a jolt in GOP." The New Hampshire Union Leader. Posted October 9, 2005 and retrieved October 11, 2005 from http://www.theunionleader.com/articles_showfast.html?article=61522.
[2421] George F. Will. "Tom Tancredo puts a jolt in GOP." The New Hampshire Union Leader. Posted October 9, 2005 and retrieved October 11, 2005 from http://www.theunionleader.com/articles_showfast.html?article=61522
[2422] Holly Bailey. A Border War. Newsweek/MSNBC.com. April 3, 2006 issue/retrieved March 27, 2006 from http://www.msnbc.msn.com/id/12017855/site/newsweek/print/1/displaymode/1098/
[2423] Holly Bailey. A Border War. Newsweek/MSNBC.com. April 3, 2006 issue/retrieved March 27, 2006 from http://www.msnbc.msn.com/id/12017855/site/newsweek/print/1/displaymode/1098/
[2424] Anne C. Mulkern. Tancredo blasts shield for religious groups. Denver Post. Posted November 15, 2005 and retrieved November 22, 2005 from http://www.denverpost.com/news/ci_3216584. good
[2425] Anne C. Mulkern. Tancredo blasts shield for religious groups. Denver Post. Posted November 15, 2005 and retrieved November 22, 2005 from http://www.denverpost.com/news/ci_3216584.
[2426] Greg Pierce. Inside Politics. The Washington Times. Published June 22, 2005 and retrieved June 24, 2005 from http://washingtontimes.com/functions/print.php?StoryID=20050621-115844-7242r.
[2427] Dan McLean. "Immigration's Tancredo's top topic." The Union Leader and New Hampshire Sunday News. Posted June 12 [sic], 2005 and retrieved July 8, 2005 from http://www.theunionleader.com/articles_showfast.html?article=56124.
[2428] Dan McLean. "Immigration's Tancredo's top topic." The Union Leader and New Hampshire Sunday News. Posted June 12 [sic], 2005 and retrieved July 8, 2005 from http://www.theunionleader.com/articles_showfast.html?article=56124
[2429] NewsMax.com. Rep. Tom Tancredo: Miami is a 'Third World Country'. Posted 11.28.06 and retrieved 8.1.07 from http://www.newsmax.com/archives/id/2006/11/28/132542.shtml.
[2430] NewsMax.com. Rep. Tom Tancredo: Miami is a 'Third World Country'. Posted 11.28.06 and retrieved 8.1.07 from http://www.newsmax.com/archives/id/2006/11/28/132542.shtml.
[2431] Tancredo the Racist Targets Miami. Published by Kenneth Quinnell. 12.15.06 and retrieved 8.1.07 from http://quinnell.us/sspb?p=237.
[2432] CNN.com. Situation Room 12.03.06. Retrieved same day @ http://transcripts.cnn.com/TRANSCRIPTS/0612/03/le.01.html
[2433] AP. Tancredo: Abolish black, Hispanic caucuses. MSNBC.com. Retrieved 1.25.07 from http://www.msnbc.msn.com/id/16812597/print/1/displaymode/1098/.
[2434] AP. Tancredo: Abolish black, Hispanic caucuses. MSNBC.com. Retrieved 1.25.07 from http://www.msnbc.msn.com/id/16812597/print/1/displaymode/1098/
[2435] Tom Tancredo Quotes. Retrieved 8.1.07 from http://www.brainyquote.com/quotes/authors/t/tom_tancredo.html.
[2436] Tom Curry. Long-shot contender hoping for N.H. upset. MSNBC.com. Retrieved 8.1.07 (Posted 3.13.07) @ http://www.msnbc.com/id/17591019/print/1/displaymode/1098/.
[2437] Tom Tancredo Quotes. Retrieved 8.1.07 from http://www.brainyquote.com/quotes/authors/t/tom_tancredo.html.
[2438] Tom Tancredo Quotes. Retrieved 8.1.07 from http://www.brainyquote.com/quotes/authors/t/tom_tancredo.html.
[2439] John Aguilar. Tancredo clarifies 'ultimate response. Rocky Mountain News. Posted July 18, 2005 and retrieved July 22, 2005 from http://www.rockymountainnews.com/drmn/local/article/0,1299,DRMN_15_3934448,00.html.
[2440] John Aguilar. Tancredo clarifies 'ultimate response. Rocky Mountain News. Posted July 18, 2005 and retrieved July 22, 2005 from http://www.rockymountainnews.com/drmn/local/article/0,1299,DRMN_15_3934448,00.html
[2441] John Aguilar. Tancredo clarifies 'ultimate response. Rocky Mountain News. Posted July 18, 2005 and retrieved July 22, 2005 from http://www.rockymountainnews.com/drmn/local/article/0,1299,DRMN_15_3934448,00.html
[2442] AP. FOXNews.com. Tancredo: If They Nuke Us, Bomb Mecca. Posted 7.18.05 and retrieved 9.29.05 from http://www.foxnews.com/printer_friendly_story/0,3566,162795,00.html.
[2443] Eric Gorski. Tancredo, interfaith group split. Denver Post. Posted November 20, 2005 and retrieved November 22, 2005 from http://www.denverpost.com/news/ci_3237338.
[2444] Eric Gorski. Tancredo, interfaith group split. Denver Post. Posted November 20, 2005 and retrieved November 22, 2005 from http://www.denverpost.com/news/ci_3237338.
[2445] Tom Tancredo Quotes. Retrieved 8.1.07 from http://www.brainyquote.com/quotes/authors/t/tom_tancredo.html.
[2446] M.E. Sprengelmeyer. Tancredo for president? Little-known Colo. Republican hits Iowa. Scripps Howard News Service. Posted July 15, 2005 and retrieved August 5, 2005 from http://www.knoxstudio.com/shns/story.cfm?pk=EARLYBIRD-07-15-05&cat=PP.

[2447] M.E. Sprengelmeyer. Tancredo tour sows national seeds. Rocky Mountain News. "Posted Aug 4, Retrieved Aug 5, 2005 from http://www.rockymountainnews.comdrmn/state/article/0,1299,DRMN_21_3976692,00.html.
[2448] M.E. Sprengelmeyer. Tancredo for president? Little-known Colo. Republican hits Iowa. Scripps Howard News Service. Posted July 15, 2005 and retrieved August 5, 2005 from http://www.knoxstudio.com/shns/story.cfm?pk=EARLYBIRD-07-15-05&cat=PP
[2449] Eunice Moscoso. Tancredo for President? Jan.12, 2007. Retrieved 1.13.07 from Atlanta Journal-Constitution. http://www.ajc.com/blogs/content/shared-blogs/washington/washington/entries/2007/01/12...
[2450] Amanda B. Carpenter. Tancredo's Jumping In. 1.12.2007 and retrieved 1.13.07 from http://www.humanevents.com/rightangle/index.php?id=19512&title=tancredo_s_jumping_in.
[2451] Anne C. Mulkern. Tancredo White House run not likely. 1.13.07 and posted April 12, 2006 @ http://www.denverpost.com/nationworld/ci_3704537.
[2452] Anne C. Mulkern. Tancredo testing presidential run. 1.13.07 and posted 1.12.07 @ http://www.denverpost.com/rapids/ci_5001411.
[2453] Colorado media Matters. Reporting on Tancredo's presidential aspirations, Post uncritically repeated spokesman's dubious comments. Retrieved 1.13.07 from http://colorado.mediamatters.org/items/200701130001.
[2454] AP. Tancredo announces presidential bid. 4.2.07 and retrieved 8.1.07 from http://www.msnbc.msn.com/id/17919814/print/displaymode/1098/.
[2455] Glen Johnson. Latest Romney Ad Hones in on Immigration. AP. Posted 7.31.07 and retrieved 8.1.07 from http://www.forbes.com/feeds/ap/2007/07/31/ap3974198.html.
[2456] World Net Daily. Miami as 3rd World? Tancredo would say it again. Posted July 13, 2007 and retrieved 8.1.07 from http://www.worldnetdaily.com/news/article.asp?ARTICLE_ID=56650.
[2457] Tom Curry. Long-shot contender hoping for N.H. upset. MSNBC.com. Retrieved 8.1.07 (Posted 3.13.07) @ http://www.msnbc.com/id/17591019/print/1/displaymode/1098/.
[2458] A Biography. Fred Thompson Biography. Retrieved 7.20.07 from http://www.anotherronaldreagan.com/Thompson_Bio.html.
[2459] A Biography. Fred Thompson Biography. Retrieved 7.20.07 from http://www.anotherronaldreagan.com/Thompson_Bio.html.
[2460] The Watergate Story. Key Players: Fred Thompson. Washingtonpost.com. Retrieved 7.20.07 from http://www.washingtonpost.com/wp-srv/onpolitics/watergate/fredthompson.html.
[2461] Susan Page. USA Today. Thompson wants to be 2008's outsider. Retrieved 6.15.07 from http://www.usatoday.com/news/politics/2007-05-30-thompson_N.htm.
[2462] Susan Page. USA Today. Thompson wants to be 2008's outsider. Retrieved 6.15.07 from http://www.usatoday.com/news/politics/2007-05-30-thompson_N.htm.
[2463] Susan Page. USA Today. Thompson wants to be 2008's outsider. Retrieved 6.15.07 from http://www.usatoday.com/news/politics/2007-05-30-thompson_N.htm.
[2464] Susan Page. USA Today. Thompson wants to be 2008's outsider. Retrieved 6.15.07 from http://www.usatoday.com/news/politics/2007-05-30-thompson_N.htm.
[2465] Mark Halperin. A New Role for Fred Thompson. Time. Posted 5.24.07 and retrieved 7.27.07 from http://www.time.com/time/printout/0,8816,1624881,00.html
[2466] A Biography. Fred Thompson Biography. Retrieved 7.20.07 from http://www.anotherronaldreagan.com/Thompson_Bio.html.
[2467] Sarah Baxter. Old girlfriends cast their vote for Thompson. Times Online. 6.24.07 and retrieved 7.20.07 from http://www.timesonline.co.uk/tol/news/world/us_and_americas/article1977478.ece?print=...
[2468] Sarah Baxter. Old girlfriends cast their vote for Thompson. Times Online. 6.24.07 and retrieved 7.20.07 from http://www.timesonline.co.uk/tol/news/world/us_and_americas/article1977478.ece?print=...
[2469] Mark Halperin. A New Role for Fred Thompson. Time. Posted 5.24.07 and retrieved 7.27.07 from http://www.time.com/time/printout/0,8816,1624881,00.html.
[2470] The Watergate Story. Key Players: Fred Thompson. Washingtonpost.com. Retrieved 7.20.07 from http://www.washingtonpost.com/wp-srv/onpolitics/watergate/fredthompson.html.
[2471] The Watergate Story. Key Players: Fred Thompson. Washingtonpost.com. Retrieved 7.20.07 from http://www.washingtonpost.com/wp-srv/onpolitics/watergate/fredthompson.html.
[2472] Susan Page. USA Today. Thompson wants to be 2008's outsider. Retrieved 6.15.07 from http://www.usatoday.com/news/politics/2007-05-30-thompson_N.htm.
[2473] Susan Page. USA Today. Thompson wants to be 2008's outsider. Retrieved 6.15.07 from http://www.usatoday.com/news/politics/2007-05-30-thompson_N.htm.
[2474] AP. Thompson says U.S. faces new challenges. MSNBC.com. 6.5.07 and retrieved 6.15.07 from http://www.msnbc.msn.com/id/19044308/print/1/displaymode/1098/.
[2475] Charlie Cook. Cook: Tennessee waltz. National Journal. MSNBC.com. 6.5.07 and retrieved 6.15.07 from http://www.msnbc.msn.com/id/190498446/print/1/displaymode/1098/.
[2476] Susan Page. USA Today. Thompson wants to be 2008's outsider. Retrieved 6.15.07 from http://www.usatoday.com/news/politics/2007-05-30-thompson_N.htm.
[2477] Michelle Cottie. Lazy Boy. Posted 4.13.07 and retrieved 7.27.07 from http://www.tnr.com/doc.mhtml?i=w070409&s=cottle041307.
[2478] Mark Halperin. A New Role for Fred Thompson. Time. Posted 5.24.07 and retrieved 7.27.07 from http://www.time.com/time/printout/0,8816,1624881,00.html

[2479] Mark Halperin. A New Role for Fred Thompson. Time. Posted 5.24.07 and retrieved 7.27.07 from http://www.time.com/time/printout/0,8816,1624881,00.html
[2480] Mark Halperin. A New Role for Fred Thompson. Time. Posted 5.24.07 and retrieved 7.27.07 from http://www.time.com/time/printout/0,8816,1624881,00.html
[2481] John Dickerson. Slate Magazine. Lazy Fred. Posted 5.31.07 and retrieved 7.27.07 from http://www.slate.com/id/2167411/.
[2482] Lorrie Morgan on Ex-beau Fred Thompson. Retrieved 7.20.07 from http://www.gactv.com/gac/nw_headlines/article/0,,GAC_26063_5551334,00.html.
[2483] Lorrie Morgan on Ex-beau Fred Thompson. Retrieved 7.20.07 from http://www.gactv.com/gac/nw_headlines/article/0,,GAC_26063_5551334,00.html.
[2484] Sarah Baxter. Old girlfriends cast their vote for Thompson. Times Online. 6.24.07 and retrieved 7.20.07 from http://www.timesonline.co.uk/tol/news/world/us_and_americas/article1977478.ece?print=...
[2485] Sarah Baxter. Old girlfriends cast their vote for Thompson. Times Online. 6.24.07 and retrieved 7.20.07 from http://www.timesonline.co.uk/tol/news/world/us_and_americas/article1977478.ece?print=...
[2486] Sarah Baxter. Old girlfriends cast their vote for Thompson. Times Online. 6.24.07 and retrieved 7.20.07 from http://www.timesonline.co.uk/tol/news/world/us_and_americas/article1977478.ece?print=...
[2487] Sarah Baxter. Old girlfriends cast their vote for Thompson. Times Online. 6.24.07 and retrieved 7.20.07 from http://www.timesonline.co.uk/tol/news/world/us_and_americas/article1977478.ece?print=...
[2488] Jonathan Martin and Mike Allen. The Politico. Fred Thompson sharpens strategy. USA Today. Posted 5.9.07 and retrieved 7.27.07 from http://www.usatoday.com/news/politics/2007-05-09-thompson-speech_N.htm
[2489] MND: Records confirm Fred Thompson worked for Pro-choice group. Posted 7.19.07 and retrieved 7.20.07 from http://mensnewsdaily.com/2007/07/19/records-confirm-fred-thomposon-worked-for-pro-choice-group/
[2490] Michelle Cottie. Lazy Boy. Posted 4.13.07 and retrieved 7.27.07 from http://www.tnr.com/doc.mhtml?i=w070409&s=cottle041307
[2491] MND: Records confirm Fred Thompson worked for Pro-choice group. Posted 7.19.07 and retrieved 7.20.07 from http://mensnewsdaily.com/2007/07/19/records-confirm-fred-thomposon-worked-for-pro-choice-group/.
[2492] MND: Records confirm Fred Thompson worked for Pro-choice group. Posted 7.19.07 and retrieved 7.20.07 from http://mensnewsdaily.com/2007/07/19/records-confirm-fred-thomposon-worked-for-pro-choice-group/.
[2493] MND: Records confirm Fred Thompson worked for Pro-choice group. Posted 7.19.07 and retrieved 7.20.07 from http://mensnewsdaily.com/2007/07/19/records-confirm-fred-thomposon-worked-for-pro-choice-group/.
[2494] MND: Records confirm Fred Thompson worked for Pro-choice group. Posted 7.19.07 and retrieved 7.20.07 from http://mensnewsdaily.com/2007/07/19/records-confirm-fred-thomposon-worked-for-pro-choice-group/.
[2495] Jeff Frecke. Fred Thompson, Pro-Choice Lobbyist. 7.6.07 and retrieved 7.20.07 from http://www.shakesville.com/2007/07/fred-thompson-pro-choice-lobbyist/.
[2496] The Watergate Story. Key Players: Fred Thompson. Washingtonpost.com. Retrieved 7.20.07 from http://www.washingtonpost.com/wp-srv/onpolitics/watergate/fredthompson.html.
[2497] Will Menaker. Ex-Watergate prober: Thompson 'was mole for the White House'. Published 7.5.07 and retrieved 7.20.07 from http://rawstory.com/news/2007/ExWatergate_prober_Thompson_was_mole_for_0705.html.
[2498] Joan Lowy. AP. Thompson helped Nixon in Watergate. Retrieved 7.20.07 and posted 7.7.07 @ http://www.presstelegram.com/news/ci_6324218.
[2499] Joan Lowy. AP. Thompson helped Nixon in Watergate. Retrieved 7.20.07 and posted 7.7.07 @ http://www.presstelegram.com/news/ci_6324218.
[2500] Joan Lowy. AP. Thompson helped Nixon in Watergate. Retrieved 7.20.07 and posted 7.7.07 @ http://www.presstelegram.com/news/ci_6324218.
[2501] Joan Lowy. AP. Thompson helped Nixon in Watergate. Retrieved 7.20.07 and posted 7.7.07 @ http://www.presstelegram.com/news/ci_6324218.
[2502] Joan Lowy. AP. Thompson helped Nixon in Watergate. Retrieved 7.20.07 and posted 7.7.07 @ http://www.presstelegram.com/news/ci_6324218.
[2503] Facing South. Fred Thompson, 'mole' for Nixon White House. Retrieved 7.20.07 @ http://southernstudies.org/facingsouth/2007/07/fred-thompson-mole-for-nixon-white.asp.
[2504] Susan Page. USA Today. Thompson wants to be 2008's outsider. Retrieved 6.15.07 from http://www.usatoday.com/news/politics/2007-05-30-thompson_N.htm.
[2505] FOXNews.com. Republicans Keep Close Watch on Possible White House Contender Fred Thompson. 4.19.07. Retrieved 5.3.07 from http://www.foxnews.com/story/0,2933,266996,00.html.
[2506] Jonathan Martin and Mike Allen. The Politico. Fred Thompson sharpens strategy. USA Today. Posted 5.9.07 and retrieved 7.27.07 from http://www.usatoday.com/news/politics/2007-05-09-thompson-speech_N.htm
[2507] Stephen F. Hayes. A Second Helping of Fred. Posted 5.3.07 and retrieved same day from http://www.weeklystandard.com/Utilities/printer_preview.asp?idArticle=13600&R=113672CDC2.
[2508] Jonathan Martin and Mike Allen. The Politico. Fred Thompson sharpens strategy. USA Today. Posted 5.9.07 and retrieved 7.27.07 from http://www.usatoday.com/news/politics/2007-05-09-thompson-speech_N.htm.
[2509] Jonathan Martin and Mike Allen. The Politico. Fred Thompson sharpens strategy. USA Today. Posted 5.9.07 and retrieved 7.27.07 from http://www.usatoday.com/news/politics/2007-05-09-thompson-speech_N.htm
[2510] Mark Halperin. A New Role for Fred Thompson. Time. Posted 5.24.07 and retrieved 7.27.07 from http://www.time.com/time/printout/0,8816,1624881,00.html

[2511] John Dickerson. Slate Magazine. Lazy Fred. Posted 5.31.07 and retrieved 7.27.07 from http://www.slate.com/id/2167411/
[2512] AP. Thompson won't tell Leno if he's running. Posted 6.12.07 and retrieved 6.15.07 from http://tennessean.com/apps/pbcs.dll/article?AID=/20070612/NEWS02/70612078/-1/NEWS020602.
[2513] Susan Page. USA Today. Thompson wants to be 2008's outsider. Retrieved 6.15.07 from http://www.usatoday.com/news/politics/2007-05-30-thompson_N.htm.
[2514] Jonathan Martin and Mike Allen. The Politico. Fred Thompson sharpens strategy. USA Today. Posted 5.9.07 and retrieved 7.27.07 from http://www.usatoday.com/news/politics/2007-05-09-thompson-speech_N.htm
[2515] Will Fred Thompson Withdraw The Troops? 4.14.07. Retrieved 5.3.07 from http://ezraklein.typepad.com/blog/2007/04/questions_for_f.html.
[2516] The Line: Debate Provides '08 Wake-up Call. Posted 7.27.07 and retrieved 8.1.07 from http://blog.washingtonpost.com/thefix/2007/07/friday_presidential_line_1.html.
[2517] Susan Saulny and David Kirkpatrick. Fred Thompson Came Up Short in June Money. Posted 7.31.07 and retrieved 8.3.07 from http://www.nytimes.com/2007/07/31/us/politics/31fred.html?....
[2518] Susan Saulny and David Kirkpatrick. Fred Thompson Came Up Short in June Money. Posted 7.31.07 and retrieved 8.3.07 from http://www.nytimes.com/2007/07/31/us/politics/31fred.html?....
[2519] AP. NewsMax.com. Fred Thompson Raises $3 Million in June. Retrieved 7.30.07 from http://www.newsmax.com/archives/ic/2007/7/30/154421.shtml?s=ic.
[2520] Mike Glover. AP. Nov.16, 2006. Ex-Bush Aide to Explore Presidential Run. Retrieved 11.17.06 from http://www.washingtonpost.com/wp-dyn/content/article/2006/11/16/AR20061116111601244_pf.html.
[2521] Luke Punzenberger. Green: Campaign Tommy Thompson Says Doyle Has Failed Wisconsin and Is Lying About Mark Green's Record. 10.27.06 and retrieved 11.17.06 from http://www.wispolitics.com/index.iml?Article=75834.
[2522] Mike Glover. AP. Thompson says he'll explore run for White House. Wilimingtonstar.com. Retrieved 11.17.06.
[2523] Tommy Thompson Preparing to Run. Posted 11.15.06 and retrieved 11.17.06 from http://blogs.abcnews.com/politicalradar/2006/11/tommy_thompson_.html.
[2524] Tony Leys. Wisconsin's Thompson studies '08 run. Des Moines Register. Published Nov.16 and retrieved 11.17.06 from http://www.dmregister.com/extras/politics/ and http://desmoinesregister.com/apps/pbcs.dll/article?AID=/20061116/NEWS09/611160412...
[2525] Tony Leys. Thompson plans Iowa campaign push. Des Moines Register. January 4, 2007. Retrieved 1.13.06 from http://www.desmoinesregister.com/apps/pbcs.dll/article?AID=/20070104/NEWS09/701040373/1001/NEWS.
[2526] Tony Leys. Thompson plans Iowa campaign push. Des Moines Register. January 4, 2007. Retrieved 1.13.06 from http://www.desmoinesregister.com/apps/pbcs.dll/article?AID=/20070104/NEWS09/701040373/1001/NEWS.
[2527] Mike Glover. AP. Nov.16, 2006. Ex-Bush Aide to Explore Presidential Run. Retrieved 11.17.06 from http://www.washingtonpost.com/wp-dyn/content/article/2006/11/16/AR20061116111601244_pf.html.
[2528] Tony Leys. Thompson plans Iowa campaign push. Des Moines Register. January 4, 2007. Retrieved 1.13.06 from http://www.desmoinesregister.com/apps/pbcs.dll/article?AID=/20070104/NEWS09/701040373/1001/NEWS.
[2529] Tony Leys. Wisconsin's Thompson studies '08 run. Des Moines Register. Published Nov.16 and retrieved 11.17.06 from http://www.dmregister.com/extras/politics/ and http://desmoinesregister.com/apps/pbcs.dll/article?AID=/20061116/NEWS09/611160412...
[2530] Mike Glover. AP. Nov.16, 2006. Ex-Bush Aide to Explore Presidential Run. Retrieved 11.17.06 from http://www.washingtonpost.com/wp-dyn/content/article/2006/11/16/AR20061116111601244_pf.html.
[2531] CNN.com. Reuters. Ex-Wisconsin governor to explore White House bid. Posted 11.16 and retrieved 11.17.06 from http://www.cnn.com/2006/POLITICS/11/16/Thompson.president.reut.
[2532] CNN.com. Reuters. Ex-Wisconsin governor to explore White House bid. Posted 11.16 and retrieved 11.17.06 from http://www.cnn.com/2006/POLITICS/11/16/Thompson.president.reut.
[2533] AP. Thompson apologizes for Jewish comments. MSNBC.com. Posted 4.17.07 and retrieved 8.1.07 from http://www.msnbc.msn.com/id/18151228/print/1/displaymode/1098/.
[2534] AP. Thompson apologizes for Jewish comments. MSNBC.com. Posted 4.17.07 and retrieved 8.1.07 from http://www.msnbc.msn.com/id/18151228/print/1/displaymode/1098/.
[2535] Tommy Thompson gets testy. Think Progress. Posted by Nico, 4.17.07 and retrieved 8.1.07 from http://thinkprogress.org/2007/04/17tommy-thompson-gets-testy/.
[2536] Tommy Thompson gets testy. Think Progress. Posted by Nico, 4.17.07 and retrieved 8.1.07 from http://thinkprogress.org/2007/04/17tommy-thompson-gets-testy/.
[2537] Tommy Thompson gets testy. Think Progress. Posted by Nico, 4.17.07 and retrieved 8.1.07 from http://thinkprogress.org/2007/04/17tommy-thompson-gets-testy/.
[2538] AP. Thompson apologizes for Jewish comments. MSNBC.com. Posted 4.17.07 and retrieved 8.1.07 from http://www.msnbc.msn.com/id/18151228/print/1/displaymode/1098/.
[2539] Craig Gilbert. Thompson apologizes to Jews for comments. Posted 4.16.07 and retrieved 8.1.07 from http://www.jsonline.com/story/index.aspx?id=591756.
[2540] Craig Gilbert. Thompson apologizes to Jews for comments. Posted 4.16.07 and retrieved 8.1.07 from http://www.jsonline.com/story/index.aspx?id=591756.
[2541] Late Night Political Jokes. April 19, 2007. Retrieved 5.3.07 from http://politicalhumor.about.com/library/bldailyfeed3.htm.
[2542] Tommy Thompson Gets Some Hometown Explaining Gaffes. Posted 5.8.07 and retrieved 8.1.07 from http://2008central.net/?p=697.

[2543] Tommy Thompson Gets Some Hometown Explaining Gaffes. Posted 5.8.07 and retrieved 8.1.07 from http://2008central.net/?p=697
[2544] Tommy Thompson Gets Some Hometown Explaining Gaffes. Posted 5.8.07 and retrieved 8.1.07 from http://2008central.net/?p=697
[2545] QC Times. Charlotte Eby. Thompson blames faulty hearing aid for misstatement on gay rights. Posted 5.10.07 and retrieved 8.1.07 from http://www.qctimes.com/articles/2007/05/10/news/state/doc4642b22422245287699870.txt.
[2546] Tommy Thompson Makes Excuses for Condoning Bigotry. Posted 5.13.07 and retrieved 8.1.07 from http://political-fallout.blogspot.com/2007/05/tommy-thompson-makes-excuses-for.html.
[2547] QC Times. Charlotte Eby. Thompson blames faulty hearing aid for misstatement on gay rights. Posted 5.10.07 and retrieved 8.1.07 from http://www.qctimes.com/articles/2007/05/10/news/state/doc4642b22422245287699870.txt.
[2548] QC Times. Charlotte Eby. Thompson blames faulty hearing aid for misstatement on gay rights. Posted 5.10.07 and retrieved 8.1.07 from http://www.qctimes.com/articles/2007/05/10/news/state/doc4642b22422245287699870.txt.
[2549] Tommy Thompson Not Anti-Gay Bigot. 5.6.07 and retrieved 8.1.07 from http://dekerivers.wordpress.com/2007/05/06/tommy-thompson-not-anti-gay-bigot/.
[2550] Patrick Marley. Lawmakers aren't claiming sick days. November 26, 2006, 17A. Other officials rack up sick leave benefits, too.
[2551] Cary Spivak and Dan Bice. Milwaukee Journal Sentinel. Dhaliwal a full-service donor for Thompson. Jan. 14, 2007, 2A.
[2552] Cary Spivak and Dan Bice. Milwaukee Journal Sentinel. Dhaliwal a full-service donor for Thompson. Jan. 14, 2007, 2A.
[2553] Cary Spivak and Dan Bice. Milwaukee Journal Sentinel. Dhaliwal a full-service donor for Thompson. Jan. 14, 2007, 2A.
[2554] Cary Spivak and Dan Bice. Milwaukee Journal Sentinel. Dhaliwal a full-service donor for Thompson. Jan. 14, 2007, 2A.
[2555] Cary Spivak and Dan Bice. Milwaukee Journal Sentinel. Dhaliwal a full-service donor for Thompson. Jan. 14, 2007, 2A.
[2556] Cary Spivak and Dan Bice. Milwaukee Journal Sentinel. Dhaliwal a full-service donor for Thompson. Jan. 14, 2007, 2A.
[2557] Cary Spivak and Dan Bice. Milwaukee Journal Sentinel. Dhaliwal a full-service donor for Thompson. Jan. 14, 2007, 2A.
[2558] Katherine M. Skiba. Thompson tests waters for presidential campaign. Dec.16, 2006. 3A.
[2559] Katherine M. Skiba. Thompson tests waters for presidential campaign. Dec.16, 2006. 3A.
[2560] Michael McAuliff. McCain jumps in ring with Rudy. New York Daily News. Posted Nov. 16 and retrieved 11.17.06. from http://dailynews.com/news/politics/story/471833p-397064c.html.
[2561] AP. McCain: GOP should return to Reagan-era approach. Published Nov.17.06 and retrieved same day from http://www.tucsoncitizen.com/daily/local/32918.php.
[2562] Mike Glover. AP. Nov.16, 2006. Ex-Bush Aide to Explore Presidential Run. Retrieved 11.17.06 from http://www.washingtonpost.com/wp-dyn/content/article/2006/11/16/AR2006111611601244_pf.html.
[2563] Tony Leys. Wisconsin's Thompson studies '08 run. Des Moines Register. Published Nov.16 and retrieved 11.17.06 from http://www.dmregister.com/extras/politics/ and http://desmoinesregister.com/apps/pbcs.dll/article?AID=/20061116/NEWS09/611160412...
[2564] National Journal Group Inc. White House 2008 Rankings. Jan. 11. 2007. Retrieved 1.13.07 from http://nationaljournal.com/racerankings/wh08/republicans/.
[2565] Katherine M. Skiba. Thompson's trial balloon below radar. Milwaukee Journal Sentinel. Dec.4, 2006. 1A/9A.
[2566] Carlson. Milwaukee Journal Sentinel, 23 A . Dec. 8, 2006.
[2567] Tony Leys. Thompson plans Iowa campaign push. Des Moines Register. January 4, 2007. Retrieved 1.13.06 from http://www.desmoinesregister.com/apps/pbcs.dll/article?AID=/20070104/NEWS09/701040373/1001/NEWS.
[2568] Tony Leys. Thompson plans Iowa campaign push. Des Moines Register. January 4, 2007. Retrieved 1.13.06 from http://www.desmoinesregister.com/apps/pbcs.dll/article?AID=/20070104/NEWS09/701040373/1001/NEWS.
[2569] Katherine M. Skiba. Thompson's trial balloon below radar. Dec.4, 2006. 1A/9A.
[2570] Katherine M. Skiba. Thompson's trial balloon below radar. Dec.4, 2006. 1A/9A.
[2571] Katherine M. Skiba. Thompson's trial balloon below radar. Dec.4, 2006. 1A/9A.
[2572] Late Night Political Jokes. April 9, 2007. Retrieved 5.3.07 from http://politicalhumor.about.com/library/bldailyfeed3.htm.
[2573] AP. Thompson apologizes for Jewish comments. MSNBC.com. Posted 4.17.07 and retrieved 8.1.07 from http://www.msnbc.msn.com/id/18151228/print/1/displaymode/1098/
[2574] AP. Thompson apologizes for Jewish comments. MSNBC.com. Posted 4.17.07 and retrieved 8.1.07 from http://www.msnbc.msn.com/id/18151228/print/1/displaymode/1098/
[2575] Katherine M. Skiba. Thompson sees home-state media as road bumps. Published 8.10.07. See http://jsonline.com/archive/index.aspx?id=AH426.
[2576] RJ Elliott. Iowa Straw Poll Results. Published 8.12.07 and retrieved 8.21.07 from http://blogcritics.org/archives/2007/08/12/023738.php.
[2577] Meg Jones. Thompson ends his quest. Milwaukee Journal Sentinel. Published 8.13.07. See http://www.jsonline.com/archive/index.aspx?id=AH426.

[2578] Richard E. Cohen and Michael Barone. "The Almanac of American Politics—2004." The National Journal Group. 2003, page 1359.
[2579] Edwin Chen. "Bush on Fund-Raising Trail for Senate and House Races." LA Times. Posted June 14, 2005 and retrieved July 1, 2005 from http://www.latimes.com/news/nationworld/nation/la-061405bush_lat,0,2826397.story?coll=la-home-headlines.
[2580] Edwin Chen. "Bush on Fund-Raising Trail for Senate and House Races." LA Times. Posted June 14, 2005 and retrieved July 1, 2005 from http://www.latimes.com/news/nationworld/nation/la-061405bush_lat,0,2826397.story?coll=la-home-headlines
[2581] Richard E. Cohen and Michael Barone. The Almanac of American Politics—2004. The National Journal Group. 2003, page 1361
[2582] Richard E. Cohen and Michael Barone. The Almanac of American Politics—2004. The National Journal Group. 2003, page 1361
[2583] Richard E. Cohen and Michael Barone. The Almanac of American Politics—2004. The National Journal Group. 2003, page 1360
[2584] Richard E. Cohen and Michael Barone. The Almanac of American Politics—2004. The National Journal Group. 2003, page 1359
[2585] Richard E. Cohen and Michael Barone. The Almanac of American Politics—2004. The National Journal Group. 2003, page 1361
[2586] Richard E. Cohen and Michael Barone. The Almanac of American Politics—2004. The National Journal Group. 2003, page 1360.
[2587] NBC News. Meet the Press. MTP Transcript for Sept.3. MSNBC.com. Retrieved Sept.6, 2006 from http://www.msnbc.msn.com/id/14568263/print/1/displaymode/1098/.
[2588] Kimberly Hefling. Santorum says family emphasized in new book. AP. Posted June 30, 2005 and retrieved July 8, 2005 from http://www.philly.com/mld/philly/news/12027272.htm.
[2589] Carrie Budoff. Senator's book puts blame on liberalism. Philadelphia Inquirer. Posted July 7, 2005 and retrieved July 8, 2005 from http://www.philly.com/mld/philly/news/12070387.htm.
[2590] Mackenzie Carpenter. Santorum book stirs debate on child care. Pittsburgh Post-Gazette. Posted July 7, 2005 and retrieved July 8, 2005 from http://www.post-gazette.com/pg/05188/534117.stm.
[2591] Carrie Budoff. Senator's book puts blame on liberalism. Philadelphia Inquirer. Posted July 7, 2005 and retrieved July 8, 2005 from http://www.philly.com/mld/philly/news/12070387.htm
[2592] Kimberly Hefling. Santorum likens abortion to slavery. AP. Posted July 6, 2005 and retrieved July 8, 2005 from http://www.buffalonews.com/editorial/20050706/1060005.asp.
[2593] AP. Clinton, Santorum Swap Child-Rearing Views. ABC 7 News. Written by Devlin Barrett. Posted July 12, 2005 and retrieved July 15, 2005 from http://www.wjla.com/news/stories/0705/242769.html
[2594] AP. Clinton, Santorum Swap Child-Rearing Views. ABC 7 News. Written by Devlin Barrett. Posted July 12, 2005 and retrieved July 15, 2005 from http://www.wjla.com/news/stories/0705/242769.html
[2595] AP. Clinton, Santorum Swap Child-Rearing Views. ABC 7 News. Written by Devlin Barrett. Posted July 12, 2005 and retrieved July 15, 2005 from http://www.wjla.com/news/stories/0705/242769.html
[2596] Brian McGrory. In sanctum Santorum. Boston Globe. Posted July 12, 2005 and retrieved July 15, 2005 from http://www.boston.com/news/local/articles/2005/07/12/in/_sanctum_santorum/
[2597] Brian McGrory. In sanctum Santorum. Boston Globe. Posted July 12, 2005 and retrieved July 15, 2005 from http://www.boston.com/news/local/articles/2005/07/12/in/_sanctum_santorum/
[2598] Anand Vaishnav. Romney begs to differ with Santorum remark. Boston Globe. Posted July 15, 2005 and retrieved July 15, 2005 from http://www.boston.com/news/local/massachusetts/articles/2005/07/15/romney_begs_to_differ_with_santorum_remark/.
[2599] Anand Vaishnav. Romney begs to differ with Santorum remark. Boston Globe. Posted July 15, 2005 and retrieved July 15, 2005 from http://www.boston.com/news/local/massachusetts/articles/2005/07/15/romney_begs_to_differ_with_santorum_remark/
[2600] The Kansas City Star. The BUZZ: Boston basher. Posted 7.14.05 and retrieved 7.15.05 from http://www.kansascity.com/mld/kansascitystar/news/politics/12127067.htm.
[2601] Brett Lieberman. Santorum hits back at Kennedy. Pennlive.com. The Patriot News. Posted July 15, 2005 and retrieved July 15, 2005 from http://www.pennlive.com/news/patriotnews/index.ssf?/base/news/1121419422185420.xml&coll=1.
[2602] Brett Lieberman. Santorum hits back at Kennedy. Pennlive.com. The Patriot News. Posted July 15, 2005 and retrieved July 15, 2005 from http://www.pennlive.com/news/patriotnews/index.ssf?/base/news/1121419422185420.xml&coll=1.
[2603] (quote was reported by Brett Lieberman of the Harrisburg Patriot-News) Found in James O' Toole. "It takes a controversy: Santorum book could be asset after initial hit, strategist says." The Pittsburgh Post-Gazette. Posted July 17, 2005 and retrieved July 22, 2005 from http://www.post-gazette.com/pg/05198/539270.stm.
[2604] Michael Kranish, Santorum blasts Mass. Senators over church scandals. The Boston Globe/ Boston.com. Posted August 1, 2005 and retrieved August 5, 2005 from http://www.boston.com/news/nation/articles/2005/08/01/santorum_blasts_mass_senators_over_church_scandal/.
[2605] Michael Kranish, Santorum blasts Mass. Senators over church scandals. The Boston Globe/ Boston.com. Posted August 1, 2005 and retrieved August 5, 2005 from http://www.boston.com/news/nation/articles/2005/08/01/santorum_blasts_mass_senators_over_church_scandal/

[2606] Michael Kranish. Santorum blasts Mass. Senators over church scandals. The Boston Globe/ Boston.com. Posted August 1, 2005 and retrieved August 5, 2005 from http://www.boston.com/news/nation/articles/2005/08/01/santorum_blasts_mass_senators_over_church_scandal/

[2607] AP. Philadelphia Archdiocese hid years of abuse by priests, grand jury say. The Milwaukee Journal Sentinel, September 22, 2005, 9A.

[2608] Jeff Miller, Call Washington Bureau, "Santorum apologizes for Hitler comment, had scolded Byrd for similar reference." The Morning Call. Posted May 20, 2005 and retrieved June 2, 2005 from http://www.mcall.com/news/local/all-a3_5hitlermay20,0,559978.story.

[2609] Jeff Miller, Call Washington Bureau, "Santorum apologizes for Hitler comment, had scolded Byrd for similar reference." The Morning Call. Posted May 20, 2005 and retrieved June 2, 2005 from http://www.mcall.com/news/local/all-a3_5hitlermay20,0,559978.story.

[2610] Jonathan Chait. The Irresistible 'Nazi' Taboo. The Los Angeles Times, Posted May 27, 2005 and retrieved June 2, 2005 from http://www.latimes.com/news/opinion/commentary/la-oe-chait27may27,0,3949760.column?coll=la-news-comment-opinions.

[2611] ABC News and Reuters. Senator Santorum calls Hitler quip 'mistake.' Posted May 20, 2005 and retrieved June 2, 2005 from http://abcnews.go.com/Politics/wireStory?id=776088.

[2612] Jeff Miller, Call Washington Bureau. Santorum apologizes for Hitler comment, had scolded Byrd for similar reference. The Morning Call. Posted May 20, 2005 and retrieved June 2, 2005 from http://www.mcall.com/news/local/all-a3_5hitlermay20,0,559978.story.

[2613] Jesse J. Holland. Santorum calls his Hitler remark mistake. AP. The Philadelphia Inquirer. Posted May 21, 2005 and retrieved June 2, 2005 from http://www.philly.com/mld/inquirer/news/nation/11701141.htm.

[2614] The Tribune-Review staff. Santorum digs up Adolf and the ADL says it stinks. The Pittsburgh Tribune-Review. Posted May 29, 2005 and retrieved June 2, 2005.

[2615] The Tribune-Review staff. Santorum digs up Adolf and the ADL says it stinks. The Pittsburgh Tribune-Review. Posted May 29, 2005 and retrieved June 2, 2005.

[2616] Nicholas Provenzo Rick Santorum's Moral Outrage. 4.25.03 and retrieved 6.29.07 from http://www.capmag.com/article.asp?ID=2698.

[2617] Nicholas Provenzo Rick Santorum's Moral Outrage. 4.25.03 and retrieved 6.29.07 from http://www.capmag.com/article.asp?ID=2698.

[2618] Nicholas Provenzo Rick Santorum's Moral Outrage. 4.25.03 and retrieved 6.29.07 from http://www.capmag.com/article.asp?ID=2698.

[2619] Rick Santorum Quotes. Retrieved 6.29.07 from http://www.brainyquote.com/quotes/authors/r/rick_santorum.html.

[2620] Maeve Reston. Santorum focusing on re-election to Senate, not White House run. Pittsburgh Post-Gazette. Posted January 26, 2005 and retrieved October 5, 2005 from http://www.post-gazette.com/pg/05026/448138.stm.

[2621] NBC News, Meet the Press. Transcript for February 27, 2005. Retrieved March 3, 2005 at http://www.msnbc.msn.com/id/7041426/.

[2622] George F. Will. Brownback's Plans for 2008. MSNBC.com & Newsweek. Posted May 29, 2005 and retrieved June 2, 2005 from http://www.msnbc.msn.com/id/8017004/site/newsweek/.

[2623] George F. Will. Brownback's Plans for 2008. MSNBC.com & Newsweek. Posted May 29, 2005 and retrieved June 2, 2005 from http://www.msnbc.msn.com/id/8017004/site/newsweek/.

[2624] Brain Faler. McCain Revives PAC—And the Speculation. Washingtonpost.com. Posted July 29, 2005 and retrieved July 29, 2005 from http://www.washingtonpost.com/wp-dyn/content/article/2005/07/28/AR2005072801908.html

[2625] Lieberman, Brett. Casey edges closer to campaign against Santorum. The Patriot News. Posted and retrieved March 3, 2005 on http://www.pennlive.com/politics/patriotnews/index.ssf?/base/news/1109845454246240.xml.

[2626] Son of former governor to challenge Santorum. The Milwaukee Journal Sentinel, March 6, 2005, 13A.

[2627] Davies, Dave. Poll: Santorum & Casey close; Ed strong. Philadelphia Daily News. Posted and retrieved March 22, 2005 on http://www.philly.com/mld/dailynews/news/local/11201074.htm.

[2628] Carrie Budoff. Bush marks date in June for Santorum fund-raiser. Philadelphia Inquirer. Posted/retrieved June 2, 2005 from http://www.philly.com/mld/inquirer/news/nation/11792157.htm.

[2629] Philadelphia Inquirer. Bush helps raise $1.5 million for Santorum at luncheon in Bryn Mawr. Posted June 14, 2005 and retrieved July 1, 2005 from http://www.philly.com/mld/philly/news/breaking_news/11892379.htm.

[2630] Rob Kall. Poll: Santorum Most Disapproved US Senator. www.OpEdNews.com. Posted June 13, 2005 and retrieved June 24 from http://www.opednews.com/kall_061605_santorum_most%20Disapproved.htm. Survey USA of Verona, NJ.

[2631] Thomas Fitzgerald. Blaming Schedule, Santorum will miss Bush's visit to Pa. The Philadelphia Inquirer. Posted and retrieved November 10, 2005 from http://www.philly.com/mld/inquirer/news/local/states/pennsylvania/counties/chester_county/13130466.htm.

[2632] Thomas Fitzgerald. Blaming Schedule, Santorum will miss Bush's visit to Pa. The Philadelphia Inquirer. Posted and retrieved November 10, 2005 from http://www.philly.com/mld/inquirer/news/local/states/pennsylvania/counties/chester_county/13130466.htm,

[2633] Dave Davies. Poll shows Ed, Santorum slipping. The Philadelphia News. Posted November 10, 2005 and retrieved same day from http://www.philly.com/mld/dailynews/news/local/13130219.htm.

[2634] Howard Fineman. Smile and say cheese Sen. Santorum. MSNBC. Posted December 14, 2005 and retrieved December 15, 2005 from http://msnbc.msn.com/id/10455461/.

[2635] Howard Fineman. "Smile and say cheese Sen. Santorum." MSNBC. Posted December 14, 2005 and retrieved December 15, 2005 from http://msnbc.msn.com/id/10455461/.

Karl McCarty: *The Last One Standing* 323

[2636] Bloomberg. McCain, Senate Rebel, Becomes Star Campaigner for Republicans. Posted December 20, 2005 and retrieved January 6, 2006 from http://www.bloomberg.com/apps/news?pid=71000001&refer=us&sid=a9iy.dNgowy8.

[2637] Michael Klein. Inqlings—Ex- Phil Doug Glanville's new base will be Chicago. The McCain watch. Posted December 8, 2005 and retrieved January 6. 2006 from http://www.philly.com/mld/philly/entertainment/columnists/michael_klein/13354339.htm.

[2638] Retrieved December 8, 2005 from http://www.ricksantorum.com/Multimedia/MMPlayer_Video.aspx?ID=1051.

[2639] Posted December 7, 2005 and retrieved January 6, 2006 from http://www.ricksantorum.com/Mutlimedia/Transcript.aspx?Id=1051.

[2640] CentreDaily.com. Handicapping the '08 presidential race. Posted Nov.14.06 and retrieved 11.17.06 from http://www.centredaily.com/mld/centredaily/news/opinion/15998697.htm.

[2641] Carrie Budoff. Santorum: No Oval office run. Philadelphia Inquirer. Retrieved Nov.17.06 and posted same day @ http://www.philly.com.mld/inquirer/news/local/16032443.htm.

[2642] Carrie Budoff. Santorum: No Oval office run. Philadelphia Inquirer. Retrieved Nov.17.06 and posted same day @ http://www.philly.com.mld/inquirer/news/local/16032443.htm.

[2643] Carrie Budoff. Santorum: No Oval office run. Philadelphia Inquirer. Retrieved Nov.17.06 and posted same day @ http://www.philly.com.mld/inquirer/news/local/16032443.htm.

[2644] His American Dream. John Heilemann. New York Magazine. Posted 12.11.06 and retrieved 12.14.06 from http://nymag.com/news/politics/25015/. 2 /11.

[2645] His American Dream. John Heilemann. New York Magazine. Posted 12.11.06 and retrieved 12.14.06 from http://nymag.com/news/politics/25015/. 4 /11.

[2646] His American Dream. John Heilemann. New York Magazine. Posted 12.11.06 and retrieved 12.14.06 from http://nymag.com/news/politics/25015/. 4 /11.

[2647] His American Dream. John Heilemann. New York Magazine. Posted 12.11.06 and retrieved 12.14.06 from http://nymag.com/news/politics/25015/. 5 /11.

[2648] His American Dream. John Heilemann. New York Magazine. Posted 12.11.06 and retrieved 12.14.06 from http://nymag.com/news/politics/25015/. 4 /11.

[2649] His American Dream. John Heilemann. New York Magazine. Posted 12.11.06 and retrieved 12.14.06 from http://nymag.com/news/politics/25015/. 4 /11.

[2650] His American Dream. John Heilemann. New York Magazine. Posted 12.11.06 and retrieved 12.14.06 from http://nymag.com/news/politics/25015/. 4 /11.

[2651] Ben Smith. Third Way Out. The New Republic. Posted June 29, 2006 and retrieved June 30, 2006 from http://www.tnr.com/user/nregi.mhtml?i=20060710&s=smith071006.

[2652] How Serious is Bloomberg? Taegan Goddard's Political Wire. Archives: 2008 campaign. Retrieved June 30, 2006 from http://politicalwire.com/archives/2008_campaign/.

[2653] How Serious is Bloomberg? Taegan Goddard's Political Wire. Archives: 2008 campaign. Retrieved June 30, 2006 from http://politicalwire.com/archives/2008_campaign/.

[2654] Quinnipiac University. July 12, 2006, New Yorkers Like Mayor's Big Talk, Quinnipiac Poll Finds; But Most Don't Think He'll Run For President. Retrieved July 14, 2006 from http://www.quinnipiac.edu/x11385.xml?ReleaseID=935.

[2655] Eamon Quinn. Bloomberg, on Ireland Trip, Rules Out White House Run. Published August 23, 2006 and retrieved August 25, 2006 from http://www.nytimes.com/2006/08/23/nyregion/23bloomberg.html?ex=1313985600&en=d9fb7cf606bd7f18&ei=5089&partner=rssyahoo&emc=rss.

[2656] September 15, 2006. Bloomberg Considers Presidential Bid. Retrieved 9.25.06 from http://www.politicalwire.com/archives/2008_campaign/.

[2657] His American Dream. John Heilemann. Posted 12.11.06 and retrieved 12.14.06 from http://nymag.com/news/politics/25015/. 1 /11.

[2658] September 15, 2006. Bloomberg Considers Presidential Bid. Retrieved 9.25.06 from http://www.politicalwire.com/archives/2008_campaign/.

[2659] His American Dream. John Heilemann. Posted 12.11.06 and retrieved 12.14.06 from http://nymag.com/news/politics/25015/. 1 /11.

[2660] His American Dream. John Heilemann. Posted 12.11.06 and retrieved 12.14.06 from http://nymag.com/news/politics/25015/. 1 /11.

[2661] His American Dream. John Heilemann. Posted 12.11.06. and retrieved 12.14.06 from http://nymag.com/news/politics/25015/. 1,2 /11.

[2662] His American Dream. John Heilemann. New York Magazine. Posted 12.11.06 and retrieved 12.14.06 from http://nymag.com/news/politics/25015/. P6,7 /11.

[2663] Bloomberg Seriously Contemplating Presidential Bid. Retrieved 12.14.06 from http://politicalwire.com/archives/2008_campaign/.

[2664] Bloomberg Seriously Contemplating Presidential Bid. Retrieved 12.14.06 from http://politicalwire.com/archives/2008_campaign/.

[2665] Jim VandeHei. From the Internet to the White House. Washington Post. Page A04. Posted and retrieved May 31, 2006 from http://www.washingtonpost.com/wp-dyn/content/article/2006/05/30/AR2006053001139.html.

[2666] Karen E. Crummy. '08 vote to have a third ticket. Denver Post. Posted and retrieved May 31, 2006 from http://www.denverpost.com/portlet/article/html/fragments/print_article.jsp?article=3881472.

[2667] Karen E. Crummy. '08 vote to have a third ticket. Denver Post. Posted and retrieved May 31, 2006 from http://www.denverpost.com/portlet/article/html/fragments/print_article.jsp?article=3881472.
[2668] Institutions. Political Parties. Fox News Opinion Dynamics Poll. June 27-28. Retrieved July 28, 2006 from http://pollingreport.com/institut2.htm.
[2669] His American Dream. John Heilemann. New York Magazine. Posted 12.11 and retrieved 12.14.06 from http://nymag.com/news/politics/25015/. 2 /11.
[2670] His American Dream. John Heilemann. New York Magazine. Posted 12.11 and retrieved 12.14.06 from http://nymag.com/news/politics/25015/. 9 /11.
[2671] His American Dream. John Heilemann. New York Magazine. Posted 12.11 and retrieved 12.14.06 from http://nymag.com/news/politics/25015/. 9 /11.
[2672] AP. Sara Kugler. Sex suit, blunt style could haunt Bloomberg. Posted 7.30.07 and retrieved 8.1.07 from http://www.chinapost.com.tw/international/2007/07/30/116466/Sex-suit,.htm.
[2673] AP. Sara Kugler. Sex suit, blunt style could haunt Bloomberg. Posted 7.30.07 and retrieved 8.1.07 from http://www.chinapost.com.tw/international/2007/07/30/116466/Sex-suit,.htm.
[2674] His American Dream. John Heilemann. New York Magazine. Posted 12.11 and retrieved 12.14.06 from http://nymag.com/news/politics/25015/. P1 /11.
[2675] Quinnipiac University. November 27, 2006—More Americans Think Well of Speaker Pelosi, Quinnipiac University National Thermometer Finds; President is low on List, But Kerry is Last. Retrieved 12.14.06 from http://www.quinnipiac.edu/x1284.xml?ReleaseId=990&ss=print.
[2676] Quinnipiac University. November 27, 2006—More Americans Think Well of Speaker Pelosi, Quinnipiac University National Thermometer Finds; President is low on List, But Kerry is Last. Retrieved 12.14.06 from http://www.quinnipiac.edu/x1284.xml?ReleaseId=990&ss=print.
[2677] His American Dream. John Heilemann. New York Magazine. Posted 12.11 and retrieved 12.14.06 from http://nymag.com/news/politics/25015/. 8 /11.
[2678] Marie Horrigan. Poll Says Bloomberg Could Be a Contender—For Governor. Congressional Quarterly. 6.26.07 and retrieved 7.20.07 from http://www.nytimes.com/cq/2007/06/26/cq_2966.html?pagewanted=print.
[2679] Marie Horrigan. Poll Says Bloomberg Could Be a Contender—For Governor. Congressional Quarterly. 6.26.07 and retrieved 7.20.07 from http://www.nytimes.com/cq/2007/06/26/cq_2966.html?pagewanted=print.
[2680] Political Figures: A-B. New York City Mayor Michael Bloomberg. Retrieved 7.27.07 from http://pollingreport.com/A-B.htm.

AFTERWORD

[2681] AP. Fred Thompson creates '08 committee. MSNBC.com. Posted 7.1.07 and retrieved 6.15.07 from http://www.msnbc.msn.com/id/18984877/print/1/displaymode/1098/.
[2682] Joel Seidman. Thompson spars with Michael Moore. MSNBC.com. 5.19.07 and retrieved 6.15.07 from http://www.msnbc.msn.com/id/18755422/1/displaymode/1098/.
[2683] AP. Thompson says U.S. faces new challenges. MSNBC.com. 6.5.07 and retrieved 6.15.07 from http://www.msnbc.msn.com/id/19044308/print/1/displaymode/1098/.
[2684] Dick Morris and Eileen McGann. Fred Thompson: Going Nowhere Fast. FOX News.com. Posted 9.14.07 and retrieved 9.20.07 from http://www.foxnews.com/printer_friendly_story/0,3566,296882,00.html.
[2685] Dick Morris and Eileen McGann. Fred Thompson: Going Nowhere Fast. FOX News.com. Posted 9.14.07 and retrieved 9.20.07 from http://www.foxnews.com/printer_friendly_story/0,3566,296882,00.html.
[2686] Mike Glover. AP. Thompson Warns of Al-Qaida Threats in the US. 9.7.07 and retrieved 9.30.07 from http://abcnews.go.com/Politics/wireStory?id=3572967.
[2687] Mike Glover. AP. Thompson Warns of Al-Qaida Threats in the US. 9.7.07 and retrieved 9.30.07 from http://abcnews.go.com/Politics/wireStory?id=3572967.
[2688] Dick Morris and Eileen McGann. Fred Thompson: Going Nowhere Fast. FOX News.com. Posted 9.14.07 and retrieved 9.20.07 from http://www.foxnews.com/printer_friendly_story/0,3566,296882,00.html.
[2689] As reported by the NBC Nightly News, September 20, 2007.
[2690] Reuters. Republican Thompson rises in 2008 polls. ABC News. Retrieved 9.20.07 from http://www.abcnews.go.com/print?id=3588286.
[2691] Reuters. Republican Thompson rises in 2008 polls. ABC News. Retrieved 9.20.07 from http://www.abcnews.go.com/print?id=3588286
[2692] CBS News. Pure Horserace: What Now For Unity '08? 9.10.07 and retrieved same day from http://www.cbsnews.com/stories/2007/09/10/politics/purehorserace/main3247388.shtml.
[2693] Libby Quaid. AP. Giuliani attacks Clinton in ad. 9.15.07 @ http://www.heraldtribune.com/article/20070915/NEWS/709150598/1006/SPORTS.
[2694] Michael Kinsley. How Dare You! Time.9.19.07 and retrieved 9.20.07 from http://www.time.com/time/printout/0,8816,1663424,00.html.
[2695] Michael Kinsley. How Dare You! Time.9.19.07 and retrieved 9.20.07 from http://www.time.com/time/printout/0,8816,1663424,00.html.
[2696]2696
[2697] Michael Kinsley. How Dare You! Time.9.19.07 and retrieved 9.20.07 from http://www.time.com/time/printout/0,8816,1663424,00.html.

[2698] Michael D. Shear. Giuliani Says He's MoveOn's 'Worst Nightmare.' Washingtonpost.com. Posted 9.18.07 and retrieved 9.20.07 from http://blog.washingtonpost.com/the-trail/2007/09/18/giuliani_says_hes_moveons_wors.html.

[2699] Political Radar. Giuliani Takes On New York Times, MoveOn.org and Clinton. Posted 9.13.07 and retrieved 9.20.07 from http://blogs.abcnews.com/politicalradar/2007/09/giuliani-takes-.html.

[2700] Libby Quaid. AP. Giuliani attacks Clinton in ad. 9.15.07 @ http://www.heraldtribune.com/article/20070915/NEWS/709150598/1006/SPORTS.

[2701] David Saltonstall. General Petraeus ad nets Giuliani big bucks from donors. 9.15.07 and retrieved 9.20.07 from http://www.nydailynews.com/news/wn_report/2007/09/15/2007-09-15_general_petraeus_ad_nets_giuliani_big_bu.html

[2702] Political Radar. Giuliani Takes On New York Times, MoveOn.org and Clinton. Posted 9.13.07 and retrieved 9.20.07 from http://blogs.abcnews.com/politicalradar/2007/09/giuliani-takes-.html

[2703] Michael Kinsley. How Dare You! Time.9.19.07 and retrieved 9.20.07 from http://www.time.com/time/printout/0,8816,1663424,00.html.

[2704] David Saltonstall. General Petraeus ad nets Giuliani big bucks from donors. 9.15.07 and retrieved 9.20.07 from http://www.nydailynews.com/news/wn_report/2007/09/15/2007-09-15_general_petraeus_ad_nets_giuliani_big_bu.html.

[2705] Dan Balz's Take. Not Waiting For the Nomination, Giuliani Makes All The World His Stage. Retrieved and Posted 9.20.07 from http://blog.washingtonpost.com/the-trail/2007/09/20/post_85.html.

[2706] Dan Balz's Take. Not Waiting For the Nomination, Giuliani Makes All The World His Stage. Retrieved and Posted 9.20.07 from http://blog.washingtonpost.com/the-trail/2007/09/20/post_85.html.

[2707] Dan Balz's Take. Not Waiting For the Nomination, Giuliani Makes All The World His Stage. Retrieved and Posted 9.20.07 from http://blog.washingtonpost.com/the-trail/2007/09/20/post_85.html.

[2708] Dan Balz's Take. Not Waiting For the Nomination, Giuliani Makes All The World His Stage. Retrieved and Posted 9.20.07 from http://blog.washingtonpost.com/the-trail/2007/09/20/post_85.html.

[2709] Transcript of the Fox News Republican Presidential Candidate Debate. 9.5.07 and retrieved 9.10.07 from http://www.nytimes.com/2007/09/05/us/politics/06text.html?ei=5070&en=41c4257e224906f4&ex=1189742400&pagewanted=print.

[2710] Transcript of the Fox News Republican Presidential Candidate Debate. 9.5.07 and retrieved 9.10.07 from http://www.nytimes.com/2007/09/05/us/politics/06text.html?ei=5070&en=41c4257e224906f4&ex=1189742400&pagewanted=print.

[2711] Transcript of the Fox News Republican Presidential Candidate Debate. 9.5.07 and retrieved 9.10.07 from http://www.nytimes.com/2007/09/05/us/politics/06text.html?ei=5070&en=41c4257e224906f4&ex=1189742400&pagewanted=print.

[2712] Transcript of the Fox News Republican Presidential Candidate Debate. 9.5.07 and retrieved 9.10.07 from http://www.nytimes.com/2007/09/05/us/politics/06text.html?ei=5070&en=41c4257e224906f4&ex=1189742400&pagewanted=print.

[2713] Transcript of the Fox News Republican Presidential Candidate Debate. 9.5.07 and retrieved 9.10.07 from http://www.nytimes.com/2007/09/05/us/politics/06text.html?ei=5070&en=41c4257e224906f4&ex=1189742400&pagewanted=print.

[2714] Transcript of the Fox News Republican Presidential Candidate Debate. 9.5.07 and retrieved 9.10.07 from http://www.nytimes.com/2007/09/05/us/politics/06text.html?ei=5070&en=41c4257e224906f4&ex=1189742400&pagewanted=print.

[2715] Transcript of the Fox News Republican Presidential Candidate Debate. 9.5.07 and retrieved 9.10.07 from http://www.nytimes.com/2007/09/05/us/politics/06text.html?ei=5070&en=41c4257e224906f4&ex=1189742400&pagewanted=print.

[2716] Transcript of the Fox News Republican Presidential Candidate Debate. 9.5.07 and retrieved 9.10.07 from http://www.nytimes.com/2007/09/05/us/politics/06text.html?ei=5070&en=41c4257e224906f4&ex=1189742400&pagewanted=print.

[2717] Face the Nation for August 19, 2007. CBS News, pdf available at CBS website. Retrieved 9.10.07.

[2718] Reuters. Republican Thompson rises in 2008 polls. ABC News. Retrieved 9.20.07 from http://www.abcnews.go.com/print?id=3588286.